The Joan Palevsky  Imprint in Classical Literature

In honor of beloved Virgil—

"O degli altri poeti onore e lume..."

—Dante, *Inferno*

The publisher gratefully acknowledges the generous support of the
Classical Literature Endowment Fund of the University of
California Press Foundation, which was established
by a major gift from Joan Palevsky.

# Crisis of Empire

TRANSFORMATION OF THE CLASSICAL HERITAGE
Peter Brown, General Editor

I. *Art and Ceremony in Late Antiquity*, by Sabine G. MacCormack
II. *Synesius of Cyrene: Philosopher-Bishop*, by Jay Alan Bregman
III. *Theodosian Empresses: Women and Imperial Dominion in Late Antiquity*, by Kenneth G. Holum
IV. *John Chrysostom and the Jews: Rhetoric and Reality in the Late Fourth Century*, by Robert L. Wilken
V. *Biography in Late Antiquity: The Quest for the Holy Man*, by Patricia Cox
VI. *Pachomius: The Making of a Community in Fourth-Century Egypt*, by Philip Rousseau
VII. *Change in Byzantine Culture in the Eleventh and Twelfth Centuries*, by A. P. Kazhdan and Ann Wharton Epstein
VIII. *Leadership and Community in Late Antique Gaul*, by Raymond Van Dam
IX. *Homer the Theologian: Neoplatonist Allegorical Reading and the Growth of the Epic Tradition*, by Robert Lamberton
X. *Procopius and the Sixth Century*, by Averil Cameron
XI. *Guardians of Language: The Grammarian and Society in Late Antiquity*, by Robert A. Kaster
XII. *Civic Coins and Civic Politics in the Roman East, A.D. 180–275*, by Kenneth Harl
XIII. *Holy Women of the Syrian Orient*, introduced and translated by Sebastian P. Brock and Susan Ashbrook Harvey
XIV. *Gregory the Great: Perfection in Imperfection*, by Carole Straw
XV. *"Apex Omnium": Religion in the "Res gestae" of Ammianus*, by R. L. Rike
XVI. *Dioscorus of Aphrodito: His Work and His World*, by Leslie S. B. MacCoull
XVII. *On Roman Time: The Codex-Calendar of 354 and the Rhythms of Urban Life in Late Antiquity*, by Michele Renee Salzman
XVIII. *Asceticism and Society in Crisis: John of Ephesus and "The Lives of the Eastern Saints,"* by Susan Ashbrook Harvey
XIX. *Barbarians and Politics at the Court of Arcadius*, by Alan Cameron and Jacqueline Long, with a contribution by Lee Sherry
XX. *Basil of Caesarea*, by Philip Rousseau
XXI. *In Praise of Later Roman Emperors: The Panegyrici Latini*, introduction, translation, and historical commentary by C. E. V. Nixon and Barbara Saylor Rodgers
XXII. *Ambrose of Milan: Church and Court in a Christian Capital*, by Neil B. McLynn
XXIII. *Public Disputation, Power, and Social Order in Late Antiquity*, by Richard Lim
XXIV. *The Making of a Heretic: Gender, Authority, and the Priscillianist Controversy*, by Virginia Burrus
XXV. *Symeon the Holy Fool: Leontius's "Life" and the Late Antique City*, by Derek Krueger

XXVI. *The Shadows of Poetry: Vergil in the Mind of Augustine*, by Sabine MacCormack
XXVII. *Paulinus of Nola: Life, Letters, and Poems*, by Dennis E. Trout
XXVIII. *The Barbarian Plain: Saint Sergius between Rome and Iran*, by Elizabeth Key Fowden
XXIX. *The Private Orations of Themistius*, translated, annotated, and introduced by Robert J. Penella
XXX. *The Memory of the Eyes: Pilgrims to Living Saints in Christian Late Antiquity*, by Georgia Frank
XXXI. *Greek Biography and Panegyric in Late Antiquity*, edited by Tomas Hägg and Philip Rousseau
XXXII. *Subtle Bodies: Representing Angels in Byzantium*, by Glenn Peers
XXXIII. *Wandering, Begging Monks: Spiritual Authority and the Promotion of Monasticism in Late Antiquity*, by Daniel Caner
XXXIV. *Failure of Empire: Valens and the Roman State in the Fourth Century* A.D., by Noel Lenski
XXXV. *Merovingian Mortuary Archaeology and the Making of the Early Middle Ages*, by Bonnie Effros
XXXVI. *Quṣayr ʿAmra: Art and the Umayyad Elite in Late Antique Syria*, by Garth Fowden
XXXVII. *Holy Bishops in Late Antiquity: The Nature of Christian Leadership in an Age of Transition*, by Claudia Rapp
XXXVIII. *Encountering the Sacred: The Debate on Christian Pilgrimage in Late Antiquity*, by Brouria Bitton-Ashkelony
XXXIX. *There Is No Crime for Those Who Have Christ: Religious Violence in the Christian Roman Empire*, by Michael Gaddis
XL. *The Legend of Mar Qardagh: Narrative and Christian Heroism in Late Antique Iraq*, by Joel Thomas Walker
XLI. *City and School in Late Antique Athens and Alexandria*, by Edward J. Watts
XLII. *Scenting Salvation: Ancient Christianity and the Olfactory Imagination*, by Susan Ashbrook Harvey
XLIII. *Man and the Word: The Orations of Himerius*, edited by Robert J. Penella
XLIV. *The Matter of the Gods*, by Clifford Ando
XLV. *The Two Eyes of the Earth: Art and Ritual of Kingship between Rome and Sasanian Iran*, by Matthew P. Canepa
XLVI. *Riot in Alexandria: Tradition and Group Dynamics in Late Antique Pagan and Christian Communities*, by Edward J. Watts
XLVII. *Peasant and Empire in Christian North Africa*, by Leslie Dossey
XLVIII. *Theodoret's People: Social Networks and Religious Conflict in Late Roman Syria*, by Adam M. Schor
XLIX. *Sons of Hellenism, Fathers of the Church: Emperor Julian, Gregory of Nazianzus, and the Vision of Rome*, by Susanna Elm

L. *Shenoute of Atripe and the Uses of Poverty: Rural Patronage, Religious Conflict, and Monasticism in Late Antique Egypt*, by Ariel G. López

LI. *Doctrine and Power: Theological Controversy and Christian Leadership in the Later Roman Empire*, by Carlos R. Galvão-Sobrinho

LII. *Crisis of Empire: Doctrine and Dissent at the End of Late Antiquity*, by Phil Booth

# Crisis of Empire

*Doctrine and Dissent at the End
of Late Antiquity*

Phil Booth

UNIVERSITY OF CALIFORNIA PRESS
*Berkeley   Los Angeles   London*

University of California Press, one of the most distinguished university
presses in the United States, enriches lives around the world by advancing
scholarship in the humanities, social sciences, and natural sciences. Its
activities are supported by the UC Press Foundation and by philanthropic
contributions from individuals and institutions. For more information,
visit www.ucpress.edu.

University of California Press
Berkeley and Los Angeles, California

University of California Press, Ltd.
London, England

© 2014 by The Regents of the University of California

First Paperback Printing 2017

Library of Congress Cataloging-in-Publication Data

Booth, Phil.
 Crisis of empire : doctrine and dissent at the end of late antiquity / Phil
Booth.
  p. cm.
 Includes bibliographical references and index.
 ISBN 978-0-520-29619-0 (pbk.: alk. paper)
 1. Church history—7th century.  2. Moschus, John, approximately
550–619.  3. Sophronius, Saint, Patriarch of Jerusalem, approximately 560–
approximately 638.  4. Maximus, Confessor, Saint, approximately
580–662.  I. Title.
BR162.3.B66  2013
270.2—dc23
                                                          2013011399

10 9 8 7 6 5 4 3 2 1
23 22 21 20 19 18

*For my parents*

CONTENTS

| | | |
|---|---|---|
| Preface | | xi |
| Abbreviations | | xiii |
| | Introduction | 1 |
| 1. | Toward the Sacramental Saint | 7 |
| | Ascetics and the Eucharist before Chalcedon | 10 |
| | Cyril of Scythopolis and the Second Origenist Crisis | 15 |
| | Mystics and Liturgists | 22 |
| | Hagiography and the Eucharist after Chalcedon | 33 |
| 2. | Sophronius and the *Miracles* | 44 |
| | Impresario of the Saints | 49 |
| | Medicine and Miracle | 59 |
| | Narratives of Redemption | 69 |
| | The *Miracles* in Comparative Perspective | 80 |
| 3. | Moschus and the *Meadow* | 90 |
| | The Fall of Jerusalem | 94 |
| | Moschus from Alexandria to Rome | 100 |
| | Ascetics and the City | 116 |
| | Chalcedon and the Eucharist | 128 |
| 4. | Maximus and the *Mystagogy* | 140 |
| | Maximus, Monk of Palestine | 143 |

|    | *The Return of the Cross* | 155 |
|    | *The Mystagogy* | 170 |
| 5. | The Making of the Monenergist Crisis | 186 |
|    | *The Origins of Monenergism* | 188 |
|    | *The Heraclian Unions* | 200 |
|    | *Sophronius the Dissident* | 209 |
| 6. | Jerusalem and Rome at the Dawn of the Caliphate | 225 |
|    | *Sophronius the Patriarch* | 228 |
|    | *Jerusalem from Roman to Islamic Rule* | 241 |
|    | *The Year of the Four Emperors* | 250 |
|    | *From Operations to Wills* | 259 |
|    | *Maximus and the Popes* | 269 |
| 7. | Rebellion and Retribution | 278 |
|    | *Maximus from Africa to Rome* | 282 |
|    | *The Roman-Palestinian Alliance* | 290 |
|    | *Rebellion and Trial* | 300 |
|    | *Maximus in Exile* | 313 |
|    | Conclusion | 329 |

*Bibliography* — 343
  *Primary Sources* — 343
  *Secondary Sources* — 355
Index — 385

PREFACE

I first encountered John Moschus's *Spiritual Meadow* in December 2003. Richard Miles had introduced me to late antiquity while a Classics undergraduate at Churchill College, Cambridge, and as a Master's student Peter Garnsey guided me through the world of late-antique monasticism and encouraged me to pursue Moschus and his circle further. This monograph is the result. It was completed in two distinct stages: first, as a doctoral student at Trinity Hall, Cambridge; and then as Junior Research Fellow at Trinity College, Oxford. The final stages of redrafting, editing, and proofreading were then carried out while holding positions funded by the Leverhulme Trust, the Isaac Newton Trust, and the A.G. Leventis Foundation, whose support I gratefully acknowledge. The thesis was generously funded by grants from Trinity Hall and from the Arts and Humanities Research Council, and was supervised by Peter Sarris, to whom I am immensely grateful for all his guidance, encouragement, and hard work. Not least, to Peter I owe also the inspiration to move outside the classical languages and genres with which I was most familiar, a decision that opened up to me entire new worlds. The thesis was examined by Rebecca Flemming and Peregrine Horden, who offered numerous comments and improvements, not least the demand for a deeper contextualization of the intellectual currents that I had identified. In Oxford I then spent three happy years converting the thesis into a monograph. I was privileged to do so in the edifying company of Bryan Ward-Perkins at Trinity, and benefited from innumerable conversations with James Howard-Johnston. To all these friends and mentors at Cambridge and at Oxford I owe an enormous personal and intellectual debt.

I must thank in addition two contemporaries who have had an immeasurable impact on the intellectual shape and content of this book. First, at Cambridge,

Matthew dal Santo, with whom I shared a PhD supervisor and whose own work on the early Byzantine cult of saints has recently appeared with Oxford University Press; and, second, Marek Jankowiak, who arrived in Oxford while I was completing the monograph and whose own book on the monothelete crisis will appear almost simultaneously with this. I cannot overstate the advantage that I have enjoyed in having two friends who shared my general approach to religious texts, who were engaged with precisely the same sources, and with whom I was not afraid to test out new ideas. Without their input, criticism, and friendship, this monograph would have been all the poorer.

Since my first encounter with the *Meadow* I have built up a considerable number of debts to others, not all of whom can be acknowledged. I am extremely fortunate to have benefited from the comments and advice of the two scholars whose work most inspired my interest in the topic and the period. Peter Brown read both the PhD thesis and an earlier version of the monograph, and his encouragement energized the long process of expanding the former into the latter; and Averil Cameron read the entire manuscript, and debated with me various points of method and of substance that helped shape and sharpen my thoughts. At Oxford, Peter Turner read some draft chapters and offered numerous new insights, pushing me toward far greater clarity in my ideas. In addition, I would like to acknowledge the important exchanges of ideas and materials that I have had with Grigory Benevitch, Jean Gascou, Derek Krueger, Richard Price, and Eileen Rubery. Pauline Allen and Bronwen Neil, whose own works on the period provide much of the backbone for this book, were kind enough to read an earlier version for the University of California Press and offered important criticisms and corrections. At the press itself, I am much indebted to Eric Schmidt and Cindy Fulton for all their guidance and professionalism. Paul Psoinos was a model copy editor and saved me from many mistakes.

I would also like to offer my sincere thanks to all those who have taken the time to teach me the numerous languages used in the period: at the RGS High Wycombe, Ian Wilson, Neil Cooper, Fran Webber and John Edwards; and, at Cambridge and Oxford, Erica Hunter, David Taylor, Tara Andrews, Theo Van Lint, and Jenny Cromwell.

The book would not have been possible without the support of my family. Most of all, I thank my wife, Emma. The love, friendship, and happiness that she has brought to my life are the underpinning of the entire book. My brothers, Laurence and Richard, provided constant encouragement, and Richard read and corrected the entire manuscript. Finally, I would like to thank my parents, Andrew and Barbara. The debt of gratitude that I owe them for their continuous love and support cannot be put into words. I dedicate this book to them.

ABBREVIATIONS

The abbreviations used throughout the notes and bibliography in this volume are as follows:

| | |
|---|---|
| *AB* | *Analecta Bollandiana* |
| *ACO* | E. Schwartz, ed., *Acta Conciliorum Oecumenicorum*. 4 vols. in 14. Berlin and Leipzig, 1914–82. |
| *ActaArch* | *Acta Archaeologica* |
| *AHC* | *Annuarium Historiae Conciliorum* |
| *AntAfr* | *Antiquités Africaines* |
| *AntTard* | *Antiquité Tardive* |
| *APB* | *Acta Patristica et Byzantina* |
| *BASOR* | *Bulletin of the American Schools of Oriental Research* |
| *BBGG* | *Bollettino della Badia Greca di Grottaferrata* |
| *BCH* | *Bulletin de Correspondance Hellénique* |
| *BHG* | F. Halkin, ed. *Bibliotheca Hagiographica Graeca*. 3rd ed. Subsidia Hagiographica 8a. Brussels, 1957. |
| *BHL* | *Bibliotheca Hagiographica Latina*. 2 vols. Subsidia Hagiographica 6. Brussels, 1898–1901. |
| *BMGS* | *Byzantine and Modern Greek Studies* |
| *BSOAS* | *Bulletin of the School of Oriental and African Studies* |
| *ByzF* | *Byzantinische Forschungen* |
| *BZ* | *Byzantinische Zeitschrift* |
| *CCSG* | Corpus Christianorum. Series Graeca. Turnhout, 1977–. |
| *CCSL* | Corpus Christianorum. Series Latina. Turnhout, 1953–. |

| | |
|---|---|
| CIL | *Corpus Inscriptionum Latinarum.* Berlin, 1853–. |
| CPG | *Clavis Patrum Graecorum.* Turnhout, 1974–. |
| CQ | *Classical Quarterly* |
| CSEL | *Corpus Scriptorum Ecclesiasticorum Latinorum.* Vienna, 1866–. |
| CSCO | *Corpus Scriptorum Christianorum Orientalium.* Louvain, 1903–. |
| SA | Scriptores Arabici |
| SAe | Scriptores Aethiopici |
| SC | Scriptores Coptici |
| SI | Scriptores Iberici |
| SS | Scriptores Syri |
| DOP | *Dumbarton Oaks Papers* |
| EHR | *English Historical Review* |
| EME | *Early Medieval Europe* |
| ÉO | *Échos d'Orient* |
| GCS | *Die griechischen christlichen Schriftsteller der ersten Jahrhunderte.* Berlin, 1897–. |
| GOTR | *Greek Orthodox Theological Review* |
| GRBS | *Greek, Roman and Byzantine Studies* |
| HThR | *Harvard Theological Review* |
| ICS | *Illinois Classical Studies* |
| IEJ | *Israel Exploration Journal* |
| JAS | *Journal of the Royal Asiatic Society* |
| JECS | *Journal of Early Christian Studies* |
| JEH | *Journal of Ecclesiastical History* |
| JHS | *Journal of Hellenic Studies* |
| JÖByz | *Jahrbuch der Österrichischen Byzantinistik* |
| JRS | *Journal of Roman Studies* |
| JSAI | *Jerusalem Studies in Arabic and Islam* |
| JThS | *Journal of Theological Studies* |
| LSJ | *A Greek-English Lexicon.* Ed. H. G. Liddell and R. Scott. 9th ed. Rev. H. S. Jones and R. MacKenzie, with supplement ed. E. A. Barber. Oxford, 1968. |
| MÉFR | *Mélanges d'Archéologie et d'Histoire de l'École Française de Rome* |
| MGH | *Monumenta Germaniae Historica.* Berlin and Munich, 1826–. |
| AA | Auctores Antiquissimi |
| SRM | Scriptores Rerum Merovingicarum |
| OC | *Oriens Christianus* |
| OCP | *Orientalia Christiana Periodica* |
| OLP | *Orientalia Lovaniensia Periodica* |
| OrSyr | *L'Orient Syrien* |
| P.Lond. | *Greek Papyri in the British Museum.* London, 1893–. |
| P&P | *Past and Present* |

| | |
|---|---|
| *PBSR* | *Papers of the British School at Rome* |
| *PG* | J.-P. Migne et al., eds. *Patrologia Cursus Completus. Series Graeca.* 161 vols. Paris, 1857–66. |
| *PL* | J.-P. Migne et al., eds. *Patrologia Cursus Completus. Series Latina.* 221 vols. Paris, 1844–1900. |
| *PLRE* | A. H. M. Jones, J. R. Martindale, and J. Morris, eds. *Prosopography of the Later Roman Empire.* 3 vols. in 4. Cambridge, 1971–92. |
| *PmbZ* | R.-J. Lilie et al., eds. *Prosopographie der mittelbyzantinischen Zeit.* 16 vols. Berlin, 1998–2013. |
| *PP* | *La Parola del Passato* |
| *PO* | *Patrologia Orientalis.* Paris, 1904–. |
| *RAC* | *Rivista di Archeologia Cristiana* |
| *RÉAug* | *Revue des Études Augustiniennes* |
| *RÉB* | *Revue des Études Byzantines* |
| *RÉG* | *Revue des Études Grecques* |
| *RHE* | *Revue d'Histoire Ecclésiastique* |
| *RN* | *Revue Numismatique* |
| *ROC* | *Revue de l'Orient Chrétien* |
| *RömHM* | *Römische Historische Mitteilungen* |
| *RQ* | *Römische Quartalschrift für Altertumskunde und Kirchengeschichte* |
| *RSBN* | *Rivista di Studi Bizantini e Neoellenici* |
| *RSR* | *Revue des Sciences Religieuses* |
| *S&C* | *Scrittura e Civiltà* |
| *SC* | *Sources Chrétiennes.* Paris, 1942–. |
| *SCO* | *Studi Classici e Orientali* |
| *SEJG* | *Sacris Erudiri* |
| *SH* | *Subsidia Hagiographica.* Brussels, 1886–. |
| *SicGymn* | *Siculorum Gymnasium* |
| *SP* | *Studia Patristica* |
| *ST* | *Studi e Testi.* Vatican City, 1900–. |
| *T&MByz* | *Travaux et Mémoires du Centre de Recherche d'Histoire et Civilisation Byzantines* |
| *ThLZ* | *Theologische Literaturzeitung* |
| *ThS* | *Theological Studies* |
| *TU* | *Texte und Untersuchungen zur Geschichte der altchristlichen Literatur.* Leipzig, 1882–. |
| *VChr* | *Vigiliae Christianae* |
| *VetChr* | *Vetera Christianorum* |
| *ZAC* | *Zeitschrift für Antikes Christentum* |
| *ZKG* | *Zeitschrift für Kirchengeschichte* |
| *ZPE* | *Zeitschrift für Papyrologie und Epigraphik* |
| *ZSlPh* | *Zeitschrift für Slavische Philologie* |

# Introduction

In the course of the seventh century, the Eastern Roman empire underwent a profound transformation. As first the Persians and then the Muslims swept over and seized the valuable provinces of the Roman Near East, the inhabitants of the now reduced empire experimented with a series of structural and cultural changes that responded to the dramatic curtailment of Roman power. The structural elements of that change—that is, the series of administrative, economic, and military reforms imposed by the emperor Heraclius and his successors—are now for the most part well known; and aspects of the cultural change (in particular, the decline in secular literature, the explosion in anti-Jewish and apocalyptic texts, and the heightened interest in, or anxieties over, religious icons), have also occupied a prominent position within scholarship. Other elements within this cultural change, however—in particular, the debasement of monasticism as the guardian of ascetic virtue, the rise of the eucharist as the central, aggregating icon of the Christian faith, and the renegotiation of competing ascetical and liturgical narratives—are less well appreciated. This book explores them in greater depth.

The story of the Christian religion in late antiquity is in many ways the story of a religion struggling and failing to overcome its ancient roots. From the conversion of Constantine onward, court theologians articulated a grand vision of a new Christian empire under a Roman emperor presented as God's pious vicegerent on earth. The Christian faith, however, had been conceived and developed in opposition to the political culture of the Roman state and, as such, carried within its intellectual inheritance the conceptual potential for a full ecclesial dissociation from the secular realm. As the pagan provincial convert was exposed to the new political ideals emanating from Constantinople, therefore, so too was he or she exposed to a Christian culture cut through with political ambiguity, one that held forth the possibility, to some for the first time, of a political identity distinct from, and even antipathetic to, that of Rome.

As the imperial authorities wrestled with the inherent ambiguities of Christian empire, so too did they struggle to mediate those divergent methodologies of Christological exegesis that had developed in the pre-Constantinian period. Emperors aspired to the spiritual and political consensus expounded in the new rhetoric of Christian rule, and in this forced or, at least, precipitated attempts to reconcile the different Christological positions. As a result of those attempts the more extreme doctrinal ideas conceived on both sides were marginalized, but the more important, and more permanent, effect was nevertheless to crystallize the different tendencies into distinct and intractable traditions with their own formulas and Fathers, languages, and hierarchies. As the imperial position became more focused on particular definitions, and as the number of official heretics ever expanded—in particular after the divisive Council of Chalcedon (451)—some alienated communities therefore began to invest in patterns of thought that never abandoned the ideal of pious Christian rule but could nevertheless conceive of an orthodox Church once again divested of the Roman empire.

We first observe this distinct shift in emphasis among miaphysite communities of the late fifth and the sixth century, when their leaders, faced with an imperial power that lurched ever more toward official condemnation, placed a distinct emphasis on eucharistic miracles as the proof of sustained doctrinal righteousness and on eucharistic participation as the touchstone of membership within the orthodox group, irrespective of the constant oscillations in imperial opinion. Within Chalcedonian communities of the same period, communities that benefited from more consistent imperial patronage, comparable concerns are notable for the most part for their absence. But when in the subsequent century the Persian and then Muslim invasions of the Eastern provinces forced Chalcedonian Christians to confront a situation in which some of their co-religionists were placed outside the confines of the Christian empire, here too Christian intellectuals began to explore more integrated ecclesiological models that also looked to the eucharist as the great aggregating icon of an embattled but unified orthodox faith and emphasized the sustained power of eucharistic communion as the ultimate proof of the Church's transcendence of the caprice of temporal politics.

A notable feature of this process of sacramental reorientation within Chalcedonian thought was an advanced attempt to reconcile long-standing ambiguities over the relationship between the charismatic and the collective, the ascetical and ecclesial, lives. Since the inception of the monastic enterprise, a profound disinterest had marked ascetic attitudes to the eucharist, both in hagiographical and in anthropological narratives. In the period after Chalcedon, however—as ideological and institutional pressures served to blur the boundaries between cleric and monk, and as the fragmentation of doctrinal consensus encouraged a differentiation between the sacramental dispensations of competing sects—commentators both Chalcedonian and anti-Chalcedonian began to assert more liturgified, more sacramentalized visions of ascetic practice, challenging the dominant strands of ascetic thought inherited from previous centuries (chapter 1). But it was not until the seventh century, and the dramatic Christian reversals that it witnessed, that elites within the Chalcedonian Church articulated a more pervasive and more comprehensive reconciliation of the competing imperatives of ascetical and sacramental theologies. Those seventh-century Chalcedonian elites thus presided over a marked and seminal shift in emphasis within the Roman East, in which the more differentiated and polycentric Christian culture of the late-antique period transformed into the more integrated and ecclesiocentric Christian culture of Byzantium.

We must nevertheless be cautious not to equate integration with simplification. Observers have sometimes been tempted to think of this period as one of collapse, of not only socioeconomic but also cultural contraction in which written sources become less diffuse, less complex, and less pluralistic. From the limited perspective of seventh-century Constantinople—which witnessed significant loss of territories and their associated revenues, dramatic social reorganization, and a marked break in the classicizing historiographical tradition—such a view might indeed be upheld. But elsewhere within the now reduced Roman empire, and even more so across former Roman territories throughout the Near East, the period was one of significant and diverse cultural production, much of it in fact driven through the political, economic, and cultural fragmentation contingent upon sporadic warfare and changes of regime. Indeed, if the historian is prepared to ignore geographic, linguistic, and generic boundaries in the circumscription of the available sources and to tread onto ground that artificial academic boundaries have for the most part preserved for theologians, then he or she is confronted with a vast amount of material. That much of this production was now religious in tone is not surprising and complements processes begun far earlier. But the striking predominance of (in particular) Christian themes and genres should not be interpreted too readily as an index of cultural regression, for in its various complexities the considerable religious literature of the period shows no signs of a marked decrease in originality, depth, or diversity. To think of this period as one of unambiguous cultural contraction, then, is not only to adopt a restricted, Romanocentric perspective but also to make monolithic a diverse (and still little-appreciated) Christian culture and to isolate a supposedly pure classicism as the sole measure of cultural efflorescence.

I have focused here on the corpus of three prominent and closely associated Palestinian monks: John Moschus, Sophronius of Jerusalem, and Maximus Confessor. Between them, these three are responsible for a quite extraordinary range and volume of Christian texts (hagiographies, poems, sermons, letters, commentaries, etc.); and there are, moreover, a multitude of further texts associated with them and their circle, not to mention a huge number of historiographical texts, in various languages, which describe the period through which they lived. I have here endeavored to encompass as much as possible of this diverse output. But at the same time I have chosen to give particular prominence to three substantial texts: Sophronius's cultic *Miracles;* Moschus's hagiographic *Meadow;* and Maximus's liturgical *Mystagogy*. Although of diverse content and purpose, these texts are conspicuous for fundamental parallels and continuities in concern, and thus they point to broader ideological anxieties engaged and developed across the entire group. Through exploring each text's distinct emphases in comparison with generic precedent and then placing it in conversation with the texts of the author's associates within the group, I here attempt both to reveal the fundamental concerns of the individual texts and to situate such concerns within the wider pattern of the group's sensibilities. What I advocate, therefore, is a more holistic approach to the cultural output of the circle, an approach through which comprehension of both individual texts and the collective corpus may be all the more enriched.

One concern that all our protagonists shared was that described above: that is, the place of ecclesiastical structures in relation to the life of the ascetic. This same tension is of course fundamental to the Christian monastic enterprise and would reappear throughout its future. In setting out to negotiate this tension, the Moschan circle—as I will sometimes call the group, after its most senior member—did not therefore resolve it but rather offered a compelling negotiation of it, a negotiation that, furthermore, constituted the first, developed, Chalcedonian attempt at its resolution. In Sophronius's *Miracles* (ca. 610–14)—when we first encounter that circle—we discover an author for whom the eucharist has an emphatic role both in differentiating Chalcedonian and anti-Chalcedonian, and in illuminating the converted. But it is nevertheless striking that Sophronius here affords both the eucharist and its associated clerical mediation a limited place in his conception of the Christian (ascetic) life, of which his narratives are an extended metaphor (chapter 2). Within both the thought of Sophronius and that of his associates, however, that quite traditional spiritual indifference to ecclesial structures was, over time, to undergo a striking alteration. Around 630 Sophronius's spiritual master, John Moschus, penned the *Spiritual Meadow*, a hagiographic text that juxtaposed traditional monastic vignettes alongside the celebration of clerics and of eucharistic miracles (chapter 3); around the same time, Sophronius's own disciple Maximus penned the *Mystagogy*, an interpretation of the eucharistic ritual that reconciled the competing visions of Evagrius Ponticus and Pseudo-Dionysius the Areopagite (chapter 4); and, in the mid-630s, Sophronius himself delivered a series of sermons in which he insisted on the regular engagement of all Christians with the sacramental structures of the orthodox Church (chapter 6).

I have attempted to demonstrate how dependent that evolution was on the context in which it occurred: both in terms of the wider imperial stage (the Persian and then Muslim invasions of the Eastern provinces) and in terms of the biographies of our three protagonists (their own westward retreat from those same invasions). The Moschan circle lived through perhaps the most dramatic period in the late-antique East, as the East Roman state oscillated between brilliant triumph and unprecedented disaster. That period witnessed, for example, the invasion of the shahanshah Khusrau II (603), his capture of Jerusalem (614), and the occupation of the Eastern provinces (610–29); the incredible resurgence of Roman fortunes, culminating in the emperor Heraclius's restoration of the captured Cross to Golgotha (630); and the explosion of the armies of the nascent caliphate into the Near and Middle East (634), signaling the end of both Roman and Persian rule in the region. These events were to have a profound effect on the lives of our three protagonists, who were forced as refugees to North Africa and Rome, there to contemplate the significance of recent events.

In the first half of this book (chapters 2–4), I argue that for these Chalcedonian authors the development of a sacramental discourse that emphasized the integration of ascetics within the Church partook of a wider Christian response to the reversals suffered at the hands of Eastern invaders, and all the ideological introspection that those same reversals demanded. Through that same discourse, Moschus, Sophronius, and Maximus emphasized the sustained unity and integrity of the orthodox Church, preserved not in the fluctuating fortunes of the Christian Roman empire but in the continued power and righteousness of the gathered eucharistic rite. For our three protagonists, therefore, the crisis of the Chalcedonian empire and the occupation of its territories compelled a far more thorough and thoughtful renegotiation of ecclesiological thought than had hitherto been attempted within ascetic circles, whether Chalcedonian or anti-Chalcedonian.

As a response to the crisis of empire, that same elevation of the eucharist and its rites would be replicated in the works of other Chalcedonian observers of the period. But in the context of our three protagonists, it came to serve a more immediate function, as Sophronius and Maximus emerged as Constantinople's leading doctrinal antagonists and looked westward to Rome for support. In the second half of this book (chapters 5–7), therefore, I examine how the ecclesiological renegotiation that the group attempted in response to Eastern crisis came also to provide the ideological underpinning for its dissidence against the emperor's attempts to achieve a new communion of the Chalcedonian and anti-Chalcedonian churches.

Contemporaneous with Heraclius's triumph over the Persians in 628, and in a bid to cement that triumph in the achievement of an elusive doctrinal consensus, the emperor and patriarch at Constantinople had promoted the doctrine of monenergism—that is, the one operation in Christ—as a means of compromising with anti-Chalcedonian communities throughout the Near and Middle East. The new initiative met with considerable success but from its inception encountered the vociferous resistance of Sophronius. Both Sophronius and Maximus had in the same period proved somewhat reluctant to accept the triumphalist Constantinopolitan rhetoric of imperial and cosmological restoration, and as that rhetoric was undone in the spectacular rise of an expansionist Islam, Sophronius developed an explicit doctrinal opposition that aimed to undo the recent unions. Here, then, the group's ever-deepening eucharistic orientation assumed a more immediate target, for Sophronius's dissidence was constructed on an ideological basis that would brook no doctrinal compromise for the sake of union and regarded such compromise as a pollution of the Church's sacramental *ordo*, a cause of sin and thus also of the divine anger manifested in Roman defeat.

In the face of Sophronius's opposition, the emperor and patriarch retreated on the question of Christological operations and instead promoted the doctrine of monotheletism—the one will in Christ—as a means of restoring peace within Chalcedonian circles. As the successes of the first caliphs became more entrenched, however, Maximus from Western exile developed and launched a further doctrinal assault upon the position of the capital, an assault that won over successive Roman popes to the antimonothelete cause and that, it appears, several times lurched into open political rebellion. In this context, the ecclesiological revisionism that I have identified as a prominent feature of the group's output came again to complement its doctrinal dissent. On the one hand, the consistent resistance to imperial doctrinal decree was validated as an assertion of ecclesial independence from secular interference, for the emperor fulfilled none of the functions of the priesthood and therefore had no right to debate or to define the faith; but on the other, the recognition of clerical privilege that had marked the circle's earlier pronouncements was extended a step further, to a recognition of Roman preeminence within the Church.

Within this circle, therefore, we witness not a devolution of the sacred from bishop or emperor to ascetic—as has sometimes been said of the period—but rather the integration of ascetic holiness around an established ecclesial pole. The ideal ascetic who emerged within the writings of Moschus, Sophronius, and Maximus was not the withdrawn outsider, standing above the demands of imperfect terrestrial institutions. He or she was a person of the Church, subordinate to its sacramental mediation, respectful of the priesthood, and mindful of the various pollutants that swirled around it. In articulating this model, our three abandoned the spiritual independence of earlier monastic generations but at the same predicted both the consistent eucharistic orientation of later centuries' most prominent Greek ascetics and the ideological basis on which those same ascetics would come to construct their own political dissent. This, then, was a new asceticism for a new age, in which ascetics at last embraced their spiritual subordination to clerics but in so doing constructed both a new vision of a Church liberated from temporal disasters and a less transient and more threatening basis from which to expose the inherent ambiguities of an empire founded in the Christian faith.

1

# Toward the Sacramental Saint

At some point in the 350s A.D., an ecclesial council was convened at Gangra in Paphlagonia. The disciplinary canons that that council produced were the first to legislate on the nascent monastic enterprise and constitute a classic expression of the anxieties that that enterprise engendered among clerics. The council had been convened to examine the activities of the Eustathians, a monastic sect whose leader had been the erstwhile ascetic mentor of Basil of Caesarea. The charges leveled at the Eustathians at the council can be categorized to constitute three central purported abuses: first, the introduction of ascetic innovations against established practice;[1] second, the disparagement or active dissolution of conventional social relations;[2] and third, the marginalization or denigration of the hierarchical and sacramental structures of the Church. From our perspective (and perhaps that of the presiding clerics) it was this last accusation that was most salient: "If anyone teaches that the house of God and the liturgies performed there [*tas en autōi sunaxeis*] are to be despised," one canon proclaimed, "let him be anathema."[3] Another legislated that "If anyone holds private assemblies outside the Church [*para tēn ekklēsian idiai ekklēsiazoi*] and in his hatred of the Church wishes to perform ecclesiastical acts [*ta tēs ekklēsias etheloi prattein*], when the priest in accordance with the bishop's will has refused permission, let him be anathema."[4] This assumption of

---

1. *Acts of the Council of Gangra*, Canons 2, 7, 8, 12, 13, 17, 18.
2. *Acts of the Council of Gangra*, Canons 1, 3, 9, 10, 14, 15, 16.
3. *Acts of the Council of Gangra*, Canon 5 [Joannou 91].
4. *Acts of the Council of Gangra*, Canon 6 [Joannou 91f.]. See also *Acts of the Council of Gangra*, Canon 4 (against those who refuse to receive communion from a priest who is married); 11 (against

clerical privilege, and with it the repudiation of the structures of the Church, represented a fundamental challenge to episcopal notions of a Christianity formed within, and mediated by, the episcopate. The Gangran legislation sought to reinforce those same notions through subordinating monks to clerical authority and ritually orienting the entire Christian community around the assemblies of the Church.

Despite sporadic legislative measures against monastic groups at both the local and imperial levels, the tensions between monks and clerics evident in the Gangran legislation nevertheless recurred throughout the late-antique Mediterranean. Clerics responded to such tensions through two principal (and quite discordant) means. The first such approach was to blur the intellectual and institutional boundaries between the two institutions, incorporating and redefining ascetic principles within the clerical ideal, and thus both clericizing monasticism and asceticizing the episcopate.[5] The second approach, however, was not so much to blur as to strengthen the boundaries between the two vocations—not so much to bring ascetics within the world but rather to force them from it. As Daniel Caner has demonstrated in a seminal monograph on monasticism in the period up to 451, ecclesial authorities across the Mediterranean responded to the emergent monastic enterprise through attempting to impose paradigms of proper ascetic practice that were more congenial to clerical claims to leadership, and thus also economic support, within Christian communities.[6] The monastic model enshrined in episcopal sermons, letters, and hagiographies emphasized that real monks were not those who wandered in cities and begged for alms—ascetic practices that in fact had a long and illustrious pedigree, in particular in Syria—but rather those who remained in the deserts and were self-sufficient, a model associated with Egypt and enshrined, of course, in Athanasius's *Life of Antony*.[7] Practices through which ascetics encroached upon the social and economic jurisdictions of clerics were thus stigmatized as impious; and in successive controversies involving the conflict of monks and ecclesiasts, those who did not conform to these normative paradigms of monastic practice were branded as heretics and relegated from the religious mainstream.

Caner regards the canonical legislation of the ecumenical Council of Chalcedon (451) as the apogee of this process, for here the ideological reorientation of

---

those who refuse an invitation to a love feast); 19 (against those ascetics who disregard the fasts prescribed by the Church); 20 (against those who condemn the assemblies in honor of the martyrs).

5. See, e.g., in the East (Cappadocian fathers): Sterk (2004), esp. 35–140. In the West (John Cassian): Markus (1990) esp. 181–97; also P. Brown (1976).

6. Caner (2002).

7. On the Syrian paradigm see Drijvers (1981); Caner (2002) 50–82. On Athanasius's *Life of Antony* and the normative Egyptian paradigm see Brakke (1995) 201–65; Caner (2002) 4–18.

monasticism anticipated at a more local level throughout previous decades was reinforced with universal episcopal and also imperial approval.[8] Crucial in this regard is the council's famous Canon 4, which summarized the monastic abuses of which the assembled bishops disapproved—meddling in ecclesiastical and even civil affairs, wandering in cities, and founding monasteries without clerical approval—and instead promoted a paradigm more congenial to the preservation of clerical privilege, in which the economic oversight of monastic communities was made an episcopal prerogative.[9] The canon thus attempted to effect the full legal and economic subordination of monasticism to the clerical establishment, presenting the former, for the first time, as a lesser institution of the latter. Caner contends that the legislation of Chalcedon marked a significant watershed in relations between clerics and ascetics, not least because it implicated their economic interests.[10] It is indeed true that the post-Chalcedonian period witnessed a distinct shift in monastic practice: in tune with episcopal demands, monks themselves began to promote models of monastic practice emphasizing that individual, withdrawn asceticism could be legitimized only by an extended period of sustained communal discipline; and in turn the power of individual ascetics went into decline, with spiritual authority increasingly the preserve of the leaders of sizable, largely coenobitic communities. If both these developments proved apposite to episcopal attempts to delimit ascetics' sphere of influence and operation, we must nevertheless be cautious not to overstate the extent of reconciliation between monastic and clerical imperatives. Significant tensions remained.

For our purposes, the most important such tensions were those that we have seen within the canonical legislation of Gangra: that is, tensions between the competing demands of individual cultivation and submission to the spiritual improvement conferred through the rites and sacraments of the Church, in particular the eucharist. Although monks themselves in the post-Chalcedonian period began to promote forms of ascetic discipline that were more congenial to the vision of their clerical superiors, and although monastic and clerical institutions were indeed ever more implicated, a significant tension remained that the Chalcedonian legislators had, in effect, ignored: that is, the discordant imperatives of the ascetical and sacramental lives. Thus, despite a heightened degree of legal, economic, and institutional integration, the relative indifference to the structures of the Church witnessed within the Gangran legislation had still not been overcome.

8. Caner (2002) 206–12, 235–41; cf. Dagron (1970) 271–75.

9. *Canons of the Council of Chalcedon* [Joannou 72–74]; with the interpretation of Caner (2002) 210f. concerning the final sentence (*Ton mentoi episkopon tēs poleōs chrē tēn deousan pronoian poieisthai tōn monastēriōn*).

10. See esp. Caner (2002) 241.

This chapter first outlines the striking eucharistic minimalism of the earliest ascetic biographies and anthropologies before tracing the attempts of various post-Chalcedonian commentators—and, in particular, anti-Chalcedonian commentators—to renegotiate that same tension. In part this renegotiation represented an extension of previous attempts to reconcile the monastic and clerical vocations, in particular in a context within which the boundaries between the two were becoming more porous. But it was also driven in the disintegration of dogmatic consensus accelerated through the Chalcedonian settlement, as anti-Chalcedonian communities began to elevate the eucharist as the central, aggregating icon of the orthodox faith and participation in its rites as the central expression of anti-Chalcedonian identity. This assertion of ritual integrity occurred at a time when sixth-century anti-Chalcedonian communities had become more alienated from the imperial Roman Church, and it was destined to be replicated within their seventh-century Chalcedonian equivalents, when foreign incursion and the perceived doctrinal deviation of Constantinople encouraged others to attempt a comparable, and indeed more comprehensive, renegotiation of the competing demands and theologies of the ascetical and ecclesial lives.

### ASCETICS AND THE EUCHARIST BEFORE CHALCEDON

It has sometimes been observed that the Eustathian practices condemned at Gangra intersect with a heretical sect described in the texts of later authors as Messalianism.[11] It is clear that in its earliest stages the heretical profile of Messalianism gathered together the various deviant monastic practices that clerics despised—wandering in cities, begging, refusing to acknowledge clerics.[12] Messalianism, however, had a further dimension that should be emphasized: that is, a perceived disengagement from the sacraments of the Church. According to Theodoret, one of the first to describe in detail the Messalian sect, their theological convictions rested on notions of inherent but displaceable sin and the possibility of restoration only through assiduous prayer. Thus, he claims, the Messalians saw no benefit in baptism;[13] but also "declared, though not separating from ecclesiastical communion, that the divine food, about which Christ the master said, 'He who eats my flesh and drinks my blood shall live into eternity' [Joh. 6:54–58], neither benefits nor harms

---

11. On those texts see esp. the comprehensive treatment of Fitschen (1998), esp. 18–88.
12. For the Messalian synthesis of radical ascetic tendencies see Caner (2002) 83–125; Plested (2004) 17–27, esp. 21; Déroche (1995) 154–225.
13. See Theodoret, *Compendium of Heretical Doctrines* 4.11 [PG 83, 429C].

[*oute oninanai oute lōbasthai*]."[14] Little wonder, then, that some commentators—both ancient and modern—have thought of the Eustathians as Messalians.[15]

For centuries it has been recognized that the various errors that Theodoret and others ascribe to the Messalians contain numerous correspondences with the corpus of Pseudo-Macarius, a late fourth-century Syrian theologian who is counted, alongside Evagrius Ponticus, as a progenitor of the late-antique mystical tradition.[16] Comparison of the two corpora indicates that Pseudo-Macarius operated within an ascetic milieu similar to, but not interchangeable with, one that observers identified as Messalian.[17] Thus he corrects the antisacramental leanings of the Messalian profile in dwelling upon the parallels between the ascetic life and the eucharistic rite, above all in Logos 52 of the so-called *Collection I*.[18] It begins with the statement "The entire visible dispensation [*oikonomia*] of the Church came about for the sake of the living and intellectual essence of the rational soul, which is made in the image of God, and which is the living and true Church of God." Because "the entire Church that we now perceive is a shadow of the true, rational man within," God granted that the Spirit be present at the altar and in baptism, and the Savior that it preside over and participate in (*epipolazein kai koinōnein*) the Church's services (*leitourgia*), so as to act on "believing hearts." Here, "the dispensation and service of the sacraments of the Church [*hē oikonomia kai diakonia tōn mustēriōn tēs ekklēsias*]" have an emphatic spiritual effect, leading the faithful to the cultivation of the inner man represented in the structures of the Church.[19] Pseudo-Macarius presents the Church's services as an illustration of the workings of the Spirit within the heart of the ascetic,[20] and emphasizes in no uncertain terms the presence of the Spirit within the sacraments, perhaps as a direct defense against accusations of an antiecclesial Messalianism.[21] Nevertheless, even in that defense,

---

14. Theodoret, *Ecclesiastical History* 4.11 [Parmentier and Hansen 229]. For the same antisacramental errors cf. the anti-Messalian lists of Timothy of Constantinople, *On the Reception of Heretics* [PG 86, 45D–52C]; John of Damascus, *On Heresies* 80 [PG 94, 729A–732B], with Stewart (1991) 52–69, esp. 63f.

15. See, e.g., Theodorus Lector, *Tripartite History* 2.74 [Hansen 37]; A. Gribomont (1957). For a full discussion see Fitschen (1998) 138–42.

16. On Macarius and his Syrian background see Stewart (1991) 9–11, 84–95; Fitschen (1998) 162–75; Plested (2004) 12–30. On the correspondences see esp. Fitschen (1998) 176–238.

17. See, e.g., Stewart (1991) 52–59; Fitschen (1998) 238; Plested (2004) 23–27.

18. Plested (2004) 40.

19. Ps.-Macarius, *Collection I* 52.1, 52.2.1–3 [Berthold vol. 2, 138–41].

20. Cf. Stewart (1991) 220. Ibid. 218–21 points also to Ps.-Macarius, *Collection I* 7.18, on the human person as temple and draws attention to important parallels between Ps.-Macarius's conception of the structures of the Church and that of the *Book of Steps*, esp. Memra 12. For the same connections between Messalian attitudes to the Church, Ps.-Macarius, and the *Books of Steps*, see Fitschen (1998) 108–28; Escolan (1999) 91–123, esp. 106; also Stewart (1991) 84–92, 162–66, 198–203, 216–23, 227–32; Golitzin (1994) 371–85; Caner (2002) 106–17.

21. As suggested in Plested (2004) 40; *contra* Fitschen (1998) 238, suggesting the Messalians are radical interpreters of the Ps.-Macarian model.

it is clear that his focus remains on the cultivation of the spiritual life and that, for the advanced ascetic, the outward structures of the Church are subordinated to the development of the inner man—in the words of Hans Urs von Balthasar, "at once something indispensable and something that must be outgrown."[22]

It is therefore incorrect to regard Pseudo-Macarius as antisacramental; but at the same time, he conforms to a pattern in which the earliest ascetic theorists marginalized a developed sacramental, and in particular eucharistic, discourse in favor of a focus upon personal, ascetic transformation. Indeed, if the Pseudo-Macarian corpus constituted one prevailing strand of late-antique ascetic thought, the other was formed through the Egyptian monk and Origenist Evagrius Ponticus. Within the Evagrian corpus, spiritual progression is on occasion conceived in sacramental terms, with practical virtues corresponding to Christ's flesh, and contemplation corresponding to his blood. Thus the famous tract *To Monks*:[23]

> Flesh of Christ is practical virtues [*Sarkes Christou praktikai aretai*]; he who eats it shall become passionless [*ho de esthiōn autas genēsetai apathēs*].
>
> Blood of Christ is contemplation of creation [*haima Christou theōria tōn gegonotōn*], and he who drinks it will thereby become wise [*kai ho pinōn auto sophisthēsetai hup' autou*].

Although in passages such as these Evagrius appears to point to the spiritual benefits conferred through communion,[24] we should be cautious not to overstate the extent of Evagrius's eucharistic orientation.[25] Contained within his quite vast corpus, there are but few comments on the eucharist; and even then, those comments are quite ambiguous as to the need for continuous submission to the rites of the Church.[26] Evagrius's approach, like that of Pseudo-Macarius, is perhaps best appreciated as a eucharistic minimalism.

It should be noted that this minimalism does not reflect a more general ambivalence toward the eucharist within Christian thought of the period, for contemporaneous with the ascetical speculations of Pseudo-Macarius and Evagrius there

---

22. Von Balthasar (1961), trans. Daley (2003) 319. Cf. Plested (2004) 40; also ibid. 109–11 and Golitzin (1994) 379–85 on the theme of the inner liturgy within the Ps.-Macarian corpus.

23. Evagrius Ponticus, *To Monks* 118–19 [Greßmann 163]. For the same sentiments cf. Evagrius Ponticus, *Commentary on Ecclesiastes* 13; *Letter of Faith* 4; *On Malign Thoughts* [PG 79, 1228C].

24. *Pace* Clark (1992) 65, talking of the "spiritualized and allegorized" nature of Evagrius's concept of the eucharist (but mistranslating the Greek, as though *autas* refers to *aretai* rather than *sarkes*). It is nevertheless clear that some contemporaries likewise interpreted the Evagrian position on the sacraments; see ibid. 63–66, 110–11, 116, 156–57; incl. *Apophthegmata Patrum (Alphabetical)*, Daniel 7 [PG 65, 156D–160A].

25. E.g., Konstantinovksy (2009) 8.

26. See, e.g., Evagrius Ponticus, *The Gnostic* 14; *The Monk* 100. For the theme of the inner liturgy cf. Evagrius Ponticus, *Gnostic Centuries* 5.53, 84.

were various Christian intellectuals who devoted far greater attention to the eucharist and to the interpretation of its rites—Ambrose of Milan, Theodore of Mopsuestia, and Cyril of Jerusalem, to name but three. In the precise same period that the great ascetic pioneers developed their complex, introspective anthropologies, so too, therefore, was there a veritable explosion of contemplation on the nature of the eucharist, the significance of its rite, and its spiritual effect on the communicant.[27] Within that tradition—which admits a remarkable degree of variation in terms of emphasis—one sometimes encounters a concern to elevate the need for moral pureness when receiving the sacrament (in particular in the homilies of John Chrysostom); but there was nevertheless little interest in accommodating the complex spiritual anthropologies developed in monastic circles. In turn, developed contemplation on the eucharistic rite remained the preserve of the episcopate.

Throughout the period before Chalcedon, therefore—and thus coterminous with the continued separation of ecclesial and monastic institutions—these two great Christian discourses remained quite distinct. The effects of that continued intellectual separation can indeed be measured further, for in the hagiographies of the same period that describe anchorites or semianchorites, the ritual structures of the Church, and in particular the eucharist, are to a large extent absent. As noted above, Athanasius's *Life of Antony* has been seen as the classic expression of the episcopal vision for proper ascetic practice: withdrawn from the world, self-sufficient, and obedient to episcopal power.[28] But as various scholars have observed, the same *Life* is also notable for its hero's total absence from the demands of the sacramental life.[29] There were of course practical difficulties for those who engaged in more singular or more withdrawn forms of asceticism in ensuring regular access to the eucharist, so that its absence might be explained in an actual indifference to communion.[30] But one must also nevertheless wonder if the emphasis upon monastic extrication from urban contexts within clerical hagiographies such as the *Life* had not also encouraged a relative ideological indifference to the regular submission of ascetics to the eucharist, which may also have demanded a regular infringement of those ascetics within the episcopal sphere.[31]

As we might expect, then, those monastic hagiographies that describe more settled or more concentrated communities are in general full of casual references

---

27. See, e.g., Mazza (1989).
28. See above, n. 7.
29. See, e.g., Dekkers (1957) esp. 33–41; Guillaumont (1989) 83f.; Callam (1996) 115.
30. See, e.g., the famous comment of John Chrysostom, *Homilies on the Letter to the Hebrews* 17.4 [PG 63, 131–32]: *ekeinoi gar [en tēi erēmōi] hapax tou eniautou metechousi, pollakis de kai dia duo etōn.*
31. For the combination of an emphasis upon episcopal subordination with indifference to the sacramental submission of ascetics see also, e.g., Theodoret's *Religious History*, with Canivet (1977) 231f.; also Guillaumont (1989) 88; Urbainczyk (2002) 115–29; Binggeli (2009) 423f.

to their ascetics' attendance of the regular service.[32] But here again we encounter a striking indifference to the spiritual effects of both the eucharist and its rites, so that in comparison to the vast amount of intellectual effort expended on material concerning the cultivation of the virtues and of mystical contemplation, speculation on the power of the eucharist is, in these texts, a marginal concern. Thus, for example, in Palladius's *Lausiac History*—a work that derives from the circle of Evagrius—we discover a specific condemnation of antisacramental attitudes in two consecutive tales in which the protagonists' descent into arrogance reaches its apogee with their refusal to attend communion and their dismissal of the eucharist as nothing.[33] But the point of these stories seems not to be an emphasis upon the spiritual benefits to be conferred through the eucharist but rather a warning against spiritual arrogance, of which absence from the communal celebration is a classic manifestation.[34] Here, then, we cannot explain indifference to the eucharist as a simple reflection of its actual absence from the ascetic life in practice (as we might for anchorites). Rather, it must reflect the same intellectual stance that we have witnessed within the earliest and most prominent ascetic theoreticians: an acknowledgment that the eucharist exists and cannot be dispensed with, but a simultaneous failure, nevertheless, to integrate regular communion within the spiritual vision.

From a later perspective, when the eucharist begins to infringe upon hagiographic narratives more and more, one text nevertheless stands out: the late fourth-century *History of the Monks in Egypt*. Once again we discover a sanction to regular eucharistic participation,[35] but here that same insistence is more balanced: on one side, with an emphasis on the spiritual benefits accrued through the host itself; and on the other, with an emphasis on the need for moral virtue on the part of the participant. Thus one tale, for example, refers to "a custom among the great [ascetics] not to provide food to the flesh before giving spiritual food [*hē pneumatikē trophē*] to the soul: that is, the communion of Christ [*hē tou Christou koinōnia*]";[36] while in another an eminent ascetic avers that "Monks, if possible, must each day partake of the mysteries of Christ [*tōn mustēriōn tou Christou koinōnein*]. For he who removes himself from the mysteries removes himself from

---

32. See, e.g., on the Pachomians, *Bohairic Life of Pachomius* 25; *First Greek Life of Pachomius* 27; *Rules of Saint Pachomius* 15; *Regulations of Horsiesius* 14. On the eucharist in Pachomius's monasteries see Guillaumont (1989) 86.

33. See Palladius, *Lausiac History* 26.1, 27.2. See also Taft (2003) 6f., and cf. *Lausiac History* 59, where separation from communion is presented as a virtue.

34. For the celebration of Evagrius and other Origenist monks within Palladius's original *Lausiac History*, and the later attempt to remove or temper it, see Gabriel Bunge's introduction in Bunge and Vogüé (1994) 20–27.

35. See, e.g., *History of the Monks in Egypt* 25.2 [Festugière 134].

36. *History of the Monks in Egypt* 2.8 [Festugière 37].

God. But he who does this frequently receives the Savior frequently. For the voice of the Savior proclaims, 'He who eats my flesh and drinks my blood remains in me, and I in him' [Joh. 6:56]. It is therefore profitable for monks constantly to remember the Savior's passion and always to be worthy to receive the heavenly mysteries [*pros tēn tōn ouraniōn mustēriōn hupodochēn*], since thus we also receive forgiveness from sin."[37]

Here, therefore, not only is the eucharist emphatically present, and its spiritual efficacy emphatically acknowledged, but its spiritual effect is also made dependent upon the moral attainment of the participant. Rather than a prevailing indifference to eucharistic communion, therefore, the *History of the Monks in Egypt*—as well as the associated vignettes within the *Lausiac History*—suggests a not insignificant debate on the spiritual status of eucharistic communion amid monastic communities, mirroring the theoreticians' attempts to counter the more extreme antisacramentalist tendencies of (at least some of) their contemporaries.[38] Although there is no developed attempt, in this earlier period, to integrate the dominant focus upon ascetic virtue and contemplation within a wider ecclesial framework, the same texts nevertheless manifest evident anxieties over ascetics' relation to the eucharist, anxieties that subsequent generations were to explore in far greater depth.

## CYRIL OF SCYTHOPOLIS AND THE SECOND ORIGENIST CRISIS

From around the Council of Chalcedon in 451, the relative hagiographic indifference to the eucharist and its rites begins to change. In part, this change must be considered as the product of real shifts on the ground: that is, on the one hand, the extension of the aforementioned phenomenon of monastic ordination, which blurred the lines between the monastic and clerical vocations;[39] and, on the other, the increasing sacramentalization and liturgification of monastic practice itself, as that practice came to be reframed within an ever-growing set of prescribed rituals.[40] In certain cases, therefore, we witness a simple continuation of the earlier inclusion within some hagiographies of casual references to monks' attendance of the eucharistic rite; but in others, one detects a definite and deliberate emphasis upon those same rituals as a prerequisite of legitimate asceticism: that is, nothing

---

37. *History of the Monks in Egypt* 8.56–57 [Festugière 68f.]. Cf. *History of the Monks in Egypt* 16 (in which the priest Eulogius insists on the purification of thoughts before receiving communion).

38. Cf. Golitzin (1994) 321.

39. On the phenomenon see Sterk (2004); Escolan (1999) 267–311.

40. For this sacramentalization and liturgification of monastic practice in this period (evidenced in a range of texts) see Patrich (1995) 229–53; and for evidence of resistance to the process see, e.g., Escolan (1999) 294–306; Frøyshov (2000).

less than an attempt to uphold a new model of monasticism itself. What we are interested in here, therefore, is not the disinterment of actual monastic practice from the scattered references contained within hagiographies so much as the delineation of the ideological model of that practice that such hagiographies seek to represent.

Post-Chalcedonian commentators offered various such models, but all shared a fundamental concern with the competing imperatives of individual and institutional ascetic endeavor. At stake was the status of the contemplative tradition represented in the corpora of Evagrius and of Pseudo-Macarius, and here we will examine two responses to it—clerical and sacramentalized on the one hand; monastic and desacramentalized on the other. The latter is contained within the collected *Lives* of the sixth-century Palestinian hagiographer Cyril of Scythopolis, in which we encounter an ascetic quite different from those exemplified in the texts of the pioneering generations, one in whom individual endeavor is subordinated to the demands of a wider institutional framework—monastic, ecclesial, and imperial. Where the most prominent monastic figures of the pre-Chalcedonian generation often found themselves in conflict with the secular authorities, Cyril's conception of the ascetic's place within the world forms a notable complement to that contained within the legislation of the emperor Justinian. Bernard Flusin has demonstrated how the stated doctrine of Cyril's heroes retrojects and repeats verbatim the official doctrinal position of the Justinianic state;[41] but these parallels in fact extend even further, to their respective political philosophies of the ascetic life.[42] Justinian's attitude to monasticism is summed up in his *Novel* 133 (published in 539), in which he proclaims the proper function of monasticism as the petitioning of God for the health of the state.[43] It is thus of great interest to note an anecdote contained within Cyril's *Life of Sabas* in which the eponymous hero encounters Justinian himself and in that encounter embodies the monastic ideal expressed within the emperor's *Novels*. The narrative describes how Sabas once traveled to Constantinople on behalf of the patriarch in order to beg for a remission of taxes following a Samaritan revolt. "While our God-protected emperor was engaged in these matters with Tribonian the quaestor in the place called Magnaura," Cyril reports, "the blessed Sabas separated himself off a little and began to recite to himself the Davidic psalms, completing the divine office of the third hour. One of his

---

41. See esp. Cyril of Scythopolis, *Life of Euthymius* 26–27 [Schwartz 39–45]; with Flusin (1983) 73–76; also Hombergen (2001) 177–206.

42. For the parallels between Justinian's legislation and the hagiographies of Cyril of Scythopolis I am much indebted to Daniel Neary's unpublished Oxford undergraduate thesis, "Cyril of Scythopolis and the Image of Justinianic Orthopraxy" (2010). For the same project, but with reference to the *Letters* of Barsanuphius and John, see Lesieur (2011).

43. Justinian, *Novels* 133.5 [Schoell and Kroll 673f.].

disciples—called Jeremiah, a deacon of the Great Laura—approached him and said, 'Honorable Father, when the emperor is showing such enthusiasm in fulfilling your requests, why do you yourself stand apart?' And the elder said to him, 'Those men, my child, do their work; let us also do ours [*ekeinoi, teknon, to idion poiousin; poiēsōmen kai hēmeis to hēmeteron*].'"[44]

Through his various *Novels* Justinian provided a secular complement to the canonical legislation on monasticism at Chalcedon, insisting too on the subordination of ascetics to bishops, and on the same principles of proper ascetic practice: in particular, social withdrawal and *stabilitas loci*.[45] Here, however, there is a new emphasis, for while Chalcedon failed to discriminate between ascetic types, in the Justinianic *Novels* it is the communal life that is regarded as the norm and duly legislated for.[46] Cyril too repeats this emphasis on coenobial training as the sine qua non of more advanced ascetic endeavor. Indeed, as Flusin has shown, throughout his various *Lives* he develops an implicit but consistent cursus honorum of the ascetic life, which complements that envisioned within the Justinianic *Novels:* first, a prolonged period of communal discipline and submission within a coenobium, then progression to a semianchoritic laura; and then, having proved one's ascetic credentials, progression again to the full anchoritic life.[47] There is, therefore, a significant recontextualization of the process of ascetic legitimization set out, for example, in the *Life of Antony:* less of a progressive withdrawal from the world, and more of a progressive rise through successive monastic institutions. Miracles within the collection serve a similar, group-oriented purpose—still associated with an individual saint, but focused on the institution and sanctioned through that same saint's progression within a hierarchical structure from which he receives sanctification, and which he in turn sanctifies.[48] Flusin has thus spoken of "une sainteté institutionnelle" in Cyril's hagiographies, a pervasive celebration of the holiness not of the ascetic as the perfect human but rather of the monastic institution as the perfect social group.[49]

---

44. Cyril of Scythopolis, *Life of Sabas* 73 [Schwartz 178]. For the encounter with Justinian see also Flusin (1983) 206–8; Hombergen (2001) 342 nn. 409, 410. See also the reported encounters with Anastasius and the empress Theodora at *Life of Sabas* 51f. [Schwartz 141–44], 71 [Schwartz 173f.].

45. See esp. Justinian, *Novels* 5, 123, and 133, but also 7.11, 22.5, 67.1, 76.1, 79, 131.7. On late-antique legislation on the monastic life see Frazee (1982); also Sterk (2004) 163–77.

46. See, e.g., Justinian, *Novels* 5.3 [Schoell and Kroll 31f.], 123.36 [Schoell and Kroll 619], 133.1 [Schoell and Kroll 667].

47. Flusin (1983) 137–54. See esp. Cyril's brief description at *Life of Euthymius* 41 [Schwartz 61] of the monk Domitian, who "earned a reputation in the coenobium, demonstrated manliness in the laura, and became eminent in the deserts." For this shift from anchoritic to coenobitic in Palestinian monasticism see also Bitton-Ashkelony and Kofsky (2000); Lesieur (2011) esp. 6–25.

48. Flusin (1983) 182–200.

49. See esp. ibid. 146f.; 153f.; also Hombergen (2001) 338–49, esp. 342f.

Within this recontextualization of the monastic life—that is, in its shift from an individual to a collective emphasis—we also encounter an apparent condemnation of the traditions of monastic contemplation enshrined within the corpus of Evagrius. The conclusion to his *Life of Sabas* records how, after its hero's death in 532, an Origenist faction among the monks of the Judean desert succeeded in sowing their doctrine among several of the leading monasteries, in securing significant episcopal appointments, and even in gaining the emperor's ear at court. It then describes how the tide in Constantinople turned against that same faction, and how the emperor and patriarch then issued a condemnation of Origen's doctrines. According to the *Life*, there then followed a period of resurgence before the rupturing of the movement when a doctrinal disagreement emerged between protoktists (who, we must assume, upheld the doctrine that Christ's soul preexisted those of other beings) and isochrists (who, we must again assume, thought that the posthumous soul might become equivalent to Christ). The *Life of Sabas* reports that, following disturbances within the capital, Justinian once again turned against his former favorites, so that Origen—as also, with him, the teaching of Evagrius and Didymus the Blind on preexistence (*prouparxis*) and universal restoration (*apokatastasis*)—was again condemned at the Fifth Ecumenical Council, in 553.[50]

We are fortunate that both sets of anathemas on Origen alleged in the *Life of Sabas* survive. The first set of nine, produced in 543, is drawn from Origen's own writings and is aimed, for the most part, at classic Origenist errors—the preexistence of the soul and universal salvation, for example.[51] The anathemas of 553, however, are of a different order.[52] Here again standard Origenist doctrines such as preexistence and *apokatastasis* are condemned; but alongside these ideas we also encounter various others not included in the condemnations of the previous decade—for example, the restoration of a primitive and undifferentiated *henad*.[53] Above all, however, there is a far more developed Christological dimension to the anathemas, including the condemnation of isochristism: the doctrine that all rational beings will become identical to Christ (attributed to the Origenists within the *Life of Sabas*).[54] In a classic book, André Guillaumont demonstrated that the same Christological position in fact derives not from Origen but rather from the

---

50. See Cyril of Scythopolis, *Life of Sabas* 83–90 [Schwartz 187–200]; cf. also idem, *Life of Cyriacus* 11–14 [Schwartz 229–31]. For the obscure fifth-century background to the apparent resurgence of Origenism in Palestine, see Perrone (2001) 246–49.

51. For the text see Justinian, *Edict against Origenism* [Schwartz 213f.]. For analysis see Guillaumont (1962) 140–43; Louth (2003) 1173f. It draws upon Origen's *Peri Archōn;* see Hombergen (2001) 23 n. 6.

52. For the text see *Fifteen Canons against Origen* [Straub 248f.]. Cf. Diekamp (1899) 90–96 (left col.).

53. *Fifteen Canons against Origen* 2 [Straub 248].

54. See *Fifteen Canons against Origen* 6–9, 12–13 [Straub 248f.]; for discussion Guillaumont (1962) 147–51. Cf. also Evagrius Scholasticus, *Ecclesiastical History* 4.38.

*Kephalaia Gnostica* of Evagrius, with which the anathemas share various doctrinal and literal correspondences.[55] Within a decade of 543, therefore, the target of anti-Origenist polemic had undergone a notable transformation—from a somewhat clichéd and anachronistic condemnation of the master himself to a more pointed and nuanced condemnation of his most prominent late-antique heir and his interpreters.

In a letter of Justinian that prompted the fifteen anathemas of 553, he cited the opinions of "certain monks at Jerusalem" as inspiring his opposition.[56] Were the Origenist monks of Cyril's hagiographies, therefore, adherents of the Christological speculations of Evagrius? There can be little doubt that his cosmological and eschatological speculations were in the air in Palestine. Thus in the Justinianic correspondence of the Gazan hermits Barsanuphius and John, we find a series of letters devoted to the controversial doctrines contained within Origenist writings, and in particular the *Kephalaia Gnostica* of Evagrius. A monk asks the pair about the Origenist doctrines of preexistence and universal salvation—making specific reference to the *Kephalaia* of Evagrius—and when both elders condemn those doctrines, he asks whether it is therefore harmful to read Evagrius's works. In his response John draws a distinction between the more speculative and more useful aspects of the Evagrian corpus: "Do not receive such doctrines. But nevertheless, if you wish, read in him what is beneficial to the soul."[57] The same monk then asks, "So how is it that some of the present fathers accept these [doctrines], and we hold them to be good monks and give them our attention?" and John responds again with specific reference to the *Kephalaia*, confessing that "certain brothers accept these things as gnostics [*hōs gnōsitkoi*]" but warning his interlocutor to avoid them.[58]

Were the Origenists of Cyril's hagiographies also adherents of Evagrius's *Kephalaia*? He does not mention Evagrius himself, and his exposition on the beliefs of the Origenists is a simple recapitulation of the anathemas of 553 (or their source). But an alternative route into the question is provided through his description of one Leontius of Byzantium as a leader of the Origenist faction within Palestine.[59]

---

55. Guillaumont (1962) 151–59; also idem (1961b). Cf., however, Perczel (2001) 262–65, arguing that the anathemata represent a later elaboration of Evagrius's position. See also Bunge (1989) 89f.; Louth (2003) 1168.

56. See Justinian, *Letter to the Synod on Origen* [*PG* 86, 991A]; cf. Diekamp (1899) 90–97 (right col.). On the precise origins of the anti-Origenist anathemata see also Richard (1970) 243–48; Flusin (1983) 83; Perczel (2001).

57. Barsanuphius and John, *Questions and Answers* 600–602 [Neyt and Angelis-Noah 812].

58. Barsanuphius and John, *Questions and Answers* 603 [Neyt and Angelis-Noah 814]. For analysis of these letters see Guillaumont (1962) 124–27; Perrone (2001) 251–55; Hombergen (2001) 222f., 284–86; idem (2004).

59. See Cyril of Scythopolis, *Life of Sabas* (e.g.) 72 [Schwartz 174–76], 84 [Schwartz 189f.]; with Hombergen (2001) 133–38.

This same person has been identified with another contemporaneous Leontius, the author of at least three extant tracts: *Against the Nestorians and Eutychians, Thirty Chapters against Severus*, and *Solution to the Arguments of the Severans*.[60] Critics remain divided as to the potential Origenist content of those same treatises: some (in particular David Evans) have suggested that Leontius's Christological pronouncements in effect recapitulate but disguise those of Evagrius;[61] whereas others (in particular Brian Daley) have defended Leontius as nothing more than a staunch proponent of the neo-Chalcedonian position, suggesting that the Origenist label applied to Leontius and his allies within Cyril's hagiographies should be appreciated not as an accurate description of the group's theological inclinations but rather as indicative of its adherence to the spirit of intellectual freedom enshrined within the Origenist tradition.[62]

In a more recent contribution, however, Daniel Hombergen has opened up a new perspective on the crisis, one less dogmatic than spiritual. Eschewing (with others) the attempt to locate the Christological or cosmological fingerprints of Origen within Leontius's thought, Hombergen points to a passage in *Against the Nestorians and Eutychians* in which Leontius cites a spiritual axiom taken from none other than Evagrius in the *Kephalaia Gnostica* and shows that the citation is embedded in a section of text that recapitulates the vision of the spiritual life as contained within the Evagrian corpus.[63] For Hombergen, therefore, Leontius's Origenism should be considered an adherence not to the more controversial and speculative Evagrian doctrines concerning Christ but rather to the contemplative tradition represented, above all, in Evagrius's writings.

In support of his spiritual reading of the crisis, Hombergen indeed demonstrates that Cyril effects a subtle *damnatio memoriae* both of Evagrius and of the contemplative ideas of which he was the champion. On the one hand, for example, he puts into the mouths of his heroes pronouncements against Origen that in fact derive from or recapitulate the later anti-Origenist anathemas of 553,[64] and he

---

60. See CPG 6813–15. For the identification of the two see, e.g., Richard (1947) 32f.; Evans (1970) 147–85; Hombergen (2001) 147–55.

61. See, e.g., Richard (1947); Evans (1970), (1980); Gray (1979) 90–103. The work of Perczel, e.g., (2000b), we should note, sides with Evans.

62. Daley (1976) esp. 366 (following Guillaumont [1962] 161f.), Daley (1995); also Lynch (1975). The *Lives* indeed presents the Origenists as the "more educated" (*logiōteroi*) and, in one place, as considering the classic Origenist doctrines of the soul's preexistence and of *apokatastasis* as "indifferent and harmless" (*mesa kai akinduna*); see Cyril of Scythopolis, *Life of Sabas* 88 [Schwartz 188]; *Life of Cyriacus* 12 [Schwartz 229]; with Hombergen (2001) 231–52.

63. See Leontius of Byzantium, *Against the Nestorians and Eutychians* [*PG* 86:1, 1285A-B].

64. See esp. Cyril of Scythopolis, *Life of Cyriacus* 11–14 [Schwartz 229–31]. For speculation on the origin of Cyril's information see Guillaumont (1962) 150f.; Flusin (1983) 81–83; Hombergen (2001) 255–87. Cf. also George Hieromonachus, *On Heresies* 9, with Richard (1947) esp. 243–48.

claims that Origen's and Evagrius's teachings were the main issue at the Fifth Ecumenical Council, which was in fact devoted to the Three Chapters.[65] But on the other hand, he also eschews an Evagrian influence within his hagiographies despite, as Flusin has demonstrated, the pervasive influence of previous monastic literature.[66] Hombergen, therefore, reinterprets the Origenist crisis as one between a more intellectualizing group—that is, those who were accepting of, selective within, or indifferent to, the spiritual doctrines of Evagrius—and a more fundamentalist group, those who repudiated the same doctrines and with them the tradition of individualistic monastic contemplation. Within that latter group is of course the hagiographer Cyril, whose *Lives* set out a radical new vision of the ascetic life, for the most part indifferent to the interior life and focused instead upon the institution. Hombergen thus places at the root of the Origenist crisis "a clash of two competitive ideals of the spiritual life: a somewhat collectivist current, focusing particularly on external aspects, and a more individualist current, concentrating primarily on the development of the interior life."[67]

This of course assumes that the Origenist label used in a range of texts was in essence a phantom, devoid of doctrinal meaning and disingenuous in intent. But as István Perczel has insisted in a string of recent publications, it is difficult to suppose that the widespread anxieties and anathemas expressed toward Evagrian (or post-Evagrian) dogma did not have some basis in an actual Evagrian circle.[68] At the same time, however, we need not assume that different observers applied the same criteria as to what constituted Origenism or that those whom contemporaries identified as Origenists did not themselves admit a vast degree of variation in their reception, reappropriation, or refusal of various Evagrian doctrines. However we wish to regard the real inspiration behind Leontius's doctrine, therefore, it is perhaps best to assume that the label "Origenist" might be applied to a wide of range of individuals who might or might not recognize that same label: from Evagrianists proper—that is, those who championed the same protological, Christological, and eschatological positions alleged and evidenced within a range of contemporaneous literature—to intellectual liberals with an interest in, or indifference to, the same theologian's dogmatic vision.

---

65. Although Origen was condemned at the council, the aforementioned fifteen anathemas were produced and ratified before it; see Diekamp (1899) 131–32, 137; Guillaumont (1962) 133–40; Hombergen (2001) 287–328.

66. See Flusin (1983) 41–86. The apparent exception is at Cyril of Scythopolis, *Life of Sabas* 3 [Schwartz 88], echoing Evagrius Ponticus, *On the Eight Evil Spirits* [PG 79, 1145A], but as Hombergen (2001) 225f. indicates, substituting the Evagrian *praktikē* for *agathoergia*.

67. Hombergen (2001) 368. For a similar suggestion see Perrone (2001) 246, 256–58. Cf. the archaeological comparison of Sabas's Great Laura with the New Laura in Hirschfeld (2001) 345.

68. See esp. Perczel (2006–7) 52–57.

Hombergen's fundamental insight on the spiritual dimension to the crisis must nevertheless be allowed to stand. That such tensions informed (though they did not determine) the crisis is indeed borne out in various texts associated with it. As we shall see, however, those tensions were more complex than a simple dichotomization of individualizing or Origenist versus institutionalizing or anti-Origenist can capture. For we shall discover that fundamental differences concerning conceptions of the spiritual life and its relation to wider institutional structures operated also within those groups that sought to suppress Evagrian doctrine and its spiritual inheritance. The hagiographer Cyril's response to such differences, therefore, was but one institutional response to the problem of monastic individualism. It competed, however, alongside others that shared the desire to subordinate ascetics but that nevertheless adopted a quite different approach, based less upon the integration of ascetic endeavor within the monastic institution and more upon its orientation around and subordination to the sacraments of the Church.

## MYSTICS AND LITURGISTS

As we have seen, a notable feature of Evagrius's thought is his minimal interest in ecclesial life, and in particular in the eucharist. Were differing approaches to the eucharist also a feature of the Palestinian Origenist crisis? Cyril's hagiographies do not suggest so, although it is nevertheless notable that all his subjects, at the pinnacle of their coenobitic careers, are ordained as priests, emphasizing their integration within a wider ecclesial context outside the hagiographic desert.[69] In certain cases, this leads to some anecdote concerning the eucharist: the *Life* of the Palestinian ascetic pioneer Euthymius, for example, contains two consecutive anecdotes in which he is, as celebrating priest, said to inspire or experience miraculous visions, and the latter of the two develops into a sermonette on the need for a pure heart while approaching the eucharist.[70] In terms of a developed sacramental (though not institutional) emphasis, however, we have progressed little from the comparable emphases contained within the *History of the Monks in Egypt*.

It is nevertheless possible that there was indeed a eucharistic dimension to the intellectual tensions that informed the Origenist crisis. In that aforementioned

---

69. In general Cyril's hagiographies are replete with references to monastic ordination, but for the specific ordination of his protagonists, all at the same stage of their careers, see Cyril of Scythopolis, *Life of Euthymius* 5 [Schwartz 13]; *Life of Sabas* 19 [Schwartz 103f.]; *Life of John the Hesychast* 3 [Schwartz 202]; *Life of Cyriacus* 7 [Schwartz 226]; *Life of Theodosius* 1 [Schwartz 236]; *Life of Theognius* [Schwartz 242]; *Life of Abraham* 2 [Schwartz 244]. On ordination within the text see Flusin (1983) 148–53; Sterk (2004) 203–6.

70. Cyril of Scythopolis, *Life of Euthymius* 28–29 [Schwartz 45–47]. For scattered reference to Cyril's monks taking the eucharist, both public and private, see Patrich (1995) 245–52.

series of letters on Origenism contained with the *Questions and Answers* of Barsanuphius and John, the elders' interlocutor makes a striking statement:[71]

> For indeed, we find even in the books of the elders that there was a certain great elder, and he said out of simplicity [*idiōteia*] that the bread of which we partake is by nature not the body of Christ but its antitype [*antitupon*]. And if he had not prayed to God on this matter, he would not have known the truth.

The statement might reference a number of spiritual tales in which monks appear to denigrate the real presence in the eucharist (and which indeed appear, in their original context, to respond to the perceived teaching of Evagrius).[72] But embedded here, amid a series of issues connected with Justinianic Origenism, one must also wonder whether this defense of the real presence does not recapitulate, in a new context, concerns over a continued Origenist deviation from proper eucharistic doctrine.

That the eucharistic minimalism we have identified within the corpora of Evagrius and Pseudo-Macarius continued to dominate the works of ascetic theoreticians is clear.[73] But one such theoretician we can also associate both with Palestine and with the Origenist crisis. According to a letter of Philoxenus of Mabbug, in the same period (ca. 510) there entered within the monastic circles of Jerusalem one Stephen bar Sudaili, a controversial ascetic who the later *Chronicle* of Michael the Syrian claims came to Palestine after a meeting with Philoxenus had resulted in a suspicion of heresy.[74] The doctrine that Philoxenus attributes to Stephen in the same letter is Origenist in inspiration: in particular, he presents him as an adherent both of *apokatastasis*—that is, the belief that all beings will, in the end, return to a primordial union with divine nature—and, in line with that, of a two-stage *eschaton*, a period of punishment or reward before the final, universal consummation. Philoxenus himself dismisses those notions, pointing out that both undermine all efforts at holiness on earth (including, we should note, both asceticism and participation in the eucharist);[75] but in his critique of Stephen's notion of a double consummation, he also refers to the latter's dependence on an Evagrian notion of motion (*kinēsis*).[76] As Irénée Hausherr long ago observed, the predominant

---

71. Barsanuphius and John, *Questions and Answers* 605 [Neyt and Angelis-Noah 824–26].
72. See above n. 24.
73. For the minimalist approach to the ecclesial sacraments in post-Evagrian ascetic theorists see, e.g., the comments of Plested (2004) 111, 114f., 197f.
74. Philoxenus of Mabbug, *Letter to Abraham and Orestes* [ed. and trans. Frothingham 28f., 44–46]; and Michael the Syrian, *Chronicle* 9.30. On Stephen see also Jacob of Serug, *Letter to Stephen bar Sudaili*. For analysis see esp. now Pinggéra (2002) 7–22; also Frothingham (1886); Hausherr (1933); Guillaumont (1961a); Widengren (1961). On the text of the letter see also Jansma (1974).
75. Philoxenus of Mabbug, *Letter to Abraham and Orestes* [ed. and trans. Frothingham 28–31].
76. Philoxenus of Mabbug, *Letter to Abraham and Orestes* [ed. and trans. Frothingham 36–37].

influence on Stephen's doctrine, as Philoxenus presents it, therefore appears to be not Origen but his spiritual heir Evagrius.[77] Philoxenus, we should note, was himself an enthusiast for Evagrius,[78] but used a Syriac version of the *Kephalaia Gnostica* that had removed or sanitized the same cosmological and eschatological doctrines of which he disapproved in Stephen.[79]

Philoxenus's Stephen has long been identified as the author of an extant ascetic tract entitled *The Book of the Holy Hierotheos*.[80] Therein the author indeed sets out the doctrines that Philoxenus refutes: he describes the fall of all beings from a primordial union with God; the ascent of the mind toward God, and its identification with Christ; its subsequent descent into hell, there to pronounce upon the souls of sinners; and its final consummation in the original Essence, in which all distinctions are dissolved and even the damned return to union.[81] The content of the treatise, therefore, confirms on the one hand both Stephen's authorship and the substance of Philoxenus's critique but on the other, as several scholars have demonstrated, the pervasive influence of Evagrian thought upon his theological scheme (including, we should note, the doctrine that resurrected souls will become Christ).[82] It is little surprise, then, that some have attributed to Stephen an obscure but nevertheless sure role in the origins of the Origenist crisis, the opening salvos of which occurred coterminous with his alleged arrival in Jerusalem.[83]

For our purposes, however, perhaps the most intriguing aspect of Stephen's work is his attitude to the eucharist. In describing the spiritual ascent of the soul toward God he writes:[84]

> Then the mind enters into the mystic and glorious holy of holies not made with hands, that it may accomplish mystically and divinely the glorious and holy mystery

---

77. See Hausherr (1933) 186f.; also Guillaumont (1961a) 1483. For the Origenist influence see Marsh (1927) 247f.; also Widengren (1961) 161–68, distinguishing the cosmological influence of Origen and the anthropological influence of Evagrius.

78. See, e.g., Harb (1969).

79. Watt (1980), *contra* Guillaumont (1962) 207–13, 231–58. For Philoxenus's sanitized Evagrianism see also Halleux (1963), e.g., 423–28; Daley (1995) 629f. For his eucharistic emphasis see Michelson (2008). For the sanitization of Evagrius in Syriac see also Guillaumont (1962) 259–90, on the Evagrian commentary of Babai the Great.

80. For the identity see Frothingham (1886) 49–55, 63–68; Marsh (1927) 222–32; and now Pinggéra (2002) 7–26.

81. For a précis of the contents see Frothingham (1886) 91–111; Marsh (1927) 204–10.

82. For this Evagrian influence on the *Book of the Holy Hierotheos* see esp. Hausherr (1933) 187–92; Pinggéra (2002) 70–73; also Guillaumont (1962) 318–23; Daley (1995) 630.

83. For the date of Stephen's arrival, ca. 509–12, see Frothingham (1886) 57–59; for Cyril's date for the outbreak of the crisis, in 514, see Diekamp (1899) 17. For the coincidence see Guillaumont (1962) 305; Hombergen (2001) 360–65.

84. Stephen bar Sudaili, *Book of the Holy Hierotheos* 3.7 [ed. and trans. Marsh 72*–74*, 78–81]. Cf. Arthur (2008) 133f. on this "spiritual and allegorical" interpretation of the eucharist.

of the holy and hallowing sacrament; which is a kind of simple and unlimited power which is extended so as to include divinely the essences that are united with it: and those glorious angels display a kind of yearning of desire to receive the eucharist and to be made partakers in the mystery thereof; and [the mind] approaches divinely the spiritual altar; and sacrifices itself, holily and divinely, in most wonderful and ineffable mystery, and is raised again, divinely and holily, in the secret of holy mystery.... Know, O my son, that the material and bodily bread which is set upon the material altar is a kind of perceptible sign—and, to tell the truth, a small and unworthy shadow—of that glorious bread which is above the heavens; and the cup of mixture also that is in our world: it too, is (only) a material sign of that glorious and holy drink of which the mind is accounted worthy in the place that is above.... A material and bodily sacrament, then, is right for those who walk according to the body; and when the question is asked, whether those minds which have been accounted worthy to receive and to give the spiritual sacrament still need the bodily sacrament, I, for my own part, would say that those who have been initiated by water have yet to be made perfect and those who are in the body must also receive bodily nourishment.

Once again, therefore, we encounter that same ambiguous attitude to the eucharist that we have seen within the writings both of Evagrius and of Pseudo-Macarius. Stephen—much like Pseudo-Macarius—is aware of potential accusations of anti-sacramentalism and is thus careful to acknowledge the place of the material eucharist within the general Christian life; but at the same time it is clear that he regards that eucharist as a mere imitation of a far more glorious and efficacious spiritual equivalent, of which the mind partakes in contemplation.

Stephen's text emerged from a context in which other contemporaries had formed a quite different perspective both on the spiritual life and on the eucharist. The *Book of the Holy Hierotheos* has often been noted for certain correspondences that it shares with the corpus of another contemporary author, the neo-Platonic theologian writing under the pseudonym of the first-century Christian convert Dionysius the Areopagite. As with the *Hierotheos* of Stephen, the writings of Pseudo-Dionysius first emerged in anti-Chalcedonian circles in the early sixth century[85]—a provenance that has inspired numerous attempts to identify him with prominent miaphysite theologians of the period[86]—and as with the *Hierotheos* again, those writings have been alleged to contain the Origenist protological and eschatological positions condemned in Justinian's fifteen anathemas.[87] (We shall

---

85. For discussion of these early references see Rorem and Lamoreaux (1998) 11–18. Arthur (2008) 104–9. Despite his apparent miaphysite origins, however, Ps.-Dionysius was quickly adopted by both anti-Chalcedonians and Chalcedonians; see Rorem and Lamoreaux (1998) 18–22.

86. For various attempts to identify him see, e.g., U. Riedinger (1956: Peter the Fuller); Esbroeck (1993: Peter the Iberian); Arthur (2008) 184–87 (Sergius of Reshʿaina). See also Lourié (2010).

87. See esp. Perczel (2001) 265–82; also idem (1999a, b); Evans (1980) 28–34; Arthur (2008) 175–87. For a more subtle approach to the question of Ps.-Dionysius's ties to other authors connected with the

return to this accusation below.) The extent and direction of dependence between Stephen and the Areopagite is a matter of much contention.[88] Karl Pinggéra, in the most recent and most extensive salvo in discussions, has argued for a distinction between a *Grundschrift* and a *Redaktionsschicht* within Stephen's extant text, the latter extending the Evagrianism of the former but offering an explicit response to the Areopagite (and redacted, Pinggéra proposes, in Justinianic Palestine).[89] These are, then, two texts that emerge in conversation with each other, and from the precise same theological milieu.[90]

Both the similarities and differences between the *Corpus Dionysiacum* and the extant version of the *Book of the Holy Hierotheos* are perhaps best represented in their treatment of a striking shared theme: that is, their mutual conception of the ninefold arrangement of celestial beings.[91] There are two crucial and informative differences: where the *Book* imagines a hierarchical ordering that is both flexible and permeable—that is, in which beings can alter their rank in ascent—in the Areopagite's vision all such ranks are fixed and immutable;[92] and where the *Book* seems to have no terrestrial equivalent to its hierarchical ranking of the angels, and thus no terrestrial mediation between the individual and God, the Areopagite situates beneath his angelic host a further hierarchical structure corresponding to the various orders of the Church.[93]

This is not the place for a full exposition of Pseudo-Dionysius's complex vision of the Church and its rituals.[94] But for our purposes, it is important to note his striking perspective on the place of monks within the world. In his *Ecclesiastical Hierarchy*, an interpretation of the various Christian rites, the Areopagite propounds a vision of the cosmos as a strictly delineated terrestrial hierarchy, the

---

Origenist crisis see the excellent Golitzin (1994) 341–45. In light of Leontius of Byzantium's alleged Origenism we may also note his complex attitude to the Ps.-Dionysian corpus, as revealed in Evans (1980); Perczel (2000b).

88. For the suggested dependence of Stephen on Ps.-Dionysius see, e.g., Marsh (1927) 210–13, 233–46; Guillaumont (1961a) 1486f., (1962) 327 with n. 89; Golitzin (1994) 343; Hombergen (2001) 362f.; Perczel (2008 [repr. 2009]) 33, 40 n. 51. For a challenge to the extent of that dependence and the suggestion of certain interpolations of Dionysian material within Stephen's text see, e.g., Frothingham (1886) 81–83; Hausherr (1933) 192–94, 198f.; Arthur (2001).

89. Pinggéra (2002) 96–155.

90. So also Perczel (2001) 279.

91. See Stephen bar Sudaili, *Book of the Holy Hierotheos* 1.12. But cf. ibid. 1.10, with Arthur (2001) 370f.

92. See the famous exposition of hierarchy at Ps.-Dionysius, *Celestial Hierarchy* 3, with Louth (2007) 170f. on his hierarchies' mediation of illumination "not of being." Cf. idem (1989) 106.

93. See Arthur (2001) 371, (2008) 18f.

94. The literature on Ps.-Dionysius is now vast. On the *Ecclesiastical Hierarchy* see, e.g., Louth (1989) esp. 52–77; Golitzin (1994) esp. 119–232.

function of which is to communicate divine illumination through its ranks, and for each rational being within those ranks to fulfill its hierarchical function and therein achieve divine union. He divides those ranks into three successive orders, defined through their closeness to God: first, the sacraments themselves; then those who initiate others in them; and then those who are initiated.[95] He divides each of these ranks into three further divisions: the sacramental, into baptism, eucharist, and oil; the clerical, into deacons, priests, and bishops; and the laical, into the uninitiated, people, and monks. These threefold divisions also correspond to a neo-Platonic triad of purification, illumination, and perfection.[96] The deacons offer purification to the uninitiated; the priests offer illumination to the people; and the bishops offer perfection to the monks.[97] On monks themselves the Areopagite comments:[98]

> However, the most exalted rank of all those being initiated [*tōn teloumenōn*] is the sacred order of monks [*hē tōn monachōn diakosmēsis*], which has been completely purified by its full power and total purity of its own operations, and inasmuch as contemplation of the sacred order [*hierourgia*] is permissible to it, it has entered into intellectual contemplation and communion [*theōria kai koinōnia*]. It is entrusted to the perfecting powers of the bishops [*hierarchai*] and through their divine illuminations and hierarchical traditions is instructed in the sacred works [*hierourgiai*] of the sacred sacraments that it has contemplated, and led, as much as it can be [*analogōs*], to the complete perfection of the sacred knowledge of them.

Ascetics, therefore, are regarded as exalted members of the congregation, but their structural and spiritual dependence upon bishops is emphatic.

For Pseudo-Dionysius, the hierarchical ordering of ecclesiastical structures has a strict soteriological function that is extinguished if subverted. This means, for example, that monks cannot exploit alternative paths to the perfection offered through the bishops or appropriate the functions of those clerical ranks above them. Instructive in this regard are the Areopagite's *Letters*, a series of dramatic mise-en-scènes that provide examples of the hierarchical principles enshrined within the wider corpus.[99] Thus in *Letters* 8, "To the Monk Demophilus," he responds to an ascetic who has presumed to dismiss a priest who forgave a penitent sinner and then storm into the sanctuary and there save the eucharist from

---

95. See esp. Ps.-Dionysius, *Ecclesiastical Hierarchy* 5.1 [Heil 104].
96. See Ps.-Dionysius, *Ecclesiastical Hierarchy* 5.3.
97. For a description of the clerical triad see ibid. 5.4–7; for the laical triad ibid. 6.1–3.
98. Ibid. 6.1.3 [Heil 116]. For the elevation of monks above the baptized see also the account of the monastic tonsure at Ps.-Dionysius, *Ecclesiastical Hierarchy* 6.3.2–5. On the Areopagite's theology of the monastic life contained here and in *Letters* 8 see in detail Roques (1961).
99. See esp. Hathaway (1969) 64–66, 86–104, on the letter to Demophilus. Cf. also Roques (1961) 296–305.

imminent defilement. The Areopagite offers a stinging rebuke that summarizes much of his thought upon the situation of monks:[100]

> Now hear my words. It is not permissible for a priest to be reproached [*euthunesthai*] by the deacons who are above you or by the ranks of monks to which you belong, even if he appears to have acted impiously against the divine or might be convicted of having done something else forbidden. For even if there is chaos and disorder [*akosmia kai ataxia*] of the most divine things and an abandonment of the ordinances and laws, that is no reason to overthrow the God-given order on God's behalf.... Do the sacred symbols [*ta hiera sumbola*] not also shout this? For the Holy of Holies [*ta hagia tōn hagiōn*] is not completely removed from all. Instead, the order of those who initiate in sacred things [*ho tōn hieroteleston diakosmos*] is close to them, then the order of priests, and following them that of the deacons. To the ranks of monks are reserved the doors of the inner sanctuary, where they are both initiated and remain, not to guard them but rather to preserve order and their recognition of being closer to the people than the priests. From here the holy principle of ordering sacred things [*hē tōn hierōn hagia taxiarchia*] has ordained them to partake of the divine things, entrusting their distribution to others—that is, of course, those within. For those who are stood symbolically, as it were, at the divine altar see and hear the divine things that are brilliantly revealed to them, and benevolently they come out beyond the divine curtains to the obedient monks [*tois hupēkoois therapeutais*], to the sacred people, and to the orders being purified, and reveal, according to worthiness, the divine things that were well protected and undefiled, until through your invasion you forced the Holy of Holies, against its will, to be exposed.

Demophilus's intervention is, therefore, not only a disruption of proper liturgical protocol but a destructive subversion of the entire divine dispensation through which ascetics receive their perfection from the sacraments and bishops set over them.

There is here an emphatic and unambiguous elevation of the eucharist, which is the supreme sacrament, "sacrament of sacraments [*teletōn teletē*]."[101] Thus the Areopagite's introduction to his exposition on the eucharistic rite:[102]

> But I proclaim that perfection [*teleiōsis*] in participating in other hierarchical symbols is possible only from the divine-ordered and perfecting gifts [*teleiōtikōn dōreōn*: i.e., of communion]. For scarcely one of the hierarchic sacraments [*teletēs*] can be completed [*telesthēnai*] without the divine eucharist as the summation of each rite [*teloumenon*], which divinely fashions a gathering to the One of the one being initiated [*tou telesthentos*] and perfects [*telesiourgousēs*] his communion with God through the God-granted gift of the perfecting mysteries [*tōn teleiōtikōn mustēriōn*].

---

100. Ps.-Dionysius, *Letters* 8.1 [Ritter 175–77]. Cf. *Ecclesiastical Hierarchy* 5.7 [Heil 109]; *Letters* 8.2–3 [Ritter 180f.]; with Louth (1989) 65–67.
101. Ps.-Dionysius, *Ecclesiastical Hierarchy* 3 [Heil 79].
102. Ps.-Dionysius, *Ecclesiastical Hierarchy* 3 [Heil 79].

In his subsequent description of the ritual, Pseudo-Dionysius insists on the moral righteousness required of the participants: thus, for the uninitiated, the rite—being a representation of the Last Supper, and a remembrance of Judas's exclusion from it—"teaches in a pure and at the same time divine manner that the approach to the divine things that is true through habit [*kath' hexin alēthēs*] bestows upon those who approach the communion that brings assimilation with them [*tēn pros to homoion autōn koinōnian*]";[103] whereas for the initiated, "if we desire communion [*koinōnia*] with him, we must look toward his most divine life in the flesh and in assimilation [*aphomoiōsis*] to its sacred sinlessness return to the godlike and unblemished state. For thus he will give to us, in a harmonious manner, the communion that brings assimilation [*tēn pros to homoion koinōnian*]."[104] The subsequent distribution of the eucharist is then said to achieve a perfect communion among those who receive and participate in it.[105]

It must be said that Pseudo-Dionysius is by no means hostile to the ascetic tradition of contemplation—that is, he does not seem to reserve the full contemplation of God for the bishop, even if the latter is, among the Church's members, the most receptive to divine illumination.[106] Instead, the need to contemplate the hidden realities of the outward structures of the Church—and thus, while remaining fixed in one's place, to be brought into closer union with God through the fulfillment of one's role in that place, ascending "into the hierarchy rather than up it"—is an imperative placed upon all the faithful.[107] The Areopagite's departure from other representatives of that tradition is, instead, to make the ecclesial liturgy the sole point around which contemplation is oriented and to emphasize the structural (and thus spiritual) subordination of ascetics to clerics.[108] His vision is, therefore, expounded from an episcopal perspective, acknowledging monks as preeminent members of the congregation but nevertheless recontextualizing ascetic advancement as an ecclesial endeavor, and thus offering a dramatic correction to the traditional monastic indifference to the structures of the Church as an effective medium of salvation. Indeed, this striking dissonance—between the institutionalized, sacramental, and hierarchical vision of the Areopagite on the one hand, and the individualized, sacramentally minimalist, and antihierarchical vision of Evagrius on the other—perhaps recaptures something of the former's purpose. If, as has been suggested above, the writings of the Areopagite emerge from the same milieu as

---

103. Ps.-Dionysius, *Ecclesiastical Hierarchy* 3.1 [Heil 82].
104. Ps.-Dionysius, *Ecclesiastical Hierarchy* 3.12 [Heil 93].
105. Ps.-Dionysius, *Ecclesiastical Hierarchy* 3.13 [Heil 93]. For Dionysius on the eucharist see the discussion of Golitzin (1994) 194–203.
106. The problem is discussed ibid. 208–14.
107. See the discussion in Louth (1989) 104–9, (2007) 154–73 (quotation at 166).
108. For the episcopal perspective see also Rorem (1989); also Golitzin (1994) 168–77.

that of Stephen bar Sudaili, then his corpus can be appreciated as a direct challenge to an Evagrian "minimalist" conception of ecclesial structures. We may thus appreciate the Pseudo-Dionysian corpus as a corrective to that same conception, in the same manner as the Pseudo-Macarian corpus serves as a corrective to the more extreme Messalian inclination that operated around it.

We must be cautious, therefore, not to overstate the degree of correspondence between the Areopagite's corpus and Stephen's *Book of the Holy Hierotheos*. Indeed, in a challenge to some recent attempts to uncover a hidden Origenism in the Areopagite's corpus, Emiliano Fiori has in a recent article demonstrated how the divergent attitudes to the sacraments revealed within the two works depend on their divergent cosmologies. Thus the *Book*, which posits the future restoration of an undifferentiated cosmos, cannot conceive a permanent place for the hierarchical order of the Church, which must be transcended;[109] while the Areopagite—who does not in fact commit to the classic Origenist notions of isochristism or *apokatastasis*—in contrast believes in both a present and a future union in which the righteous retain their individualism and that is realized in and through the hierarchical, sacramental order of the Church.[110] Thus the Areopagite is committed not to the abolition of terrestrial hierarchies but rather to their transfiguration.

The most important conclusion from comparison of the two authors, therefore, is not their similarity but rather their distinct difference, for the pair offer quite antithetical approaches to the nature of the cosmos and the place of the individual within it. Those antithetical approaches, moreover, are arranged along the same dividing lines that we have identified elsewhere in the same period: on the one side, ascetical enthusiasts emphasizing spiritual independence and the endeavor of the individual; on the other, the representatives of institutions emphasizing spiritual submission and integration within wider structures.[111] It is in this sense that Alexander Golitzin has seen in Pseudo-Dionysius a response to sustained concerns about Messalian practice and belief;[112] and it is in this sense also—and not in a clandestine commitment to the more controversial aspects of Evagrian doctrine—that he should be connected to the Origenist crisis in Palestine.

---

109. Fiori (2011) esp. 33f. Cf. Clark (1992), e.g., 247 (on Evagrius).

110. Fiori (2011) 34–38 (using the Syriac text). On Ps.-Dionysius's departure from Origen on this point see also Golitzin (1994) 283; and for his reframing of Evagrian thought ibid. 322–48, esp. 340f., 346–48 (on the placement of Evagrius's asceticism within an ecclesial context).

111. For this tension between Stephen and Ps.-Dionysius, between the mystical and the liturgical, see also Arthur (2008) 129–36; cf. also Perczel (2008 [repr. 2009]) 33, who regards Stephen's treatise as "a radical rethinking of the *CD* [*Corpus Dionysiacum*] in terms of Origenistic theology" (but who does not refer to the distinct sacramental imbalance between the two).

112. See Golitzin (1994) 349–92 (demonstrating also the importance of Ephrem, the *Book of Steps*, and Ps.-Macarius as predecessors to the Areopagite's sacramental thought).

This tension between Pseudo-Dionysian and Evagrian schemes is not a modern observation, for it was obvious also to the former's first translator into Syriac, Sergius of Resh'aina (d. 536).[113] Among his manifold interests Sergius, we should note, was an enthusiast for Evagrius, and was perhaps a commentator on the latter's controversial *Kephalaia Gnostica*—one of his contemporaries, at least, went so far as to describe him as practiced "in the doctrine of Origen."[114] Indeed, Sergius attached to his translation of the Areopagite's corpus an existing autograph treatise *On the Spiritual Life* that recapitulated the thought of Evagrius and then proceeded to set out how the Dionysian corpus might be reconciled to that same thought.[115] Sergius here sees in the progression of the Areopagite's texts the Evagrian program of spiritual progression from action to contemplation, so that, for example, the *Ecclesiastical Hierarchy* is related to the Evagrian stage of *praktikē* or virtuous action, and the *Divine Names* to the final, divine contemplation.[116] This short introduction, then, should perhaps be appreciated as the first serious attempt to reconcile the two competing visions. It was an attempt that later generations were to replicate.

It is perhaps unsurprising to discover that the Areopagite's ideas also found a particular resonance within Palestine, and in none other than Scythopolis. The city indeed appears as something of a crucible for the same intellectual tensions that we have explored here, tensions that revolved around the competing imperatives of the individual and the institution. At the end of 552 the bishop of Scythopolis—one Theodore, a former Palestinian monk of the Origenist faction—submitted to the emperor Justinian a *libellus* in which he recanted various Origenist errors (errors that mirror the anti-Evagrian anathemas of 553);[117] and, as we have seen, the hagiographies of Cyril of Scythopolis point toward a comparable interest in the suppression of Origenism and, with it, the traditions of individual contemplation enshrined within the Evagrian tradition.

Pseudo-Dionysius's first substantial commentator was another Scythopolite, the sixth-century bishop John (most probably Theodore's predecessor).[118] As Paul

---

113. For Sergius's Syriac translation and its potential importance to reconstructions of Ps.-Dionysius's original text see Perczel (2000b) and (2008 [repr. 2009]) esp. 32f.

114. Ps.-Zachariah of Mytilene, *Chronicle* 9.19 [Brooks vol. 2, 136]. See also Perczel (2008 [repr. 2009]) 33f., on the connections between Sergius's translation and Stephen bar Sudaili, *The Book of the Holy Hierotheos* 3.

115. See Sergius of Resh'aina, *On the Spiritual Life* 116–17 [ed. Sherwood (1961) 148f.; trans. Perczel (2008 [repr. 2009]) 31]. See also Sherwood (1952b). For the Evagrian influence upon Sergius's thought in this prologue see Guillaumont (1962) 226 with n. 101.

116. See Perczel (2008 [repr. 2009]) 31.

117. See Theodore of Scythopolis, *Libellus on the Errors of Origen* [*PG* 86, 231B–236B]. For discussion of Theodore see Diekamp (1899) 125–29; Guillaumont (1962) 151 n. 91; Flusin (1983) 20f.

118. For John's career and dates see Perrone (1980) 245f.; Flusin (1983) 17–29; Rorem and Lamoreaux (1998) 23–45. Binns (1994) 141f., 247f., places him after Theodore; but see Hombergen (2001) 365 n. 528.

Rorem and John Lamoreaux have noted in their compelling book on John's commentaries, besides Christological observations, it is above all a concern for the preservation of hierarchical order within the Church that characterizes John's comments on the texts.[119] Within that same concern John, like Pseudo-Dionysius, demonstrates an acute concern with the subordination of monks to their clerical superiors. Thus when he comes to the Areopagite's aforementioned *Letters* 8, to the rebel monk Demophilus, he reaffirms the structural relegation of monks to clerics, noting that "even if he sins, a priest must not be corrected by a deacon or a monk, or indeed by the laity . . . for [they are] above the order of monks and the liturgists—that is, deacons."[120] For John, the monastic rebellion that Demophilus epitomized was a resonant topic: "And so note," he concluded in the opening scholion on the letter, "that these evils also took place in those times [*kaka tauta kai epi ekeinōn tōn chronōn egeneto*]."[121]

Contained within John's scholia we also encounter a somewhat ambiguous and selective approach both to Origen and to Evagrius.[122] Indeed, it has been suggested that the same prevarication places John within the Origenist camp in Palestine—that is, within the circle of those who pursued a spirit of intellectual liberalism—and moreover explains the otherwise quite remarkable silence of Cyril's *Lives*, in which his fellow Scythopolite does not feature.[123] I would propose a quite different explanation, however: if we accept that the label "Origenist" signifies more than mere dedication to theological experiment and in fact implies (at least) an interest in the Evagrian tradition of spiritual contemplation, then it becomes problematic to place John within the same camp, since the liturgical vision that he promotes is in itself antagonistic to the presumptions of singular monastic practice.[124] Both Cyril and John, in effect, share the same desire to situate monasticism within a broader institutional context and thus also to deemphasize more singular spiritual endeavor; but each approaches the same tension from a quite different perspective, corresponding to their respective vocations, monastic and clerical. Thus, while Cyril (as Flusin has demonstrated) is careful to acknowledge the theoretical subordination of his heroes to the patriarch of Jerusalem, it is above all the institution

---

119. Rorem and Lamoreaux (1998) 62–65.

120. *PG* 4, 548A–B; with Rorem and Lamoreaux (1998) 257, 276.

121. *PG* 4, 544C; with Rorem and Lamoreaux (1998) 256, 276. Note also the injunction against false ascetics ("Lampetians or Messalians or Adelphians or, to repeat, Marcionists") at *PG* 4, 169D, with Golitizin (1994) 357; Rorem and Lamoreaux (1998) 179.

122. Cf., e.g., the critique at *PG* 4, 172C–176C, 545C; and the positive assessments ibid. 76D–77A, 337D, 549B. For comment see Rorem and Lamoreaux (1998) 39, 44, 56f., and esp. 89–97; also Flusin (1983) 25–28; Perrone (2001) 250f.

123. Hombergen (2001) 366f.

124. See also the apparent correspondences between John's critique of Evagrius and the anathemas of 553, with the comments of Flusin (1983) 27–29; Rorem and Lamoreaux (1998) 90f.

of monasticism that for him constitutes the perfect terrestrial society;[125] in contrast, for John (as for Pseudo-Dionysius) that same society is realized in the entire worshipping community, gathered around the altar of communion. In the end, despite their common purpose, the views of Cyril and John on the place of monasticism within the Christian cosmos are quite antithetical. It is perhaps unsurprising, then, that the former might prove hostile to the latter, refusing him the (inapposite) title "Origenist" but nevertheless condemning him through silence.

Within the Justinianic Near East, then, and in particular in Palestine, we witness something of the intellectual tensions that remained within and around monastic circles, tensions that the Chalcedonian legislators had failed to address. While the bishops gathered in 451 had lent an ecumenical impetus to preexistent notions of monks' legal and economic dependence on their clerical superiors, those same bishops did not—indeed could not—legislate against the spiritual independence long enshrined within the dominant traditions of ascetic thought, in particular that of Evagrius. Those traditions were, as we have seen, indifferent (though not hostile) to the hierarchical and sacramental structures of the Church and located salvation in complex processes of ascetical self-transformation and spiritual contemplation, for the most part detached from wider dependences. In time, however, that independence would in turn be challenged, as various post-Chalcedonian authors attempted a theological renegotiation of ascetics' relation to the wider world. Two authors are of particular note: first, Cyril of Scythopolis, whose hagiographies sought to reorient monastic practice around the monastic institution, deemphasizing the individualistic, contemplative tradition and demonizing its adherents or admirers as Origenists; and second, Pseudo-Dionysius, whose liturgical vision presented nothing less than the full institutional, cosmological, and spiritual dependence of monks upon the external realities of the Church.

## HAGIOGRAPHY AND THE EUCHARIST AFTER CHALCEDON

If, as we have seen, the eucharistic minimalism of earlier ascetic thought is complemented in the general eucharistic minimalism of the earlier hagiographies, is the post-Chalcedonian shift toward a more sacramentalized vision of the ascetic life—so evident in the works of the Areopagite and his commentator—also paralleled within the period's hagiographies? This might of course be expected, for the process of monastic ordination that various authorities promoted, and that served as a prominent medium through which ascetic charisma was integrated within

---

125. See Flusin (1983) 201–4. It should be noted that Cyril twice uses the Dionysian word *hierarchia* but not in a Dionysian sense; see Cyril of Scythopolis, *Life of Sabas* 11 [Schwartz 95] and *Life of Cyriacus* 3 [Schwartz 224].

ecclesial structures, was in this period far more advanced. But, to repeat, we are interested here not in fleeting references to monastic participation in rituals or sacraments but rather in the deliberate and developed attempt of hagiographers to articulate a new, more sacramentalized vision of the ascetic life. Thus, for example, Cyril of Scythopolis reports his heroes' ordination but, coterminous with his moral elevation of monasticism above the clerical vocation, devotes minimal attention to the eucharist. In the same period, however, we do discover elsewhere hagiographic visions of ascetics-*cum*-priests that include an unprecedented eucharistic emphasis. Those visions are contained within the *Lives* of the stylites.[126]

Eucharistic participation presented a particular problem both to pillar saints themselves, stood atop their remote columns, and to those ecclesiasts who would attempt to subordinate them to regular submission to a priest.[127] It is nevertheless notable that despite these difficulties, the hagiographers of these saints, rather than relegating a eucharistic emphasis in order to focus on their heroes' superior ascetic prowess as in most earlier hagiographies, chose in fact to dwell upon communion in order to demonstrate their subjects' integration within the wider Church. Within a context in which significant ideological constraints had been placed upon the practice of more singular ascetic feats, and in the light of the rather extreme ascetic singularity that stylites represented, it was no doubt now crucial that these same hagiographers demonstrate their heroes' consciousness of, and place within, local ecclesial structures.

One such hagiographer is the anonymous author of the *Life* of Daniel the Stylite, that fifth-century disciple and imitator of Symeon the Elder who established a column outside Constantinople during the reign of the emperor Leo I.[128] Within the *Life* Daniel's integration within the surrounding world is above all emphasized in political terms, in the patronage of successive emperors, the saint's predictions concerning the future of the state, and the supplications of foreign diplomats before him;[129] but his radical ascetic practice is also offset through his integration within the local church through ordination and a subsequent emphasis upon the reciprocal bond that tied him to the Constantinopolitan patriarch. Soon after Daniel established himself in the capital, the *Life*

---

126. On stylites in general see Delehaye (1923); Harvey (1988); Sansterre (1989); Frankfurter (1990); Kaplan (2001).

127. Binggeli (2009) 421f.

128. For analysis of the text see the magisterial treatment of Lane Fox (1997); also Hesse (2001); Kaplan (2001); Vivian (2003); Déroche and Lesieur (2010) 283–90.

129. Imperial patronage and friendship: *Life of Daniel the Stylite* 35, 38, 42, 44, 48, 49, 50 (calling the emperor Leo "inseparable" [*achōristos*] from Daniel), 51, 54–57, 68. Foreign diplomats: ibid. 51. Political prophecies: ibid. 53, 56, 65, 68, 85, 91. On the quite extraordinarily uncritical attitude of Daniel's hagiographer toward successive emperors, in particular on the question of doctrine, see Lane Fox (1997) 205–8. On Daniel's role as prophet and political validator ibid. 222–24.

reports, the emperor commanded the patriarch Gennadius to make Daniel a priest. The latter's column then provides the stage for a quite remarkable scene expressing the mutual cohesion of saint and patriarch, for after the ritual of ordination Gennadius ascends on a ladder and the pair receive communion from each other's hands.[130] Although in the earliest stages of his career Daniel had fallen under criticism from local Constantinopolitan priests, he now becomes the patriarch's companion and supporter.[131] Thus, during the reign of the usurper Basiliscus, and in the context of an imperial edict abrogating Chalcedon, the patriarch Acacius summons Daniel, and the saint descends from atop his column and travels to the cathedral church, uniting with Acacius and writing to rebuke the emperor as a new Diocletian.[132] Daniel then presides over the reconciliation of emperor and patriarch in church.[133]

In Daniel's *Life*, however, as in the *Lives* of Cyril of Scythopolis, the saint's or saints' reported ordination above all emphasizes a commitment to the wider Christian ministration; the celebration of the eucharist itself, however, infringes little upon the narrative.[134] We can nevertheless contrast this relative absence with another *Life* of the post-Chalcedonian period, that of the sixth-century Antiochene stylite Symeon the Younger, an imitator of his more illustrious fifth-century namesake.[135] Like Daniel, Symeon is portrayed as the spiritual patron of an emperor (Justin II) and, like Daniel again, his life is presented as one of progressive integration within the wider ecclesiastical establishment.[136] In his early career atop his column, he is frequented and feted by the bishops of Seleucia and Antioch, and ordained as a deacon;[137] at some later stage, under pressure from his monks and the local population, he becomes a priest;[138] and throughout his life, he predicts the

---

130. *Life of Daniel the Stylite* 43 [Delehaye 39–41]. For Gennadius's deference to the saint see also *Life of Daniel the Stylite* 58.

131. For these tensions see esp. ibid. 19.

132. Ibid. 70–73.

133. Ibid. 83. It should be noted that I make no claim as to the truth of these vignettes; on which see the comments of Lane Fox (1997) esp. 200f.

134. For an exception see *Life of Daniel the Stylite* 96. For the saint at the center of the liturgy see also ibid. 58, with Binggeli (2009) 434f.

135. On Symeon and his *Life* (ca. 600) see van den Ven (1962) vol. 1, 11*–191*; Déroche (1996).

136. Justin II: *Life of Symeon the Younger* 203, 206–11. It is notable that the author excludes from his narrative the patronage of the emperor Maurice, referred to in Evagrius Scholasticus, *Ecclesiastical History* 5.21. van den Ven (1962) vol. 1, 92*–96*, 107*f., explains this through ignorance; but cf. Déroche (1996) 73–75, arguing that the author writes under Phocas. It is also possible that the silence reflects a more general ambivalence toward Maurice's (unpopular) rule.

137. See *Life of Symeon the Younger* 19, 25, 34. Cf. ibid. 71, where the ghost of Ephraim of Antioch appears to Symeon to recount how much he admired him.

138. See ibid. 132–35. The chronology is confused, since Symeon celebrates the eucharist before explicit mention of his elevation to the priesthood; see ibid. 105, 127.

careers of the great and the good of the Eastern patriarchal scene—Anastasius of Antioch and John the Faster, for example.[139]

At the same time, Symeon's hagiography is notable for the constant intrusion of liturgical acts and contexts upon the narrative.[140] Its hero's life is marked with visions of the eucharistic celebration;[141] he composes liturgical troparia;[142] and his ascetic practice is defined in the constant performance of the monastic office.[143] Most striking, perhaps, is a notice that places the stylite at the heart of liturgical life:[144]

> When Pentecost arrived and the synaxis had been completed, [Symeon] commanded the approaching crowds to be dismissed, and on the following Sunday, after the morning hymns, he commanded the brothers to close the gates of the monastery and to come together to him. And as he spread incense he ordered everyone to perform genuflections and then did so himself. He threw himself upon his face and in tears prayed for one hour along with them, and at the end of the prayer everyone said *Amēn*, and he told them to remove his leather cowl. In prayer he forgave them for their ignorance concerning every quarrel, speaking to them that Gospel saying. [There follows a brief sermon]. And when he had said these and many other things that turned and led them on the way to the eternal life, he entrusted them to the Lord, and having pronounced the Lord's prayer that lies in the Gospel of John on behalf of his disciples, he placed his hands upon them and blessed them all. He spoke a universal prayer for the world and for the men who hate us in vain. [There follows another brief sermon]. And when he had prayed thus he gave himself to those outside the sanctuary's railing, and receiving him they set him upon an empty throne and lifted unto his chest the holy Gospels, and as he went around he spoke a prayer in every place within the monastery and in the guardhouse. With great prudence the truly holy Martha, his mother according to the flesh, took the honorable and life-giving Cross and processed before him singing, "Save us, Son of God, who was crucified for us. Lord, glory to you, *hallelujah!*" And so the brothers raised the slave of God in their own hands like a holy vessel [*hōs skeuos hagion*], and singing hymns to God they bore him into the holy church of God that had been built by him. They prostrated themselves before him and asked that he recommend them to the Lord, and led him up both in peace and with hymns and installed him on his holy column.

---

139. See ibid. 202–5. We should, however, note signs of significant tensions with local ecclesiasts: e.g., ibid. 72, 116, 195, 225, 239.

140. Harvey (1998) 535.

141. *Life of Symeon the Younger* 35, 112, 135, 256. At ibid. 35 the author claims that the eucharist "vivifies for the safeguard of the soul and the body, for the observance of the commandments, the remission of sins, and the eternal life" [van den Ven 34].

142. *Life of Symeon the Younger* 105–7.

143. See, e.g., ibid. 17, 37, 39, 121.

144. Ibid. 113 [van den Ven vol. 1, 91–93]. For the physical centrality of Symeon's column to the church that surrounded it see also the comments of van den Ven (1962) vol. 1, 191*–221*; Binggeli (2009) 433–35.

In an important but perhaps neglected article on the hagiographies of Symeon and his synonymous predecessor, Susan Ashbrook Harvey has noted the "extraordinary emphasis on the integration of the stylite's ascetic practice into the liturgical life of the worshipping community, both monastic and civic." Pointing to the rituals of prostration, prayer, and psalmody through which these stylites are said to have practiced their labors, and through which their supplicants are said to have approached them, Harvey argues that the "stylite's defining ritual context" was not a "ritualized activity [an individual ascetic practice]"—as in Peter Brown's classic interpretation—but the "eucharistic liturgy of the gathered body of the church, the collective presentation of the Christian salvation drama."[145] In these texts, Harvey suggests, the ascetic endeavors of the individual stylite are brought within, and made relevant through, the communal ritual contexts in which they are practiced.

In the *Life of Symeon the Younger*, the remarkable emphasis on the ascetic's ecclesiastical, sacramental, and liturgical context in part represents, no doubt, its hero's actual sacerdotal status.[146] But placed next to the *Life of Daniel the Stylite* and the *Lives* of Cyril of Scythopolis—whose subjects are also all priests, but where the liturgical aspect is far less developed—that emphasis appears also to indicate the hagiographer's desire to underline his hero's orientation around, and integration within, liturgical structures. In a context of ascetic redefinition, in which the models of the pioneering generation more and more proved discordant with the ideological constraints that beset ascetics both from outside and from within, these post-Chalcedonian authors presented their heroes as an integral part of a far wider worshipping community. But for the author or authors of the *Life of Symeon the Younger*, that same project involved a far more pervasive assertion of the stylite's ecclesial credentials and, in particular, the placement of his ascetic practices within a distinct liturgical context. Thereby (in the memorable words of Harvey) "liturgy transfigured the ascetic body of the stylite into the ecclesial body of the church," reconciling "the poles of charismatic and institutional authority" and presenting "a ritual practice dependent upon mutually inclusive ascetic and liturgical meanings."[147]

The elaboration of this more sacramentalized, more liturgified vision of the ascetic life occurs also within another, interrelated context: less, however, in relation to tensions over the boundaries of the clerical and monastic vocations, and

---

145. Harvey (1998) 525; cf. P. Brown (1971).
146. For the ordination of stylites see also Binggeli (2009) 436–38. For Symeon the Elder's submission to the eucharist (in particular at Lent) see Theodoret, *Religious History* 26.7; *Syriac Life of Symeon Stylites* 28–29, 54. Cf. on his earlier life, e.g., ibid. 10. See on Symeon and the eucharist Golitzin (1994) 386–89; Harvey (1998) 530–34; Binggeli (2009) 424–26. In contrast to Daniel and to Symeon the Younger, there is no contemporary indication that Symeon the Elder himself became a priest, despite the later assumption of Evagrius Scholasticus, *Ecclesiastical History* 1.13.
147. Harvey (1998) 525.

more in relation to tensions over doctrine and the formation of schismatic communities. The canonical reinforcement of a normative paradigm of ascetic practice had, of course, been marginal to Chalcedon's actual purpose, which had been a decisive intervention in the doctrinal dissent concerning Christ's "one" nature or "two" natures. The Chalcedonian definition, however, failed to convince large numbers of clerics and monks, and led to the gradual formation of distinct, anti-Chalcedonian communities committed to a "one nature" Christological confession. In the post-Chalcedonian period, hagiographers within those same communities—confronted with a swathe of Chalcedonian bishops and oscillating if not oppositional imperial opinion—began to elevate the eucharist within the texts that celebrated their ascetic heroes, placing the sacrament and its rites at the center of new religious identities and shifting the orientation of their communities from the pious Christian emperor and his empire to the pious, "true" Church, the rites of which remained unsullied despite alienation from the secular authorities.

A wonderful example is provided in the *Plerophoriae* of John Rufus, a collection of anti-Chalcedonian vignettes composed in Palestine about 515.[148] Rufus was a priest at Antioch who broke communion after the second deposition of the anti-Chalcedonian Peter the Fuller, and thence traveled to Palestine, where he entered the ascetic circle of Peter the Iberian (whose *Life* he also composed), later, perhaps, becoming bishop of Maiuma.[149] Within the *Plerophoriae* we find a plethora of stories concerning the eucharist and its rites, in striking contrast to the relative minimalism of earlier hagiographic collections. The change of tone reflects a change of circumstance. For Rufus, the differentiation between efficacious and nonefficacious, true and false, eucharists is the ultimate dividing line between anti-Chalcedonian and Chalcedonian, true and false, doctrines. Frequent visions or miracles associated with the eucharist therefore serve to establish the righteousness of the anti-Chalcedonian position; while communion serves as the ultimate statement of membership within the orthodox group.[150]

The Chalcedonian eucharist is therefore presented as polluted; its anti-Chalcedonian equivalent, as exalted. Rufus relates, for example, how a woman at Alexandria once hesitated to commune after the circulation of the so-called counterencyclical (that is, the proclamation of the emperor Basiliscus that withdrew his previous support for the anti-Chalcedonians). Then in a vision she perceived a

---

148. For the date see Horn (2006) 19–21. There has been a spate of recent volumes on the Christian communities of late-antique Gaza. See also Hevelone-Harper (2005); Bitton-Ashkelony and Kofsky (2004), (2006). On John Rufus see Horn (2006) 12–44; Steppa (2002); Menze (2003).

149. Details on John Rufus's life are dependent on his own words, esp. at his *Life of Peter the Iberian* 79, 81, and *Plerophoriae* 22. Evidence for his elevation to the bishopric of Maiuma comes only in the title to the *Plerophoriae* [Nau 11]. For discussion of his life see Steppa (2002) 57–61; Horn (2006) 30–44.

150. See also Menze (2003) 226–31.

great church with two altars: one grand but somber, with a Chalcedonian bishop celebrating the eucharist; and the other small but ordained in gold and gems, where a small child (the Savior) was offering the sacrifice and proclaiming, "Receive communion at this altar."[151] Chalcedonian bishops are here presented as dishonoring the host or unable to transform it: thus in one tale Timothy of Alexandria relates how, at the time of Chalcedon, he had a vision in which he approached the altar to receive communion and discovered the bread to be stale, a portent that presaged "the abandonment of God's grace from the churches"; in another Zachariah of Maiuma had a vision in which he perceived himself in a Chalcedonian church at Beirut and saw the priests offering the cup but treating it as miserable; while in one more, also situated at the moment of the circulation of the counterencyclical, one Abba John has a vision in which he perceives the altar of the Church to have been stripped and the eucharistic elements scattered on the floor.[152]

It is therefore unsurprising that Rufus throughout the collection rails against indiscriminate participation in the Chalcedonian eucharist. We read of a monk, Constantine, who at the time of Chalcedon was unsure whether to commune at the shrine of Saint John the Baptist at Sebaste, and thus to become an apostate; the saint himself then appears and warns the monk not to abandon the Church and not to lose his soul—"For," John proclaims, "everywhere you go I will be with you."[153] In the subsequent notice, another monk, Zosimus, goes from Sinai to Jerusalem and en route rests at the shrine of Jacob near Bethel; he is reassured that taking communion there is not a problem, but once again the saint appears, rebukes him, and orders him to hate "the renegades."[154] Here, then, Rufus confronts a situation in which the Chalcedonian possession of prominent saints' shrines presented a significant concern, in particular, as Cornelia Horn has demonstrated, amid the manifold sacred sites of Palestine.[155] His position is nevertheless unambiguous: preservation from doctrinal pollution is more important than worship at specific sites.[156] Thus, for example, he holds forth the vignette of a nun who goes from the Mount of Olives to the Church of the Ascension at Jerusalem but is there closed in during a Chalcedonian celebration. When it has finished, she returns to her cell but soon after falls ill and on her deathbed proclaims, "People are saying to me, How could

---

151. John Rufus, *Plerophoriae* 86 [trans. Nau 76].

152. John Rufus, *Plerophoriae* 66, 73, 83. Cf. also ibid. 23, where John has a vision of Basil of Seleucia's return from Chalcedon, in which a terrible figure stops Basil at the point of celebrating the eucharist and drags him from the church.

153. John Rufus, *Plerophoriae* 29 [trans. Nau 38].

154. John Rufus, *Plerophoriae* 30 [trans. Nau 38].

155. Horn (2006) 325–31 (on the theme in Rufus). For a specific warning in regard to taking the Chalcedonian eucharist in Jerusalem cf. Severus of Antioch, *Select Letters* 1.4.7.

156. Cf. also John Rufus, *Plerophoriae* 28, 74, 79. For discussion of this theme see Steppa (2002) 156–58; Horn (2006) 304–31.

you be counted among the orthodox, you, who decided to stay put during a celebration of the renegades and watch the unworthy partake of the holy mysteries?"[157]

As will be evident, there is a distinct anticlerical tone to Rufus's collection, an indignant sense that most (though not all) bishops had abandoned the true faith at Chalcedon.[158] Where Chalcedonian priests challenge or persecute anti-Chalcedonian monks there are disastrous consequences for the former,[159] and Rufus draws a sharp distinction between the pure world of anti-Chalcedonian ascetics and the corrupt world of Chalcedonian bishops.[160] One anti-Chalcedonian relates how he once saw, in a vision, a mob of bishops sealing in a lit furnace a small child (Christ), with the hero of the Latrocinium, Dioscorus of Alexandria, alone abstaining from their plans;[161] another reports still another vision, in which he perceives Saint Paul standing amid a group of bishops and proclaiming to them, "Not one of you has been found to be pure."[162]

Given that an alternative, anti-Chalcedonian Church had still to be realized at the time of the *Plerophoriae*'s composition, this repudiation of the episcopate has some significant practical consequences that Rufus attempts to address. Thus, when during a persecution at Alexandria a monk can find no orthodox priests to celebrate the eucharist, his entreaties to God precipitate the miraculous revelation of a piece of the sacrament in his hand; and when a secular pilgrim hesitates to receive from his own hand a host that has been preconsecrated and that he carries with him, his doubts are assuaged when he discovers it bleeding.[163]

In light of his celebration of anti-Chalcedonian asceticism, his perspective on the corrupted episcopate, and the evident difficulties in accessing the orthodox eucharist, it is quite remarkable that Rufus chose not to marginalize the sacramental structures of the Church but instead placed them at the center of his vision. The differentiation between true and false eucharists becomes a central marker of the wider differentiation between true and false doctrines, and orthodox communion becomes the superlative expression of anti-Chalcedonism.[164] Thus Rufus records

---

157. John Rufus, *Plerophoriae* 80 [trans. Nau 74]. For further tales involving the revelation or assistance of saints see, e.g., *Plerophoriae* 37, 51, 57, 60, 74.

158. For this tension see also Steppa (2002) 138–40; Menze (2003) 220–23; Horn (2006) 217–21.

159. See, e.g., John Rufus, *Plerophoriae* 47–48.

160. Chalcedonians can be designated even under the convenient shorthand of "the party of the bishops." See esp. ibid. 39 [trans. Nau 47] ("Claudian of Eleutheropolis was from the party of the bishops"); 70 [trans. Nau 67] ("Evagrius, who had been an adherent of the bishops, converted to orthodoxy").

161. John Rufus, *Plerophoriae* 14 [trans. Nau 15f.].

162. John Rufus, *Plerophoriae* 60 [trans. Nau 63].

163. John Rufus, *Plerophoriae* 77–78. For the phenomenon of autocommunion see also Binggeli (2009) 425–29; Caseau (2002). For discussion of the intrusion of anti-Chalcedonian ascetics on the sacramental prerogatives of Chalcedonian clerics in Rufus see Steppa (2002) 156f.; Horn (2006) 222–25.

164. Se, e.g., John Rufus, *Plerophoriae* 20, 89; Steppa (2002) 153f.

how a man in Cilicia who received the sanctified eucharist from Peter the Iberian married a woman who was devout but also a Chalcedonian and how that woman then fell into such a grave illness that the doctors despaired for her life; the wife, however, then had a vision in which angels revealed to her the heaven preserved for enemies of Chalcedon, and upon waking she received the anti-Chalcedonian host and was healed.[165] Here, therefore, as elsewhere within the collection, it is the act of communion, more than a mere mental conversion, that is the most important expression of one's adherence to one or other camp.[166]

The texts of Rufus's anti-Chalcedonian contemporaries are also conspicuous for this same elevation of the eucharist. The various *Letters* of Severus of Antioch, for example, demonstrate a constant concern for both sacramental protocol and the preservation of the eucharist from heretical pollution. Like Rufus, Severus in several places addresses the problem of absent priests, sanctioning autocommunion but also chastising those who consider the worthiness of the celebrant to affect the oblation itself.[167] A series of his *Letters*, furthermore, reiterates the point that anti-Chalcedonians must not commune with their Chalcedonian adversaries: one should commune with those who are like-minded, or else invite damnation (even monks, Severus insists, are not exempt from this imperative); nor should one admit heretics to the eucharistic service, lest the gift of pure communion be polluted.[168]

Volker Menze's recent monograph on the formation of the Syrian Orthodox Church has highlighted this eucharistic discourse as one of the central means through which anti-Chalcedonian authorities responded both to the doctrinal fragmentation of the episcopate and to their creeping alienation from Constantinople.[169] It thus had both a practical and an ideological dimension: for those living in Chalcedonian areas, issues of sacramental protocol were no doubt real and immediate

---

165. John Rufus, *Plerophoriae* 38. Cf. also ibid. 39 for a similar vision and a subsequent act of communion.

166. See also, e.g., ibid. 1, 6, 36, 58.

167. See Severus of Antioch, *Select Letters* 1.3.1–4. Also the letter of Severus falsely attributed to Basil of Caesarea discussed in Voicu (1995).

168. See esp. Severus of Antioch, *Select Letters* 1.4.1–10. Cf. also ibid. 7.3 and *Letters* 44–45. On the eucharist and on sacramental protocol see also ibid. 30, 53, 104, 105, 107. For problems of sacramental protocol in other anti-Chalcedonian authors of the period see also, e.g., John of Ephesus, *Lives of the Eastern Saints* 5 [Brooks 102]; *Ecclesiastical Canons* 1–7; Ps.-Zachariah of Mytilene, *Chronicle* 10.4; John of Tella, *Canons*, e.g., 8, 13, 17; John of Tella, *Rules to Deacons*, edited in Menze (2006), with discussion. For an in-depth discussion of anxieties over the eucharist in Syrian circles, and in particular the respective prerogatives of laity, monks, and clerics, see the excellent discussions in Escolan (1999) 291–311; Menze (2004). For the place of the eucharist in fifth-century and sixth-century Christological debates see also Gray (2005) and (with reference to the Nestorian controversy) Chadwick (1951); Hainthaler (2005).

169. See Menze (2008) esp. 145–93.

concerns that authorities were forced to confront; but at the same time, in elevating the anti-Chalcedonian eucharist and disparaging that of their opponents, those same authorities used the same sacramental emphasis as a means of establishing the ritual boundaries of their doctrinal group, without limiting participation to one particular social group (monks, clerics, seculars, etc.). It is, therefore, of little surprise that from the reign of the Chalcedonian emperor Justin I anti-Chalcedonian leaders, who had until then distributed the eucharist to the faithful through a disparate network of established or exiled clerics, began instead to ordain the leaders of an alternative, anti-Chalcedonian Church.[170] Those ordinations were an intractable step on the path to the full fragmentation of the Eastern Church.

The intrusion of the eucharist within hagiographies such as the *Plerophriae* places the sacrament and its rites at the center of anti-Chalcedonian self-perception. In setting out this new vision, anti-Chalcedonian authors were also preparing the ground for a gradual dissociation of Christian faith and empire, in which the emphasis upon eucharisitc righteousness would come to provide the basis for self-definition in an imminent future in which both imperial politics and foreign incursion encouraged the exploration of new, post-Roman identities.[171] But for our purposes here, we should note that a more immediate effect of this shift is to transport the eucharist—to a far greater degree than in the past—into hagiographic narratives, implicating hagiographic heroes within a broader ecclesial framework from which ascetics are not absent or excused. The presence of the eucharist therefore has a somewhat different purpose here than in, for example, the *Life of Symeon the Younger* (where doctrinal references are conspicuous for their absence).[172] But the result is nevertheless the same: far from operating outside sacramental imperatives, in this post-Chalcedonian period some prominent ascetics are now presented as integrated within, and subordinated to, a far broader, sacramentalized world with the eucharist at its navel.

In a range of post-Chalcedonian literature we witness a series of interrelated tensions: between the individual and the institution, between asceticism and eucharist, between monasticism and Church. Although the process of ideological reorientation expressed and enforced within the Chalcedonian legislation had no doubt done much to reconcile the monastic and clerical vocations, it is evident that significant tensions remained. Not least, and despite legal and economic integration,

---

170. On John of Tella's ordinations and establishment of "eucharistic communities" in this period see Menze (2006) esp. 71–89.

171. For these broader processes within sixth-century miaphysite circles see Wood (2010).

172. See Déroche (1996) 76. *Life of Symeon the Younger* 226 concerns a Gothic Arian, a nonpartisan in Chalcedonian terms. The same politic silence is also mirrored in other texts; see Booth (2011a) and above n. 129.

no intellectual solution had been offered to the traditional ascetic indifference to the eucharist, an indifference so evident in the writings of the earliest ascetic theoreticians and hagiographers.

Throughout the post-Chalcedonian period various Christian commentators attempted to address those same tensions: the hagiographers of pillar saints emphasized the full liturgical integration, even ordination, of their heroes; anti-Chalcedonian commentators began to place the eucharist at the center of the orthodox monastic (and broader Christian) life; and, perhaps above all, the Areopagite set out a radical new vision that contextualized the ascetic tradition within the structures of the Church and made monks dependent upon the spiritual perfection offered through the eucharist and its episcopal mediators. Dissenting voices could still nevertheless be heard, and it is, above all, in the Palestinian Origenist crisis that we catch precious glimpses of a disparate group of monks who still clung to the mood of spiritual and moral freedom that had defined the earliest ascetic thinkers, against those who would subordinate monks to the demands of successive institutions (coenobium, church, and empire).

It is indeed in Palestinian circles that we will pursue such tensions in the remainder of this book, in the writings of three monastic authors trained in the coenobia and laurae of the Judean deserts: John Moschus, Sophronius of Jerusalem, and Maximus Confessor (fl. ca. 610–60). These three authors were Chalcedonian in doctrine, and when we first encounter the group, in Sophronius's *Miracles of Cyrus and John*, we discover an author who recapitulates the anti-Chalcedonian eucharistic emphasis notable, for example, in the *Plerophoriae* of Rufus, elevating communion as the preeminent expression of conversion to orthodox doctrine. This sacramental differentiation of orthodox and heretic, Chalcedonian and anti-Chalcedonian, would continue to dominate the cultural output of Sophronius and his circle, but whereas the former would in the *Miracles* prove indifferent to the spiritual demands of communion outside contexts of conversion, in later decades, the same group would attempt a far more comprehensive and more urgent reevaluation of Chalcedonian ecclesiological perception. As the empire was pitched into a geopolitical crisis that placed some Chalcedonian communities under "barbarian" rule and that forced Chalcedonian Christians to explain evident divine disfavor, the same circle set about exploring a new model of the Christian life, pursuing a far more profound and pervasive renegotiation of the conceptual divide between asceticism and eucharist than had hitherto been attempted, either in Chalcedonian or in anti-Chalcedonian circles. Therein, Moschus, Sophronius, and Maximus abandoned long-standing monastic claims to spiritual independence of ecclesial realities but at the same time asserted a more integrated model of the orthodox Christian community, guaranteeing its righteousness even as the Christian empire proved ephemeral.

2

# Sophronius and the *Miracles*

John Moschus was born (ca. 550) at Aegae, in Cilicia, during the reign of Justinian I.[1] According to the short biographical prologue attached to some manuscripts of his opus, the *Spiritual Meadow*, he became a monk in the coenobium of Theodosius, in the Judaean desert.[2] Soon, however, he appears to have retreated to the Laura of Pharon, farther north, where Moschus himself claims to have spent a decade, and where several tales place him roughly in the period 568–78.[3] It was perhaps here that he first encountered the sophist Sophronius, an educated Damascene who would become his disciple and lifelong companion.[4] At the beginning

---

1. For his Cilician origins see John Moschus, *Spiritual Meadow* 171 [PG 87:3, 3037C], which says of one Zoilus that "we shared the same upbringing." The F manuscript adds to his name *ho Aigeotēs*, thus confirming Moschus's own origins; see Chadwick (1974) 56; Pattenden (1975) 41 n. 1; Maisano (1982) 247. See also the references to Cilician monasteries at John Moschus, *Spiritual Meadow* 27–29, 31–32, 51, 57–58, 81–87, 90, 100; and to Cilician ascetics ibid. 3, 22, 41, 59, 61, 115, 123, 166, 182–83.

2. See *Prologue to the Spiritual Meadow* [Usener 91]; and the references to Theodosius's higoumen as "our father" at 92–94. For the authorship of the *Prologue to the Spiritual Meadow* see below pp. 106–8.

3. See John Moschus, *Spiritual Meadow* 40 [PG 87:3, 2893D], *Emeina gar en autēi etē deka*; with the chronological reconstruction of Schönborn (1972) 63f.; Chadwick (1974) 55f. For tales involving this community and its members see John Moschus, *Spiritual Meadow* 41–42, 45, 62–67, 139–40.

4. For Sophronius as Moschus's disciple see Sophronius, *Miracles* 70.8; *Prologue to the Spiritual Meadow* [Usener 92]. Moschus himself refers to Sophronius with various terms of respect ("'lord," "brother," "son," "companion," "sophist"); see John Moschus, *Spiritual Meadow* preface, 69, 77, 92, 102, 110–11, 113, 135, 157, 162; Clugnet (1905) 51–54 no. 8. For speculation as to their meeting see, e.g., Chadwick (1974) 59, suggesting the aristocratic pilgrim Sophronius may have selected Moschus as a spiritual guide in Palestine. For Sophronius's origins in Damascus see his own comments at *Miracles* 70.4 and

of the reign of the emperor Tiberius II (r. 578–82), the pair visited the monasteries of Egypt, and upon their return Sophronius was in turn initiated as a monk of Theodosius.[5] Thereafter, it appears, Moschus settled for another decade in the Laura of the Aeliotes, perhaps on Mount Sinai,[6] and then spent the 590s in the Palestinian Nea Laura of Saint Sabas, where the biographical prologue places him in the same period.[7] Upon the invasion of the Persians (603), however, he and Sophronius retreated from Palestine to "the region of Antioch the Great" and thence to Alexandria.[8]

At some point during this second sojourn in Alexandria, Sophronius contracted a painful disease of the eyes and was, according to his own witness, "tortured for many months" by a "sea of pain."[9] When Hippocratic physicians proved unable to alleviate his affliction and warned that blindness would soon result Sophronius set out for the shrine of Saints Cyrus and John at Menuthis, having

---

in the *Epigrams* 1 [*PG* 87:3, 3421C–D]. For their relationship see Chadwick (1974) 59; also the recent observations of Krueger (2011) esp. 28–38.

5. For the Egyptian visit see John Moschus, *Spiritual Meadow* 78; also Nissen (1938) 354–56 no. 1; and *Prologue to the Spiritual Meadow* [Usener 92], stating that Moschus had been sent "on service" (*eis diakonian*); cf. the *Synaxarium of Constantinople* (cited in Schönborn [1972] 57), stating that Sophronius went for the purposes of *paideia*. For Sophronius's intention to become a monk at this stage see John Moschus, *Spiritual Meadow* 110, also 69; and for his initiation ibid. 102, with the interpretation of Chadwick (1974) 57. For Sophronius as a monk of Theodosius see Sophronius, *Miracles* 70.4 and *Epigrams* 1 [*PG* 87:3, 3421C–D]. The contention of Chadwick (1974) 59 that "Sophronius's decision to renounce the world was taken in consequence of his cure at Menouthis" places it too late. Cf. Schönborn (1972) 65f., and John Moschus, *Spiritual Meadow* 92, 102, 111, 135, preceding the pair's departure from the East and referring to Sophronius with the monastic titles "Abba" and "Brother."

6. See John Moschus, *Spiritual Meadow* 67 [*PG* 87:3, 2917C]: *Emeina gar en autēi etē deka*. For further tales associated with this laura John Moschus, *Spiritual Meadow* 45, 62–68. For its location on Sinai see ibid. 134 [*PG* 87:3, 2997C], where Patriarch John of Jerusalem (575–93) is said to be constructing a nearby reservoir *eis to Sina*. Binns (1994) 50, however, locates the laura in Judaea, for the Latin of the *PG* gives *in Sigma*, so that he reads "in [the shape of] Sigma," thinking that "the semi-circular shape of a sigma, as it was then written, would have become the distinguishing feature of a new reservoir." (The F manuscript on which the *PG* Latin is based also gives *Sigma*; see Maisano [1982] 246.) The reason for referring to its shape, however, is still unclear, and Binns is incorrect that Sinai was nevertheless "far outside" the jurisdiction of Jerusalem's patriarch. It is perhaps preferable, therefore, to follow the reading in the *PG*, with Chadwick (1974) 57, and to locate Moschus on Sinai in this period, where numerous tales of the *Spiritual Meadow* are situated, and where he himself later wished to be buried; see John Moschus, *Spiritual Meadow* 122–27; *Prologue to the Spiritual Meadow* [Usener 92].

7. *Prologue to the Spiritual Meadow* [Usener 91].

8. Ibid. Cf. Sophronius, *Miracles* 70.4 [Marcos 395], in which Sophronius says that he came to Alexandria "for a reason which it is not necessary to recall in writing." For Moschus's presence in Antioch see John Moschus, *Spiritual Meadow* 39, 88–89. It is probable that before departing for Alexandria the pair visited Seleucia and Cilicia, where two tales in the *Spiritual Meadow* place them; see John Moschus, *Spiritual Meadow* 79–80.

9. Sophronius, *Miracles* 70.4 [Marcos 395].

heard of the saints' reputation for miraculous healing.[10] There, through a series of strange visions, he was eventually cured,[11] and thereupon determined to record the saints' miracles as a record and thanks.[12]

The *Miracles of Cyrus and John*—which appears to have been composed between 610 and 614—consists of seventy short miracle narratives, composed in a basic narrative style but nevertheless punctuated with frequent rhetorical flourishes.[13] Unusually for a hagiographer, Sophronius makes no pretenses as to the simplicity of his style, for while "not unaware that in the sacred telling of the miracles, a loose and relaxed style is more appropriate," he nonetheless adopts "an intense one, so that through this the fervor, gracefulness, and intensity of the holy men toward the healing of the sick may be known."[14] The narratives are divided into three distinct groups, in accordance with the geographical origins of the subject: supplicants within the first group (*Miracles* 1–35) are Alexandrians; within the second group (*Miracles* 36–50) they are Egyptians and Libyans; and within the third group (*Miracles* 51–70) they are from farther afield: Palestinians, Constantinopolitans, Romans, and so on.[15] While all the miracles follow the same basic narrative pattern, and all involve cures bestowed upon individuals, there is nevertheless considerable variation among the vignettes. Some supplicants are heretics, for example, and others pagans; some diseases are derived from natural causes but others from sin, demons, or magic; and some cures

---

10. For the disease (*epichusis* or *platukoria*) see Sophronius's words at *Prologue to the Miracles* 9 and *Miracles* 70.1–7.

11. See Sophronius, *Miracles* 70.8–2. At ibid. 70.8 [Marcos 396] Saint Cyrus appears to Sophronius "in the divine habit of a monk and in the same form as John [Moschus], the patient's spiritual father and teacher, who was with him at the martyrs' tomb and praying for his disciple and child." Moschus appears again at Sophronius, *Miracles* 70.13. For this particular miracle, which includes Sophronius's renunciation of Homer, see now Agosti (2011).

12. For the text as a memorial see Sophronius, *Prologue to the Miracles* 1. For the text as the payment of a debt owed to the saints see ibid. 8 and *Miracles* 70.2.

13. Sophronius tells us that the text was composed during the patriarchate of John the Almsgiver (610–20); see *Miracles* 8.2, 11.6. It was written while Sophronius was still in the city (see, e.g., *Miracles* 32.2, which refers to Alexandria as "here"), and so the date of the text depends on the date of his withdrawal; see below p. 101. Because of the absence of references to the Persian sack of Jerusalem—esp. ibid. 65.5—it is tempting to place it in the earlier half of the decade. For the Greek text I have used the critical edition of Marcos (1975), with the majority of the textual corrections suggested by Duffy (1984b) and (1987), and by the excellent commentary of Gascou (2006), with French translation. For the *Prologue* attached to Sophronius's *Miracles* I have used the text of Bringel (2008).

14. Sophronius, *Prologue to the Miracles* 6 [Bringel 7]. On the opposition between an "intense" (*suntonos*) and "relaxed" (*aneimenos*) style here see Milazzo (1992).

15. For Sophronius's explanation of this division see *Prologue to the Miracles* 6 and the moments of transition at *Miracles* 1.1, 35.13, 36.1, 50.7, 51.1. For the biblical and mystical significance of the numbers 7, 10, and 70 see Sophronius, *Prologue to the Miracles* 4–5.

occur instantaneously through dreams yet others through certain prescriptions.[16] Nearly all, however, occur within the context of the saints' shrine at Menuthis, situated northeast of Alexandria in an area now submerged in Aboukir Bay.[17]

According to the details included in the *Prologue* that Sophronius attaches to the *Miracles* (and that appear in two anonymous *Lives*), Cyrus and John were martyred at Alexandria during the Diocletianic persecutions.[18] Following the saints' execution the Christian community transferred their relics to the Church of Saint Mark, where they remained until the reign of Theodosius II. Then, according to Sophronius, an angel appeared to the patriarch Cyril and commanded him to transfer the saints' relics to the Church of the Evangelists at Menuthis, in order to combat a popular pagan shrine within the region (possibly the famed cult of Isis). There the saints not only set the goddess to flight but also submerged her temple under sand and sea.[19]

Sophronius's account of the shrine's establishment is seemingly authenticated by three extant sermons on the saints transmitted under Cyril's name.[20] Critics of the Cyrillian tradition have nevertheless challenged that attribution, pointing instead to an alternative history of the shrine suggested in a Syriac source, the early sixth-century *Life of Severus* by Zachariah of Mytilene. Therein, in a digression devoted to religious activity at Menuthis in the late fifth century, Zachariah not only describes a (continuing) cult of Isis but conspicuously fails to mention Saints Cyrus and John, a failure that perhaps suggests that the shrine was in fact established later, and by an anti-Chalcedonian patriarch (hence Sophronius's revisionism).[21] In a magisterial study, however, Jean Gascou has not only challenged once again the Cyrillian attribution of the sermons but has also pointed to potential distortions within the account of Zachariah, whose picture of an un-Christianized Menuthis conveniently suits his purpose of demonstrating the antipagan zeal of the anti-Chalcedonians at

---

16. For detailed typologies of the various diseases and remedies within the text see Marcos (1975) 87–146.

17. For the archaeology of the site (wrongly identified as Canopus) see Goddio (2007) 29–68, with the correction of Stolz (2008). For the early Byzantine jewelry and coins from the site see Goddio and Clauss (2006) 259ff. (with discussion by Stolz) and Petrina [née Stolz] (2012). As Stolz (2008) 204 points out, the description of the site given in Goddio (2007) 29–31 is strikingly consistent with that in Sophronius, *Prologue to the Miracles* 29. For a description of the shrine as based on Sophronius, *Miracles* cf. Marcos (1975) 42–49; Montserrat (1998) 268–70.

18. Sophronius, *Prologue to the Miracles* 18. For the relation of the anonymous *Lives* to Sophronius's *Prologue to the Miracles* see Gascou (2007) 246–51.

19. Sophronius, *Prologue to the Miracles* 23–29. In antiquity Menuthis was famed for a cult of Isis, although Sophronius calls the resident pagan goddess "Menuthis"; see ibid. 24 [Bringel 26].

20. See *PG* 77, 1100–1105.

21. See esp. Duchesne (1910); Wipszycka (1988). On the relation of the Cyrillian orations and the *Life of Severus* see also Sansterre (1991) 71–74; Alan Cameron (2007) 23–28.

Alexandria.[22] Instead, Gascou has suggested that the shrine was first promoted in the late fifth century by the monks of the Metanoia, a monastery at nearby Canopus.[23]

For our purposes, it is sufficient to note that Sophronius's account of the shrine's establishment is but one among several potential foundational stories (both then and now). Indeed, Gascou's deconstruction of the Cyrillian tradition has pointed to yet more competing myths within the saints' hagiographic dossier and, furthermore, to several rival centers of their cult at Alexandria. Thus, for example, the Constantinopolitan synaxarion assigns the saints' *inventio* not to Cyril but to his predecessor Theophilus, while the Coptic synaxarion locates their final resting place not at Menuthis but at Mark's (where an Arabic miracle of Cyrus similarly situates the saint's thaumaturgic activity).[24] Immediately, then, the biographical details within Sophronius's *Prologue* appear not as innocent statements of an uncontested tradition but as polemical claims designed both to promote Menuthis as the preeminent cultic center and to situate that center within a doctrinally clean history associated with the Chalcedonian Cyril.

This chapter, similarly, approaches the *Miracles of Cyrus and John* as a polemical text composed within a context of, and in opposition to, numerous competing discourses. It focuses, however, not on rival cultic centers or traditions within wider Alexandria but rather on competing models of cultic practice and belief internal to the Menuthis shrine itself. The saints' clientele at Menuthis was both socially and culturally diverse, consisting of rich and poor, orthodox and heretic, believer and apathete.[25] All these supplicants brought to the shrine their own expectations of the saints, their own suppositions as to how best they might be appeased. Amid that polyphony, Sophronius's text attempts not merely to celebrate the saints' cult but to impose and to perpetuate particular models of proper cultic practice and belief. Such models, however, compete not only vertically (with the expectations of a culturally diverse clientele) but also horizontally (with the rival visions of other impresarios of the saints' cult). Thus, the *Miracles* does not so much describe the Menuthis cult as offer the vision of a specific commentator, a vision which can moreover reveal much about his particular ideological concerns.[26]

I argue here that Sophronius's narratives of individual illness, saintly intervention, and final restoration are far more than mere entertaining tales. The funda-

---

22. Gascou (2007); Alan Cameron (2007) 23. Cf. Montserrat (1998) 261–66, who attempts to reconcile the two traditions by arguing that the cult was disused under Cyril's successor and rival Dioscurus and later revived in opposition to a resurgent paganism at Menuthis.

23. Gascou (2007) 276ff.

24. Ibid. 266–68, 273–75. For these rival centers see also Leontius of Neapolis, *Life of John the Almsgiver* 23 [Festugière 374]. Variant traditions concerning a saint's (or saints') origins are not uncommon; see Esbroeck, (1981) on Cosmas and Damian; Davis (2001) 41–47 on Thecla.

25. See also Montserrat (1998) 276–78.

26. *Pace* Maraval (1981) 394 n. 8.

mental questions that Sophronius is forced to address within those narratives—
questions of cosmology, anthropology, soteriology—present his text not simply as
a celebration of the saints but as a theological system that promotes both a model
of proper cultic practice and a particular theological anthropology. Thus, when
Sophronius's subjects move from corruption (disease) through judgment (saintly
intervention) to redemption (cure), they simultaneously replicate the soteriological movement of mankind. In expounding upon the mechanisms by which that
movement is achieved, therefore, Sophronius sets out both a scheme for saintly
appeasement and a strategy for salvation. From the perspective both of cultic practice and of soteriology, therefore, it is remarkable that the *Miracles of Cyrus and
John* attributes minimal significance to liturgy and ecclesiastical hierarchy. In contexts where the saints' supplicant is an anti-Chalcedonian heretic, the Chalcedonian eucharist here assumes a central function as a marker of conversion; but for
an orthodox patient, the sole prerequisite of success before the saints is Christian
virtue—perseverance, resistance to temptation, obedience—independent of communion. On the one hand, therefore, Sophronius recapitulates the concerns of his
anti-Chalcedonian counterparts in the preceding period, who had elevated the
eucharist as the central icon of the orthodox faith; but, on the other, he also recapitulates the eucharistic minimalism of Evagrius, Pseudo-Macarius, and their
heirs, failing to conceive a permanent place for communion—and, with it, the
outward realities of the Church—within the spiritual life. At both the practical and
the theological level, Sophronius substitutes sacrament for asceticism, subordinating communion with Christ through the eucharist to communion with Christ
through virtuous imitation.

## IMPRESARIO OF THE SAINTS

Although the Persians did not cross the Euphrates until 610,[27] an anacreontic poem
of Sophronius suggests that he and Moschus had come to Alexandria earlier, during
the reign of Phocas (602–10).[28] If so, he and Moschus must there have witnessed

---

27. The main sources for the invasion to this point are Ps.-Sebēos, *History* 31–33; Theophanes, *Chronicle* A.M. 6096–98; Agapius, *Universal History* [Vasiliev 448f.]; Michael the Syrian, *Chronicle* 10.25; *Anonymous Chronicle to 1234* 86–87; *Anonymous Chronicle to 724* [Brooks 145f.]; *Chronicle of Seert* 79; *Khuzistan Chronicle* [Guidi 20f.]; Jacob of Edessa, *Chronicle* [Brooks 324f.]. For discussion of the sources and chronology of the initial Persian advances, beginning from 603, see Flusin (1992b) vol. 2, 67–83; Howard-Johnston (1999b) 197–202; less critical is Stratos (1968–78) vol. 1, 58–66.

28. Sophronius, *Anacreontics* 21 (full title "On the Grandfather Menas, Steward of the Ennaton at Alexandria, Wrongly Accused under Phocas of Having Received Theodosius the Son of Maurice" [Gigante 128]) appears to place him in Alexandria during the reign of Phocas, for in addition to its subject it also contains a rare positive description of the emperor at ll. 99–103 [Gigante 132]. Cf. also the fleeting reference to the pro-Phocan Alexandrian patriarch Theodore at Sophronius, *Miracles* 8.2.

nothing less than civil war, although both the *Miracles of Cyrus and John* and the *Spiritual Meadow* give no hint of it. In September 608, as a series of simultaneous provincial riots tore through the cities of the empire, an usurper, Heraclius, had launched from North Africa a coup against the emperor Phocas. That coup proceeded in two directions: Heraclius himself went across the sea to assail the capital while his cousin Nicetas went overland to seize Alexandria and thus to deprive Constantinople of the *annona*.[29] On the basis of our extant sources, we would know little of this Egyptian phase of the campaign—the pro-Heraclian *Paschal Chronicle*, for example, simply records that "in this year [609] Africa and Alexandria revolted"—if it were not for the fortuitous survival of the *Chronicle* of John of Nikiu, which describes a protracted civil war in which Nicetas, having first seized Alexandria, gained the upper hand over Phocas's hated lieutenant Bonosus in a dramatic battle before the city's gates.[30] In the course of the war, we ascertain from elsewhere, the pro-Phocan patriarch of Alexandria, Theodore, was put to the sword.[31]

In his place was elected the Cypriot aristocratic layman John, to be known to tradition as "the Almsgiver." The principal sources that later describe John's life—two anonymous paraphrases of a *Life* by Moschus and Sophronius themselves, and a continuation of that same *Life* by Leontius of Neapolis—all attempt to excuse the election of their hero (who as both a layman and an outsider was ineligible to be patriarch). Thus the former sources claim that John's virtuous life on Cyprus made him celebrated throughout the empire and that "under strong pressure from the emperor Heraclius and through the particular instigation of Nicetas [*hupo tou basileōs Hērakleiou lian ekbiastheis eisēgēsei malista Nikēta*] . . . but also with the approval of the entire Alexandrian populace he was raised as archbishop to the patriarchal throne";[32] while the latter source goes even further, stating that John's accession was "truly by divine decree [*psēphōi ouraniōi*] and not 'from men neither through men' [Gal. 1:1]."[33] The origins of John's association with Heraclius and Nicetas cannot be established conclusively—the former had perhaps encountered him

---

29. See the apparently widespread but no doubt apocryphal tale that whoever of the pair made it first to the capital would be crowned emperor: e.g., in Theophanes, *Chronicle* A.M. 6101; Agapius, *Universal History* [Vasiliev 449f.]; Michel the Syrian, *Chronicle* 10.25; *Anonymous Chronicle to 1234* 90; Nicephorus, *Short History* 1; *Anonymous Chronicle to 741* 6; *Anonymous Chronicle to 754* 1.

30. See John of Nikiu, *Chronicle* 107–9. For Bonosus and the events surrounding the coup in more detail, see Booth (2011b).

31. So *Paschal Chronicle* [Dindorf 699]: "And in this year Africa and Alexandria revolted. And the patriarch of Alexandria was killed by enemies." John of Nikiu, *Chronicle* 107 records that Theodore, whose patriarchate Theophanes places 606/7–608/9, was an imperial appointment. For a parallel situation in Jerusalem see *Paschal Chronicle* [Dindorf 699]; Strategius, *On the Fall* 4.

32. *Anonymous Life of John the Almsgiver* 4 [Delehaye 20f.].

33. Leontius of Neapolis, *Life of John the Almsgiver* 1 [Festugière 347], repeating in the same chapter that John "was enthroned by divine command" [Festugière 348]. For comment see Borkowski (1981) 54f.; Déroche (1995) 137f.

en route to Constantinople via the islands[34]—but soon that association would be confirmed through solemn oaths of friendship and mutual dependence, for at the beginning of his patriarchate John was, or became, the ritual brother (*adelphopoiētos*) of Nicetas,[35] a relationship that was further formalized when the patriarch became the latter's children's godfather (*sunteknos*).[36] Based on a rereading of an awkward passage within Leontius's *Life*, Claudia Rapp, moreover, has made the tantalizing suggestion that John, along with Nicetas, became the *sunteknos* of Heraclius's son and designated successor Heraclius Constantine at the latter's baptism in the capital in 612/13.[37] John, therefore, was a political appointee and an intimate of the emperor's cousin Nicetas, if not also of the wider imperial household.

From the *Lives* that derive from that of Moschus and Sophronius, written for the patriarch's funeral in 620, the Almsgiver appears as an active Chalcedonian. Thus the fifth chapter of those *Lives* informs us that upon his election as patriarch John suppressed the widespread use of the theopaschite addition to the Trisagion, for although he discovered a mere seven chapels (*euktēria*) maintaining the orthodox rites, "through much diligence he provided that that number be increased to seventy, and there sanctioned the celebration of the immaculate offering [*tēn amōmēton proskomidēn*]."[38] As Vincent Déroche has pointed out, this means not that John found the numbers of Chalcedonian churches in decline and realized a rapid reversal of that same process (as is often said) but rather that he enforced the exclusion of the theopaschite addition from Chalcedonian churches that had adopted it.[39] That concern to preserve the strict doctrinal and liturgical boundaries between Chalcedonian and anti-Chalcedonian communities was also manifested, the same texts claim, in the patriarch's attitude to ordinations, for he demanded

---

34. For Heraclius's route via the islands see John of Nikiu, *Chronicle* 109. During the Heraclian revolt coinage bearing the Heraclii was issued on Cyprus; see Grierson (1950). For a suggested sojourn on Cyprus see Olster (1993b) 127; Borkowski (1981) 37f.; but cf. Kaegi (2003) 48. Borkowski (1981) 40 and Rapp (2004) 130 suggest that the aristocrat John may have offered financial support to Heraclius during his rebellion. For Heraclius's connection to Cyprus see also the famous inscription dated to 631 in Sodini (1998).

35. *Anonymous Life of John the Almsgiver* 4 [Delehaye 20f.]; *Epitome of the Life of John the Almsgiver* [Lappa-Zizicas 274], with Rapp (2004) 127–29.

36. See Leontius of Neapolis, *Life of John the Almsgiver* 10 [Festugière 357], with further indications of codependence in Rapp (2004) 128 with nn. 31, 32.

37. Rapp (2004) 132f. For Heraclius Constantine's baptism, with the explicit presence of Nicetas, see Nicephorus, *Short History* [Mango 64].

38. *Anonymous Life of John the Almsgiver* 5 [Delehaye 21]; the version at *Epitome of the Life of John the Almsgiver* 5 [Lappa-Zizicas 275] has minor differences, including "six or seven" rather than simply "seven."

39. See Déroche (1995) 138. As Déroche points out, that same uncritical acceptance of the theopaschite Trisagion would earn John's Chalcedonian contemporary Arcadius of Cyprus the rebuke of Sophronius; see below p. 221.

from those aspiring to clerical position "written confessions [*libellous*] for the preservation of the orthodox faith and the protection of all the proclamations set forth in the canons." "Those priests who repudiated certain heresies, gave written confessions of their repentance, confessed the teaching of the orthodox faith, and both received the four ecumenical holy councils and anathematized all the heresies along with the heresiarchs, these [John] welcomed with open arms and restored as communicants in the catholic Church."[40]

John's patriarchate was nevertheless remembered as a time of peace in anti-Chalcedonian circles, and it is probable that the emperor had charged him with that precise goal: that is, maintaining religious concord following the turbulent period of Heraclius's rebellion.[41] It is thus of considerable interest to note that the later *Life* of Leontius of Neapolis (composed ca. 641–42), which is conceived as an explicit continuation of that by Moschus and Sophronius, presents the pair as the patriarch's most trusted advisors and doctrinal disputants.[42] Thus one chapter of that *Life* states that "Toward the purpose of this celebrated man, which was wholly divine, God sent to him John [Moschus] and Sophronius, who were wise in the divine [*theosophoi*] and of everlasting memory [*aeimnēstoi*]." "They were truly useful counselors," Leontius continues, "and he listened to them unquestioningly as if to fathers and celebrated them as especially noble and courageous soldiers for piety. They put their faith in the power of the Spirit and the Archshepherd; they launched an unceasing war with the Severans and the other impure heretics who were in the province; and like fine shepherds delivered many villages, but more churches, and in like manner monasteries, like sheep from the mouths of these beasts. And because of this the all-holy [patriarch] showed them above all especial honor."[43]

---

40. Anonymous *Life of John the Almsgiver* 5 [Delehaye 21]; the version at *Epitome of the Life of John the Almsgiver* 5 [Lappa-Zizicas 275], interestingly, has "five synods." For the same use of "four synods" (a common usage, which does not imply rejection of the fifth council) cf., e.g., John Moschus, *Spiritual Meadow* 40; Gregory the Great, *Letters* 6.65. For discussion of John's doctrinal and liturgical activities see Déroche (1995) 137–42.

41. See Maspero (1923) 328, citing an Arab translation of Leontius of Neapolis's *Life of John the Almsgiver* (perhaps via Coptic) and the patriarch's presence in Jacobite calendars. See also the two anti-Chalcedonian unions achieved in Egypt under John's patriarchate, referred to together in the *Anonymous Chronicle to 724* [Brooks 146] and analyzed below pp. 104–5.

42. See Leontius of Neapolis, *Life of John the Almsgiver*, prologue, including "The others who have already before me spoken about this wondrous man and archbishop John wrote in an extremely fine and lofty manner [*kallista te kai hupsēlotata*], since they were truly capable in deed—I mean of course John and Sophronius, who feared God, loved virtue, and were truly champions of piety" [Festugière 343]. Leontius's *Life of John the Almsgiver* can be dated through the reference ibid. 5 to the death of Constantine III (April 641) and its apparent commissioning by the archbishop Arcadius of Cyprus (died ca. 642); see below p. 261 n. 138.

43. Leontius of Neapolis, *Life of John the Almsgiver* 33 [Festugière 383]. Cf. also ibid. 5 [Festugière 349f.], where Sophronius offers spiritual comfort to the patriarch, with the presence of Moschus indi-

In another remarkable tale we are told that "Certain heretics called Theodosians came to his holiness seeking to ridicule him, who was wise in the things of God, as inexperienced in the sophistic and rhetorical arts, and to show him contempt as a fool." Upon arriving the heretics confront him and ask, "How is it that, when you are patriarch, you believe in the faith and do not dogmatize about it but entrust your soul and your faith to the lips of others?" —making allusion, Leontius explains, "to John [Moschus] and Sophronius, the true lights." With divine inspiration, the Almsgiver then asks his accusers if they have experienced everything that they believe or proclaim, and they confirm that "If we are not convinced of something through actual experience of it, then we not do believe in or proclaim it." The patriarch then proceeds to ask whether they believe that the All-holy Spirit is present and descends upon the holy font and holy oblation (*epiphoitai kai katerchetai to panagion pneuma eis tēn hagian kolumbēthran kai eis tēn hagian anaphoran*), and when they answer yes, he asks, "What, then? Have you seen it with your own eyes?" "Even if we have not seen it," they respond, "our fathers have." "Well look, then," John retorts, "you too believe from others in what you have not known or seen. And so why do you reproach me that I believe in something that I do not know how to proclaim and dogmatize about?"[44]

In combination, the two *Lives* thus present the patriarch as a committed Chalcedonian, keen to preserve the liturgical and doctrinal boundaries between Chalcedonians and anti-Chalcedonians, but nevertheless avoiding active persecution

---

cated in the statement that Sophronius acts *keleustheis hupo tou epistatountos* and with the additional, parenthetical explanation that "both happened to be there, nobly struggling against the demonic and heretical mania of the godless Acephali"; and ibid. 16 [Festugière 364], in which, "because of the innumerable heretics who lived in the county" ("Theodosians, Gaianites, Barsanuphites, and other impious heretics") John "appointed those aforementioned men of eternal memory—that is, John and Sophronius, favored with the grace of God and illuminated through the divine wisdom of the blessed new Noah, Modestus, who occupied the seat of the city of Christ, who had not acquired a unique ark but who restored all the holy arks of God." On John and his relationship to Moschus and Sophronius see further Usener (1907) 80-107; Chadwick (1974) 49-59; Rapp (2004). On Leontius of Neapolis and his hagiographies see Mango (1984); Déroche (1995); Krueger (1996). Though not considered here, it should be noted that John the Almsgiver is the author of a much-neglected *Life of Tychon*; see Usener (1907).

44. Leontius of Neapolis, *Life of John the Almsgiver* 37 [Festugière 386f.]. It is tempting to suppose that such disputations occurred at the Ennaton, which appears in *Anonymous Life of John the Almsgiver* 9, *Epitome of the Life of John the Almsgiver* 9, Sophronius, *Anacreontics* 21, and in John Moschus, *Spiritual Meadow* 145-46 (with Maisano [1982] 246 for the former), 171, 177, and the additional tale at Paulus Evergetinus, *Synagōgē* 850f. These authors all present the Ennaton as Chalcedonian, but for the presence there of anti-Chalcedonians (both Syrian and Egyptian) in the precise same period see, e.g., *History of the Patriarchs* [Evetts 473-84]; and Hatch (1937) and Baars (1968) 1 on the biblical translations completed there by the Syrian scholars Thomas of Heraclea and Paul of Tella ca. 615-17. For the existence of disputations between Chalcedonians and anti-Chalcedonians in Egypt in this period cf. also Anastasius of Sinai, *Hodegos* 1.1 [Uthemann 9].

and instead engaging with doctrinal dissenters through debate and through Moschus and Sophronius. Although this picture is constructed in retrospect, it nevertheless finds a complement in Sophronius's *Miracles of Cyrus and John*, composed in the first half of John's patriarchate. For here too we discover that same combination of concerns: on the one hand, a strict sacramental differentiation between orthodox and heretic; but on the other, a relative moderation in the denunciation of heretics and explicit promotion of Chalcedon.

Although Chalcedon receives but one explicit mention within the extant Greek text, in a series of central tales Sophronius nevertheless presents the saints as opponents of the enemies of the Chalcedonian settlement.[45] From these it becomes clear that the Menuthis shrine's clientele was less homogenous in its doctrine than he may have cared for. At Alexandria, of course, the Chalcedonian shrine of Menuthis competed against the far grander and more celebrated anti-Chalcedonian cult of Menas at Mareotis.[46] We should not suppose, however, that all Alexandrian Chalcedonians patronized Menuthis and, vice versa, all anti-Chalcedonians Mareotis.[47] Whereas all Christian shrines regularly and very publicly proclaimed their particular doctrinal affiliation (through choice of clergy, the diptychs, the creed, etc.), such shrines were, it seems, nevertheless frequented by Christians of various doctrinal stripes, and those opposed to the official doctrinal position of a shrine could put into play various strategies of subversion or resistance through which to circumvent a shrine's official confession.[48]

Sophronius's *Miracles of Cyrus and John* indeed describes those strategies in vivid detail. In *Miracles* 36, for example, a heretic Theodore comes to the saints and is encouraged by them to participate in the orthodox eucharist. "No, I shall not come," he says. "For I am of another doctrine and not of the confession of the Church. Today I await my mother, who is bringing the gifts of my own communion." Having refused to commune within the Chalcedonian Church, Theodore then requests the saints' permission to take some oil from their tomb. "For many who are not in communion still do this," Sophronius says, "taking the oil

---

45. See below n. 223.

46. For this shrine see Grossmann (1998). For the rivalries between different local cults (or different shrines of the same saints) see, e.g., *Egyptian Miracles of Cosmas and Damian* 18; *Miracles of Cosmas and Damian* 12; *Miracles of Thecla* 4, 29. On the latter Davis (2001) 78f. This competition is also expressed in claims to the precise same miracles; see, e.g., Sophronius, *Miracles* 30.13, and cf. *Miracles of Cosmas and Damian* 2 and 24 and Delehaye (1925) 48f. (here attributed to Menas). On the potential competition between different saints in the same shrine see also Nesbitt (1997) 13f.; Davis (2001) 133–36.

47. On the rivalry between Menuthis and Mareotis see Sophronius, *Miracles* 46.1, 51.7.

48. For this phenomenon elsewhere see, e.g., *Miracles of Thecla* 10, 14; *Miracles of Cosmas and Damian* 17; *Ecclesiastical Canons* 3–4; with Booth (2011a). For pagan supplicants see *Miracles of Thecla* 11, 40, with Dagron (1978) 80–94; *Miracles of Cosmas and Damian* 9. Cf. *Egyptian Miracles of Cosmas and Damian* 23.

that burns in the candle instead of the holy body and blood of Christ, God and Savior of us all."[49] Theodore, therefore, simply circumvents the shrine's sacramental system by substituting the Chalcedonian eucharist for his own imported host and for the oil from the saints' tomb. Similarly, in Sophronius's *Miracles* 38 the heretic Stephanus is healed by the saints and converts to the Chalcedonian faith. His slave asks him, "Look, my lord, here we have obeyed the saints' commands and have communicated with the catholic Church. But when (God willing) we take to the road home, shall we abide by their orders, or return again to how it was before?" Stephanus replies, "While we are here we act as the martyrs see fit, but when we depart from them we shall revert back to our own dogmas as before, and to the faith that our fathers handed down to us."[50] In all instances, the saints punish all those who refuse to profess a (permanent) Chalcedonian confession.

In presenting the saints as Chalcedonians, Sophronius at the same time claims for himself a special cultic insight. His actual status within the saints' cult at Menuthis, however, was no doubt more casual (and contested) than he might confess. A prominent ascetic and advisor to the Alexandrian patriarch, he nevertheless held no discernible position within the shrine's staff. That ambiguous status in turn transfers to the text itself, for whereas certain features—such as the formulaic narrative endings that conclude most miracles[51]—perhaps indicate the text's liturgical function (or at least its intention for that function), other characteristics point to an author engaged in an attempt to establish his own preeminence, and that of his text, within the cult.[52] Indeed, the context of cultic competition with which the *Miracles of Cyrus and John* engages is immediately apparent: "Let each man honor the saints in his own way," Sophronius says in his *Prologue*, "triumph in their gifts by various means, and herald their good deeds in multiple ways: some with the erection of mighty temples and others with the adornments of various marbles; some with compositions of resplendent pebbles, others with bright arts of painters; and some with offerings of gold and of silver, others with silk or silken robes. To put it simply, let all strive toward the honor of the martyrs, according to each man's capacity and desire. And in these things let each seek to outdo the other and display the love that

---

49. Sophronius, *Miracles* 36.15 [Marcos 325].
50. Sophronius, *Miracles* 38.6 [Marcos 334]. For a similar tale cf. Sophronius, *Miracles* 37, with Maraval (1981) 388f.
51. See, e.g., Sophronius, *Miracles* 8.15 [Marcos 256]: "Let us now do the same things as he, and sharing with him the singing of hymns to [the saints], let us move our account on to the miracles that were similarly performed upon his wife by the martyrs." On these formulaic endings see Krueger (2004) 64–70.
52. For a multiplicity of cultic authorities both official and unofficial within a single shrine see esp. *Miracles of Thecla* 41, and the (often derogatory) references to other contemporary rhetors ibid. 19, 21, 30, 38–40.

is within them for the saints." Sophronius then proclaims his own project superior, for he will honor the saints with the word (*logos*), "more precious than any earthly substance, inasmuch as it pours forth not only from the material tongue but also from the spirit."[53] In particular, Sophronius appears to vie with one Christodorus, a cleric and the shrine's steward (*oikonomos*), a patriarchal appointment.[54] In *Miracles* 8, Sophronius describes him as "worthy of remembrance not only through the virtue that he obtained (for he was very much a lover of virtue and of learning) but also because of the earnestness and diligence that he showed toward the saints, and the favor of the martyrs toward him."[55] Yet the cumulative picture is somewhat less sycophantic. At one point, for example, Christodorus's secretary (*notarios*), Menas, is revealed (and punished) as an anti-Chalcedonian heretic, perhaps thus implicating the orthodox credentials of the steward himself.[56] Elsewhere, furthermore, Christodorus is presented as irresolute and ignorant. In *Miracles* 31, for example, upon the completion of a miracle, "Christodorus was amazed," Sophronius tells us, "for he was completely unaware of what was happening."[57] In similar circumstances in the subsequent miracle Sophronius claims (somewhat unnecessarily), "But Christodorus was ignorant (for he learned everything later from a child)."[58] Sophronius thus sets his own cultic insight (through mastery of his narratives and their meanings) against the ignorance of the shrine's preeminent cleric.[59]

53. Sophronius, *Prologue to the Miracles* 7 [Bringel 8].

54. For Christodorus's status as a cleric see his performance of liturgical functions at Sophronius, *Miracles* 31.4, 32.7. Although he is never called *presbuteros*, see the descriptions of his predecessor George at Sophronius, *Miracles* 51.11–12, described also as "leader of their congregation" (51.6: *hēgoumenon tēs autōn homēgureōs*), who "for some time miraculously presided over the temple" (ibid.: *chronon tina tou naou thaumastōs hēgēsamenos*). See also ibid. 51.10: "For [the saints] raised him in their temple like ancient Samuel, and made him virtuous, and promoted him bit by bit in the clergy, when he was of the appropriate age for each stage. And when he was able to manage it, they judged him worthy of their administration." *Pace* Marcos (1975) 49, 52; Gascou (2006) 178 n. 1063. The steward appears in Sophronius, *Miracles* 8, 9, 10, 32, 35, 39, 40, 67, and his secretary ibid. 39.10. They no doubt controlled the treasury (*gazophulakion*) referred to ibid. 40.6. Two deacons are mentioned within the text: a John (ibid. 11.2) and a Julian (ibid. 36.13, 36.19, 36.23). It is unclear, however, whether these two were exact contemporaries. Ibid. 67 refers, more ambiguously, to *hoi tōi neōi diakonoumenoi* (67.4), *hoi tēn hupēresian tou temenous poioumenoi* (67.5), and *hoi tēn leitourgian tōn hagiōn poioumenoi* (67.7). It appears that clerical members of the saints' staff are implied. These were aided by janitors (67.5, 67.7) and *philoponoi* (5, 35.6, 56.2); see Wipszycka (1970).

55. Sophronius, *Miracles* 8.1 [Marcos 253]. Cf. also Sophronius, *Miracles* 9 and 10, which concern Christodorus's wife and daughter, respectively.

56. See ibid. 39.10.

57. Ibid. 31.7 [Marcos 308].

58. Sophronius, *Miracles* 32.8 [Marcos 311].

59. Cf. the author of the *Miracles of Thecla*, a priest who was twice excommunicated by the local bishop and turned to abuse; see *Miracles of Thecla* 12 (against the bishop Basil), *peroration* (against the bishop Porphyrius). The author, therefore, is a controversial figure on the margins of the saint's official cult, in which context the *Miracles of Thecla* also circulated and was performed. See also Krueger (2004) 79–93.

That claim to special cultic status is constructed also through the collection's proclaimed methodology. The seventy miracles that Sophronius selects are, he says, "brought together from the innumerable mass, like a few countable drops compared to an inestimable sea."[60] Yet, he says, "I shall not recall those miracles that happened long ago, nor shall I relate those that occurred in the too distant past, lest I refuse the aid of time, and the haters of God are able to reject them. I shall instead write down the things that occurred in my own time, some of which I saw personally, and others of which I heard about from others who had seen them. Indeed the majority of those who suffered (or rather were cured) are still alive with us, look upon the sun, and engage in present business. They provide witness of the truth to me and have reported these things to me with their own mouths (both for the glory of God and for the honor of the saints). But some had already gone to the Lord and were released from affairs here below. These had announced the things that had happened to them to many people and thus left behind for me reliable witnesses of the things that were said—that is, those who had both seen and heard them happen."[61] Against "pagans" who might doubt the truth of his narratives, Sophronius again reiterates his personal experience of the saints' miracles: "Whereas before I had only heard about [the saints'] grace (like all those who are separated from their temple by a great distance), now also I became a witness to the truth of the things that I had heard. For I went to them on account of a disease of the eye (as was said previously), and I myself was cured and saw others reaping their cures."[62] Sophronius thus claims both for himself and for his narratives an authority based both in personal experience and in meticulous (verifiable) investigation.[63]

Sophronius presents the saints as the eager patrons of his project. The truth (and thus authority) of his narratives is thus established both by detailed inquiry on the ground and by divine verification from above. His text is presented as the cult's official history, inspired by the saints and mediated through the pen of their select impresario:[64]

> Not knowing what to do, I fled to the martyrs and asked them what needed to be done in their service. And they welcomed the purpose of my zeal and did not dishonor it for its rashness but committed to me the task of writing and agreed to confer their help. And so they often appeared to me as I wrote, fulfilling their promise. At one point they provided me with ink and pen; at another they took my parchment

---

60. Sophronius, *Prologue to the Miracles* 31 [Bringel 34]. Cf. *Miracles of Thecla* 44.
61. Sophronius, *Prologue to the Miracles* 31 [Bringel 34].
62. Sophronius, *Prologue to the Miracles* 33 [Bringel 36].
63. For similar statements of the methodology see *Miracles of Thecla* prologue, 44; John of Thessalonica, *Miracles of Demetrius* prologue, 3; *Miracles of Artemius* prologue.
64. Sophronius, *Prologue to the Miracles* 3 [Bringel 3–4]. For the cooperation of the saints cf. Sophronius, *Miracles* 8.1; also *Miracles of Thecla* 31; Cyril of Scythopolis, *Life of Euthymius* 60 [Schwartz 83], with the analysis of Krueger (2004) 77–78.

and corrected my errors. Sometimes also they took pleasure in my tales, and their faces lit up with joy, for they experienced in the telling the pride that we often feel when we come to words or to passages that are rather pleasing. Countless times they rebuked me while I was engaged in other pursuits and chastised me for being negligent. They said, "For how long will you leave the truth unfulfilled?" and they called the present writing, the encomium in their honor, the truth.

Imbued with divine approval, Sophronius's text assumes an extraordinary supernatural status of its own: "There is vast benefit in the recounting of miracles. In like manner it benefits all those who hear it and strengthens their souls with their bodies. To their souls it bestows a more abundant faith and to their bodies an aversion from somatic disease, and equally to both bodies and souls a pure and long-desired cheer and a pleasure full of spiritual exultation that a speech is not able to convey to its audience."[65] The *Miracles of Cyrus and John*, then, is so implicated within the saints' cult that it recapitulates within its audience the saving power of the saints.

Sophronius's purpose in composing his *Miracles of Cyrus and John*, therefore, is complex. Far from simply celebrating Cyrus and John, he attempts also to establish Menuthis both as a Cyrillian foundation and as the preeminent Alexandrian center of the saints' cult (as Gascou has observed). At the same time, and in the face of a doctrinally diverse clientele, the *Miracles* presents orthodox (Chalcedonian) faith as essential to a successful supplication and chastises those heretics or pagans who attempt to circumvent that same imperative. Through constructing that normative paradigm of cultic belief, moreover, Sophronius claims a special status as commentator on the saints' cult. Against rivals who honor the saints in various ways, he offers his text as the highest form of praise and positions himself as superior to other cultic authorities. His *Miracles*, therefore, cannot be conceived in simplistic terms as the shrine's official memory but rather as one of several competing visions of the saints' cult (both written and oral), visions through which rival authorities attempted to impose their own particular interpretations of the cult's history, doctrine, and practice.[66] Thus, just as the dominant Cyrillian foundational

---

65. Sophronius, *Miracles* 20.1 [Marcos 280]. Cf. Sophronius, *Miracles* 18.4. 32.11–12.

66. Sophronius indeed hints at other miracle writers ibid. 35.1. An alternative Alexandrian collection of the *Miracles of Cyrus and John* does indeed survive within an unpublished manuscript at Athos (*BHG* 479i). The first miracle is situated in Heraclius's twenty-fourth year, between October 634 and October 635, although the collection itself is later; see Gascou (2007) 247. It is tempting to speculate that the composition of a new group of the saints' miracles represents an attempt to dethrone Sophronius as the preeminent impresario of the saints' cult, in particular if the author was a devotee of Cyrus of Alexandria, whom Sophronius confronted in the summer of 633; see below p 209. The collection is now the subject of a much-anticipated study by Vincent Déroche. The existence of various (nonextant) literatures is well attested for other cults; see, e.g., the alternative miracles or encomia of Cosmas and Damian described at *Miracles of Cosmas and Damian* 26; *Egyptian Miracles of Cosmas and Damian* 10; Lucius (1904) 258 n. 4 (for the *Suda*'s witness to a collection

myth cannot be regarded simply as the Menuthis cult's official history, neither can Sophronius's text be viewed uncritically as the shrine's official literature.[67] The *Miracles*, like other equivalent collections, should instead be considered as a polemical text composed within a context of, and in opposition to, numerous competing discourses.

## MEDICINE AND MIRACLE

The attitudes that Sophronius and other such miracle writers attempted to instill within their audiences were not limited to questions of religious adherence but embraced a whole range of issues both practical and theological.[68] Within their narratives, those authors instructed supplicants in various aspects of a cult's existence, including the most immediate and mundane of demands—not chattering at night, in one memorable tale.[69] Here, however, we first focus on one particular concern of all such authors: that is, the provision of appropriate attitudes to Hippocratic medicine. Over time the authors of saints' miracles became increasingly hostile to secular medicine, but the *Miracles of Cyrus and John*, while punctuated by intermittent assaults on secular physicians, in fact partakes of a long-established (and orthodox) Christian tradition that attempted not to suppress but rather to include Hippocratic medicine within Christian narratives.[70] Sophronius's complex but careful integration of that medicine reveals him as the most thoughtful of all miracle authors, and at the same time presents his text not as a simple hagiographical narrative but rather, in the words of Christoph von Schönborn, as "a sort of 'implicit catechism.'"[71]

Where in earlier collections of healing-saint miracles the failure of doctors to cure a disease is presented as a matter of fact rather than an occasion for comment,[72]

---

by one Christodorus of Thebes); or Basil of Seleucia's *Acts of Thecla*, described in Photius, *Bibliotheca* 168 [Henry vol. 2, 161].

67. Pace Maraval (1981) 394 n. 8.
68. On this "pedagogic function" see also Maraval (1981).
69. See *Miracles of Artemius* 8, in which a patient at the shrine chatters incessantly and keeps all the other supplicants awake; the saint then appears and threatens to double his disease if he does not leave.
70. See, e.g., Amundsen (1982); Miller (1985) 53–61; Larchet (1991); Temkin (1991). For this integrative tradition see also, on hospitals and monasticism, Miller (1985) 50–67, Crislip (2005); on holy men and medicine Horden (1982) and (1985), Harvey (1984). In the seventh century it is best represented by Anastasius of Sinai's *Questions and Answers*, in which, for example, a doctor heals a number of patients at a shrine of Epiphanius (ibid. 96). On Anastasius and medicine see Déroche (1993) 105f.; Haldon (1992) 137–39.
71. Schönborn (1972) 225.
72. See, e.g., the incurable diseases at *Miracles of Thecla* 11, 24, 25, 38; *Miracles of Cosmas and Damian* 21, 22. In these collections the doctors and the saints can be seen even to collaborate; see *Miracles of Thecla* 11, 24; and esp. *Miracles of Cosmas and Damian* 19a, a wonderful description of a surgeon in

Sophronius's *Miracles of Cyrus and John* is punctuated by (sometimes savage) indictments of secular physicians. The theme is established in the preface and continues unabated to the final, autobiographical notice in which Sophronius describes his own miraculous cure.[73] As in the earlier miracle collections, such criticism is often directed at perceived abuses on the part of physicians. Thus in the opening miracle a patient's doctors, though unable to diagnose the disease, "nevertheless investigated it thoroughly in their desire to be paid, so that they might procure the payment of all payments in silver and a glory better than their credit."[74] In *Miracles* 32, again, certain doctors "practiced their art upon [the patient], knowing that he would not prevail or banish the illness but nevertheless deceiving the poor man in hope of payments."[75] This critique of medical avarice continues throughout the collection, but most damning, perhaps, is *Miracles* 69. Sophronius describes how a patient who becomes blind was "no longer able to be a bother to the doctors, not only since he learned that he would no longer see but because he ran out of money with which to service them."[76] In contrast Saints Cyrus and John are *anarguroi*, "the silverless ones."[77]

Sophronius often expounds also upon the uselessness of medical procedures. Confronted with the failure of doctors to relieve a patient in *Miracles* 19, for example, he says, "Thus [the doctors] show [the disease's] natural perversity, which no fine-powdered or efficacious remedy, no green-anointed plaster, no antidote ascribed to Philo, nor any other natural aid, either unmixed or made from the combination of different elements, has been able to calm up to this very day."[78] The same is repeated at *Miracles* 23: "But the doctors could offer no help to Gennadius, even though they used many unguents, various scourings, bloodletting, purges, and all their other aids."[79] Sophronius reserves his most venomous assault, however, for those most celebrated of ancient medical authorities, Hippocrates and Galen. In *Miracles* 13 (a case of leprosy) Sophronius tells us that "here Hippocrates, Galen, and nature's bastard brother Democritus were of course useless, and with

---

action (under impulsion from the saints). Cf., however, the references to the simple remedies supplied by the saint (or saints), perhaps implying that doctors provide the opposite, at *Miracles of Thecla* 8, 18, 23; also *Miracles of Cosmas and Damian* 23. On the status of medicine within these texts see Dagron (1978) 107f.; Johnson (2006) 147ff.; Csepregi (2002) 107–12.

73. See Sophronius, *Prologue to the Miracles* 9 and *Miracles* 70.7.
74. Ibid. 1.11 [Marcos 246].
75. Sophronius, *Miracles* 32.4 [Marcos 309].
76. Sophronius, *Miracles* 69.5 [Marcos 392]. For similar statements see also Sophronius, *Miracles* 6.2, 24.3, 28.6, 29.10, 40.4.
77. An epithet primarily associated with Cosmas and Damian but used at Sophronius, *Miracles* 21.5 [Marcos 283].
78. Sophronius, *Miracles* 19.2 [Marcos 279].
79. Sophronius, *Miracles* 23.1 [Marcos 285]. Cf. Sophronius, *Miracles* 5.1, 12.5, 30.5.

them those who take pride in their words and offer us their names in place of grand remedies."[80] And again *Miracles* 19: "But the doctors, and their founders Hippocrates and Galen, clever pride of their profession, are not ashamed to proclaim [that profession] inferior, and not only refuse to wage war on the cancerous disease but even crown it the victor."[81] Throughout the collection, a doctor's consultation of Hippocrates and Galen, and the application of their recommendations, often prove futile.[82]

While antagonism toward the medical profession thus pervades Sophronius's collection, it can nevertheless be mitigated by contextualization. It should be noted from the outset that the *Miracles of Cyrus and John* makes no attempt to oppose or to obfuscate rational causes of disease, for Sophronius readily recognizes the natural derivation of most somatic disorders. Thus in *Miracles* 15, elephantiasis is described as "an inhuman disease, which of all the bodily illnesses is the greatest and most bitter."[83] In *Miracles* 58, a rich and noble man falls into "a difficult illness, for the properties of nature do not spare such men, even if they think they are different from their fellow man because of the aforementioned advantages."[84] And, again, in *Miracles* 64, a mute is said to suffer from a "congenital illness, not one derived from some other disease over time but produced in him from birth itself."[85] This recognition of natural etiology allows also for the recognition of Hippocratic medicine. Thus in a discussion on dropsy Sophronius states that doctors "are not able to provide any benefit, neither great nor small, to anyone who falls into this condition, nor to bestow any reassurance from their profession, which they do in the case of nearly all other illnesses, healing some perfectly.[86] Furthermore, whereas certain (perhaps most) doctors are corrupt charlatans, others nevertheless provide genuine relief. For example, Sophronius describes one Theodore, "a doctor, and of good standing in terms of his profession, and because of this very famous. But through magic he became immobile, and not knowing the cause of his disease, he hurried to heal himself, doing those things that he thought would cure him and that when he had applied had helped those suffering not from magic but from a slackness of the limbs."[87]

---

80. Sophronius, *Miracles* 13.2 [Marcos 270].
81. Sophronius, *Miracles* 19.2 [Marcos 279].
82. See Sophronius, *Miracles* 17.3; 22.2; 30.6; 54.6.
83. Ibid. 15.1 [Marcos 272f.].
84. Sophronius, *Miracles* 58.1 [Marcos 373].
85. Sophronius, *Miracles* 64.3 [Marcos 383]. Cf. also Sophronius, *Miracles* 21.1, 23.1, 65.2.
86. Sophronius, *Miracles* 20.2 [Marcos 281].
87. Sophronius, *Miracles* 55.1 [Marcos 370]. Sophronius often acknowledges a hierarchy of medical ability; see Sophronius, *Miracles* 8.9, 9.2, 11.1, 21.3, 25.3, 28.6, 30.2, 32.12, 48.2, 54.5, 60.2, 70.4.

As the final example makes evident, however, not all diseases are of natural derivation. Some are induced through magic or through demons, and others still are the product of the subject's spiritual condition.[88] The *Miracles of Cyrus and John*, in fact, sets out an explicit etiological system that distinguishes diseases derived from nature and those derived from sin. The crucial passage concerns a patient suffering from a disease of the testicles:[89]

> But [the patient] was perhaps ashamed at such an illness, and wanted to keep his infirmity hidden; but we have been commanded to feel shame not at the diseases of the body but rather those of the soul. . . . And the Lord said that those sent into eternal shame were not those weighted down by bodily diseases, for he himself has borne our infirmities and our illness [cf. Is. 53:4; Matt. 8:17], but rather those who are sick in the soul and the doers of evil. For some illnesses are involuntary, those of the body and known in relation to the body. Others are voluntary and products of our will [*gnomēs hēmeteras kuēmata*], those that damage the beauty of the autonomous and intelligent soul [*psuchēs autexousiou kai noeras to kallos*].

Sophronius thus makes a critical distinction between (unwilled) somatic disease as the product of nature and (willed) psychological disease as the product of sin.[90] Thus in the first miracle Sophronius describes how an arrogant young man, Ammonius, was afflicted with scrofula. However, "when [the saints] saw that the young man was proud and carried away toward arrogance in the conceit that comes from wealth, they cured the swelling of his soul before they put an end to the inflammations on his bodily neck."[91] In this particular instance, Ammonius's psychological sickness (arrogance) is not connected with his physical disease (scrofula), for their remedies are separate.[92] Often, however, the two are presented as interdependent, for certain (somatic) diseases are said to be the direct product of divine chastisement for (psychological) sin.[93]

---

88. For instances of magic see Sophronius, *Miracles* 12, 21, 27, 35, 55, 63, 68. For demonic diseases, both through possession and assault, see ibid. 3, 9, 14, 26, 34, 35, 36, 40, 41, 44, 49, 54, 56, 57, 63, 65, 67. In certain cases magic and the demonic are equated; see ibid. 35.12, 63.1.

89. Ibid. 16.1-2 [Marcos 274f.]. On this passage see also Maraval (1981) 391.

90. For an informative contrast to this position see the words of Sophronius's disciple Maximus Confessor in the *Dispute at Bizya* 3 [Allen and Neil 78]; also Maximus Confessor, *Centuries on Love* 1.64.

91. Sophronius, *Miracles* 1.6 [Marcos 244]. For a similar tale of a dissolute youth cf. Sophronius, *Miracles* 12.2-3 (drawing on the metaphor of the chariot in Plato's *Phaedrus* 246a-254e).

92. See Sophronius, *Miracles* 1.7-8.

93. Thus in the same miracle, ibid. 1.10 [Marcos 245], Sophronius tells us that Ammonius "forgot his previous correction [*paideia*] and was corrected [*paideuetai*] again with an illness of the body." For the punishment of skeptics, pagans, and astrologers with illness cf. Sophronius, *Miracles* 28.6, 29.9-10, 30.5, 32.4; with Maraval (1981) 384-86, Dagron (1992) 60f. In most instances heresy seems not to produce disease but rather to prevent cure; see, e.g., Sophronius, *Miracles* 12.6 [Marcos 266], in which

In all such instances (demons, magic, sin) the consequent diseases lie beyond the competence of Hippocratic medicine. Thus in *Miracles* 63 when a patient is afflicted by a demon (itself induced through magic), Sophronius offers the typical statement that "The affliction was beyond their [the doctors'] art, for the disease was curable by God alone and his divine healers, those to whom he has bestowed whatever abilities they wish."[94] The saints, however, are able to alleviate all diseases: they are *hoi sōmatōn kai psuchōn iatroi*, "the doctors of bodies and souls," "skilled in divine medicine, and not in what makes Hippocrates, Galen, and Democritus its founders—for these men speak from the earth."[95] That superior competence, furthermore, includes those natural infirmities that are nonetheless incurable by man, so that while in certain cases the competences of Hippocratic and divine medicine overlap, that of the former is in the final analysis a mere subset of the all-encompassing power of the saints.[96]

The careful integration of Hippocratic medicine within Sophronius's scheme makes further aspects of the *Miracles of Cyrus and John* less problematic. His regular use of Hippocratic terminology (for example), his knowledge of medical procedures, and his frequent expositions on Hippocratic theory appear not disingenuous but entirely consistent with the broader integrative vision.[97] Sophronius's epithet, "the Sophist," of course implies a degree of medical education, and such erudition is indeed evident throughout his text. Indeed, a tale contained within Moschus's *Spiritual Meadow* perhaps allows us to establish a more concrete link with the Alexandrian medical establishment, for Moschus recalls how, during their first sojourn in Alexandria, he and Sophronius "went to the house of Stephanus the Sophist to study." (Or, in the so-called F manuscript of the *Meadow*, "to the

---

a patient's dogma "stands in the way of the provision of a complete health." Where heretics prove intransigent, however, or revert back to their previous dogma, the martyrs either intensify their disease or inflict a new one. For the former see Sophronius, *Miracles* 12.8; 39.5; for the latter see ibid. 37.7, 38.7–9, 39.10.

94. Sophronius, *Miracles* 63.3 [Marcos 381].

95. Sophronius, *Miracles* 43.3 [Marcos 347]. Cf. Sophronius, *Miracles* 22.3 [Marcos 284]: "If the blessed martyrs heal from God, then terrestrial doctors heal from man and from the earth." For the saints as healers of both bodies and souls cf. *Miracles of Thecla* 18; *Miracles of Cosmas and Damian* 2, 6, 9, 11, 23, 25; *Miracles of Artemius* 7.

96. For statements of the saints' superiority see, e.g., Sophronius, *Miracles* 18.3, 41.6.

97. For the various diseases within the text, with equivalent references in Dioscorides, Galen, Aetius of Amida, Alexander of Tralles, Paul of Aegina, and other medical authors, see Marcos (1975) 108–11. For such phrases as "the Asclepiadae call this . . ." see, e.g., Sophronius, *Miracles* 1.3, 15.2, 20.2, 22.1–2, 32.4, 36.4. For the use of Hippocratic terminology and theory (esp. with reference to the humors) see, e.g., ibid. 4.2, 5.1, 8.6, 9.9–10. Sophronius often presents both doctors and patients employing humoral theory; see ibid. 18.3, 35.4, 54.5, 70.5.

house of Stephanus the Philosopher.")[98] Wanda Wolska-Conus has argued that this Stephanus is identical with that celebrated medical commentator of the same name, a contemporary of Sophronius and active in late sixth-century Alexandria.[99] Although that conclusion is regrettably speculative, Wolska-Conus's general conclusions—that Sophronius was not hostile to secular medicine, and furthermore that he "knew medicine such as had been taught at Alexandria in the sixth and seventh centuries"—remain valid.[100]

Once this complex scheme is recognized, it allows Sophronius's sporadic opposition to the medical profession to be appreciated more fully. As several scholars have emphasized, suspicion of, and hostility to, the medical profession is a common motif in ancient literature, unique neither to Christian hagiography nor to Christian texts.[101] It is furthermore notable that nowhere in the *Miracles of Cyrus and John* is medicine subjected to critique as a system of knowledge (unlike, for example, astrological predestination), for natural diseases and natural cures are both recognized as elements of divine creation, and Sophronius himself employs Hippocratic reasoning.[102] The criticism of secular medicine occurs only in contexts where doctors prove corrupt or attempt to overreach their own competence.[103]

As in earlier collections, the superior competence of Saints Cyrus and John over secular physicians is established also through assimilation.[104] Thus the saints are frequently described as *iatroi*, their shrine is an *iatreion*, and sometimes the pair appears in the form of doctors.[105] Indeed, in addition to the standard supernatural cures familiar from other collections (in particular the application of oil from the

---

98. John Moschus, *Spiritual Meadow* 77 [PG 87:3, 2929D]. For the translation of *hina praxōmen* as "in order to study" see Schönborn (1972) 58f. For the textual variation see Maisano (1982) 243; and below p. 91 n. 5.

99. Wolska-Conus (1989) 47–59. For Stephanus see also *PLRE* vol. 3; Temkin (1991) 228–30.

100. Wolska-Conus (1989) 59. It is of interest to note the appearance of a Sophronius among Stephanus's intellectual circle in another text, the astrological *Apotelesmatikē pragmateia* attributed to Stephanus himself; see Papathanassiou (2006) esp. 196–98, identifying the text's Sophronius with Sophronius of Jerusalem (and thus placing him with Stephanus in Constantinople in September 621).

101. See, e.g., Horden (1982) 9f.; Duffy (1984a) 24f.; Miller (1985) 64; Haldon (1997) 44.

102. For the critique of astrological predestination see Sophronius, *Miracles* 28.2–5; see also Maraval (1981) 389f.

103. See esp. Sophronius, *Miracles* 67.10–11 [Marcos 389], in which the saints round upon a janitor who has admitted a "quack" (*iatriskos*) to their shrine in an attempt to save a suicide.

104. For the saints' shrine as *iatreion*: *Miracles of Thecla* 25; *Miracles of Cosmas and Damian* 9, 10, 12, 22. For Cosmas and Damian acting as doctors on their rounds, or performing surgeries, see ibid. 1, 17, 23. For the principle of superiority through assimilation see the discussion of Davis (2001) 76–77. Cf. Déroche (1993) 103 n. 22.

105. "Doctors": Sophronius, *Miracles* 1.5, 4.3, 7.1, 8.5, 10.6, 23.1, 50.6, 52.2; *iatreion*: ibid. 10.6, 17.3, 42.4, 67.10. See also ibid. 33.8 ("in the form of doctors," as master and apprentice), 62.4 (like doctors on their rounds). On assimilation to doctors cf. also Montserrat (2005) 238–40; Déroche (2000) 155–60. The latter argues that the authors of miracle collections, even though in competition with secular

saints' shrine or physical contact with the saint in a dream),[106] the saints often prescribe material remedies drawn from a natural *materia medica* indistinguishable from that of Hippocratic medicine,[107] and that induces physiological effects that Sophronius describes using the lexicon of Hippocratic humoral theory.[108]

Despite this recognition of Hippocratic medicine, and the frequent references to (quasi-Hippocratic) material cures (and their quasi-Hippocratic effects), Sophronius is nevertheless highly sensitive to potential accusations of the saints' reliance upon Hippocratic method. Indeed, an entire tale is devoted to the refutation of that very charge. In *Miracles* 30 the iatrosophist Gesius is said to have "mocked the martyrs Cyrus and John as if they cured human disease from medical skill rather than from the highest divine power. For when he saw the remedies that they prescribed for the sick, which I have in part described, he pronounced them to be the teachings of the doctors. This aid, he said, was derived from Hippocrates, and these others too could be found in his writings; another remedy, he proclaimed, was from Galen, and lay in his corpus; another application, he said, was clearly from Democritus, and he recalled the very place where. And having heard of a plaster he immediately boasted that it was from some doctor, maintaining that everything spoken by the saints had been patched together from one doctor or another. And always he looked for the natural causes of illnesses and of the qualities of the things dispensed, [claiming] that these had been prescribed according to medical logic and [only thus] brought about the purging of the conditions."[109] Then, however, Gesius is afflicted in his upper back ("as if from some divine anger") and "not knowing the cause of the disease, he who had cured others did not know how to cure himself."[110] "But when

---

medicine, were forced to assimilate it to some degree, not only for the reassurance of patients and persuasion of the medically minded but also because such authors could not stretch the limits of what the public would accept.

106. Oil: Sophronius, *Miracles* 1, 3, 7, 22, 50, 65; direct intervention in a dream: ibid. 11, 12, 14, 16, 19, 21, 33, 53.

107. See ibid. 4.4 (citron fruit), 5.4 (dried fig), 8.14 (cooked peas), 10.7 (honey), 13.6 (camel dung mixed with water), 17.4 (salted cumin), 51.8 (Bithynian cheese), 53.2 (roasted pepper), 59.4 (raw leeks). The same is true of more exotic products: powdered crocodile meat (24.5), for example, or an unguent of salted quail (43.4). Such remedies (powders, unguents) are furthermore prescribed in technical language that reeks of the lexicon of secular medicine; see the cure ibid. 6.3 [Marcos 252], said to be a "compound [*sunthēma*] made from parsnip and honey and mixed through rubbing [*dia tripseōs*] with a bread to become from both a single plaster [*kataplasma*]." On the closeness of Sophronius's cures to both contemporary technical and popular medicine cf. Marcos (1975) 136–52; Wolska-Conus (1989) 47–59; Montserrat (2005) 235f. For Byzantine *materia medica* see Scarborough (1984); Stannard (1984).

108. See, e.g., Sophronius, *Miracles* 20.4, 25.6, 36.8–10.

109. Ibid. 30.4 [Marcos 303].

110. Sophronius, *Miracles* 30.5 [Marcos 303]. Cf. Sophronius, *Miracles* 52.1 [Marcos 365] on the chief doctor (*archiētros*) Zosimus: "And he who had promised a cure to others was not able to help himself."

he had done all the things that his profession recommended, and that Galen and Hippocrates and the swarm of other doctors had taught him, the disease had still not diminished."[111]

In due course Gesius is persuaded to visit Saints Cyrus and John, whose solution for his illness is somewhat ironic: "Take the packsaddle of a donkey," they say, "and put it on, setting it around your aching shoulders, neck and arm. And during the middle of the day walk around our entire temple, and shout loudly 'I am a moron and utterly stupid.' And having done as we command, immediately you will obtain a cure for your body."[112] Presented with this cure, Gesius is "unable to make sense of what combination and of what natural and essential quality these things are", but nevertheless eventually complies and is duly cured.[113] Then the saints demand, "Why do you want all the remedies that we bestow upon the sick to be discoveries of long-dead doctors? Tell us, where did your Hippocrates record the aid for your disease? Where did your precious Galen speak of it? Where did Democritus pronounce these things? Where have any of the other celebrated doctors recalled it? If you can find these things being said by them, then indeed you have spoken truly about them; but if you find no proof of them speaking such things, know then that you are mistaken about them."[114] Such qualifications indeed occur throughout the collection.[115]

For Sophronius, then, as for other miracle authors, the desire to emphasize the superior competence of the saints over Hippocratic rivals demands a clear differentiation of their modes of healing. If a somatic disease is of natural derivation, then it is curable by both doctor and saint (although, perhaps, using different remedies); where it proves to be the product of supernatural forces, however, or where secular physicians are unable to alleviate it, the saints alone are able to cure it. The purpose, then, is not to eliminate Hippocratic medicine as a system of somatic

---

111. Sophronius, *Miracles* 30.6 [Marcos 303].
112. Sophronius, *Miracles* 30.8 [Marcos 304].
113. Sophronius, *Miracles* 30.9 [Marcos 304].
114. Sophronius, *Miracles* 30.12 [Marcos 305]. On Gesius, a famous fifth-century physician and therefore symbolic of the entire medical profession, see *PLRE* vol. 2; with Montserrat (2005) 239.
115. See, e.g., Sophronius, *Miracles* 10.6, 11.1, 22.3, 23.1, 27.7, 47.3–4. At *Miracles* 15.6 [Marcos 274] Sophronius tells his audience, "And I shall write of the remedy through which the martyrs easily cured this affliction, lest any officious doctor think the saints applied some Hippocratic principle, and thus contemptuously mock their ineffable power and proclaim Hippocrates or Galen as the author of the cure rather than the martyrs who actually performed it." Sophronius describes the cure as "glass, which [the saints] converted into its old form, sand, after trituration [*meta tēn leiōsin*]" [Marcos 274]. Paul of Aegina 6.22 uses the phrase *hualos chnoōdēs* (lit. "fine-powdered glass") to describe an absorbent of some kind. Speaking of the disease *aigilōps* (an ophthalmic ulcer) he writes: "And fine-powdered glass sprinkled over these miraculously dries them up, as does *Aloe vera* mixed with powdered frankincense" [Heiberg vol. 2, 62]. *Pace* Montserrat (2005) 238, who refers to the cure's "bizarre nature."

healing but rather to establish its subordination to the superior competence of the saints.

Recent research has emphasized the coexistence of several competing epistemologies in late-antique therapeutic culture and a subsequent pluralism of therapeutic options dependent upon a "hierarchy of resort."[116] Indeed, Sophronius and other miracle writers describe a culture in which a visit to the saints was considered only where medicine had failed, even in those instances where the saints had cured a patient before.[117] In various instances, patients demonstrate an ability to draw on several nonexclusive systems of etiological explanation (nature, sin, demons, magic, etc.), and where one system proved unsatisfactory, another was substituted for it without contradiction.[118]

In acknowledging the pluralism of therapeutic options available to late-ancient patients, and in integrating such options within his intellectual scheme, Sophronius both recognizes and legitimizes the pragmatic realities of the therapeutic process. At the same time, his careful integration of secular medicine stands in stark contrast to the tone of another contemporary collection, the *Miracles of Artemius*, where medical practice is repeatedly lambasted without qualification,[119] and where there is a heightened desire to differentiate the saint's mode of healing from that of Hippocratic doctors.[120] Both emphases are concerned most obviously with competition, for the emphasis both upon Artemius's specialization in diseases of the genitals, and upon his successful, sometimes painless surgeries, present incubation as a credible alternative to the painful, potentially fatal, and all-too-real operations performed under the knife.[121] In an important contribution John Haldon

---

116. P. Brown (1981) 114f.; Horden (1982) 12; Haldon (1997) 44; Chirban (2010).

117. See Sophronius, *Miracles* 1.10, 8.9–10; 40.5.

118. For this process of etiological differentiation see, e.g., ibid. 26.2, 30.6–7, 41.3, 45.2, 54.5. In certain instances Sophronius professes some confusion as to the cause of a disease; see ibid. 23.1: "Thus the illness was terrible and unusual. Whether it was magic that produced it or some natural symptom, I do not know. For I was able to learn only of the disease and its treatment" [Marcos 285]; also Sophronius, *Miracles* 52.1.

119. Criticism of doctors is ubiquitous. For accusations of incompetence see, e.g., *Miracles of Artemius* 3, 4, 20; for rapaciousness, ibid. 23, 32, 36.

120. For this desire see the descriptions of the saint's cures and surgical procedures within the various rhetorical excursuses that punctuate the center of the collection ibid. 24–32, and that explicitly attempt to distance the saint from accusations of dependence on medical procedure—e.g., ibid. 24 [Crisafulli and Nesbitt 143]: "So, where are the boastful Hippocrates and Galen, and the countless other doctors? Inasmuch as this kind of gynaecological disease is only a ruptured groin, such people maintain that one ought first to cut with force the patient's folded skin wherever the outer membrane has been made to bulge because of the swelling. [Artemius] attended to none of these things." On the antimedical nature of Artemius's cures see also Déroche (1993) 104. For the simultaneous assimilation of the saint to doctors, as in other collections, however, see *Miracles of Artemius* 2, 6, 22, 38–42.

121. Cf. Miller (1985) 65f.; Déroche (1993) 105–7.

has, however, argued that the "need to stress divine intervention and heavenly authority" within this collection (and in the seventh-century *Miracles of Demetrius* and eighth-century *Miracles of Therapon*) reflects "not just a concern to underline the effectiveness of the saint as patron, nor again a simple desire to emphasise the power of divine intervention in some general competition with Hellenistic medicine," but rather promotes "a powerful hidden agenda ... determined by the wider political and cultural contexts of the times." While confessing that the precise etiology of disease is rarely discussed within the *Miracles of Artemius*, Haldon argues that "the impression gained ... is that, whatever the ability or competence of doctors, maladies caused by spiritual infirmity can only be cured through recourse to the saint; maladies of uncertain origin are best dealt with by the saint, on the ground that impurity or weakness of spirit may well underlie them." He thus observes how "explanations for sickness and its causes had a very specific political dimension, for the state or polity could also be seen metaphorically and allegorically in terms of the human body. The latter was a microcosm of the wider world. The question of the application of the correct cure could thus become a particularly acute issue—differences of opinion on how the human body became open to illness and disease, and what treatment was best prescribed, when transferred to the political level, would result in radically different suggestions for dealing with the maladies of state and society."[122] Heightened hostility to Hippocratic medicine thus represents a more pronounced differentiation of natural (rational) and supernatural (antirational) systems of causation, a differentiation driven by the perceived causes of, and supposed solutions for, the crisis of empire.

Haldon's seductive argument, however, demands some qualification. For the proposed political metaphor to work, diseases within the *Miracles of Artemius* must all be (or must at least all be implied to be) the product of sin and divine punishment. Yet it is notable that the same text, like all other miracle collections, in fact preserves a dual etiological system in which certain diseases are attributed to natural derivation and others to supernatural derivation: some hernias, therefore, are said to be produced through lifting weights or stretching,[123] whereas others are presented as a punishment for sin.[124] No doubt all healing collections might

---

122. Haldon (1997) 52. For the same argument applied to the *Miracles of Therapon* see Haldon (2008). For a similar argument applied to Gregory of Tours's Western narratives, see Van Dam (1993) 86–94.

123. See *Miracles of Artemius* 7 (lifting a weight), 21 (shouting and lifting a weight), 28 (falling out of bed), 30 (stretching while running), 32 (weight falling on stomach), 40 (heavy lifting). Cf. also *Miracles of Cosmas and Damian* 22, in which the patient is said to be afflicted with "a certain humor from bad regimen" (*chumos tis ek ponēras diaitēs*) [Deubner 157].

124. See *Miracles of Artemius* 17 and 37, in which patients who doubt the saint are afflicted with hernias. The same threat is made ibid. 8; the cause of a doubter's hernia ibid. 15, however, is ambiguous. On sin within the *Miracles of Artemius* see now also Alwis (2012), who argues that the frequent reference to inflammation (*phlegmonē*) of the testicles within the text is "a metaphor for passion or

still be read as political metaphor, for the message of all is to some extent the same: that the appeasement of God provides the solution to all maladies, whatever their precise origins. But in all the texts considered here (including the *Miracles of Artemius*), that same metaphor does not demand outright opposition to a rational system of causation (even if such opposition does occur in terms of modes of healing).[125] Indeed, the maintenance of an etiological framework that recognizes both the natural and the supernatural derivation of diseases is crucial for Sophronius, for it provides him with the intellectual basis to construct an alternative metaphor, more soteriological than political. Here the suffering body, as we shall see, is not so much a microcosm of empire; it is instead the summation of postlapsarian man.

### NARRATIVES OF REDEMPTION

In order to understand the soteriological analogies that the *Miracles of Cyrus and John* constructs around its narratives of divine healing, let us revisit once again Sophronius's conception of disease. *Miracles* 16 distinguishes between involuntary illnesses, "those of the body and known in connection to the body" and voluntary illnesses, "products of our will," "deliberately chosen and not of necessity" (*tōn tēs psuchēs proairetikōn kai ouk anankaiōn pathōn*)."[126] This memorable distinction between somatic and psychological disease is an inheritance from the Greek philosophical and medical traditions, but it is presented here within a broader Christian scheme.[127] Thus somatic disease is presented as a product not only of creation but of postlapsarian creation. "Her affliction was terrible," Sophronius tells us of a patient in *Miracles* 21, "for it was not natural like those many diseases that are caused by an excess of humors or generated by other occurrences, and that the body by necessity is allotted to serve after the transgression in Paradise."[128] Such diseases, therefore, are emblematic of mankind's broader corruption in the Fall. Thus in *Miracles* 14 Sophronius says, "Having tasted at origin from the tree of disobedience in Paradise, [the body] was naturally subjected to diseases, and while it

---

excess." For that metaphor cf. Sophronius, *Miracles* 1.6 [Marcos 244]: The saints "cured the swelling [*tēn phlegmonēn*] of his soul before they put an end to the inflammations on his bodily neck."

125. Haldon's argument is most applicable to John of Thessalonica, *Miracles of Demetrius* 3, in which the author describes the onset of a plague. Plague, however, was exceptional and demanded an exceptional explanation. Thus the protagonist of the previous miracle is "bright in birth, and even more resplendent in faith" but nevertheless suffers a "rupture of blood through the stomach" [Lemerle 69]. The latter must therefore be natural.

126. Sophronius, *Miracles* 16.1–3 [Marcos 275].

127. For such traditions see Temkin (1991) 8–17.

128. Sophronius, *Miracles* 21.1 [Marcos 282].

lives it is a slave to corruption and to the pitfalls and properties of corruption, until the common resurrection of all."[129] Hence Sophronius's insistence that somatic diseases are unwilled and without blame, for such are an immovable element of mankind's postlapsarian nature.

Psychological diseases, however, are a product not of nature but of demonic temptation (and thus also the will). "Illness of the immortal soul," Sophronius continues in *Miracles* 14, "is against nature, and is a kind of alteration of its nature, which is incorruptible by the grace of God its creator, and a disease similar to corruption, born in the abuse of demons and instituted by their hatred against us."[130] As the fallen nature of mankind retains the free will to resist such evil, however, willing submission makes us responsible and is therefore a sin.[131] In *Miracles* 35 Sophronius claims that "The father of hatred among men and the teacher of hatred toward one's brother [i.e., the Devil], he who from the beginning had deceived man and stripped him of whatever divine grace there was within him, is not satisfied with his own madness and anger toward men, and ceaselessly assaults them with a great number of disasters and misfortunes, as the divine Job says. But he continuously rouses them against each other, spreads among them the seeds of hatred toward one's fellow man, and incenses them toward hatred of one another, so that they even choose him as an ally in their wrath, in the first place doing themselves a great harm (for the death of the soul is born from that consent) and thus also their brothers, whom we have been ordered to love as ourselves."[132] Sophronius's distinction between somatic and psychological disease, therefore, captures the complex moral position of postlapsarian humankind.

Appreciated thus, Sophronius's narratives take on a broader significance as Christian narratives of redemption. Indeed, the *Miracles of Cyrus and John* often presents the progression of its subjects from (voluntary or involuntary) sickness to health as parallel to the movement of humankind from (voluntary or involuntary) corruption to salvation. In *Miracles* 34, for example, Sophronius recalls the pilgrimage to Menuthis of one Dorothea and her two young sons, describing how the elder child fell sick after swallowing an egg: "When the author of evil [i.e., the Devil] saw them under a tree," he tells us, "at once he remembered that ancient plan that he

---

129. Sophronius, *Miracles* 14.2 [Marcos 271].

130. Sophronius, *Miracles* 14.2–3 [Marcos 271f.]. Cf. Maximus Confessor, *Centuries on Love* 2.16 [Ceresa-Gastaldo 96]: "Passion is a movement of the soul contrary to nature."

131. See Sophronius's spirited defense of free will in the refutation of astrological predestination at *Miracles* 28.2–5.

132. Sophronius, *Miracles* 35.2 [Marcos 319]. See also Sophronius, *Miracles* 27.2 [Marcos 292]: "For we wretched men are accustomed to avenge ourselves on our fellow man not only with tortures and murderous instruments and swords, if he has done some wrong toward us, or being ruled by jealous hatred of our brother, even if he has done nothing wrong to us, still then to set upon him with poisons, abandoning our natural love for our neighbor."

hatched against us under a tree, through which, in Adam and Eve, he killed the entire human race with his malign weapons, and through which it was commanded to slave under death. Hence he revealed to the boys a wind-egg of the serpent through which he had contrived our own destruction and showed it to the lads as it lay beside the tree trunk, which was neither good to eat, nor was it beautiful to look at, even if it appeared so to the boys, as it had to Eve, on account of the immaturity of their age, which had not obtained the trained eyes of the soul [*gegumnasmena ta tēs psuchēs aisthētēria*] in order to discriminate between good and evil."[133] Here, then, the temptation and subsequent sickness of the child is an explicit recapitulation of the temptation and subsequent corruption of Adam and of Eve.[134]

To those corrupted by the Fall, the saints bestow both health and the promise of future salvation. Thus, in *Miracles* 38, when a heretic patient informs his slave that he will rejoin his sect upon his return home, the saints punish him by renewing his former illness. "But the Christ-imitating saints," we read, "in the excess of their love of man and desire that all men be saved [*sōthēnai*] and come to knowledge of the truth, showed the cause [of his illness] in a dream, so that he might come to recognition, and in recognition repent, and repentant be saved [*sōtheiē*]."[135] The soteriological analogy, therefore, is further enabled by the ambiguity of recurrent words in the Greek. The saints offer not only health (*sōtēria*) and release (*lutrōsis*) but salvation (*sōtēria*) and redemption (*lutrōsis*).[136]

In curing the sick, therefore, the saints both inhabit and prefigure the redemptive role of Christ. In several instances their activities are an explicit recapitulation of cures performed by Christ within the Gospels. At the end of *Miracles* 5, for example, the patient whom the saints cure picks up his mat and runs into Alexandria, "imitating by this deed the sick man who lay in the sheep pool, whom Christ cured after thirty-eight years and ordered to pick up his mat [John 5:1–15]."[137] Again in *Miracles* 46, the saints dispatch a blind man to wash his face in the pool of Siloam at Jerusalem, in direct imitation of Jesus in the Gospel of John. "For these [saints]," says Sophronius, "are imitators of the Savior, and use his words, in their haste to demonstrate, through all their cures, whence they draw their grace."[138]

---

133. Sophronius, *Miracles* 34.2 [Marcos 315].
134. On this innocence of youth and the training of the soul cf. also Sophronius, *Miracles* 44.2.
135. Ibid. 38.9 [Marcos 334f.]. Cf. Sophronius, *Miracles* 37.7 [Marcos 331f.]: The patient "knew the cause, and knowing he repented, and repentant he obtained forgiveness, and with forgiveness he was corrected, and corrected he saw once again."
136. See also Sophronius, *Miracles* 66.5–6, in which a healed patient undergoes a quasi resurrection.
137. Sophronius, *Miracles* 5.7 [Marcos 251].
138. Sophronius, *Miracles* 46.3 [Marcos 352]. Cf. Sophronius, *Miracles* 11.9, 23.3, 25.1, 37.9. See also ibid. 70.1–2, in which Sophronius presents the telling of his own miracle as a recapitulation of the news spread by the leper healed by Jesus at Mark 1:40–45. For similar statements cf. also *Miracles of Cosmas and Damian* 14, 15, 26.

Cyrus and John, therefore, are "imitators of Christ" (*Christomimētoi*),[139] "bearers of Christ" (*Christophoroi*);[140] their involvement on earth is a *sunkatabasis*, "condescension."[141] Imitation, however, extends beyond the saints' action to their metaphysical union, for in his *Prologue* Sophronius describes the posthumous pairing of the saints in the language of the (Chalcedonian) union of divine and human natures in the Incarnation.[142]

In addition to replicating both the historical deeds of Christ and his divine-human union, the saints also prefigure his eventual judgment:[143]

> I remember saying in what preceded that I would write two or three tales through which the intensity and astringency of the saints would be made known, for the help of those who are rather indifferent, and for the benefit of those who are more steadfast, so that each might learn that [the saints] know how not only to reward the best but also to punish the worst. And in this they mimic Christ, their Master, who spreads out his kingdom to all but does not concede it entirely to all, but to those who heed it in his message and maintain both faith in what they do and his commands. But to those who are not such, he gives the sleepless worm, eternal hell, and external darkness. [Cf. Mark 9:43–48; Isaiah 66:24.] And to those on the right he says, "Come, receive your inheritance," and to those on the left he shouts, "Go from me into the eternal fire." [Cf. Matthew 25:35–41.] And through the prophet Isaiah he similarly said to all, "If you desire it and you hear me, you will eat the good things of the earth; if you do not desire it and you do not hear me, you will receive the sword. For the mouth of the omnipotent Lord told these things [Isaiah 1:19–20]." And let nobody reproach the saints as austere nor suspect them to be cruel or harsh when they follow in their master's footsteps in doing good to the prudent and punishing the wicked.

In approaching the saints, therefore, the sick anticipate their appearance before Christ upon the Last Day. Indeed, in several places within the *Miracles of Cyrus and John*, the saints themselves emphasize that it is not they who decide who shall be healed or when, but rather Christ, their master.[144] Before both the saints and Christ,

---

139. Sophronius, *Miracles* 38.9.
140. Ibid. 30.8.
141. See ibid. 9.3, 23.2, 62.1.
142. See esp. Sophronius, *Prologue to the Miracles* 11 [Bringel 11]. Sophronius, *Prologue to the Miracles* 12–13 proceeds to describe how the divergent celestial and terrestrial persons and careers of the saints (Cyrus as monk, John as doctor) were brought into perfect union through Christ. Cf. also Schönborn (1972) 225ff., who applies a similar analysis to Sophronius's patriarchal sermon *On Saints Peter and Paul*. Cf. below p. 233 n. 26.
143. Sophronius, *Miracles* 29.1–2 [Marcos 298]. See also Sophronius, *Miracles* 27.3, 34.7. Cf. *Miracles of Thecla* 28 [Dagron 364]: "For in knowing how to treat well those who have done some good in their lives and to punish the impious and those who dare the unholy, [Thecla] imitates, I think, the example of Christ king."
144. See esp. Sophronius, *Miracles* 36.25–26, in which a patient sees an image in which the saints are supplicating Christ. Cf. ibid. 42.5–6 [Marcos 345]: "It is not us [the saints], O women, who are the

those with somatic diseases are without blame, for such diseases are a product of our natural (and blameless) corruption in the Fall. Indeed, such diseases might even be conceived as a boon—"virtues and heavenly *praxeis* (*aretai gar ekeinai kai praxeis ouranoi*)," as Sophronius states in *Miracles* 13.[145] Those with diseases of the soul, however, are sinners, for such diseases are products of the will. Thus *Miracles* 16: "We shall give an account and stand in judgment at the tribunal of Christ, whenever the Judge descends from heaven to distribute to each according to his deeds, but not according to diseases of the body. 'For we all must stand at the tribunal of Christ, so that each may receive his rewards for what he did while in the body, whether good or bad' [II Cor. 5:10]."[146]

In order to appease both the saints and (by extension) Christ, supplicants must first demonstrate the virtue of their souls. For Cyrus and John, says Sophronius, "pay greater attention to the sinlessness [*apatheia*] of souls than the curing of bodies."[147] As a basic precondition of the saints' approval, therefore, patients must demonstrate a resolute faith (*pistis*) in God and the martyrs.[148] In *Miracles* 2, Sophronius thus relates the tale of one Theodore: "He also was from the same city of Alexandria but had a modest fortune, led a life free from anxiety [*bios amerimnos*], and best of all, enjoyed contentment with his lot [*autarkeia*]."[149] Theodore falls into an affliction of the eyes, and the doctors tell him it is incurable. And so "he went to the shrine of the martyrs, clothing himself in a single and unshakable hope, sincere faith in them and the vision that comes from them to those who believe in them thus. And so coming to the holy temple of the martyrs, he reaped the fruit of believing in them with his whole soul [*tēs eis autous holopsuchou pisteōs*]. For having spent the shortest time there, he obtained the fruit that had not been cultivated for a long time but tended in simplicity of faith."[150]

By contrast, other supplicants must undergo an extraordinary test of endurance in order to prove their commitment to the saints. In *Miracles* 69 a blind Roman patient comes to the saints, but makes "the unshakable resolution" not to enter their temple until he has first set aside his disease. "For he sat before the doors of

---

lords of health, but Christ the provider and guide. . . . We offer prayers for everyone alike and cure and immediately release whoever our Lord and Savior, Jesus Christ, orders us to." For a similar statement cf. *Miracles of Cosmas and Damian* 3. On such passages, which occur in all miracle collections, see also Maraval (1981) 388; Déroche (1993) 108–10.

145. See Sophronius, *Miracles* 13.1 [Marcos 269], speaking of Paul's illness at Gal. 4:13–14.
146. Sophronius, *Miracles* 16.4 [Marcos 275].
147. Sophronius, *Miracles* 1.6 [Marcos 244]. Cf. the use of *apatheia* at Sophronius, *Miracles* 69.3 and 70.8, in which it appears instead to mean "freedom from [somatic] disease."
148. See, e.g., ibid. 33.8, 46.2.
149. Ibid. 2.1 [Marcos 247].
150. Sophronius, *Miracles* 2.2–3 [Marcos 247]. On the importance of faith (and the rejection of doubt) within the *Miracles* see also Maraval (1981) 384–87.

the temple, and lay, ate, and slept there. He was burned in summer and froze in winter. He was soaked by violent rains and scorched by fierce rays, since he had the sun blazing over his head during the day and the deliverance of the moon during the night. And he had thus completed eight years in the open air and had not dishonored his own promise, nor even considered dishonoring it up until then, or to abandon it, even if he remained blind for the rest of his life. Hence those who knew him judged him worthy of praise for such constancy of thought and steadfast judgment; and the martyrs judged him worthy of a final cure."[151] Such asceticism is a demonstration of resistance to the demons that assault the soul.[152] Thus in *Miracles* 13 a leper comes to the shrine in hope of a cure. "But when a not inconsiderable amount of time had passed and still he had gained no profit, he grew despondent. For the saints manage their cures with a certain economy. Evidently he was suffering from a diabolical mind that wanted to prevent his cure and to eradicate the sympathy of the saints, and he was no longer able to remain in the temple. For the disease of accidie [*tēs akēdias to pathos*] is serious and greatly opposed to souls that love God, able to do them great injury unless they quickly extinguish it as an illusion of the midday demon [*hōs daimoniou phasma mesēmbrinou*]."[153]

Recalcitrant sinners are brought to obedience either through persuasion or through punishment.[154] Speaking of the obstinate heretic Theodore in *Miracles* 36, Sophronius describes how "When he had heard all these sworn pronouncements, he nevertheless remained disobedient and unchanged [*apeithēs kai ametathetos*]. The martyrs, therefore, since they were not able to persuade him using words, tried with the goads of illness."[155] Those diseases that manifest on patients' bodies (i.e., that occur as a form of divine *paideia*) are both punitive and positive. (*Paideia* itself means both "punishment" and "education.")[156] "For the saints," says Sophronius, "do this to help, as does the common teacher of all, so that those who undergo their

---

151. Sophronius, *Miracles* 69.6–7 [Marcos 393]. Cf. Sophronius, *Miracles* 48.4 (two-year wait), 48.8 (three-year wait).

152. Cf. ibid. 1.12–13 [Marcos 246], in which the saints cure the "vainglory" (*to kenodoxon*) of a patient's soul through ordering him to wear a sackcloth ("which the very poor wear because it is very cheap") and to carry drinking water on his shoulders "to the weaker brothers."

153. Sophronius, *Miracles* 13.3 [Marcos 270]. Cf. Sophronius, *Miracles* 42.4 [Marcos 344], in which the saints' surgery is said to "keep off all accidie and disease." For the importance of patience cf. *Miracles of Cosmas and Damian* 1; *Miracles of Artemius* 27.

154. On "persuasion" and "punishment'" see Sophronius, *Miracles* 12.7–8 [Marcos 266] on the heretic Julian: "Sometimes also [the saints] disputed with him over dogma, proclaiming the truth heralded in the Church, and swore that here was the true proclamation of our God, Christ. But when they had done all these things and more, and could not persuade Julian, who did not want to be persuaded, again they renewed his former illness."

155. Sophronius, *Miracles* 36.8 [Marcos 324].

156. On the "spiritual meaning" of illness within the patristic tradition more broadly see Larchet (1991) trans. Breck and Breck 55–77.

punishments might be able to become conscious [of their sin] and thus demonstrate the proper repentance."[157] In such cases, Cyrus and John "are sympathetic toward those who suffer and bestow their healings quickly upon them, unless they are unworthy of such things, or in need of a greater correction [*paideia*] through some irrationality and hidden sin that only the ruler of all knows, and those to whom he has imparted the knowledge because of their worthiness."[158] But, Sophronius says in *Miracles* 17, the saints bestow healing "on all those who approach them without envy, turning nobody away from their gift, unless someone is particularly loathsome and unworthy of their goodwill, or through lack of faith has become unworthy, or obtained through evil deeds an incontrovertible will [*boulēsis*]."[159] Such instances occur twice within the narrative.[160] Elsewhere, the outward scars of a disease remain as an "edifying proof" of a patient's reluctance to believe.[161]

The route both to the immediate approval of the saints and to future resurrection, therefore, is through adoption of the virtues and resistance to sin. Christ himself provides the paradigm for humankind to follow: "The Lord first revealed to us the road of justice and first discovered the way to complete withdrawal from the diseases of the soul [*tribon tēs apo tōn psuchikōn pathōn teleias anachōrēseōs*], saying to all in his mercy, 'Learn from me' [Matthew 11:29]."[162] Being without sin, Christ's will is in perfect accordance with that of God. Sophronius thus quotes Christ's words within the Gospel of John, "'I have food to eat that you do not know' (by 'food' meaning the salvation and sweet redemption of those who believe in him). 'For my food,' he says, 'exists so that I may do the will [*thelēma*] of the Father who sent me and complete his work' [John 4:34]."[163] The will of mankind, however, while free, is subject to temptation and to sin, a product of our imperfect postlapsarian condition.[164]

Within both the shrine and the broader Christian life, the *Miracles* emphasizes, eventual redemption is achieved through ascetic discipline: the faithful forbearance

---

157. Sophronius, *Miracles* 29.1 [Marcos 298].
158. Sophronius, *Miracles* 35.5 [Marcos 320]. Cf. Sophronius, *Miracles* 42.6 [Marcos 345]: "Certain people arrive here in need of a greater correction (*paideia*), and others again others deserve to be healed quickly."
159. Sophronius, *Miracles* 17.1 [Marcos 276].
160. See Sophronius, *Miracles* 28 and 49. Cf. ibid. 17.2 [Marcos 276]: "And I will recall one or two in the present narrative who received no help from the saints. So that knowing their zeal for faith and hatred of base deeds, men may hurry to please them both in life and in faith." [Marcos 276].
161. See Sophronius, *Miracles*. 37.10 [Marcos 332f.]. Cf. Sophronius, *Miracles* 13.7-8. For incredulity preventing cure cf. *Miracles of Thecla* 25; *Miracles of Cosmas and Damian* 21.
162. Sophronius, *Miracles* 16.4 [Marcos 275].
163. Sophronius, *Miracles* 11.9 [Marcos 264]. For comment see Schönborn (1972) 196–98.
164. On this aspect of Sophronius's theology see Schönborn (1972) 141–47. It should be noted, however, that there is no indication within Sophronius's *Miracles* that the author thinks in corresponding terms of either "one" or "two" Christological wills, as I was tempted to think in Booth (2009). Cf. below pp. 197, 265

of natural corruption and constant resistance to the demons that assault the soul. The adoption of the "ascetic life [*bios monēros*]," Sophronius tells us in *Miracles* 65, "is for [the saints] a much-desired repayment from those they have cured," and furthermore, "they receive such people with joy, and immediately release them in good health."[165] The *Miracles of Cyrus and John* summons its audience to follow the example of Christ and the saints, to renew fallen humanity through obedience to divine will, withdrawal from sin (*anachōrēsis*), and the pursuit both of spiritual perfection (*apatheia*) and the life free from care (*bios amerimnos*).

In the preceding chapter we saw how the dominant late-antique strands of Christian ascetic theory (the vocabulary of which Sophronius repeats in the *Miracles*) were eucharistically minimalist: that is, that such theories subordinated divinization through the objective power of the eucharist to divinization through individual spiritual endeavor. While Sophronius recapitulates such emphases in presenting ascetical self-transformation as the principal route to success at the shrine (and thus also to salvation), he nevertheless preserves a prominent place for the objective effects of the eucharist. In order to be healed, pagan and heretic supplicants at Menuthis must not only cleanse themselves of sin but also illuminate their souls through communion. In *Miracles* 12 the saints repeatedly appear to the anti-Chalcedonian heretic Julian, "warning him to renounce that dogma and to embrace the communion of the catholic Church. And often they carried a goblet full of the holy body and blood of the Lord and ordered him to approach it, seemingly taking communion themselves and summoning Julian to commune with them."[166] In *Miracles* 37 Sophronius describes how the blinded heretic John came to the saints' shrine in search of a cure. "John was sleeping on a bed," he tells us, "and as he slept he saw himself stood before the tomb of the saints, and he begged for the strength back in his eyes. And as he did this he seemed to see the saints seated before their own tomb in the form and shape of priests. They rose from their seats, and taking John's hand led him to the divine altar. Standing him there, they offered him the bread that had become the holy and life-giving body of Christ. And after partaking of this, they took again from the mystical table a goblet full of divine milk, and gave it to him to drink. . . . After this they dismissed John and addressed him with these words: 'See, young man, you have learned the way of true life. In future partake of Christ's mysteries here.' For John was of the same doctrine as Theodosius and Severus, and had obtained the rank of subdeacon in their sect."[167] Waking up John then "immediately partook of the mysteries where he was commanded, setting aside all his previous doctrine and embracing the soul-aiding preaching of the Church. When he had done this as

---

165. Sophronius, *Miracles* 65.4 [Marcos 385].
166. Sophronius, *Miracles* 12.7 [Marcos 266].
167. Sophronius, *Miracles* 37.3–4 [Marcos 330f.].

was ordained, on the third day he saw light with his eyes, which followed the immediate illumination of his soul [*phōtismos tēs psuchēs*]."[168]

In the subsequent miracle, the saints once again demand that a heretic, Stephanus, partake in the orthodox eucharist. Cyrus appears in a dream and says to the patient, "Truly, brother, I want more than anything to hear you saying, as you approach the temple, 'Amen, amen, Lord.'" Then Stephanus "knew that he was talking about partaking in the mysteries of Christ." "For," Sophronius interjects, "this is what we say in response to the priests when they distribute the life-giving and salvific body and blood of Christ God, bearing witness with our own voice and confessing that it is true and called true that it is given by them for our spiritual nourishment [*trophē pneumatikē*] and release from sins [*aphesis hamartiōn*]."[169] Stephanus partakes of the Chalcedonian eucharist and is cured of his blindness, yet the disease returns when the saints punish him for intending to revert to his former dogma. Then, "when the divine martyrs saw him sincerely promising and hurrying with all his might to honor his agreement with them concerning the faith, again they appeared to him in a dream, standing at the altar of Christ and offering bloodless sacrifice, which they brought and presented to him. And as he again partook of it they showed him the Church, Bride of the Savior, flashing in bright clothes, divinely ornamented and with an incomparable beauty that it is not possible to describe in human words. And coming forward to the august altar, she herself again took the mysteries of Christ that lay there and offered them to Stephen. And when the saints asked her if what was given sufficed for perfection [*pros teleiōsin*], she replied with these words: 'I want him to abound in divine gifts, and to acquire more than what is given. For now I have received him as one who is enlightened, and from now on he shall be called my son.' And having spoken thus to the martyrs, she hung from his neck a golden cross that shone with radiant precious stones about his chest, providing this as a proof of the illumination [*phōtisma*] that had been given to him."[170] Sophronius refers to the event as an "initiation" (*mustagōgia*).[171]

---

168. Sophronius, *Miracles* 37.5–6 [Marcos 331]. Cf. Sophronius, *Miracles* 36.22 [Marcos 327]: The heretic Theodore "immediately entered the sanctuary [*phōtistērion*] and partook of the mysteries of Christ, and in partaking of the mysteries illuminated his soul."

169. Sophronius, *Miracles* 38.4 [Marcos 333f.].

170. Sophronius, *Miracles* 38.10–11 [Marcos 335]. Cf. 39.10–11 [Marcos 338]: "For as [the heretic Menas] slept, he saw the saints at the blessed sanctuary and mystical, heavenly table, as if participating in the holy mysteries. They turned, and when they saw that he was not following, they turned to him, and holding rods in their hands they struck him hard and revealed to him the reason for his punishment: 'When you see us entering into communion,' they said, 'why do you not partake with us? If you want to stay in our home, follow what we ordain. Where we enjoy the Master's nourishment, there you also participate.' And they pointed to the holy table with outstretched fingers. . . . When he woke up, he was racked with pains and had bruises as if he had been struck while awake, which bore witness to the will of the saints. Whence he got up and immediately took communion and threw off the pains of his trials. And having illuminated his soul with the grace of true faith, he gained the goodwill of the saints

Conversely, those pagans and heretics who approach the eucharist without abandoning sin are punished. In *Miracles* 31 Sophronius relates the tale of one Theodore, who "while in the temple of the saints, after partaking in the life-giving mysteries of Christ—and whence motivated I do not know: either with something urging him on to anger or inflamed by some great mania and burning with the movement of simmering blood around the heart—the wretched, sorry man insulted the Divine by blaspheming, not by simple words or by abusing him as if he were a fellow slave but by sucking up air through the nostrils and making a noise like some terrible thunder, which forced everyone who was present, who saw it, and who unwittingly heard it, straightaway to shudder."[172] Sophronius then comments: "Many Christians do this, [not] realizing that they are blaspheming, as I see it; for they are completely unaware of what they are doing. If they understood it properly, they would not do it after a myriad tortures. Perhaps it is not pointless to describe this evil. For perhaps when some learn its nature, and that it is an invention worthy of pagan impiety, they will protect themselves against such folly. Porphyry says that when the pagans offer their polluted sacrifices to idols, they sneeze violently and produce such a noise through a forceful, powerful inhalation of the breath, [thinking that they thus] compose a sacred hymn.... This, then, is the nature of such noises, which exist for the service of demons, and which force those who produce them imperceptibly to celebrate the impure demons."[173] Returning to his tale, Sophronius thus relates how "Theodore used this loathsome and demon-pleasing noise after [taking] the food of immaculate communion, and immediately was deprived of his sight and blinded, finding a vengeance to accompany his blasphemy."[174]

The same emphasis upon ritual purity occurs most emphatically within the next miracle, which again concerns a pagan. The silver seller Agapius is convicted of idolatry in Constantinople but flees to Alexandria, "thinking that he could here lie low and be hidden."[175] When he is then afflicted with paralysis ("the work of justice"),

---

for the future." See also the extra text of Sophronius, *Miracles* 39.5, preserved in Latin at *PG* 89:3, 3574A (with Gascou [2006] 146f.), referring to the eucharist in the context of the heretic Peter's conversion.

171. Sophronius, *Miracles* 38.11 [Marcos 335].
172. Sophronius, *Miracles* 31.1 [Marcos 306].
173. Sophronius, *Miracles* 31.2–3 [Marcos 306f.]. On paganism in the text see also Sophronius, *Miracles* 54.6 (a woman who refuses to eat pork "because of the death of Adonis"), with Marcos (1975) 142 n. 101, and cf. the *Miracles of Cosmas and Damian* 2, in which the saints force a Jewish woman to eat pork.
174. Sophronius, *Miracles* 31.3 [Marcos 307]. On this phenomenon see Gascou (2006) 108 n. 618. For Sophronius's concern for ritual purity cf. the Hellenophile Gesius's baptism at Sophronius, *Miracles* 30.2 [Marcos 302; cf. *Odyssey* 4.511]: "And when he rose out of the divine bath he impiously pronounced that line of Homer, 'Ajax perished when he tasted the bitter water.'"
175. Sophronius, *Miracles* 32.1–2 [Marcos 308].

some people advise him to go to Saints Cyrus and John for a cure. Fearing lest in his unwillingness he be unveiled as a pagan ("for the wretched man was pretending to be a Christian"), Agapius acquiesces and travels to their shrine.[176] "Not long after," says Sophronius, "who he was became known to the [other] patients, for as in the manner of heresy he refused to partake of the life-giving mysteries, and much murmuring against him arose among those in the temple. When he realized this, wanting to avert suspicion, he partook of the holy mysteries of Christ. And swiftly after his participation in them, a savage demon fell upon him, exactly as Satan attacked the traitorous Judas after he took the bread that the Savior gave, having dipped it. . . . Tortured by the demon and continuously under its spell, even while asleep, if indeed he did sleep, he was convicted of approaching the mysteries not with faith but with hypocrisy."[177] Those around Agapius realize that the demon will soon kill him, and they remove him from the temple to travel to Alexandria to die. "But when he had left the saints' temple, and traveled a short distance, he breathed his last in much pain, and thus obtained a death worthy of his impiety, for the demon choked him on the road."[178]

For Sophronius the eucharist is the central marker of membership within the Chalcedonian Church. It has, moreover, a powerful and emphatic spiritual effect: it provides "illumination of the soul," "spiritual nourishment," "release from sins." There is, however, a central paradox, for although Sophronius of all miracle authors devotes most space to the eucharist, and although he regards eucharistic participation as the central medium through which the boundaries of the orthodox group are constructed, it is nevertheless notable that mention of the eucharist within the *Miracles of Cyrus and John* occurs only in those cases where the supplicant is a heretic or a pagan (*Miracles* 12, 31, 32, 36–39). Eucharistic communion thus provides an initial moment of spiritual enlightenment in a context of conversion, but in no other instances (where the orthodox credentials of a supplicant are assumed) is there any mention of participation in the shrine's eucharistic rituals. For most subjects, therefore, the purification of the soul (and thus appeasement of the saints) is achieved not through communion with Christ in the eucharist but through communion with Christ in ascetic imitation.[179] Although the eucharist occupies a privileged position as a fundamental expression of orthodox belief, as a permanent mode of spiritual enlightenment (and thus also as a strategy for saintly appeasement) it here seems ineffective.[180]

---

176. Sophronius, *Miracles* 32.5–6 [Marcos 309f.].

177. Sophronius, *Miracles* 32.9 [Marcos 311].

178. Sophronius, *Miracles* 32.10 [Marcos 311]. On ritual purity see also *Egyptian Miracles of Cosmas and Damian* 32, in which a supplicant prepares for the eucharist through fasting.

179. Cf. however Sophronius, *Miracles* 56.3–4, in which the saints offer a "blessing" (perhaps the eucharist) to a patient in the shrine's toilets.

180. On the similarity of the eucharist to baptism in Sophronius's *Miracles* see Déroche (2002) 171 n. 16; Csepregi (2006) 107.

## THE *MIRACLES* IN COMPARATIVE PERSPECTIVE

The general restriction of the eucharist within the *Miracles of Cyrus and John* is symptomatic of a broader marginalization of clerical personnel and ecclesial context within Sophronius's scheme. Enigmatic dreams, it should be noted, are exceptional, and only once do we glimpse a possible clerical arbitration of divine access through dream interpretation.[181] Indeed, while certain of the shrine's clerics are included as subjects of the saints' miracles, such clerics are for the most part conspicuous for their absence from surrounding narratives. Furthermore, where ecclesiastical rituals do appear, it is in dreams, and the rites themselves are appropriated by the saints. In the face of recalcitrant pagans or heretics, therefore, it is not clerics but the martyrs who appear as priests with the cup of communion, spreading incense in the manner of the steward or reading from the Gospels in the form of a deacon.[182] Furthermore, when such supplicants awake and partake of the eucharist, they do so directly, seemingly without clerical mediation.[183]

In a text that celebrates the direct intercession of the saints within the lives of individuals, the absence of clerics and mediating rituals is perhaps unsurprising. Nevertheless, once we situate Sophronius's text next to other healing-saint collections produced within the same period, his presentation of the saints' cult's practice appears not as a simple description of patients' experience at the shrine but as a particular model promoted over potential others, and in competition with other potential impresarios. Several of such collections survive: thus at Seleucia we have the *Miracles of Thecla* (444–76);[184] at Constantinople, the *Miracles of Cosmas and Damian* (ca. 527–623)[185] and *Miracles of Artemius* (658–68);[186] and at Thessalonica, the *Miracles of Demetrius* (ca. 610).[187] Like Sophronius, these authors too insist on

---

181. See Sophronius, *Miracles* 11.8 (John the Deacon acts as interpreter). On the problem of dream interpretation in the various miracle collections see Déroche (2000) 160–62.

182. See Sophronius, *Miracles* 12.7, 32.7, 36.13, 37.3, 37.9. For the saints as clerics cf. *Miracles of Cosmas and Damian* 18. On the *Miracles of Artemius*, however, see Woods (2000).

183. See also the saints' performance of a quasi baptism in the shrine's bath complex at Sophronius, *Miracles* 52.3–4; cf. ibid. 8.15. For the appropriation of liturgical acts by other saints cf. *Miracles of Cosmas and Damian* 21; *Miracles of Artemius* 32, 41.

184. For the date see Dagron (1978) 17–19. It should be noted, however, that not all the miracles within the *Miracles of Thecla* concern incubation.

185. For the dates of the first three collections (*Miracles of Cosmas and Damian* 1–26), see Booth (2011a).

186. For the text's date and composition (which still requires further examination) see Haldon (1997) 33–35; *pace* Nesbitt (1997) 7f.

187. For the date see Lemerle (1979–81) vol. 2, 79f. Like the *Miracles of Thecla*, however, not all miracles contained within John of Thessalonica's *Miracles of Demetrius* concern incubation. For further miracle collections of the period see Déroche (1993) n. 1, to which we can perhaps add at least some of the miracles associated with St. George; see Festugière (1971) 259–67; Hoyland (1997) 89–91.

basic virtue as a precondition of their saint or saints' patronage (although their schemes, we should note, are less developed). Besides the need for faith in the saint, emphasized within all collections, the *Miracles of Thecla* 4 makes explicit reference to the need for supplicants to adopt a "worthy life." For, the text tells us, "the holy megalomartyr will never approach someone who is slovenly and impious."[188] The *Miracles of Cosmas and Damian* too, like the *Miracles of Cyrus and John*, emphasizes the importance of obedience to, and faith in, the saints: "See now, most faithful ones," interjects one author at the end of *Miracles of Cosmas and Damian* 16, "how many difficulties disobedience [hē parakoē] brings about, and what better, what greater benefits the virtue of obedience [hē tēs hupakoēs aretē] produces."[189] The *Miracles of Artemius*, too, makes explicit reference to sin as an impediment to cure.[190]

Alongside these demands for basic virtue, however, these collections also comment on the clerical and liturgical structures of their shrines. In the *Miracles of Thecla* clerics are celebrated as special recipients of the saint's favor, and the cult itself is integrated within a far broader ecclesiastical world. Thus the text describes a remarkable succession of high-level clerics: Dexianus, bishop of Seleucia (3, 7, 8, 32), Menodorus, bishop of Aegae (9), Basil, bishop of Seleucia (12), Marianus, bishop of Tarsus (29), Maximus, bishop of Seleucia (30), John, bishop of Seleucia (44), and Porphyrius, bishop of Seleucia (*peroration*). "The archpriests and priests," the author informs us in *Miracles of Thecla* 6, "are more honorable than all men."[191] Both Dexianus and Menodorus, furthermore, prior to election to their respective sees, are said to have been administrators (*paredroi*) within the saint's shrine.[192] The cult is presented, therefore, both as the playground of an ecclesiastical elite and as a training ground for local clerical honors.

Furthermore, where the *Miracles of Cyrus and John* makes little or no reference to liturgical contexts—that is, contexts that might require clerical intercession—the *Miracles of Cosmas and Damian* contains a general exhortation to participate in the eucharist, added, almost as an afterthought, to *Miracles of Cosmas and Damian* 5:[193]

---

188. *Miracles of Thecla* 4 [Dagron 296].

189. *Miracles of Cosmas and Damian* 16 [Deubner 141]. Cf. for similar statements *Miracles of Cosmas and Damian* 6 [Deubner 111] and 26 [Deubner 167f.].

190. See the words of patients at *Miracles of Artemius* 5 (Crisafulli and Nesbitt 86: "I was diseased in the testicles and waited upon saint Artemius in the Church of Saint John the Baptist at Oxeia, and my sin prevented me from being healed") and 35 (Crisafulli and Nesbitt 184–86: "My children, my sins are impeding me; I am not worthy to obtain a cure on account of my deeds.").

191. *Miracles of Thecla* 6 [Dagron 300].

192. See *Miracles of Thecla* 7, 9, 32; Dagron (1978) 75; Davis (2001) 55f.

193. *Miracles of Cosmas and Damian* 5 [Deubner 108f.]. For the eucharist within this collection cf. also *Miracles of Cosmas and Damian* 10, with Csepregi (2006) 103f. Elsewhere in the collection conversion is guaranteed not by the eucharist but by baptism; see *Miracles of Cosmas and Damian* 2, 9.

Therefore you learn, friends of Christ, what you knew—that is, the operations of the saints Cosmas and Damian, which most of us have enjoyed, lest we neglect to come together as far as we are able in their church, which benefits all. For those who are strong of body who fulfill this procure security for themselves, and those among them judged worthy of a cure by the saints who compete with them fulfill a debt and perform an act of gratitude, in particular whenever their hands look to the needs of those in want and they participate more frequently in divine communion—I mean the awesome mysteries. For those who live with these virtues not only serve God, who is well pleased with such sacrifices, but also found their own souls on rock, souls whose foundations the winds of life are not able to shake, for they have been founded on the secure rock of faith.

The same text sets two miracles at the saints' regular vigil,[194] and furthermore, it contains one narrative that dramatically underscores the potential of liturgical acts to heal. Therein, a deaf and dumb woman comes to the shrine and implores the saints to intervene. "Before being healed," the anonymous authors tell us, "she sang in her mind the Trisagion, and through and by this she was healed with the grace of Saints Cosmas and Damian. For when the lamplight service [*to luchnikon*] had finished in their home and the Trisagion was being pronounced as was the custom, suddenly she who was deaf heard the psalmody and who was mute cried out with the psalm singers, and sang with them the Trisagion."[195] The *Miracles of Thecla*, too, contains a long and detailed description of the liturgical celebrations at the saint's feast,[196] referring to the "spiritual benefit" (*ōpheleia tēs psuchēs*) that those celebrations bestow.[197]

The later *Miracles of Artemius* presents an even more ritualized vision of a shrine's practice (although the eucharist itself is, we should note, absent).[198] In Sophronius's scheme, the sole acts that he prescribes to his audience (through inclusion in the narratives of most miracles) are the offering of prayers to the saints in preparation for a cure and the offering of thanks upon that cure's completion.[199]

---

194. See ibid. 10, 26. The vigil is also mentioned during the preface to the third collection as the context for healed supplicants to recount how they had been healed [Deubner 154].

195. *Miracles of Cosmas and Damian* 7 [Deubner 112]. See also, on the importance within the text of prayer (though not preparatory rituals), Csepregi (2002) 96.

196. See *Miracles of Thecla* 33 [esp. Dagron 376–78]. The same miracle also contains a reference to the objective effect of the eucharist, in which attendees at the saint's annual festival are said to come "to participate in the mysteries, to be sanctified in both body and soul like a new initiate" [Dagron 376]. See also *Miracles of Thecla* 26, which describes the celebration of an annual vigil for the saint at Dalisandus, and 41, which again concerns the saint's feast.

197. Ibid. 29 [Dagron 368]. Cf. also *Miracles of Thecla* 19 [Dagron 340–42]. On such acts in the *Miracles of Thecla* see Dagron (1978) 103.

198. For this absence see Csepregi (2006) 118, who links it to the simultaneous absence of pagans and heretics from the collection.

199. On the importance of prayer see esp. Sophronius, *Miracles* 40.4.

But such acts in themselves confer no spiritual benefit (and are thus not prerequisite to success before the saints). In the *Miracles of Artemius*, however, many miracles refer to the performance of the "customary rites" (*ta ethē*) as a preparation for incubation itself, rites that seem to involve the simple dedication of a votive lamp (*kandēlē*) with wine and oil, or of a candle (*kēros*).[200] Furthermore, the author offers a spirited defense of the efficacy of that practice when, in *Miracles of Artemius* 34, a sick girl who often lights lamps on behalf of her mother is saved from death by the saint. In a dream she sees angels coming to collect her, but Artemius objects and claims her for himself, thus saving her. The author then comments: "These things were revealed to the girl not because the martyr was opposed to the divine command (for this could not be) but in order that she might know that the Lord of Life had long since granted her to him, and lest she think that that the constant lighting [of lamps] be reckoned vain by the saints."[201]

The ritualized context that the *Miracles of Artemius* constructs is maintained further through frequent references to the shrine's weekend vigil. *Miracles of Artemius* 33, for example, takes its setting as the time of the Sabbath, "with the Lord's Day dawning and the spiritual vigil being celebrated, when the *kathisma* had been sung, after the three evening antiphons."[202] The patient has a dream in which the saint commands him to apply a wax salve as a cure. When the patient wakes, "It was then the hour when the midnight rites [*ta mesonuktika*] are fulfilled, and the time when the holy wax salve is distributed with the adoration of the honorable and life-giving Cross."[203] The patient performs his adoration, receives the holy salve, and is cured.[204]

Artemius's night vigil is indeed the defining act of worship for those devoted to his shrine. Thus the subject of *Miracles of Artemius* 15 is described as "a certain man in voluntary service, an attendant to one of the elite, who frequented the night vigil of the Forerunner on the Sabbath."[205] In *Miracles of Artemius* 18 the protagonist is "a certain man who attended the night vigil of the Forerunner from

---

200. See, e.g., *Miracles of Artemius* 4 [Crisafulli and Nesbitt 84]: "And when he reached the Church of the Forerunner he made a votive lamp according to the prevailing custom with wine and oil." Cf. *Miracles of Artemius* 12, 21, 38, 45. On votive lamps see Nesbitt (1997) 22.

201. *Miracles of Artemius* 34 [Crisafulli and Nesbitt 180]. Cf. also *Miracles of Cosmas and Damian* 3.

202. *Miracles of Artemius* 33 [Crisafulli and Nesbitt 174].

203. *Miracles of Artemius* [Crisafulli and Nesbitt 176].

204. For further references to ritual context see *Miracles of Artemius* 29, set during the vigil; 37 [Crisafulli and Nesbitt 194], in which a patient is said to have completed "the night office" (*tēn pannuchon humnōidian*); 39 [Crisafulli and Nesbitt 204], which refers to "the doxology of the lamplight service" (*tēn epiluchnion doxologian*). The lamplight service is also mentioned in *Miracles of Cosmas and Damian* 7.

205. *Miracles of Artemius* 15 [Crisafulli and Nesbitt 102]. The position *ep' eleutherikēi huporgiai* is no doubt equivalent to that of *philoponos* within Sophronius, *Miracles*.

a young age, and who still now sings the verses of the sainted, humble Romanus."
In the same miracle, Theodosius "the church singer" (*psaltēs*) and Abraamius "the treasurer of the society of those who attend the night vigil" (*arkarios tou philikou tōn tēs pannuchidos*) also make appearances, as does one Theophylact, who also "frequented the night vigil."[206] In *Miracles* 36 the author recalls how a woman, Sophia, brought her herniated son to the shrine. "This child, Alexander," we are told, "while he waited there to be cured, assisted ably at the time of the synaxis—that is to say, the holy martyr's festival—hanging lamps and distributing water and [performing] other necessities." When Artemius subsequently appears to the mother, he tells her, "I want nothing from you except this alone—if your son recovers, frequent the night vigil that is celebrated here."[207] When the boy is duly cured, Sophia gives to the church "as much as possible, and in accordance with the saint's supervision she enrolled herself in the night vigil there."[208]

The near-total absence from Sophronius's narratives of liturgical context—or, at least, its sublimation into the realm of the saints—seems therefore quite remarkable. Where the *Miracles of Artemius* prescribes the performance of certain preparatory rituals (*ta ethē*) as an efficacious method of appeasing the saint, the *Miracles of Cyrus and John* demands only resolute faith and resistance to the passions. Furthermore, where the *Miracles of Thecla*, the *Miracles of Cosmas and Damian*, and (in particular) the *Miracles of Artemius* all emphasize the special healing power and spiritual benefit of liturgical contexts, in the *Miracles of Cyrus and John* such contexts are lacking (even if the presence of the patient at the shrine itself is an apparent necessity).[209] Sophronius's silence both on ritual acts and on ritual contexts should not, however, be interpreted as a comment on the absence of such things from the shrine itself, for the *Miracles of Cyrus and John* in fact hints at more ritualized regimes that conditioned the experiences of supplicants at the shrine.[210] Rather, that absence points to the author's own ambiguous attitude

---

206. *Miracles of Artemius* 18 [Crisafulli and Nesbitt 114–20]. On this society see also Nesbitt (1997) 24.

207. *Miracles of Artemius* 36 [Crisafulli and Nesbitt 190].

208. *Miracles of Artemius* [Crisafulli and Nesbitt 192]. See also *Miracles of Artemius* 23, the subject of which is a "certain priest" of the saint's church; 30, in which the subject becomes a warden of the church (*prosmonarios*); and 38, concerning George, who became a reader (*anagnōstēs*). For the clergy at the shrine see also Déroche (1993) 100.

209. See Montserrat (2005) 234, who claims that only two miracles occur outside the shrine (Sophronius, *Miracles* 8, which occurs en route to Mareotis, and 14, which occurs at the entrance to the saint's shrine). To this we may add Sophronius, *Miracles* 33.5, 33.7, 53.3, and perhaps also 9 (which takes place upon seeing the shrine rather than within it) and 11 (which happens at a house next door to the shrine). See also the statement of the saints' omnipresence ibid. 8.4 and 35.11, although such claims are a platitude of the genre; cf. *Miracles of Thecla* 10, 15, 26; *Miracles of Cosmas and Damian* 13.

210. Beyond references to the eucharist and sanctuary see the unique reference at Sophronius, *Miracles* 68.6 [Marcos 391], in which the saints prescribe to a patient the repetition of "a certain written

toward such acts as an efficacious method of improving the soul and thus appeasing the saints. Indeed, Sophronius's silence is all the more remarkable when we consider that his miracle narratives are informed by, and integrated within, a far broader theological scheme. He presents his narratives not as simple tales for the straightforward edification of his audience but rather as analogies for the entire Christian existence. In order to be healed (and thus also to be saved), the text emphasizes, one must strive to improve the soul, but that improvement is achieved not through participation in ritual (beyond the initial illumination offered to converts in the eucharist) but rather through the adoption of the virtues, resistance to the passions, and willing obedience to God (in imitation of Christ and his saints). In comparison with ascetic self-transformation, engagement with the external realities of the Church, as a continuous mode of spiritual enlightenment, here seems insignificant.

According to Leontius of Neapolis's *Life of John the Almsgiver*, the patriarch at Easter used to deliver sermons in which, under inspiration from Sophronius, he railed against the participation of heretics in the Chalcedonian eucharist:[211]

> [We have shown] how much of an immovable zealot was the hieromyst for the orthodox faith, and a great despiser, in particular, of the leaders of heresies. And just as the divinely inspired disciples did for Paul, thus the celebrated [John] put forward Sophronius as a warrior of doctrine and pious dogmas. Often he commanded and bore witness, especially in his festal letters to the people, the point that they should never, at any time, share or approach communion with those of a different faith [*hē tōn heteropistōn koinōnia*], or rather defilement [*koinōsis*].... "How, [he proclaimed], when we have been joined to God through the orthodox and catholic church and faith ... will we not have a share in the punishment that awaits the crowds of heretics in the world to come, if we defile the orthodox and holy faith and pervert it through communion with heretics [*dia tēs koinōnias tōn hairetikōn*]? ... And so I entreat you, my children, do not touch upon such oratories: no, I beg, not for communion, nor for prayer, nor for sleeping [*eis parakoimēsin*]."

The tone of the sermon—which, as Déroche has suggested, may have come from the pen of Moschus and Sophronius themselves—of course resonates with a central theme of the *Miracles of Cyrus and John*: that is, the importance of eucharistic participation in constructing the boundaries between orthodox and heretic.[212] Where other cultic authors comment on the eucharist in passing, Sophronius

---

psalm of those sung in their honor." It is telling, however, that in contrast to the *Miracles of Cosmas and Damian* 7, where psalmody suffices to heal, here Cyrus and John also prescribe a little cake (*pastellon*). For other scattered (but rare) references to ritual see Marcos (1975) 33–39.

211. Leontius of Neapolis, *Life of John the Almsgiver* 49 [Festugière 398f.].
212. For the suggestion Déroche (1995) 125.

affords it a central place within his collection (conceptually and literally), pointing to the necessity of eucharistic communion as the central expression of adherence to Chalcedonian doctrine.[213] Therein he recapitulated, and perhaps responded to, the parallel emphasis developed within anti-Chalcedonian texts such as the *Plerophoriae*.

The importance of the eucharist to Sophronius's vision must nevertheless be qualified. In constructing narratives that celebrated supernatural experiences of the saints, the authors of all miracle collections were aware of the centrifugal pull that unrestricted, unmediated supernatural access might exert.[214] While the celebration of the saints of itself precluded a pervasive emphasis on terrestrial mediation—thought not, it should be noted, in equivalent Western collections[215]—those same authors nevertheless attempted to counteract that pull through the imposition of certain centralizing imperatives. In the *Miracles of Thecla*, the *Miracles of Cosmas and Damian*, and the *Miracles of Artemius*, as we have observed, that qualification is achieved through subtle emphases on clerical structures: in the *Miracles of Thecla*, continuous reference to the local clerical establishment and the special place accorded to the saint's feast; and in the *Miracles of Cosmas and Damian* and *Miracles of Artemius*, intermittent references to ecclesial contexts and to the special favor that such contexts confer. Each of these authors thus constructed a particular model of proper cultic practice that contextualized the dream experience within the liturgical rhythms and hierarchical structures of the shrine itself.[216]

In Sophronius's *Miracles*, however, those same emphases are conspicuous for their absence. Sophronius's text, we must remember, is the longest and most complex of all miracle collections,[217] imbued with an intricate soteriological metaphor through which the progression of its narratives parallels the movement of the Christian life through corruption to redemption. The remarkable absence of ecclesiastical structures from the *Miracles of Cyrus and John*, therefore, appears not as an accident of genre but rather as a deliberate exclusion, a comment on the ambiguous status of those structures within Sophronius's comprehension of the spiritual life. Of all miracle authors, Sophronius is the most concerned to integrate the eucharist within his scheme: it provides an initial moment of spiritual

---

213. This literal centrality is also remarked upon in Csepregi (2006) 109.

214. Cf. Booth (2009).

215. See Van Dam (1993) 89–105 on the miracles composed by Gregory of Tours; and esp. Moreira (2000) 134. On the clerical monopoly of the holy in the West, in contrast to the East, see P. Brown (1971) 95 and (1976).

216. On the potential modification of praise for the saints under pressure from clerical authorities see also Déroche (2000) 164, with n. 71.

217. See also Déroche (2000) 164, who notes also Sophronius's attempts to include the eucharist within his scheme. Maraval (1981) 393 claims also that Sophronius "seeks to elevate the tone" of the genre.

enlightenment and is, furthermore, the quintessential expression of membership within the Chalcedonian Church. But despite its elevated status, the relevance of eucharistic communion as a permanent mode of spiritual progression is at best ambiguous. For Sophronius, the appeasement of Christ involves engagement not with the outward structures of the Church but rather with resistance to the passions and obedience to God in Christlike imitation. His theological vision in effect replicates the eucharistic minimalism that we have observed among the earliest ascetic generations.

In the end, therefore, Sophronius presents a Chalcedonian group defined less through mutual orientation around the orthodox eucharist and more through shared doctrine and ascetic endeavor. That endeavor nevertheless embraces all orthodox Christians, irrespective of social or geographical status, for Sophronius includes within his scheme Christians of all imaginable callings, from the highest to the lowest,[218] from the nearest to the farthest.[219] That inclusive emphasis is important, for it will appear again and again in the texts produced within his circle.[220] Indeed, in subsequent decades it would come to complement a striking modification of that same circle's attitudes to eucharistic participation, through which Moschus, Maximus, and indeed Sophronius would attempt further to close the conceptual gap between asceticism and eucharist, adding to Sophronius's doctrinal emphasis an urgent imperative that all orthodox Chalcedonians, including monastics, partake of the unrivaled spiritual gifts conferred through regular communion.

In the course of time, Sophronius's attitudes to heretics would also undergo a significant evolution. At the time of the text's composition, we should recall, Sophronius is said to have been a prominent doctrinal disputant of the patriarch John, entrusted with engaging with local dissenters. (Thus we may read as somewhat

---

218. For the critique of wealth within the text see esp. Sophronius, *Miracles* 24, but also 6.2, 21.5, 69.5. On the saints as lovers of the poor see ibid. 46.5, 56.1. On this theme see also Maraval (1981) 392; Déroche (2006); Holman (2008). Despite Sophronius's rhetoric, all miracle collections imply that the rich were given preferential treatment at incubatory shrines (by being allowed to sleep closer to the saints' tombs); see *Miracles of Cosmas and Damian* 21; Sophronius, *Miracles* 24.4; *Miracles of Artemius* 17.

219. For the international flavor of the saints' clientele see Sophronius, *Miracles* 51.1, with Montserrat (1998) 274–76. For international visitors see also Leontius of Neapolis, *Life of John the Almsgiver* 1.

220. Nor, it should be said, is that inclusive vision particular to the genre, for it can be contrasted, for example, with the *Miracles of Thecla*, where the saint's clientele is also elite (*pace* Dagron [1978] 73–79). See, e.g., *Miracles of Thecla* 13, 15, 18–20, 30, 35–40, 42–44. The sole named poor supplicant within the text must even be assimilated to his superiors before he can be cured; see ibid. 23 [Dagron 348]: "For even if this man was counted among the poor and the artisans, he was nevertheless judged worthy of a miracle by the martyr and counted by her as equal in rank to the most powerful and far-famed." Cf. also John of Thessalonica's *Miracles of Demetrius*, in which named supplicants are always of significant social status (clerics, bureaucrats, et al.); see Skedros (1999) 115–20; and, on the shrine's iconography, ibid. 97–100, 147; Cormack (1985) 78–94.

autobiographical the striking scene in *Miracles of Cyrus and John* 12 in which the saints are said to "dispute over dogma" with the recalcitrant anti-Chalcedonian Julian.)[221] In the *Miracles of Cyrus and John*, there can be little doubt as to the author's adherence to Chalcedonian doctrine or to the errors of the Theodosians, Severans, Julianists, Apollinarians, and Gaianites whom he critiques.[222] Nevertheless, it should also be noted that explicit reference to Chalcedon occurs in but one tale, and in comparison to some later texts—the *Spiritual Meadow* of his master John Moschus, for example, or his own sermons—his attitude to heretics appears as somewhat moderate.[223] Indeed, at the end of that short but central sequence of vignettes that concerns the conversion of heretics, Sophronius even offers a remarkable defense of his failure to expand on the theme: "I want to recall even more miracles of those who have communicated upon the order of the martyrs and learned the true faith," he informs his audience, "but I content myself with those that have been said, lest anyone think I write the saints' miracles because of my faith [*pisteōs heneka*]."[224] We thus encounter in the *Miracles* the same stance that Leontius of Neapolis, at least, attributes to Sophronius's patron, John the Almsgiver: a firm adherence to Chalcedonian doctrine and to the protection of its rites from heretical pollution, but a simultaneous commitment to conversion through engaged dialogue. From a later perspective—when, as we shall see, Sophronius's attitude both to heretics and to doctrinal dialogue becomes far more aggressive, and when the man himself becomes the emperor's principal doctrinal antagonist—that stance here seems quite remarkable.

Both changes of attitude—that is, the move toward a more developed understanding of the spiritual benefits conferred through the eucharist and the simultaneous hardening of attitudes both to heretics and to doctrinal dialogue—proceeded hand in hand with the deepening crisis of the Eastern empire. Although the *Miracles of Cyrus and John* itself maintains a stubborn silence on the looming shadow of Khusrau's invasion, as Sophronius set down his pen in Alexandria the Persian campaign from which he and Moschus had fled had entered a more ambitious phase. Perhaps taking advantage of Heraclius's revolt against the emperor Phocas, in 610 Persian armies had crossed the Euphrates and invaded the provinces of the Mediterranean seaboard. One force passed from Armenia into Asia Minor and in 611 captured Caesarea in Cappadocia. To the

---

221. See Sophronius, *Miracles* 12.7 [Marcos 266].

222. For these heresies see, respectively, Sophronius, *Miracles* 12.6, 12.11, 12.17, 36.7, 37.4.

223. For the reference to Chalcedon see ibid. 39.5, with more text preserved in the Latin at *PG* 87:3, 3574A (also mentioning the council). Schönborn (1972) 66 n. 47, and Flusin (1992a) 65, both note the (comparatively) moderate stance in this period. On the doctrine of the text see also Maraval (1981) 389; *contra* Montserrat (2005) 231.

224. Sophronius, *Miracles* 39.11 [Marcos 338].

south, a separate Persian force overran Antioch and surrounding cities and then extended operations southward to Phoenicia, where Damascus capitulated in 613. From there that same force seized control of Caesarea, the metropolis of Palestina Prima, and in 613 the emperor Heraclius suffered a significant defeat at Antioch, breaking the Roman resistance.[225]

The Persian capture and occupation of Jerusalem that followed that defeat were to send shock waves throughout the Christian world and force Sophronius and his associates to retreat to the Latin West. Here, alienated from the East and dependent upon Western aristocrats for patronage, those same associates began to explore an alternative model of the Christian Church, a model that made a far more advanced attempt to reconcile the clerical and monastic vocations and with them their competing eucharistic and ascetical theologies. In its immediate context, that model partook of a broader process of ideological realignment through which Chalcedonian Christians, much like their anti-Chalcedonian equivalents in the period before, attempted to comprehend a situation in which the coinherence of empire and Church had been destabilized. But as the crisis in the East deepened and assumed a doctrinal dimension, and as the alienation of Sophronius and his colleagues from Constantinople became more entrenched, so would that new vision come to be deployed for far more subversive ends. Sophronius, in the *Miracles of Cyrus and John*, writes during the calm before the storm. But *Miracles* 69 nevertheless portends an imminent future in which he would challenge the authority of the emperor, recognize the preeminence of Rome, and question the ideal of a Christian empire:[226]

> This man [John] was a Roman, not born in a city that is subject to the tribute of the Romans but having Rome itself, which rules first among them, as his fatherland and city. For truly Rome desired that this be added to its own glory—that is, to take pride in the miracles of Cyrus and John as things that are the more sacred, knowing these things to be brighter by far than crowns and scepters and the purple. For such things have their origin on earth, and are once more dissolved into earth.

---

225. The main sources for these events are Ps.-Sebēos, *History* 33–34; *Anonymous Chronicle to 724* [Brooks 146]; Theophanes, *Chronicle* A.M. 6099–6105; Agapius, *Universal History* [Vasiliev 450]; Michael the Syrian, *Chronicle* 10.25, 11.1; *Anonymous Chronicle to 1234* 92. For the narrative in greater detail see, e.g., Stratos (1968–78) vol. 1, 103–7; Foss (1975) and (2003); Flusin (1992b) vol. 2, 67–83; Kaegi (1973) and (2003) 67–78.

226. Sophronius, *Miracles* 69.2 [Marcos 391f.]. In this light we should also note the reason stated for the papal librarian Anastasius Bibliothecarius's translation of the *Miracles of Cyrus and John* into Latin: that Sophronius was a fine example of resistance to "the rulers of the Christian world" (cited in Neil [2006b] 54).

3

# Moschus and the *Meadow*

To move from Sophronius's *Miracles of Cyrus and John* to the *Spiritual Meadow* of John Moschus is to step into another world: from the hustle and bustle of an Alexandrian cult to the stillness of the Eastern deserts, from the complexities of the mundane to the simplicities of a world rendered black and white, and from the high-minded rhetoric of the sophist to the simple *koinē* of the monk. The differences in presentation are nevertheless deceptive, for the reader will discover fundamental strands of shared interest: like Sophronius's *Miracles*, Moschus's *Meadow* questions the relation of asceticism to the sacramental structures of the Church; like the *Miracles*, it insists on strict adherence to Chalcedonian doctrine as the basis for spiritual endeavor; and like the *Miracles* again, it seeks to extend the demands of ascetic virtue to Christians of all vocations.

The text—a vast hagiographic collection of more than two hundred short biographies, *apophthegmata*, and anecdotes gathered from across the Eastern provinces—stands in the grand tradition of late-antique *gerontika*: that is, anthologies that memorialized the deeds and words of the eastern Mediterranean's ascetic stars. Moschus's collection focuses for the most part on the monks and monasteries of the Judaean desert, but it also includes tales gathered from various authorities and locations across the Christian East. According to the biographical prologue, Moschus arranged it not according to "the sequence of the things heard and seen," but rather according to "the resemblance between them."[1] Certain groups of tales therefore belong together—those associated with Abba Palladius, for example, or those concerning Romans—but otherwise the narra-

---

1. *Prologue to the Spiritual Meadow* 34–37 [Usener 92].

tive appears to proceed at random, oscillating from place to place, person to person.[2]

An immediate consequence of Moschus's open, delinearized narrative is that where later scribes have added their own narratives to, or subtracted others from, manuscripts of the *Spiritual Meadow*, it is difficult to know which are in fact from his pen.[3] Thus where an unattributed tale refers to an Eastern context of the sixth or seventh century, or where such a tale sits within a manuscript alongside recognizably authentic tales (that is, tales with multiple attributions to Moschus or with references to the presence of Sophronius), it is tempting to regard it as an original component of the text. There are, furthermore, a huge number of manuscripts both in Greek and in several other Eastern languages (among which an Arabic and an Old Church Slavonic version are of particular importance).[4] It is perhaps unsurprising, therefore, that the text still lacks a modern critical edition—the unenviable task has occupied Philip Pattenden since the 1970s.

In the current absence of an edition the student of the *Spiritual Meadow* must therefore depend upon the Greek text contained within Migne's *Patrologia Graeca* (noting, however, the important variations contained within the Florentine F manuscript, and set out in an appendix to Riccardo Maisano's excellent Italian translation of the text).[5] The *Patrologia Graeca*'s edition, however, is not without its difficulties—certain tales within it derive from other

---

2. For those tales that appear to belong together see, e.g., John Moschus, *Spiritual Meadow* 69–76 (concerning Abba Palladius), 147–51 (concerning Roman bishops). For Moschus's method see the comment at *Prologue to the Spiritual Meadow* 30–34.

3. The problem was already apparent in the ninth century to Photius, *Bibliotheca* 199 [Henry vol. 3, 96f.]: "Read a book composed of 304 tales.... The compiler has given the book the name *Meadow*.... And in all the books in which the tales are preserved you will not find an equal number, but in some they are divided into 342, with the number increased in part by the division of some chapters, and in part by the addition of tales."

4. On the Greek manuscripts see Nissen (1938); Mioni (1950), (1951); Chadwick (1974) 41–44; Pattenden (1975), (1984), (1989); Maisano (1982) 50–56; Lackner (1982); Munitiz (1983); Palmer (1993b) 50–62. For other versions: (Arabic) Gvaramia (1965); also Levi della Vida (1946); (Slavic) Wijk (1933); Golysenko and Dubrovina (1967); (Armenian) Bousset (1923) 150–69; (Ethiopic) Arras (1967) vol. 2, 184–91; (Georgian) Abuladze (1960); Garitte (1964) vol. 2, 171–85; (Latin) *PL* 129 301C–302A, 369C–371A (in Anastasius Bibliothecarius's translation of the *Acts* of the Seventh and Eighth Ecumenical Councils); also Huber (1913). These various versions are discussed usefully by Chadwick (1974) 44–46; Maisano (1982) 50, 56f.

5. *PG* 87:3, 2852–3112 [henceforth John Moschus, *Spiritual Meadow* 1–219]. For the variations see Maisano (1982) 239–49; and for the F manuscript Pattenden (1975) 40f. I have also used the Greek critical text of *Spiritual Meadow* 120–22, 131–32, set out in Pattenden (1975) 49–54. It should be noted that the Latin translation that accompanies the Greek in the *PG* edition, that of Ambrogio Traversari in the fifteenth century, was also made from the F manuscript (hence its sometimes preferable readings); see Chadwick (1974) 41f.

authors, and it is clear that the text is not comprehensive.⁶ On the basis of the manuscript Parisinus graecus 1596, which contains large sections of the Migne collection, François Nau suggested three convincing addenda, all of which complement existing tales: the first appears to concern the same Marcellus of *Meadow* 152; the second describes the patriarch Amos, whose consecration Moschus attends at *Meadow* 119; and the third includes a reference to "the sophist Sophronius and I" at the Lithazomen—the location also for *Meadow* 69.⁷ In similar vein, on the basis of the Venetian codex Marcianus graecus II.21, which again contains large sections of the *Meadow*, Elpidio Mioni has pointed to further tales not included within the *Patrologia Graeca*'s edition but that appear once again to derive from the pen of Moschus: one perhaps belongs to the series of stories associated with Abba Palladius, and another concerns a debate between Sophronius and the monastic elder Joseph at the Ennaton.⁸ While we can be more or less confident that such tales constitute genuine components of the *Meadow*, other tales within the same manuscripts are more problematic. From Marcianus graecus II.21, for example, Mioni attributed to Moschus a tale that concerns the elder John at the Laura of Heptastomus (a Sabaitic foundation known from the *Lives* of Cyril of Scythopolis).⁹ While that tale is located in the deserts east of Jerusalem (as are most of the *Meadow*'s), and while it concerns a specific protagonist (as do most of the *Meadow*'s), it in fact derives not from Moschus but rather from his fellow Palestinian monk Strategius;¹⁰ another that Mioni attributes to Moschus seems in fact to belong to the hagiographic corpus of Daniel of Scetis.¹¹ In both Marcianus graecus II.21 and Parisinus graecus 1596, furthermore, large portions of the Migne collection are interspersed with vari-

---

6. Thus John Moschus, *Spiritual Meadow* 203, 211, 212, 216, 218, and 219 in fact come from the sixth-century *Reflections* of Abba Zosimas; see Chitty (1966) 164 n. 6. On the possible interpolation of *Spiritual Meadow* 45, 81, and 180, which all involve icons, see Brubaker (1998) 1239–44. On *Spiritual Meadow* 52, 115, 195, 205, and 217 as possible later additions from other texts see also Chadwick (1974) 46, but cf. Maisano (1984) 10–17, who argues for a deliberate appropriation of preexisting material as a means of legitimization.

7. For the published texts see, respectively, Nau (1902b) 613f. (see also Mioni [1951] 76 no. 131); Nau (1903b) 92f. (cf. idem [1903a] 88–89 no. 59; see also Mioni [1951] 82); Clugnet (1905) 51–54 no. 8 (see also Nau [1902a] 612–13; Mioni [1951] 76 no. 118).

8. For these texts see Paulus Evergetinus, *Synagōgē* 429f. (see Mioni [1951] 77 no. 132), 850f. (see Mioni [1951] 75 no. 112).

9. See Mioni (1951) 78 no. 149. For the foundation of the Laura of Heptastomus see Cyril of Scythopolis, *Life of Sabas* 49 [Schwartz 129f.], and for its archaeology Hirschfeld (1990) 40f. The tale has been published in Greek at Paulus Evergetinus, *Synagōgē* 670f. Cf. also Conybeare (1910) 506 n. 18.

10. Strategius, *On the Fall* 6.

11. See Mioni, (1951) 78 no. 152, citing Paulus Evergetinus, *Synagōgē* 658f. See *BHG* 2102c, with the discussion in Dahlman (2007) 49–51.

ous tales that include such vague historical personages as two friends at Apamea; a *scholasticus* at Ascalon; and a pillar saint in part of Asia. In such instances it is near impossible to know if the tale derives from Moschus himself, and in general caution must be advised (even if that did not prevent Wilhelm Bousset, Theodor Nissen, and Mioni from attributing large numbers of such stories to him).[12] Until the publication of Pattenden's edition, the contours of the original *Meadow* must remain unclear.

It is perhaps not unreasonable to suggest that the *Spiritual Meadow* is the most underappreciated of late-antique hagiographic collections.[13] In part that neglect must be attributed to the regrettable lack of a critical text, but it has no doubt been further compounded by a recent scholarly emphasis upon the *Meadow*'s comparative lack of historical interest: that is, its lack of historical detail in comparison to earlier hagiographies and the relative distance of its subjects from contemporary society. This chapter does not challenge such interpretations in themselves: the *Meadow* is indeed less detailed and more anecdotal than previous hagiographies; its subjects are indeed more detached. Rather, it attempts better to understand those features of the *Meadow* through resituating the text within the context of its production and through placing it in conversation not only with previous hagiographies but also with a range of other texts produced within Moschus's own Palestinian circle. Viewed from this perspective, the *Meadow*'s distinct themes (social and geographical breadth, doctrinal polemic, elevation of the eucharist) and its distinct form (anecdotal technique, delinearized narrative, colloquial language) take on new significance not as evidence of introversion or decline but rather as expressions of a wider ideological reorientation through which Moschus and his monastic colleagues, in a context of profound Christian crisis, attempted to overcome the limited social and sacramental vision of the ascetic pioneers and thence to articulate a new vision of a unified, orthodox, and ritualized Church immune to the caprice of political fortune.

---

12. See esp. the thirteen published tales in Nissen (1938) 354–72; and the twelve in Mioni (1951) 83–94. Of these I find only Nissen's first tale (354–56) convincing, since it bears some resemblance to John Moschus, *Spiritual Meadow* 112. Nissen's nos. 8 and 13 also open with the precise topographic and prosopographic details that characterize other tales in the *Spiritual Meadow*, and both concern the monasteries of the Judean desert, but in their present form (at least) they are to my mind too long to be from the hand of Moschus. On the basis of Marcianus gr. II.21 and Parisinus gr. 1596 Mioni and Bousset also ascribed to Moschus many more tales, some of which belong to other authors, and most of which are spurious; see Mioni (1951) 71–82, esp. 82 n. 2; Bousset (1923) 14f., 182–85. For further suggested addenda, see also *BHG* 1442a–y.

13. As often stated by those who study it: e.g., Baynes (1947) 404, 414; Chadwick (1974) 41; Pattenden (1975) 38. There are, however, some notable recent contributions on the text; see Palmer (1991), (1993a, b), (1994a, b), (1997a, b); Maisano (1984); Pasini (1985); Penkett (2003). The superlative treatment is without doubt Chadwick (1974).

## THE FALL OF JERUSALEM

The dramatic events that unfolded at Jerusalem in 614 were to shock the Christian world. "In this year around the month of June," the anonymous author of the Constantinopolitan *Paschal Chronicle* (ca. 630) wrote, "a disaster worthy of unceasing grief befell us. For along with many other cities of the East, Jerusalem was captured by the Persians, and many thousands of clerics, monks, and virgin nuns were slaughtered there. The tomb of the Lord was set ablaze, and the famous temples of God, and put simply, all the honorable places were razed to the ground. The Persians took the holy wood of the Cross along with sacred vessels that were beyond number, and the patriarch Zachariah even became a prisoner. And these things happened not over a long period of time or even a whole month, but in mere days."[14]

From the account of the Armenian historian Pseudo-Sebēos (ca. 660), it appears that the inhabitants of Jerusalem submitted to the Persians without resistance, accepting their rule in return for peace.[15] Then, however, and despite the continued complaisance of the general population, certain elements had rebelled against and murdered the new administrators, thus inviting upon themselves the devastating vengeance of the Persian general Shahrbaraz.[16] The subsequent body count at Jerusalem varies according to the source: in the Palestinian monk Strategius's extensive prose narrative *On the Fall of Jerusalem* (ca. 630) it stands, depending on the manuscript, between 33,067 and 66,509;[17] in Pseudo-Sebēos, at a more sober 17,000 (corrupted to 57,000 in Thomas Artsruni);[18] and in the derivatives of Theophilus of Edessa, at a striking 90,000.[19] The numbers provided in texts must therefore be treated with extreme caution, and although archaeological evidence

---

14. *Paschal Chronicle* [Dindorf 704–5]. For the date, cf. e.g., *Anonymous Chronicle to 724* [Brooks 146], giving A.G. 925 (A.D. 613/4).

15. For Persian policy in the East in this period (recently reassessed as moderate rather than oppressive) see Altheim-Stiehl (1992c); Foss (2003); Gariboldi (2009).

16. See Ps.-Sebēos, *History* 34 [Abgaryan 115f.]. Ps.-Sebēos attributes the rebellion to the *mankunk'* ("young men"), perhaps the circus partisans (sometimes referred to as or at least including *neoi*); for this interpretation see Alan Cameron (1976) 76. Strategius's narrative does not refer to an earlier submission to the Persians but describes a refusal to surrender that he attributes to "agitators and their leaders" ("perturbatores et duces eorum") opposed to the policy of rapprochement adopted by the patriarch Zachariah; see *On the Fall* 5 [Garitte, *Prise* vol. 2, 8]. For Shahrbaraz's initial attempts to ensure the peaceful surrender of the Jerusalemites see also Sebēos, *History*, fr. 2 [Abgaryan 430]; *Khuzistan Chronicle* [Guidi 25]. For the fragments of the genuine Sebēos see the useful study of Mahé (1984).

17. Strategius, *On the Fall* 23 [Garitte, *Prise* 53; Garitte, *Expugnationis . . . Recensiones* vol. 1, 54, 103; vol. 3, 147, 190]. For comparison of the versions of Strategius see the useful table in Flusin (1992b) vol. 2, 160. And cf. the anonymous *De Persica Captivitate* [PG 86:2, 3236A–B]. For the date of the latter text and its relation to Strategius's *On the Fall* see Flusin (1992b) vol. 2, 135f.

18. Ps.-Sebēos, *History* 34 [Abgaryan 116]; Thomas Artsruni, *History* 2.3 [Patkanean 89].

19. Theophanes, *Chronicle* A.M. 6106 [de Boor 301]; Michael the Syrian, *Chronicle* 11.1 [Chabot vol. 4, 403]; *Anonymous Chronicle to 1234* 83 [Chabot vol. 1, 226].

provides little or no confirmation of the picture of widespread damage to Jerusalem's Christian structures,[20] we should not dismiss as willful exaggeration Christian claims to significant violence against the city's population, however short-lived.[21] Although the Persians no doubt had to be conscious of potential repercussions among the significant Christian population within Iran, the Jerusalemites' rebellion nevertheless demanded an unambiguous response.

According to the various sources that pertain to the punishment, the killing of Jerusalem's people was accompanied also by the imprisonment of its patriarch Zachariah, the forced deportation of part of its population, and the seizure of Christendom's most sacred relic, the True Cross. According to a tradition preserved in the *Khuzistan Chronicle* and in Ṭabarī's *Annals*, upon the Persian approach the Cross had been buried in a garden, but Pseudo-Sebēos reports that in their search for the relic, the Persians tortured and decapitated certain clerics until the Christians revealed its place of concealment.[22] The Cross was then removed to Persia, where according to Strategius's evocative account its captors forced their Christian prisoners to trample upon it before the gates of Ctesiphon.[23]

For the monks of the Judaean deserts, the assault upon the city and captivity of the Cross assumed a still greater piquancy. Around 630 Antiochus Monachus, archimandrite of the celebrated laura of Saint Sabas, composed a compendium of monastic knowledge (the *Pandects*), to which he attached a letter as a preface. That preface described how, as the Persians approached Jerusalem, opportunist tribesmen had launched an assault upon the monks of his laura, hoping to uncover hidden monastic wealth:[24]

---

20. For recent attempts to tie archaeological evidence to the assault see Avni (2010: mass graves, esp. at Mamila); Magness (2011: breach in walls). For the broader but meager archaeological evidence that may be tied to the conquest, including an inscription recording Modestus's restoration of the Church of the Ascension, see also Schick (1995) 33–39 and cf. now Stoyanov (2011) 11–23; Bowersock (2012) 31–51; also on the numismatics Ben-Ami and Tchekhanovets (2008); Ben-Ami, Tchekhanovets, and Bijovsky (2010); Bijovsky (2010). It is possible that the lack of firm archaeological data should be attributed to the actions of Modestus in restoring damaged buildings, referred to in a number of sources; see below n. 32.

21. *Pace* Howard-Johnston (2010) 164–67.

22. See *Khuzistan Chronicle* [Guidi 25]; Ṭabarī, *Annals* [de Goeje vol. 2, 1002]; Ps.-Sebēos, *History* 34 [Abgaryan 116].

23. Strategius, *On the Fall* 18 [Garitte, *Prise* vol. 2, 37]. For the journey of the Cross from Ctesiphon to Jerusalem see also the various tales contained within the hagiographic corpus of Anastasius the Persian edited by Flusin (1992b) vol. 1.

24. Antiochus Monachus, *Letter to Eustathius* [PG 89:1, 1424C]. Antiochus claims that "The number of dead was forty-four, and they are celebrated on 15 May" [1425D]. The synaxaria, however, give the date as 16 May; see Patrich (1995) 326 n. 3. The *Pandects* is often dated to ca. 620 but must in fact be later (ca. 630–34); see below p. 204.

For Ishmaelites descended upon our laura one week before the attack upon the holy city, and pillaged all the church's holy vessels, and most of the fathers fled at once. But the more steadfast slaves of the Christ remained in the laura, not wanting to leave the place. The barbarians however seized them, and mercilessly beat them for many days, thinking they would find some money among those who know nothing of this world. Having finally abandoned this purpose, they were maddened and began to cut them all limb from limb. And when we returned from Arabia we discovered that their discarded bodies had been left for many days unburied.

Farther east, toward the Jordan, another monastic text of the same period records similar events. The monk Strategius's narrative *On the Fall of Jerusalem* records how, during the Persian siege, "evil enemies came and seized the blessed elder John" at the Laura of Heptastomus "and killed him";[25] while Antony of Choziba's *Life of George of Choziba* (ca. 631) recalls that "when the Persians invaded and surrounded the holy city, then both the brothers in the coenobium and those in cells left, some fleeing to Arabia with the higoumen, others entering into caves, and others hiding in Calamon.... But the Saracens inspected the wadi, and searched the heights for people among them. They discovered the elder [George] and many of the other fathers, and took them to another wadi, where they killed from their number Abba Stephan, the elder from Syria, who was around one hundred years old or more, and a holy martyred father. The others they put into captivity."[26]

The monastic communities of the Judaean deserts were therefore confronted with a double disaster: first, the capitulation of Jerusalem to the Persians; and second, the reported murder or imprisonment of several prominent monks at the hands of opportunist raiders.[27] It is evident that large numbers of the region's monks were too traumatized to return to their former communities. In his preface to the *Pandects* Antiochus Monachus describes the attempts of the new patriarchal *locum tenens* Modestus to persuade the former residents of Saint Sabas to resettle their laura: on the first occasion, the monks remained within their laura for two

---

25. Strategius, *On the Fall* 6 [Garitte, *Prise* vol. 2, 13]. It is, however, possible that the "enemies" referred to are the Persians rather than Bedouin raiders.

26. Antony of Choziba, *Life of George of Choziba* 7 [Houze 129f.]. For the ransoming of captives from the Arabs (described as *Madiēneoi*) see also *Anonymous Life of John the Almsgiver* 9 [Delehaye 23f.]. The latter describes how John sent Theodore bishop of Amathus, Anastasius archimandrite of the Monastery of Antony the Great, and Gregory bishop of Rhinocura to deliver the ransom; but the later, independent *Epitome of the Life of John the Almsgiver* 9 [Lappa-Zizicas 276] records an intriguing extra detail, for it claims that all this was done through the mediation of "Nicomedes, higoumen of Saint Sabas." The same Nicomedes is also mentioned in Antiochus Monachus, *Letter to Eustathius* [PG 89:1, 1424C], and perhaps in the *Life of John Eremopolites* [Halkin 16].

27. See also Flusin (1992b) vol. 2, 21f. n. 30, on numismatic evidence for the abandonment of the Monastery of Martyrius coterminous with the Persian presence. Cf. Schick (1995) 32f.

months, until "rumor of a barbarian incursion" forced their retreat closer to Jerusalem; on the second, Antiochus reports, some remained "but for a short time, out of fear of the Saracens who neighbored us."[28]

At the same time, the Persian occupation of Palestine must have interrupted the regular pilgrimage trade on which the communities of the Judaean desert had come more and more to depend. The late sixth and seventh centuries had witnessed a dramatic reorientation of those communities from the deserts close to Jerusalem to the pilgrim-centered milieu near the Jordan, an indication of their increasing economic dependence upon small-scale pilgrim donations (rather than aristocratic or imperial largesse).[29] The Persian occupation of Palestine and the concomitant opening of more marginal zones to the attentions of nomadic raiders cannot but have caused severe disruption to those same donations. In his aforementioned preface to the *Pandects*, for example, the Sabaite archimandrite Antiochus Monachus praises the efforts of the patriarchal *locum tenens* Modestus to repair Jerusalem's most prominent sacred sites, and states that "because of this we also have good hopes for the future, and in particular that people will come from other regions to worship at the holy places."[30] Indeed, Pseudo-Sebēos attributes to Modestus a letter to the Armenian catholicus Comitas in which the former, with evident relief, celebrates the recent arrival at Jerusalem of pilgrims from Armenia through whom, Modestus states, God "has consoled us in his great compassion for all our afflictions" [II Cor. 1.3-4].[31] The return of foreign pilgrims no doubt signaled the restoration both of peace and of divine favor; but for some, at least, it must also have marked the welcome restitution of a regular source of income.

Modestus's rapid restoration of Jerusalem's sacred sites and monasteries is celebrated in a number of sources, including one inscription from the Church of the

---

28. Antiochus Monachus, *Letter to Eustathius* [*PG* 89:1, 1424D-1425B]. It is evident that certain monks of Choziba felt similar fears; see Antony of Choziba, *Life of George of Choziba* 8 [Houze 134-35].

29. For this dependence see Hirschfeld (1992) 102-11. For the reorientation and the flourishing of the Jericho milieu see Binns (1994) 52-53, *contra* Flusin (1992b) vol. 2, 39-46, who argues (to my mind unnecessarily) for a stagnation of Judaean monasticism in this period. For the elaboration and expansion of holy sites around Jericho cf. the accounts contained within Theodosius, *On the Topography of the Holy Land* 20; Piacenza Pilgrim, *Itinerary* 9-14; Adamnan, *On the Holy Places* 13-19. For pilgrim donations in this region see John Moschus, *Spiritual Meadow* 13, 107, 157; Antony of Choziba, *Life of George of Choziba* 25; idem, *Miracles of the Blessed Theotokos at Choziba* 1; with Olster (1993a). For the intimate association of biblical text, sacred site, and monasticism in this region see also *Spiritual Meadow* 1 (on John the Baptist and the Monastery of Sapsaphas), 11 (on Elijah and the "Twelve Stones" [at Galgala]); for the archaeology of the same sites in this period, which were both designed to meet the needs of pilgrims, see Hirschfeld (1990) 35-36, 50-52; (1992) 55f. For the reading "Sapsaphas" rather than "Saphas" see Maisano (1982) 240.

30. Antiochus Monachus, *Letter to Eustathius* [*PG* 89:1, 1428B].

31. Ps.-Sebēos, *History* 35 [Abgaryan 116; trans. Thomson 70].

Ascension.[32] Nevertheless, confronted with the Persian occupation certain Palestinian ascetics abandoned the Eastern provinces altogether and retreated to the West. John Moschus and Sophronius were still in Alexandria when news first arrived of Jerusalem's reported devastation. In its wake came a veritable flood of refugees, each no doubt bearing news of events in Palestine.[33] According to the biographical prologue attached to certain manuscripts of his later work, the *Spiritual Meadow*, "when [Moschus] heard of the capture of the holy places and the cowardice of the Romans, he sailed [from Alexandria] with his most intimate disciple Sophronius to the great city of the Romans [*epi tēn tōn Rhōmaiōn megalēn polin*], and as they retreated they sailed via various islands."[34]

As Moschus and Sophronius retreated from the Persian advance, so too did the latter begin to reflect on the fate of Jerusalem. To this period of retreat we should perhaps ascribe three anacreontic poems that share Jerusalem as their theme: *On the Ascension; On the Desire to See the Holy City and the Sacred Places;* and above all, *On the Capture of Jerusalem*.[35] The final poem commences with a *recusatio*—not, however, because its author proclaims his abilities too meager but rather because its substance defies adequate human expression.[36] Sophronius proceeds to describe how the Persians appeared in Rome's Eastern provinces and then approached Jerusalem; how the Christians in surrounding towns abandoned their homes and sought out the safety of the holy city; and how the Persians then laid siege to it and penetrated the defenses, slaughtering the Christian

---

32. See Antiochus Monachus, *Letter to Eustathius* [PG 89:1, 1428B]; Strategius, *On the Fall* 24 [Garitte, *Prise* vol. 2, 55]; Leontius of Neapolis, *Life of John the Almsgiver* 18 [Festugière 365f.]; Ps.-Sebēos, *History* 35–36 [Abgaryan 116–21]; *Palestinian-Georgian Liturgical Calendar* [Garitte 110–11]; Eutychius, *Annals (Alexandrian Recension)* 28, 30 [Breydy 120, 128]; and the manuscript variations of Theophanes's *Chronicle* A.M. 6120 [de Boor 328 n. 26]. Leontius of Neapolis's *Life of John the Almsgiver* 16 [Festugière 364] calls Modestus "the new Noah," "not because he had obtained a single ark, but because he had restored all the holy arks of God." For the epigraphic evidence see the discussion of Schick (1995) 33–47, at 35, 42. The *Khuzistan Chronicle* [Guidi 27], it should be noted, attributes the reconstruction to Khusrau's celebrated Christian minister Yazdin—a remnant, no doubt, of Persian propaganda but perhaps also indicative of the official permission granted to Modestus.

33. For this flood see Leontius of Neapolis, *Life of John the Almsgiver* 6–7, 11 [Festugière 350–53, 357–59]. Cf. also the *Anonymous Life of John the Almsgiver* 6–13 [Delehaye 21–25]; Jacob of Edessa, *Chronicle* [Brooks 324].

34. Prologue to the Spiritual Meadow 25–29 [Usener 92].

35. Sophronius, *Anacreontics* 19, 20, and 14, respectively. On the famous description of Jerusalem in *Anacreontics* 19 and 20 see H. Donner (1981); Wilken (1992) 226–31; Wilkinson (2002) 13f., 157–63. On Sophronius's attachment to Jerusalem see also the epigram attributed to him in the *Anthologia Graeca* 1.123, with Alan Cameron (1983) 291f.

36. Sophronius, *Anacreontics* 14.7–14 [Gigante 102]. It should be noted that the *Anonymous Life of John the Almsgiver* 9 [Delehaye 23]—in fact a paraphrase of a *Life* by Moschus and Sophronius, now lost—attributes a similar dirge upon the disaster to John the Almsgiver (in imitation of the prophet Jeremiah).

population and seizing "holy spoils" (*hagia skula*).[37] The progression of the poem is encapsulated in the ascending doublets that punctuate the text: from "Come, children of the blessed Christians, grieve for the lofty Jerusalemites" and "Weep, nations of the blessed Christians, for the holy Jerusalemites are slain"; to "Christ, may you see to it that Persia is soon seen burning in revenge for the holy places," and "Christ, may you subdue the ill-starred children of God-hating Persia by the hands of the Christians."[38]

As such lines make evident, the poem is nearly Manichaean in its moral vision. The Persians are presented both as barbaric, wielding "murderous swords" and "accomplishing all with cruelty,"[39] and demonic, blaspheming against God and inspired through "the mania of demons."[40] The Christians of Palestine, in contrast, are the passive victims of Persian aggression, an *hieros dēmos* that flees before the Persian armies; Jerusalem is inhabited "as a heaven," and its virgins "appear like angels upon the earth."[41] The devastation is thus conceived both as the clash of unfettered, barbarous aggression against settled civilization and as the sacrificial slaughter of an angelic Christian nation at the hands of demonic pagans. The Jerusalemites here, therefore, are blameless, and in ascribing Persian success to demonic inspiration Sophronius externalizes its cause and thus postpones the need to reconcile events to divine Providence. There is no introspection, no appeal to collective Christian sin as the cause of divine anger. Jerusalem's destruction cannot be appeased in the moral restoration of its population; it must instead be appeased through the sanctified violence of the pious Christian empire.

In Palestinian circles Sophronius's rationalization of events as the triumph of demonic rage was somewhat unique—indeed, he too would later abandon it. Other Palestinian observers instead reverted to a familiar biblical paradigm and pointed to the sins of Jerusalem's population as the cause of its devastation. Strategius's narrative *On the Fall of Jerusalem* (ca. 630)—which provides an extensive account of Jerusalem's capitulation and the exile of the patriarch Zachariah—time and again points to collective sin as the cause of Christian reversals, although its author, like other contemporaries confronted with large-scale catastrophes,

---

37. Sophronius, *Anacreontics* 99 [Gigante 107]. It is possible that the *hagia skula* include the Cross, although it is notable that Sophronius makes no explicit mention of it. For early Palestinian references to its seizure, however, see, e.g., Strategius, *On the Fall*, e.g., 13 [Garitte, *Prise* vol. 2, 23f.]; Antony of Choziba, *Life of George of Choziba* 6 [Houze 127]; Antiochus Monachus, *Confession* [PG 89:1, 1852B]; idem, *Pandects* 107 [PG 89:1, 1764C]; *De Persica Captivitate* [PG 86:2, 3236A].

38. Sophronius, *Anacreontics* 14.5–6, 23–24, 73–74, 91–92 [Gigante 102–7].

39. Sophronius, *Anacreontics* 14.28, 93 [Gigante 103, 107].

40. Sophronius, *Anacreontics* 14.25f. [Gigante 103].

41. Sophronius, *Anacreontics* 14.33 [Gigante 104]. For the analysis of this poem I regret that I have not had access to Lavagnini (1979).

struggles to reconcile the mass fate of a large population to notions of divine justice.[42] Strategius's introduction to the Persian assault commences with the capture of two Phoenician monks whom the Persian general spares and leads into Palestine. The Persians then question those monks as to whether Jerusalem will be delivered into their hands and are at first told that the right hand of God protects the city. Then, however, the pair witness Jerusalem's angelic protectors abandoning the walls "because we abandoned obedience to God and despised his commands," and proclaim to their Persian captors an imminent triumph.[43] For Strategius, therefore, the Persian devastation of Jerusalem was, in his own words, "a rod of education and medicine for guilt."[44] Other Palestinian contemporaries shared his assessment. In the same period, the monk Antony of Choziba recalled how his hero, George, before the Persian advance upon Jerusalem, "bemoaned and bewailed the people's confusion, but more their ignorance and sinfulness," and called upon God to smite them. Thereupon the elder perceived a rod of fire stretching in the air from Jerusalem to Bostra—"And the saint knew that something grave would correct the people."[45]

Dramatic reversals demanded explanation, and the simplistic, dichotomized perspective of Sophronius's *On the Capture of Jerusalem* could not explain the failure of God to protect his chosen people. Persian success challenged Christian claims to God's special favor and demanded the readjustment of triumphalist narratives to account for defeat. Palestinian observers therefore explained that defeat as divine punishment for collective Christian sin. From this perspective, the devastation of Jerusalem was the manifestation not of Persian triumph but rather of Christian failure.[46]

## MOSCHUS FROM ALEXANDRIA TO ROME

After abandoning Alexandria, it appears that Moschus and Sophronius spent some time on Cyprus, the home of their patron John the Almsgiver, for a tale within Moschus's *Spiritual Meadow* purports to record their presence at the empo-

---

42. See, e.g., the letter of Zachariah (supposedly) preserved in Strategius, *On the Fall* 22 [Garitte, *Prise* vol. 2, 46–50]; and esp. the discussion in *De Persica Captivitate* [PG 86:2, 3236C–3240A].

43. Strategius, *On the Fall* 5 [Garitte, *Prise* vol. 2, 10f.]. In the subsequent section Strategius once again presents a monk as the prophet of Jerusalem's fate; see ibid. [Garitte, *Prise* vol. 2, 12], where John of Heptastomus reports to his disciple a vision of the city's imminent destruction. (Here, however, because of "the lawless clerics of this place.") The Greek text of this anecdote is published at Paulus Evergetinus, *Synagōgē* 670f.

44. Strategius, *On the Fall* 2 [Garitte, *Prise* vol. 2, 5].

45. Antony of Choziba, *Life of George of Choziba* 7 [Houze 129].

46. On the theme of human sin and divine punishment more broadly in this period see also Flusin (1992b) vol. 2, 129–49; Olster (1994).

rium of Tadai (or Dadē) on the island.⁴⁷ It was here, perhaps, that the pair composed that aforementioned *Life* of their Cypriot patron and Alexandrian patriarch John the Almsgiver, for although, as we have seen, that original *Life* does not survive, a later redaction preserves a final chapter in which "John and Sophronius" present their work as a funeral oration (*epitaphios logos*) and "tombside speech" (*epitumbion prosphthegma*).⁴⁸ The implication, therefore, is that the *Life* was first recited at the patriarch's funeral on Cyprus, in November 620.⁴⁹

Although the *Prologue to the Spiritual Meadow* indicates an immediate retreat from Alexandria upon the Persian conquest of Jerusalem, it is possible that Moschus and Sophronius remained in Alexandria throughout the 610s and came to the island with their patron upon the abandonment of Alexandria in 619.⁵⁰ Although (as we noted in the previous chapter) the patriarch had been a political appointment of Heraclius, and had even become both the ritual brother, and godfather to the children, of the emperor's cousin Nicetas, both the later redactions of

---

47. John Moschus, *Spiritual Meadow* 30. The reading "Dadē" (*Dadē*) is offered in the F manuscript; see Maisano (1982) 241. See also John Moschus, *Spiritual Meadow* 108 [PG 87:3, 2969C]: "When we were on the island of Samos we went to the coenobium that is called Charixenos." For the possible presence of Maximus Confessor with the pair, see below p. 105.

48. *Epitome of the Life of John the Almsgiver* 16 [Lappa-Zizicas 278]. Two further redactions are the so-called *Anonymous Life* and Symeon Metaphrastes, *Life of John the Almsgiver* 1–6 [PG 114, 896A–901B]. For the *Anonymous Life of John the Almsgiver* and its relation to that produced by John and Sophronius see Delehaye (1927) 5–17; Lappa-Zizicas (1970) 265–74; Rapp (2004) 121f. John and Sophronius's *Life* was known to the Cypriot hagiographer Leontius of Neapolis, who produced his own *Life* of the patriarch as a supplement to it; see Leontius of Neapolis, *Life of John the Almsgiver*, prologue [Festugière 343]. For Leontius's direct use of John Moschus's *Spiritual Meadow* for both his *Life of John the Almsgiver* and his *Life of Symeon the Holy Fool* see below p. 334 n. 16. For Sophronius's links with Cyprus, which were perhaps forged in this period, see Sophronius, *Letter to Arcadius*; George of Resh'aina, *Life* 7–14 [Brock 305–9].

49. For this date see Borkowski (1981) 55f., and esp. Déroche (1995) 118; *contra* Grumel (1958) 443, placing it in 619. The claim that John's patriarchate lasted ten years, made in Nicephorus, *Chronography* [de Boor 129], and Theophanes, *Chronicle* A.M. 6101–10, can be justified if one places John's election coterminous with Heraclius's coronation in October 610 and his death late in 620. For Sophronius's presence at his funeral see also Sophronius, *Epigrams* 2 and 3, both claiming to be epitaphs on the patriarch's tomb. The authenticity of the latter poems—in which the name of the Almsgiver's father is given differently versus the texts derived from Moschus and Sophronius's own *Life*—is defended in Pattenden (1982); but cf. Alan Cameron (1983) 288–90.

50. The date of the fall of Alexandria is dated with precision to June 619 in the *Anonymous Chronicle to 724* [Brooks 146], a date that complements the papyrological evidence; see esp. Altheim-Stiehl (1992a, b, c); MacCoull (1986). Narrative evidence for the Persian invasion is scant, but for the siege of Alexandria see *Khuzistan Chronicle* [Guidi 25f.]; *History of the Patriarchs* "Andronicus" [Evetts 484–86], and for the advance through the Nile Delta, Theodore of Paphos, *Life of Spyridon* 20 [van den Ven 81–83]. For the date of John's flight see also Déroche (1995) 118 n. 64. The destruction of monasteries at Pelusium is described in (Ps.-)Abū Ṣāliḥ, *Churches and Monasteries* [Evetts 168]. See also the documents associated with Pisentius of Coptus, described in Sayed (1984) esp. 314–17. The suggestion that Moschus and Sophronius remained in Alexandria until 619 is made in Jankowiak (2009) 127 n. 425, 136.

Moschus and Sophronius's *Life* and the continuation of Leontius of Neapolis nevertheless attempt to assert the independence of the Almsgiver from the influence of his imperial patrons. In the former, for example, the patriarch refuses to ordain a dissolute monk whom Heraclius has sent to him for election;[51] while the latter contains two remarkable anecdotes in which John admonishes Nicetas for his attempts to generate more revenue for the public fisc—in the first instance, through confiscating patriarchal wealth; and in the second, through manipulating the market.[52] The purpose of such vignettes is of course to assert both the freedom of the patriarch from secular interference and the subordination of the secular to the sacred;[53] but as Vincent Déroche has observed in his indispensable monograph on Leontius, both *Lives* nevertheless contain significant indications that relations between patriarch and imperial administration did indeed become more strained as time progressed—in particular, it seems, in the context of the Persian invasions.[54] In those texts dependent upon the lost *Life* of Moschus and Sophronius, we are told that "when [John] heard of the utter devastation of the Roman state at the hands of the Persians, he wanted to travel to the emperor and to negotiate for peace [*presbeusai ta peri eirēnēs*]" but that the people of Alexandria prevented him from leaving. The Persians, however, then threatened Alexandria itself, and John, upon discovering "a certain murderous plot being hatched against him" (*epiboulēn tina meletōmenēn kat' autou phonikēn*), decided to return to his home island.[55] Within the same texts, two curious incidents mark the patriarch's return to Cyprus: first, the arrival of "a certain general called Aspagurius" who had been "sent to Constantia" and who declared war when its citizens refused to receive him (John is said to broker a peace before the outbreak of hostilities);[56] and second, the arrival from Alexandria of the general Isaac, the city's alleged betrayer (*ho tote stratēgos*

---

51. See *Anonymous Life of John the Almsgiver* 5; *Epitome of the Life of John the Almsgiver* 5.

52. Leontius of Neapolis, *Life of John the Almsgiver* 10, 13. Cf. also the brief mention ibid. 12. Mango (1984) 35f. doubts the authenticity of these scenes on the ground that Nicetas could not have been Augustalis; but, as Déroche (1995) 119 n. 66, 142–53, notes, Nicetas does not need to have occupied that post in order to have wielded the powers described in Leontius's *Life*. The fiscal crisis of the state is well known, and I find no reason to doubt the basic plausibility of the anecdotes; for parallel attempts to extract money elsewhere see below p. 109.

53. See Déroche (1995) 294–96.

54. Ibid. 137f.; *pace* Rapp (2004) 128f., emphasizing the continuous bonds of ritual friendship that bound John and Nicetas together.

55. *Anonymous Life of John the Almsgiver* 13 [Delehaye 25]; paraphrased at *Epitome of Life of John the Almsgiver* 13 [Lappa-Zizicas 277].

56. Ibid. Although Aspagurius's name indicates that he was a Persian, Grierson (1950) 82f. has argued that the general was one of Heraclius's and that the episode has been displaced from the period of his revolt against Phocas, an explanation also adopted in Borkowski (1981) 55. Cf., however, Foss (1975) 724f., pointing to accounts of Persian naval activity in this period, esp. *Anonymous Chronicle to 724* [Brooks 147]; to which should be added Michael the Syrian, *Chronicle* 11.3; *Anonymous Chronicle to 1234* 96 [Chabot vol. 1, 230]; Ps.-Sebēos, *History* 38.

*tēn Alexandreōn polin prodous*), who then formed an (unsuccessful) intrigue to assassinate the patriarch.[57]

Leontius of Neapolis's *Life* hints at similar tensions surrounding the patriarch's retreat from Alexandria: "When through God's consent, or rather punishment, Alexandria too was about to be delivered to the godless Persians," we read, "the shepherd [John] recalled what was said, 'Whenever they chase you from one city flee to another' [Matt. 10:23], and fled to his own homeland: that is, to Cyprus and to his home city." As he sailed, however, the emperor's cousin Nicetas (also on board) suggested that he instead travel to Constantinople and there "bestow your god-obedient prayers upon our glorious rulers." John, according to Leontius's account, consented, but when the vessel then reached Rhodes, he saw in a dramatic vision "a certain eunuch of radiant appearance, holding a golden scepter in his right hand, standing beside him and saying 'Come, I beg you, the king of kings seeks you out.'" "You, master," John reports to Nicetas upon waking, "called me to go to the emperor here on earth, but the celestial emperor has anticipated [this] and summoned my humbleness." The patriarch then reports his vision to Nicetas, and the latter, with all due respect and enthusiasm, encourages John to return to Cyprus.[58]

Both the *Life* by Leontius and its predecessor by Moschus and Sophronius therefore represent John's later life as mired in political intrigue (though both attempt also to obfuscate it): the aborted visit to Constantinople to negotiate a peace with Heraclius; the "murderous plot" at Alexandria; the apparent decline of an imperial summons to Constantinople (dressed up as a miraculous intervention); a negotiated peace with the hostile (probably Persian) general Aspagurius at Constantia; and a further assassination attempt at the hands of the refugee general Isaac. The most obvious cause of these tensions was the machinations that appear to have surrounded the surrender of Alexandria to the Persians. We might have possessed a detailed description of those tensions in the *Chronicle* of John of Nikiu, but an unfortunate lacuna has removed almost the entire reign of Heraclius. Our two narrative sources for the Persian capture of Alexandria are, therefore, late and somewhat anecdotal, but it is worth noting that in both the city is opened up to the Persians from within—either (in the *Khuzistan Chronicle*) through betrayal or (in the *History of the Patriarchs of Alexandria*) through the willing capitulation of its inhabitants.[59] The patriarch John, we may imagine, represented an Alexandrian (and later Constantian) faction that wished to negotiate an independent peace

---

57. *Anonymous Life of John the Almsgiver* 15 [Delehaye 25]; paraphrased at *Epitome of Life of John the Almsgiver* 15 [Lappa-Zizicas 278].

58. Leontius of Neapolis, *Life of John the Almsgiver* 52 [Festugière 402f.]. Cf. the comments of Déroche (1995) 234f., with n. 22.

59. See *Khuzistan Chronicle* [Guidi 25f.], attributing the betrayal of the city to an Arab student, Peter. Cf. *History of the Patriarchs* "Andronicus" [Evetts 485].

with the Persians (e.g., Aspagurius), against the wishes of the emperor Heraclius and his representatives (e.g., Nicetas and, later, Isaac). The obscure conspiracies that conclude the extant hagiographies, and Leontius's somewhat forced apologia for his hero's refusal of a summons to the capital, are thus perhaps best explained as products of political tensions arising from the surrender of Alexandria.[60]

It is possible that the apparent political estrangement described in both *Lives* was compounded in, or informed through, a simultaneous disagreement over doctrine. Although it must have been a quite remarkable event on the Alexandrian religious scene, it is notable that no redactions of John's *Life* refer to a spectacular union achieved at Alexandria, which Marek Jankowiak has now fixed in the second half of 617.[61] That union reestablished communion between the anti-Chalcedonian patriarch Anastasius and his Antiochene counterpart, Athanasius (the so-called Camel Driver) at a moment when the anti-Chalcedonian churches had been plunged into crisis through the Persian advance. Nicetas, no less, was its broker. The two patriarchates had been in official schism since relations had broken down some decades earlier, under the patriarchs Damian and Peter. But in a letter of Athanasius the Camel Driver embedded in the *Chronicle* of Michael the Syrian, the patriarch describes that while at Alexandria—perhaps, like Moschus and Sophronius, as a refugee from the Persian invasions[62]—one of the province's prominent anti-Chalcedonians, "le très magnifique stratège Patricius" (in Chabot's translation), came up from Arsinoe to Alexandria, "close to the glorious patrician Nicetas, with whom we had conferred on the matter from the beginning, and in whom we could not have had more hope," and asked to engage the Antiochene patriarch in discussion aimed at peace. There, the same letter reports, after numerous discussions with the Antiochene bishop Thomas (acting under Athanasius's orders), the pair reached an accord, and the respective patriarchs entered into communion.[63] For his part Anastasius, in another letter embedded in Michael's *Chronicle*, also praised the emperor's cousin as the union's genius.[64]

---

60. For the same problem of local surrender in the context of the Muslim conquests see, e.g., Kaegi (1992) 252–54.

61. See Jankowiak (2009) 18–20, pointing esp. to *Anonymous Chronicle to 724* [Brooks 146], placing it in A.G. 929 (A.D. 617/8). Michael the Syrian, *Chronicle* 10.27 [Chabot vol. 4, 402] dates the union to "921 of the Greeks" (A.D. 609/10), although Chabot vol. 2, 399 n. 1, corrects the Syriac to "921" from an original "927" (A.D. 615/6), to bring it into line with a second "921" on the same page.

62. The presence of anti-Chalcedonians among the refugees from the Persian invasions should of course be expected and is implied in the *Anonymous Life of John the Almsgiver* 5–6, 12; also Jacob of Edessa, *Chronicle* [Guidi 324].

63. See also the patriarchs' synodical in Michael the Syrian, *Chronicle* 10.26, and the letters of Anastasius to Athanasius and of Athanasius to the bishops of Syria ibid. 10.27.

64. Michael the Syrian, *Chronicle* 10.27 [Chabot vol. 4, 402]. I have cited Chabot's translation since it is possible instead that we should read "patrician Strategius." The union is also afforded a prominent position in Anastasius's biography in the *History of the Patriarchs* "Anastasius" [Evetts 481–83], although Nicetas is not mentioned.

As Jankowiak has emphasized, Nicetas's arbitration of the anti-Chalcedonian schism provides a crucial index of the imperial impulse toward accommodation over doctrine in this decade, an impulse that thus manifested from the earliest stages of Heraclius's reign and that would reappear throughout it.[65] As we have seen in the previous chapter, it is probable that the emperor's selection of John the Almsgiver as patriarch of Alexandria was intended to further this same aim, and there are significant indications both in the patriarch's hagiographies and in Sophronius's *Miracles of Cyrus and John* that dialogue with anti-Chalcedonians was high on the Alexandrian agenda. Was the patriarch, therefore, complicit in the union of 617? Were Moschus and Sophronius? We cannot know, although we should note that in the 630s Sophronius, at least, referred to the union with obvious distaste,[66] and that a later text associated with his disciple Maximus Confessor presented the Almsgiver as an opponent of imperial doctrinal maneuvers in this same decade (although, as we shall see, in a quite different context).[67] It is therefore possible that the attitudes of the Almsgiver and his entourage to the imperial doctrinal program underwent, in the course of the 610s, a significant revision, as the crisis of empire deepened in the East and as attempts at accommodation moved from dialogue to the actual facilitation of anti-Chalcedonian union.[68]

The sources for the Almsgiver's later career permit no more than speculation. Nevertheless, for our immediate purposes, it is important to note Moschus and Sophronius's intimate association with, and alleged doctrinal influence upon, a prominent political and ecclesiastical actor—an actor who had, it seems, fallen foul of imperial opinion in the face of imperial political (and perhaps doctrinal)

---

65. See Jankowiak (2009) 18–23, pointing also to a union with the Tritheists referred to in the *Anonymous Chronicle to 724* [Brooks 146] and placed in A.G. 930 (A.D. 618/9); also Olster (1985). Note also the staunch opposition of one of John's Chalcedonian predecessors, Eulogius, to a comparable union of Gaianites and Theodosians; see Photius, *Bibliotheca* [Henry vol. 4, 111–13].

66. Sophronius, *Synodical Letter* 2.6.1 [Riedinger 482; repr. Allen 144]. Cf. Sophronius, *Synodical Letter* 2.6.2 [Riedinger 482; Allen 144], in which Sophronius proceeds to anathematize "the Syrians John, Sergius, Thomas, and Severus, who are still living this accursed life and waging mad war on piety." According to Michael the Syrian, *Chronicle* 10.26 [Chabot vol. 4, 399], a Severus and a Thomas signed the Alexandrian union on the Syrian side and are perhaps to be identified with the Severus of Samosata and Thomas of Heraclea eulogized at Michael the Syrian, *Chronicle* 11.8 [Chabot vol. 4, 417–20] and 10.25 [Chabot vol. 4, 391]; see Allen (2009) 145. Sophronius's anathemas, however, are perhaps better understood as being aimed at the protagonists in the later union with Heraclius at Mabbug; see below pp. 205, 237.

67. *Disputation with Pyrrhus* [PG 91, 332B–333A]. The context is that of official monenergism; see below p. 197f.

68. Cf. Déroche (1995) 139, observing that the *Anonymous Life of John the Almsgiver* 5, which is framed with vignettes concerning the Triasagion and the ordination of heretic priests, describes John's refusal to elect a monk whom the emperor sent, perhaps implicating the orthodox credentials of the emperor himself.

machination. We shall encounter this nexus of politics, doctrine, and dissidence—and the Moschan circle's implication within it—several times again. and in circumstances that are far clearer. But for now, the full political and doctrinal crises set in motion through the rise and success of the Persians, and then of the Muslims, and the simultaneous imperial endorsement of an emergent and controversial Christological doctrine, remained in the future. For Moschus and Sophronius a more immediate concern, perhaps, was the death of their erstwhile patron. New sponsors had to be sought.

Moschus's movements subsequent to the sojourn on Cyprus, however, have proved a subject of considerable disagreement. Although the biographical prologue claims that Moschus's eventual destination was "the great city of the Romans," in 1977 Keetje Rozemond proposed that that same city was not Rome on the Tiber, as one would expect, but New Rome: that is, Constantinople. She observed that the route described in the prologue appears "too northerly for the purpose of sailing to Rome," and pointed to two further instances of the phrase *tōn Rhōmaiōn* where the author in fact meant "of the Greek Byzantines."[69] A further complication, that the prologue then refers to Moschus *epi tēs Rhōmēs genomenos* and *en tēi Rhōmēi*, was countered with the observation that Sophronius used the description *anax Rhōmēs* to refer to the emperor Heraclius within an anacreontic poem produced within the same period;[70] "Rome," therefore, could also mean "New Rome."[71] In 1988 the same argument was refined in an extensive article by Enrica Follieri, who concurred that the prologue's *tōn Rhōmaiōn megalē polis* was indeed New Rome. She cited several more examples of Constantinople's designation as *Rhōmē*, and furthermore argued that Moschus and Sophronius—who, as we shall see, are sometimes referred to under the shared surname of Eukratas—there resided in a "Monastery of the Eukratades" (*monē tōn Eukratadōn*) mentioned in the acts of a Constantinopolitan council of 536.[72]

In 1998, however, Andrew Louth mounted an important critique of the emerging consensus.[73] He pointed out that all but one of Follieri's examples for the alternative application of *Rhōmē* were from verse, in which *Kōnstantinoupolis* would have been an obvious metric inconvenience.[74] The use of *Rhōmē* within the prose of the biographical prologue is therefore problematic to Follieri's posi-

---

69. See *Prologue to the Spiritual Meadow* 18, 26 [Usener 91f.].
70. See Sophronius, *Anacreontics* 14.18 [Gigante 103].
71. Rozemond (1977), (1984). Rozemond's position is supported in Maisano (1982) 38.
72. Follieri (1988). For the reference to the council see *Acts of the Council of 536* [Schwartz 34, 46, 129, 144, 158, 164, 173]; cf. Janin (1953) 117.
73. For the influence of Follieri's arguments see, e.g., the various references in Lapidge (1995a).
74. Louth (1998); *contra* Follieri (1988) 12, who points (in support of Rozemond) to Sophronius, *Anacreontics* 18.75 [Gigante 75], for the description of Heraclius as *pais Rhōmēs*. Cf. the epigrammatic evidence cited in Bowersock (2009) 43f.

tion, for in the prose texts of the period Constantinople is never referred to as "Rome." In Sophronius's *Miracles of Cyrus and John* and Moschus's *Spiritual Meadow*, for example, the imperial capital is *Buzantion*[75] or *Kōnstantinoupolis;*[76] whereas *Rhōmē* always refers to Rome on the Tiber.[77] Although Follieri has claimed that "the *usus scribendi* of John Moschus and of Sophronius cannot be invoked to corroborate that of the unknown author of the prologue," such comparisons are in fact crucial, since the prologue can be shown to emanate from within the Moschan circle. It includes references to "our father Sabas" and "our sainted father Theodosius," references that point to a Palestinian monk as its author.[78] Philip Pattenden, furthermore, has noted that the manuscripts of the *Meadow* that preserve the prologue (the so-called alpha group) are also those to which an early editor has added various prosopographical and topographical marginalia, so that the evidence "points to one and the same writer for the *Vita* and the additional alpha material." The precise nature of those marginalia, Pattenden argues, would necessitate an exacting knowledge both of Moschus's travels and of his acquaintances.[79] For the author of the prologue we must therefore look for a Moschan disciple who shared his master's *xeniteia* throughout the Mediterranean. In his exceptional article on Moschus of 1974, Henry Chadwick resisted the obvious conclusion: "The author of this prologue seems to speak of Sophronius as other than himself, or one would be quickly tempted to think of Sophronius as the editor and 'publisher' of the Meadow."[80] That objection, however, evaporates once one recalls the sustained use of the third person in the final autobiographical notice of Sophronius's *Miracles of Cyrus and John*.[81] The prologue, furthermore, contains striking verbal echoes of Sophronius's later sermon *On the Nativity of Christ*, for where the former refers to *barbarikē tis ataxia* and the *turannikē epanastasis tōn legomenōn Agarēnōn*, the latter refers in its title to

---

75. Sophronius, *Miracles* 11.5, 32.2, 60.1, 60.5 [Marcos 263, 308, 376, 377]; John Moschus, *Spiritual Meadow* 174, 188 [PG 87:3, 3041C, 3065D].

76. Sophronius, *Miracles* 53.1 [Marcos 366]; John Moschus, *Spiritual Meadow* 38, 43, 75, 76, 79, 93, 97, 112, 145, 147, 148, 153, 173, 178, 186, 188, 201 [PG 87:3, 2888D–2889A, 2897A, 2928A, 2928C, 2936D, 2952B, 2956C, 2976D, 3008C, 3012A, 3012D, 3021B, 3041B, 3048D, 3064B, 3065C, 3089A].

77. Sophronius, *Miracles* 69.2, 69.8 [Marcos 391, 393]; John Moschus, *Spiritual Meadow* 147, 148, 150, 151, 192 [PG 87:3, 3012A–B, 3012C, 3013C, 3016D, 3072A]. See also Sansterre (1983) vol. 2, 111 n. 57.

78. Prologue to the *Spiritual Meadow* 9–10, 16, 58–59, 69 [Usener 91–93].

79. Pattenden (1989) 49.

80. Chadwick (1974) 49.

81. See, e.g., Sophronius, *Miracles* 70.4. Pattenden (1989) 49 moves tantalizingly toward the same conclusion: "The second writer was very probably one of Moschus' disciples and perhaps Sophronius himself—but that is another story." If Sophronius were the editor, it would explain why John Moschus's *Spiritual Meadow* is soon attributed to him; see, e.g., John of Damascus, *On Images* [PG 94, 1280A, 1316D].

*hē tōn Sarakēnōn ataxia kai phthartikē epanastasis* and then alludes to *toxon to Agarikon*.[82]

While the attribution of the *Spiritual Meadow*'s biographical prologue to Sophronius must remain tentative—the prologue itself refers to twelve further disciples, any one of whom may well have penned it—the derivation of the text from within the Moschan circle nevertheless confirms the significance of Moschus's *Meadow* and Sophronius's *Miracles of Cyrus and John* as comparable texts.[83] Moschus and Sophronius did not use *Rhōmē* to refer to the Eastern capital; nor did the author of the prologue, a close associate of Moschus, perhaps Sophronius himself. Even if Moschus did indeed retreat to Constantinople for a period of time—a possibility that should not be discounted—the prologue is nevertheless unequivocal: Moschus's ultimate destination was *Rhōmē*: that is, Rome on the Tiber.

If the reason for leaving Palestine, Antioch, and then Alexandria had indeed been the Persian threat, as the biographical prologue to the *Spiritual Meadow* claims, then Constantinople would indeed have been an odd choice of destination: for in the same period in which Moschus and Sophronius are reported to have set out from Alexandria, a large Persian force had menaced Constantinople from Chalcedon,[84] and in subsequent years the capital remained in a perilous position—culminating, of course, in the spectacular but failed attempt of the Avars and their allies to seize it in 626.[85] In contrast, the West offered relative peace and isolation from the Persian threat—little surprise, then, that Heraclius was rumored to want to relocate his capital to North Africa in the precise same period.[86]

---

82. See *Prologue to the Spiritual Meadow* 45, 55 [Usener 92f.]; Sophronius, *On the Nativity* 3 [Usener 501, 508]. The coincidence is noted by Follieri (1988) 22 n. 100, 26, but on the basis of the prologue's failure to mention Sophronius's elevation to the patriarchate of Jerusalem in 634, she contends that the prologue was written by a Palestinian monk in the second half of the seventh century (ibid. 24–26). For Vailhé (1903) 366 and Maisano (1982) 59f., however, that silence implies that the prologue was composed after Sophronius's arrival in Palestine in September 634 but before his elevation to the patriarchate in or just before December. Other explanations are possible, however: if Sophronius was indeed the author, he may have felt it inappropriate to refer to his own elevation as patriarch in a piece dedicated to his master; if another Moschan disciple was the author, he must have written at a time when the orthodox credentials of Sophronius as patriarch were assailed, so that mention of his tenure as patriarch was controversial.

83. For the twelve "co-disciples" of Sophronius who brought Moschus's remains from Rome to Palestine see *Prologue* 49–50 [Usener 93]. As John Moschus's *Spiritual Meadow* does not mention these disciples, it is possible that the group formed in exile.

84. See Theophanes, *Chronicle* A.M. 6107–8; *Acts of Anastasius the Persian* 8; Nicephorus, *Short History* 6; *Paschal Chronicle* [Dindorf 706], with the discussion of Whitby and Whitby (1989) 159 n. 422, 201–2 *contra* Ericsson (1968). The entry of Theophanes, *Chronicle* A.M. 6100 (A.D. 607/8), referring to a Persian presence at Chalcedon, probably confuses the later event. For discussion see Flusin (1992b) vol. 2, 83–93.

85. For the siege see below p. 141.

86. For this rumor see Nicephorus, *Short History* 8, with the discussions of Van Dieten (1972) 8f. with n. 29; Kaegi (2003) 88f.

There is, however, a further reason for supposing that Constantinople was not Moschus's eventual destination, for alongside the expatriation of monks in the mold of Moschus and Sophronius, the Persian occupation of Rome's Eastern provinces had precipitated an economic crisis that limited the potential of the capital's secular and sacred hierarchies to offer financial support. The emperor Heraclius was confronted with a dramatic curtailment of public revenue and was thus compelled to put in place various measures to reduce expenditure: in 615, the debasement of the coinage, in effect halving public salaries;[87] and in 618, the suspension of state-provided bread subsidies (a reaction, no doubt, to the threat then posed to the precious Egyptian *annona*).[88] The perilous financial position of the public fisc is also indicated in several stories that point to imperial efforts to elicit loans of ecclesiastical monies from the patriarchs. As we noted above, Leontius of Neapolis's *Life of John the Almsgiver* reports that the emperor's cousin Nicetas approached the patriarch and asked him to donate the wealth of the Alexandrian Church to the public purse, in order to alleviate the empire's dire financial position;[89] and Theophanes' *Chronicle* claims that in April of the tenth indiction (622), on the eve of his final campaign against the Persians, Heraclius seized monies from religious establishments and melted down various liturgical vessels seized from Hagia Sophia in order to mint a large amount of gold and silver coinage.[90] (A similar report appears in Nicephorus's *Short History*.)

For our purposes, the crisis of the public fisc is important for the problems it presented both to religious refugees and to those who would receive them. In 617 the emperor Heraclius published a piece of legislation that attempted to limit the access of such refugees to the distributions of the Constantinopolitan Church,

---

87. *Paschal Chronicle* [Dindorf 706]. For further comment see Hendy (1985) 494f.; Whitby and Whitby (1989) 158–59 n. 441.

88. *Paschal Chronicle* [Dindorf 711]. For comment see Whitby and Whitby (1989) 164 n. 449. For the empire's economic position in this period and imperial attempts at fiscal reorganization see also Van Dieten (1972) 7–10; Howard-Johnston (1999a) 34f. Loss of revenue to the Persians is also alluded to at George of Pisidia, *Heraclias* 1.161–64 [Pertussi 247], and perhaps reflected in contemporary rumors of lost public treasure; see John of Nikiu, *Chronicle* 110, and Fredegar, *Chronicle* 63 (both Phocas); Nicephorus, *Short History* 8, and *Khuzistan Chronicle* [Guidi 26] (both Heraclius). For the latter tale, of treasure lost to the Persians because of the caprice of the winds at Alexandria, in the Arabic tradition see also Butler (1902) 78 n. 1.

89. Leontius of Neapolis, *Life of John the Almsgiver* 10 [Festugière 356]. To my mind there is no reason to doubt the basic plausibility of the tale, even if its inclusion was in part intended to emphasize the disastrous consequences of such seizures to Heraclius's successors, as suggested in Déroche (1995) 150–52, 294–96. Leontius of Neapolis, *Life of John the Almsgiver* 13, also points to a perilous fiscal position, for it reports imperial attempts to manipulate the market.

90. Theophanes, *Chronicle* A.M. 6113 [de Boor 302f.]. Cf. also Nicephorus, *Short History* 11 [Mango 54]: "At this time [of Heraclius's marriage to Martina] the valuables [*keimēlia*] of the churches were being sold off and expended in order to raise tribute for the barbarians." Nicephorus perhaps refers to the expensive peace agreed to with the Avars, described at *Short History* 13.

indicating that the influx of religious mendicants from the provinces was a significant financial strain.[91] But it also, perhaps, provides a further context for the westward retreat of Eastern ascetics such as Moschus and Sophronius. If the pair did indeed travel to Constantinople before their ultimate withdrawal to the West, they may well have encountered an emperor and patriarch unwilling or unable to provide them with patronage. One indeed wonders whether the pedagogic purpose of the *Life of John the Almsgiver* that Moschus and Sophronius composed in this same period—with all its tales of the patriarch's benevolence toward the displaced—is not, in part, the provision of an appropriate paradigm for episcopal beneficence in a context of severe socioeconomic disruption.[92]

After their retreat from Alexandria via the "various islands" of the eastern Mediterranean, the pair appear to have headed for North Africa. *Meadow* 196 commences with the statement that "The following was told to us by George, the prefect [*huparchos*] of the province of Africa, a man who loved Christ, who loved monks [*philomonachos*], and who loved the poor."[93] This George, whom the *Spiritual Meadow* describes as an Apamean,[94] is perhaps to be identified with that same George, "prefect of the city of the Carthaginians" (*eparchos tēs Karthagennēsiōn poleōs*), who supervised Heraclius's forced baptism of Jews in North Africa in 632, and whose prefecture began at some point after 627.[95] Although it is possible that the *Meadow*'s apparent awareness of George's elevation to the prefecture is a later addition,[96] the presence in North Africa of Sophronius is nevertheless confirmed in the corpus of Maximus Confessor, who in *Opuscula* 12 refers to "the divine

---

91. Heraclius, *Novels* 2 [Konidaris 74]. The legislation is discussed in brief by Hatlie (2002) 221, who assumes that it applied to both clerics and monks.

92. For John's munificence to refugees (in particular monks) *Anonymous Life of John the Almsgiver* 6, 12; cf. Leontius of Neapolis, *Life of John the Almsgiver* 6, 11.

93. John Moschus, *Spiritual Meadow* 196 [*PG* 87:3, 3080D]. For the title *huparchos* or *eparchos* outside the capital see Guilland (1981).

94. John Moschus, *Spiritual Meadow* 196 [*PG* 87:3, 3080D]: "He was from Apamea, in the province of Syria Secunda." It is of interest to note that the F manuscript here adds "from the estate [*ktēma*] called Thorax"; see Maisano (1982) 248 (with Traversari's Latin at *PG* 87:3, 3079D). The addition (almost certainly from the hand of Sophronius) betrays an intimate knowledge of George's background. For George see also *PLRE* vol. 3, "Georgius 50," "Georgius 51"; *PmbZ* "Georgios" 1962; Winkelmann (2001) 204f.; and for his association with Maximus below p. 151f.

95. See *Doctrine of Jacob*, preface 1.1–2 [Déroche 71, with 70 n. 1]. Cf. the conclusion to Maximus's letter in Devreesse (1937). For his possible predecessor, Gregory, in 627 see Pope Honorius, *Letters* 9 [*PL* 80, 478D].

96. The suggestion is made at Schönborn (1972) 77 n. 83, since it problematizes his conviction that Moschus was interred in Palestine in 619 rather than 634. However, as the information concerning George's eparchate appears in the Greek of the *PG* edition—and is therefore not one of the addenda contained within the α group of manuscripts—it appears to be part of the original text; for this differentiation see Pattenden (1989) 46–49; and above at p. 107.

Sophronius, who spent time in the province of Africa with me and with all the foreign monks ["in Afrorum regione mecum et cum omnibus peregrinis monachis moras agebat"]."[97] It appears, therefore, that before his ultimate withdrawal to Rome, Moschus—along with various Eastern contemporaries, including Sophronius and Maximus—first retreated to North Africa.

For the historian of Moschus and his circle, the 620s is an opaque decade. As the Persian occupation of Palestine became more entrenched, and Heraclius's war with Khusrau continued, we must presume that Moschus spent the entire period as a refugee—in particular, perhaps, in North Africa, where later we can place some of his associates.[98] What made Moschus travel onward to Rome we cannot know: perhaps he admired Rome's long-standing status as a defender of Chalcedonian doctrine; and perhaps also he wanted to honor the tombs of Saints Peter and Paul, like that Abba John the Persian whom he memorialized in the *Spiritual Meadow*.[99] He was, nevertheless, to prove something of a pioneer. The precise place in which Moschus resided in Rome is unknown, although it is tempting to suppose that he settled among that group of Cilician monks and compatriots known to have colonized the site of Aquae Salviae around this same period.[100] In a recent article Robert Coates-Stephens has nevertheless pointed to a more tantalizing option. Most scholars now agree that a monastic institution at Cella Nova in Rome was populated with Palestinian monks around the time of the Lateran Council (649) and that, at the same time or soon after, it was renamed for the Palestinian ascetic hero Saint Sabas.[101] On the basis of various textual, archaeological, and epigraphic data, however, Coates-Stephens has argued that the site was a continuation of a much earlier settlement, a "xenodochium de Via Nova" referred to in the correspondence of Gregory the Great and established by him for the reception of religious notables at Rome.[102]

---

97. Maximus Confessor, *Opuscula* 12 [*PG* 91, 142A]. In their petition to the Lateran Synod the assembled Eastern monks also refer to their collective presence in North Africa; see below at p. 299.

98. I see little reason to accept the contention of Schönborn (1972) 71 that Sophronius returned to Saint Theodosius in Palestine between 619 and 628 (altered to 626 in Allen [2009] 19).

99. John Moschus, *Spiritual Meadow* 151.

100. For this community see *Acts of the Lateran Council* [Riedinger 50f.], with the discussion of Sansterre (1983) vol. 1, 13–17; and below pp. 297-99. The *Georgian Appendix to the Spiritual Meadow* 12 also places one "Abba Paul the Cilician" at Rome in this period. See also below n. 116 on Theodore of Tarsus.

101. For discussion see Sansterre (1983) vol. 1, 22–31; Coates-Stephens (2007) 223–31. For Maximus's settlement of Cella Nova with other "Nestorian" monks from North Africa see George of Resh'aina, *Life* 19, 24; and below p. 290.

102. Coates-Stephens (2007) 231–56. For the identification of Cella Nova and Saint Sabas, as well as the link to Gregory, see esp. John the Deacon, *Life of Gregory the Great* 1.9 [*PL* 75, 66A], discounting the tentative suggestion of Rubery (2011) 27 that Cella Nova should be associated with the Via Nova and thus with Santa Maria Antiqua.

The settlement of Moschus himself at Cella Nova is, of course, pure speculation, but in that connection it is nevertheless of considerable interest to note the prominent role of Moschus and his Eastern associates in the promotion of Gregory's early cult. While Gregory's own reception in native Roman circles was somewhat unenthusiastic,[103] the *Spiritual Meadow* incorporates two admiring anecdotes centered on him. In the first a Roman priest named Peter—perhaps that same Peter who serves as interlocutor in Gregory's *Dialogues*, where the tale first appears—records how the pope once excommunicated a monk for contravening a rule concerning monastic possessions. Soon after, that same monk died, still under the punishment of exclusion, and Gregory, aggrieved, gave an order that his archdeacon should read a prayer of redemption over the monk's tomb. That night the dead monk appeared to the same archdeacon and related that he had now been released from prison. "And so," Moschus concludes, "it was known to all that in the hour that the archdeacon read the prayer over the tomb, in that same hour his soul was released from excommunication and liberated from judgment."[104]

The *Spiritual Meadow*'s other anecdote celebrating Gregory, which concerns his generosity toward a Palestinian monk at Rome, is worth quoting in extenso:[105]

> We came to Abba John the Persian at Monidia, and he told us the following about the most blessed Gregory the Great [*ho megalos Grēgorios*], bishop of Rome: "I went to Rome to worship at the tombs of the holy apostles, Peter and Paul. One day, as I stood in the middle of the city, I saw Pope Gregory about to go past me, and so I thought I would prostrate myself before him. When those who were in his entourage saw me, one by one they began to say to me, 'Abba, do not prostrate yourself.' But I did not know why they said this to me. Besides, I considered it out of place not to prostrate before him. And so when the pope came near and saw that I was going to prostrate myself—may God be my witness, brothers—he prostrated himself on the ground first and did not stand up before I had been pulled up. And he embraced me with much humility, and gave me three nomismata by hand, and ordered that I be given a cloak, and that all my needs be provided for. And so I glorified God who had bestowed upon him such humility, charity, and love."

---

103. See Llewellyn (1974); Thacker (1998) 71–74.

104. John Moschus, *Spiritual Meadow* 192 [*PG* 87:3, 3072A–C]. Cf. Gregory the Great, *Dialogues* 4.57; also Anonymous of Whitby, *Life of Gregory* 28. The story is repeated in Georgius Monachus, *Chronicle* [de Boor and Wirth 748–49], and variant versions have been attributed also to Anastasius II of Antioch and Ps.-Anastasius of Sinai; see Pitra (1868) vol. 2, 276–77; Nau (1903a) 84–85 no. 54. Havener (1988) 21 argues convincingly that the Greek version contained in the *PG* edition of John Moschus's *Spiritual Meadow* is a secondary rendering of an original by Anastasius II, the translator also of Gregory's *Pastoral Rule*. (See Gregory the Great, *Letters* 12.24.) He also makes the tantalizing suggestion that Moschus, as a refugee at Antioch in the early 600s, may have heard the tale from Anastasius directly. For the same tale cf. Heid (2002) 167–70.

105. John Moschus, *Spiritual Meadow* 151 [*PG* 87:3, 3016D–3017A]. For analysis see Havener (1988) 19–20; Degórski (2009) 413–14.

Like the aforementioned tale concerning the excommunicated monk, this tale made it into Gregory's later, Latin hagiographic corpus. Where, however, the former derived from Gregory's own *Dialogues*—and was known in several other Greek versions—the anecdote concerning the pope's beneficence toward an Eastern monk, when it appeared in John the Deacon's Latin *Life*, was expressly said to have come from a Greek original.[106] It contains, furthermore, the earliest extant usage, in either Latin or Greek, of the pope's famous sobriquet, "the Great" (here, *ho megalos*).[107]

Remarkably, the celebration of Gregory was not limited to Moschus alone but extended to others within his circle. In the 1960s Gérard Garitte published an appendix of spiritual tales contained within a Georgian manuscript of the *Spiritual Meadow* that he regarded as the product of a single author and dated its compilation, on internal evidence, roughly to the period 590–668.[108] The career of the author appears to mirror that of Moschus in several obvious ways: he was interested in the monasteries of Palestine and was perhaps a monk of Saint Sabas; he knew Sophronius in his later guise as patriarch of Jerusalem and regarded him as a champion of orthodox doctrine; and he had traveled in the Latin West, to Rome and Ravenna.[109] Jean-Marie Sansterre has therefore suggested that he was one of those twelve disciples of Moschus described within the prologue to the *Meadow*.[110] We shall return to the contents of the text, but for our immediate purposes we note that the Palestinian author of the Georgian appendix, like Moschus, chose to include an anecdote centered on Gregory the Great. Thus we are told that while in Rome one "Abba Paul the scribe, from Cilicia," related how in the time of Gregory "the Wonder Worker" some Franks came to him and requested a relic of Saint Peter in order to place it in a new church named for the apostle. The pope, wishing to fulfill their request, cut a rag from the altar cloth in the apostle's (Roman) church, and placing it in a box with a prayer, he left it at Peter's tomb for three days. The Franks accepted the box with delight but, upon returning home and opening

---

106. John the Deacon, *Life of Gregory the Great* 4.63 [*PL* 75, 213C-D]: "ex Graecorum relationibus ad me nuper interpretatis." It should be noted that the Greek tale of Gregory and the pauper-angel printed in Abicht and Schmidt (1896) 152–55 contains various Latinisms and is undoubtedly a translation from Latin; cf. John the Deacon, *Life of Gregory the Great* 1.6, 9–10; 2.23. For Gregory's Greek hagiographic corpus see also Delehaye (1904); Halkin (1955). For Gregory in John Moschus's *Spiritual Meadow* see Degórski (2009) 412–18.

107. For this point Havener (1988) 20.

108. See Garitte (1966) 398–406. Cf. idem (1964) 179–85.

109. See *Georgian Appendix to the Spiritual Meadow* 12–13 (set in Italy), 14–19 (set amid the monasteries of Palestine), 18–19 (referring to Sophronius), 30 (referring to "our Laura of Sabas"). It should also be noted that author shares Moschus's predilection for topographical and prosopographical precision, as well as a pervasive interest in the eucharist; on the latter see below p. 329.

110. Sansterre (1983) vol. 1, 57–61.

the box, discovered the small rag contained within, and enraged at the apparent deception returned to Rome to confront the pope. He wanted to reassure them, and so he led the Franks in a procession of clerics and others to the Church of Peter, where he opened the box and cut the rag with scissors. To the great dread and regret of its doubters, the rag began to bleed.[111]

This striking tale was later integrated into another source that shares a connection with Moschus: Gregory's first full hagiography, composed by an anonymous monk of Whitby in the early eighth century.[112] As Alan Thacker has argued, these correspondences suggest that both authors drew upon a common corpus of written Gregorian material emanating from the pope's own circles in Rome;[113] but he also suggests that the composition of the Whitby *Life* occurred on the back of the pope's promotion in England by Theodore of Tarsus, the archbishop of Canterbury (668–90).[114] Theodore had been consecrated in 668, but prior to that he had been resident in Rome.[115] Like Moschus, Theodore was a Cilician ascetic who had settled in Rome in the aftermath of the Persian invasions;[116] like Moschus, he seems to have known Sophronius and Maximus Confessor;[117] and like Moschus again, he appears to have been acquainted with Clement's lost *Hypotyposeis* (even more remarkable since it was also cited in the works of Maximus and, it seems, Sophronius).[118] Theodore of Tarsus, therefore, can be considered as a relative intimate of

---

111. See *Georgian Appendix to the Spiritual Meadow* 12 [Latin trans. Garitte 406–8]. The same tale also survives in Arabic; see Sauget (1973). The story is reminiscent of a similar tale told by Gregory himself of Pope Leo at *Letters* 4.30.

112. See Anonymous of Whitby, *Life of Gregory the Great* 21.

113. Thacker (1998) 61–67, making the mistake, however, that the *Georgian Appendix to the Spiritual Meadow* derives from John Moschus's *Spiritual Meadow* itself rather than from an author close to Moschus who continued to write after the latter's death.

114. Thacker (1998) 75–77.

115. For his election see the account in Bede, *Ecclesiastical History* 4.1.

116. For Theodore's biography see the reconstruction in Bischoff and Lapidge (1994) 5–81; Lapidge (1995b). Ibid. 19–21 suggests that Theodore was resident either in Saint Sabas or in the community of Cilicians at Aquae Salviae, preferring the latter because of Theodore's links to Anastasius the Persian, on which see below p. 298f.

117. See Canterbury Commentator, *First Commentary on the Pentateuch* 35 [Bischoff and Lapidge 310], citing Sophronius as an authority on the etymology of the toponym "Emmaus" (which does not appear in his extant works). For the correspondence between Theodore's and Maximus's corpora see Bischoff and Lapidge (1994) 225; Lapidge (1995b) 24. For Theodore's potential role in the Lateran Council of 649 see below p. 294 n. 71.

118. See John Moschus, *Spiritual Meadow* 176 [PG 87:3, 3045C-D], with Echle (1945); cf. Canterbury Commentator, *Second Canterbury Commentary on the Gospels* 82 [Bischoff and Lapidge 412]. It is possible that the author of the *Second Canterbury Commentary* cites directly from Moschus's *Spiritual Meadow*, as suggested in Bischoff and Lapidge (1994) 226. The same scholars also suggest a direct connection between *Spiritual Meadow* 176 and Theodore of Canterbury, *Iudicia* 2.4.4 [Finsterwalder 317], both of which cite Gregory Nazianzus as an authority on baptism by tears. For Maximus's

the Moschan circle. Like Moschus himself and the author of the Georgian appendix to the *Spiritual Meadow* he was, moreover, among the most prominent promoters of Gregory the Great's early cult.

It is possible that the enthusiasm of Moschus and his Eastern colleagues represents nothing more than simple admiration for a pope whose connections with the Chalcedonian East had been extensive (and included an intervention in a monastic dispute in Jerusalem).[119] It is nevertheless tempting to speculate that the celebration of Gregory's memory by Moschus and his monastic colleagues reflects the same pope's status as the founder of their new community at Cella Nova (soon to be Saint Sabas, the modern San Saba). In this regard it is perhaps significant, therefore, that Moschus included within the *Spiritual Meadow* a seemingly original tale that celebrated Gregory's generosity toward a Palestinian monastic pilgrim at Rome. At the least, the anecdote indicates that tales of Roman beneficence toward Eastern pilgrims circulated in Moschus's monastic circle; but within the context of the *Meadow*'s composition at Rome, it perhaps also constitutes something of a foundation myth for the community at Cella Nova, a retrospective (and portentous) celebration of papal patronage of Eastern monks in exile.[120]

---

citation of Clement's *Hypotyposeis* see Maximus Confessor, *Scholia on Ps.-Dionysius's "On the Divine Names"* [PG 4, 228A] and *Scholia on Ps.-Dionysius's "On Mystical Theology"* [PG 4, 421B–C]. The latter passage reads: "But I have read 'seven heavens' also in the *Disputation of Papiscus and Jason* ascribed to Aristo of Pella, which Clement of Alexandria in the eighth book of *Hypotyposeis* says Saint Luke wrote." Sophronius, *On the Circumcision* 23–27 [Duffy 4], also refers to the *Dialogue of Jason and Papiscus* and ascribes it to Saint Luke, perhaps indicating that he too knew the *Hypotyposeis*. For analysis of this newly discovered sermon by Sophronius see Duffy (2011), noting the connection with Clement, Moschus, and Maximus.

119. For these connections in more depth see Booth (2013a); also Dal Santo (2009a, b) and (2012). Apparent shared acquaintances between Gregory and Moschus include Amos of Jerusalem (Gregory the Great, *Letters* 8.6; John Moschus, *Spiritual Meadow* 119, 149; Nau [1903b] 92f.) and, perhaps, Eulogius of Alexandria (Gregory the Great, *Letters*, e.g., 5.41, 6.61, 7.31, 7.37, 8.28-9, 9.176, 10.14, 10.21, 13.42-3; John Moschus, *Spiritual Meadow* 195). The authenticity of the latter passage, however, has been challenged by Chadwick (1974) 46, although it is notable that Eulogius's name is preserved in the F manuscript, and thence in Traversari's Latin at PG 87:3, 3078A; see Maisano (1982) 248. Schönborn (1972) 59f., 64f., nevertheless speculates that Sophronius and Moschus would have encountered Eulogius during their first (and perhaps second) sojourn at Alexandria; see Sophronius's brief epigram on a *xenodochium* that Eulogius constructed, PG 87:3, 4009B, but with Alan Cameron (1983) 290f. for doubts over authorship. Eulogius is mentioned also at Sophronius, *Miracles* 1, 8, 9, 62; John Moschus, *Spiritual Meadow* 77, 146–47. For Gregory's intervention, involving monks of the Nea Monastery, see Gregory the Great, *Letters* 7.29 (also 11.46). In this connection it is interesting to note the condemnation of Amos as "a hater of the monks" in the tale attributed to Moschus at Clugnet (1905) 51–54 no. 8.

120. Cf. Havener (1988) 20, speaking of "the attitude of openness between Eastern Christianity and the Latin church so clearly expressed in this story."

## ASCETICS AND THE CITY

In the preface to the *Spiritual Meadow*, Moschus conceives his text as a memorial to the pious men and women who distinguished themselves in his lifetime, and from whose lives and deeds he has made a choice selection.[121] Nevertheless, as his apposite title *Meadow* makes evident, the virtues of his various heroes assumed various manifestations.[122] The *Meadow*, therefore, constitutes a self-conscious celebration of Christian virtue that, from the outset, signals to the reader its own transgression of the standard paradigms of hagiographic holiness. It transcends those paradigms to explore the possibilities of virtue outside the limited confines of the desert and thus to embrace the entire continuum of Christian space. Moschus, therefore, articulates a grand vision of collective Christian virtue in an age in which collective Christian sin was weighing on the minds of his close contemporaries.

It is notable that the Persian capture of Jerusalem makes no explicit mark upon the *Spiritual Meadow*—indeed, the casual reader may well assume that Moschus writes before it.[123] Moschus presents the monastic world of the late sixth and the seventh century as a paradise, a self-sufficient environment in which pious monks can depend upon God to provide all their needs. Monks here are marked with miraculous signs and powers, have the saints as their constant companions, and straddle the divide between life and death. The action, therefore, seems distant and detached—far removed from the urgent, vivid histories of Moschus's Palestinian contemporaries. In part the disruptions of the present are not the *Meadow*'s most immediate concern, for the text seeks not to dwell on present failure but to celebrate the ascetic stars of the pre-Persian East. Moschus's purpose, therefore, is both to memorialize the characters and communities of the Eastern deserts in the age before disaster, and to defend that same generation from accusations of moral decadence. Intimations of imminent failure were, perhaps, inappropriate.

I would nevertheless suggest that the crisis of the Christian empire in the East, and its rationalization as the product of collective Christian sin, so evident in Palestinian circles, had a profound effect on the hagiographic vision of the text. While

---

121. John Moschus, *Spiritual Meadow*, prologue [PG 87:3, 2852A–B], with the important variations in the F manuscript at Maisano (1982) 240.

122. The title *Meadow* is a traditional classical title for miscellanies of various descriptions; see Johnson (2006) 179–85.

123. A tale attributed to Moschus by Mioni (1951) 89–90 (no. 7) references the Persian capture of Jerusalem but lacks the prosopographical and topographical details that in general seem to characterize Moschus's method (*pace* Chadwick [1974] 62, who regards it as "probably part of the authentic text"). Mioni (1951) 74 no. 104 also attributes to Moschus another story of a virgin's martyrdom at the time of the Persian invasion, published in Cerulli (1946) 456f. and (1947) 378f. But the tale in fact derives from Strategius, *On the Fall* 12 [Garitte, *Prise* 30–33].

presenting the monastic deserts of the sixth and seventh centuries as a paradise, Moschus transcends the traditional confines of the genre to articulate a new, less introspective vision, a vision that represents the converse of simultaneous resorts to the paradigm of collective Christian sin. Alongside more traditional anecdotes of pious monks in their desert retreats, he places those that celebrate less traditional Christian heroes: urban ascetics, pious clerics, and virtuous *kosmikoi*. The *Spiritual Meadow* thus explores the existence of holiness outside the limited confines of the hagiographic desert, and articulates a vision of the Christian collective that sees the potential realization of God's will not in monasticism alone, but in various Christian vocations.

In order to appreciate the *Spiritual Meadow* as a product of the distinct circumstances of the period after the Persian capture of Jerusalem, it is perhaps expedient first to explore the alternative approach that regards it as a timeless, disengaged catalogue of Christian ascetic virtue. In a comparison of the hagiographies of Moschus, Cyril of Scythopolis, and John of Ephesus, for example, Susan Harvey has emphasized Moschus's failure to provide an "historical framework," with the result that "the reader might often wonder where and when the stories take place." Drawing attention to the paradisiacal themes that pervade the text, she notes the detachment of the *Meadow*'s monks from "the events of their time, events that penetrate the desert air only for didactic purposes." Given the "general malaise" that affected Palestine in this period, she argues that Moschus's "focus is other-worldly not by luxury of circumstance but by conscious intent." For Harvey the *Meadow* self-consciously presents "an asceticism of impenetrable timelessness, in which the temporal world is a place to be shunned, while one's faith is played out between oneself and one's God." It is "a majestic vision of ascetic devotion to God, unbounded by time or place."[124]

We need not dwell here on the paradisiacal themes that pervade Moschus's text, which are characteristic of the genre. In the miraculous desert, monks wield power over lions;[125] miracles provide for basic needs;[126] and those intent on plunder or murder are immobilized or killed.[127] For these advanced ascetics, the divide between

---

124. Harvey (1990) 140–45.

125. For further tales in which lions are subjected to monks within the *Spiritual Meadow*, see 2, 18, 58, 92, 101, 107, 125, 163, 167, 181. For the theme see Goddard Elliott (1987) 162–67; Layerle (2005) 159–63.

126. Food: John Moschus, *Spiritual Meadow* 28, 179. (The latter tale appears to be a shortened form of the *Life of Mary of Egypt*, set in Palestine and attributed to Sophronius in most manuscripts. Although the attribution has been challenged—see Schönborn [1972] 116; Kouli [1996] 66, with bibliography—the *Life* includes the eucharistic emphasis that I would regard as characteristic of the hagiographies of the period, and in particular of the Moschan circle. It is possible that it therefore emanates from a pen close to Moschus and Sophronius. Cf. Cyril of Scythopolis, *Life of Cyriacus* 18 [Schwartz 233]). Water: John Moschus, *Spiritual Meadow* 16, 53, 81, 173–74, 214–15. For the disastrous effects of attempting to circumvent this miraculous economy ibid. 80, 85.

127. Ibid. 15, 20–21, 70, 99, 155.

life and death becomes blurred.[128] That interstitial status is confirmed, above all, in the constant infringement of supernatural beings upon the narratives—demons, angels, and saints, and, in particular, the Virgin.[129] Monks themselves can wield supernatural powers;[130] and in this miraculous economy visions become the currency of revelation, in particular during a state of *ekstasis* (here a positive term).[131] Moschus thus presents the ascetic wilderness as a paradise in which desert monks have restored the prelapsarian state of Adam and in which historical events—wars, barbarian incursions—are referred to in the vaguest of terms. Such events, we must concur with Harvey, "penetrate the desert air only for didactic purposes."[132]

Her simultaneous characterization of that desert as "remote in both place and time" nevertheless demands some qualification. Although the paradisiacal themes that permeate the *Spiritual Meadow* may indeed present its action as distant and exotic, it nevertheless appears characteristic of Moschus's method to give the names and locations of the actors in his tales. At the beginning of most notices, he introduces first his interlocutors and then the tale itself, so that a typical example begins, for example, "Abba Gerontius, higoumen of the monastery of our sainted father Euthymius, told me the following";[133] or "When we were at the Ennaton in the coenobium Tougara, Abba Menas the coenobiarch told us the following about the sainted Pope Eulogius."[134] Although certain tales then proceed to describe such vague historical personages as "a monk" or "a priest," a larger number nevertheless concern named individuals at specific locations. Thus whereas *Meadow* 1, for

---

128. Monks foreseeing their own demise: ibid. 5, 7, 35, 86, 90, 91, 93, 94, 127, 129, 167. Continued activity after death: 11, 40, 84, 88, 92, 192, 195 (cf. 77–78). Bodies remain fresh: 87, 89.

129. Demons: ibid. 19, 45, 55, 60, 62, 63, 66, 115, 119, 152, 159, 160, 177, 182, 198; Nau (1902b) 613f., (1903b) 92f., Paulus Evergetinus, *Synagōgē* 429f., with Palmer (1994a). Angels: John Moschus, *Spiritual Meadow* 4, 10, 25, 43, 66, 108, 143, 178, 198, 199. Saints: John the Baptist (John Moschus, *Spiritual Meadow* 1, 3, 46, 119; Nau (1903b) 92f., Demetrius (43), John (46), Eleutherius (145), Julian (146), Peter (147, 149). Persons of brilliant appearance (*vel sim.*): 19, 26, 38, 66, 69, 105, 128; Clugnet (1905) 51–54 no. 8. Virgin: ibid. 45–48, 61, 75, 175, 180. On the popularity of the Virgin in Palestine this period see also Antony of Choziba, *Miracles of the Blessed Theotokos at Choziba*. On her cult more generally in this period, see the pioneering work of Averil Cameron (1978), (1979a), (2004).

130. Power over fire: John Moschus, *Spiritual Meadow* 69, 87, 92, 104, 123, 183.

131. Visions: ibid. 26, 30, 37, 49–50, 102, 104, 106, 139. *Ekstasis* (often involving visions of heaven or hell): ibid. 16, 19, 44, 65–6, 105, 128, 130.

132. Harvey (1990) 140. For such events see, e.g., John Moschus, *Spiritual Meadow* 50 (earthquake at Phoenicia), 131–32 (plague at Caesarea). In both cases the vignettes serve to demonstrate the miraculous foresight or *parrhēsia* of local monks.

133. See John Moschus, *Spiritual Meadow* 21 [PG 87:3, 2868B]. The F manuscript adds "and the sophist Sophronius" to "told me"; see Maisano (1982) 241.

134. John Moschus, *Spiritual Meadow* 146 [PG 87:3, 3009B]. For Moschus and Sophronius at the Ennaton see above p. 53 n. 44.

example, concerns the conflict of "an elder" from the Monastery of Abba Eusturgius with "the archbishop of Jerusalem,"[135] *Meadow* 3 concerns a more concrete person: a Cilician priest called Conon at the coenobium of Penthus. The localizing effect that such references create is reinforced, furthermore, in the intermittent intrusion of Moschus and Sophronius themselves within the narratives. Thus *Meadow* 4 begins, "We visited Athanasius at the laura of our sainted father Sabas, and the elder told us the following tale" and *Meadow* 69, "I and Lord Sophronius the Sophist, before he renounced the world, visited Abba Palladius in Alexandria."[136] Although the moral axioms that Moschus seeks to impart within his tales are not—indeed cannot be—dependent upon particular protagonists or contexts (so that such details are to some extent irrelevant), those tales are nevertheless articulated and (for the most part) situated within a distinct historical context: not that of the grand political events of the time, to be sure, but nevertheless that of the anchorites, archimandrites, and patriarchs of the post-Justinianic Mediterranean. The chronological frame may to us be unfamiliar, but a chronological frame it is nonetheless.

The *Spiritual Meadow*, therefore, is not a timeless collection devoid of historical references, but a catalogue of timeless Christian virtues as recreated in the Eastern provinces of the late sixth and seventh centuries. It contains but the slightest hint of the disastrous reversals that occurred in the period preceding the *Meadow*'s composition and that precipitated its author's own retreat from the East. I would nevertheless argue that those same disasters had a profound influence upon the text—not in terms of long, historical descriptions of invasion, occupation, and exile, but rather in terms of its hagiographic vision. The focus remains on desert monasticism, to be sure; but alongside these more traditional celebrations of isolated asceticism Moschus places those that explore less traditional heroes. In the same manner as his Palestinian monastic contemporaries pointed to the moral imperatives now incumbent upon all Christians (for all Christians were complicit in the causes of crisis), so too does Moschus transcend the limited confines of the hagiographic deserts to present pious Christians of all vocations: anchorites and urbanites, popes and paupers, soldiers and *kosmikoi*.

John Binns has attempted to explain the distinct form of the *Spiritual Meadow* through reference to the context of its production. He, like Harvey, emphasizes the antihistorical nature of Moschus's enterprise, in contrast to the earlier hagiographies of Cyril of Scythopolis. "Cyril," according to Binns, "wrote history, describing how the monks [of the Judaean desert] helped to shape the Church of the

---

135. John Moschus, *Spiritual Meadow* 1 [PG 87:3, 2852C]. We should note, however, that in the so-called F manuscript the protagonists of *Spiritual Meadow* 1 are named as "a certain elder ... named John" and "Elias the patriarch of Jerusalem"; see Maisano (1982) 240.

136. John Moschus, *Spiritual Meadow* 4 [PG 87:3, 2856B] and 69 [PG 87:3, 2920A].

empire"; "Moschus," however, "tells stories."[137] Binns proceeds to explain that difference as a product not of conscious intent (as for Harvey) but rather of the shifting circumstances of Judaean monasticism in the period after Justinian. Pointing to the reorientation of the movement from Jerusalem to the Jordan in the late sixth and seventh centuries, Binns maps Moschus's "anecdotal style" onto the monks' gradual extrication from the "ecclesiastical and political life of the province." The distinct form of the *Meadow*, therefore, and its lack of attention to grand political narratives, is "a result of a change in the self-awareness of the monks." "Their horizon has shrunk and their world is smaller.... Moschus' monasteries are self-contained and inward-looking."[138]

Although Binns recognizes the crucial importance of context to appreciating the distinctive qualities of the *Spiritual Meadow*, he nevertheless limits that context to the (supposed) extrication of the Judaean monasteries from political life, without reference to the broader material and ideological context within which the *Meadow* was produced. At the same time, Binns focuses upon the text's dominant monastic content, and therefore marginalizes perhaps its most radical element—the inclusion of Christians of all social statuses, from all regions of the Mediterranean. In the *Meadow* the reader encounters the Christian community in all its diversity, from the pope at Rome to a beggar on the streets of Antioch. It is of course correct that Moschus focuses for the most part on the monastic desert. But it should also be noted that the miraculous interventions that characterize that desert also pervade the *oikoumenē*. And while Harvey is no doubt right that Moschus articulates an ascetic ideal that is more detached than those contained within other collections, that same ideal is attainable for Christians of various vocations, irrespective of location.[139] The detachment of Moschus's subjects from wider social relations is therefore mitigated in and through the text itself, which both projects and celebrates a model of the Christian community that is wholly and self-consciously inclusive.[140] Moschus's monasteries may indeed be "self-contained and inward-looking," but the *Meadow* itself is the precise opposite: boundless and panoramic.

---

137. Binns (1994) 52. For a more critical assessment of Cyril's "history" see Hombergen (2001), and more generally Flusin (1983).

138. Binns (1994) 52–53.

139. This detachment should not be pushed too far, however. See, e.g., the various tales that emphasize almsgiving as the superlative virtue at John Moschus, *Spiritual Meadow* 9, 16, 61, 85, 175; Paulus Evergetinus, *Synagōgē* 850f. On this theme see also Baynes (1947) 410–12; Chadwick (1974) 72f.; Pasini (1985) 354f.; Palmer (1993b) 297ff. For further tales in which monks use their powers to aid surrounding society see John Moschus, *Spiritual Meadow* 28, 56, 81, 83, 114.

140. *Pace* Harvey (1990) 140: "Moschus does include stories of worthy ascetics living in urban settings; but these tend to be bishops, or holy men on business, who remain as detached in their city as in the desert."

In most late-antique hagiographies, the desert is presented as the sole legitimate context within which to practice asceticism, and there were, indeed, powerful imperatives toward the preservation of that same desert setting—both the ideological program of clerics keen to distance monks from their spheres of influence and the legitimization of ascetic practice that social separation itself came to express.[141] The *Spiritual Meadow* preserves that same dominant emphasis upon desert ascetics and desert existence, but it is nevertheless crucial to note the intermittent inclusion of anecdotes that assume or explore legitimate forms of urban asceticism. In one of the *Meadow*'s more autobiographical anecdotes, for example, Moschus recalls that:[142]

> My companion Sophronius and I were in Alexandria and one day went to the Church of Theodosius. A certain bald man wearing a sackcloth down to his knees appeared in front of us. He appeared as if he were mad [*salos*]. And so Abba Sophronius said to me, "Give me some obols, and you will see the virtue of the man who approaches." I gave him five obols. And taking them he gave them to the apparent madman, who took them without speaking. We then secretly followed behind him, and when he turned off the street, he stretched out his right hand, which held the obols, to heaven, held it up on high, and made a prostration to God. And setting the obols on the ground, he went away.

Not dissimilar is *Meadow* 127, in which one Amma Damiana relates how she once took a kinswoman (also a relative of the emperor Maurice) to the Church of Saints Cosmas and Damian in Constantinople, and how that kinswoman did not want to accept an offering of two small coins that an old Galatian woman gave as alms to each supplicant. Reluctantly, she accepted the coins from the old woman, who said to her, "Take these and eat." The noblewoman then dispatched one of her maids to buy vegetables with the money, and when she then ate them, she pronounced them "as sweet as honey." "And she was amazed and glorified God for giving such grace to his servants."[143]

This theme of concealed urban holiness appears again elsewhere in the text. *Meadow* 37 relates how the *comes Orientis* Ephraim (future patriarch of Antioch) had a dream in which he saw a local laborer prostrate with a column of fire reaching above him to heaven. Ephraim then summoned the laborer and asked him who he was, but when the laborer replied that he was a simple pauper, Ephraim insisted that he reveal the truth. The laborer then revealed that he was in fact a bishop, fleeing from his diocese at the behest of God and now suffering affliction

---

141. For this see esp. Goehring (1993), (2005); also Dagron (1970); Browning (1983); Rapp (2006).
142. John Moschus, *Spiritual Meadow* 111 [*PG* 87:3, 2976A–B].
143. John Moschus, *Spiritual Meadow* 127 [*PG* 87:3, 2992A–B].

and toil in Antioch. "How many hidden servants God has," Ephraim proclaimed, "and known to him alone!"[144]

In another tale an unnamed Scetiot monk travels to Alexandria and there witnesses a novice entering a tavern. When that novice later leaves, the elder intercepts him and confronts him with a barrage of questions: "Lord Brother, do you not know that you wear the holy habit? Do you not know that you are a novice? Do you not know that the snares of the devil are many? Do you not know that monks are harmed through the eyes, ears, and mouth when they spend time in cities? You fearlessly enter taverns; you hear things that you would not want to hear, see things that you would not want to see, and you indecently fraternize with women. Please, I beg you, flee into the desert, where you may be saved as you desire." The novice then replies to him, "Come, good Elder, God requires nothing but a pure heart." Then the elder stretched out his hands to heaven and said, "Glory unto God, that I have spent fifty years in Scetis and not obtained a pure heart. This man fraternizes in taverns but has."[145]

Moschus does not attempt to subvert the traditional conception of cities as corrupting.[146] (Indeed, he includes several tales that depend upon the standard literary dichotomy of desert versus city.) Nevertheless, the repetition of tales that concern urban monks serves to demonstrate the possibility of sustained ascetic virtue in the city, even if the latter remains a morally perilous context. In *Meadow* 171, for example, Moschus celebrates the lives of two Alexandrian ascetics with whom he was acquainted, Theodore the Philosopher and Zoilus the Reader:[147]

> Some fathers went to Lord Cosmas the *Scholasticus* and asked him about Abba Theodore the Philosopher and Zoilus the Reader, saying, "Which of the two persevered further in his ascetic labors?" And he said to them, "Both had the same kind of food, the same kind of bed, and the same kind of clothes but abstained from all excess and were humble, poor, and self-controlled. But Abba Theodore the Philosopher went barefoot and was greatly afflicted in the eyes, and had learned the Old and New Testaments by heart. Except he had as consolation the company of the brothers and conversation with friends, a great distraction whenever he was on business or teaching. As for Zoilus the Reader, not only was his *xeniteia* worthy of praise but also his solitude, his immeasurable toil, and his restraint in speech. He had no friends, no family; he never spoke with anyone, and he took no part in any worldly activity. He

---

144. John Moschus, *Spiritual Meadow* 37 [PG 87:3, 2888C]. For this refrain cf. below p. 334.

145. John Moschus, *Spiritual Meadow* 194 [PG 87:3, 3076C–3077A].

146. For those tales or apophthegmata that are antiurban in character, see also John Moschus, *Spiritual Meadow* 97, 110, 152, 159, 168, 179, 187, 204, 208; Nau (1902b) 613f. On this theme in John Moschus's *Spiritual Meadow* see also Palmer (1994b).

147. John Moschus, *Spiritual Meadow* 171 [PG 87:3, 3037D–3040B]. For Cosmas the *Scholasticus* see also John Moschus, *Spiritual Meadow* 172.

admitted no relief and accepted from nobody even a welcome service. He cooked and washed for himself and took no solace from reading. He was ready to serve others and gave no heed to heat nor cold nor bodily affliction, always being free from laughter, sadness, accidie, and leisure. Because of the roughness of his clothing he was consumed, unhumbled, by a mass of lice. But in comparison with the first he had no mean distraction in his freedom of movement, having total license to travel, day or night. But his immeasurable toil cheated this license, and he avoided overfamiliarity with those in the world."

Both men are ascetics in Alexandria: Zoilus, however, preserves the life of the desert ascetic, shutting himself off from the world, whereas Theodore is a teacher and lives among others. But, the text emphasizes, "Each will receive his own reward according to his toil and to the measure of his resurrection, his intellectual and spiritual purity, his fear of God, and his charity, his service, his contrition, his unwavering psalm singing and prayer, his earnest faith, and the satisfaction of God, which is hidden and concealed from man."[148] For Moschus, therefore, presence within cities, and even active social engagement, is no impediment to ascetic virtue.

This same respect for the life of social engagement extends also to the clerical vocation. Alongside those more traditional tales that point to the virtues of desert existence, Moschus places repeated stories that celebrate the virtues of patriarchs, bishops, and priests. In part, this of course reflects a situation in which monasticism had come to form the first rung on the ecclesiastical cursus honorum. Thus the *Spiritual Meadow*'s clerics have often been ordained from within monasticism itself and, as the *Prologue to the Spiritual Meadow* informs us, Moschus himself at some point became a priest.[149] (When is unknown.) The presence of clerical heroes within Moschus's text should not, however, be taken as purely descriptive, for it represents something far more significant: a conscious decision to depart from hagiographic precedent in the elevation of clerics alongside their counterparts within monasticism.

One anecdote notes with approval, for example, the meekness of the patriarch Theodotus of Antioch, who shared his litter with a lesser cleric;[150] another describes in gruesome detail the death of a Thessalonican archbishop who "set the priestly dignity at naught" (he is discovered face down in a latrine);[151] and still another

---

148. Ibid. [*PG* 87:3, 3040B].

149. *Prologue to the Spiritual Meadow* [Usener 91], where John Moschus's *Spiritual Meadow* is said to be *hupo Iōannou tou en hosiai mnēmēi presbuterou genamenou kai monachou epiklēn Moschou eponomazomenou*. For instances of monastic ordination see John Moschus, *Spiritual Meadow* 94, 104, 108, 109, 123, 124, 134, 139, 182. On the phenomenon more broadly in late antiquity see Sterk (2004).

150. John Moschus, *Spiritual Meadow* 33.

151. Ibid. 43. For the same theme see ibid. 145.

praises the compassion of Apollinarius, Chalcedonian patriarch of Alexandria.[152] *Meadow* 34 celebrates the kindness of Alexander, patriarch of Antioch, to those who abused him and records the memorable witticism "There is nothing more profitable for me than to sin against Alexander."[153] Of Moschus's ecclesiastical heroes others are more celebrated still. *Meadow* 191 and 197 describe the lives of the patriarchs John Chrysostom and Athanasius, while at *Meadow* 121 one Abba Athanasius of the Laura of Sabas relates an anecdote—via several people but beginning with Adelphius, bishop of Arabissus—concerning Chrysostom's exile at Cucusus.[154]

Among these assorted stories of ascetics-*cum*-priests and virtuous patriarchs, the bishops of Rome are a conspicuous presence. In a series of consecutive tales Moschus relates several anecdotes centered on Rome and its popes.[155] Three such tales—the first of which is told via Gregory the Great in his guise as papal ambassador or *apocrisiarius* in Constantinople—center on Pope Leo,[156] and the series then progresses to an anecdote that concerns a misunderstanding between Pope Agapetus and the virtuous bishop of Romilla or Roumella (near Rome). It concludes with that aforementioned tale of Gregory the Great's generous provision of monies to a monastic pilgrim from the East.[157]

These stories of virtuous Chalcedonian champions serve to situate Moschus and his Chalcedonian contemporaries within a (vertical) continuum of holiness stretching deep into the patristic past;[158] at the same time, however, those same stories also serve to situate contemporaries within a (horizontal) panorama stretching across both social and geographical boundaries. Indeed, Moschus's exploration of various paradigms of holiness extends further still, to virtuous secular Christians living in the world. One tale records the life of a certain soldier John at Alexandria, who spent "from dawn until the ninth hour" within a monastery, wearing a sackcloth, weaving baskets and chanting verses. "At the ninth hour," however, "he took off the sackcloth that he wore and put on his military uniform—that is, his own clothes—and thus retired to his own camp."[159] Elsewhere the grazer

---

152. Ibid. 193; the same story is attributed to John the Almsgiver in Leontius of Neapolis, *Life of John the Almsgiver* 35. For further tales of ecclesiastical virtue see John Moschus, *Spiritual Meadow* 34–36, 94, 128, 145, 149–51, 197.

153. John Moschus, *Spiritual Meadow* 34 [PG 87:3, 2884B].

154. John Moschus, *Spiritual Meadow* 128 [PG 87:3, 2992B–2993B].

155. John Moschus, *Spiritual Meadow* 147–51.

156. John Moschus, *Spiritual Meadow* 147–49 [PG 87:3, 3013B–C]. For these tales on Leo see also Schönborn (1975) 476–78.

157. John Moschus, *Spiritual Meadow* 150–51. The reading *Rhoumēlla* rather than *Rhōmilla* is offered in the F manuscript; see Maisano (1982) 246.

158. For this same emphasis within John Rufus's *Plerophoriae*, see Steppa (2002) esp. 88–111.

159. John Moschus, *Spiritual Meadow* 73 [PG 87:3, 2925C]. For an alternative version of this story see Nau (1902b) 616. For holy soldiers in John Moschus, cf. *Spiritual Meadow* 20.

or *boskos* Abba Jordanes relates how three anchorites visited Abba Nicolaus in the Betasimum Valley ("in a cave between Saint Elpidius and the monastery called 'The Strangers'") and there discovered a man of the world (*kosmikos*). Nicolaus then bade him to speak to the visitors, and he replied:

> "What help can a man of the world be to you? Why, I can't even help myself!" And the elder said to him, "At any rate you must say something." Then the man of the world said, "For twenty-two years apart from Sundays and Saturdays the sun has not seen me eat. I was a hired laborer on the estate of a wealthy man who was unjust and greedy. I spent fifteen years with him laboring night and day, but he would not pay me wages, but every year seriously mistreated me. But I said to myself, 'Theodore, if you put up with this man, in place of the wages that he owes you, he will guide you to the kingdom of heaven.' And I kept my body pure from women up unto this day."

The anchorites, Moschus reports, were "greatly edified."[160] Holiness here, therefore, appears not as the preserve of a limited few in the distant monastic deserts but is available to all, irrespective of place or vocation.

Tales centered on pious *kosmikoi* are a particular feature of that series of tales associated with the Thessalonican Abba Palladius at the Alexandrian Lithazomen. The series begins with two anecdotes on suburban asceticism; the first concerning the cell of the Mesopotamian ascetic David, which was positioned against the walls of Thessalonica, and which appeared aflame at night, and the second concerning another Mesopotamian monk at Thessalonica, an urban dendrite called Adolas (or Addas), who was saved from the murderous intentions of a pillaging barbarian when the latter was immobilized in mid-strike.[161] Then, however, Palladius relates several tales that focus on less traditional figures: a condemned murderer at Arsinoe who upbraids a monk for his lack of moral effort, a Christian lad in Alexandria who is almost executed on a false accusation of murder, the aforementioned Alexandrian soldier John, a pious merchant who entrusts his wife and child to the protection of the Theotokos when on business in Constantinople, and a ship's master whose ship, upon leaving its harbor, stops because one of its passengers has committed infanticide. Certain stories, therefore, celebrate the pious in unexpected places; others serve to demonstrate the presence of the miraculous amid the mundane. But the effect is nevertheless the same: the clichés of the hagiographic desert are extended to the entire continuum of Christian social space, breaking down those traditional barriers that had restricted holiness and the miraculous to the terrestrial but nevertheless distant realm of the withdrawn ascetic.

---

160. Ibid. 16 [*PG* 87:3, 2864A–B]. For a further tale that perhaps concerns *kosmikoi* see John Moschus, *Spiritual Meadow* 129, in which the F manuscript (Maisano [1982] 245) reads *kosmikoi* for *boskoi*.

161. John Moschus, *Spiritual Meadow* 69–70. The variant *Addas* is offered in the F manuscript; see Maisano (1982) 243.

The language, authorial stance, and dislocated structure of the text reinforce that same sense of universalism. Unlike Sophronius in the *Miracles of Cyrus and John*—who, we will recall, adopts an explicitly "intense" style—Moschus presents his text in a simple, unadorned language that suits the social breadth of his vision. It includes vernacular Greek in instances of direct speech and has proved a precious resource for philologists.[162] This quotidian language, however, should not be read as an indication of Moschus's lack of education—the considerable intelligence of his immediate circle suggests as much, not to mention the rhetorical sophistication of the *Spiritual Meadow*'s prologue, which includes a quotation from Euripides.[163] Rather, as Geoff Horrocks has emphasized, his self-conscious adoption of a low-level narrative reflects nothing more than the desire to communicate to as wide an audience as possible.[164]

That desire is reflected also in Moschus's self-positioning as author. He, like Sophronius in the *Miracles of Cyrus and John*, inserts himself throughout his own text but unlike Sophronius nevertheless devolves the authorial voice to one or more authorities: "We visited Abba A, and he told us that Abba B had heard this about Abba C."[165] The purpose of this technique is in part, no doubt, to establish the truth of the tale itself through presenting a chain of reliable authorities (much like the Islamic *isnād*). But the effect is also to create a multivocal text that retains Moschus as the selector of his own stories but that defers the act of authorship to various authorities. The *Spiritual Meadow* presents itself not as the personal memoir of a monastic traveler but as the collected wisdom of a pan-Mediterranean Church.

The same effect is reinforced in the *Spiritual Meadow*'s distinct lack of structure, for in oscillating from person to person, place to place, the text disrupts and suppresses its autobiographical element (much to the frustration of historians). At the same time, however, that same oscillation serves to juxtapose Christians of various vocations and from various regions. Thus a tale of the Palestinian Father Gerasimus and his lion is placed next to a tale set on Samos concerning a priest;[166] the celebration of Theodotus, patriarch of Antioch, next to an anecdote concerning the repentance of an actor at Tarsus in Cilicia;[167] and the tale of the pious laborer at Antioch next to a tale of the emperor Anastasius at Constantinople.[168]

---

162. See, e.g., Hesseling (1931); Mihevc-Gabrovec (1960); Horrocks (1997) 185–88.
163. See John Moschus, *Spiritual Meadow*, prologue [PG 87:3, 2852B]: "I have plucked the finest flowers and fashioned a wreathed crown from this virgin meadow [*plekton stephanon akēratou leimōnos*]"; cf. Euripides, *Hippolytus* 73–74: *soi tonde plekton stephanon ex akēratou leimōnos, ō despoina, kosmēsas pherō*. For the rhetorical sophistication of the prologue see also Maisano (1982) 250.
164. Horrocks (1997) 164, 186f. On this broad appeal see also Pasini (1985) esp. 356–62.
165. John Moschus, *Spiritual Meadow* 6 [PG 87:3, 2857A].
166. John Moschus, *Spiritual Meadow* 107–8.
167. Ibid. 32–33.
168. Ibid. 37–38.

The reader is transported from the imperial bedchamber to the humble cell of the hermit, from the quiet deserts of the Dead Sea to the streets of papal Rome. The effect of this dislocated structure, therefore, is to juxtapose the socially and geographically disparate, and thus to present a grand vision of a diverse but nevertheless unified Christian commonwealth stretching across the Roman empire.[169]

This grand vision, which embraces high and low as well as near and far, finds little comparable in earlier hagiographies.[170] However, when the *Spiritual Meadow* is placed alongside the texts of Moschus's Palestinian contemporaries— the narrative of Strategius, for example—its broad social vision appears not as a simple hagiographic innovation but as one element within a far broader response to the Eastern crisis of empire and, in particular, to the Persian capture of Jerusalem. That event compelled Jerusalem's ascetics to defend their own movement from accusations of moral failure (hence the explosion in Palestinian encomia such as the *Life of George of Choziba*, the *Acts of Anastasius the Persian*, and the *Meadow*);[171] but it also compelled them to explain events in a manner that preserved Christian claims to divine favor. Sophronius, in the poem *On the Capture of Jerusalem*, had conceived of the Persians as an unreined, uncivilized force inspired through demonic rage; but other Palestinian contemporaries—such as the Sabaite monk Strategius—pointed to collective Christian sin as the cause of disaster and called for a collective moral restoration to reverse it. Moschus's *Meadow* responds to that call. It celebrates the words and deeds of desert monks, cocooned in their comfortable quasi paradise; but alongside such notices it also explores new, less traditional paradigms and thus holds forth the prospect that holiness, in fact, might not be the sole preserve of monasticism, nor even of the desert. The *Meadow* celebrates urban asceticism; it lauds the virtues of the clerical vocation; it even points to pious *kosmikoi*. At the same time, as the text leaps between various persons to encompass the whole social spectrum of the late-antique world, it also leaps between various places to encompass vast tracts of the eastern Mediterranean. Moschus's magnum opus is, therefore, both the final memorial of Greek monasticism's golden age and, at the same time, an index of its crisis.

---

169. For the structure of John Moschus's *Spiritual Meadow* see also Maisano (1982) 45.

170. For an anti-Chalcedonian precedent for Moschus's theme of concealed urban sanctity, however, see the so-called *Greek Life of Daniel of Scetis*, the dominant theme of which is the hidden holiness of those in the world (including the Alexandrian holy fool Mark); see Dahlman (2007) 70–89 (with ibid. 56–58 on the text's probable miaphysite origins); and cf. John of Ephesus, *Lives of the Eastern Saints* 17, 52. For an anti-Chalcedonian celebration of urban asceticism see also John Rufus, *Plerophoriae* 88.

171. For this point see also Flusin (1992b) vol. 2, 219f.

## CHALCEDON AND THE EUCHARIST

For all its differentiation of Christian virtue, the socially inclusive community that the *Spiritual Meadow* presents to its audience is nevertheless delineated by strict boundaries defined both through doctrine and through ritual. Just as Sophronius in the *Miracles of Cyrus and John* presents a socially diverse clientele at Menuthis but attempts to impose upon that clientele the imperative of adherence to Chalcedon, so too does Moschus in the *Meadow* define his diverse heroes through their shared commitment to the Chalcedonian settlement; and just as Sophronius elevates communion as the central expression of conversion to the orthodox group, so too does Moschus present eucharistic participation as the ultimate statement of recognition of Chalcedon. There is here, however, a noticeable change of emphasis, for where Sophronius' in his *Miracles* does not conceive a further role for the eucharist within his conception of the Christian life, Moschus's *Meadow* affords to it a far more prominent, more diverse, and more permanent position.

The bishops whom the *Spiritual Meadow* celebrates are either those celebrated within the Chalcedonian tradition—Elias of Jerusalem, Flavian of Antioch, or Gennadius of Constantinople, for example—or those who proved staunch defenders of the Chalcedonian definition in Moschus's own time and within whose circles he and Sophronius operated.[172] In one tale Abba Sergius, an anchorite near the Dead Sea, perceives the future election of Gregory, archimandrite of the Palestinian laura of Pharon, to the patriarchal throne of Antioch;[173] and the subsequent tale records simply that "Certain of the elders said about Abba Gregory the Patriarch of Antioch that he was upright in these virtues: almsgiving, the forgiveness of sins, and tears. He had a great sympathy for sinners. And of these things we too had much experience."[174]

Another prominent Chalcedonian within the *Spiritual Meadow* is Eulogius, patriarch of Alexandria and friend to both Gregory of Rome and Gregory of Antioch.[175] A series of three consecutive notices centered on the patriarch both reflect and reinforce Eulogius's well-earned reputation as a staunch defender of Chalcedonian

---

172. For Gennadius of Constantinople see John Moschus, *Spiritual Meadow* 145; for Elias and Flavian see ibid. 35.

173. John Moschus, *Spiritual Meadow* 139. For Gregory's origins in the Judean monasteries cf. Evagrius Scholasticus, *Ecclesiastical History* 5.6.

174. John Moschus, *Spiritual Meadow* 140 [PG 87:3, 3004B]. For Gregory of Antioch see also John Moschus, *Spiritual Meadow* 40, 42. For the closeness of Moschus to the circle around the patriarch Gregory see also Chadwick (1974) 47f., who points to the various similarities between the anecdotes of the *Spiritual Meadow* and those contained within the *Ecclesiastical History* of Evagrius Scholasticus, Gregory's own disciple.

175. For the association of Eulogius and Gregory the Great see above n. 119; for Eulogius's association with Antioch and with the patriarch Gregory see John of Ephesus, *Ecclesiastical History* 1.40, 3.29; Photius, *Bibliotheca* 226 [Henry vol. 4, 111].

doctrine.[176] In one, Abba Menas, head of the coenobium of Tougara in the Ennaton complex outside Alexandria, relates the aforementioned anecdote that he had heard from the Roman *apocrisiarius* and future pope Gregory while in Constantinople. According to that tale, when Pope Leo had composed his celebrated letter to Flavian, patriarch of Constantinople—better known as the dogmatic *Tome* recognized at Chalcedon—he placed it "on the tomb of Peter, head of the apostles [*tou koruphaiou tōn apostolōn Petrou*]" and supplicated the "first of the disciples" thus: "If I as a man have erred, you, yourself, who have been entrusted with the Church and the throne by the Lord and God and Savior, our Jesus Christ, correct it." "Then," we read, "after forty days the apostle appeared to the pope as he prayed and said to him, 'I have read it and corrected it.' And indeed, [Leo] took the letter from the tomb of Saint Peter, opened it, and discovered it had been corrected by the apostle's hand."[177]

This association of Eulogius and Leo continues also in the final tale within this series. At *Meadow* 148 Theodore of Dara (in Libya) relates that when he had been a *sunkellos* of Eulogius in Alexandria, he saw in a dream a large, solemn-looking man who said, "Announce me to the sainted Pope Eulogius." When Theodore then asked the visitor how he wished to be announced, the latter replied, "I am Leo, the Roman pope." Upon hearing his guest announced, Eulogius sprang up and ran to meet him, and the two patriarchs embraced each other. Then Leo said to Eulogius, "Do you know why I have come to you?" and when his colleague responded that he did not, Leo retorted:[178]

> I have come to thank you, because you so finely and strongly defended my letter, which I wrote to our brother Flavian, patriarch of Constantinople. You have made clear my own purpose and shut up the mouths of the heretics. But you should know, brother, that it is not only me whom you have pleased with this divine labor of yours,[179] but also the head of the apostles, Peter, and, above all else, the truth itself that we proclaim and that is Christ, our God.

The same vision appeared to Theodore three times, and thus convinced he related its contents to Eulogius. The latter wept and raising his hands to heaven in thanks said, "I thank you, Christ Master, our God, that you have judged me worthy to become a herald of your truth and that through the prayers of your servants Peter

---

176. Eulogius's output survives in meager fragments; see CPG vol. 3, 319–21 nos. 6971–79. However, Photius ascribes to him various works (noted at CPG vol. 3, 320 no. 6976), of which the most relevant for our purposes is the large *Defense of the Council of Chalcedon*; see Photius, *Bibliotheca* 103 [Henry vol. 5, 11–39]. See also the (negative) account of Eulogius's doctrinal activities in *History of the Patriarchs* "Anastasius" [Evetts 479f.].

177. John Moschus, *Spiritual Meadow* 147 [PG 87:3, 3012A–B].

178. John Moschus, *Spiritual Meadow* 148 [PG 87:3, 3012D–3013A].

179. I have changed *enthen* for the preferable *entheon* [PG 87:3, 3013A], as per Traversari's Latin *divinum* [PG 87:3, 3014A], not noted in Maisano's F manuscript variations.

and Leo, and just as the widow's two mites [cf. Mark 12:41–44; Luke 21:1–4], your goodness has welcomed our insignificant purpose."[180]

Such tales, therefore, serve both to assert the truth of the Chalcedonian definition and to celebrate Eulogius, erstwhile patriarch of Alexandria, as its most staunch and pious defender. At the same time, however, it is not Alexandria that is presented as the principal guardian of the true faith but rather Rome, via its two most prominent champions, Saint Peter and Pope Leo.[181] In the *Spiritual Meadow*, therefore, the representatives of Rome are conspicuous not merely by their presence—as, for example, in the aforementioned tales concerning Gregory the Great—but also by their status as the foremost founders and defenders of the Chalcedonian faith.

If the vision of the Christian community that the *Spiritual Meadow* constructs can be said to be socially inclusive—in its exploration of paradigms of sanctity beyond the confines of monasticism—then it is nevertheless doctrinally exclusive, demanding a strict adherence to dyophysite doctrine as a necessary prerequisite to virtue.[182] Membership within the orthodox group is therefore defined from within by Chalcedonian doctrine, and from without by a catalogue of anti-Chalcedonian heresies.[183] Of all those considered heretics, however, it is the Severans who pro-

---

180. John Moschus, *Spiritual Meadow* 148 [PG 87:3, 3013A].
181. For this celebration of Peter and Leo see esp. Degórski (2009) 418–20.
182. See, e.g., the general injunctions against heretics found at John Moschus, *Spiritual Meadow* 12 [PG 87:3, 2861A]: "Do not consort with heretics." and 74 [PG 87:3, 2025D]: "The elder [Palladius] issued us a warning and said, 'Believe me, my children, schisms and heresies have done nothing for the holy Church, except to turn us even more from love of God and each other.'" For the theme of heresy within the text see also Chadwick (1974) 68ff.; Pasini (1985) 374–77; Palmer (1993b) 378–82 and (1997b). Moschus's attitude is conveyed at John Moschus, *Spiritual Meadow* 38 [PG 87:3, 2888D–2889A], which repeats the famous anecdote of John Malalas, *Chronicle* 16.20 [Thurn 334f.], concerning the vision of the emperor Anastasius in which an angel pronounces a shortening of his life. But where in Malalas's account the punishment is applied "because of your greed" (*dia tēn aplēstian sou*), in Moschus's version, where it follows a report of the emperor's deposition of the Constantinopolitan patriarchs Euphemius and Macedonius, it is applied "because of your faithlessness" (*dia tēn apistian sou*). Cf. *Paschal Chronicle* [Dindorf 610]; Theophanes, *Chronicle* A.M. 6010 [de Boor 163f.], the latter also giving *dia tēn kakopistian sou*. At John Moschus, *Spiritual Meadow* 35, the death of Anastasius is associated instead with his exile of the pro-Chalcedonian patriarchs Elias of Jerusalem and Flavian of Antioch.
183. See, e.g., the vision of hell at John Moschus, *Spiritual Meadow* 26 [PG 87:3, 2872C–2873A], in which are "Nestorius and Theodore, Eutyches and Apollinarius, Evagrius and Didymus, Dioscorus and Severus, Arius and Origen, and certain others." The F manuscript omits *Theodoron . . . Euagrion kai Didumon*; see Maisano (1982) 241. Nestorius: John Moschus, *Spiritual Meadow* 46, and the tale attributed to Moschus at Nissen (1938) 354, the opening of which (*En tais archais Tiberiou tou basileōs kai pistotatou kaisaros apēlthomen eis Oasin, hētis diakeitai ek dusmōn tēs anōteras Thēbaidos kata tēn erēmon*) resembles that of John Moschus, *Spiritual Meadow* 112 (*En tais archais Tiberiou tou basileōs kai pistotatou kaisaros apēlthomen eis Oasin*) [PG 87:3, 2976B]. Evagrius: *Spiritual Meadow* 177 [PG 87:3, 3048A–B]. We note, however, that Moschus recognizes the Evagrian spiritual distinction between

vide the *Spiritual Meadow*'s particular bête noire—a reflection, perhaps, of Moschus's own experience in disputing with them on behalf of John the Almsgiver but now, we should note, with a far more aggressive and pervasive condemnation than is perceived in the *Miracles of Cyrus and John*.[184]

At *Meadow* 213 "a certain elder" speaks of the divine miracles that occur "even now in the Church of God because of the godless heresies that have been and are still produced, and in particular because of the schism of the headless Severus and the other heretics, for the assurance and edification of weaker souls and the conversion of those same [schismatics], should they so wish."[185] An apposite example of this miraculous confirmation of the Chalcedonian faith is provided at *Meadow* 36, where the Chalcedonian patriarch of Antioch, Ephraim (527–45), decides to confront a stylite near Hierapolis whom he discovered to be an adherent of "Severus's excommunicates and the Acephali." When Ephraim attempted to persuade the stylite "to commune with the holy, catholic, and apostolic Church," the monk challenged him to a trial: "Let us light a fire, Lord Patriarch," he proclaimed, "and let us both enter into it. Whoever comes out unharmed, he is the orthodox one, and we ought to follow him." Ephraim then proceeded to light a fire, and when the monk refused to come down, he threw into the fire his episcopal cape (*ōmophorion*), which emerged after three hours "intact, unharmed, and without blemish" (*sōon, ablabes kai akeraion*). "Then," the tale concludes, "when the stylite saw what had happened, he was enlightened [*eplērophorēthē*] and anathematized Severus and his heresy, and came into the holy Church, and received communion [*ekoinōnēsen*] from the hands of the blessed Ephraim, and glorified God."[186]

Such miracles, therefore, serve to establish both the truth of Chalcedonian doctrine and the proper sectarian divisions between competing Christian factions. From the anti-Chalcedonian perspective, we have also observed this same concern in the *Plerophoriae* of John Rufus, in particular in relation to Jerusalem's sacred sites.[187] That precise same tension appears also within the *Spiritual Meadow*, and Moschus too attempts to enforce the strict sacramental boundaries of the orthodox. His approach is epitomized in a pair of wonderful anecdotes at *Meadow* 48 and 49. In the first an apparition of the Virgin prevented one "Cosmiana, wife of Germanus the patrician," from worshipping at the tomb of Christ, and when

---

"practical" and "contemplative"; see, e.g., John Moschus, *Spiritual Meadow* 40 [PG 87:3, 2893D]: "The meaning of the two swords is the practical and the contemplative [*to praktikon kai to theōrētikon*]. If someone has the two virtues, he is perfect."

184. See above p. 87f.

185. John Moschus, *Spiritual Meadow* 213 [PG 87:3, 3105B–C].

186. John Moschus, *Spiritual Meadow* 36 [PG 87:3, 2884C–2885C]. For similar trials by fire cf. John Rufus, *Plerophoriae* 46–47; with Steppa (2002) 129.

187. See above pp. 38-40.

Cosmiana realized that it was because she was a heretic, she sent for a deacon, "and when the holy chalice arrived, she partook of the holy body and blood of our great God and Savior, Jesus Christ, and thus she was judged worthy of worshipping without impediment at the holy and life-giving tomb of our Lord, Jesus Christ."[188] In the second tale it is said that the *doux* of Palestine, one Gebemer, suffered a similar fate when he once came to worship at the same church, for when he tried to enter, "he saw a ram charging at him, wanting to impale him." This vision occurred several times, until the Guardian of the Cross (*staurophulax*) Azarias convinced Gebemer to look within his soul for the reason. Realizing that the vision appeared because of his communion with the Severans, the *doux* "asked the Guardian of the Cross that he might partake of the holy and life-giving mysteries of Christ, our God. And when the holy chalice arrived, he communicated. And thus he entered and worshipped, and no longer saw the vision."[189]

We observe, therefore, that in the three stories of anti-Chalcedonian converts that we have set out above—that is, those of the Hierapolitan pillar saint, Cosmiana, and Gebemer—the process of conversion is driven through miraculous intervention but nevertheless culminates, much as it does in Sophronius's *Miracles of Cyrus and John*, in eucharistic communion. Here, however, we should note a crucial difference, for whereas Sophronius suppresses the existence of clerical structures of sacramental mediation—that is, it is the saints themselves who appear as priests to administer the eucharist, or else patients themselves commune without the explicit supervision of a priest—here Moschus insists on the presence of a consecrated cleric and, in two of our instances, even names the celebrant (Ephraim, patriarch of Antioch, and Azarias, *staurophulax* at the Church of the Anastasis). As in the *Miracles*, therefore, participation in the eucharist is here the central profession of membership within the orthodox Church; but in contrast, it is here also a simultaneous submission to clerical mediation.

The *Spiritual Meadow* also diverges from Sophronius's *Miracles of Cyrus and John* in its inclusion of several miracles centered on the eucharist itself, miracles that serve once again to differentiate the truth of orthodox belief from a mass of heretical pollutants (in particular Severanism). *Meadow* 29 concerns the rivalry of a Chalcedonian and a Severan stylite near Aegae in Cilicia, which culminates when the former asks the latter to send to him "a portion of his communion" (*merida tēs autou koinōnias*). The Severan thought that his rival would now convert, but when the orthodox monk received the Severan portion, he instead cast it into a cauldron with its orthodox equivalent, and the latter alone "remained intact and dry."[190] Like

---

188. John Moschus, *Spiritual Meadow* 48 [PG 87:3, 2904A–B].

189. John Moschus, *Spiritual Meadow* 49 [PG 87:3, 2904B–2905A]. Lampe (1961) 1489 lists the instance of *phrangelitēs* as a hapax and suggests "lictor."

190. John Moschus, *Spiritual Meadow* 29 [PG 87:3, 2876C–2877A].

the anecdotes associated with the Severans Cosmiana and Gebemer, the one that concerns the Severan stylite in Cilicia also forms one half of a complementary pair. Thus in the subsequent vignette, a monk at Tadai (or Dadē) on Cyprus reports to Moschus and Sophronius how, when he was "in the world," he had a wife, and both of them were Severans. Once he discovered that his wife had gone to their Chalcedonian neighbor to take communion (*koinōnēsai*), and upon going round to prevent her, and discovering her at the point of eating, he grabbed her throat and made her spit out the portion (*meris*). A flash of lightning descends and takes the communion, and after two days the narrator sees a black-faced man wearing rags who proclaims, "You and I alike have been condemned to one punishment." When the man asks him who he is, he replies, "I am he who struck the Creator of all, our Lord, Jesus Christ, on the jaw at the time of the Passion [cf. John 18:22]."[191] Offense against the Chalcedonian eucharist, this memorable tale emphasizes, is identical to offense against Christ.

For Moschus, therefore, miracles associated with the Chalcedonian eucharist provide the ultimate proof of the righteousness of the corresponding doctrine; at the same time, participation in the eucharistic celebration provides the ultimate statement of membership within the Chalcedonian group. It is therefore unsurprising to discover that Moschus (much like Rufus and Sophronius before him) inveighs against those who partake of communion in either doctrinal camp. In one tale Abba Theodore, higoumen of the Palaia Laura, relates an anecdote concerning two Syrian brothers in which the elder brother is informed, in a dream, that his sibling "has fornicated with the innkeeper's wife." When the younger brother is questioned, he responds: "I am not aware of having done something bad, except that I found some monks in our village who were of Severan dogma, and not knowing if this is evil, I used to take communion with them [*ekoinōnoun autois*]."[192] Thus, just as Sophronius in the *Miracles of Cyrus and John* rails against those anti-Chalcedonians who receive, in place of the eucharist, the sanctified oil from the saints' tomb, so too does Moschus point to the dangerous moral consequences of indiscriminate participation in the non-Chalcedonian eucharist. In *Meadow* 178 one "Abba George, priest of the coenobium of the Scholarii," relates how a great elder at Monidia "toiled much but was careless concerning the faith, and used to take communion without discrimination [*metelambanen adiakritōs*]

---

191. John Moschus, *Spiritual Meadow* 30 [2877B–2880A]. For a similar tale see John Moschus, *Spiritual Meadow* 79, in which a Severan businessman (*pragmateutēs*) tries to burn the reserved communion that his Chalcedonian agent keeps within a box—"according to the local custom" (*kata to ethos tēs chōras*)—and then discovers that the portions (*merides*) have sprouted miraculous roots. The tale constitutes a rare witness to the practice of home communion in Chalcedonian circles; see Taft (2003) 3; Caseau (2002) 91 on John Moschus, *Spiritual Meadow* 30.

192. John Moschus, *Spiritual Meadow* 188 [*PG* 87:3, 3065B–3068A].

wherever he found himself." An angel appears to the elder and asks him, "If you die, how do you want us to bury you? As the Egyptian monks bury [their dead], or as the Jerusalemites do?" The elder is confused at the vision, but then a colleague asks him, "Where do you participate in the holy mysteries?" (*Pou metalambaneis tōn hagiōn mustēriōn?*) When he responds, "Wherever I find myself," the other elder then admonishes him: "No longer should you communicate outside of the holy, catholic, and apostolic Church, where the four holy synods are named: the synod of 318 at Nicaea; the synod of 150 at Constantinople; the first synod of 200 at Ephesus; and the synod of 630 at Chalcedon." When the angel returns and repeats the question, the elder responds, "I want [to be buried] as the Jerusalemites do." Then at once the elder died, the tale concludes, lest he "destroy his labors and be judged with the heretics."[193]

Advancement within the spiritual life, therefore, means nothing if one does not acknowledge the Chalcedonian Church and submit oneself to its rites. Those indifferent to doctrine, or opposed to Chalcedon, may seem to be pious, but their estrangement from the orthodox rites ensures their ultimate condemnation. This fundamental point is underlined in an anecdote in which one Abba Theodulos tells how he encountered in Alexandria a Syrian monk "who owned nothing except a hair shirt, a cloak, and a few loaves of bread" and who "stood all the time in one corner, reciting the psalms [*stichologōn*] day and night, and not acknowledging anyone." When Sunday arrived Theodoulos asked the stranger if he would come to Saint Sophia to "participate in the holy and solemn mysteries" (*hina metalabēis tōn hagiōn kai septōn mustēriōn*), but the latter replied that he was "an adherent of Severus, and not in communion with the Church." Theodulos then has something approaching a crisis of (doctrinal) faith and begs God to reveal to him which doctrine is correct. When he next sees the monk, he perceives "a dove hovering above his head, covered with soot as if from a butcher, plucked and festering." "Then I knew," he concludes, "that the blackened, festering dove that had appeared to me was his faith."[194]

Communion within the Chalcedonian Church is, therefore, the sine qua non of the virtuous life, and advanced ascetics are not excused. *Meadow* 17 describes a great elder who "did not drink wine or eat bread, unless it was made from bran," but nevertheless concludes with the observation that "he took communion three times a week" (*metalambanen de triton tēs hebdomados*);[195] *Meadow* 86 tells of a Cilician anchorite who lived as a grazer (*boskomenos*) but who, "on the Lord's Day used to come and partake of the holy mysteries [*metelambanen tōn hagiōn*

---

193. John Moschus, *Spiritual Meadow* 178 [*PG* 87:3, 3048B–3049A].

194. John Moschus, *Spiritual Meadow* 106 [*PG* 87:3, 2965A–C].

195. John Moschus, *Spiritual Meadow* 17 [*PG* 87:3, 2865A]. The F manuscript places the elder at the Laura of Peter; see Maisano (1982) 241.

*mustēriōn*]";[196] and at *Meadow* 100 one Theodore ("who became bishop of Rhossus") records his pilgrimage to Sinai with the Pontic priest Peter, whose extreme fasting is nevertheless punctuated with the food of communion.[197] The celebration of advanced ascetics is also accompanied, therefore, by the simultaneous recognition of their regular participation in the eucharist.

That recognition, of course, may be appreciated as a simple comment on actual ascetic practice of the period. This I do not dispute. But in light both of the earlier hagiographic indifference to an ascetic eucharist that is present but not emphasized and of Moschus's persistent interest in the sacraments, his decision to include such qualifications cannot but assume a far greater significance. Besides these simple and somewhat spontaneous statements, for example, he demonstrates an acute awareness of the practical tension between the decentralizing imperatives of withdrawn asceticism and the centralizing demands of regular submission to the eucharist. In certain anecdotes, the miraculous interventions that in general characterize his conception of both the hagiographic desert and the *oikoumenē* provide a convenient solution: in one anecdote, one Abba Stephen the Cappadocian relates how once during the eucharistic celebration on Mount Sinai, at the point of the sacrifice being offered (*tēs hagias anaphoras epiteloumenēs*), he (and he alone) saw two naked anchorites appear to take communion and then depart on foot across the Red Sea;[198] and in another a certain higoumen also on Mount Sinai, George, is one Holy Saturday overcome with the desire "to celebrate the Holy Resurrection in the Holy City and to partake of the holy mysteries [*metalabein tōn hagiōn mustēriōn*] in the Holy [Church of the] Anastasis of Christ, our God"—he is then in an instant transported to Jerusalem to receive communion from the hands of the patriarch Peter (524-52), much to the latter's amazement.[199]

Thus where Sophronius in the *Miracles of Cyrus and John* marginalizes the permanent significance of the eucharist to the spiritual life (coterminous with an apparent indifference to clerics and their prerogatives at Menuthis), Moschus in the *Spiritual Meadow* insists on both universal and regular participation (coterminous with his celebration of the episcopate and priesthood). At the same time, Moschus's evident interest leads him to include several anecdotes that center on the eucharistic celebration and on issues of eucharistic protocol. Certain tales, for example,

---

196. John Moschus, *Spiritual Meadow* 86 [PG 87:3, 2944B]. For *boskoi* see the famous discussion of Evagrius Scholasticus, *Ecclesiastical History* 1.21; with the discussion in Binns (1994) 108; Wortley (2001); Penkett (2003).

197. John Moschus, *Spiritual Meadow* 100 [PG 87:3, 2960A-B].

198. John Moschus, *Spiritual Meadow* 122 [Pattenden (1975) 51f.].

199. John Moschus, *Spiritual Meadow* 127 [PG 87:3, 2988C-2989A]. The tension between withdrawn asceticism and the demands of participation in the eucharist is perhaps also played out in stories of angels officiating at desert altars; John Moschus, *Spiritual Meadow* 4, 10, 199. For the same tension see also Déroche (2002) 177f.

emphasize the importance of moral virtue on the part of the participant;[200] still others focus on the virtues of the presiding cleric. The persecuted priest whose holiness is then established in the eucharistic celebration is indeed a distinct topos of the collection. The congregation of one Cilician priest reports him to his bishop for postponing and rearranging the eucharistic service, but when the bishop then confronts the priest over his apparent disregard for liturgical procedure, the priest reports that he only begins the synaxis when he perceives "the Holy Spirit overshadowing the holy altar";[201] another accused priest on Samos is vindicated when a celestial apparition releases him from prison to perform the eucharistic service;[202] and the bishop of Romilla (near Rome) proves his holiness before Pope Agapetus (535–36) when he establishes that the presence at the altar of a certain deacon is preventing the usual descent of the Spirit (*epiphoitēsis*).[203]

Moschus therefore—unlike certain contemporaries both Chalcedonian and anti-Chalcedonian—attaches a particular significance to the holiness of the eucharistic celebrant,[204] and it is that same significance that leads him to explore those circumstances in which a priest proves unworthy to perform the liturgy. The Arab ascetic Julian, we are informed at *Meadow* 96, was once outraged at Macarius, patriarch of Jerusalem (544–52, 564–75), and refused to communicate with him. The reasons for this outrage are obscure, but it appears that Macarius had perhaps refused to depose a sinful priest within Julian's coenobium and that he as a result was concerned not to receive communion from that priest's hands. He related the matter to Symeon the Younger on the Wonderful Mountain, outside Antioch, and the great stylite said to him, "Do not withdraw, nor wish to distance yourself from the holy Church. For by the grace of our Lord, Jesus Christ, Son of God, he means no evil. In any case know this also, brother: that whoever administers the eucharist [*proskomisei*] in your coenobium, you have there an elder called Patricius. This elder stands outside the sanctuary, below all the others, near to the church's west-

---

200. See John Moschus, *Spiritual Meadow* 150 (in which the spirit does not descend upon the liturgy until a certain deacon has been dismissed) and 192 (in which a supposed sinner is excluded from communion). For the importance of ridding oneself of sin see also ibid. 161 [PG 87:3, 3029A], in which a demon taunts a monk for making a mistake in his work: "But I said to him, 'Why do you say this?' And he replied, 'Because for three Sundays you have taken communion while at enmity with your neighbor.'"

201. John Moschus, *Spiritual Meadow* 27 [PG 87:3, 2873C].

202. John Moschus, *Spiritual Meadow* 108.

203. John Moschus, *Spiritual Meadow* 150 [PG 87:3, 3016B].

204. It should be noted that there is no agreement among authorities both Chalcedonian and non-Chalcedonian as to whether liturgical efficacy is dependent on the spiritual condition of the celebrant. For such an association see, e.g., John Rufus, *Plerophoriae* 20; *Life of Symeon the Younger* 132. For the opposite approach see, e.g., Severus of Antioch, *Select Letters* 1.3.1–4; Anastasius of Sinai, *Tales* B1, B7 [Nau (1903a) 69f., nos. 43, 49]; idem, *On the Holy Synaxis* 20–21. On this theme see also the comments of Déroche (2002) 173–75.

ern wall. He himself also says the holy eucharistic prayer [*legei tēn hagian euchēn tēs proskomidēs*], and the sacred offering [*hē hagia anaphora*] is reckoned his."[205]

A comparable problem is explored in a celebrated episode at *Meadow* 25, an episode that appears also in Antony of Choziba's contemporary *Miracles of the Blessed Theotokos at Choziba*.[206] In Moschus's version, one "Abba Gregory, former member of the Scholarii," records how a brother at the Monastery of Choziba "learned [the words used at] the offering of the holy eucharistic prayer [*tēn proskomidēn tēs hagias anaphoras*]." One day, as the same monk was returning to his monastery with the elements, "he said the offering as if reciting psalms," and when the Chozibite priest Abba John ("later bishop of Caesarea in Palestine") made the oblation, "he did not see the accustomed coming [*epiphoitēsis*] of the Holy Spirit." John was distressed and, assuming that he had committed some sin that prevented the presence of the Spirit, burst into tears and threw himself upon the floor of his church. At that point, however, an angel appeared to him from God and explained: "Since the brother who brought the blessings [*tas eulogias*] on the road pronounced the holy eucharistic prayer, they were sanctified and perfected." As in the previous anecdote, therefore, an ascetic's recitation of the eucharistic prayer is enough to ensure the consecration of the elements. Here, however, Moschus records a quite different result: "From then on the elder established a rule that nobody should learn the eucharistic prayer unless he had been ordained, and that it should not be pronounced at any time except in a consecrated place."[207]

Numerous scholars have before noted Moschus's conspicuous interest in issues of sacramental protocol.[208] Elsewhere the *Spiritual Meadow* includes an anecdote in which a certain pious priest in Cilicia postponed and rearranged the eucharistic service because he could not begin until he perceived the presence of the Spirit; in one tale a virtuous elder perceived angels when he performed the eucharistic rites, even though he had learned the necessary prayers (in all innocence) from heretics;[209] and George, the prefect of Africa, records how some children at Apamea once enacted the entire eucharistic service as a game, electing from their number representatives of the relevant clerics, performing the entire rite word for word, and then, on the point of communion—when, we must assume, the eucharist had been consecrated—being blasted with a celestial fire that almost killed them.[210]

---

205. John Moschus, *Spiritual Meadow* 96 [PG 87:3, 2953B–2956A].
206. Antony of Choziba, *Miracles of the Blessed Theotokos at Choziba* 5 [Houze 366–68].
207. John Moschus, *Spiritual Meadow* 25 [PG 87:3, 2369D–2872A]. See also Déroche (2002) 173.
208. Chadwick (1974) 69f.; Maisano (1982) 47; Krueger (2009); also Déroche (1995) 262. Here I focus on the eucharist, but Moschus is also interested in issues of baptismal protocol; see John Moschus, *Spiritual Meadow* 176, 197, 198.
209. Ibid. 27, 199.
210. Ibid. 196. Note the numerous variations in the F manuscript, in Maisano (1982) 248. A similar tale, told by "Abba Basil, priest and anchorite who became a monk of the New Laura," is attributed to

This emphasis upon the eucharist, and the concomitant exploration of issues of sacramental protocol, is rare in monastic texts (and, in particular, in Chalcedonian texts). As we have seen, the dominant emphasis on social withdrawal in the hagiographies associated with the pioneering generations had undermined the use of urban contexts but had also demanded that superior ascetics, and in particular anchorites, be seen to operate beyond the constraints of the sacramental system.[211] Moschus's striking celebration of the eucharist as the definitive emblem of the Chalcedonian Church thus marks a notable departure but can nevertheless be seen to complement his wider program. Eucharistic miracles attest to the truth of Chalcedonian doctrine, while participation in communion establishes the concrete ritual boundaries between orthodox and heretic. At the same time, the celebration of the orthodox eucharist unifies a diverse Church, bringing it together in shared celebration and subordinating all to its incomparable power. That, of course, leads Moschus to pursue various unresolved problems of sacramental procedure. Should the pure, or sinners, participate in the eucharist? Can sinful or nonecclesiastical celebrants consecrate the host? The *Spiritual Meadow* offers pragmatic rather than theological solutions to these problems. Yet the inclusion of such tales in itself points to a heightened interest in ecclesiastical ritual—a new desire to elucidate the complex interactions of sin, asceticism, and sacrament.

This chapter has examined the *Spiritual Meadow* of John Moschus as one constituent element within a broader Palestinian reaction to the Persian invasion and its various political, administrative, and economic consequences. In response to the dramatic Persian capture of Jerusalem and the reported massacre of part of its population, Moschus's monastic contemporaries in Palestine conceived of Persian success as divine punishment for collective Christian sin. That understanding of events demanded a reevaluation of long-standing notions of holiness, for withdrawn monks, despite their introverted moral prowess, had failed to assuage divine wrath. From his exile in Rome, Moschus constructed a new hagiographic vision, one that still celebrated traditional vignettes of distant desert existence but nevertheless devolved Christian virtue to other, less obvious heroes. At the same time, he delimited that broad social vision in the strident demand for Chalcedonian doctrine as the basis of proper faith and in the elevation of eucharistic par-

---

Moschus by Nissen (1938) 361–65 (no. 8). It develops into the famous story of the young Jewish convert placed in a furnace by his father, but in its current form, at least, it is too long and too late to belong to the *Spiritual Meadow*. A different version of the same tale is attributed to Moschus by Mioni (1951) 93–94 (no. 12). For other versions see, e.g., John Rufus, *Plerophoriae* 14; Cyril of Scythopolis, *Life of Sabas* 5 [Schwartz 89f.]; Evagrius Scholasticus, *Ecclesiastical History* 4.36; Gregory of Tours, *Glory of the Martyrs* 9; Georgian Appendix to the *Spiritual Meadow* 22.

211. See above p. 13.

ticipation as the ultimate proof of membership within the orthodox group, distinguishing the pious from external pollutants and proclaiming a diverse Church unified under the shared imperatives of a single sacramental order.

In this distinct eucharistic emphasis, Moschus's text shares obvious parallels with the *Miracles of Cyrus and John* of his disciple Sophronius. In Sophronius's text, as in the *Spiritual Meadow*, participation in the eucharist serves to differentiate between orthodox and heretic, between true and false doctrines (in direct response, no doubt, to the claims of anti-Chalcedonian authors). But where in his disciple's narratives that same sacramental emphasis is coupled with an apparent indifference to repeated communion as a spiritual imperative and a concomitant marginalization of its clerical mediators, in the *Meadow* Moschus, while exploring various pressing issues of sacramental protocol, also points to the need for continuous submission to the eucharist and celebrates the clerical vocation alongside the ascetic. We should avoid thinking of this dissonance as the product of simple generic determination or personal preference, for as we shall see, the striking shift partakes of a wider pattern within the circle's output. As the crisis of empire deepened, so too would Sophronius and his own disciple Maximus also come to articulate more sacramentalized, more integrated models of the Christian life.

As we have seen, this distinct shift of emphasis was predicted in anti-Chalcedonian circles of the preceding period.[212] Both processes can be said to have occurred within a context in which the relation between orthodox Church and empire had been destabilized: in the Chalcedonian case, when the Persian occupation of the Near East had encouraged, in particular among Palestinians, a process of profound spiritual and political introspection; and in the anti-Chalcedonian case, when the emperors at Constantinople had turned against anti-Chalcedonian communities in the provinces. Although there is no indication in Moschus's *Spiritual Meadow* of the doctrinal crisis soon to engulf his circle, the emphasis upon the sustained sacramental unity and integrity of the Church evident within the *Meadow* would therein serve, as it had for previous generations of anti-Chalcedonians, as a distinct complement to its dissent from imperial doctrine. In the subsequent decades, Moschus's Palestinian heirs would develop further his insistence on the need for regular participation in the eucharist, his recognition of the clerical hierarchy through which it was mediated, and his celebration of Rome and its popes as the guardians of the orthodox faith. Those same ideological emphases, however, would then be deployed within a dramatic new context, one in which the emperor and patriarch at Constantinople placed the weight of imperial power behind a doctrine that proved anathema to Moschus's disciples and in which those same disciples' hopes of a permanent return to the East were dashed in the rapid and brilliant success of a nascent Islam.

212. See above pp. 37-42.

4

# Maximus and the *Mystagogy*

Throughout the 620s, as Moschus and Sophronius had retreated westward to North Africa and Rome, the provinces that the pair had abandoned remained under Persian occupation, and Constantinople itself came under considerable threat. In 622, having established his dominion across the Levant and Egypt, the Persian shahanshah Khusrau II launched a bold assault upon Anatolia, and soon after Heraclius was compelled to abandon an ambitious counteroffensive into Persia and to rush westward. The reason, perhaps, was the creeping menace of the Avars, who soon after attempted to capture him at a supposed summit in June 623 and thence proceeded to ravage Constantinople's hinterland.[1] The Persians had, in the meantime, continued their pressure both on Anatolia and on the Aegean, but in 624 a crucial but expensive peace concluded with the Avars permitted the emperor to resume his previous counteroffensive, catching the Persians off guard and penetrating into Persarmenia and Atropatene, ravaging the same regions in

---

1. For the narrative of events presented here I am dependent on, and much indebted to, the critical reconstruction presented in Howard-Johnston (1994), (1995), (1999b) 213–21, and (2004); I follow the latter but for a different vision of the 625 campaign, placing it in winter 624/5, see Zuckerman (2002b). I am much indebted to James Howard-Johnston for a preview of his forthcoming monograph on the Last Great War, but see also Stratos (1968–78) vol. 1, 135–236; Kaegi (2003) 100–191. In what follows I nevertheless present the main sources. For this stage of Heraclius's campaign see George of Pisidia, *Persian Expedition* 1-3, with ibid. 3.305–40 for the sudden westward retreat, which Howard-Johnston (1999a) 14f. links to the reported Avar siege of Thessalonica in *Anonymous Miracles of Saint Demetrius* 2. For the attempt to capture the emperor and subsequent action around the capital: *Paschal Chronicle* [Dindorf 712f.]; Nicephorus, *Short History* 10; Theophanes, *Chronicle* A.M. 6110. See also Theodore Syncellus, *On the Virgin's Robe*, with Averil Cameron (1979b).

the process.² In 625, after Heraclius had wintered in Albania, the Persians regrouped and launched three armies into the field to encircle the Roman force. But through a series of brilliant maneuvers, Heraclius avoided being entrapped and even managed to inflict successive humiliating defeats upon his pursuers.³

The Persian campaign now entered a different, more daring phase. In an attempt to force Heraclius to retreat to Constantinople, Khusrau launched a two-pronged assault into Anatolia, in coordination with an Avar assault upon the capital from Thrace. Once again, however, the emperor did the unexpected. Rather than retreat to the capital, he instead rushed into Anatolia and there confronted one of the advancing armies, inflicting a crushing defeat.⁴ The other Persian force—under the general Shahrbaraz, conqueror of Jerusalem—now advanced upon and seized Chalcedon, and there awaited the arrival of the Avar allies. There the Persians stood as menacing but for the most part passive observers upon the dramatic siege of Constantinople in 626, in which a vast eighty thousand Avar confederates are estimated to have taken part. Despite their impressive numbers, the capital's considerable defenses held out against the Avar siege engines and a Slavic naval assault—an outcome that some within the walls attributed to the miraculous intervention of the Virgin.⁵ Confronted with its failure to progress, the loose federation of Avar allies dissolved, leaving the Persians isolated on the Asian side of the Bosporus. His capital secured, Heraclius now once again headed eastward, to Iberia, where in 627 he confirmed a crucial strategic alliance with the Turks.⁶ Together the combined armies defeated a final Persian force in the plain of Nineveh, opening an unobstructed path to the Persian capital, Ctesiphon.⁷ Soon

---

2. For the peace see Theophanes, *Chronicle* A.M. 6111; Nicephorus, *Short History* 13. For the 624 campaign see *Paschal Chronicle* [Dindorf 713f.]; George of Pisidia, *Heraclias* 2.160-230; Theophanes, *Chronicle* A.M. 6114 ; Ps.-Sebēos, *History* 38 [Abgaryan 124]; Movsēs Daskhurants'i, *History* 10 [trans. Dowsett 78-80].

3. See Ps.-Sebēos, *History* 38 [Abgaryan 125]; Theophanes, *Chronicle* A.M. 6115-16; Movsēs Daskhurants'i, *History* 10 [trans. Dowsett 81].

4. See esp. Theophanes, *Chronicle* A.M. 6116-17; Ps.-Sebēos, *History* 38 [Abgaryan 125].

5. For the siege see esp. *Paschal Chronicle* [Dindorf 716-26]; Theodore Syncellus, *On the Siege*; George of Pisidia, *Avar War*; Nicephorus, *Short History* 13; Theophanes, *Chronicle* A.M. 6117; also in brief Agapius, *Universal History* [Vasiliev 458]; Michael the Syrian, *Chronicle* 11.3; *Chronicle to 1234* 98 [Chabot vol. 1, 231]. For discussion see Van Dieten (1972) 12-21; Howard-Johnston (1995); and the extensive commentary in Whitby and Whitby (1989) 169-81.

6. See Theophanes, *Chronicle* A.M. 6117; Movsēs Daskhurants'i, *History* 11-12 [trans. Dowsett 81-88]; Nicephorus, *Short History* 12; Agapius, *Universal History* [Vasiliev 462f.]; Michael the Syrian, *Chronicle* 11.3; *Anonymous Chronicle to 1234* 98 [Chabot vol. 1, 233]; with Zuckerman (1995).

7. Theophanes, *Chronicle* A.M. 6118; Ps.-Sebēos, *History* 38 [Abgaryan 126]; *Chronicle of Seert* 87 [Scher 541]; Movsēs Daskhurants'i, *History* 12 [trans. Dowsett 89]; Agapius, *Universal History* [Vasiliev 452, 463f.]; Michael the Syrian, *Chronicle* 11.3; *Anonymous Chronicle to 1234* 99 [Chabot vol. 1, 233f.]; *Khuzistan Chronicle* [Guidi 27f.].

after, while wintering in Atropatene in 628, Heraclius received the news of a successful domestic coup against the beleaguered Khusrau and a letter in which his successor sued for peace.[8] From the desperate position of 622, it has been a quite remarkable turnaround of fortunes.

Although it is difficult to suppose that news of these events did not spread like wildfire, we cannot know for certain whether Moschus, when he composed the *Spiritual Meadow* around 630, was aware of these events within the East. The triumph of Heraclius—soon to be compounded in the wholesale withdrawal of Shahrbaraz from the eastern provinces and the spectacular return of the Cross to Jerusalem—nevertheless held forth the promise of a restoration of the status quo ante bellum and with it a reunification of the fragmented monastic movement of Jerusalem. During the Persian occupation, that movement appears to have been beset with significant tensions. Some of its members, of course, had remained in exile alongside the patriarch Zachariah, who according to a letter surviving in Greek and appended also to the narrative of Strategius seems to have been concerned that those who remained in Jerusalem not think themselves superior to their captured compatriots.[9] Among those who had avoided deportation, furthermore, there was now a quite profound divide: between those, like Modestus, who remained under Persian rule within Palestine and those, like Moschus and Sophronius, who had preferred retreat. We might imagine some tension between these two groups, but the extant sources permit no more than speculation. Thus we could read as somewhat polemical the words that Antiochus Monachus, in postconquest Palestine, placed in the mouth of the *locum tenens* Modestus, who in the wake of the Bedouin raid upon Saint Sabas "called upon us all not to abandon our place, but nobly to remain amid trials, remembering the words of the Lord, 'The gate that leads to life is small, and the road is narrow' [Matt. 7:14], and that of the Apostle, that 'We must pass through many hardships to enter the kingdom of heaven' [Acts 14:22]."[10]

Amid those who chose to enter exile in the West, we now encounter a member of the Moschan circle who has hitherto remained in the background: Maximus Confessor. Maximus's output has thus far not been contextualized alongside that of Moschus and Sophronius. A persistent but unsubstantiated legend of Maximus's Constantinopolitan origins—based on a tissue of medieval misdirection and modern misunderstanding—has inhibited the venture, for it has obscured the fact

---

8. See *Paschal Chronicle* [Dindorf 727–29]; Ps.-Sebēos, *History* 38f. [Abgaryan 128f.]; Theophanes, *Chronicle* A.M. 6118; Agapius, *Universal History* [Vasiliev 452, 464f.]; Michael the Syrian, *Chronicle* 11.3; *Anonymous Chronicle to 1234* 100 [Chabot vol. 1, 234]; *Khuzistan Chronicle* [Guidi 28f.]; *Chronicle of Seert* 92 [Scher 551]; Eutychius, *Annals (Alexandrian Recension)* [Breydy 125–27, 130–31]. For the recent revision of Khusrau's chronology see Tyler-Smith (2004).

9. See Zachariah, *Letter*; cf. Strategius, *On the Fall* 22. For Zachariah in later texts see *Georgian Appendix to the Spiritual Meadow* 24–25 and Anastasius of Sinai, *Tales* B5.

10. Antiochus Monachus, *Letter to Eustathius* [PG 89, 1425A].

that Maximus was a product of Palestinian monasticism. This need to establish Maximus's proper origins is, we should note, far more than a pedantic quest for historical correctness, for once we reconceptualize Maximus as both a Palestinian and, indeed, as a member of the Moschan circle, we can better appreciate his own intellectual and cultural formation, and thus counteract the still pervasive treatment of the man and his thought in isolation.[11] Indeed, once we contextualize certain prominent features of Maximus's corpus alongside the output of his closest associates, those features appear less as the products of an exceptional mind—although exceptional it no doubt was—and more as an expression of religious sensibilities evident within the Moschan circle at least since Sophronius's *Miracles of Cyrus and John*.

Like Moschus, Maximus in exile composed several texts that demonstrate both a profound respect for the clerical vocation and at the same time an acute interest in the reconciliation of ascetical and eucharistic narratives. As we have seen, for all the legal and socioeconomic integration of monasticism within the wider Church in the fourth to sixth centuries, in the same period ascetic attitudes toward its hierarchical and sacramental structures remained ambiguous at best, in particular in Chalcedonian circles. Within the anecdotal narratives of the *Spiritual Meadow*, Moschus had signaled a new interest in exploring ascetics' orientation around, and subordination to, those same structures, and now his associate Maximus would provide those narratives with a theological complement. Maximus's *Mystagogy*, composed in exile at some point in the 630s, attempted nothing less than the full intellectual integration of the ascetic enterprise within a eucharistic scheme. Where Pseudo-Dionysius the Areopagite's vision had paid scant attention to the complex anthropologies of the monastic pioneers, Maximus would, for the first time, reconcile the narratives of the great ascetic theoreticians to the external realities of the terrestrial Church. In doing so, he sacrificed the spiritual independence of monks from the illumination offered through the Church. But at the same time, he offered a radical new vision of a Church united against all external threats and elevated above the shifting sands of Eastern geopolitics.

## MAXIMUS, MONK OF PALESTINE

According to a later Greek *Life*, Maximus had been born to noble parents of Constantinopolitan origin. In his youth, according to that same tradition, Maximus exhibited all the characteristics of the hagiographic *senex puer*, and soon came to the attention of the emperor Heraclius, who summoned him to the palace and elevated him to the position of first secretary of imperial records (*hupographeus*

---

11. See Flusin (1992b) vol. 2, 52–54, for the importance of the question of Maximus's origins to understanding the intellectual culture of Palestine in this period.

*prōtos tōn basilikōn hupomnēmatōn*). Maximus, the *Life* claims, nevertheless valued philosophical contemplation far more than terrestrial gain, and when he perceived the innovations in the faith that the monotheletes had introduced, he retired from the administration and took up a life of sequestered asceticism at a monastery in nearby Chrysopolis, where he soon assumed—against his will—the position of higoumen. Then, however, when monothelete doctrine became more entrenched within the capital, Maximus decided to retreat to "older Rome," knowing it to be "unblemished with this stain."[12]

Although this account was for a long time canonical, within the available sources there were nevertheless hints of an alternative tradition of Maximus's origins, for the hostile *Chronicle* of Michael the Syrian and the *Anonymous Chronicle to 1234* both claim that Maximus was, in fact, from Ḥeṣfin, in the Golan.[13] Then in 1973 Sebastian Brock published the Syriac text from which Michael and the anonymous chronicler had (ultimately) derived their information. Contained within a single manuscript in the British Museum, its author—one George of Reshʿaina, who claims to be a disciple and admirer of Sophronius—states that Maximus was born at Ḥeṣfin, the scion of an illicit union between a Persian slave girl and a Samaritan linen maker. Soon after Maximus's birth, George claims, his parents died, and the local priest Martyrius—who had, wonderfully but inexplicably, christened him Moschus (*mwsky*)—took him to the Palestinian Palaia Laura, where the abbot Pantaleon received him into the novitiate and changed his name to Maximus.[14] It was thus in Palestine, the *Life* claims, that Maximus had his monastic formation, and not in Constantinople.

How then can we explain this startling divergence? We should first note that the Greek *Life* of Maximus exists in three recensions, and that the earliest of those recensions came from the pen of a Constantinopolitan author writing in the tenth century (perhaps Michael Exaboulites, a Studite monk).[15] The basic soundness of that dossier's account of Maximus's origins has been assailed from several direc-

---

12. *Greek Life of Maximus (Recension 3)* 1–7 [Neil and Allen 38–50, quotations at 44, 50]. For analysis of the three recensions of the *Greek Life of Maximus* see Neil (2001).

13. See Michael the Syrian, *Chronicle* 9.9 [Chabot vol. 4, 426]; *Anonymous Chronicle to 1234* 130 [Chabot vol. 1, 264–67]. Both authors claim to have used an anti-Maximianist text of Shemʿun of Qenneshre. For comment see Brock (1973) 337–40.

14. For the name *mwsky* see George of Reshʿaina, *Life* 3 [Brock 303]. Brock translates *mwsky* as "Moschion" (ibid. 314), but the Syriac allows both possibilities. The fascinating coincidence is noted by Chadwick (1974) 46 n. 2: "In this hostile, confused but important text Maximus was a bastard Palestinian named Moschus (Mwsky), monk of the Old Lavra. Are Sophronius's two friends merged here?"

15. See Lackner (1967) 315f.; Neil (2001) 47; Roosen (2010) 435–51, esp. 450f. Cf. Winkelmann (2001) 171–73 no. 171. See also Khoperia (2003) 403f. and 408–10 for some extra (but spurious) biographic material preserved in a tenth-century Georgian *Life*, seemingly derived from a lost recension of its Greek counterpart. On Georgian sources for Maximus's life see also eadem (2000), (2001).

tions: even before Brock's publication of the alternative *Life*, Wolfgang Lackner, for example, demonstrated that parts of the narrative of Maximus's birth and childhood were in fact based upon details contained within the *Vita A* of Theodore the Studite;[16] while Marie-France Auzépy has pointed to the parallel processes through which the lives of two other controversial Palestinian monks (Stephen the Sabaite and Cosmas the Hymnographer) were also transformed and thus sanitized in medieval Constantinopolitan sources.[17] Others have pointed to certain anachronisms contained within the Greek *Life*'s narrative: it is doubtful, first of all, that Maximus would have abandoned the capital because of monotheletism, since the monothelete crisis proper did not begin until about 640; there is no indication that he ever became a higoumen, whether at Constantinople or elsewhere; and, moreover, the administrative title that the *Life* attributes to Maximus—*hupographeus prōtos tōn basilikōn hupomnēmatōn*, or *prōtoasēkrētis* in several *passiones*—is not otherwise attested until after Maximus's lifetime.[18]

Various attempts have nevertheless been made to trace the *Life* back to an earlier model.[19] While all such attempts have been discredited, in an impressive recent paper Bram Roosen has once again reopened the difficult question of Maximus's Greek hagiographic corpus. Concluding that the various versions of the Greek *Life* are, in their description of Maximus's descent from Constantinopolitan aristocrats, indeed dependent on the *Vita A* of Theodore the Studite,[20] he nevertheless presents the convincing contention that a set of various interdependent *passiones*—which also contain the claim that Maximus was before his tonsure *prōtoasēkrētis* in the imperial administration—derive from a lost *Urpassio*, but furthermore that this *Urpassio* was composed in Palestine in the early eighth century, and in parallel with a Greek *Life* of Pope Martin I, Maximus's eventual Roman collaborator.[21] The notion that Martin and Maximus's *passiones* were produced in parallel, we should note, is more asserted than argued; and the dating of the former (and thus of the latter) is based on nothing more than a terminus post quem provided through a reference to the Council in Trullo (691/2).[22] Their mutual dependence, therefore, remains

---

16. Lackner (1967) 294–98. Cf. Roosen (2010) 446–51.

17. Auzépy (1994) esp. 204–17.

18. For this point see Lackner (1967) 291 n. 3; for discussion of the title idem (1971). For the *passiones* see Roosen (2010) 411–33, with n. 58.

19. The state of the debate is summarized in Allen (1985); also Conte (1989) 249–62; Neil (2001) 51–53.

20. See esp. Roosen (2010) 450f.

21. Ibid. 427–33.

22. For the references to the council in Trullo see *Greek Life of Pope Martin* 14. For the proposed date of the *passio* of Martin—which survives in a single manuscript—see Roosen (2010) 428 with n. 74, citing Conte (1989) 248; and thence Neil (2006c) 108. Conte's dating is somewhat insecure, however, for it is based on a vague reference at *Greek Life of Pope Martin* 14 [Peeters 262] to heresy "even now,"

unclear, and it is moreover possible that the posited *Urpassio* and the Greek *Life* of Martin are much later in date than Roosen has supposed. For our purposes it must nevertheless be noted that Roosen is careful to avoid the claim that the *Urpassio*'s supposed information on Maximus's Constantinopolitan career is accurate. He prefers instead to accept the Palestinian narrative of Maximus's origins and even makes the tantalizing suggestion that the *Urpassio* responded to the Syriac *Life*.[23] Although we therefore have an important corrective to previous conceptions of Maximus's hagiographic corpus—one that asserts the importance of the various *passiones* over the *Life*—the conclusion in effect repeats recent skepticism toward the Greek account of Maximus's earliest career. The most learned and extensive modern investigation of the Greek corpus, therefore, has been unable to vindicate the contested sections of the *Life*.

The scholars who have in the past defended that *Life*'s account of the Confessor's Constantinopolitan origins have nevertheless held a trump card, for whatever problems may beset it, it is claimed, the corpus of Maximus himself still contains "unimpeachable evidence" that he was indeed *prōtoasēkrētis* in the Heraclian administration.[24] Investigation, however, reveals this to be false, for in the passage from Maximus's *Letters* often cited to establish that point, he simply makes the observation that "it is a better and more honorable thing to have the last rank beside God rather than to hold first place beside the emperor here below of those on the earth."[25] The context, we should note, is not autobiographical.

Others, however, have argued that further indications within Maximus's wider corpus demonstrate his implication within Constantinopolitan monastic circles, for the title of the surviving Latin translation of the *Ambigua ad Iohannem* describes its recipient as "archbishop of Cyz" (read, in the Greek retranslation, as Cyzicus on the Propontis). Thus, it is claimed, this John was archbishop of Cyzicus, and it was there, in a monastic house dedicated to Saint George no less, that

---

which he suggests refers to the first outbreak of official iconoclasm (730–40). Neil (2006c) 109 suggests that the text should in fact be dated to "the resurgence of monotheletism under Philippikos Bardanes (711–13)." Cf. Sansterre (1983) vol. 1, 138f., and Chiesa (1992) 223 n. 28, both preferring a date around the second quarter of the eighth century.

23. Roosen (2010) 431–33, with n. 86, citing Boudignon (2004). Roosen (2010) 432 argues, with Conte (1989) 245–48, that the *passio* of Martin and the so-called *Urpassio* were produced in Palestine, *contra* Mango (1973) 703f., and Sansterre (1983) vol. 1, 138f. and 181f., who both argue for a Roman origin for the *Greek Life of Pope Martin*. Cf. Neil (2006c) 108f. for criticism of Conte's reasoning for a Syro-Palestinian origin for the text.

24. Louth (1996) 4 with 199 nn. 6, 11, transforming the "slight hint" highlighted in Lackner (1971) 63. The error now risks becoming canonical; see, e.g., Neil and Allen (2003) 12, noting the same passage; or Törönen (2007) 13, noting Louth. Others reject the Syriac *Life* without argument: see, e.g., Bathrellos (2004) 65 n. 12 and Ekonomou (2007) 79 with n. 2.

25. Maximus Confessor, *Letters* 12 [*PG* 91, 505B]. On this same passage cf. the relative caution of Larchet (1998a) 36; Winkelmann (2001) 239.

Maximus and John conducted the famous theological discussions noted in the same text's preface.[26] There are two immediate problems with this narrative: first, that there is no indication of where those discussions in fact took place; and second, that the monks of Saint George who are supposed to have resided there appear but once or twice in Maximus's correspondence—once in a letter to John Cubicularius and perhaps again in a letter to the obscure "Kurisikios"—but never is mention made of their situation in or near the capital.[27] The attendant contention that Maximus at some point resided at Cyzicus is, therefore, speculation.

It has, furthermore, often been argued that the same "John of Cyz" was the recipient of Maximus's Letters 6, 28, 29, 30, and 31, addressed in the manuscripts to "Archbishop John," "Bishop John," or the aforementioned "Bishop Kurisikios" (the latter being taken as a corruption of Kuzikēnos).[28] In respect of the latter, we should note that the designation Kuzikēnos never occurs within the Letters, and it is in fact possible that the "Cyz" of the Latin Ambigua represents a later attempt to render explicable the otherwise obscure "Kurisikios." Indeed, even if we accept that one "Bishop John of Cyzicus" was in fact the recipient of the Ambigua and one or more of these letters, we need not then assume that he was a resident or bishop of that same town. One other John of Cyzicus (Iōannēs ho Kuzēkēnos) appears in the literature of the period; he features as an interlocutor in Moschus's Spiritual Meadow but is higoumen of the monks of Abba Abraham on the Mount of Olives.[29] The prosopographical information contained within the Letters has, then, been read through the lens of the narrative of Maximus's origins contained within the Greek Life; but once that same narrative is revealed as problematic, so too can we appreciate the often speculative nature of inferences based upon the Letters. The so-called internal evidence for Maximus's Constantinopolitan career is, therefore, a chimera.

A different avenue for those who wish to defend the preeminence of the Greek Life has nevertheless been to emphasize Maximus's considerable erudition and acquaintance with two members of the court: such things point to Constantinople, it is claimed, and to Constantinople alone.[30] In a recent article Christian Boudignon

26. Maximus Confessor, Ambigua to John [Jeauneau 17]. For this imaginative reconstruction see, e.g., Larchet (1996) 12f.; (1998a) 41–45; Sahas (2003) 98f.

27. See Maximus Confessor, Letters 3 [PG 91, 408C] and 31 [PG 91, 625C]. We should also note that no "Monastery of George" is otherwise attested at Cyzicus until the eleventh century; see Janin (1975) 223. Cf. Boudignon (2004) 26–28. On John Cubicularius see PmbZ "Iohannes" 2692; Winkelmann (2001) 215f.

28. See, e.g., Sherwood (1952a) 27; Larchet (1998a) 41–45.

29. John Moschus, Spiritual Meadow 187 [PG 87:3, 3064D–3065A]. It is also notable that Photius, Bibliotheca 192B [Henry vol. 3, 82f.], in describing the works of Maximus, knows of one letter "To the Sophist John," two "To the Bishop John," and one "To the Bishop Kurisikios." He does not mention any to John of Cyzicus. See also Dalmais (1982) 28f.; Boudignon (2004) 23–26; Jankowiak (2009) 114–16.

30. See Larchet (1996) 8–12, esp. 10f.

has convincingly challenged both (rather dubious) claims. Starting from the prosopographical information contained within Maximus's *Letters*, Boudignon points to the frequent association of Maximus's correspondents not with Constantinople but with Alexandria, where Sophronius had studied and where Maximus too may have acquired or sharpened his theological acumen, perhaps even in Sophronius's entourage.[31] Furthermore, as Boudignon points out, Maximus's acquaintance with certain members of the Constantinopolitan elite does not demand that Maximus himself be from the capital, an origin to which he, like his opponents, never refers.[32] We should abandon the notion that to be an ascetic and to be connected demand that one be from the capital. Moschus and Sophronius had themselves been implicated within the highest echelons of the Heraclian elite—through their association with John the Almsgiver—and, as we shall see, Maximus too belonged to their immediate circle. It is unsurprising, therefore, that he too may also have cultivated relationships with various persons at the Constantinopolitan court, irrespective of his origins.[33]

It therefore seems quite clear that the account of Maximus's origins contained within the Greek *Life* is a fabrication, a medieval attempt to sanitize a controversial figure who would in fact prove a persistent thorn in the Constantinopolitan side.[34] The *Life* of George of Resh'aina, in contrast, inspires confidence both in its closeness to events and in its intersection on various incidental points of detail with other sources of the period.[35] We must of course allow for some distortion for the purpose of polemic—the account of Maximus's ignoble origins is perhaps intended as a slur,[36] as too perhaps is the allegation of his teacher's Origenism[37]—but the

---

31. Boudignon (2004) 15–22. I would suggest that Larchet's position in n. 30 above (and to a lesser extent Boudignon's) underestimates the considerable and sustained intellectual sophistication of the Palestinian monastic movement; see, e.g., Maximus Confessor, *Letters* 13 [*PG* 91, 533A], on Sophronius and his "host of divine books."

32. Boudignon (2004) 35f.

33. For the same point from a different perspective, cf. Boudignon (2004) 40, explaining Maximus's connections not through his masters but through his disciples, Anastasius and (perhaps) Theocharistus.

34. For this sanitization see also the Greek *Life*'s reworking of Maximus's trial literature (removing references to his denial of the emperor's sacerdotal status) discussed in Dagron (1996) 182–84.

35. See below and the commentary on Brock (1973) 320–29; also Conte (1989) 280–84.

36. Although cf. *Life of Theodore of Sykeon* 3.

37. See George of Resh'aina, *Life* 7, with Larchet (1996) 11f. It is notable that the Palaia Laura, where the latter *Life* places Maximus's novitiate, appears to have assumed a leading role in the refutation of Origenism during the sixth century; see Cyril of Scythopolis, *Life of Cyriacus* 11–15 [Schwartz 229–31]. Michael the Syrian, *Chronicle* 11.9, says the same monastery was one of two Judean monasteries that gave birth to dyotheletism (the other being the Nea Laura). For Maximus's refutation of Origenism see, e.g., Sherwood (1955); Dalmais (1961), (1966); Daley (1982); Argárate (2003); Cooper (2005) 65–95; and of extreme anti-Origenism Benevitch (2009).

hostile tone of the text does not somehow demand an all-embracing dismissal of its narrative.[38] It is difficult to suppose, for example, that George's general presentation of Maximus as a prominent Palestinian monk constitutes some form of defamation, or that it would be desirable or even possible (before an informed audience of contemporaries) to displace his entire monastic career. Maximus's placement within a Palestinian context is, furthermore, far more consistent both with his own theological inclinations—his interest in Origenism, for example, or his enthusiasm for the Areopagite—and with his recognized acquaintances: not least, of course, Sophronius, whom George of Resh'aina claims to have fallen under Maximus's (nefarious) influence while the latter was still a monk in Palestine.[39]

That Maximus and Sophronius were indeed intimates is confirmed in Maximus's own corpus. In his *Letters* 8, composed in 632 and addressed, in one manuscript, "To the Monk Sophronius," Maximus begged once again to be received under his correspondent's protection; and in *Letters* 13, composed in 633 or 634, he referred to his "beloved master, father, and teacher, Lord Abba Sophronius".[40] While we cannot pinpoint the precise beginnings of that relationship in chronological terms, Maximus's intimate association with both Sophronius and John Moschus is corroborated in a curious coincidence concerning a particular surname. In the manuscript tradition of the *Spiritual Meadow*, Moschus sometimes bears the alternative surname *Eukratas*, a name repeated in an aforementioned title to *Letters* 8—"To the Monk Sophronius, Surnamed Eukratas" (*pros Sophronion monazonta ton epiklēn Eukratan*)—and in the longest recension of Leontius of Neapolis's *Life of John the Almsgiver*, where Moschus and Sophronius are together referred to as "the Eukratades" (*hoi Eukratades*).[41] It is therefore remarkable that Maximus, in a letter dated 641 (and thus after Moschus and Sophronius's deaths), refers to the presence with him in North Africa of "the blessed slaves of God and our Fathers, those surnamed Eukratades" (*hoi eulogēmenoi douloi tou Theou kai Pateres hēmōn, hoi epiklēn Eukratadēs*), whom we must assume to be the disciples of the Palestinian pair.[42] Indeed, one of Maximus's own associates was, according to a later text, one Sergius Eukratas.[43]

---

38. See, e.g., Allen and Neil (2002) 12 n. 43. Cf. the more nuanced position in Larchet (1996) 9.

39. George of Resh'aina, *Life* 6–7. For the importance of Palestine in shaping Maximus's thought see also Louth (1997) 339; Bathrellos (2004) 41.

40. *Letters* 13 [PG 91, 533A].

41. See Devreesse (1937) 32, citing Vaticanus gr. 504 fol. 150v; Leontius of Neapolis, *Life of John the Almsgiver* 23 [Festugière 373]. Cf. Photius, *Bibliotheca* [Henry vol. 3, 82], where the patriarch in a discussion of Maximus's corpus refers to "two letters 'To Sophronius the Monk, Surnamed Eukratas,'" (*duo de pros Sophronion monazonta ton epiklēn Eukratan*).

42. *Letters* 12 [PG 91, 461A].

43. See *Record* 6. It is possible that this is the same Sergius, disciple of Maximus, referred to in George of Resh'aina, *Life* 17, where he is listed along with Anastasius as a disciple. In *Record* 9 [Allen

Maximus's evident closeness to the monastic circle of Moschus and Sophronius, alleged within George of Resh'aina's hostile *Life* and corroborated both in Maximus's *Letters* and in his striking association with the surname Eukratas, does not confirm but again complements the notion that his monastic career originated in the deserts of Palestine and not on the shores of the Bosporus. Indeed, it is conceivable that Maximus had been within Sophronius's entourage since the time of the *Miracles of Cyrus and John*. As we have seen, Boudignon's research on Maximus's correspondence suggests an extended period amid the educational institutions of Alexandria; but it also appears that Maximus, like Moschus and Sophronius, spent some time amid the Greek islands, for among his earliest correspondents he counts one Marinus, a monk, perhaps to be identified with that Marinus, priest of Cyprus, to whom he would later address several theological tracts.[44] In the previous chapter we noted that certain scholars have wished to locate Moschus and Sophronius in Constantinople following their flight from Alexandria via the Aegean, residing there in a "monastery of the Eukratades" (*monē tōn Eukratadōn*) mentioned several times in the *Acts* of the Constantinopolitan Council of 536 (whence their surname).[45] The prospect that Moschus and Sophronius did indeed make a brief retreat to the capital in this period and there earned their common epithet cannot be discounted; and neither can a parallel retreat of Maximus, whose acquaintance with certain members of the court—his correspondents John Cubicularius and Constantine Sacellarius—may indeed have

---

and Neil 64] Sergius says to Maximus, "Often I came to your cell at Bebbas, and listened to your teaching." As suggested in Garrigues (1976a) 411, 421, and Sansterre (1983) vol. 2, 86 n. 195, this "Bebbas" is perhaps a corruption of "Sabas," which would place Sergius Eukratas at Rome; cf. John the Deacon, *Life of Gregory the Great* 1.9 [*PL* 75, 66A], describing "Cella Nova, where now is the oratory dedicated to [Gregory's] name, and the famous monastery of the confessor of Christ Saint Baba." An alternative option is the Laura of Besses in the Judean desert, a reading supported in a Georgian version of the text; see Jankowiak (2009) 315 with n. 100. In the trial literature, however, he appears alongside Troilus, one of Maximus's accusers, and is said at *Record* 6 [Allen and Neil 60] to be "The one set over the imperial table" (*Sergios ho Eukratas ho epi tēs trapezēs tēs basilikēs*), suggesting perhaps that he had abandoned Maximus. Cf. Sergius Magoudas at *Record* 2 and one Constantine ibid. 10, with Brandes (1998b) 201 and n. 386; Jankowiak (2009) 286f.

44. See Maximus Confessor, *Letters* 20 [*PG* 91, 597B–604B], which Sherwood (1952a) 34 dates to the period 628-30. For the theological tracts see Maximus Confessor, *Opuscula* 1, 2, 7, 10, 19, 20 [*PG* 91, 9–56, 69–89, 133–37, 216–45]. For the identification of all addressees see, e.g., *PmbZ* "Marinos" 4775; Winkelmann (2001) 235f.; but cf. the caution of Sherwood (1952a) 34. The conventional dating for *Letters* 21, "To the Bishop of Cydonia" (on Crete), which Sherwood (1952a) 30 places in 627–33, would also link Maximus with the islands before his arrival in North Africa. His own account of a theological dispute with Severan bishops on Crete [*PG* 91, 49C], however, includes a reference to a discussion on the two energies and two wills, and the sojourn thus seems to belong to a later period. *Pace* Larchet (1998b) 19, that same dispute is therefore less likely to be the occasion for *Opuscula* 13.

45. See *Acts of the Council of 536* [Schwartz 34, 46, 129, 144, 158, 164, 173].

been cultivated during a sojourn within Constantinople itself.[46] Whatever his precise route, however, it is certain that Maximus soon traveled westward to North Africa, where the aforementioned *Letters* 8 places him after Pentecost 632.[47]

It is possible, therefore, that the monastic triumvirate of Moschus, Sophronius, and Maximus had been together for a far longer period than the Constantinopolitan tradition of Maximus's origins permits: acquaintance in Palestine; withdrawal to Antioch and then to Alexandria; flight (perhaps) to the capital, and then the Aegean; retreat to North Africa. That the three monks shared this experience is of course speculative; but it is nevertheless not impossible, and there is evidence enough in the sources to support it. But however we wish to reconstruct the movements of the group in the 620s, it is clear that toward the end of that obscure decade Sophronius and Maximus, and perhaps also Moschus, were united as refugees in North Africa.

In our previous discussion of Moschus and Sophronius's westward retreat, we noted the potential importance of networks of patronage in influencing their movements. After the death of John the Almsgiver, the writings of the pair for the most part obscure their dependence upon such networks. But in the case of Maximus, the survival both of a portion of his correspondence and of various texts associated with his later persecution permit us to perceive to a far greater extent his implication within, and dependence upon, the highest echelons of the North African political elite. It thus provides a further context in which we may understand Moschus and Sophronius's own retreat to the province.

First among Maximus's patrons there was the eparch or prefect George, in all likelihood that same *philomonachos* whom the *Spiritual Meadow* describes as an Apamean.[48] George appears throughout Maximus's correspondence, either as a direct recipient (*Letters* 1) or in a scattering of voluptuous praise. In his *Letters* 1, addressed to George while the latter was embroiled in crisis at Constantinople (to which we shall return in a subsequent chapter), Maximus framed a theological discussion of the ascetic life with praise for his addressee's various virtues and in conclusion referred to the eparch's "manifold benefits toward me" and included, alongside his own salutation, that of "all the honorable fathers who are inhabiting this province because of you."[49] In two further letters related to that same crisis,

---

46. John Cubicularius is the recipient of Maximus, *Letters* 2–4, 10, 12, 27, 44, and 45; Constantine Sacellarius, of *Letters* 5, and perhaps also 24 and 43 (which are identical). Cf. the attempts of some scholars to reconcile the Syriac and Greek *Lives* through placing Maximus's reported monastic career in the capital after his retreat from Palestine; see, e.g., Dalmais (1982); Bausenhart (1992) 12–14.

47. See Devreesse (1937). On the presence of Sophronius and Maximus in North Africa see also Averil Cameron (1982) 38–48.

48. See p. 110.

49. *Letters* 1 [*PG* 91, 392A].

Maximus poured forth to his correspondent John Cubicularius a great list of George's virtues, among which, we should note, was his status as "protector of monks" (*monachōn kēdemōn*)—a traditional Christian virtue, to be sure, but one with great resonance in the context of Maximus and his monastic colleagues' westward exodus (and not dissimilar to the *Meadow*'s remembrance of George as *philomonachos*).[50] It is apparent that the relationship of the eparch and Maximus was close: elsewhere in the *Letters* the latter acts as a middleman between George and his other correspondents, and in one instance he even writes upon the eparch's behalf, a quite remarkable expression of their closeness.[51] The earliest of those letters seems to date to before 633 and thus to the earliest stages of Maximus's exile in North Africa.[52]

It therefore seems clear that the eparch George had assumed, in North Africa in the 630s, the principal role as the exiled monks' protector; and that Maximus, in return, had adopted a position as his spiritual and doctrinal advisor (recapitulating, in effect, the role which Leontius of Neapolis attributes to Moschus and Sophronius on behalf of John the Almsgiver). George, however, was but one among several prominent Africans whose patronage and favor Maximus cultivated in this period. According to an accusation aired at his later trial, Maximus had in 633/4 acted as advisor to one Peter, once "general of Numidia in Africa" (*stratēgos Noumidias tēs Aphrikēs*), who later, it appears, became the African exarch at Carthage, and to whom Maximus dedicated a computational treatise.[53] It is moreover possible—as Boudignon has suggested—that the Theocharistus "the magnificent *illustris*" (*megaloprepestatos illoustrios*), who appears in Maximus's correspondence as a bearer of a letter from North Africa to John Cubicularius, is identical with that Theocharistus who also appears as an associate of Maximus in the same trial literature, and who is presented as the brother of the Italian exarch Plato.[54] In

---

50. *Letters* 44 [*PG* 91, 641C–648C, at 645D]. For further praise cf. *Letters* 16–17 [*PG* 91, 576D–577A, 584BC], 45 [*PG* 91, 648C–649C].

51. See *Letters* 17–18.

52. This is *Letters* 17, not naming George but speaking of "the blessed slave of God, the all-praised eparch" [*PG* 91, 584C]; for one George as eparch in this period cf., however, *Doctrine of Jacob* 1.2 [Déroche 70–71]. For the date of *Letters* 17 see Sherwood (1952a) 36; Larchet (1998a) 58.

53. See *Record* 1 [Allen and Neil 48]. For Peter's later status see Duval (1971). *Contra*, e.g., Winkelmann (2001) 251, Zuckerman (2002a) 173f. makes an important distinction between this patrician Peter, who is also the recipient of Maximus's *Comptus Ecclesiasticus* (640/1), and Peter the Illustrious, who is the recipient of Maximus's *Opuscula* 12 and *Letters* 13 and 14. Jankowiak (2009) 105f. n. 342 reasserts the identification, but at the time of *Opuscula* 12 (ca. 643–45) Peter as exarch would have been too eminent to bear the title *illustris*. It is more probable, therefore, that the two Peters are distinct.

54. See Maximus Confessor, *Letters* 44 [*PG* 91, 644D, but mistaking *Theocharistos* for an adjective]; *Record* 3 [Allen and Neil (2002) 52]. For the date of *Letters* 44 (late 630s) see below p. 255f., with n. 116. For Theocharistus as brother of the Italian exarch of Africa see Brandes (1998b) 192f.; Boudignon (2004) 38–40. Cf. again Allen and Neil (2002) 177 n. 15, for whom the exarch is ecclesiastical, not secular. (This is not convincing.) On Theocharistus see further below n. 143.

the West, therefore, the earlier association of the Moschan circle with the provincial elite—in particular with Nicetas, via John the Almsgiver—was continued in Maximus's cultivation of its highest secular dignitaries.[55]

It is thus possible that the group's association with the great and the good of North Africa predated their own arrival in the province (as well as informed it): John the Almsgiver, of course, was the ritual brother of the North African Nicetas, Heraclius's cousin, and it is difficult to suppose that Moschus and Sophronius had not at some stage encountered him—if, that is, we can trust the picture of all three presented in Leontius's *Life of John the Almsgiver*. Indeed, a further clue as to the implication of the group within both the North African and the broader Heraclian elite occurs within the literature that purports to record Maximus's later persecution and relates to his disciple Anastasius, whom George of Resh'aina indeed calls a North African.[56] According to one text, Maximus had acquired his most prominent disciple in 618—a claim that, we should note, does not fit well with the Constantinopolitan tradition of Maximus's origins and career—and in another the emperor Constans calls the same Anastasius "the secretary [*notarios*] of our late grandmother [*mammē*]."[57] As Boudignon has again observed, this presents us with two distinct options for Anastasius's former patron: Eudocia, the wife of the emperor Heraclius and mother to Constans's father, Heraclius Constantine; or the wife of Nicetas, mother to Gregoria, Constans's mother.[58] Either would of course implicate Maximus's disciple within the highest circles of the African and imperial elites; but if Anastasius were the *notarios* not of Eudocia but of the wife of Nicetas, one might explain better his association with Maximus, for all three figures might then have been present at Alexandria in the 610s: Maximus with Moschus and Sophronius, moving amid the circles of the patriarch John; and both Anastasius and his patroness with Nicetas, the latter, perhaps, in the role

---

55. See esp. Boudignon (2004) 37–41. For this Western patronage we should also note *Georgian Appendix to the Spiritual Meadow* 13 [Garitte 408], in which the author (who is a Palestinian monk and perhaps a disciple of Moschus) recalls that "We once went from Rome to the place called Ravenna, and Gregory the son of Boethius summoned us into the palace; for he was the leading administrator ["in loco principis"] and a friend to us from the very beginning." Here a Byzantine deacon recounts to them a tale set "in temporibus Heraclii," suggesting that Gregory's exarchate should be placed after 641. See Jankowiak (2009) 344 with n. 183, suggesting ca. 645.

56. See George of Resh'aina, *Life* 19. On the career of Anastasius the Disciple see *PmbZ* "Anastasios" 237; Winkelmann (2001) 191–94. It is unclear whether Anastasius was bilingual, but if as some suspect he is the author of the Latin addition to Maximus Confessor, *Letter to Anastasius the Disciple* [Allen and Neil 122], then he must have been; see below p. 321 n. 193.

57. *Dispute at Bizya* 13 [Allen and Neil 114]. At *Record* 11 [Allen and Neil 70], the trial being held in 655, Maximus claims that his disciple Anastasius has been with him for thirty-seven years.

58. Boudignon (2004) 31–34; *pace* Allen and Neil (2002) 183 n. 45, suggesting the grandmother may have been Martina. For Gregoria see Nicephorus, *Short History* 9; *PLRE* vol. 3, "Gregoria 3."

of Augustalis (or at least as the preeminent imperial representative in the province).[59]

Little is known of Nicetas's career after the retreat from Alexandria, but a single source suggests that he once again assumed a prominent position in North Africa. In 1902 François Nau published a Greek spiritual tale that is set "in the time of Nicetas the Patrician, in Carthage in Africa" (whereas an alternative version has "In the time of the emperor Heraclius and the patrician Nicetas").[60] This suggests, of course, that Nicetas had returned to administer the province in the 620s. The same vignette, we should note, is centered on "the slave of God Thalassius who adorned the whole of Africa" and presents him as the spiritual leader of the monks at Carthage.[61] This same person appears to be identical with that Thalassius the Libyan (or Thalassius the African) who authored the Greek *Centuries on Charity* and who is the dedicatee or recipient of several works of Maximus dating roughly to the decade 630–40.[62] If the description of Thalassius as "the African" is accurate, then he must have been a bilingual North African; but if not, then he may have been a recent émigré from the East.[63] Whatever the case, the apparent presence of Nicetas in the province, and his recognition in a contemporaneous Greek tale associated with Maximus's circle, perhaps provides us with a further level of context in which to understand Maximus's own westward retreat.

The association of Anastasius with the imperial household during the first decade of Heraclius's reign perhaps also allows us to resolve another problematic passage relating to Maximus's life. In a text that describes an event later in Maximus's career, the so-called *Dispute at Bizya*, the Constantinopolitan consul Paul comes under an imperial command to retrieve the aged monk from exile (in the editors' translation)

---

59. See above p. 102 n. 52.

60. See Nau (1902a) 83–87, at 84. For the alternative version *BHG* 1318a. This tale—not from John Moschus's *Spiritual Meadow* or Anastasius of Sinai's *Hodegos*, as in *PLRE* vol. 3, "Nicetas 7"—is the basis for the notion that Nicetas later became prefect or exarch in Africa. A later connection between Maximus and the Heraclii is also suggested in the name of his later African protector, the patrician and exarch Gregory; see below p. 285 n. 29.

61. For a recent but somewhat forced interpretation of this tale, with useful translation, see Kaegi (2010) 78–81, falsely attributing it to Anastasius of Sinai.

62. "Thalassius" is the recipient of Maximus Confessor's *Centuries on Theology and Economy* and *Questions to Thalassius*, where the addressee is described as "the most holy slave of God, Lord Thalassius, priest and higoumen" [Laga and Steel vol. 1, 17]. For the same cf. Maximus Confessor, *Letters* 9, 26, 40–42 ("To the Priest and Higoumen Thalassius"). None of these works can be dated to after 634, but Maximus Confessor, *Letter to Thalassius* [*PG* 129, 583D–586B], dates to ca. 640. For Maximus Confessor's *Centuries on Charity* see *PG* 91, 1428A–1469C; for the identification with the author of this work see, e.g., Larchet (1998a) 48–50. On Thalassius see also *PmbZ* "Thalassios" 7253; Winkelmann (2001) 269f.

63. In that case he may also be identified with the Thalassius identified as a signatory to the petition of Greek monks submitted to the Lateran Council in 649; see below p. 298.

"with much honor and coaxing, both because of his age and infirmity, and the fact that he is our ancestor and was honored among them [*dia te to gēras kai tēn astheneian kai to einai auton progonikon hēmōn, kai genomenon autois timion*]."[64] The passage has of course been cited as a potential proof that Maximus was indeed a Constantinopolitan aristocrat and administrator within the Heraclian regime.[65] But for adherents of both schools of Maximus's origins the adjectival *progonikos* is problematic, for there is never a suggestion, even in the Greek *Life*, that Maximus was related to the imperial household. Boudignon has indeed suggested that *progonikos* represents something less definite than the noun *progonos*, and he translates the crucial sentence as "il pourrait être notre grand-père," with *autois* then indicating Nicetas and his wife.[66] Even if the translation of *progonikos* as "like a grandparent" must remain uncertain, it should nevertheless be clear that the same sentence does not constitute a vindication of the Greek *Life*. From the earliest stages of his career, Maximus was a member of an eminent circle of Palestinian ascetics with ties to the most prominent members of the Heraclian political and religious elite. Constans's acknowledgement of him as *progonikos* seems to be a simple recognition of that status.

It will be evident to the reader that much within Maximus's career must remain uncertain. Nevertheless, from the mass of circumstantial detail two clear points emerge: first, that Maximus was (like Moschus and Sophronius) a Palestinian monk, and not a Constantinopolitan aristocrat (even if he spent some time within the capital); and second, that despite his non-Constantinopolitan origins he soon operated (like Moschus and Sophronius) in close contact with the highest representatives of the Roman state. Understanding Maximus in this guise—as the disciple of and heir to his masters—allows us to arrive at a far better comprehension both of his career and of his output. For soon, from exile in North Africa, he too would add his voice to Moschus's attempt to reconceptualize the position of the monk, and therein to assert a new asceticism without social boundaries but nevertheless delimited by strict sacramental imperatives.

## THE RETURN OF THE CROSS

Although the Moschan circle had languished in the West for most of the 620s, after the collapse of Khusrau's regime in 628 an event was to occur in Palestine that held forth the promise of total restoration, both political and cosmological: Heraclius's restoration of the True Cross.

After the dethronement of Khusrau, his successor, Kavadh Shiroe, had attempted to negotiate a settlement with Heraclius, who in turn demanded the

---

64. *Dispute at Bizya* [Allen and Neil 106f.].
65. See, e.g., Garrigues (1976b) 35; Flusin (1992b) vol. 2, 52 n. 19.
66. Boudignon (2004) 31f.

return of the Cross, captured during the Persian seizure of Jerusalem in the previous decade.[67] Most sources attribute the restoration of the relic not to Kavadh Shiroe, however, but rather to Shahrbaraz, that same Persian general who had led the assault upon Jerusalem.[68] At the death of Kavadh Shiroe and the accession of his infant son, Ardashir (October 628),[69] it appears that Heraclius and Shahrbaraz agreed to a settlement.[70] The precise terms of the peace are not recorded but can nevertheless be inferred: Shahrbaraz would cede the Eastern Roman territories that Khusrau had conquered and, furthermore, restore the Cross to Roman hands; Heraclius, meanwhile, would support his counterpart's claim to the Persian throne. The Roman emperor therefore assigned certain of his soldiers to Shahrbaraz, and the combined force then marched into Persia, where the general besieged Ctesiphon and assumed the role of regent for the infant Ardashir.[71] He then fulfilled his

67. For this demand see Nicephorus, *Short History* 15.
68. For Shahrbaraz as the restorer of the Cross see Nicephorus, *Short History* 17; Ps.-Sebēos, *History* 40; Sebēos, *History*, fr. 2; *Anonymous Chronicle to 1234* 103; *Khuzistan Chronicle* [Guidi 30]; Strategius, *On the Fall* 24; *Chronicle of Seert* [Scher 556]; Agapius, *Universal History* [Vasiliev 208]. For alternative traditions, however, see Theophanes, *Chronicle* A.M. 6118 (restoration attributed to Kavadh Shiroe); Ṭabarī, *Annals* [de Goeje et al. vol. 2, 1064] (restoration attributed to Boran); Mari, *History* [Gismondi 61] (restoration attributed to Ardashir). The various traditions are discussed in detail by Flusin (1992b) vol. 2, 295–97.
69. If we follow the claim in Ṭabarī, *Annals* [de Goeje et al. vol. 2, 1062], that Ardashir had ruled for one year and six months (his death being dated to 27 April 630; see Nöldeke [1878] 388 n. 4, 432–33, although placing the beginning of sole rule in June 629). For Ardashir's accession the month September is provided in Strategius, *On the Fall* 24 [Garitte, *Prise* vol. 2, 54], although there is an obvious discrepancy in his indictional dating for the year ("tenth indiction"), and the text states, furthermore, that he ruled for only three months. Three of the Arabic recensions of Strategius, we should note, give April (Garitte, *Expugnationis . . . Recensiones* vol. 1, 55, 104; vol. 3, 190).
70. Cf., however, the anecdote that Shahrbaraz defected at the siege of Constantinople (626), having read a royal command for his execution that Heraclius intercepted and then showed to him; see Theophanes, *Chronicle* A.M. 6118; Michael the Syrian, *Chronicle* 11.3; *Anonymous Chronicle to 1234* 98; Agapius, *Universal History* [Vasiliev 461f.]; Ṭabarī, *Annals* [de Goeje et al. vol. 2, 1008f.], although with Ṭabarī, *Annals* [de Goeje et al. vol. 2, 1061f.], placing Shahrbaraz's defection at the accession of Ardashir; *Chronicle of Seert* [Scher 540f.]. Cf. Nicephorus, *Short History* 12. Howard-Johnston (1999b) 223 suggests that such stories represent "a pi ece of deliberate disinformation, circulated to further Roman interests as the war reached a climax." Other sources place the alliance in the period of Ardashir's accession but disagree as to its initiator: for Shahrbaraz see Sebēos, *History*, fr. 2 (with the claim that Ardashir attempted to assassinate him); Nicephorus, *Short History* 17. For Heraclius, Ps.-Sebēos, *History* 40, although ibid. 39 [Abgaryan 127] also states that Shahrbaraz (here called "Choream") "did not come to help Khusrau" when Heraclius threatened Ctesiphon, and furthermore later refused an order from Kavadh Shiroe to return from the Roman East to Persia. For that same refusal cf. Michael the Syrian, *Chronicle* 11.3, where, however, it is attributed not to Shahrbaraz but to his troops.
71. For the military support see *Chronicle of Seert* [Scher 556] and Sebēos, *History*, fr. 2, both referring to one David as a leader of the force. For the latter see Thierry (1997) 172–76. For Heraclius's assistance of Shahrbaraz cf. Ps.-Sebēos, *History* 40, where Shahrbaraz requests a "small army" from Heraclius; *Anonymous Chronicle to 1234* 103; *Khuzistan Chronicle* [Guidi 30]. The report of Strategius,

promise to Heraclius and restored the Cross to the Romans who had assisted the mission.[72] In July 629 the settlement was formalized at a meeting at Arabissus Tripotamus and celebrated in the construction of a church to Peace, the marriage of Shahrbaraz's daughter to Heraclius's son, and the return of certain sacred relics captured at Jerusalem—the Sponge, and later the Lance—through Shahrbaraz's son Nicetas, whom the Romans in turn elevated to the rank of patrician.[73] Soon after, Heraclius entered Constantinople with the Cross (perhaps on 1 August), where at the Feast of the Cross on 14 September, it was elevated in an elaborate and emotive ritual in Hagia Sophia.[74]

---

*On the Fall* 24 [Garitte, *Prise* vol. 2, 54], that Heraclius dispatched against Ctesiphon a force under the eunuch Narses should perhaps be placed under Kavadh Shiroe; see Flusin (1992b) vol. 2, 285. The regency of Shahrbaraz, suggested ibid. 293–309, is necessary if he returned the Cross before 21 March 630, and thus before his own accession, reported to have taken place on 27 April 630 (unexplained in the revision of Pourshariati [2008] 173–83, with nn. 960 and 972).

72. For this detail see Sebēos, *History*, fr. 2; *Khuzistan Chronicle* [Guidi 29f.], which describes Shahrbaraz as an "adherent" (*dabīqā*) of Heraclius; *Chronicle of Seert* [Scher 556]. Cf., however, Ps.-Sebēos, *History* 40, where Heraclius dispatches "reliable men" to collect the Cross only after Shahrbaraz's successful coup. Thomas Artsruni, *History* 2.3 [Patkanean 97], adds the additional detail that the Cross was "still in its original wrapping." For Heraclius's later reception of the Cross at Mabbug, see Michael the Syrian, *Chronicle* 11.7; *Anonymous Chronicle to 1234* 103.

73. For the interdynastic marriages see Nicephorus, *Short History* 17, with the observations of Mango (1985) 117. Nicetas was perhaps that "son of Shahrbaraz" given to Heraclius as a hostage upon the Persian's defection; see *Anonymous Chronicle to 1234* 98. For Nicetas's return of the relics see *Paschal Chronicle* [Dindorf 705] with the persuasive argument of Klein (2001), which moves the notice from 614 to 629; also Speck (2000). For the meeting at Arabissus Tripotamus (in Cappadocia) see *Anonymous Chronicle to 724* [Brooks 147]. The most authoritative chronological reconstructions of the period retain the stated date of that meeting (July 629) but place it before Shahrbaraz's coup; see Flusin (1992b) vol. 2, 290, 307; Howard-Johnston (1999a) 28f.; following Ps.-Sebēos, *History* 40, where Shahrbaraz and Heraclius meet in person to formalize peace prior to the former's coup. But that position leaves scant time if we wish to honor the various reports of a reception of the Cross at Constantinople in September 629, prior to its restoration at Jerusalem in March 630. (See subsequent note.) I would therefore prefer to place Shahrbaraz's coup before the formalization of peace in July 629. This would allow time for two further Armenian traditions that place Heraclius in Armenia distributing pieces of the Cross; see Flusin (1992b) vol. 2, 309f.

74. See *Paschal Chronicle* [Dindorf 705], with Klein (2001). Klein's argument finds a complement in Sebēos, *History*, fr. 2 [Abgaryan 432], which claims that the Cross came from Ctesiphon "via the highway of Georgia" and was elevated in Hagia Sophia on 14 September; see also Mahé (1984). Eutychius, *Annals (Alexandrian Recension)* 30 [Breydy 127], also claims that Heraclius set out for Jerusalem from Constantinople, as does Theophanes, *Chronicle* A.M. 6120. Agapius, *Universal History* [Vasiliev 208], claims that the Cross went directly from Persia to Constantinople "and remains there until this day." In fact it appears that once restored to Jerusalem the Cross remained there until the Arab occupation of Palestine; see Theophanes, *Chronicle* A.M. 6125; Ps.-Sebēos, *History* 41; also Ps.-Shapuh, *History* [Darbinjan-Melikjan 71]. Nicephorus, *Short History* 18 [Mango 66], reports that the Cross was elevated in Hagia Sophia by the patriarch Sergius after the Cross's reception at Jerusalem, but nevertheless he places the ceremony in Hagia Sophia "in the second indiction" (September 628 to August 629)

The Cross subsequently remained in the capital for several months while the emperor and his entourage, no doubt, finalized detailed plans for its dramatic restoration to Jerusalem. The event was planned as an elaborate set piece on the grandest scale, suffused with various levels of significance. As contemporaries were aware, this was the first time that a Christian Roman emperor had visited Jerusalem.[75] The date of that visit—21 March—was selected with precision, for it was no coincidence that contemporaries associated it with the creation of the celestial bodies and thus with the beginning of time.[76] The restoration of the Cross would therefore at once proclaim on the temporal plane the emperor's dramatic removal of the Persians from the Levant and on the cosmological plane a new historical era.

It is probable that the emperor and his entourage were also aware of the potential eschatological significance of the act. Even before the explosion of apocalyptic speculation that accompanied the rise and expansion of Islam, texts of the post-Justinianic period pointed to a widespread expectation that Christ's final advent was imminent.[77] It is impossible to ascertain if the emperor was aware of the tradition (soon to be enshrined in the *Apocalypse of Pseudo-Methodius*) that predicted that a Last Roman Emperor would place his crown upon Golgotha and thus effect the final age of man; it is possible that Heraclius instead inspired it.[78] But perhaps in the late 620s, and under the patronage of the Constantinopolitan patriarch Sergius, Theophylact Simocatta had attributed to the Persian king Khusrau II a curious prediction: "The Babylonian race will hold sway over the Roman state for three cycles of seven years. But after this Romans will enslave the Persians in the fifth cycle of seven years. When these things have happened, the day that has no evening will dwell among men, and the expected end will hold sway, when the things of destruction are dissolved and those of the better life rule."[79] This dramatic prediction was, no

---

and therefore supports the argument that the Constantinopolitan ceremony occurred before that at Jerusalem (in March 630, the third indiction). For the potential date of 1 August for an initial reception of the Cross in the capital, provided in certain liturgical texts, see also Mango (1990) 185.

75. See *Return of the Relics of Anastasius the Persian* 1 [Flusin 99].

76. For 21 March as the date of the creation of the heavenly bodies (*phōstēres*), and indeed the spring equinox, see *Paschal Chronicle* [Dindorf 26–27]. It has also been argued that the incomplete *Paschal Chronicle* most probably culminated in the restoration of the Cross to Jerusalem; see Whitby and Whitby (1989) xi f., 190f. For this same theme of (re)creation see also Theophanes, *Chronicle* A.M. 6119, which associates Heraclius's six-year campaign in Persia with the six days of Creation; cf. George of Pisidia, *Heraclias* 3, frs. 54a, 54b [Pertusi 292].

77. See, e.g., Eustratius Presbyter, *Life of Golinduch* 15; Antony of Choziba, *Life of George of Choziba* 18. For the political context of eschatological speculation see the compelling argument in Magdalino (1993).

78. For the myth of the last Roman emperor see esp. Ps.-Methodius, *Apocalypse*, with Alexander (1985) 151–84. On apocalyptic in the wake of the Arab invasions see Hoyland (1997) 257–335.

79. Theophylact Simocatta, *History* 5.15 [de Boor and Wirth 216f.].

doubt, constructed after the fact, but its message to contemporaries was nevertheless clear: the emperor's campaigns against the Persians were waged on a cosmological scale; their completion would realize the advent of the *eschaton*.[80]

Accounts of events at Jerusalem itself are few and confused but nevertheless lend the impression of an imperial *adventus* on a scale to rival those of centuries past. According to the account of Pseudo-Sebēos, the emperor arrived with an impressive retinue of soldiers and courtiers, bearing the Cross and certain sacred vessels once removed to the capital. His procession into Jerusalem was accompanied with "an outpouring of lamentation, wailing, and tears" inspired in "the terrible fervor of the compassion of [the inhabitants'] hearts, and the gut-wrenching grief of the emperor, the princes, all the soldiers, and the inhabitants of the city."[81] The actual restoration, however, appears to have been prefaced with a dramatic mise-en-scène, for Nicephorus reports that Heraclius presented the sealed relic—which had been "preserved just as it had been taken"—to the patriarchal *locum tenens* Modestus, who then proclaimed the seal to be intact, the relic within "untouched and unseen by the profane and murderous hands of the barbarians."[82] The theatrics are perhaps explained in the desire to avoid the considerable inconvenience of having to confront the Cross's desecration, but Cyril Mango has suggested that the confirmation of the relic's intactness represented something far grander: an act of rapprochement that proclaimed both the new political alliance of the Roman and Persian empires and, furthermore, their imminent spiritual unification in Christ—Shahrbaraz's son and designated successor, the patrician Nicetas, was a Christian.[83]

The multiple levels of potential historical and theological meaning that Heraclius's restoration of the Cross to Jerusalem presented to contemporaries were perhaps best expressed in a poem composed to celebrate the occasion. The court poet George of Pisidia's *On the Restoration of the Cross* compares the entrance of the emperor to Jerusalem to the entrance of Christ: "Prepare new palm branches," it commands Golgotha, "for the meeting of the new victor" (*pros tēn apantēn tou neou nikēphorou*).[84] "Now, O emperor," it proclaims, "you hold the power of

80. On this eschatological theme within contemporary literature, both Christian and Jewish, see also Sivan (2000); Reinink (2002); Van Bekkum (2002); and esp. now Stoyanov (2011) 45–75.

81. Ps.-Sebēos, *History* 41 [Abgaryan 131]. Cf. Strategius, *On the Fall* 24 [Garitte, *Prise* vol. 2, 55], who also places the empress Martina in the imperial retinue. Cyril Mango has suggested that Jerusalem's Golden Gate may well have been constructed for the occasion; see Mango (1992) 7–16.

82. Nicephorus, *Short History* 18 [Mango 66]. On the Cross's return to Jerusalem see now also Woods (2007), on the evidence of Adamnan's *On the Holy Places* (with some misgivings on the date of the Cross's return expressed at 411 n. 18).

83. See Mango (1985) 105–17, with further discussion in Stoyanov (2011) 65 with n. 79. The claim of the relic's intactness is also made in Strategius, *On the Fall* 24 [Garitte, *Prise* vol. 2, 55], contradicting the earlier narrative of the relic's desecration.

84. George of Pisidia, *On the Restoration* 7–8 [Pertusi 225].

mystical rule among us, and all the country, city, and cosmos exalt with one voice the grace bestowed upon you."[85] George summons the emperor Constantine to appear once again in Rome to praise his successor, who has surpassed his own achievement. Constantine, he claims, recovered the Cross at Jerusalem; Heraclius, however, has recovered the Cross from the furnaces of Persia and restored it once again to its proper place. The emperor is also a new David, restoring to Jerusalem a powerful relic, and his enemies perceive his Cross "as a new ark, but more than the ark," for "the power of the Cross dispatched against [the barbarians] weapons that were alive."[86] For George, the restoration of the Cross is an act of universal restoration, news of which was received in Constantinople "on an appropriate occasion," for it was announced at the Feast of Lazarus, with all its associations of resurrection.[87]

The restoration of the Cross at Jerusalem was, therefore, a multivalent event that proclaimed to contemporaries both an era of renewal and an imminent *eschaton*. Heraclius was presented as a new David, a warrior-king restoring to Jerusalem a sacred relic; a new Constantine, honoring the Cross and (re)establishing the Eastern Christian empire; and, perhaps, the Last Roman Emperor, precipitating the advent of Christ.[88] Pseudo-Sebēos, Nicephorus, and George of Pisidia present the occasion as one of universal Christian celebration, a dramatic and finite affirmation of the Christian empire and its fundamental place within the providential scheme of God.

An anacreontic poem of Sophronius nevertheless presents the Cross's restoration in a rather different manner. The poem *On the Holy Cross* appears to have been composed soon after the restitution, for it opens on a note of evident relief: "The time of the impious has passed—rejoice, good faith! The cloud of the godless has lifted—lyre, celebrate our joy in song!"[89] The presentation of the Persians here repeats that of the poem *On the Capture of Jerusalem*, for the subsequent stanza speaks of "the doom of Babylon," "races of the impious," and "peoples of the lawless."[90] There is, however, a substantial difference, for where that earlier piece had conceived of the Persian devastation of Jerusalem as the triumph of demonic rage against a blessed, blameless people, *On the Holy Cross* situates events within a different and rather more developed interpretive frame. "God came forth to punish

---

85. George of Pisidia, *On the Restoration* 43–46 [Pertusi 227].

86. George of Pisidia, *On the Restoration* 73–77 [Pertusi 228].

87. George of Pisidia, *On the Restoration* 101–13 [Pertusi 229]. For the emperor Heraclius's association with David see also Spain Alexander (1977).

88. On these various levels of symbolism, see also Mango (1985); Flusin (1992b) vol. 2, 312–19; and esp. Drijvers (2002); Stoyanov (2011) 65–69. On George of Pisidia see the various contributions of Mary Whitby (1994), (1998), (2002).

89. Sophronius, *On the Holy Cross* 1–2 [Gigante 114].

90. Sophronius, *On the Holy Cross* 5–8 [Gigante 114].

dreadful sins," Sophronius opines. But then "God came forth to save, brimming with pitiful compassion."[91] The invaders here are conceived as the agents not of demonic but of divine anger, for it was Christ who allowed them "to despoil his own city."[92] The Persian, therefore, is "God-sent" (*theēlatos*), and the cause of Jerusalem's devastation is presented not as demonic evil but as collective Christian sin.[93]

It has been suggested that the conception of Roman defeat as the consequence of shared sin was a political convenience for the emperor Heraclius, for it shifted attention from explanations conceived in terms of his own moral or political failures to those that placed the burden of responsibility upon the entire Christian community.[94] That is no doubt correct, but I would suggest that the same explanation had a further consequence that was less apposite to imperial ideology, for it rendered ambiguous the role and position of the emperor in the process of restoration. In the poem *On the Capture of Jerusalem*, Sophronius's call for vengeance presupposed imperial involvement as the instrument of divine vengeance. Through internalizing the causes of crisis in the later poem *On the Holy Cross*, however, he imagined restoration not in militaristic vengeance but in moral reversal. Within the scheme of collective sin, therefore, either the emperor must become the moral redeemer of the collective or else he is irrelevant.

It is therefore notable that the role of the emperor in subsequent sections of Sophronius's poem is, as Bernard Flusin has observed elsewhere, somewhat minimal.[95] As we have seen, in George of Pisidia's comparable piece, the emperor remains the constant focus of attention: he is a new David, a new Constantine; the agent of both temporal and cosmological renewal. In distinct contrast, Sophronius reduces the emperor's significant role in the Persian campaigns to that of a mere observer. He describes how the Cross, upon arrival in Ctesiphon, killed Khusrau, causing the wielder of the sword to die himself "through murderous swords."[96] "Then," Sophronius claims, "the seed of peace spread over all the land," and "under the glorious peace that went out to mortals from God, the son of great Rome [*megalēs pais Rhōmēs*] indeed rejoiced most mightily."[97] Now those citizens who had fled from the cities of their fathers through fear of persecution returned. "And let the blame of the monstrous Hebrews be turned upon their heads," the poem

---

91. Sophronius, *On the Holy Cross* 17–20 [Gigante 114f.].
92. Sophronius, *On the Holy Cross* 32 [Gigante 115].
93. Sophronius, *On the Holy Cross* 36 [Gigante 115].
94. See esp. Olster (1994) 44.
95. Flusin (1992b) vol. 2, 318: "S'il agit bien là d'Héraclius, et non de tout Romain, l'allusion est furtive, et le rôle qu'on lui reconnaît, minime et passif."
96. Sophronius, *On the Holy Cross* 55–64 [Gigante 116].
97. Sophronius, *On the Holy Cross* 73–76 [Gigante 117]. For this passage, in which "Rome" means either the Roman empire or Constantinople, see also above p. 106.

concludes. "For the wood of God has come into the city of God. The Cross has come into the land of the pious! Rejoice, races of pious men!"[98]

George of Pisidia imagines Heraclius in the role of grand redeemer. In comparison, Sophronius reduces the role of Heraclius in the Cross's restoration to a single, fleeting reference. Where his Constantinopolitan counterpart presents the emperor as the sole agent of peace, Sophronius attributes that peace to the sacred power of the Cross itself and to God's implied compassion for previous sin. As Averil Cameron has suggested, the differences in presentation are no doubt explained, in part, through the different perspectives and rhetorical ends of the poets: as a Constantinopolitan panegyricist, George emphasizes the central position of the emperor; as a provincial ascetic and homilist, Sophronius instead focuses on the Cross's "devotional and soteriological rather than its public and political significance."[99] That Sophronius chose to minimize the political aspects of the Cross's return nevertheless seems significant. His recognition of Heraclius's achievement is muted, and although the tone is one of exultation, the grand claims to cosmological renewal are a conspicuous absence. Once the doctrinal disputant of a Heraclian patriarch, but a refugee from the East since the reign of Phocas, it is understandable that Sophronius might prove unwilling to invest in the exaggerated rhetoric of his Constantinopolitan counterpart. The return of the Cross to Jerusalem was, of course, a cause for celebration; but its significance on both the political and the cosmological planes remained to be seen.[100]

The imperial rhetoric of triumphant restoration in fact leaves little trace within Palestinian literature of the period.[101] Indeed, in a letter written to the sacellarius Constantine (or to John Cubicularius, or both) Maximus too referred to the peace in terms that were far from triumphalist, and that sought to place the emperor's achievement in its proper perspective:[102]

> But since your letter contained news of a peace on earth [*eirēnēs kosmikēs euangelia*], it transformed the grief of my soul into joy. For this we must be completely

---

98. Sophronius, *On the Holy Cross* 89–90 [Gigante 117].

99. Averil Cameron (1992a) 264.

100. Cf. also the hint of dissent contained within the *Miracles of Anastasius the Persian* 7 [Flusin 131], in which an "unbelieving woman" at Caesarea refuses to meet the saint's relic on the basis that "I will not worship a relic [*leipsanon*] that has come from Persia." I am grateful to Marek Jankowiak for this point.

101. For an example see *Return of the Relics of Anastasius the Persian* 1 [Flusin 99]; also Strategius, *On the Fall* 24 [Garitte, *Prise* vol. 2, 54f.], nevertheless noting disquiet over the emperor's marriage to his niece Martina (on which the *Paschal Chronicle* is also strikingly silent; cf. Nicephorus, *Short History* 11, 20).

102. Maximus Confessor, *Letters* 24 [*PG* 91, 608C–609A]. The letter is repeated nearly verbatim in Maximus's corpus as *Letters* 43 but addressed to different correspondents, perhaps through error. Sherwood (1952a) 32 dates the letter to 628/9 and suggests that Maximus may have been in North Africa, since he is "far off" from his correspondents (*PG* 91, 608C and 637C).

well disposed to God for bestowing it as was fitting, so that we do not seem ungrateful for his beneficence, having offered a meager reward for his good deed. Instead we shall all be completely well disposed, having used the peace as we should, and having set aside the fondness that wickedly exists in us for the world and for its ruler [*kai tēn pros kosmon kai ton kosmokratora kakōs hēmin enuparxasan athetēsantes philian*], let us end the war that has been stirred up against God through the passions, even if it is now late. And when we have made an unbreakable treaty of peace with him, in the destruction of the body, let us cease from our enmity toward him.

For Maximus here, therefore, Heraclius's triumph in war was not the occasion for retreat into admiration for the emperor; it was a prompt to renew that greater war against the passions that had fomented God's anger in the first place.[103] Like Sophronius, Maximus invests in the rhetoric of sin and political disaster; like Sophronius again, he is nevertheless cautious to equate political restoration with forgiveness.

We thus encounter in both Sophronius and Maximus somewhat sober commentators on the emperor's success. Nevertheless, the retreat of the Persians from the East seems to have inspired an expectation of a potential reversal of that monastic exodus in which Moschus, Sophronius, and Maximus had all partaken. Sophronius, it appears, did indeed return from North Africa in this period (perhaps to witness in person the return of the Cross); and Maximus, too, harbored hopes that he and others might return from their exile. Soon after Pentecost 632, and thus some time after Heraclius's entrance into Jerusalem, he addressed from North Africa that aforementioned letter "To the Monk Sophronius, Surnamed Eukratas," in which he expressed sorrow at his separation from his master, with whom he nevertheless remained unified in spirit. "Since I had been considered worthy to have such desire toward your most holiness from the beginning," Maximus proclaims, "I seem always to see you present and perceive you conversing with me. And there is no time and place that can keep me from your memory, which constantly indicates your presence in spirit and drives out all the foul thoughts within me that do not bear the sweet smell of the divine grace within you. And I am convinced that that memory does not merely imagine your most holiness but actually perceives you to be present, and I make its occurrence a certain guarantee [*plērophoria*] of your presence."[104] "Because of this," Maximus con-

---

103. Cf. later in Maximus Confessor, *Letters* 24 [*PG* 91, 609A–B]: "For as long as we are at war with and enemies of God, even if we attach to ourselves the name of 'believers,' then for so long we might wish to be slaves to the passions of dishonor; and there will be no benefit for us from peace on earth while the soul is badly disposed, in revolt against our own maker, and refusing to live under his kingdom." For analysis see also Sahas (2003) 101.

104. Maximus Confessor, *Letters* 8 [*PG* 91, 440D–441A].

tinues, "I go around in grief and sullen, desiring and seeking you, the good pastor and teacher, who know how to settle me, the wandering sheep, to a place of pasture."[105] The relationship expressed within the text is, it seems, that of master and disciple.[106]

Maximus then encourages Sophronius to summon him back to his protection: "But for the rest, honored father, fulfill the reed of the teaching [*tēs didaskalias ho donax*] of the divine Spirit, and like a shepherd and with love of man call him who wanders, shepherdless, upon the mountains of ignorance and hills of evil."[107] "And so, honored father," he concludes, "do not desist from shepherding me in your sympathy with words of truth, caught as I am by wild beasts. . . . Call me to you and give me shade beneath your wings, if truly all fear of actual barbarians [*pas phobos barbarōn aisthētōn*] has passed, on whose account I made so long a voyage in fear of my life [*hōs philozōos*]."[108]

It should be noted that the date of the letter is problematic for those who adhere to the Constantinopolitan tradition of Maximus's origins, for if—as is sometimes supposed—he had fled from the capital around the time of the Avar siege, in 626,[109] then he proved somewhat overcautious in still fearing that threat in 632, when it had long since diminished. At the same time the tone of the letter, in which Maximus from exile wishes to be reunited with his master, is once again difficult to reconcile to that same tradition, since on its evidence the association of the two monks must have been forged before Maximus's arrival in North Africa. There are two obvious solutions: to refuse the attribution to Sophronius as addressee altogether,[110] or to posit his presence in the capital[111]—but both depend upon the redundant need to reconcile the traditional attribution of the letter to Maximus's supposed Constantinopolitan origins. We can, of course, avoid all such difficulties if we instead recognize that Maximus and Sophronius had been acquainted as ascetics within Palestine; and that Sophronius, in the wake of the Persian withdrawal from the occupied provinces, had returned from his Western retreat to his former Eastern haunts, perhaps even to Palestine. On this reading, therefore, the "barbarians" to whom Maximus referred in *Letters* 8, and from whom he con-

---

105. Maximus Confessor, *Letters* 8 [*PG* 91, 441B–C].
106. On the relationship of the two see also Boudignon (2002) 326–29 and (2004) 17–22.
107. Maximus Confessor, *Letters* 8 [*PG* 91, 441D–444A].
108. Maximus Confessor, *Letters* 8 [*PG* 91, 445A]. The "actual" is used to correspond with an implicit earlier "metaphorical," on which see p. 231, with n. 20.
109. See, e.g., Garrigues (1976b) 38; Larchet (1996) 13.
110. See, e.g., Sherwood (1952a) 28; Larchet (1998a) 43f.
111. Rozemond (1977) 64f., but nevertheless upholding George of Resh'aina's account of Maximus Confessor's origins. Follieri (1988) 32f. also accepts George's account but suggests that he and Sophronius may both have fled to Constantinople in the 610s. (Hence the relationship expressed in Maximus Confessor, *Letters* 8.)

fessed earlier to have fled, were either the Persians or, as Boudignon has suggested, the Bedouin tribesmen who had raided the Judaean desert in 614.[112]

Despite Maximus's apparent caution as to the permanence of Eastern peace in *Letters* 8, his request that Sophronius once more receive him appears as part of a broader attempt at this time to encourage the reunification of Eastern communities in diaspora. Thus, in the same manner as he had exhorted his own master to once again protect him, in a series of similar letters—all written, it appears, around 632—Maximus encouraged other correspondents to once again gather in the servants of Christ, repeating that same image of the shepherd and the wandering sheep used in *Letters* 8 to Sophronius. In *Letters* 28, addressed in the manuscripts to the aforementioned bishop "Kurisikios," Maximus opens with the recipient's (recent?) election to the "high priesthood" (*archierōsunē*) and refers to him as "head" (*kephalē*) of God's Church; as such, he exhorts him "to gather into one the dispersed children of God," to call "to those near and far," and to bind them to him. There is, however, a condition for the refugees' return, familiar from Maximus's own confession in *Letters* 8, for he here again seeks reassurance that "the expectation of enemies" has passed, for on this account those same refugees "were banished far from the land that had borne them."[113]

Just as Maximus had requested Sophronius once more to receive him—if the barbarian threat had indeed vanished—so too, therefore, did he encourage the bishop, or archbishop, "Kurisikios" to receive back his scattered sheep. That request, it furthermore seems, was a success, for in *Letters* 29—addressed to the same recipient, and which appears as the obvious sequel to *Letters* 28—Maximus claims that his correspondent, "having fulfilled the reed of the teaching [*tēs didaskalias ho donax*] of the Holy Spirit," has now collected around him "the flock that, against its will, had traveled from its fatherland" but was now returned to its pasture having crossed "the vast expanse of sea." "Kurisikios" is "the fine and wise pastor," who should receive his flock "still inaccessible to wolves but even destructive to them, being rich in the manifold goods of the soul."[114] Here, furthermore, Maximus places among the returned exiles a specific individual, for he reports that the recipient has now received one "sanctified Lord Abba George the Priest, a sacred man, who has obtained a life equal to his word."[115]

This same George, it seems, also appears in two further short epistles published as *Letters* 30 and 31 and related again to *Letters* 8, 28, and 29. In those letters—both

---

112. For the former reading, there is of course the complication that the Persian withdrawal occurred much earlier, in 629, although it is possible that Maximus still feared renewed warfare. Boudignon (2004) 17f. provides a neat solution, although I am doubtful of the supposed evidence for Maximus's awareness of Arab activities in 632; see p. 231, with n. 20 below.

113. Maximus Confessor, *Letters* 28 [*PG* 91, 620C–621A].

114. Maximus Confessor, *Letters* 29 [*PG* 91, 621C–D].

115. Maximus Confessor, *Letters* 29 [*PG* 91, 621C–624A].

addressed "To the Bishop John"—Maximus once again repeated the call that his correspondent, if the danger of enemies now indeed were vanished, draw in his scattered sheep. "Call to yourself with ways and words of sympathy," he proclaims in *Letters* 30, "those who wish to return to you and desire in their prayers to be shepherded by you . . . if the foul expectation of enemies has completely passed, on account of which they endured so great a flight." *Letters* 31, like *Letters* 29, appears as a sequel to its predecessor. Once again the recipient's task has been fulfilled, for Maximus reports that "the true servant of God, the daughter and mother, Mistress Eudocia, the nun, has come to you with her holy flock." "For the rest," he continues, "take pleasure and delight that you have received the more honorable part of your flock; and especially that you have received our lord the sanctified George the Priest, the truly divine field [*geōrgion*] and the most esteemed cultivator [*geōrgon*] of the divine and great George, equal in work and deed before God and all the people, according to his knowledge of the cultivation of souls [*kata tēn psuchōn geōrgikēn epistēmēn*], and because of this beloved to all those who love the Lord."[116] It seems certain, therefore, that this George is identical with the same "sanctified George the Priest" who appears in *Letters* 29.

We note, therefore, the numerous correspondences of language, metaphor, and content between *Letters* 8 and *Letters* 28–31 (not least the strange phrase "reed of teaching," which occurs in *Letters* 8 and 28).[117] Indeed, for those scholars who have wished to challenge the attribution of Maximus's *Letters* 8 to Sophronius, these correspondences have suggested a single recipient for all five.[118] There are, however, subtle differences that separate *Letters* 8 from the other four. As well as being far more extensive, in the former Maximus begs for a personal reacquaintance, and the image of the shepherd is pastoral without being episcopal; while in the latter, he begs for the reception of others, and the image of the shepherd is, in line with the recipients' episcopal (or archiepiscopal) status, ecclesiastical.

Thus in *Letters* 28 "Kurisikios" is encouraged to fulfill his clerical calling through gathering in his scattered children, "in accordance with the grace of the high priesthood," as "an imitator of goodness," and as "a mark [*charaktēr*] of divine goodness." "And since you have become head of the honorable body of the holy Church of God [*kephalē tou timiou sōmatos tēs hagias tou Theou Ekklēsias*]," Maximus continues, "unite its members [*melē*] to one another through the design of the Spirit. And since you have been made herald of the divine teachings, call with loud voice those near and far, and bind them to you with the ineluctable chain of the Spirit's love."[119]

---

116. Maximus Confessor, *Letters* 31 [*PG* 91, 625B–C].

117. Cf. also within the pastoral metaphor the references to wolves at Maximus Confessor, *Letters* 8 [*PG* 91, 444A] and *Letters* 29 [*PG* 91, 621D], noted also in Sherwood (1952a) 29; Larchet (1998a) 44 n. 1.

118. See Sherwood (1952a) 29; Larchet (1998a) 41–45.

119. Maximus Confessor, *Letters* 28 [*PG* 91, 619D–621A].

In the two letters addressed to John, we encounter even more extensive statements as to the function of priesthood. Thus in *Letters* 30 Maximus compares the role of the priesthood to that of God, "who draws up [*helktikos*] all those who wish to observe his laws and suffer to embrace the pious life." He declares the priesthood "to be a picture that in image possesses a fitting imitation," that too "draws up [*helktikē*] those under the same nature." The bishop John, therefore, is the "image of God on earth," who must fulfill his clerical function in reintegrating his scattered flock.[120] That task fulfilled, Maximus in *Letters* 31 once again extols the virtues of the priesthood:[121]

> Just as a beam of light gently draws in the healthy vision, which naturally rejoices at the light and the giving in return of its own light, thus also the good priesthood [*hierōsunē*], since it is for those upon the earth the type through all things of the blessed divinity, attracts into itself every soul according to its God-loving and divine habit [*hexis*] and shares its own knowledge, peace, and love, so that, once it has brought each power [*dunamis*] of the soul to the limit of its own operation, it may place beside God those who have been deified in all things and initiated by it in the mysteries [*dia pantōn theōthentas tous hup' autēs mustagōgoumenous*]. For the end of the rational operation in the soul is true knowledge; of the affective [operation], love; and of the irascible [operation], peace; just as [the end] of the true priesthood is both to be deified and to deify through these things.

"Kurisikios" and John—the recipients of *Letters* 28–31—are therefore clerics and, unlike in *Letters* 8 "To the Monk Sophronius," Maximus here adapts his metaphor to acknowledge that same status.

But were, as some have suspected, the bishops "Kurisikios" and John in fact the same person?[122] The similarities between their letters are undeniable. But unless we assume that Maximus wasted considerable effort in duplicating not one but two letters destined for the same individual, then we must maintain their traditional distinction. From comparison with *Letters* 8, moreover, we ascertain that Maximus was quite prepared to repeat certain images, even certain phrases, in letters to different correspondents. It therefore seems to me far more expedient to explain the similarities between *Letters* 28–29 and 30–31 not in the suggestion of a single recipient but in their composition within the same context and, furthermore, in their mutual destination to recipients of comparable clerical rank.

From the common reference to the presence of "Abba George the Sanctified," we know that those correspondents were located in the same place. Where? It should now be clear that the tissue of modern inference that construes "Kurisikios" as "Kuzikēnos" and "Bishop John" as "Archbishop John of Cyzicus" is founded

---

120. Maximus Confessor, *Letters* 30 [PG 91, 624B].
121. Maximus Confessor, *Letters* 31 [PG 91, 624D–625B].
122. Sherwood (1952a) 27f.; Larchet (1998a) 41–43. Cf. also Boudignon (2004) 23–26.

upon several questionable leaps of the imagination. Once we point, however, to the obvious deficiencies in the Constantinopolitan tradition of Maximus's origins, then the information contained within Maximus's correspondence can be liberated from the need to place it within the context of the capital. Thus the "Abba George the Sanctified," whom some scholars have elaborated as "Abba George, higoumen of the house of Saint George at Cyzicus," need not be a Constantinopolitan at all but was perhaps from the eastern provinces, whence Maximus himself had fled.[123] As we have seen, the "barbarian" threat from which he retreated was in all likelihood that of the Persians—or else the Arab tribesmen who had exploited their presence to raid the eastern deserts. It is therefore preferable to locate the episcopal correspondents "Kurisikios" and John not in the capital but within the East, along with Sophronius, and to explain the similarities in circumstance between the various letters as the product of their separate recipients' shared status and location. In the wake of the Persian withdrawal and the reestablishment of Roman power, therefore, Maximus dispatched three letters to eminent associates in which he sought their reassurance that the danger had indeed passed, and encouraged them, like good shepherds, to gather in their errant sheep. *Letters* 29 and 31 provide confirmation that some ascetics, at least, did indeed return to their former provinces. To ascertain from George of Resh'aina's Syriac *Life of Maximus Confessor*—which places its subject in Syria on the eve of the Muslim conquest—Maximus himself did the same soon after.[124]

We perhaps will never know the precise identities of the bishops "Kurisikios" and John, whose letters from Maximus so resemble that sent to Sophronius. But it is worth noting that one scholar has suggested a tantalizing prospect. Starting from the premise that the recipients of *Letters* 28–31 are in fact one and the same, Keetje Rozemond has argued that the striking similarities of circumstance between this group of letters and that dispatched to Sophronius—including, as we have seen, certain turns of phrase—suggest that their recipient John/"Kurisikios" was

---

123. For the frequent assertion that this same man was higoumen of the monastery of Saint George at Cyzicus see, e.g., Sherwood (1952a) 27; Larchet (1998a) 43. It is of note that Maximus Confessor refers to him as "most esteemed cultivator [*geōrgon*] of the divine and great George" in *Letters* 31 [PG 91, 625C], suggesting that he served a monastic community named after Saint George (perhaps that same referred to in Maximus Confessor, *Letters* 3 [PG 91, 408C], on whose behalf Maximus received blessings from John Cubicularius). He is therefore in all likelihood distinct from that "George the Priest" who was higoumen of Theodosius in the 630s and 640s; see below p. 232f., with n. 21. Rather than place "Abba George the Sanctified" in Cyzicus, it is more tempting to place his original community in Apamea, the home town of the African eparch George (John Moschus, *Spiritual Meadow* 196). Moschus and Sophronius too spent some time near the town (above p. 45), and the *Georgian Appendix to the Spiritual Meadow* 12 places there a "Monastery of Saint George" whose monks the author knew.

124. George of Resh'aina, *Life* 17–18. As Brock (1973) 325 notes in terms of Maximus's career, "Perhaps . . . one should envisage two stays in Africa."

none other than Sophronius's partner in crime John Moschus. ("Kurisikios" she explains as the Greek translation of an Armenian surname derived from his native Cilicia.) It is of course possible that Moschus was indeed one, the other, or both of Maximus's correspondents, although the circumstances of the letters would require an otherwise unattested election as bishop and a likewise unattested return to the East from Rome. Rozemond, however, went even further, for on the basis of two obscure references to Moschus in later texts—one in John of Damascus, the other in a manuscript of the *Spiritual Meadow*—she suggested that between 614 and 634 Moschus, in the face of Zachariah's capitulation to the Persians, had been elected as patriarch of Jerusalem in exile, and was thus also the recipient of Maximus's *Letters* 6, "to John the Archbishop."[125] Modestus, she therefore suggested, was the patriarchal *locum tenens* not of Zachariah, who had surrendered Jerusalem, but of Moschus, his fellow monk of Theodosius.[126]

This thesis is of course seductive. It should be resisted, however, for the evidence for Moschus's patriarchate is late and obscure, and the sources of the period contain not the slightest confirmation. Rozemond's bold idea nevertheless draws attention to a significant point, for as we shall see, in the same period in which Maximus was encouraging the reintegration of expatriated Eastern communities, his own province of Palestine had been plunged into crisis and lacked an archbishop. For that reason, we are forced to inquire whether Maximus's otherwise obscure correspondent "Kurisikios," elected to the *archierōsunē*, was in fact, as Rozemond suspected, an irregular patriarch or episcopal figurehead elected in a context of conflict.[127] Whether this person may also be identical with the otherwise unknown "John the Archbishop" of *Letters* 6 must also remain unclear.

Although the evidence allows nothing more than speculation, this same group of letters—which, because of the similarities with *Letters* 8, we can date with confidence to around 632—nevertheless provides some invaluable insight into the mind of Maximus at that time. As Adam Cooper has noted in a compelling piece of scholarship on Maximus's thought, it is in these same letters that we encounter some of the Confessor's most comprehensive statements on the priesthood.[128] Therein, as we have seen, he lavished praise on his clerical correspondents, referring to the priesthood as an icon of God, and elaborating on the function of deification that it offered. These letters, indeed, served as a complement to the implicit

---

125. Maximus Confessor, *Letters* 6 [*PG* 91, 424C].
126. Rozemond (1977); also eadem (1984). Rozemond's position is supported in Maisano (1982) 39f.
127. For this same suggestion cf. Jankowiak (2009) 114–19.
128. Cooper (2005) 169–73. He points also to a statement at Maximus Confessor, *Letters* 21 [*PG* 91, 604D], according to which "God ordained the priesthood to stand in his place on earth" in order that "he not cease to be seen bodily, and his mysteries appear to those able to see." Sherwood (1952a) 30 cautiously dates the letter 627–33. For Maximus Confessor's views on the priesthood see also *Letters* 21 [*PG* 91, 604B–605C].

acknowledgment of clerical mediation set out in the contemporaneous *Spiritual Meadow* of Moschus and further elaborated within Maximus's own writings of the period. Here in the *Letters*, Maximus expected orthodox clerics to act as the lightning rods around which scattered communities might reform; but in another text he would go even further, orienting the entire Christian existence around the eucharistic rite.[129] Confronted with the crisis of empire and his own displacement, Maximus's interpretation of that rite asserted a vision of the terrestrial Church that proclaimed its undiminished power to unite and to perfect, irrespective of political reversals. To that interpretation we now turn.

## THE *MYSTAGOGY*

In 1937 Robert Devreesse drew attention to an unpublished section of Greek text that provided the original conclusion to Maximus's *Letters* 8 (that "To the Monk Sophronius, Surnamed Eukratas"), dated to 632.[130] Therein Maximus reports upon a recent mass baptism of African Jews and Samaritans, which the prefect (*eparchos*) carried out at Pentecost on the command of the emperors at Constantinople.[131] As with the return of the Cross to Jerusalem, the forced baptism of unbelievers was perhaps intended as another prominent act in an eschatological drama scripted at Constantinople;[132] and as with the return of the Cross once again, it was received among our circle with profound ambivalence.

Within his letter Maximus informs Sophronius that he has heard that the baptism occurred throughout the entire empire and reports that it leaves him with a terrible fear, for several reasons. First he declares himself anxious "lest this great and truly divine mystery be polluted when it has been given to those who have not previously displayed a disposition concordant with faith"; second, he contemplates

---

129. Cf. Cooper (2005) 177.

130. Devreesse (1937). Cf. the comment on an alternative version of the text in Schönborn (1972) 77 n. 84.

131. The same forced baptism is described in the *Doctrine of Jacob* 1.2; Michael the Syrian, *Chronicle* 11.4; Fredegar, *Chronicle* 4.65. Fredegar is perhaps the earliest witness to the later widespread legend of Heraclius's dream concerning the impending victories of a circumcised race, to which he attributes the emperor's forced baptism of Jews; see, e.g., *History of the Patriarchs* "Benjamin" [Evetts 492f.] and Hoyland (1997) 218 n. 12 for comment and further references. For immediate precedents cf. the alleged forced baptisms under Maurice (John of Nikiu, *Chronicle* 99) and Phocas (*Chronicle of Zuqnin* [Chabot vol. 2, 148f.] nevertheless ascribing the action to one "George the Prefect [*huparka*]" and placing it in A.G. 928 [A.D. 616/7]). For the persecution of Jews under Heraclius see also Eutychius, *Annals (Alexandrian Recension)* [Breydy 128f.]. The arguments against the authenticity of Maximus Confessor's letter in Speck (1997) 441–67 do not convince; cf. Larchet (1998a) 43f.; Winkelmann (2001) 58f. no. 21, 191; Stoyanov (2011) 69 n. 191 (with literature).

132. See Magdalino (1993) 19; Stoyanov (2011) 68–70. This event, as with the restitution of the Cross, also had distinct Constantinian overtones; see Dagron (1996) 158.

"the danger to the soul" lest somehow, with "the bitter root of their ancestral faithlessness" still buried deep, the converts themselves may undergo some terrible judgment; and third, he is suspicious of apostates mixing with the faithful and corrupting the faith, which he reads as "a clear and unambiguous sign" of an imminent apocalypse.[133] In response to an imperial initiative to baptize non-Christians, therefore, Maximus expresses some grave doubts as to the pollution of the sacrament (here, baptism) and to the (negative) eschatological consequences of that initiative for the Christian faithful, thus perhaps inverting the intended signification of the act. Here, then, we discover—perhaps for the first time in Maximus's corpus—an explicit expression of political dissent grounded in the same conception that we have encountered within Sophronius's *Miracles of Cyrus and John* and the *Spiritual Meadow* of John Moschus: that is, the pressing need to preserve the sacraments and doctrine of the Church from external pollutants. This nexus of the political, doctrinal, and sacramental would, indeed, come to define Maximus's later opposition to the emperor.

Measuring the shifts over time in Maximus's thought of the period is not a simple task, and significant difficulties surround the dating of his corpus (not least, that the still standard date list depends on the discredited Greek *Life*).[134] Nevertheless we should pause here over three works that can be dated with some confidence to the period of the 610s or 620s: the *Book on the Ascetic Life*, the *Centuries on Love*, and the *Exposition on the Lord's Prayer*.[135] The *Book on the Ascetic Life* consists of two rough halves: a dialogue between an elder and a novice on the ascetic life; and then an extended tirade on the urgent need for compunction and love in a context of moral decline (informed, no doubt, through the Persian occupation of the East).[136] For our purposes, however, it is the first half that is of most immediate interest, for it is notable that here Maximus expounds a traditional monastic vision, in which the eucharist does not feature. The emphasis is indeed upon communion with Christ, but that communion is presented not as participation in the eucharist—which is not mentioned at all—but rather as imitation through the cardinal Christian virtues.[137] The general scheme is, of course, familiar from Sophronius's *Miracles of Cyrus and John*.

The *Centuries on Love* is presented as an addition to the *Book on the Ascetic Life* and consists of four centuries of advanced monastic wisdom in the Evagrian tradition. Across four hundred entries on the spiritual life the eucharist is again conspicuous for its absence, and we discover instead something of that internalizing,

---

133. See Devreesse (1937) 35. For Jews and Judaism in Maximus Confessor's thought see Laga (1990). On Maximus and the reign of the Antichrist see also below p. 278, with n. 1.
134. Sherwood (1952a).
135. See the discussion ibid. 26, 31.
136. See, e.g., Maximus Confessor, *Book* 660–69 [Van Deun 77].
137. See, e.g., Maximus Confessor, *Book* 1–6.

spiritualizing approach to the structures of the Church that we earlier encountered within the corpus of Pseudo-Macarius:[138]

> He who anoints his mind for the sacred contests and drives from it passionate thoughts has the characteristics [*logon epechei*] of a deacon; he who illuminates it with knowledge of beings and utterly destroys false knowledge, of a priest; and he who perfects it with the holy myrrh of knowledge of the worshipful and holy Trinity, of a bishop.

That same approach is also apparent in the *Exposition on the Lord's Prayer*. In the prologue to the text Maximus states that the Word "fashions an imparting of divine life in making himself edible [*edōdimos*], as he himself knows, and those who have taken from him such great perception of mind. Thus in the tasting of this food, they know with a true knowledge that the Lord is good, since in order to deify he intermixes [*metakrinōn*] those who eat with a divine quality, as clearly he both is and is called bread of life and of power."[139] That Maximus understands this "bread" and "eating" in a metaphorical sense is confirmed within his later exposition on the verse "Give us this day our daily bread," wherein he refers to "the bread" as "celestial" and "supersubstantial" and contrasts it with "sensible food." He states that "living a life according to our vows, we shall receive—as a supersubstantial and lifegiving bread [*kathaper arton epiousion te kai zōtikon*] to feed our souls and to preserve the vigor of the good things bestowed upon us—the Word, who said, 'I am the bread that has come down from heaven and that gives life to the world' [Joh. 6:51], and who becomes all things for us in proportion [*analogōs hēmin*] with the virtue and wisdom with which we have been nourished, becoming embodied in various ways [*poikilōs sōmatoumenos*], as only he knows, in each of the saved."[140]

On its own, this emphasis upon the spiritual nourishment given through the bread of the Word, and the manifold means through which it is achieved, is of course quite traditional.[141] But from the perspective of both the previous eucharistic

---

138. Maximus Confessor, *Centuries on Love* 2.21 [Ceresa-Gastaldo 100]. It is nevertheless notable that we also find in this text the assertion that "the supreme states of pure prayer are two" (*tēs kitharas proseuchēs duo eisin akrotatai katastaseis*), one for the active and one for the contemplative; see Maximus Confessor, *Centuries on Love* 2.6 [Ceresa-Gastaldo 92], with Thunberg (1965) 387-89. For the same differentiation in Maximus Confessor's later *Mystagogy*; see below pp. 178-84., and cf. Anastasius of Sinai, *Questions and Answers* 24 [Richard and Munitiz 50f.].

139. Maximus Confessor, *Exposition on the Lord's Prayer* 128-34 [Van Deun 34].

140. Maximus Confessor, *Exposition on the Lord's Prayer* 549-57 [Van Deun 59]. Cf. for the precise same sentiment Maximus Confessor, *Centuries on Theology and Economy* 2.56 [PG 90, 1149A-B], a passage that Combefis inserted into the *PG* edition of the *Exposition on the Lord's Prayer* at PG 90, 897B-C.

141. For the theme of noneucharistic communion with Christ in Maximus Confessor's thought see Larchet (1996) 424-26; Cooper (2005) 196f. For an explicit statement see also Maximus Confessor, *Questions to Thalassius* 35 [Laga and Steel 238-41], with Blowers (1995) 145-49. Cf. also Maximus Confessor, *Ambigua to John* 44 [Jeauneau 219-22]. For the suggested date of these texts (respectively 628-30 and ca. 630-34) see Sherwood (1952a) 31f., 34f.

minimalism of ascetic thought and of Maximus's later position within the *Mystagogy*, the total and unqualified separation of the ascetic life from sacramental realities here seems quite striking. Like ascetic theoreticians before him—and Sophronius in the earlier *Miracles of Cyrus and John*—Maximus in his earliest works conceives of a communion with Christ in virtuous imitation and thus also of an ascetic life liberated from the imperatives of eucharistic communion proper (with all its implications of submission to clerics). In the course of his exile from the eastern provinces, however, this position was to undergo a dramatic revision. While the emphasis upon Christlike imitation through the virtues would of course remain, regular eucharistic participation within the Church would now be presented as the principal mode of divine union, detached from which all others were in vain.

For the later vision we now turn to the *Mystagogy*—Maximus's interpretation of the eucharistic ritual. Maximus, it must be noted from the outset, is the first monastic theologian to compose such an interpretation; comparable texts from previous centuries—including that of the Pseudo-Areopagite—are the conspicuous products of bishops, who no doubt needed, more than most, to explain the purpose and meaning of the central Christian ritual. Furthermore, although those same bishops were for the most part of provable ascetic bent, there is minimal attempt within their works to implicate liturgical and ascetic discourses: that is, to explain how the two great engines of Christian salvation might interrelate—even, as we have seen, in the vision of Pseudo-Dionysius, where monks are nevertheless acknowledged as advanced members of the congregation.[142] Liturgical interpretation was the preserve of bishops; ascetic speculation, that of monks. It is difficult, therefore, to explain Maximus's interpretation of the eucharistic rite in simplistic terms as something that theologians do. It is instead something quite radical: the attempt of a monastic theologian to reconcile two monolithic currents of Christian thought. It is a text that demands, therefore, contextualization.

Because of the absence of more localizing references, the *Mystagogy*—like so much of Maximus's corpus—is difficult to locate within a precise chronological framework. On the basis of the absence of pregnant Christological references and a perhaps (from a later perspective) unguarded reference to the union of participants "according to a single identity of will" (*kata mian gnōmēs tautotēta*), most critics have nevertheless supposed that Maximus composed it before the outbreak of the monothelete crisis (ca. 640), prior to his refinement of the language of *gnōmē* and perhaps as an exile in North Africa.[143] Although the dating is not crucial to our

---

142. See above pp. 26-28.
143. For the reference see Maximus Confessor, *Mystagogy* 24.957 [Boudignon 60]. For a proposed date (628–30) see Sherwood (1952a) 32, noting theological affinities with Maximus Confessor, *Letters* 6 (on which see Sherwood [1952a] 25). Boudignon (2002) 317 states that the text was "écrit sans doute à Carthage dans les années 630," although without any supporting argument. The text is dedicated to

argument, this would make it more or less contemporaneous with Moschus's *Spiritual Meadow*, a text with which, as we shall see, it shares a remarkable number of concerns.

The *Mystagogy* represents the pinnacle of Maximus's theological thought, his "total vision."[144] It comprises four main sections, all attributed to the teachings of a certain "old man"[145] and explicitly conceived as a supplement to the Pseudo-Dionysian *Ecclesiastical Hierarchy* (on which in the same period Maximus had also composed an extensive commentary).[146] Those four sections are: an exposition on the imagery of the physical church building (chaps. 1–7), a commentary on the symbolism of successive liturgical rituals (chaps. 8–21), a reinterpretation of that symbolism from the perspective of the contemplative (rather than the active) soul (chaps. 22 and 23), and a final conclusion, summing up the entire teaching on the rite (chap. 24).

The first of these, the exposition on the symbolism of the church, begins with a now familiar theme, the essential unity of the Christian community:[147]

> As has been said, the holy church is an image of God because it realizes [*energousa*] the same union of the faithful with God. Even though they are different in their characteristics [*idiōmasi*], and from both different places and different customs [*kai topōn kai tropōn*], therein they are made one through faith. God is disposed to realize [*energein pephuken*] this [union] in respect of the essences of beings without confusion [*asunchutōs*], but in assuaging and reconciling their difference, as has been shown, in relation and union to himself as cause, beginning, and end [*pros heauton hōs aitian kai archēn kai telos*].

Here Maximus repeats a theme that pervades his corpus: that is, the union of constituent parts that remain distinct (also present, of course, in the Chalcedonian

---

Theocharistus, a figure who appears to be the same as that "Theocharistus, brother of the [Italian] exarch" who appears in *Record* 3 [Allen and Neil (2002) 52]. If this is also the person who appears in Maximus Confessor, *Letters* 44 [PG 91, 644D], as the bearer as a missive from North Africa to the capital ca. 634–40, then it encourages us to think that the *Mystagogy* was composed in the West at that same time. For the date of *Letters* 44 see below p. 255 n. 116. For Theocharistus cf. Boudignon (2004) 38–41, also identifying him with the Theocharistus who appears among the signatories of the monastic *libellus* submitted at the Lateran Council of 649; see *Acts of the Lateran Council* [Riedinger 57].

144. Thunberg (1985) 113. For discussions of Maximus Confessor's *Mystagogy* from which I have drawn much inspiration see esp. Bornert (1966) 83–124; Riou (1973) 123–200; Thunberg (1985) 113–29; Larchet (1996) 399–436; Louth (1996) 74–77; Mueller-Jourdan (2005); Cooper (2005) 165–205; Törönen (2007) 143–52.

145. For this artifice see Boudignon (2002).

146. See Maximus Confessor, *Mystagogy* 54–58 [Boudignon 6]. Maximus's scholia on the *Ecclesiastical Hierarchy* are confused with those of John of Scythopolis; but for the identification of his comments on the *Divine Names* see Suchla (1980).

147. Maximus Confessor, *Mystagogy* 1.199–206 [Boudignon 14].

logic of the Christological natures).[148] From its diverse and "almost infinite" members the church effects an unconfused and inseparable union of the faithful, thus imaging "by imitation and type" (*kata mimēsin kai tupon*) the operation (*energeia*) of God, who too "leads all beings to a common and unconfused identity [*eis tautotēta adiaphoron te kai asunchuton*] of movement and existence."[149] "In accordance with faith," Maximus states, the church gives to all "a single, simple, complete, and indivisible condition that does not allow one to contemplate the many unspeakable differences between each, even if they exist, on account of the universal relationship and combination [*suneleusis*] of all things with it."[150] Thus divine and ecclesial activities are inseparable, in that both effect an unconfused and inseparable union—God of the cosmos, the church of the faithful.

For Maximus, the realization of that union is inseparable from the physical realities of liturgy and ecclesial architecture.[151] In the separation of sanctuary and nave he sees symbolized three principal divisions: cosmological, anthropological, and psychological.[152] The bipartite church, then, is first of all an image of the cosmos, likewise divided into sensible and intelligible.[153] However, just as the cosmos "circumscribes the difference of its parts, which comes from natural properties [*ex idiotētos phusikēs*], in relation to what is one and indivisible in itself,"[154] with the intelligible imprinted on the sensible and vice versa,[155] so too is ecclesial space an ultimate and unconfused unity:[156]

> For although [the church] is one house in construction, it partakes of difference in the character of the shape of its arrangement [*tēi kata tēn thesin tou schēmatos poiai idiotēti*] in being divided into a place assigned to priests and ministers alone, which we call a sanctuary [*hierateion*], and one that all the faithful are free to enter, which we call a nave [*naos*]. Again, it is one according to its hypostasis [*kata tēn hupostasin*] and is not split in its parts on account of the difference of those parts from each other.

---

148. For this theme see esp. Törönen (2007), although countering the notion that a "Chalcedonian logic" determines this same theme (esp. 2–6) *contra* von Balthasar (1961; trans. Daley 65-74); Thunberg (1965), e.g., 21f.; Louth (1996) 49–51.

149. For the quotations see Maximus Confessor, *Mystagogy* 1.164 [Boudignon 12], 1.131 [Boudignon 10], 1.138–40 [Boudignon 11]. For this activity by imitation and by imprint see Thunberg (1985) 117.

150. Maximus Confessor, *Mystagogy* 1.174–78 [Boudignon 12f.].

151. Cooper (2005) 167, *contra* Thunberg (1985) 113. See also Riou (1973) 146; von Balthasar (1961; trans. Daley 315ff.).

152. For reasons of space and relevance I here omit some further symbolism observed by Maximus: see Maximus Confessor, *Mystagogy* 6 [Boudignon 31] ("How and in What Manner the Holy Scripture Is Said Also to Be a Man"), 7 [Boudignon 33] ("How the Cosmos Is Said to Be a Man, and in What Manner Man Also a Cosmos").

153. See Maximus Confessor, *Mystagogy* 2.229–33 [Boudignon 16].

154. Maximus Confessor, *Mystagogy* 2.234–37 [Boudignon 16].

155. See Maximus Confessor, *Mystagogy* 2.241–44 [Boudignon 16].

156. Maximus Confessor, *Mystagogy* 2.211–25 [Boudignon 15].

Rather, in their relation to the oneness of itself, it releases these parts from their nominal [*en tēi klēsei*] difference, showing to each other that both are the same thing and revealing that one is to the other in turn what each is to itself. The nave is a sanctuary in potency [*kata tēn dunamin*], in being consecrated by the relation of the mystagogy toward its end [*tēi pros to peras anaphorai tēs mustagōgias hierourgoumenos*], while conversely the sanctuary is a nave in operation [*kata tēn energeian*], since it possesses the principle [*archē*] of the continuous mystagogy. Thus [the church] remains one and the same in both.

According to this final sentiment, the division of ecclesial space exists, in Cooper's words, "in a single reality whose primary, final, subjective singularity is brought about by the ordered, reciprocal penetration of its parts and their ritually determined orientation to their final state."[157]

Maximus now applies precisely that same logic to the anthropological divisions symbolized in the ecclesial separation of nave, sanctuary, and altar. Thus "the holy church of God is a man, since it has the sanctuary as a soul, the divine altar as a mind, and the nave as a body."[158] Furthermore, the tripartite architectural and anthropological division also represents a corresponding separation of the spiritual life into moral philosophy (*hē ēthikē philosophia*), natural contemplation (*hē phusikē theōria*), and mystical theology (*hē mustikē theologia*).[159] Thus just as the church symbolizes man, so "man is a mystical church," who—in the ascetic-mystical movement from virtuous observance of the commandments through natural contemplation to the silent dwelling with God—progresses "through the nave, which is his body," "through the sanctuary of his soul," and "through the altar of the mind."[160] For Maximus, however, ascetic virtue is not simply the precursor to mystic contemplation but its inseparable companion. As Hans Urs von Balthasar has said, here "action and knowledge ... penetrate each other inseparably and push each other toward a constantly fuller degree of integration. Action, in the end, is only the revelation of knowledge, just as knowledge is the bright interior of action."[161] The liturgical revelation of the church's architectural singularity thus discloses the same singularity in both man and the spiritual life. Here, therefore, the indissoluble tripartite union of body, soul, and mind—of *praxis, phusikē*, and *theologia*—is imaged in the essential indivisibility of nave, sanctuary, and altar.

That architectural indivisibility similarly images a psychological synthesis that accompanies the anthropological integration of the active and the contemplative. In the separation of sanctuary and nave Maximus sees further symbolized the

---

157. Cooper (2005) 199.
158. Maximus Confessor, *Mystagogy* 4.263–66 [Boudignon 18].
159. Maximus Confessor, *Mystagogy* 4.269–73 [Boudignon 18].
160. Maximus Confessor, *Mystagogy* 4.273–84 [Boudignon 19].
161. See von Balthasar (1961; trans. Daley 334).

separation within the soul of the intellectual and vital faculties, with their corresponding powers of (contemplative) mind (*noos*) and (active) reason (*logos*).[162] According to Maximus, "to the soul belong—in its mental aspect—mind, wisdom, contemplation, knowledge, and enduring knowledge, all directed to truth; and in its logical aspect, reasoning, prudence, action, virtue, and faith, all directed to the good."[163] As we have seen, however, the purpose of the spiritual life is not a transition from the active to the contemplative but rather a progression toward their final synthesis: "a rational mind, a prudent wisdom, an active contemplation, a virtuous knowledge, and along with them an enduring knowledge that is both most faithful and unchangeable."[164] Maximus concludes:[165]

> When it is likened in contemplation to the soul, to all these things the holy church of God will clearly accommodate itself. Through the sanctuary it symbolizes all the things of the mind, and that have been shown to be from the mind in their procession [*kata proodon*]; through the nave it makes clear the things of reason, and that have been shown to be from reason in their distinction [*kata diastolēn*]; and all these things it gathers for the accomplishment of the sacrament and mystery [*mustērion*] upon the divine altar. Whoever has been able sensibly and wisely to be initiated [*muēthēnai*] into the things that are accomplished in church, he has rendered his soul divine and a true church of God. Because of this, perhaps, that of which it is wisely the symbolic model because of the variety of divine things within it—the church made with human hands—has been given to us to guide us to what is better.

Maximus proposes, then, that the coinherence and interpenetration of the parts within ecclesial space reveals a parallel coinherence and interpenetration of the parts within cosmos, man, and soul. In the same manner as the church's two (or three) parts are, in the end, inseparable but unconfused, so too are the constituent elements of those things that it images. In the progression toward God, however, those divisions are not dissolved but rather cease to function as opposites. Thus the lesser partners—the somatic, the active, and the sensible—"are not to be eliminated as impure but to be transcended as insufficient."[166]

If ecclesial architecture represents the principle of simultaneous union and distinction within the cosmos, man, and the soul, then the eucharistic rite dramatizes the progression through which their coinherence is revealed. In the passage of the

---

162. Maximus Confessor, *Mystagogy* 5.285–92 [Boudignon 19f.].
163. Maximus Confessor, *Mystagogy* 5.323–27 [Boudignon 22].
164. Maximus Confessor, *Mystagogy* 5.431–33 [Boudignon 27]. Cf. also Maximus Confessor, *Mystagogy* 5.412–19 [Boudignon 26f.].
165. Maximus Confessor, *Mystagogy* 5.495–506 [Boudignon 31]. On these passages of *Mystagogy* 5 see the analysis of von Balthasar (1961; trans. Daley 336–39).
166. Croce, as cited in Nichols (1993) 38; also Louth (1996) 77; Cooper (2005) 64. I regret that I have not had access to Louth (2009).

liturgical drama Maximus therefore sees imaged those processes through which the constituent elements of the things represented in ecclesial space—cosmos, man, and soul—come into ever closer (but still unconfused) union. On one level, it therefore predicts the final consummation to be realized in the *eschaton*, mirroring in its signification the chronological progression from the Incarnation through the Second Coming to the World to Come;[167] but on another, it also parallels that process through which the elements of cosmos, man, and soul can be brought into greater union in the present—that is, the life of the ascetic.[168] The eschatological and the spiritual movements are, in the end, inseparable: both proceed from the Incarnation and toward God, and at their pinnacle reconcile the nominal divisions of soul, man, and cosmos.

In exploring the parallel with the spiritual life—which is the dominant theme of the text—Maximus adds a further distinction, however, dividing the meaning of the rite according to the spiritual condition of the participant, whether active or contemplative. Both interpretations of the ritual recognize two distinct stages of proceedings, divided at the dismissal of the catechumens.[169] The most part of the text interprets the rite from the perspective of the active participant and sees represented in the dismissal of the uninitiated the classic Evagrian shift from *praxis*, or active virtue, to *theōria*, or contemplation. Thus following the entrance of the bishop and his ascent to the throne (which represents Christ's Incarnation and Resurrection), the various acts that precede the exclusion of the catechumens—the divine words and chants, the salutations of peace, the reading of the Gospel—represent the progressive components of an active ascetic *praxis* that culminates in the attainment of passionlessness (*apatheia*).[170] Then with the dismissal of the uninitiated and the closing of the doors there is effected, according to this interpretation, the passage from the sensible to the intelligible world,[171] so that subsequent rituals—the divine kiss, the profession of faith, and the like—represent the progressive ascent of the soul toward God, culminating in silent contemplation of the divine and a final deification represented in the taking of the eucharist itself.[172]

---

167. See, e.g., the comment at Maximus Confessor, *Mystagogy* 24.936–47 [Boudignon 59].

168. See Riou (1973) 163: "Après la montée ascétique de la première partie, [la seconde partie] se présente comme une ascension spirituelle, actualisant dans une initiation mystique le second avènement du Christ dans la gloire." Riou ibid. neatly describes the two phases as "l'anamnèse rituelle et ascétique de la première parousie [du Christ]" (159) and "l'anticipation sacramentelle et mystique de la second parousie" (163).

169. Riou (1973) 159, 163. For the division see Maximus Confessor, *Mystagogy* 15.714–19 [Boudignon 44f.].

170. See Maximus Confessor, *Mystagogy* 8–14.

171. Ibid. 15.

172. Ibid. 16–22.

Following this extended exposition, however—which dominates the text—the penultimate chapter then reconsiders the entire rite from the perspective of the contemplative. For these advanced Christians, the closing of the doors represents not—as for the noncontemplatives—the shift from *praxis* to *theōria* but rather the movement within the latter from natural to theological contemplation. Thus, rather than indicating the gradual obedience to the commandments and progression in virtue—a state that contemplatives have already achieved—the first half of the rite represents the progressive perception of the principles (*logoi*) of creation and of Providence; and while the second half again represents the shift from the material to the immaterial, here the successive rites represent a more elevated state of progression, which nevertheless culminates in the same contemplation of the Godhead and, in the end, deification.[173]

In the concluding chapter Maximus offers a short précis of the rite's meaning from the perspective of the active participant, and then an extended recapitulation of his entire interpretation.[174] On one level, as has been said above, the rite dramatizes the chronological progression from the Incarnation to the *eschaton*, so that, for example, "the descent of the bishop [*archiereus*] from the throne and the dismissal of the catechumens in general signifies the Second Coming from heaven of the great God and our Savior, Jesus Christ, and the separation of the sinners from the saints, and the righteous recompense according to the worthiness of each."[175] At the same time, however, Maximus offers alongside that eschatological interpretation a further level of meaning corresponding to the different stages of the spiritual life, and distinguishing within that two levels of interpretation corresponding to the two aforementioned classes of Christian, "the active and virtuous ones" (*hoi praktikoi kai euaretoi*) and "the contemplative and gnostic ones" (*hoi theōrētikoi kai gnōstikoi*).[176] Thus, for example, the divine readings represent both "the steadfast disposition to virtue of those who are active" and "the contemplative habit of the gnostics";[177] the reading of the Gospel signifies "for the active, the mortification and conclusion of both the Law and thought according to the flesh, and for those who have knowledge, the collection and ascent of the many different principles toward the most essential principle;"[178] and the closing of the doors means "for those at the active stage, the transfer from active virtue to contemplation [*apo praxeōs eis theōrian*] of those who have shut down their senses and become outside the flesh and the cosmos through the repudiation of activities in themselves,

---

173. Ibid. 23.
174. For the short précis see ibid. 24.900–947 [Boudignon 56–59].
175. Maximus Confessor, *Mystagogy* 24.997–1001 [Boudignon 62].
176. Maximus Confessor, *Mystagogy* 24.956–58 [Boudignon 60].
177. Maximus Confessor, *Mystagogy* 24.976–81 [Boudignon 61].
178. Maximus Confessor, *Mystagogy* 24.992–95 [Boudignon 61].

and the ascent from the mode of the Commandments to their principle, and the connatural kinship and union of these Commandments, according to their own principles, in relation to the powers of the soul, and the habit that is requisite for theological thanksgiving; for those who have knowledge, [it means the transfer] from natural contemplation to the simple contemplation of the things pertaining to the mind [*apo tēs phusikēs theōrias eis tēn tōn noētōn haplēn katanoēsin*], according to which they no longer pursue the divine and ineffable Word by sense or any sensory data, and the union in the soul of its powers, and the simplicity that by the mind apprehends in single form [*henoeidōs*] the principle of divine Providence."[179]

Both the active and the contemplative now move in parallel toward a final union, via different but ever-converging paths. So the Trisagion represents for the active, "the brilliance of life equal to the angels [*isangelos*], as far as it is attainable for men, and the vigor of the theological hymnology"; whereas for the contemplative it signifies "thoughts, hymns, and perpetual movements concerning the Godhead that are equal to the angels, so far as possible for men."[180] Thus far, Maximus has offered divergent interpretations for each of the liturgical acts, according to the spiritual state of the observer. But in the final liturgical acts, and in particular, it seems, in the taking of the eucharist, this distinction is at last dissolved:[181]

> The blessed invocation [*epiklēsis*] of the great God and Father and the declaration of the "One is Holy" and what follows, and participation in the holy and life-giving mysteries demonstrate the adoption, union, kinship, divine likeness, and deification that will come about wholly and upon all the worthy [*epi pasi kai epi pantōn tōn axiōn*], through which God himself will be all in all [I Cor. 15:28] in those who are saved, and as an archetypal beauty is conspicuous as cause in those who are likewise in agreement with him through virtue and knowledge by grace.

In the same manner as Maximus does not privilege soul over body, contemplation over action, or mind over reason, he does not in the final analysis elevate the fate of the contemplative Christian over that of the active. The separation of action and contemplation is, therefore, not a simple concession to the relative spiritual states of the faithful but a genuine parallelism in which both active and contemplative move toward the same consummation—in the words of von Balthasar, "predominant emphases within a single overarching ideal."[182] In Maximus's hands, therefore, the eucharistic liturgy is not simply a symbol of the passage from this world to the next; it is at the same time a recapitulation of the entire spiritual life, in both its active and its contemplative dimensions.

179. Maximus Confessor, *Mystagogy* 24.1021–33 [Boudignon 63f.]. Cf. Gregory of Nazianzus, *Orations* 2.7.
180. Maximus Confessor, *Mystagogy* 24.1043–47 [Boudignon 64].
181. Maximus Confessor, *Mystagogy* 24.1048–56 [Boudignon 64f.].
182. Von Balthasar (1961; trans. Daley 334).

Within this intricate, threefold interpretation, however, Maximus's emphasis on liturgical acts as a representation of their spiritual or eschatological counterparts may seem to reduce the liturgical drama to the realm of shallow theater. For Maximus, however, the eucharistic rite is not a simple performance designed to enlighten or to educate its participants. It is rather an efficacious rite that realizes, if temporarily and incompletely, the cosmic, anthropological, and psychological unity that it anticipates. Nowhere is that more apparent than in Maximus's central description of communion itself (where, we will remember, distinctions between the active and the contemplative interpretations are no longer relevant):[183]

> After which, as the culmination of everything, comes the distribution of the sacrament [hē tou mustēriou metadosis] that transforms into itself and, through grace and participation [methexis], shows as similar to the causal good those who worthily share in it, and who are lacking in nothing of what is attainable and possible for men, so that they can also be and be called gods by adoption [thesis] through grace, because of himself God in his entirety has filled them all in their entirety and has left no part of them devoid of his presence.

Here, then, we encounter something quite radical. In contrast to the eucharistic minimalism of earlier ascetic theoreticians, participation in the eucharist is, for Maximus, the pinnacle of the spiritual life, the divinization of man both represented and realized; it is (in Lars Thunberg's words) "the sacramental integration of the whole human person before and toward its final and ultimate goal, which is the Trinitarian God, the image and likeness of whom it carries and manifests."[184] In the consummation achieved in communion the cosmological, anthropological, and psychological divisions imaged in the architectural context are transcended: as the parts comprising ecclesial space are revealed as an unconfused union in virtue of their mutual orientation around the sacrament, so too are the various divisions that that space represents. Here, then, we witness nothing less than "an effective transformation of the world into transfigured, divinized existence."[185]

It is therefore unsurprising that Maximus—again in utter contrast to previous monastic authors—insists that all Christians frequent the church and participate in the sacrament. While the explicit divinizing effect that Maximus attributes to the eucharist promotes it above the liturgical acts that precede it, however, we need not suppose that those same acts cannot be efficacious in themselves.[186] As

---

183. Maximus Confessor, *Mystagogy* 21.768-75 [Boudignon 48f.].
184. Thunberg (1985) 126f. Cf. Riou (1973) 167: "C'est donc dans la communion, sommet de la liturgie et de la vie mystique qu'on retrouve une préoccupation profondément mystérique et non seulement anticipatrice et représentative."
185. Von Balthasar (1961; trans. Daley 322). Cf. Cooper (2005) 204.
186. Larchet (1996) 407, 430-32.

Jean-Claude Larchet has argued, the ritual representations of which he speaks in fact share an ontological relation to the things represented—it is legitimate to speak, therefore, of "un symbolisme efficace" pervading the rite.[187] Nevertheless, the movement from the representative to the real, from the less to the more efficacious, is dependent in degree upon the spiritual attainment of each participant.[188] Thus the text's final chapter:[189]

> For this same reason the blessed old man believed it necessary that every Christian (and he did not stop from exhorting them) should frequent the holy church of God and never abandon the synaxis accomplished within it, because of the holy angels who are present there and who record each time those who enter and present themselves to God, and make supplications on their behalf, and because of the grace of the Holy Spirit that is always invisibly present, but especially and in a peculiar way at the time of the holy synaxis, when it transforms and changes each person who is found there and, to speak truly, remolds him into something more divine in proportion to his capacity [*epi to theioteron analogōs heautōi*] and leads him to what is revealed through the mysteries accomplished there—even if he himself does not perceive it, if he is among those who are children in Christ [I Cor. 3:1] and is not able to look into the depths of what is happening—and effects the grace that is revealed in it through each of the divine symbols of salvation being accomplished, and that proceeds according to the series and order from the preliminaries to the completion of everything.

Thus, in the same manner as the meaning of each rite is dependent upon the spiritual state of the participant (whether active or contemplative), so too is its effectiveness in accomplishing in that participant the eschatological and spiritual realties represented. Contrast with Pseudo-Dionysius's vision is here telling: where the latter elevates monastics as superior members of the congregation, the illumination received is more passive and unilateral, with little acknowledgment of monks' own discrimination between different spiritual stages; for Maximus, in contrast, there is no differentiation within the congregation based on social (rather than spiritual) rank, and the illumination received is more active and bilateral, dependent upon the complex conception of spiritual development long elaborated within monastic circles.[190] It is, in effect, a reconciliation of liturgical and ascetic theologies.

---

187. Ibid. 404f. See also von Balthasar (1961; trans. Daley 324); Bornert (1966) 117f.

188. See Larchet (1996) 407.

189. Maximus Confessor, *Mystagogy* 24.883-99 [Boudignon 55f.]. Cf. for a similar sentiment Maximus Confessor, *Mystagogy* 24.1076-82 [Boudignon 66]: "Therefore let us not abandon the holy Church of God, which encompasses such great mysteries of our salvation in accordance with the holy arrangement of the divine symbols completed there, through which it fashions in Christ each of us who live especially well, in proportion to his capacity [*analogōs heautōi*] and brings into the light the charism of adoption given through holy baptism in the Holy Spirit and perfected in Christ."

190. For this contrast with Ps.-Dioynius see Roques (1961) 306; Riou (1973) 149f.; also Dalmais (1962) 282f.

Although the perspective is here ascetical—as opposed to episcopal—there is for Maximus no "monastic movement" to be distinguished among the faithful; rather, the ascetic imperative is imposed upon all members of the Christian Church ("asceticism for all," as Andrew Louth has said of Maximus's thought).[191] At the same time, the explicit celebration of the active life recognizes that not all Christians can or may wish to attain to the level of the contemplative. Instead, Maximus places the life of active virtue in parallel with the life of detached contemplation, positing within the Church two separate routes to the same enlightenment—realized both in the eucharist and in the *eschaton*—and thus also integrating and sanctioning nonmonastic modes of Christian holiness, clerical and secular. As von Balthasar has commented: "This way of conceiving the twofold Christian ideal moves in a very different direction from the whole of monastic theology from Evagrius to John Climacus; it is one of the great surprises in all of Maximus's work."[192]

I would nevertheless suggest that the same emphasis appears less surprising once Maximus's thought is contextualized alongside that of his closest Palestinian associates. In the earlier *Miracles of Cyrus and John*, as we have seen, Maximus's master Sophronius had too demonstrated an acute interest in the interface of asceticism and sacrament, and in the extension of the former to a vast and varied congregation. But it is above all in the *Spiritual Meadow* of Moschus, composed at around the same time as the *Mystagogy*, that Maximus's magnum opus finds its most striking complement. Like the *Meadow*, the *Mystagogy* extends the imperatives of the ascetic life to the entire Christian congregation; like the *Meadow*, it celebrates both the ascetic and the clerical vocations; and like the *Meadow* again, it places the eucharist at the center of the Christian existence. Here at last, then, we can see how the debate on Maximus's origins becomes more important than a pedantic wrangling over proper source criticism. For even if we choose to ignore the dramatic political and economic changes of the period as somehow unimportant to his thought, then establishing the contours of Maximus's immediate intellectual circle nevertheless remains crucial. At the least, therefore, liberating him from his supposed origins in Constantinople allows us to place his thought in conversation with the cultural output of his closest Palestinian contemporaries. Far from appearing as a singular departure in monastic sensibilities ex nihilo, Maximus's interpretation of the eucharistic rite can be appreciated as a striking continuation of the concerns so long evident in the writings of the Moschan circle.

I do not think it a coincidence, moreover, that Maximus chose to write such a text when he did. If, as I have argued in the previous chapter, the dominant themes

---

191. Louth (1996) 35.
192. Von Balthasar (1961; trans. Daley 334).

of Moschus's *Spiritual Meadow* can be appreciated as a response to the ideological crisis fomented within Palestinian circles through the Persian occupation of the eastern provinces, then Maximus's text can also be understood as a product of that crisis. Although a precise date for our text proves elusive, it derived from the pen of a man who had, at the least, fled from the East in the face of "barbarian" aggression and settled as a refugee in the distant West. It is perhaps unsurprising, therefore, that in that same period he, like his associate John Moschus, chose to compose a text that seemed at once to undermine monastic claims both to moral independence from the Church and to elevation above the Christian herd; but at the same time to declare in dramatic fashion the undiminished power of the Christian faith and the continued union of its diverse but equal members.

It has often been said that Roman provincials' experience of the Persian occupation in the 610s and 620s helped to facilitate the Muslim conquests in the subsequent decade, for on the one hand, it exposed them to the (benign) realities of "barbarian" rule, and on the other, it weakened their ideological commitment to inclusion within the Roman empire.[193] Given their flight from the occupied provinces, we cannot assess Moschus, Sophronius, and Maximus's attitudes in respect of the first explanation; but our exploration of Maximus's thoughts in this crucial period has offered some vindication of the second. Alienated from the East because of foreign incursion, and in parallel with Moschus in the same period, Maximus abandoned the traditional monastic ambivalence to the structures of the Church and set out a new vision that reconciled the ascetic and the sacramental lives, presenting an orthodox Church in which all members were united around and dependent upon the eucharist. In doing so, he had abandoned that spiritual self-determination that stood as the last bastion of late-antique monastic independence, but in return he had been able to set out an ecclesiological model that provided the intellectual complement to the universalizing spirit that pervades Moschus's *Spiritual Meadow*.

Like Moschus, Maximus in the *Mystagogy* shifted from the earlier ambivalence of Sophronius's *Miracles of Cyrus and John* to acknowledge the unrivaled and continuous spiritual enlightenment offered through the Church. He therein presented its essential independence from the vagaries of terrestrial politics, and the text cannot but be seen as the product of a context in which Persian success had shattered the comfortable coinherence of Chalcedonian Church and empire. Now Chalcedonian Christians were forced to confront the realities of a situation in which some of their coreligionists were placed outside the empire, and to fend off accusations—so often defended within anti-Jewish texts of the period—that reversals on the

---

193. See, e.g., Foss (2003) 170.

political sphere translated to a crisis of the faith itself.[194] Heraclius's restoration of the Cross to Jerusalem, with its manifold associations, had attempted to restore the relation of Church and state, and to proclaim a new era of terrestrial regeneration. But Sophronius and Maximus had greeted his achievement with profound ambivalence, unwilling to invest in the Constantinopolitan rhetoric of renewal. That ambivalence perhaps reflects their suspicions as to the permanence of the peace; but it was nevertheless consistent with the paradigm in which Persian success had been explained, for if collective sin had been the cause of divine displeasure, then collective purification had to be its solution. For both, therefore, the success of Heraclius, and the restoration of the Christian empire, remained to be seen.

Both Sophronius and Maximus nevertheless soon seized the chance to return to the regained territories. But as Maximus from North Africa was encouraging prominent Eastern acquaintances to gather back in those communities scattered through "barbarian" invasion, a new crisis was brewing, precipitated through the precise same peace that had allowed him to conceive of a potential return to the status quo ante bellum. For the emperor Heraclius, in his ambition to reunite the eastern provinces under Roman rule, had not limited his ambition to the political plane but had also extended it to the doctrinal. Although neither Moschus's *Spiritual Meadow* nor Maximus's *Mystagogy* indicates an awareness of the Christological controversies soon to engulf their authors' circle, the ecclesiological vision of both provided an inextricable complement to that circle's imminent doctrinal dissidence. From the earliest stages of its extant output—that is, from Sophronius's *Miracles of Cyrus and John* and Sophronius and Moschus's *Life of John the Almsgiver*—it is evident that the circle, though engaged in theological dialogue with opponents, nevertheless conceived of a strict doctrinal and sacramental differentiation of orthodox and heretical communities; but now its commitment to that same differentiation would be tested to a far greater extent, as the emperor and patriarch at Constantinople moved toward doctrinal conciliation and even communion with anti-Chalcedonian communities throughout the East. In this context, the Moschan circle's emphasis on the eucharistic rite would come to be articulated in a dramatic new fashion: less as a reactive statement of the sustained righteousness of the Christian Church and more as an aggressive defense of its independence from secular interference.

194. See, e.g., *Trophies of Damascus* 3.4 [Bardy 222]: "But this is the most miraculous thing, that the Church though embattled has remained unconquerable and unquenchable, and while all strike against it, the foundation has remained unmoved. For while the head and the empire stand, so the body is easily renewed." Also *Disputation against the Jews* [PG 89, 1221C-D]: "Do not say that we Christians today suffer and are taken prisoner. For what is greater is that although our faith is persecuted and embattled by so many, it stands and does not cease, and neither is the empire abolished, nor our churches closed. But in the midst of the peoples who rule and persecute us, we have churches, erect crosses, found churches, and perform masses [*thusias epiteloumen*]." For anti-Jewish polemic in this period see, e.g., Dagron and Déroche (1991); Kaegi (1992) 220–27; Olster (1994) 116–79; Déroche (1999); Sivan (2000); Averil Cameron (2002).

5

# The Making of the Monenergist Crisis

Before Heraclius departed from Jerusalem after his restoration of the Cross, he thanked Modestus for his reconstruction of Jerusalem's churches and elevated him to the patriarchate.[1] He then distributed imperial largesse to the communities of the Judaean desert, thus reviving a form of imperial euergetism that appears to have lapsed since the reign of the emperor Maurice.[2] According to several sources, however, Modestus's patriarchate soon came to an abrupt end, for on a mission to Damascus to obtain further monies for church reconstruction he died (or was poisoned), perhaps on 15 April 631 (thus thirteen months after the restoration of the Cross).[3] Thereupon the Palestinian Church was

---

1. For Modestus's elevation to the patriarchate in March 630 see Strategius, *On the Fall* 24 [Garitte, *Prise* vol. 2, 55]; Eutychius, *Annals (Alexandrian Recension)* 30 [Breydy 129]; *Translation of the Relics of Anastasius the Persian* [Flusin 101].

2. See *Translation of the Relics of Anastasius the Persian* 1 [Flusin 99]; cf. Eutychius, *Annals (Alexandrian Recension)* 30 [Breydy 129f.]. Ps.-Sebēos, *History* 40, also refers to the emperor's distribution of alms. For the lapse see the comment of Flusin (1992b) vol. 2, 316f.

3. See Strategius, *On the Fall* 24 [Garitte, *Prise* vol. 2, 55, and *Expugnationis . . . Recensiones* 56, 104f., 191], these versions containing the accusation of poisoning en route to seek funds and placing his death on 15 April at a place on the borders of Palestine called Sozos (in the Georgian) or Arsūf (in the Arabic). Note, however, the variations in the C manuscript of Strategius in Arabic, where Modestus is not said to have died en route to Syria (although the mission is mentioned), and his death is said to have occurred after seven months as patriarch [Garitte, *Expugnationis . . . Recensiones* 150]. Eutychius, *Annals (Alexandrian Recension)* [Breydy 130f.], also reports the mission to procure monies in Syria but does not refer to poisoning and places Modestus's death nine months into his patriarchate. It appears that the author of the C manuscript (A.D. 1231–32) of Strategius has added details taken from Eutychius's *Annals* to the end of the Arabic translation [Garitte, *Expugnationis . . . Recensiones* 149f.]. It is tempting

thrown into crisis, and the patriarchal throne remained vacant until late in 634, when Sophronius himself would succeed to it. For the intervening period, later sources refer to "irregular" Palestinian consecrations performed through a *locum tenens*, Sergius of Joppa. In a *libellus* submitted to the Lateran Council of 649, one Stephen of Dora, a lieutenant of Sophronius, would allege that Sergius, "assuming the role of representing the see of Jerusalem [*tēn topotērēsian tou en Hierosolumois thronou labōn*] after the withdrawal of the Persians, not from ecclesiastical procedure [*akolouthia*] but from secular power [*apo kosmikēs exousias*], ordained several bishops there, in contravention of the canons, as suffragans of the see of Jerusalem";[4] and in a letter that Pope Martin dispatched to the East in the aftermath of that same council, he too would refer to the irregular ordinations that occurred before, during, and after Sophronius's tenure as patriarch.[5] It thus seems that a significant faction of Palestinians (though not all) refused to recognize Sergius and those whom he appointed. We are, therefore, provided with a potential context in which we may situate Maximus's references, within his *Letters*, to a new and otherwise unknown archbishop "Kurisikios" and his appeals to that same person, along with other prominent figures, to reunite the scattered communities that had fled from the Persians. The Palestinian opponents of Sergius, perhaps, had appointed their own leaders.

The origins of this Palestinian conflict, which leaves but a bare trace within the sources, should, it seems, be located in the Constantinopolitan promotion of the Christological doctrine of monenergism (that is, the single operation in Christ). Contemporaneous with the political reunification of the eastern provinces under

---

to speculate—as in Jankowiak (2009) 119f.—that the death of Modestus was somehow connected to religious tensions within the province, but if we presume that Modestus approved Heraclius's religious initiatives before his elevation, there is nevertheless no hint of hostility to him in later sources; see, e.g., Leontius of Neapolis, *Life of John the Almsgiver* 16; Anastasius of Sinai, *Tales* B4.

4. *Acts of the Lateran Council* [Riedinger 46]. The Latin version of the *Acts* adds "and although he himself had scarcely been confirmed, he presumed to ordain others" [Riedinger 47]. There appears to be a chronological contradiction in Stephen's account: the reference to the Persians suggests that Sergius's appointment occurred before Sophronius's patriarchate, but the appointed bishops are said to appeal to Paul of Constantinople (641–53) for confirmation. Thus several scholars argue that Sergius was elected after Sophronius's death: see, e.g., Van Dieten (1972) 50; Winkelmann (2001) 101f. no.74, 260; Levy-Rubin (2001) 296. The two accounts can be reconciled, however, if one assumes that Sergius's appointments remained in place throughout Sophronius's patriarchate and that their appeal occurred in response to the later attempts of Pope Theodore to remove them. Flusin (1992b) vol. 2, 361, and Jankowiak (2009) 113f. also favor the earlier date.

5. See Pope Martin, *Letter to John of Philadelphia* [PL 87, 159A–B]. Cf. also idem, *Letter to Pantaleon* [PL 87 172BD]. In both Martin recognizes that the irregular consecrations that occurred on either side of (but not during) Sophronius's patriarchate happened "on account of the difficulties of the time" ("propter temporis angustiam"). On promonenergist/promonothelete parties in Palestine see below at p. 233f.

Roman rule, the emperor Heraclius and the Constantinopolitan patriarch began to promote one side of a theological discussion that had simmered beneath the surface of Chalcedonian speculation since the *Tome* of Leo. That imperial program, which aimed at the reconciliation of anti-Chalcedonians to the council, achieved some remarkable and spectacular success, and it cannot be a coincidence that, at the moment of his greatest political success, the emperor was also able to convince others of the righteousness of his doctrinal program. For some, no doubt, God had demonstrated his support for Heraclius in unambiguous terms.

The converse of this equation between terrestrial success and divine favor was, of course, that of terrestrial failure and divine displeasure. If, as some passages in their works of the period suggest, Sophronius and Maximus demonstrated a rather striking ambivalence in respect of the proclaimed restoration that the emperor had achieved, then soon that same reservation was to receive a more concrete confirmation. The apparent tensions that beset the see of Jerusalem after the death of Modestus point toward preexisting concerns among Palestinians toward the imperial program of doctrinal accommodation. But from 633 Sophronius launched a more patent doctrinal opposition toward Constantinople and its allies. As we shall see, however, his opposition cannot be understood in reductionist terms as the simple application of some developed, preexistent commitment to the opposite doctrine. Although it may well have elaborated existing principles, that opposition was articulated and expanded within the context of the debate itself and cannot but have been informed through the dramatic political and cultural context in which it was formed. I do not intend here, therefore, to apologize for Sophronius as a champion of "orthodox" doctrine; but nevertheless I want better to understand his opposition, not least because its intellectual basis was perhaps not obvious or organic. As we shall see, placing Sophronius's opposition within the context both of his own experiences in the previous decades and of the dramatic political events sweeping over the Near East allows us to arrive at a far more comprehensive understanding of his dissidence, and indeed of the impossible task that opponents faced in their attempts to appease him.

## THE ORIGINS OF MONENERGISM

At least from the late 620s, concomitant with Heraclius's reunification of the eastern provinces, the emperor and patriarch began to promote the doctrine of the single operation in Christ (or monenergism) as a means of appealing to moderate anti-Chalcedonian communities within those same provinces.[6] Recon-

---

6. Readers should note that the impressive monograph of Lange (2012), which no doubt adds much to the issue of monenergism's origins, regrettably appeared too late to be considered here.

structing the origins of monenergist doctrine, however, is a task beset with various methodological difficulties. It is evident, for example, that Christian theologians of the fourth and fifth centuries did not consider the Christological operation to be a significant or at least pressing problem; and the issue of the Christological will (a related discussion that matured in the 640s) had been raised within the Cappadocian response to Apollinarianism, but then receded.[7] Nevertheless, in order to demonstrate that their respective theological positions were consistent with patristic Christological thought, monenergists and dyenergists of the seventh century scoured the tradition for texts that supported their theologies (and were often forced, of course, to recruit or reinterpret the precise same passages).

A single example from a church in Rome should suffice to demonstrate something of the nature of their efforts. Soon after the Lateran Council in 649, at which both monenergism and monotheletism (the interrelated doctrine of the "one will") were condemned, there was commissioned in Santa Maria Antiqua in the forum a fresco depicting four Fathers of the Church—Leo the Great, Gregory of Nazianzus, Basil of Caesarea, and John Chrysostom—each holding a script emblazoned with (supposed) antimonenergist or antimonothelete quotations from one of their works.[8] (The same quotations, we should note, also appear in the patristic testimonies contained within the *Acts* of the Lateran Council.)[9] The quotation from Leo is the celebrated passage from his *Tome*—"For each nature does what is proper to it with the cooperation of the other: that is, the Word performing what appertains to the Word, and the flesh carrying out what appertains to the flesh."[10] It was indeed a pertinent quotation, for in appearing to present the two natures as the agents of Christ's actions it underscored two operations but nevertheless raised the specter of Nestorianism.[11] At the same time, moreover, it offered two distinct readings as to the nature of Christ's actions, for in its first part it emphasized a so-called *communicatio operationum* or theandric operation (where all acts are both divine and human);[12] whereas in the latter it seemed to contradict that same conviction in distinguishing between separate operations (where different acts can be ascribed either to the divine or to the

---

7. See, e.g., Daley (2002a, b).
8. For the frescoes see Rushforth (1902). The citations are usefully set out in Rubery (2011) 12.
9. See, respectively, *Acts of the Lateran Council* [Riedinger 298, 270, 270, 312].
10. Here, however, in the Greek version derived from the *Acts of the Council of Chalcedon* [Schwartz 14]. For the Latin cf. Pope Leo, *Letters* 28 [PL 54, 767A-B].
11. I stress "appearing" because the preceding and subsequent passages in the *Tome* place due emphasis on Christ as the subject of the natures; see Hovorun (2008) 141f.; *contra* Bathrellos (2001) 205-8. Nevertheless it must be noted that the latter focuses on Leo's formula as cited in the crisis, not its broader context in situ.
12. I borrow the phrase from Hovorun (2008) 122.

human nature).¹³ It thus stood at the center of the debate, and each side emphasized different aspects—and even altered the text itself—according to their own convictions.¹⁴

As a recent publication by Eileen Rubery makes clear, the relevance of the other, earlier quotations is more questionable. That from Gregory Nazianzus refers to the "one will" of the Godhead, and that from Basil also identifies the will of the Father and of the Son.¹⁵ While it is unsurprising that the former, at least, was claimed for the monothelete cause as well,¹⁶ in the original, of course, these citations from the Cappadocians had little to do with Christological debates; their context, and principal meaning, was trinitarian.¹⁷ In similar vein, the fourth and final citation, from Chrysostom, does indeed refer to the "two operations"—but even from the passage quoted it is evident that the context is not Christological but hagiological; the sermon from which it is excerpted is, furthermore, spurious.¹⁸ Thus in a dyenergist and dyothelete fresco celebrating patristic adherence to its doctrine, we are presented with a quite remarkable selection of texts: a pertinent but nonetheless contested passage from Leo; two Cappadocian citations taken out of context (and even containing the phrase "one will"); and a spurious quotation of Chrysostom that is non-Christological. This, then, is a telling barometer of those citations that someone, at least, considered best to represent the patristic interest in the question of the operation (or operations) and the will (or wills).¹⁹

Similar difficulties beset our evidence for later, post-Chalcedonian discussions on the operation or operations. Although various recent studies have attempted to illuminate the same discussions as the forerunners of later debates on the opera-

---

13. For this ambiguity see, e.g., the criticism of Severus of Antioch, *Against the Impious Grammarian* 3.29, with Chesnut (1976) 31; Hovorun (2008) 16f., 141f. Also Uthemann (1997) 379–83; Price (2010) 222 (drawing attention to Pope Leo's clarification of his position in *Letters* 124.5 [*PL* 54, 1065B]). For anxieties over the *Tome*'s position on the operations see, e.g., the initial reaction to monenergism of Cyrus of Alexandria, *First Letter to Sergius* [Riedinger 590; repr. Allen (2009) 160–62]. Cf. the response of Sergius of Constantinople, *First Letter to Cyrus* [Riedinger 528–30; repr. Allen (2009) 164–66], disavowing the existence of "two operations" in the Fathers.

14. For the problematic status of this statement during the monenergist/monothelete crisis—and the attempts of theologians on both sides to alter it in accordance with their beliefs—see the excellent discussion of Bathrellos (2004) 176–87; also Allen and Neil (2002) 9f. with nn. 27–29.

15. Cf. Gregory of Nazianzus, *Orations* 30.12 [Gallay vol. 6, 250]; Basil of Caesarea, *On the Holy Spirit* 21 [*PG* 32, 105A-B]. For the former in both monothelete and dyothelete texts see below n. 27 and p. 101 n. 101.

16. I infer this from the fleeting comment of Brock (1985) 39 on the monothelete florilegium; see also *Disputation with Pyrrhus* [*PG* 91, 316C–317A]; Maximus Confessor, *Opuscula* 7 [*PG* 91, 81C-D]. See also Rubery (2011) 14–18.

17. See ibid. 18f.

18. Ps.-Chrysostom, *Sermon on the Apostle Thomas* [*PG* 59, 500], with Rubery (2011) 21.

19. *Pace* Rubery (2011) 21f.

tion (or operations), those studies almost without exception ignore a significant methodological problem: that is, the frequent entrenchment of the relevant passages within later partisan texts. Extant sources for these earlier discussions, so crucial to understanding the origins of the debate, thus survive for the most part in texts produced within the circles of seventh-century dyenergists and are thus embedded in later polemical contexts, often without independent attestation and in some cases demonstrably distorted or falsified.[20] At the same time, those sources, in the main florilegia, set out a vision of previous theological thought in which the doctrine of the two operations is shown to be a simple extension of the orthodox tradition—there can thus be limited appreciation of the context in which theological speculation on the Christological operation or operations in fact arose.

Some examples can again illustrate some of the challenges involved. In later literature, the dyenergists/dyotheletes distinguish between two recent theologians, both called Theodore: Theodore the Monk and Theodore of Pharan (on Sinai). The former was cited in one of Maximus's *Opuscula* with approval, and from that citation appears to be identical with another Sinaitic theologian, Theodore of Raithou, whose popular neo-Chalcedonian tract, the *Preparation*, survives in various manuscripts independent of antimonenergist and antimonothelete literature.[21] Theodore of Pharan, however, whom opponents placed in the earlier patriarchal reign of Sergius of Constantinople (610–38), was regarded as the font of the monenergist error, and excerpts from his otherwise unknown *Letter to Sergius of Arsinoe*, which argues for the "one operation" and "one will" of Christ were read out during the third session of the Lateran Council and condemned.[22] Maximus cites (with disapproval) another work of the monothelete Theodore of Pharan—"a treatise [*skedos*] on essence, nature, hypostasis, person, and other chapters"—but as Werner Elert long ago observed, this too is in fact the *Preparation* of Theodore of Raithou.[23] Maximus, it therefore seems, cites different passages from the same work and, depending on his opinion of them, ascribes them to different Theodores. Theodore of Pharan,

20. See, e.g., Richard (1966); Madden (1982); Paramelle (1996) esp. 263; Neil (1998) 99f. and (2006c) 130f.; with Winkelmann (2001) 153f. no. 151. In the opposite direction see the accusation at *Dispute at Bizya* 4. On the psychology of forgery in the monothelete controversy see Wessel (2001) esp. 215–19; and for the mutual destruction of opponents' writings see Brandes (2003) 109f.

21. Maximus Confessor, *Opuscula* 26 [*PG* 91, 276A–B]. Cf. Theodore of Raithou, *Preparation* [Diekamp 200ff.]. For the correspondences see, e.g., Theodore the Monk's *phusis esti, kata men philosophous, archē kinēseōs kai ēremias* [*PG* 91, 276A] with Theodore of Raithou's *phusis de estin archē tēs hekastou tōn apērithmēmenōn toutōn kineseōs te kai ēremias* [Diekamp 202].

22. *Acts of the Lateran Council* [Riedinger 120–22]. Cf. also the *libellus* of Stephen of Dora contained therein [Riedinger 38] and passim within the *Letters* of Pope Martin [*PL* 87, 120–204].

23. Maximus Confessor, *Opuscula* 10 [*PG* 91, 136C–D]. Cf. Theodore of Raithou's *Preparation* [Diekamp 205f.], with Elert (1951) esp. 71–76, and Van Dieten (1972) 26f. Cf. Jankowiak (2009) 26–30, pointing also to the citation of Theodore of Raithou in the dyenergist/dyothelete *Doctrina Patrum* [Diekamp 41f.], despite the attribution of operation to hypostasis within that same passage.

Theodore the Monk, and Theodore of Raithou, however, are one and the same person, a neo-Chalcedonian and protomonenergist and protomonothelete on Sinai. Texts on which the historian might depend to demonstrate the progression of monenergist and monothelete thought from the earlier neo-Chalcedonian movement have been broken up and distorted, ascribed to separate theologians according to their "good" or "bad" content.

Similar methodological difficulties beset attempts to trace the debate on operations among Chalcedonian theologians of the sixth century. Two prominent figures should hold our attention here: the emperor Justinian I (527–65) and the patriarch Anastasius I of Antioch (559–70, 593–98). In the later *Acts* of the (prodyenergist, prodyothelete) Sixth Ecumenical Council an unknown treatise of Justinian, *Against the Nestorians and Acephali*, was cited in defense of the doctrine of the two operations. Commenting on Leo's controversial statement on the natural activities in the *Tome*—"For each nature does what is proper to it with the cooperation of the other"—the extract states, "At once the heretics leap up and say that it is not necessary to speak of different operations, of the divinity and humanity of Christ, but rather that there is one operation—and once more they in this way blaspheme in accordance with the madness of Apollinarius. For all the holy fathers have taught us to believe in the passion and impassibility of the one and same, and have instructed us to confess different operations of the one and same, our Lord, Jesus Christ."[24] Here, then, an emperor, no less, appears as a protochampion of dyenergism: emphasizing the singleness of Christ's acting person but nevertheless distinguishing the two operations.[25]

The problem for the historian who wishes to assess Justinian's actual contribution to the debate on the Christological operations is that elsewhere he is presented as a champion of the opposite cause. Although the eventual triumph of dyenergist and dyothelete doctrine entailed a pervasive expurgation of monenergist and monothelete texts (besides negative citations in their enemies' own works), in the 1980s Sebastian Brock published a precious monothelete florilegium that—much like the *Acts* of the Sixth Council, from the opposite perspective—attempts to demonstrate the adherence of the "one operation" and "one will" to previous Chalcedonian tradition.[26] It is therefore striking that the florilegium contains an extract from another otherwise obscure treatise of Justinian, *Against the Agnoetae*, which speaks

---

24. *Acts of the Sixth Ecumenical Council* [Riedinger 350].

25. Cf. *Acts of the Sixth Ecumenical Council* [Riedinger 352–56] for another text of Justinian (*Letter to Zoilus of Alexandria*) citing the famous formula of Leo, and disavowing "one natural operation." For discussion of both texts see Uthemann (1997) 389.

26. Brock (1985), Winkelmann (2001) 170f. no. 170b. The extracts on the operations and wills taken from one George the Monk and contained within the Syriac ms. BM Add. 14535, referred to at Brock (1985) 36, 44 with n. 21—see also Winkelmann (2001) 84 n. 49—are now being studied by Maria Conterno.

of "the entire will" of God in Christ.²⁷ It thus presents the emperor as a protomonothelete, placing him alongside other (alleged) opponents of the two operations and wills (Pope Vigilius, the patriarch Menas, Anastasius I of Antioch, and Symeon the Younger).²⁸ Both sides, therefore, were involved in similar games of retrospective recruitment, adding the weight of imperial pronouncements to their own positions and citing otherwise unknown texts to do so.²⁹

For similar reasons, the precise contribution of the patriarch Anastasius I of Antioch must remain a matter of doubt. One important treatise, the *Definitions*, survives in a line of independent transmission;³⁰ but two further crucial contributions—the *Defense of the Tome of Leo* and *On Operations*—can be accessed only through fragmentary citations in later florilegia, texts designed precisely to establish both the antiquity and the orthodoxy of dyenergist thought. Thus while the *Definitions* demonstrates a profound interest in the meaning of "operation" and "will,"³¹ the explicit application of that speculation to the Incarnation is visible only in the *Defense* and in *On Operations*, from which the patriarch appears as a staunch proponent of the "two operations" (and was cited as such).³² In order to evaluate the precise character of Anastasius's thought, therefore, we must depend on excerpts that have been filtered through parties who had all reason to fragment or reconstruct the past to their advantage (and who, in other cases at least, did so without hesitation).³³

As we have seen, furthermore, the adherence of Anastasius to the "two operations" was a matter not of established fact but rather of polemical contention, for in Brock's aforementioned florilegium Anastasius is in fact cited as a defender of

---

27. Brock (1985) 38f., indicating that the passage proceeds into a quotation from Gregory of Nazianzus's second oration to the Son. (One presumes the much-contested statement from *Orations* 30.12; see above n. 15.)

28. For Justinian as monenergist see also the *Discussion between the Emperor Justinian and the Nestorian Paul of Nisibis*, speaking of "the single hypostatic operation" of the Logos (but not as the crux of the text); for discussion see Guillaumont (1969–70) 52f.; Uthemann (1997) 390f. The florilegium's text from Symeon the Younger—the *Memra to Barlaha the Stratēlates*—which denies the two operations, is also unknown from elsewhere; see Brock (1985) 42f.; Winkelmann (2001) 52, no. 8b.

29. *Pace* Bathrellos (2004) 91–94, who questions the authenticity of the various passages within the monenergist/monothelete florilegium but is willing to accept otherwise unknown passages from post-Chalcedonian authors, including Justinian and Anastasius of Antioch, when cited by the dyenergists/dyotheletes. For the use of patristic authorities by both sides within the conflict cf. the accounts of Bausenhart (1992) 183–95; Tannous (2006) 4–13.

30. See the introduction of Uthemann (1980) 306–41.

31. See Anastasius I of Antioch, *Definitions* 116–26.

32. For the *Defense of the Tome of Leo* (CPG 6952) see *Acts of the Lateran Council* [Riedinger 314, 436]; *Acts of the Sixth Ecumenical Council* [Riedinger 362–64] For *On Operations* (CPG 6953) see *Acts of the Lateran Council* [Riedinger 435f.]; *Doctrina Patrum* [Diekamp 78–80, 134–36].

33. See above n. 20.

monenergism. The florilegium includes two excerpts from an unknown *Letter to Marinus of Apamea* in which Anastasius insists that if Christ is one without confusion, he must then have a single operation and a single will.[34] Indeed, that Anastasius was perhaps less consistent in his thought than later florilegial citations reveal is implied in a later defense of his dyenergist credentials by none other than Maximus himself. At some point around 640, the Confessor composed a dogmatic treatise for the priest Marinus in which he responded to the latter's concerns over Anastasius's striking use of the phrase "one operation in Christ" in a lost antitritheist tract *Against Diaetetes*.[35] Maximus argued that Anastasius in fact meant "nothing other than the indissoluble union of the natural energies, and the result from them: that is, the work and action," thus claiming that "one operation" in fact meant two.[36] Whatever the merits of Maximus's interpretation—which in effect excuses all previous uses of "one operation"—his failure to challenge the existence of the phrase indicates that Anastasius, as one might infer from Brock's monothelete florilegium, was less consistent in the application of dyenergist phraseology than Maximus and his allies in a later context would have cared for. Anastasius was, we can be sure, interested in the Christological operations; but where he would position himself in later Chalcedonian discussions must remain unclear.[37] Both sides claimed him for their own.

Despite these methodological misgivings, it seems to me that two salient points emerge: first, that no Chalcedonian consensus existed on the question of the Christological operations in the period before the outbreak of the controversy proper (hence the apparent inconsistencies within the same authors); and second, that however much distortion or falsification was involved in later periods, the universal desire to recruit or reframe the theological speculation of earlier Chalcedonians demonstrates that such people were at least interested in the issue of Christ's operation (or operations) and will (or wills), however much such interest remained undeveloped. We can, therefore, dismiss one oft-repeated but much-maligned accusation—that is, that the emperor Heraclius and patriarch Sergius of

---

34. Brock (1985) 40–42.
35. The text (CPG 6956) is cited in fragments in Maximus Confessor, *Opuscula* 20 [PG 91, 229C, 232B–C], and also in the later antimonothelete *Doctrina Patrum* [Diekamp 191, 204–5], although the citations there do not concern the energies. Otherwise it does not survive.
36. Maximus Confessor, *Opuscula* 20 [PG 91, 229B-233B, at 229C]. For this defense of Anastasius in more detail see Uthemann (1997) 400–404; Hovorun (2008) 116f. For similar logic see Maximus's defense of Cyril of Alexandria's use of "one operation" at *Disputation with Pyrrhus* [PG 91, 344B–345C], with Bausenhart (1992) 292–303. Later, at *Dispute at Bizya* 4 [Allen and Neil 90–92], he dismisses the same citation as a forgery of Timothy Aelurus but then interprets it as dyenergist nonetheless, further rejecting his opponent's claim that "You must accept the words at face value" (*haplas gar tas phōnas anagkēn echeis dexasthai*). Cf. also *Opuscula* 7 [PG 91, 85C–88A], 8 [PG 91, 101A–112A].
37. For Anastasius see also Winkelmann (2001) 48f. nos. 6 and 7, 188.

Constantinople "invented" monenergism as a means of appealing to moderate anti-Chalcedonians within the beleaguered eastern provinces.[38] Although the pair must of course have perceived the potential political advantages to be derived from a doctrine that emphasized the singularity of the acting subject in the Incarnation, to regard that same doctrine as a political expedient ex nihilo is to lend too much credence to the rhetoric of its opponents. The evidence for the earlier post-Chalcedonian period is sufficient to state that the debate on the operations, at least, was not a Heraclian invention but an organic development from discussions surrounding the Chalcedonian definition and the *Tome* of Leo's somewhat ambiguous position on the agent in the Incarnation.[39]

Indeed, Cyril Hovorun has demonstrated the use of monenergist formulas in a range of sixth-century anti-Chalcedonian authors, in particular in Severus of Antioch, for whom the famous formula of the *Tome* of Leo was nothing less than Nestorianism.[40] Hovorun has furthermore suggested that the Justinianic discussion on theopaschism "represented an early attempt to raise the question of *energeia* as a self-sufficient theological problem and to use it as a meeting point for the Chalcedonian and anti-Chalcedonian traditions."[41] At the same time, and from

---

38. For this erroneous but still common view see, e.g., Allen and Neil (2002) 3, 8f.; Sánchez Valencia (2003); Ekonomou (2007) 81–85. Cf. also the somewhat imaginative argument of Nevo and Koren (2003) 59–65 that Heraclius's proposal of monotheletism was a deliberate ploy designed to tempt both Chalcedonian and anti-Chalcedonian Christians within the eastern provinces into heresy, and thus was also "a step towards the final aim of abandoning responsibility for the Christians in the areas which Byzantium had decided not to defend" (59).

39. See above p. 189f.

40. Hovorun (2008) 15–41; on Severan monenergism and monotheletism see also Chesnut (1976) 20–34; Grillmeier and Hainthaler (1995) 162–70. See also, however, the intriguing neo-Chalcedonian response to Severus's monenergism contained within Eustathius Monachus's sixth-century *Letter on the Two Natures* 11–12, 29–30 (respectively quoting and responding to Severus of Antioch, *First Letter to Sergius* [Lebon 86f.] and *Sermon on the Nativity* [Brière and Graffin 300–302]); and the rebuttal of Severan accusations concerning the *Tome* of Leo and its apparent "two operating subjects" contained within Eulogius of Alexandria's *Against Severus and Timothy*, as described in Photius, *Bibliotheca* 225 [Henry vol. 4, 105]. Sergius of Constantinople, *First Letter to Cyrus* [Riedinger 530; repr. Allen (2009) 166] claims that Eulogius's *Defense of the Tome of Leo* (CPG 6952) did not speak of "two operations," which fits its description in Photius. Cf., however, the potential attempt to recruit him in Ps.-Eulogius, *On the Trinity and the Incarnation*, on which see Winkelmann (2001) 50 no. 7. For a sixth-century Chalcedonian interest in the operations see also the alleged dyenergist quotation from John of Scythopolis cited in *Acts of the Lateran Council* [Riedinger 314]; *Acts of the Sixth Ecumenical Council* [Riedinger 366–68]; *Doctrina Patrum* [Diekamp 85f.]; with Rorem and Lamoreaux (1998) 33–35; Winkelmann (2001) 48 no. 5; also John's scholion on Ps.-Dionysius's fourth epistle at PG 4, 536A, with Rorem and Lamoreaux (1998) 253 n. 9. Cf. also Ephraim of Antioch as cited in *Acts of the Sixth Ecumenical Council* [Riedinger 356–62]; and the defense of Leontius of Byzantium and Leontius of Jerusalem's dyenergist /dyothelete credentials in Bathrellos (2004) 39–54.

41. Hovorun (2008) 41–50, at 41.

the Chalcedonian perspective, Karl-Heinz Uthemann has demonstrated that monenergist and monothelete doctrine represented an extension of the concerns of various earlier neo-Chalcedonian theologies;[42] whereas Demetrios Bathrellos, in response to Uthemann, has pointed to passages in the neo-Chalcedonian theologians par excellence, the Leontii, that may in fact be seen to express an implicit (but never explicit) commitment to the "two operations" formula.[43] In respect of the latter argument, it is of course possible to highlight references that can be interpreted as expressing an implicit commitment to the two operations; but to do so is to suppose that those authors could have had some full conception of the problem before the terms themselves were defined, and thus also to risk recapitulating the games of retrospective recruitment pursued within the course of the crisis itself. Bathrellos's reaction to Uthemann's argument nevertheless serves to demonstrate a more important point: that however we may wish to interpret the implications of the various references in these post-Chalcedonian theologians, the issue of the operations, whether one or two, was an ever more conspicuous but undeveloped issue in their thought. The official promotion of the single operation under Heraclius, therefore, represented not so much a *novitas* as the crystallization of a theological discussion present in the Chalcedonian Church for at least a century.

We must therefore be cautious to separate the origins of Constantinopolitan support for the doctrine from the doctrine's actual origins, even if the former served to condense the latter. Much like the doctrine itself, however, the origins of the imperial interest in monenergism are obfuscated in later polemic, and we must again depend for much of our narrative on the retrospective accounts of Maximus and his allies. Thus in a text that purports to record a dispute between Maximus and the deposed monothelete patriarch Pyrrhus in North Africa in 645, in which the latter had accused Sophronius of stirring up "this inopportune discussion on the energies," Maximus responded:[44]

> I am completely at a loss as to what defense you may give for having so gravely accused a blameless man. Tell me truly. When Sergius wrote to Theodore of Pharan, sending him the *libellus* of Menas through the intermediary Sergius Macaronas, bishop of Arsinoe, and urged him to tell him his thoughts on the "one operation" and "one will" used in that *libellus*, and when Theodore replied to him approving these things, where then was Sophronius? Or when Sergius wrote to Paul the One-eyed, the Severan, in Theodosiopolis, and sent to him the *libellus* of Menas and his own

---

42. Uthemann (1997).

43. Bathrellos (2004) 51–54, *contra* Uthemann (1997) 373–89, though acknowledging (and then interpreting) some ambiguities in the thought of Leontius of Jerusalem and confessing that in the same period "the question of Christ's energies was still somewhat nebulous, and perhaps potentially controversial" (59). Winkelmann (2001) 47f., we should note, regards the Leontii as protomonenergists.

44. *Disputation with Pyrrhus* [PG 91, 332B–333A].

accord with Theodore of Pharan? Or when he wrote to George, surnamed Arsas, a Paulianist, [to request] that their citations [chrēseis] about the "one operation" be sent to him, and put this in a letter, in order to effect a union between them and the Church through them? The blessed John [the Almsgiver], patriarch of Alexandria, seized this letter from Arsas and hence wanted to depose him because of it but was prevented by the sudden incursion of the Persians into Egypt. Or when Sergius replied to Cyrus of Phasis, when he had been asked by the latter about "one operation" or "two operations," and sent him also the so-called *libellus* of Menas?

According to the *Disputation*, therefore, the conflict had its immediate origins in the machinations of the patriarch Sergius, who had sought out theological opinion on the single operation and promoted it as a potential basis for union from the earliest period of Heraclius's reign (that is, before the Persian incursion into Egypt in the late 610s).[45] This account, we should note, provides the standard guide to Constantinopolitan maneuvers in modern scholarship.[46]

One of the most striking of Maximus's claims is, of course, the presentation of Moschus and Sophronius's quondam patron John the Almsgiver as protoscourge of monenergism. On the basis of that claim, it is perhaps tempting to speculate that Sophronius while in Alexandria had imparted his own antimonenergist principles to his patron and that toward the end of the latter's life those principles were manifested, as the *Disputation* suggests, in the Almsgiver's actions against George Arsas. In the *Miracles of Cyrus and John*, Sophronius had indeed made some statements that might be read as expressing a commitment to "two operations" in Christ (corresponding to the two natures). Thus in *Miracles* 29 he had said, "And the Savior said to the Jews who did not believe in him, 'If I do not do the deeds of my Father, do not believe in me; but if I do those deeds, even if you do not believe in me, believe in my deeds' [John 10:37–38]. And he gave to us a constant and firm intelligence and a discretion that does not lie in order to make out the doers from the deeds [*apo tōn ergōn tous energountas*]"; in *Miracles* 37 he had said, "'For what kind of communion is there between light and darkness?' [2 Cor. 6:14], as the divine Paul said. For just as light does not suffer to remain in communion with darkness, nor either is darkness able to dwell with light. For since they have a contrary nature [*enantian tēn phusin*] in all things, they also possess a contrary operation [*enantian energeian*]"; and in *Miracles* 41 a patient's healed tongue is said to "operate according to its nature" (*poioumenē kata phusin heautēs tēn energeian*).[47]

---

45. For the chronology of the Persian invasion of Egypt see Altheim-Stiehl (1992b).
46. See, e.g., Van Dieten (1972) 25–27; Bausenhart (1992) 277–84; Winkelmann (2001) 50–55; Allen and Neil (2002) 8f.; Ekonomou (2007) 86; Hovorun (2008) 58–60 and (2010) 219; Jankowiak (2009) 23–30.
47. Sophronius, *Miracles* 29.6, 37.9, 41.9 [Marcos 299f., 330, 343]. For these correspondences see also Schönborn (1972) 210f. For the first passage from John 10 cf. *Disputation with Pyrrhus* [PG 91, 348D–349A].

The evidence nevertheless demands significant caution. Although Sophronius in the *Miracles of Cyrus and John* expressed some principles that from a later perspective may seem to express a commitment to the "two operations," that commitment is obscure at best and is stated in the main in non-Christological contexts.[48] Indeed, the lack of explicitness in itself perhaps belies a general awareness or even existence of a broader "monenergist problem" in this period, and we should beware of later partisan genealogies that attempt to establish both the age and breadth of the antimonenergist resistance. Although the issue of the Christological operations was, to be sure, in the air in Chalcedonian circles in the 610s, the debate proper would not erupt until much later. Besides the *Disputation's* account here, there is no indication that the resistance had begun in earnest under the patriarchate of the Almsgiver.

Certain further details within the *Disputation's* account find some corroboration elsewhere. Although the correspondence between Sergius of Constantinople and Theodore of Pharan, for example, is not referred to in other sources, Theodore of Pharan's (or rather of Raithou's) *Letter to Sergius of Arsinoe* was read out and condemned at the Lateran Council;[49] we ascertain from Brock's aforementioned monothelete florilegium and from elsewhere that the *libellus* of the Constantinopolitan patriarch Menas was indeed a central (but much-contested) monenergist and monothelete text;[50] and a period of intense correspondence on the energies between Sergius and several of the figures referred to in Maximus's account is attested in a so-called dossier of monenergist texts read out at the (antimonenergist and antimonothelete) Lateran and Sixth Ecumenical councils in 649 and 680/1.[51] That dossier contains a letter from Cyrus of Phasis (in Lazica) to Sergius in which he explains how, having once encountered the emperor Heraclius, he expressed some doubts as to the apparent contradiction of the *Tome* of Leo contained within the emperor's prohibition of "two operations" in a previous ordi-

---

48. *Pace* Schönborn (1972) 210f.; Hovorun (2008) 152.

49. *Acts of the Lateran Council* [Riedinger 120]; cf. *Disputation with Pyrrhus* [PG 91, 332B-333A]. For Arsinoe as a center of ecumenicism in this period cf. above p. 104. and below p. 206f.

50. For the *libellus* see Winkelmann (2001) 45–46 no. 1 (dating it to 552). For its citation in the monothelete florilegium Brock (1985) 37f.; cf. Sergius of Constantinople, *First Letter to Cyrus* [Riedinger 528; Allen (2009) 164] and *First Letter to Honorius* [Riedinger 546; repr. Allen (2009) 192]. After a protracted investigation the *libellus* was condemned as a fake at the Sixth Ecumenical Council; see *Acts of the Sixth Ecumenical Council* [Riedinger 532]. *Pace* Bathrellos (2004) 90f. n. 171, from the *Dispute at Bizya* 4 [Allen and Neil 90] and *Disputation with Pyrrhus* [PG 91, 328A-B] it appears that earlier dyotheletes thought it genuine, since Maximus therein condemns its contents but not its authenticity. See also Bausenhart (1992) 262–64.

51. "Monenergist dossier" is the title attributed to the texts in the useful reedition and translation of Allen (2009). It should be noted, however, that the latter does not include Cyrus of Alexandria, *Third Letter to Sergius* as contained in *Acts of the Lateran Council* [Riedinger 172].

nance against one Paul, "the highest head of the nonbishops," and how the emperor himself then alleviated those same doubts through instructing him to read a report of the Constantinopolitan patriarch Sergius on the energies, composed in response to the emperor's own ordinance against Paul.[52] In a later document within that same dossier—that is, Sergius's so-called *First Letter to Honorius* (winter 634/5)— these earlier explorations into a doctrine of the Christological operations are again referred to and given further context. Therein the patriarch reports to the pope how Heraclius, on campaign against the Persians in Armenia, had entered into a theological discussion with, and bested, the Severan Paul, referring in the course of that discussion to the single operation. "After some time," Sergius continues, the emperor came to Lazica, where Cyrus of Phasis reminded him of his discussions with Paul and requested that he elucidate the issue of the operations, at which point the emperor referred him to the Constantinopolitan patriarch.[53] According to these accounts, therefore, the issue of monenergism was an imperial initiative that had arisen and been further elucidated during two separate discussions in the Caucasus. The two reported meetings have been placed in 624 and 626.[54]

The problem for the historian wishing to reconstruct the earliest stages of imperial support for monenergism, however, is that the texts that describe those stages all appear in later antimonenergist citations (whether in the *Disputation* or in the conciliar material). There is therefore a distinct risk of circular argumentation, for the sources that corroborate these earliest discussions all emanate from the same partisan circle. Although it seems indisputable that both the issue of the Christological operations and the impulse toward dialogue between different schisms were indeed topical, for independent attestation of imperial maneuvers on monenergism we must look to other sources, and to the period of Heraclius's political triumph against the Persians in the late 620s, when the emperor attempted to complement his restoration of the eastern provinces with a concomitant program of

---

52. See Cyrus of Alexandria, *First Letter to Sergius* [Riedinger 588–92; repr. Allen (2009) 160–62]. For the ordinance against Paul cf. Sergius of Constantinople, *First Letter to Cyrus* [Riedinger 528–30; repr. Allen (2009) 162–66]. The account of monenergism's origins at *Synodicon Vetus* 128—which assumes that Sergius convened a council having received Cyrus's letter—depends on the same dossier of documents from the Sixth Ecumenical Council. (So also Duffy and Parker [1979] 107 n. 154.) On the identity of Paul, a prominent Armenian bishop exiled to Cyprus—rather than the leader of the Cypriot Severans—see esp. Jankowiak (2009) 36–40; *contra*, e.g., Van Dieten (1972) 28 n. 93.

53. Sergius of Constantinople, *First Letter to Honorius* [Riedinger 534–36; repr. Allen (2009) 182–84].

54. It is traditional to place the first meeting in 622/3; see, e.g., Van Dieten (1972) 28–30; Winkelmann (2001) 54f. no. 12, 57 no. 18; Allen (2009) 25–27. But see now Jankowiak (2009) 30–36. We should also note that *Synodicon Vetus* 129 [Duffy and Parker 108] alleges a subsequent council proclaiming one will and one energy "upon the return of Heraclius to the royal city Constantinople," but this council is not known from elsewhere and is perhaps an inference from the *Acts of the Sixth Ecumenical Council*.

ecclesial reunification. That program, it appears, met with some considerable and unprecedented success.

## THE HERACLIAN UNIONS

The imperial interest in the reconciliation of anti-Chalcedonians within the Caucasus, alleged within the later record of the Sixth Ecumenical Council, is corroborated within the Armenian tradition, for in the same period in which the Cross was restored to Jerusalem, numerous sources report an official reconciliation of the Armenian Church with the doctrine of Chalcedon.[55] After his brief account of the restoration of the Cross at Jerusalem, Pseudo-Sebēos reports that a Roman general forced the catholicus Ezr to travel to the emperor and that when he had received a statement of faith from him (which anathematized Nestorius but not Chalcedon), the pair shared communion.[56] Other Armenian sources place that meeting at Theodosiopolis, but where it suffices for Pseudo-Sebēos to narrate the union and then move on, such sources report a considerable domestic resistance. Thus according to a series of independent sources—most importantly, the anonymous *Narration on Armenian Affairs*, the *History* of John Catholicus, and the *History* of Stephen Orbelian—when the council of Armenian bishops approved the dyophysite Christology of Chalcedon, one John Mayragomec'i and several prominent clerics denounced the catholicus, and entered into schism.[57]

This same pattern of official union and domestic opposition, so familiar to students of the post-Chalcedonian Christological controversies, was repeated also in Nestorian Persia. A doctrinal union between the Chalcedonians (in the Roman empire) and Nestorians (in the Sasanian) at this time should, perhaps, not elicit surprise: the Sasanian queen Boran, having deposed Shahrbaraz from the throne,

---

55. For the date—ca. 631—see Jankowiak (2009) 83.

56. Ps.-Sebēos, *History* 41, with Howard-Johnston (1999b) 228, placing the event in 631, with Winkelmann (2001) 63f. no. 25; *contra* Garitte (1952) 303, placing it 632/3. For the same council in the so-called *Anonymous Chronicle* see Greenwood (2008) 244.

57. See *Narration on Armenian Affairs* 119–43, with the accounts of John Catholicus and Stephen Orbelian set out and translated in Garitte (1952) 288–98, with extensive citations from other Georgian and Armenian authors ibid. 278–350. Opposition within Armenia is also evidenced in a letter of Athanasius the Camel Driver to Ezr's deposed predecessor Christopher—on whom see Ps.-Sebēos, *History* 40—in which Athanasius praises Christopher for not indulging in Ezr's "madness." That letter is contained within an Armenian version of Michael the Syrian's *Chronicle;* see Van Dieten (1972) 223f. For an Armenian interest in the monothelete crisis see also the account of ecclesiastical history contained within the *Anonymous Chronicle*, set out in Greenwood (2008) 245–48; cf. the *Discourse* of the late seventh-century catholicus Sahak III, which includes a long defense of the "one operation" and "one will," and even cites Pope Honorius; see Esbroeck (1995) esp. 402–6 (noting also the interest in the Trisagion and eucharist ibid. 421–36). For Heraclius's efforts at doctrinal union in Georgia cf. Sumbat Davitidze, *Lives and Times of the Georgian Bagratids* cited in Kaegi (2003) 220.

and dependent on a perhaps doubtful imperial blessing for the removal of her predecessor, had good reason to desire a closer religious union between the two empires; and, furthermore, as Hovorun has made clear, Nestorius himself (following Theodore of Mopsuestia) had spoken of a single (prosopic) operation and will in Christ.[58] Conditions were thus ripe for reconciliation. According to an account preserved in the Nestorian *Chronicle of Seert*, then, upon her accession Boran, fearing reprisals from the Romans, had dispatched the catholicus Isho'yahb II and his bishops to guarantee the peace.[59] (Contacts between the Nestorian episcopate and Heraclius in 630 are, we should note, also attested in a number of other, independent, sources.) The emperor then examined the catholicus as to his confession, and having reckoned it orthodox, twice received the eucharist from his hands and honored him with splendid gifts. As in Armenia, however, the union appears to have aroused some significant resistance: when the catholicus returned to Persia, according to the *Chronicle*, his own bishops reprimanded him for sacrificing the faith to the allure of imperial largesse.[60]

It is notable that the *Chronicle of Seert* makes a specific statement concerning the doctrinal content of the accord: "And the patriarch left the land of the Romans loaded with honors," it reports, "and Isho'yahb's profession of faith was in accord with that of Sergius, patriarch of Constantinople, in the recognition of the one will and one operation [*fī al-i'tirāfi bimašī'ati wāḥidati wa-fi'li wāḥidi*]."[61] Although, as has been said, such a profession was not discordant with that of Nestorius himself, no other source refers to the "one operation" (or "will") as the basis for the union, and the same formulas are a conspicuous absence in two later confessions attributed to the catholicus himself.[62] It is possible, therefore, that a monenergist or monothelete formula was not in fact a constituent of the agreement, and that later polemic has lent to it a retrospective prominence. Nevertheless, the accretion of

---

58. Hovorun (2008) 9–15. Maximus and his allies recognized that Nestorius had assigned operation to person; see *Disputation with Pyrrhus* [PG 91, 313B, 336D–337A], with Bausenhart (1992) 253f.

59. *Chronicle of Seert* 93 [Scher 557–59]; cf. the similar account in Mari, *History* [Gismondi 61f.]; and 'Amr ibn Mattā, *The Tower* [Gismondi 52f.; repr. Sako (1983) 56f.]. See also *Khuzistan Chronicle* [Guidi 30]; Thomas of Marga, *Books of Governors* 2.4–6; *Translation of the Relics of Anastasius the Persian* 2–3 [Flusin 99–101]. Excluding the latter, these sources are usefully collated in Sako (1983) 29–58. See ibid. 67–70, Flusin (1992b) vol. 2, 319–27, and Jankowiak (2009) 75–79 for discussion, dating the embassy to the summer of 630. It should be noted that this significant Nestorian union is absent from the source register of Winkelmann (2001).

60. *Chronicle of Seert* 93 [Scher 560f.]. Cf. Sako (1983) 70–72, however, expressing some doubts as to the text's account of resistance.

61. *Chronicle of Seert* 93 [Scher 560].

62. See 'Amr ibn Mattā's fourteenth-century *The Tower* [Gismondi 53–54; repr. Sako (1983) 59f.], which claims to transmit the profession of faith given to Heraclius, but in which operation and will are a conspicuous absence. Cf. also Isho'yahb II, *Christological Letter*, with the discussion of Sako (1983) 101–36, in which there is again no explicit mention of operation or will.

evidence from elsewhere within the Roman East suggests that monenergist doctrine, if not monotheletism, was indeed a component of Constantinopolitan attempts at doctrinal union, even if subsequent polemic has elevated it to a position that some contemporaries, at least, may not have perceived.

Perhaps the best-documented of these initiatives occurred at Hierapolis in the winter of 629/30, where several sources attest to a meeting between the emperor and the anti-Chalcedonian patriarch Athanasius (the "Camel Driver").[63] Here again the sources place a monenergist formula at the center of discussions. According to Theophanes—or rather his source, which narrates the entire monenergist and monothelete crisis within a single notice under A.M. 6121 (A.D. 628/9)—Athanasius at that time approached Heraclius while the latter was at Hierapolis (the ancient Syrian Mabbug) and promised to accept Chalcedon in return for his elevation to the throne of Antioch. (This, of course, was the Chalcedonian throne, vacant since the murder of Anastasius II in 608.)[64] At the same time, however, knowing that to confess one operation was in fact to confess one nature, Theophanes' source claims, Athanasius also inquired about the pronouncement of one or two operations and wills, and when the emperor wrote to Sergius of Constantinople and Cyrus of Phasis to seek their opinion on this "novel language," he found them in agreement with Athanasius over the "one operation," and thus began to promote the doctrine.[65]

The account in the *Chronicle* of Michael the Syrian is far more detailed. The *Chronicle* contains several entries that purport to record the attempted rapprochement. One such notice, which precedes the narrative of the meeting with Athanasius, records a letter of the emperor to the anti-Chalcedonians in which he refers to the "one operation" (*ma'bdāyūtā ḥdā*);[66] another, again preceding the report on

---

63. For the various dates offered in scholarship see Winkelmann (2001) 61–63 nos. 24 and 24a. The date of the union depends upon the date of the death of Anastasius of Antioch. *Anonymous Chronicle to 724* [Brooks 144], *Anonymous Chronicle to 819* [Chabot 11], *Anonymous Chronicle to 1234* 104, and Michael the Syrian, *Chronicle* 11.5, together give July 631, and are followed by, e.g., Flusin (1992b) vol. 2, 312 n. 81, *contra* Van Dieten (1972) 220–26; I follow Jankowiak (2009) 63–65. For analysis of the meeting see Van Dieten (1972) 35f., 219–32; Hage (2004); Jankowiak (2009) 62–74. With Kaegi (2000), Jankowiak (2009) 44–48, 72–74, convincingly places within the context of the meeting George of Pisidia, *Against Severus*, which cites the *Tome* of Leo (*kai thateron drai thaterou koinōnias*) and then proceeds to ascribe different activities to the human or divine nature (e.g., *hupnoi men, hōs anthrōpos, hōs Theos palin / phrattei thrasunthen tou thanatou to stoma*); see *Against Severus* 622–49 [PG 92, 1168B–1169B]. Pace MacCoull (1998) and Jankowiak, George cannot therefore be considered a champion of monenergism (or monotheletism).

64. For the Chalcedonian patriarchs of Antioch in the seventh century, elected again after 639, see Brandes (1998c).

65. Theophanes, *Chronicle* A.M. 6121 [de Boor 329f.]; cf. *Greek Life of Maximus* (Recension 2) 8 [PG 90, 76D–77A]. A similar account of monotheletism's origins is preserved in Anastasius of Sinai, *Against the Monotheletes* 1 [Uthemann 56]—the latter, however, placing the meeting at Antioch.

66. Michael the Syrian, *Chronicle* 11.1 [Chabot vol. 4, 403f.].

the meeting at Hierapolis, records (without precise context) a long, dogmatic *libellus* from Athanasius to the emperor, in which the former denounces both the Council of Chalcedon and, in particular, the *Tome* of Leo, making explicit reference to that controversial passage in which the pope distinguished between the human and the divine operations.[67] The account proper of that meeting then recounts how Heraclius, returning from Persia—and having been refused communion at the hands of the anti-Chalcedonian bishop of Edessa, we should note[68]—arrived at Hierapolis and there entered into doctrinal discussions with Athanasius and twelve of his bishops. Those discussions complete, the emperor then demanded that the patriarch give him communion and accept a Chalcedonian confession that recognized the one operation and will. When he refused, the *Chronicle* reports, Heraclius in anger attempted to enforce Chalcedon throughout the empire and began a persecution of miaphysites in Syria. That persecution, we are informed, met with some success, with several prominent monastic communities converting to Chalcedon.[69]

From independent attestation in the *Chronicle of Seert* and in the Armenian version of Michael's *Chronicle*, it does indeed appear that Athanasius refused communion.[70] Nevertheless Michael, in recognizing the conversion of certain monastic communities, also acknowledges that same pattern of mixed domestic acceptance and resistance that we have seen in Armenia and in Persia. If imperial attempts at doctrinal unification achieved somewhat mixed results within anti-Chalcedonian circles, then, the same attempts appear to have aroused some significant disquiet within their Chalcedonian equivalents. In the *Doctrina Patrum* (a late seventh-century or early eighth-century patristic anthology), for example, there survive excerpts from a *Treatise of Bishop Eubulus of Lystra against the*

---

67. Michael the Syrian, *Chronicle* 11.2 [Chabot vol. 4, 405–8].

68. On Heraclius at Edessa see Jankowiak (2009) 60–62.

69. Michael the Syrian, *Chronicle* 11.3 [Chabot vol. 4, 408–10]. See also the brief reference to the meeting in *Anonymous Chronicle to 1234* 103 [Chabot vol. 1, 238], with the same account as Michael the Syrian's *Chronicle* concerning the refusal of communion to Heraclius at Edessa, at *Anonymous Chronicle to 1234* 102 [Chabot vol. 1, 236]. Events at Edessa are also referred to in Agapius, *Universal History* [Vasiliev 467], who calls the recalcitrant bishop Qurrah rather than Isaiah (as in Michael the Syrian and the *Anonymous Chronicle to 1234*). For the subsequent persecution reported in Michael the Syrian's *Chronicle* see also the *Anonymous Chronicle to 1234* 99 [Chabot vol. 1, 236f.].

70. *Pace* Van Dieten (1972) 228–32, favoring its short-lived realization. See *Chronicle of Seert* 88 [Scher 544–45], and for the Armenian version of Michael the Syrian's *Chronicle*, in which Athanasius praises the deposed catholicus Christopher for not joining Ezr's "madness," see Van Dieten (1972) 223f. The account in the *Chronicle of Seert* 88 suggests that Athanasius remained in self-imposed exile in Phoenicia while the emperor was at Mabbug, but Michael the Syrian, *Chronicle* 11.5 [Chabot vol. 4, 414], places Athanasius's burial (and thus perhaps place of permanent exile) in the Monastery of Garoumaye, on which see Jankowiak (2009) 69 n. 221. On the Armenian versions of Michael the Syrian see Haase (1915); Schmidt (1996).

Libellus [*chartēs*] *Delivered to the Most Pious Emperor Heraclius by Athanasius the Pseudo-Bishop of the Severans, When He Was Pressed by Him*.[71] The title thus corroborates later accounts to the effect that Heraclius requested a doctrinal confession from the anti-Chalcedonian patriarch of Antioch but also indicates, furthermore, that the same confession had compelled a Chalcedonian bishop in Asia Minor to respond.

For our purposes, however, the most significant indication of an incipient Chalcedonian resistance comes from the monastic deserts of Palestine. We have encountered the *Pandects* of the Palestinian archimandrite Antiochus Monachus before, since its dedication describes in detail the Bedouin assault on the Judaean monasteries at the time of the Persian invasion. It also contains, however, a wonderful passage that comments on the disruption that rumors of a potential reconciliation with the anti-Chalcedonian patriarch of Antioch had caused and the specter of divine punishment that that same reconciliation seemed once more to represent:[72]

> Our iniquities have multiplied and surpassed our heads, and we were not educated by the Chaldaean scourge, nor did their yoke tame our unpliant necks, but we are emboldened still more in our sins. For the sake of this, and with the assent of God, Satan brought a blow down upon us, a blow able to touch our innards, marrow, and bones. We have heard that a certain forerunner of the Antichrist has come to the East, wanting to obtain the throne of Antioch, and he is called Athanasius, or rather, immortal death, for he espouses the doctrines of Apollinarius, Eutyches, Severus, and Jacob. This report [*akoē*] has caused considerable disturbance [*ou metriōs etaraxe*] among the orthodox inhabitants of the holy city and the monasteries around it.

Antiochus's account appears to have been written after the Persian withdrawal from Palestine, for he speaks of the Persian ("Chaldaean") "scourge" in the past tense. Rumors of Athanasius's aspiration to the Chalcedonian patriarchate of Antioch—an aspiration also alleged in the *Chronicle* of Theophanes—thus circulated after 629, and furthermore, those same rumors caused considerable consternation in Jerusalem, in particular among its monastic communities. Once again, therefore, we catch a precious glimpse of some of the tensions that may have informed the religious scene at Jerusalem in the early 630s, concomitant with Heraclius's restoration of the Cross and the apparent patriarchal interregnum following the death of Modestus, when one Sergius of Joppa, a *locum*

---

71. See *Doctrina Patrum* [Diekamp 141–48]. The question of the latter's date is bound up with that of authorship; for discussion see Winkelmann (2001) 134f. no. 126. The text is an antimonenergist, antimonothelete compilation often attributed to one of the Anastasii, Maximus Confessor's disciples. We should note that the issue of the Christological energies does not appear in the fragment cited, and nothing more is known of Eubulus.

72. Antiochus Monachus, *Pandects* 130 [PG 89:1, 1843B–C].

*tenens* whom opponents regarded as an imperial stooge, began a round of "irregular" consecrations.

The Palestinian interest in the union at Hierapolis is perhaps also evident in a letter that Sophronius composed late in 634, in which he anathematized four living Syrian bishops whose names—John, Sergius, Thomas, and Severus—are conspicuous for their appearance as signatories in Michael's *Chronicle*.[73] It is nevertheless impossible to ascertain if Sophronius and Maximus (perhaps also Moschus) had earlier become aware of imperial maneuvers that aimed at the doctrinal reconciliation of the anti-Chalcedonians—not least, of course, the Antiochene patriarch Athanasius, whom Moschus and Sophronius will have remembered, perhaps even known, as an architect of the anti-Chalcedonian union at Alexandria in 617. But when the new initiative achieved perhaps its most spectacular success at Alexandria, Sophronius, now returned from his exile in the West, was compelled to act against it.

Details of the Alexandrian accord and of Sophronius's resistance to it are again for the most part dependent upon later partisan sources—the writings of his disciple Maximus and documents embedded in the *Acts* of the Sixth Ecumenical Council. The latter include a text that claims to detail the doctrinal basis for a union, dated to June 633, between "the Theodosians" (that is, Egyptian Severans) and Cyrus of Phasis, now acting (like Sergius of Joppa in Palestine) as *topotērētēs* or *locum tenens* of the Chalcedonian throne of Alexandria.[74] The nine chapters of faith contained therein are for the most part standard neo-Chalcedonian fare, including the dual use of "from two natures" and "in two natures."[75] Two such chapters, however, are remarkable for their evident preoccupation with an issue that was not quite so standard—that is, of course, the Christological operations. Thus chapter 3 of this so-called *Pact of Union* states that "If someone does not confess both the sufferings and the miracles of our same and one Lord Jesus Christ, the true God, but [calls them] of one or of the other, let him be anathema"; while chapter 7, the most extensive and perhaps most important of the chapters, defines Christ as "suffering humanly in the flesh like a man but remaining impassible like

---

73. See Sophronius, *Synodical Letter* 2.6.2 [Riedinger 482; repr. Allen (2009) 144]. Cf. Michael the Syrian, *Chronicle* 11.3 [Chabot vol. 4, 409f.]. On this reading Sophronius's John is John bishop of Cyrrhus, Sergius is Sergius of 'Arac(?), Thomas is Thomas of Heraclea, bishop of Mabbug, and Severus is Athanasius's brother Severus, bishop of Samosata. See further Jankowiak (2009) 136–38; Allen (2009) 145 nn. 173–76; and above p. 105 n. 66.

74. I owe this point to Jankowiak (2009) 89f. See *Pact of Union* [Riedinger 594; repr. Allen (2009) 168], referring to the union achieved *para Kourou eleōi theou episkopou ton topon epechontos . . . tou apostolikou thronou tautēs tēs Alexandreōn philochristou poleōs*.

75. See *Pact of Union* 6 [Riedinger 598; repr. Allen (2009) 170]. For an examination of the contents of the *Psēphos* see, e.g., Léthel (1979) 36–49; Ohme (2008) 314f., 332f. The *Synodicon Vetus* 130 alleges an Alexandrian synod to decide the nine chapters, but perhaps assumes such a council from the *Acts of the Sixth Ecumenical Council*, to which the author had access.

God in the sufferings of his own flesh, and the same one Christ and Son effecting both divine and human things 'with one theandric operation' [*energounta ta theoprepē kai anthrōpina "miai theandrikēi energeiai"*], according to Dionysius among the saints."[76] Here, then, the emphasis on the single operation serves to underline the single subject of the Incarnation, assuaging the aforementioned anti-Chalcedonian anxieties—so evident, for example, in the texts of Severus of Antioch—over the perceived Nestorianizing tendencies of the *Tome* of Leo, which risked dividing Christ in distinguishing between his different acts, divine and human, and in presenting as the subject of the operations (at least in its most famous excerpt) the natures themselves rather than the person.[77]

As elsewhere in the restored eastern provinces, the Egyptian union appears to have met with remarkable success. The correspondence contained within the "monenergist dossier" cited at the Sixth Ecumenical Council includes a letter sent from Cyrus to his colleague in Constantinople in which he informed the latter of the achievement: "For I make it clear," he said to Sergius, "that all the clerics of the dogma of those called Theodosians in this Christ-loving city, Alexandria— together also with those who are notable in public and military service, and again those who pay into the public coffers [*tois eis dēmon telousin*]—stretching into the thousands, on the third day of the month of June, in our most holy, catholic church of God, partook of God's spotless mysteries with us."[78] The claim of the letter at first appears extravagant but nevertheless finds some independent attestation in a number of Coptic sources. A *Life* of the anti-Chalcedonian patriarch Benjamin embedded in a later Arabic compilation, the *History of the Patriarchs of Alexandria*, indeed describes how its hero, upon Cyrus's arrival in Egypt, entered into exile in the south, and how "countless numbers" of the orthodox, either through persecution or through blandishment, ascribed to the Chalcedonian faith, including two high-profile bishops, Cyrus of Nikiu and Victor of Fayyūm. The text then proceeds to recount the persecution of those anti-Chalcedonians who refused to recognize the new accord. It concludes: "Heraclius appointed

---

76. *Pact of Union* 7 [Riedinger 598; repr. Allen (2009) 170–72]. It should be noted that in the *Acts of the Lateran Council* [Riedinger 12], Cyrus is stated simply as asserting "one operation." On the citation from Ps.-Dionysius see below p. 212.

77. Cf. also Sergius of Constantinople's response in his *Second Letter to Cyrus* [Riedinger 136–38; repr. Allen (2009) 178]. Sergius cites the *Pact of Union*'s statement that "The same and one Christ operates things befitting God and human things with one operation," apparently omitting the adjective "theandric" (cf. *Pact of Union* [Riedinger 598; repr. Allen (2009) 172]). He then adds, "For every divine and human operation proceeds from one and the same enfleshed God, Word. In accordance with this pious conception the archbishop of Rome, Leo of holy memory, also thought and taught when he said, 'Each form operates with the communion of the other.'"

78. Cyrus of Alexandria, *Second Letter to Sergius* [Riedinger 592; repr. Allen (2009) 174]. Cf. also the claim of Sergius of Constantinople, *First Letter to Honorius* [Riedinger 536–38; repr. Allen (2009) 186].

bishops throughout the land of Egypt, as far as the city of Antinoe, and tried the inhabitants of Egypt with hard trials, and like a ravening wolf devoured the reasonable flock, and was not sated. And this blessed people who were thus persecuted were the Theodosians."[79]

The *History of the Patriarchs of Alexandria*—which in these sections depends on an original Coptic compilation composed around 715[80]—thus points to the remarkable success of the new initiative, which witnessed a reported communion stretching from Alexandria to Antinoe and including at least two converts from high-profile bishoprics. Indeed, Victor of Fayyūm's prominent role in supporting the new accord is confirmed in two further sources: first, a sermon of the patriarch Benjamin *On the Dinner at Cana*, which refers to one "Victor"—no doubt ours—as a famous Judas,[81] and second, the Coptic *Life* of Samuel of Kalamon, which places its subject in the reign of Heraclius and, although composed later, appears to integrate genuine sources of the period.[82] The *Life* records how "Cyrus the Colchian came southward in the land of Egypt, persecuting in every place" and forcing monks to subscribe "to the polluted *Tome* of the impious Leo and take communion from his hands [*nftreusunage hnnefčij*]." "After this," the text claims, Cyrus "came to the region of the Fayyūm with great pretension, and Victor the bishop of the Fayyūm came out to meet him with great joy and the vainglory of this world, and he was glorified until they came to the city of Fayyūm."[83] Cyrus, so the text continues, then realized that if he could convert the monasteries, so too would the rest of the population convert. Thus "he went out to all the monasteries, and the monks he found he forced to subscribe to the *Tome* of Chalcedon and they took communion from his hand."[84]

---

79. *History of the Patriarchs* "Benjamin" [Evetts 490–92]. The success of Cyrus's initiative is confirmed in a subsequent section, which reports the postconquest efforts of Benjamin to reintegrate "the people whom Heraclius, the heretical prince, had led astray" and "the bishops who had denied their faith"; see *History of the Patriarchs* "Benjamin" [Evetts 497f.]. On the extent of the reported communion it is of interest to note that, according to the *Chronicle* of John of Nikiu, the Arab invaders did not encounter fierce doctrinal resistance to Heraclius until they reached Antinoe; see his *Chronicle* 115 [Zotenberg 203]. On the union see also Moorhead (1981).

80. See Den Heijer (1989) 121–24, 142f.

81. See Benjamin, *Sermon on the Feast of Cana* [De Vis 64]. For the same sermon cf. the study of Müller (1968).

82. See Hoyland (1997) 286.

83. Isaac the Presbyter, *Life of Samuel* 9 [Alcock 9].

84. Isaac the Presbyter, *Life of Samuel* 9 [Alcock 9]. Cf. the earlier implication of the submission of Scetis to Cyrus at ibid. 8 [Alcock 7]: "As to the things that happened then in Scetis, we will be silent." We should note, however, that the account of Samuel's persecution at Scetis draws clear inspiration from the Justinianic persecution of Daniel of Scetis as described in the Coptic tale published in Guidi (1900–1901) 535–52; for comment see also Dahlman (2007) 56–58. Zaborowski (2003) 106 points to a further parallel in the *Life* of Apa Longinus.

For our purposes the most extraordinary aspect of this account, indeed of all the accounts of Cyrus's initiative, is its emphasis upon large-scale monastic conversions.[85] Several post-Chalcedonian emperors had, of course, attempted to compromise on anti-Chalcedonian doctrine; and several anti-Chalcedonian patriarchs, including those at Alexandria, had accepted those same compromises. But the success of these imperial initiatives had time and again come up against the intransigence of local monastic communities, which severely limited the doctrinal maneuverability of their respective bishops, whatever the political will on the broader stage. In the 630s, however, various sources point to something quite remarkable: the communion not only of high-profile anti-Chalcedonian bishops with the Chalcedonian patriarch at Alexandria but also of monastic communities. Although Coptic sources would soon remember the late reign of Heraclius as a time of persecution and celebrate those who resisted the emperor's attempts at conversion, those same sources also point to the remarkable success that the new Alexandrian initiative in fact enjoyed within Lower and Middle Egypt.[86]

The Heraclian program of doctrinal reunification, then, was comparable to the triumph over Persia in its ambition, scope, and success. Indeed, it was perhaps that same triumph that served as the ideological prop for the new doctrinal initiative: God had shown the emperor clear favor in his magnificent victories within the temporal plane—How, then, could one challenge his authority within the celestial? Thus, in an explosion of diplomatic activity throughout the early 630s, a series of disparate anti-Chalcedonian churches were brought back into official communion with Constantinople—some of them, at least, on the basis of the monenergist theology developed in both anti-Chalcedonian and neo-Chalcedonian circles in the sixth century. We should not, of course, overstate the success or permanence of the venture, for in those same regions where we can observe official reconciliation we also see evidence of significant domestic resistance. But in the end, the fatal blow to the fragile new consensus came not from the circles of anti-Chalcedonian provincial intransigents, as it had so often to imperial initiatives of the past. It came instead from a Chalcedonian. It came from Sophronius.

---

85. Cf. also *History of the Patriarchs* "Benjamin" [Evetts 497f.].

86. For the sustained success of the venture see also John of Nikiu, *Chronicle* 120 [Zotenberg 212], which reports that upon his return from exile to Alexandria in 641, Cyrus first retreated to a "Church of the Theodosians [*tābodosawyān*]" and then retrieved "the glorious Cross from the monastery of the Theodosians [*dabra tābodosawyān*]." The current translations, of Zotenberg (1883) 454 and Charles (1916) 192f., mask this fact, assuming (incorrectly) that Cyrus as a Chalcedonian patriarch cannot have fraternized with Severans (thus both offer "Tabenessiots"). After the Muslim conquest, however, it appears that both Nikiu and the Fayyūm, at least, returned to the anti-Chalcedonian fold; see Isaac the Presbyter, *Life of Samuel of Kalamon* 30–31; *Book of the Consecration* [Coquin 106, 112, 128].

## SOPHRONIUS THE DISSIDENT

We must not make the mistake of thinking that Sophronius's intervention at Alexandria was somehow akin to the deus-ex-machina political interventions of the monastic past. As the erstwhile advisor to John the Almsgiver—a patriarch whom both Chalcedonians and anti-Chalcedonians appear to have admired—Sophronius was an established figure on the political and religious scene at Alexandria, with significant experience of theological discussion with the anti-Chalcedonian communities in and around the city. It is unsurprising, therefore, that the new union attracted his attention.

In a letter to the Roman pope Honorius embedded in the aforementioned "monenergist dossier," and sent it seems in the final months of 634, the Constantinopolitan patriarch Sergius set out to explain to his correspondent the course of events thus far.[87] Recalling the union with the Theodosians, he described how Sophronius "was in Alexandria at the time and in the company of the aforementioned most holy pope" and how, when he examined the profession of faith that formed the basis of the union, he "opposed and contradicted the chapter on the single operation [*to tēs mias energeias kephalion*], since he thought it right in all instances to declare as doctrine two operations [*duo energeias*] of Christ, our God."[88] Maximus too, who had perhaps now returned eastward and was thus a witness to the scene, would describe the dramatic confrontation of his master with the Alexandrian patriarch: "Therefore the divine and great Sophronius then came to Alexandria," he told his correspondent, "and from the very first reading (for Cyrus had even given to him those nine impious chapters for approval) he let out a great cry of grief and poured forth torrents of tears, fervently begging, beseeching, demanding, spread out on the ground at [Cyrus's] feet, that he proclaim nothing of these things from the pulpit against the universal Church; for he said that these were clearly the impious doctrines of Apollinarius."[89]

Despite the Alexandrian patriarch's reported appeals to accommodation for the sake of communion, Sophronius is now said to have traveled to the imperial

---

87. For the letter Winkelmann (2001) 77f. no. 43. I cannot concur with his date of late 633 or the beginning of 634, for Sergius of Constantinople, *First Letter to Honorius* [Riedinger 538; repr. Allen (2009) 186], mentions the election of Sophronius to the patriarchate, which did not occur until late 634 (eighth indiction). See below p. 231f., with n. 21.

88. Sergius of Constantinople, *First Letter to Honorius* [Riedinger 538; Allen (2009) 186]. It is this same phrase of Dionysius that Sophronius defended in his *Synodical Letter* [Riedinger 456; repr. Allen (2009) 114]. The presence of Sophronius in Alexandria has also been read into Maximus Confessor's *Letters* 13 [PG 91, 533A]. For discussion see Sherwood (1952a) 39f.; Larchet (1998a) 51f.; Boudignon (2004) 16f.

89. Maximus Confessor, *Opuscula* 12 [PG 91, 143C–D]. For the return of Maximus to the East, see above p. 168.

capital to intervene in person with the patriarch Sergius.⁹⁰ In his aforementioned letter to Pope Honorius, Sergius claims that after debating with Sophronius on the Christological operation (or operations) he realized that "from such wrangling the dissensions of heresies always come about" and thus decided "to devote all effort to stopping and cutting short this superfluous war of words [*tēn perittēn tautēn logomachian*]." Thus, the letter claims, in a quite remarkable concession to Sophronius Sergius wrote to the patriarch of Alexandria that he should "no longer in future permit someone to proffer 'one operation' or 'two operations' in Christ, our God, but rather, exactly as the holy and ecumenical synods have handed down, that he should confess that one and the same only-begotten Son, our Lord, Jesus Christ, true God, operated both divine and human things [*energein ta te theia kai ta anthrōpina*], and that every operation, being fitting both for God and for man [*pasan theoprepē kai anthrōpoprepē energeian*], proceeds without division [*adiairetōs*] from one and the same incarnate God, the Word." It was further agreed, Sergius continues, that Sophronius himself "would in future start no discussion concerning the one operation or two operations," and the patriarch provided him with a letter describing the resolution, should others inquire of it.⁹¹ Then, when the emperor himself from Edessa requested that Sergius send to him the aforementioned *libellus* of Menas, the patriarch explained to him the commotion that had occurred and the subsequent agreement to follow the faith of the Fathers: that is, "to confess that the only-begotten Son of God is truly God and man together, that he operates divine and human things, and that from one and the same incarnate God, the Word, as we have said, proceeds every divine and every human operation, without partition and without division. For the God-bearing Leo taught us this explicitly when he said, 'Each nature does [*energei*] what is proper to it in communion with the other.'"⁹² Heraclius, no doubt deflated, appears to have concurred.⁹³

---

90. See Sergius of Constantinople, *First Letter to Honorius* [Riedinger 540; Allen (2009) 186–88]. Sophronius's appeal before Sergius is also referred to in the *Disputation with Pyrrhus* [*PG* 91, 333A–B].

91. Cf. also Pope Honorius, *Second Letter to Sergius* [Riedinger 624; repr. Allen (2009) 208], for a reported papal letter to Sophronius and Cyrus disavowing further discussion on the one or double operation. It does not survive; see Conte (1971) 417 nos. 60 and 61.

92. Sergius of Constantinople, *First Letter to Honorius* [Riedinger 540–46; Allen (2009) 186–92]. For the letter given to Sophronius, which is perhaps equivalent to the *Psēphos* (below), see also Pope Honorius, *First Letter to Sergius* [Riedinger 548; repr. Allen (2009) 194].

93. For Heraclius's apparent agreement see the rather ambiguous statement that concludes Sergius's account in his *First Letter to Honorius* [Riedinger 546; repr. Allen (2009) 192]: "In response to these things we received an all-pious ordinance [*keleusis*] of his all-benign Authority, which contained things befitting his god-guided Serenity." For the documents mentioned within the letter, which with one exception do not survive elsewhere, see Winkelmann (2001) 74–76, nos. 37–39. That exception is the so-called *Psēphos* of Sergius; see below pp. 213–15.

That both emperor and patriarch decided to retreat is, one suspects, testament both to the precarious nature of the theological peace and to Sophronius's considerable reputation. What, however, was the reason for the latter's opposition? The most immediate cause, and that presented in the sources, was his refusal to accept the "one operation" set out in the *Pact of Union*. There is, however, a distinct problem with this explanation alone, for as we have observed above, there was in fact little Chalcedonian and no patristic consensus on the question of the Christological operations. Thus Sergius, in that aforementioned letter to Pope Honorius describing his confrontation with Sophronius at Constantinople, describes how he requested his opponent "to bring forth testimonies of the holy and select Fathers— or rather those whom we all clearly confess as common teachers and whose dogmas the holy churches of God recognize as law—which precisely and in the very words prescribe to speak of two operations in Christ." "This," Sergius then stated, "he was utterly at a loss to do."[94]

Sophronius, it is said elsewhere, would later produce a florilegium of six hundred patristic citations supporting the "two operations."[95] (It does not survive.) But his outright commitment to a developed "two operations" formula at the earliest stage of the crisis, in 633, is far from self-evident. In the *Miracles of Cyrus and John* (ca. 610–14), as we have seen, Sophronius had expressed some ideas and used some biblical quotations that might be used to argue for a commitment to the two operations; and, in Alexandria in the same period if not before, he had perhaps come into contact with the Aristotelian principle sometimes expressed in the writings of Alexandrian philosophers, that operation was a function of nature (so that one operation in effect entailed one nature).[96] At the same time, he may have

---

94. Sergius of Constantinople, *First Letter to Honorius* [Riedinger 540; repr. Allen (2009) 188]. In contrast to the dearth of patristic support for dyenergism, Sergius claims that at Alexandria Cyrus presented to Sophronius "certain testimonies of our holy Fathers where they had spoken of the single operation here and there [*sporadēn*] in certain of their own writings" (*First Letter to Honorius* [Riedinger 538; repr. Allen (2009) 186]). See also Sergius's statement that "The expression 'one operation,' even if it was said by some of the holy Fathers, nevertheless alienates and bewilders the ears of some" (*First Letter to Honorius* [Riedinger 542; repr. Allen (2009) 188–90]). In the same letter he confesses that earlier pronouncements did not have the Christological operations as their immediate context: Sergius of Constantinople, *First Letter to Honorius* [Riedinger 544; repr. Allen (2009) 190]. Cf. also Honorius's statement in response that "neither the Gospel nor the apostolic writings nor synodical judgments" appear to have defined "one operation" or "two operations" (Pope Honorius, *First Letter to Sergius* [Riedinger 554; repr. Allen (2009) 200]).

95. See *Acts of the Lateran Council* [Riedinger 40]. It is perhaps this same dyenergist florilegium that is described in Photius, *Bibliotheca* 231 [Henry vol. 5, 65–67]. See also Conte (1971) 418f. no. 65; Winkelmann (2001) 82f. no.46.

96. On this see Hovorun (2008) 108–11, 150f. On Sophronius's possible association with Stephanus of Alexandria see above p. 63f. For Maximus's association with Alexandrian scholastics see Boudignon (2004) 15.

suspected that the quotation from the Areopagite—speaking of "one theandric operation"—was incorrect or falsified, for the original seems in fact to have posited a "new theandric operation."[97] Indeed, a later text cited at the Lateran Council (649) claimed that Sophronius protested against nothing else within the *Pact of Union* except this very phrase.[98] Sophronius himself, in a letter produced in late 634 or soon after, would make the same point.[99]

It is possible that Sophronius would have recognized the reaction that later Chalcedonians attributed to anti-Chalcedonian contemporaries of the union at Alexandria: "It isn't we who have come into communion with Chalcedon, but rather Chalcedon with us."[100] As the doctrinal disputant of John the Almsgiver, he must have engaged in numerous discussions with Egyptian miaphysites, and in the *Miracles of Cyrus and John* he had characterized them—somewhat hypocritically—as hopelessly intransigent.[101] For Sophronius, therefore, schooled in the Christological arguments and perceived recalcitrance of anti-Chalcedonian communities in Egypt, the recent union may have smacked of doctrinal compromise, an inapposite capitulation to the anti-Chalcedonian cause. We might therefore explain Sophronius's reaction in some preexisting but nevertheless obscure commitment to the doctrine of two operations and the belief that to confess one operation would be to contravene a philosophical or theological axiom.[102]

---

97. Various scholars have pointed out that the reading "new" is corroborated in the fragmentary Severus of Antioch, *To John* 17–22, although it is seldom acknowledged that this survives only in the prodyothelete, prodyenergist *Doctrina Patrum* [Diekamp 309] and is thus suspect; for a comparable attempt to present Severus as a dyenergist see also *Acts of the Lateran Council* [Riedinger 146]. For discussion see, e.g., Rorem and Lamoreaux (1998) 13–15 (noting other phraseology untypical of Severus in the passage); Hovorun (2008) 18–20, 111–16. Ibid. 112 n. 71 cites the Armenian text of Ps.-Dionysius in the *Armenian Version of Dionysius the Areopagite* [Thomson 233] for the reading "new," but this is little more than a translation from John's Greek.

98. See the citation from a "dogmatic tome" of the Constantinopolitan patriarch Pyrrhus in *Acts of the Lateran Council* [Riedinger 152]. Cf. *Acts of the Lateran Council* [Riedinger 142–44, 148]; also *Acts of the Sixth Ecumenical Council* [Riedinger 216, 606–8]. It is also notable that at *Acts of the Lateran Council* [Riedinger 12] Cyrus's support for "one theandric operation" in the *Pact of Union* is caricatured as supporting "one operation." For further references to the Areopagite's text in the course of the monenergist/monothelete crisis see also *Disputation with Pyrrhus* [PG 91, 345C–348C]; Maximus Confessor, *Ambigua to Thomas* 5 and *Opuscula* 7 [PG 91, 84D–85A]; Anastasius the Disciple, *Letter to the Monks of Cagliari* 14.

99. See Sophronius, *Synodical Letter* 2.3.16 [Riedinger 456; Allen (2009) 112–14]. This does not necessarily mean that the original Ps.-Dionysian position was closer to that of the dyenergists; see, e.g., Pelikan (1987) 18–21.

100. Anastasius of Sinai, *Against the Monotheletes* 3.1.63–4; cf. Theophanes, *Chronicle* A.M. 6121.

101. For Sophronius's derogatory statements on the Egyptians as a *dusmetatheton ethnos* see *Miracles* 39 [Marcos 337], with some further venom (perhaps interpolated) in Anastasius Bibliothecarius's Latin at *PG* 87:3, 3574A–B.

102. See Booth (2009) for the suggestion of an intersection between Sophronius's view of sainthood in his *Miracles* and his later Christology. I am now, however, far less confident that Sophronius's

One crucial point must nevertheless be emphasized: whatever the extent of Sophronius's opinions on the question of the Christological operations, and whatever the claims of the participants in the polemic, there was no preexistent Chalcedonian consensus on the matter. Even if he was committed to an a priori notion of the two operations, therefore, it would not have been a contravention of official Chalcedonian doctrine to concede or suppress that same notion and to recognize the alternative, more irenic course. Indeed, although he had challenged the doctrinal basis of the Alexandrian union, it is notable that in Constantinople Sophronius agreed to uphold a principle of doctrinal silence, a principle that he himself would soon abandon and that his disciple Maximus would, after his master's death, often deride in others. Sophronius's opposition, therefore, is best considered not as an organic extension of some developed, preconceived commitment but rather as the formation of a theological position that developed and hardened over time.

We can indeed perceive something of this process in the corpus of Maximus Confessor, who would later in his career come to regret some of his earlier pronouncements on the question of the operations. In the mid-640s, for example, Maximus in *Opuscula* 1 defended his earlier use, in the *Ambigua to John* (ca. late 620s), of the phrase "one operation of God and the saints"—not Christological, of course, but unthinkable in a later context.[103] Indeed, even in the immediate aftermath of the outbreak of the monenergist crisis, Maximus composed an effusive letter to the priest and higoumen Pyrrhus in which he lauded the doctrinal concord that the patriarch Sergius had agreed to with Sophronius and enshrined, it seems, in a document that Maximus calls the *Psēphos*.[104] "What more shall I say to

---

position in the text can be regarded as protodyenergist, although it is nevertheless clear that the debate on sixth-century energies was not limited to Christ but extended also to questions of sainthood; see esp. Eustratius Presbyter, *On the State of Souls after Death*, with Constas (2002) 275. From the later perspective, then, it is possible that Sophronius may have perceived that the divine suppression of the human energy perceived in monenergism not only compromised a Christocentric soteriology but also undermined the full ontology of synergized saintly activity after death. The issue of the saintly and divine wills is later raised in Maximus Confessor's *Opuscula* 1 [PG 91, 24C–28A] and 20 [PG 91, 233A–236A]; *Ambigua to John* 3 [Jeauneau 25f.]; and in the *Disputation with Pyrrhus* [PG 91, 292B–293B].

103. See *Ambigua to John* 3 [Jeauneau 26], "una et sola operatio Dei et dignorum"; cf. *Opuscula* 1 [PG 91, 33A–B]. For their respective dates see Sherwood (1952a) 31f., 53–55. Pace Sherwood (1952a) 37; Larchet (1998b) 24; Winkelmann (2001) 72f. no. 35, I see no reason to accept the contention that Maximus's antimonenergist *Opuscula* 5 was written before the publication of Sergius's *Psēphos*. His earliest antimonenergist text appears to be *Ambigua to Thomas* 5, arguing against the reading "one theandric operation" within the Areopagite (and thus dating to late 633 or after); see Sherwood (1952a) 39.

104. It is safe to assume that this document is summarized in Sergius of Constantinople, *First Letter to Honorius* [Riedinger 542–44; repr. Allen (2009) 188–90], since Sergius's words there are repeated nearly verbatim in the text of the *Ekthesis*, as read out in the *Acts of the Lateran Council* [Riedinger 158–60]. On the question whether this document contained a statement on the wills see below p. 240 n. 58. The theological position of the letter is explored in Carcione (1985a, b).

you, blessed father," he proclaims, "when I see that you have become the begetter [*gennētōr*] of such words as these, through which, as if from some lofty mountain of knowledge, you have made known the *Psēphos* on divine dogmas, which has been brought forth and published, like divine tablets [given] through the new Mediator and great Moses over us and priest of priests, and leader of the divine priesthood in the whole *oikoumenē*?" "This," Maximus continued, "the holy and sole honored Trinity pronounced through the aforementioned archpriest [Sergius] as if through an instrument, and bound the churches to a greater harmony, that they set at naught the widespread innovation in the faith [*tēn peri tēn pistin kainotomian*] that happed in the city of Alexandria."[105] Maximus proceeded to set out his own position on the Christological operations, in striking concordance with the irenic position of Sergius set out within the *Letter to Honorius*. "The *Psēphos* that has been given," he claimed, "has preserved complete the opinion that the God-bearing Fathers transmitted to the holy churches to believe." "For he operated divine things humanly [*sarkikōs*]," Maximus stated during a subsequent excursus on the Christological doctrine, "because [he operated] through the flesh, which is not without share of the natural operation [*phusikēs energeias*]; and [he operated] human things divinely [*theïkōs*], because [it was] according to his volition and free will [*kata thelēsin exousiastikōs*], but he did not accept the experience of human passions according to circumstance. For neither [did he operate] divine things divinely, since he was not naked God; nor human things humanly, since he was not a mere man. For this reason the miracles were not without passion; and the passions were not without miracles. But the former, if I may make so bold, were not passionless; and the latter were manifestly miraculous. And both wonders, because also divine,[106] proceeded from the one and same incarnate God, Word, who in action through both gives faith in the truth of those things from which and that he is. For what is constituted from certain things without confusion in union according to natural combination [*kata sunodon phusikēn*] also maintains unchanged the natures from which it exists, and preserves its component powers undiminished, in the fulfillment of a single deed."[107] Maximus's thought, therefore, here coincided with the part of the *Tome* of Leo that spoke of each nature doing "what is proper to it with the cooperation of the other"; it thus also complemented Sergius's position in the *Psēphos*.[108]

105. Maximus Confessor, *Letters* 19 [*PG* 91, 593B-C].
106. The editor, we should note, here adds *kai anthrōpina* in parentheses [*PG* 91, 593A].
107. Maximus Confessor, *Letters* 19 [*PG* 91, 592D-594B].
108. See Sergius of Constantinople, *First Letter to Honorius* [Riedinger 542–44; repr. Allen (2009) 188–90]. For a comparable statement concerning the operations, dating perhaps to this same period, see Maximus Confessor, *Letters* 15 [*PG* 91, 573B]. The lack of stricter definition, to my mind, situates the same statement in the earlier part of the range of Sherwood (1952a) 40, who gives ca. 634–40 (noting the similarities to the statement within *Letters* 19, "To Pyrrhus").

Although Maximus at no point within that letter referred to the "two operations," he nevertheless requested from his correspondent a clarification of the relevant theological terms that had given rise to the dispute: "But rather I summon you to make clear to me, through your honorable letters and so that I may understand their power when written, the definition of 'operation' [*hē energeia*], and what senses 'operation' has [*kai posachōs hē energeia*], and besides this what *to energēma* is. And which of these do we say in order to differentiate the work [*to ergon*] and the practice [*tēn praxin*]? For I have not yet been able to understand precisely why and how it is necessary to accept speaking and thinking of 'the one operation' [*tēn mian energeian*]."[109] Maximus's etiquette—and the fleeting reference to the "natural operation" of the flesh—seems to disguise a deep suspicion of the monenergist "innovation."[110] But his request for further clarification constitutes a precious witness to the still nascent nature of discussions and moreover indicates a theologian for whom the solution to the question of the Christological operations was far from explicit. Both the outright commitment to the "two operations" formula and the ardent assault upon monenergist doctrine that would characterize his later writings are here conspicuous for their absence.[111]

Indeed, in a theological tract composed about 646–48 and sent to the clerics, monks, and people of Sicily, Maximus was forced in the face of anonymous detractors to defend his earlier position in the letter to Pyrrhus. Therein he reports that his correspondent had sent him "a huge tome" in which he had done Maximus great honor and inquired after his opinion on "one operation" or "two operations." In response, Maximus claimed, he too had shown Pyrrhus great respect, for "the divine Word commands us to love and to bless those who think differently or write against us." "And at the same time my concern," he continued, "was not to exasperate but rather to appease [*homolazein*] the man with praises to him, that he may come to concord with the things that I piously taught, in accordance with the teaching of the holy Fathers. Whence also I confessed thus to have understood, in the letter that I wrote to him, the things that he had written to me, encouraging him in this manner, as I said, and summoning him to assent with the pious word that would effect for him the greatest salvation if he acquiesced and confessed with

---

109. Maximus Confessor, *Letters* 19 [*PG* 91, 596B].

110. As argued in, e.g., Van Dieten (1972) 36f.; Doucet (1983) 65–67; Bausenhart (1992) 113f.; Larchet (1996) 299–302; Bathrellos (2004) 65, 129f.; *contra* Léthel (1979) 59–64. It is important, however, to avoid argumentative extremes: it is incorrect to state that Maximus was not at this stage perturbed at monenergism; but at the same time it cannot be said that he proved "a dyothelite and dyenergist throughout," and here "followed the same lines of the dyoenergite Christology that he would confess consistently for the rest of his life" (Bathrellos [2004] 129f.).

111. For the lack of controversy around the concept *energeia* in Maximus's early work cf. his *Letters* 2 [*PG* 91, 401C–D], where it is "noch kein belasteter Begriff": Winkelmann (2001) 56 no. 16. This is perhaps Maximus's earliest letter; see Sherwood (1952a) 25; Larchet (1998b) 38.

us as we had written—that is, two natural operations of the one and same Christ, God."[112] In this later letter, therefore, Maximus reinterpreted his earlier remarks as if they had been explicitly dyenergist. They had not.

At the same time, the words of praise that he had so lavished on his correspondent were excused as a mere expression of humble Christian love for one's opponents. Pyrrhus, who appears from Maximus's letter to hold a profound interest in the question of the Christological operations, appears once to have been a Palestinian archimandrite: a further indication of the considerable interest of the province's ascetics in the new initiative, as well as the divisions that it caused.[113] At the time of writing, however, it is more probable that he was ensconced within the capital, where he was, according to Nicephorus, *archōn* and higoumen of the monasteries of Chrysopolis and a friend to the patriarch Sergius.[114] Thus, as Marek Jankowiak has pointed out, we have here an intriguing situation: a prominent disciple of Sergius writing to a prominent disciple of Sophronius in an attempt, we must presume, to shore up the new accord between their masters.[115] If the former had perhaps hoped that the latter would abide by the terms of the *Psēphos* and abandon the discussion, then Maximus's response no doubt proved a bitter disappointment.[116]

As we shall see in the subsequent chapter, Pyrrhus would later become Sergius's successor as patriarch of Constantinople and the leading proponent of monotheletism. From the perspective of the 640s, when Maximus answered his Sicilian critics, therefore, his gushing praise for a prominent protomonothelete (and

---

112. Maximus Confessor, *Opuscula* 9 [*PG* 91, 132A–B]. For the date see Sherwood (1952a) 55. Jankowiak (2009) 182f. convincingly identifies the "tome" with that "dogmatic tome" of Pyrrhus read out in *Acts of the Lateran Council* [Riedinger 152], which refers to Sophronius in respectful terms and thus seems to belong to the earliest stages of the conflict.

113. See Pertusi (1958) 14–21; Flusin (1992b) vol. 2, 384–89; also Boudignon (2004) 29f. and (2007) 262–65.

114. Nicephorus, *Chronography* [de Boor 118]; cf. the account of Pyrrhus's election in Nicephorus, *Short History* 26, claiming that Pyrrhus "had lived with Sergius" [Mango 74].

115. Jankowiak (2009) 105.

116. We might suppose that Maximus adopted a somewhat inconsistent position in regard to the *Pact of Union*—if, that is, we situate his *Letters* 13 within the immediate aftermath of June 633, as several scholars do (on the basis, however, of the false identification of the addressee, Peter the Illustrious, with Peter the Dux of Numidia); see, e.g., Sherwood (1952a) 39f.; Larchet (1998a) 51f.; Sahas (2003) 101f.; Jankowiak (2009) 105f. Therein Maximus inveighs against some converted Severans who have apostatized from Chalcedon (*PG* 91, 512B–C) and locates Peter in a place where Sophronius is also (*PG* 91, 533A). It is tempting, therefore, to place the letter in the second half of 633, perhaps before Maximus became aware of his master's recourse to Constantinople, and to presume that the Severans concerned are those recently reconciled to Cyrus. But the lack of localizing references, the chronological difficulties, and the obscurities of the actual career of Peter the Illustrious preclude a proper resolution. At the least, however, the letter must predate Sophronius's election as patriarch in late 634 (since Maximus calls him "Abba").

indeed his predecessor Sergius) and his failure to commit to a more definite position on the question of the two operations must have presented an acute embarrassment.[117] That embarrassment nevertheless reinforces our impression that both Sophronius's and Maximus's opposition was not the simple product of some developed, preformed commitment but rather was a position that evolved in the course of the crisis itself. Indeed, in a compelling section of his monograph Bathrellos has underlined the subtle transformation of Maximus's thought on the operations in the course of his career.[118] Thus in his *Opuscula* 8—which Polycarp Sherwood places around 640—Maximus interpreted those few patristic passages where a theologian had spoken of the "one operation" but also argued that both "one operation" and "two operations" must be understood to protect the Chalcedonian definition: "For he who understands thus and does not embrace both equally and properly, applying the former to the union and the latter to the natural difference, falls either completely into division or in all likelihood into confusion."[119] And again in *Opuscula* 7—which Sherwood places around 642—he repeated the notion that monadic expressions contained within the Fathers, though not supporting monenergism, should nevertheless be embraced for their opposition to division in Christ.[120] As we shall see, this striking stance—in which both "one" and "two" are confessed in order to guard against division and confusion—would in the 650s be adopted at Constantinople, in a desperate plea to restore the Chalcedonian consensus; but at that stage, Maximus and his allies had abandoned the same stance and launched a bitter assault upon those who upheld it. Thus for example in his *Opuscula* 9—composed around 646–48, and the same in which he excused his earlier letter to Pyrrhus—he defended himself against accusations that he had once confessed "three operations" (that is, one at the level of the union and two at the level of nature) and dismissed as erroneous a patristic passage from Heraclianus of Chalcedon that opponents claimed to legitimize the simultaneous expression of "one" and "two."[121]

In order to comprehend in full this transformation it is, of course, necessary to explore the wider ideological imperatives that may have informed it. Indeed, this need becomes all the more pressing once we appreciate that, besides the alternative

---

117. For the date (646–48) see Sherwood (1952a) 55; also Winkelmann (2001) 119f. no. 102. For analysis see also Uthemann (1997) 404–13.

118. Bathrellos (2004) 195–201.

119. Maximus Confessor, *Opuscula* 8 [*PG* 91, 105A], with Bathrellos (2004) 197. For the date see Sherwood (1952a) 43f.; Winkelmann (2001) 93 no. 63.

120. Maximus Confessor, *Opuscula* 7 [*PG* 91, 88B–89D]. Cf. also the apology for Anastasius of Antioch's monenergist phraseology in *Opuscula* 20 [*PG* 91, 229B–233B]; and n. 36 above.

121. Maximus Confessor, *Opuscula* 9 [*PG* 91, 125C–128B]. His detractors claimed that this had occurred in a letter to Marinus, which may refer to either the aforementioned sections of *Opuscula* 7 [*PG* 91, 88B–89B] or *Opuscula* 20 [*PG* 91, 229B–233B]. For the shift in position cf. also below p. 322.

commitment to the phrase "one operation" or "two operations," there seems in fact little consistent theological substance separating the two doctrinal camps. Although, as Hovorun's monograph makes clear, theologians from both sides in the conflict were somewhat inconsistent in their opinions on the operations, both sides were committed to the doctrine of two natures; both sides admitted that a single Christ did both divine and human things; and both sides thought in terms of divine-human ("theandric") acts.[122] The difference appears to have been one of emphasis: the monenergists chose to emphasize the singleness of each of Christ's actions (protecting against Nestorianism), whereas the dyenergists upheld the duality of the natural operations that informed them (protecting against miaphysitism). As Richard Price has concluded in a provocative investigation of the two theologies, "the difference between monenergism and dyenergism seems a matter of terminology rather than of substance."[123]

How, then, can we explain the considerable dissent between the two camps? One emphatic difference between Sophronius and his opponents in Constantinople and Alexandria was a matter less of doctrine than of doctrinal politics.[124] In an important article Heinz Ohme has observed how the Alexandrian *Pact of Union*, Sergius's submission to Sophronius, and the publication of the *Psēphos* are all notable for their (often explicit) expression of the principle of *oikonomia*, or doctrinal accommodation.[125] This accommodation, however, should be considered not only as a simple political machination—political though it no doubt was—but also as the expression of a theological principle present in the Church for centuries and expressed in our period in the writings of Eulogius, Chalcedonian patriarch of Alexandria (580-608). Within the later *Bibliotheca* Photius describes a now lost tract in which Eulogius explores the concept of *oikonomia*, upon which a recent anti-Chalcedonian union of Gaianites and Theodosians had been based. Eulogius distinguishes three situations in which a genuine "accommodation" may be founded (insisting, as a precondition, that the representatives of the patriarchal sees be its arbitrators): first, when the true faith is not harmed (under this heading, he also includes an "opportune accommodation" [*proskairos oikonomia*] designed to allow the true faith to recover its strength when under assault); second, when the faith is orthodox but articulated in different words, even if ill expressed; and third, when certain people ignore a promulgated decree (*ekkēruktos psēphos*)

---

122. See Hovorun (2008) esp. 165.
123. Price (2010) 223. For the skeptical tradition that informs Price's position, regarding monenergism as more verbal than real, see the useful précis of literature in Bathrellos (2004) 66-69.
124. Ohme (2008), arguing that "der monenergetisch-monotheletische Streit—durchaus im Kern!—auch ein Streit um die Anwendungsmöglichkeit und Bedeutung der *oikonomia* in Lehrfragen war" (309). Cf. Hovorun (2008), e.g., 70 for a similar observation. On the concept of *oikonomia* more broadly Dagron (1990).
125. Ohme (2008).

against them, so long as the faith, again, is not harmed.[126] For Eulogius, of course, the anti-Chalcedonian union met none of these conditions, but Sergius of Constantinople and his allies may well have considered monenergist doctrine to have fulfilled one or more. The promulgation of that doctrine, therefore, was not a simple political expedience; it represented the application of an ecumenical principle in which the purpose of union was elevated above differences in regard to words.[127]

In contrast, Sophronius and his allies distinguished themselves in their vociferous opposition to the precise same principle. Thus Sergius's *Letter to Honorius* describes how the Alexandrian patriarch Cyrus, upon Sophronius's hostile reaction to the *Pact of Union*, pleaded with him to accept the initiative, pointing out that the Fathers, "for the sake of gaining salvation of more souls, often appear to use God-pleasing accommodations and agreements [*thearestois oikonomias chrēsamenoi phainontai kai sumbasesi*] and in this did not undermine the exactitude [*akribeia*] of the orthodox dogmas of the Church." Sophronius, however, rejected the notion that the principles of *oikonomia* and *akribeia* were not at odds, and when he repeated his intransigence before the patriarch Sergius, the latter thought it "harsh" (*sklēron*): "For how was it not harsh and most excessively onerous [*sphodra barutaton*]," he explained, "when it was poised to undo and overturn that whole unanimity and unity that had so finely come about in the city of Alexandria and all the provinces under her, which at no point up to now have received even the simple name of our inspired and celebrated father Leo or memorialized the holy and great and ecumenical synod in Chalcedon, but now with bright and loud voice proclaim this in the divine liturgies [*en tais theiais mustagōgiais*]?" Here, then, we are presented with the voice of the doctrinal politician, willing to compromise for the sake of preserving a greater good: that is, a universal union of the faithful.[128]

Throughout these texts Sophronius in contrast appears as a staunch opponent of all attempts at accommodation. (This Andreas Stratos once labeled "senile persistence.")[129] His opposition to such accommodation indeed finds some independent corroboration, for in a letter that Sophronius sent to Arcadius, the archbishop of Cyprus, around this time he set out an explicit statement to that effect.[130] As

---

126. Photius, *Bibliotheca* [Henry vol. 4, 111–13]. For comment see also Ohme (2008) 325–32.
127. For this sympathetic perspective on Sergius's efforts see also Van Dieten (1972) 52f.
128. For *oikonomia*, the *Pact of Union*, and Sergius of Constantinople's *First Letter to Honorius* see also Ohme (2008) 310–13.
129. Stratos (1968–78) vol. 1, 300. The latter's assessment of Maximus is equally damning, accusing him of a "resolute obstinacy" coupled with "monastic and senile stubbornness"; see ibid. vol. 3, 121.
130. The editors date Sophronius's *Letter to Arcadius* to the period of Sophronius's patriarchate, but the internal evidence to that effect is ambiguous; see Albert and Schönborn (1975) 176 n. 48 and 189 n. 4. The absence of charged Christological references, to my mind, situates the letter before the outbreak of the monenergist crisis; cf. Brock (1973) 322 and below p. 239 n. 55. For discussion of the *Letter* see also Conte (1989) 288–91.

Jankowiak has argued, repeated references suggest that Arcadius had assumed a prominent position as a trusted confidant of the emperor and as the arbiter of his irenic policies toward the anti-Chalcedonians: thus when Heraclius issued that imperial decree against the aforementioned Severan Paul in Armenia, it was to Arcadius that the same decree was dispatched, an indication that the exiled bishop Paul had been placed under the archbishop's guardianship;[131] and later, when the anti-Chalcedonian bishop of Edessa refused communion to the emperor, he too is said (in the *Universal History* of Agapius) to have been sent to Cyprus.[132] The immediate issue addressed within the *Letter to Arcadius*—the use of the popular anti-Chalcedonian addition to the Trisagion—can thus be seen to condense a fundamental point of disagreement between two prominent figures on either side of the monenergist debate: that is, the extent to which theological, and indeed liturgical, rigor should be sacrificed for the sake of union.[133]

In the introduction to the extant fragment of the *Letter to Arcadius*, which survives in a sole Syriac manuscript, Sophronius refers to a "recent" development that had seen the "high-placed positions" become "favorable to a certain accommodation": that is, a degree of doctrinal liberalism for the sake of union.[134] Sophronius, however, declares himself opposed to such a principle and proceeds to set out a long statement of Chalcedonian doctrine that, we should note, includes a passing reference to the confusion of Christological activities (*sū'rāye*) that results from a confusion of the natures.[135] It is nevertheless striking that the question of the operations is otherwise absent from the letter as it stands, and although it is possible that Sophronius avoids referring to it in accordance with the terms agreed upon with Sergius late in 633, his future conduct in fact suggests that he was soon more than willing, even after the *Psēphos*, to agitate against the "one operation" formula. I would suggest, therefore, that the relative absence of the debate on operations situates the letter in a period before the crisis had crystallized (and thus before June 633), when Sophronius and his circle were aware of imperial maneuvers aimed to achieve a reconciliation with anti-Chalcedonians but had still to formu-

---

131. See Cyrus of Alexandria, *First Letter to Sergius* [Riedinger 588; repr. Allen (2009) 160]; cf. Sergius of Constantinople, *First Letter to Cyrus* [Riedinger 528; repr. Allen (2009) 164]. This decree cannot have been sent before the beginning of Arcadius's bishopric in 625, at the earliest; see Sodini (1998) 629f.; Winkelmann (2001) 55 no. 14; and above p. 199. For the role of Arcadius see Jankowiak (2009) 36–40, 62, 142, and the words of his successor Sergius below p. 261 n. 138.

132. Agapius, *Universal History* [Vasiliev 467]. Cf. also above p. 203 n. 68.

133. Cf. Jankowiak (2009) 139–42.

134. Sophronius, *Letter to Arcadius* 1 [Albert and Schönborn 188]. *Pace* Winkelmann (2001) 67–69 no. 29 and Jankowiak (2009) 141, the accommodation to which Sophronius refers need not have in view events after his encounter with Sergius. (It may suggest, for example, the union at Mabbug.)

135. Sophronius, *Letter to Arcadius* 32 [Albert and Schönborn 222, with 223 n. 71]; also Winkelmann (2001) 68.

late a doctrinal response. The position that regards Sophronius's silence in the *Letter to Arcadius* as deliberate presupposes a developed position on the operations that he then suppresses. As we have seen, it is possible that at the time of composition no such position existed.

The actual theme of the letter repeats an issue that we have encountered repeatedly in the writings of the Moschan circle: that is, the need to preserve the rites of the Church from heretical intrusion. In their *Life of John the Almsgiver*, as has been said above, Moschus and Sophronius praised the patriarch's efforts in eliminating the theopaschite addition to the Trisagion from the Alexandrian churches (an indication, perhaps, that its use was widespread within Chalcedonian circles), and in the *Letter to Arcadius*, too, Sophronius sets out a detailed theological refutation of that same addition.[136] That Sophronius felt compelled to set out that refutation in correspondence with a prominent Chalcedonian bishop suggests once again that some Chalcedonian clerics, at least, were less anxious over the recognition of controversial formulas than Sophronius and his Palestinian circle, but it also underlines to how remarkable an extent anxieties over liturgical acts, and the preservation of those acts from anti-Chalcedonian pollution, had come to dominate the output of that same circle.

It is therefore of considerable interest to note the distinct sacramental dimension to the reported accords that the emperor and his agents had achieved with the various anti-Chalcedonian communities. Each of the stories that reports an act of union involves the sharing of communion: the emperor is thus said to commune with the Armenian catholicus Ezr; he receives communion twice from the hands of the Nestorian Ishoʻyahb; he demands the eucharist from the anti-Chalcedonian patriarch of Antioch Athanasius; and the unions at Alexandria and elsewhere within Egypt are celebrated in a shared mass. As we have seen throughout the previous chapters, if there was an act most probable to attract the attention of the Moschan circle, it was sharing communion with (perceived) heretics. In the 610s, Sophronius's *Miracles of Cyrus and John* had constructed strict sacramental boundaries between orthodox and heretic, warning against the indiscreet participation of one group in the rites of another; Moschus's *Spiritual Meadow* had then repeated those warnings and regaled its audience with tales of the miraculous punishments that befell those heretics who dared to approach or insult the Chalcedonian host; and now, in the same period, Maximus Confessor had placed the eucharistic rituals at the center of his whole vision for the cosmos—past, present, and future. We should not be surprised, therefore, if reports of an unprecedented program of interconfessional communion raised the suspicions of this same circle.

---

136. Sophronius, *Letter to Arcadius* 2 and 33–54. For Sophronius's concerns over the theopaschite addition see esp. ibid. 33 [Albert and Schönborn 222]. Cf. below p. 239 n. 55.

Within Sophronius's doctrinal dissent, therefore, we also witness the conspicuous consolidation of two further positions: first, that doctrinal precision should not be sacrificed for the sake of union; and second, that the Chalcedonian rites should be preserved from heretical pollutants. Here, then, we have arrived at a far more complex appreciation of Sophronius's protest in Alexandria, a protest in which evolving doctrinal, political, and sacramental perceptions all interwove. Even before the union with the Theodosians, Sophronius had posited a strict sacramental differentiation of orthodox and heretic, and had furthermore expressed both consternation at the inclusion of an anti-Chalcedonian formula within an orthodox rite (the Trisagion) and disillusionment at the recent inclination of the "high-placed positions" toward *oikonomia*. Whatever the extent of his preconceived commitment to the "two operations," therefore, these considerations alone could explain his subsequent decision to elaborate an explicit doctrinal resistance, further deepening his commitment to the principles of doctrinal and liturgical *akribeia*. A theologian who had begun his public career as the doctrinal advisor to a prominent Heraclian appointee, therefore, now set himself on a dramatic collision course with Constantinople.

At some point in the late 620s (on a conventional dating) Maximus replied to a missive of the Constantinopolitan official John Cubicularius, a missive that had put to its recipient a perhaps controversial question: "How is it that God has judged it right that men be ruled by other men?"[137] Maximus replies that the Fall has introduced an unnatural disorder into both man and the entire cosmos. As we cherish this wretched life even amid our sufferings, Maximus states, God has conceived the law of rule over men (*ton tēs basileias tois anthrōpois nomon*) lest we should become "like the fishes of the sea, killing each other without discrimination."[138] He has thus permitted that men, although otherwise equal in nature, be divided into ruler and ruled, in order that in this he may both marshal those who are obedient to the laws of nature and punish those who in their arrogance refuse to acknowledge them, thus maintaining righteousness through reason and fear. For Maximus, therefore, "whichever ruler [*basileus*] endeavors to maintain the law of rule in this way truly is revealed as the lieutenant [*deuteros*] of God upon earth, as a most pious servant of the divine will, who as a righteous heir of rule from God rules also over men."[139] "But," Maximus concludes, "whichever [ruler] has rebutted this law and has deigned to rule for himself, and not for God, will no doubt bring about the opposite of these things. In his tyranny [*turannikōs*] he will shake from

---

137. Maximus Confessor, *Letters* 10 [*PG* 91, 449A-453A, at 449A (as reported question)]. On this letter see also Sahas (2003) 110f.
138. Maximus Confessor, *Letters* 10 [*PG* 91, 452A].
139. Maximus Confessor, *Letters* 10 [*PG* 91, 452D].

himself good men and will set himself far apart from all council and co-rule [*boulēs kai dunasteias*]. Then he will draw to himself the wicked and establish them as the lords of his entire domain. This is the final pit of destruction for both rulers and ruled. Let God provide that we be ruled willingly by him, through the fulfillment of his life-giving Commandments, and that we worthily honor those who rule in his name on earth, as guardians of his divine ordinances."[140]

Maximus's vision of the emperor's temporal role is to some extent traditional. In the pattern of post-Eusebian *Kaiserkritik*, he presents the emperor as a divine vicegerent on earth, a pious ruler whose terrestrial function consists in the maintenance of peace and the elevation of the ruled toward God (though not, we should note, in the espousal of doctrinal diktats). In contrast to most political commentators, however, Maximus also explores the converse of that vision. The ruler who himself neglects to observe God's ordinances cannot also maintain them in his empire; he will gather to himself the wicked and corrupt, and he will drag down all to eternal damnation. The condition of the empire is, therefore, the moral barometer of the emperor himself.[141]

At the time of Heraclius's triumph over Persia, both Maximus and Sophronius had offered a somewhat restrained recognition of the emperor's achievement. If that restraint indicates a certain suspicion over the permanence or even the realization of peace, then such suspicion was soon to be confirmed, as we shall see, in the spectacular conquests of a nascent Islam, which swept over Palestine in the precise same period, almost to the month, when Sophronius began his opposition. This cannot be a coincidence. Although Sophronius and his colleagues avoided the direct condemnation of the emperor throughout the subsequent crisis, ascribing the doctrinal "innovations" of Constantinople to malevolent advisors, there can be little doubt of the association of sin and disaster in their minds.[142] But that sin, which had been and remained the cause of the reversals that now beset the Christian empire, had now assumed a more concrete form: the pernicious doctrine of monenergism, an unwarranted capitulation to the errors of the anti-Chalcedonians.

If the immediate difference over Christological doctrine was also complemented in a fundamental difference over doctrinal and sacramental politics, then we must recognize that the complex ideological intransigence of Sophronius and his allies was assumed within and informed through a broader context. The intellectual apparatus for Sophronius's dissent, as we have seen, had long been in

---

140. Maximus Confessor, *Letters* 10 [*PG* 91, 452D–453A].

141. For discussion of this political philosophy and its relation to the notion of collective sin see Olster (1994) 30–50.

142. For the explicit connection between errant doctrine and disaster see (on the monothelete side) George of Resh'aina, *Life* 23; and (on the dyothelete) Anastasius of Sinai, *Against the Monotheletes* 1.84–112; Theophanes, *Chronicle* A.M. 6121.

formation: the commitment to Chalcedonian doctrine, and frustration with the perceived recalcitrance of anti-Chalcedonian interlocutors; a preference, perhaps, for "two operations" over "one operation"; and the elevation of communion and its attendant rites as the inviolable bedrock of the orthodox Church. But it was, I suggest, the charged political context—as the expansion of the emergent caliphate plunged the Roman empire once more into crisis—that at last forced his hand, precipitating a dangerous public opposition to Constantinopolitan doctrine and thence the further elaboration of the "two operations" position. In hindsight, therefore, the emergence of Sophronius and his allies as the capital's principal antagonists may not seem so surprising. This circle had experienced more than most the effects of imperial failure in the 610s and 620s, and it is thus less remarkable that as Sophronius and his circle hesitated over the emperor's proclaimed restoration, news of his irenic doctrinal initiatives amid and even communion with anti-Chalcedonians, based at least in part upon an untested formula, elicited a critical response from that same circle, given public voice at the precise same moment when divine displeasure once again manifested in Christian reversals in the East.

Sophronius's opposition to monenergism was therefore a multifaceted phenomenon for which we must avoid reductionist explanation. Although that opposition manifested as a doctrinal disagreement, doctrine alone cannot suffice to explain it, for there was no established Chalcedonian position on the Christological operations, and the two sides were, after all, not so distinct. Rather than recognize the considerable achievement of Sergius and his allies in bringing various anti-Chalcedonian groups into communion with Chalcedon and renegotiate such preconceived notions as he and his circle may have held on the "two operations," Sophronius instead launched a full campaign to dissolve the union and must be considered as a principal cause of its undoing. Recognizing that Sophronius's doctrinal dissent was informed through a wider ideological and material context is not to present doctrinal issues as irrelevant to the Palestinian opposition, a mere rhetorical gloss on other, more "real" motivations. It is instead to acknowledge that perceptions of doctrinal difference, and the subsequent elaboration of the theological opposition, were informed as much through the political context as through the doctrinal imperatives of the past. In the same manner as the development and promotion of Chalcedonian monenergism cannot be separated from its political implications or purpose, nor either can the articulation of its doctrinal opposite be separated from the evolving political vision of those Palestinian intellectuals who developed it. Little wonder, then, that as the crisis of empire deepened, so too did the circle's dissent.

6

# Jerusalem and Rome at the Dawn of the Caliphate

The Heraclian regime's grand claims to political and cosmological restoration were soon to prove premature, and therein no doubt was confirmed the evident reticence of Sophronius and Maximus toward its claims to restoration. While memories of the Persian occupation still remained fresh, the armies of the nascent caliphate swept over the former territories of the Eastern Roman empire. In the same period, an increasing number of Eastern ascetics once again traveled westward, to North Africa and Rome. As Constantinople then struggled to realize doctrinal consensus among Chalcedonian communities through abrogating monenergism and promoting instead monotheletism (the doctrine of Christ's single will), from his eastern bolthole Maximus began to expand upon a doctrine of the two wills. Through sustained diplomatic pressure applied at Rome, he and his circle had ensured successive popes' support for that same doctrine, and in this new context Maximus began to reinforce long-standing Roman claims to ecclesial preeminence. Here, then, Moschus's earlier celebration of the Roman popes within the *Spiritual Meadow*, and Maximus's previous recognition of clerical privilege within the *Mystagogy*, assumed a more far-reaching and polemical aspect, both as a further tool in the galvanization of the Roman-Palestinian alliance and as a potent weapon in the doctrinal conflict with the capital.

Since the Council of Chalcedon, the churches of New and Old Rome had found themselves in frequent conflict. For our purposes, two phenomena are worth emphasizing. First of all, and in particular before the establishment of permanent papal *apocrisiarii* in the capital, in that same period Rome had on occasion availed herself of Eastern monastic communities in conflicts with the capital, communities that had, for their part, appealed to Roman intervention as a means of circumventing their theoretical subordination to the Eastern patriarchates. Thus, for example, during the Acacian schism, the Constantinopolitan monks of the Acoemetae—who had perhaps benefited from an influx of Roman monies,[1] and who had disposed themselves as effective Roman agents in the capital[2]—attached a provocative papal deposition to the Constantinopolitan patriarch's robe during the mass, an act that several expiated with their lives.[3] In the end, Rome sacrificed the Acoemetae on the altar of ecclesiastical politics, condemning them as Nestorians when the popes sought reunion with the capital;[4] but their dramatic actions nevertheless underline the continued willingness of Rome to deploy Eastern ascetics to its political advantage, as well as the potential for Eastern ascetics to make recourse to Rome when confronted with Eastern patriarchal opposition.

It was during this same schism with the capital that our second phenomenon occurred, for it was then that a Roman pope first articulated a developed claim to the separation of the powers of Church and state. Such a separation was also, of course, articulated in the East, but there the emphasis was placed upon the coinherence of the two institutions: that is, in Gilbert Dagron's useful formulation, the separation of functions rather than of powers (so that there was no concomitant denial of the emperor's elevated religious status in, for example, presiding over the empire, convoking and enforcing councils, or appointing bishops).[5] Now, in the West, it was articulated with more force, and with the potential for a far more pervasive limitation of imperial power. When still a deacon, Gelasius in a letter to the

---

1. See *Life of Marcellus Acoemeta* 12, which reports in the mid-fifth century the beneficence of a rich recruit whose father was a member of the "senate of the Romans." On the *Life* see Dagron (1968). See also in the same period the establishment of the Studius monastery and its population with members of the Acoemetae, at Theodorus Lector, *Tripartite History* [Hansen 108]; Theophanes, *Chronicle* A.M. 5955. Later tradition remembered him as a Roman; see Nicephorus Callistus, *Ecclesiastical History* 15.23 [*PG* 147, 68B] and the *Life of Theodore the Studite (A)* 29 [*PG* 99, 145A]. On the foundation of Studius see also Hatlie (2007) 106–10. For the history of the community more generally see Baguenard (1988) 219–40.

2. See Evagrius Scholasticus, *Ecclesiastical History* 3.19-21.

3. See ibid. 3.18; Liberatus, *Breviarium* 18; cf. Theophanes, *Chronicle* A.M. 5980. For a discussion of the various sources see Baguenard (1988) 222–24; and for the complexities of the affair Blaudeau (2006) 481–85. For desperate imperial attempts to curb the considerable influence of the Acoemetae—and, it appears, their economic independence also—see the fascinating account at Ps.-Zachariah of Mytilene, *Chronicle* 7.7–8, which recalls the removal of the monks' imperial stipend and the cutting off of their water supply. For the general context see Frend (1976).

4. See Pope John II, *Letter to Illustrious Men*, in *Acts of the Fifth Ecumenical Council* [Schwartz vol. 2, 210]: "Aquimatos vero, qui se monachos dicunt, qui Nestoriani evidenter apparuerunt, Romana etiam eos damnat ecclesia." Cf. also Pope John II, *Letter to Justinian*, in *Codex Justinianus* 1.1.8 esp. 21, 31–33. For the subsequent decline of the community see Hatlie (2002) 217f.; cf. idem (2007) 141f.

5. See Dagron (1996) 312f. For the tradition East and West prior to Acacius see Dvornik (1966) 746–98. The classic example is Justinian, *Novels* 6, preface [Schoell and Kroll 35f.]. Cf. Justinian, *Novels* 7 [Schoell and Kroll 53] and 137 [Schoell and Kroll 695]; with Dvornik (1966) 815–39.

emperor Zeno called him "a son, not a hierarch, of the Church" ("filius est, non praesul Ecclesiae"), reminding him that "in religious matters, it becomes him not to teach but to learn." "For," Gelasius continued, "God wished the administration of the Church to belong to priests, and not to the powers of the world."[6] In a subsequent (and famous) letter to Zeno's successor Anastasius, Gelasius as pope formulated this same discrimination in greater depth. "There are two things, august emperor, by which this world is principally ruled," he proclaimed, "the sacred authority of the priests ["auctoritas sacrata pontificum"] and imperial power ["regalis potestas"]." Gelasius then continued to point to the emperor's submission to the eucharist, and potential exclusion from it, as evidence of the distinction, while recognizing that priests, for their part, live within the God-given empire and are obedient to its (secular) laws.[7]

On its own, there was little novel in Gelasius's pronouncement (except, perhaps, the legalistic distinction of *auctoritas* and *potestas*). Nevertheless, it is significant for three reasons: first, because it expressed Western anxieties over the emperor's religious status that would deepen in the coming decades (in particular, during the Three Chapters crisis); second, because it pointed to the potential of Christians removed from the "orthodox" empire—in this case, through the Ostrogothic takeover—to reconceptualize the relationship of Church and state (in particular, we should note, with reference to the extrication of the Church's sacramental system from the secular sphere); and third, because it formed a significant weapon within the rhetorical arsenal of later popes, complementing existing claims to papal preeminence over matters of the faith (and in the end forming the papal thesis of the "two powers"). For centuries, the Roman Church had a claim to special status within the Church on apostolic (association with Peter and Paul), historical (the arbitration, for example, of the teachings of Paul of Samosata), and canonical grounds (the recognition of its preeminence at the councils of Constantinople and Chalcedon). But from the time of Pope Leo, such claims had also assumed a more patent theological dimension: that is, in a far more vociferous emphasis on the biblical promise of Christ to Saint Peter, and on the pope's status as the successor to, and representative of, the head of the apostles.[8] Unlike in the East, therefore, Gelasius's separation of the secular and sacred spheres formed the basis of an ecclesiological vision that conceived not of those spheres' coinherence but rather of their incoherence. It thus complemented a conception of the pope as the preeminent

---

6. Pope Gelasius, *Letters* 1 [Thiel 292f.].

7. Pope Gelasius, *Letters* 12 [Thiel 350f.]; cf. also, on Melchizedek as "emperor-*cum*-priest," Pope Gelasius, *Tractates* IV [Thiel 567f.]. For comment on both passages see, e.g., Dvornik (1966) 799–809; Dagron (1996) 309–11. For Gelasius and his pontificate Ullmann (1981), and ibid. 162–216 on his ecclesiological stance in respect of the East.

8. See, e.g., Ullmann (1960) and (1981) 61–87; Wessel (2008) 285–97; Neil (2009) 39–44.

power within the Church, and at the same time threatened to relegate the special religious significance to which emperors aspired.[9]

If in the late fifth and sixth centuries these two phenomena—the Roman reception of disenfranchised Eastern ascetics and the papal articulation of an ecclesiological model alien to Eastern realities—had proved nothing more than a consistent irritant in the Eastern capital, then in the course of the monenergist and monothelete crises studied here both were to manifest with far greater, more menacing force. As the Muslims extended their remarkable series of victories in both East and West, the emperor and the Constantinopolitan patriarch were confronted with a doctrinal alliance that in its unification of Italian bishops and Palestinian ascetics stretched across the Mediterranean, lending to both parties the pretense of ecumenicism. At the same time, under Maximus's leadership, the Palestinians within that alliance had begun to propagate ideas that recognized long-standing claims to papal preeminence within the Church and that would in the near future challenge the established relationship of Church and state in undermining the sacerdotal aspirations of the imperial office. In leading and conceiving that dissent, Maximus drew upon the same ecclesiological vision that he, Moschus, and Sophronius had developed during previous decades; but now that same vision was turned to more subversive ends, as the ideological underpinning for the doctrinal dissidence launched against Constantinople.

## SOPHRONIUS THE PATRIARCH

In 2002 Stefan Heid published two recensions of a remarkable spiritual tale associated with Sophronius as patriarch of Jerusalem: recension A of that tale purports to be "about Sophronius archbishop of Jerusalem," whereas recension B instead claims to be from the pen "of Sophronius, our sacred father, archbishop of Jerusalem." The subsequent vignette records how a pious man once died and "the patriarch" wanted to inter him under "the Great Church" but there uncovered twenty bodies. In both tales, these are said to be priests (*hiereis*), but since they are also described as "brothers" (*adelphoi*), we are perhaps encouraged to consider them also as monks. Ignorant of the reason for their presence there, the patriarch and his clerics supplicate God to uncover the cause, at which point a miracle prompts one of the bodies to announce them as those who, distracted through terrestrial concerns, disparaged or neglected "the office of the church" (*tēn akolouthian tēs ekklēsias*) and were as a result excommunicated. The patriarch then asks the length of their neglect of the office, and when the corpse replies, "Twenty years," he and

---

9. For the divergence of Western and Eastern ecclesiologies and its effects in this period see Dvornik (1964) 33–72. For the papal perspective (up to Justinian) see also idem (1966) 809–15; for papal-Constantinopolitan relations in the sixth century Sotinel (1992) and (2005).

his clerics petition God on their behalf, and at once the corpses are released from "the chain" of condemnation. "And so we here also, brothers," concludes recension A, "who are members of the Church of the entire inhabited earth, let us not disparage the whole office of the Church, so that we may find mercy into eternity." (Recension B, we should note, develops into a sermonette on the liturgical hours that comprise that "office" and the liturgical obligations of different Christians).[10]

Whether or not this tale can indeed be considered a genuine text of Sophronius, or whether he is indeed "the patriarch" described, need not detain us here.[11] For our purposes, what is remarkable is Sophronius's association with a tale that recapitulates the precise same concern that we have seen to be so conspicuous within his circle: that is, the integration of ascetic practice within the broader rhythms of liturgical life. It is, therefore, all the more remarkable that there exists another text associated with both Sophronius and Moschus, again concerning the monastic performance of liturgical rites.[12] Embedded in the eleventh-century *Hermeneia* of Nicon, and entitled *Narration of the Abbots John and Sophronius*, the text dates from the seventh or eighth century.[13] It stages a conversation on the Liturgy of the Hours between the eponymous pair and one Nilus of Sinai, and it is concerned above all with the differences between the monastic and cathedral offices. Therein Moschus and Sophronius express their surprise that Nilus does not include within his office certain hymns, but the latter responds that these are the preserve of "psalmists, readers, deacons, and priests, and those who have received ordination."[14] Like the Areopagite, he offers a view of the Church in which each ecclesial rank has a defined role and inveighs against monks who appropriate the privileges of clerics (even when a priest is absent). "Why do we make ourselves shepherds," he asks his interlocutors, "when we are sheep? Why do we become the head when we are feet? Why do we undertake to be generals, when we are ranked among the soldiers?"[15] Instead, Nilus insists, monks should preserve tradition, offering prayers to God and reading from the Bible, and not presuming to usurp

---

10. See Heid (2002), situating the tale within a wider context of contemporary stories concerning the ecclesiastical power to bind and loose. For the interrelation of the recensions see ibid. 156, 159f.

11. *Pace* Heid, ibid. 156–59, rehearsing the various options for the tale's setting (Antioch, Jerusalem, Constantinople) but suggesting that the context is in fact "the Great Church" at the capital, that Sophronius is indeed the author, having composed it during his sojourn there in 634, and that the anonymous patriarch is Sergius, having been subjected to *damnatio memoriae*. The position is speculative, and the precise authorship and context must remain obscure.

12. For this coincidence cf. ibid. 160.

13. For the text see Longo (1965–66), with discussion of dating and authorship at 236–38. For further comment see Taft (1986) 198–200, 274–76 and (2000); Patrich (1995) 237–39; Frøyshov (2000) 235f.

14. *Narration of Abbots John and Sophronius* 2–4 [Longo 253–55].

15. *Narration of Abbots John and Sophronius* 4–5. Ibid. 7 offers the biblical example of Ozia, who presumed to usurp the functions of the priesthood and was struck with leprosy as punishment [2 Chron. 26].

the role of clerics. "For," he continues, "day and night angels stand inseparably at the altar, and they know him who sings psalms in vainglory, arrogance, and ostentation.... For they recognize those who approach piously, with fear and affection and temperance, constraining themselves toward the purification of the mind, conscience, and heart from shameful thoughts and bad ideas.... And if we are not such, why do we appropriate the role of priests?"[16] The monk, he concludes, should not make the church or cell into a stage.[17]

Again, we need not concern ourselves with the question of whether "Moschus and Sophronius" are in fact the authors of this text (which is improbable). What is important for our purposes is that here—as in Heid's aforementioned spiritual tale—the names of Moschus and Sophronius have become associated with evident tensions between ascetic and ecclesial practice. The concern here, of course, is liturgical rather than sacramental—and the context is the heightened assimilation of monastic and ecclesial liturgies realized above all in the Sabaitic office in Palestine. The Nilus narrative nevertheless recapitulates an issue that runs parallel to ascetic reticence toward participation in the eucharist: that is, a wider concern at the intrusion of ecclesial rituals, and in particular the singing of psalms, within the life of the ascetic (especially, the anchorite or semianchorite).[18] It is striking, therefore, that here Moschus and Sophronius are represented as the agents of the opposite imperative: that is, the liturgical integration of monastic and ecclesial practice. As we have seen in Moschus's *Spiritual Meadow*—and shall again see in the patriarchal sermons of Sophronius—that same imperative, in its eucharistic dimension, indeed pervades the pair's output. It was an emphasis that progressed hand in hand with the ever-deepening crisis of the Eastern Roman state and the imperial Chalcedonian Church.

For historians of the monenergist and monothelete theological controversies, for the most part interested in its intellectual dimension, it is all too easy to forget that the opening salvos of the crisis occurred coterminously with the dramatic expansion of Islam within and from Arabia. Toward the end of his life the prophet Muhammad had demonstrated a significant interest in the conquest of the Levant, and in the late 620s several Islamic raiding parties had pressed upon the provinces of the Roman East. Late in 633—and thus simultaneously with the promulgation of Sergius's *Psēphos*—the first caliph, Abū Bakr, had launched a more ambitious campaign, and in February 634 Muslim soldiers defeated a Roman force near Gaza, leaving rural Palestine open to their advance.[19]

16. *Narration of Abbots John and Sophronius* 8–11 [Longo 260–64].
17. *Narration of Abbots John and Sophronius* 13.
18. See Frøyshov (2000) 234f.
19. For these early campaigns see the critical reconstruction of Howard-Johnston (2010) 373f., 465f.; also F.M. Donner (1981) 111–48; Kaegi (1992) 88–111. For the defeat at Gaza see *Anonymous Chronicle to 724* [Brooks 147]; Theophanes, *Chronicle* A.M. 6124; Michael the Syrian, *Chronicle* 11.4;

It is impossible to ascertain at what stage Moschus, Sophronius, and Maximus became aware of these initial Islamic successes—attempts to read a reference to Muslim expansion into Maximus's *Letters* 8, written in 632, do not convince.[20] Although for the crucial months between the *Pact of Union* and the losses in southern Palestine we cannot evaluate the extent of the circle's awareness of the Muslim invaders' victories over Roman forces—and with them the dramatic unraveling of the Heraclian ideological edifice—I would nevertheless suggest that it was no coincidence that Heraclius's program of doctrinal reunion came undone at the precise same time that his program of political reunion, with all its claims of cosmological renewal, was shown to be vapid. If, as was suggested above, success on the terrestrial plane provided the ideological prop for the doctrinal campaign—in underlining the divine favor in which the emperor was held—then reversals within the same plane had the opposite implication. As Maximus had made clear in his earlier *Letters* 10, the condition of the empire was the moral measure of the emperor, and from this perspective Heraclius must have appeared a mortal sinner. It was the Muslim success, therefore, that in the end confirmed the gathering suspicions of Sophronius and his circle—who had languished in the West for so much of Heraclius's reign, and who pointed to sin as the cause of disaster—as to the heretical nature of the emperor's doctrinal initiatives and prompted their public resistance to them.

After securing the dramatic volte-face of Sergius on the "one operation" formula, Sophronius appears to have traveled to Rome and there to have collected the corpse of his mentor, Moschus. According to the biographical prologue attached to the *Spiritual Meadow*—of which Sophronius is the most probable author—when Moschus was about to die he summoned his "beloved disciple" to him and, having handed over the *Meadow,* he instructed him not to leave his remains in Rome but to take them to be interred on Sinai or, if "barbarian" disorder prevented that, at the coenobium of Theodosius, near Jerusalem. Then Sophronius, along with twelve of his co-disciples, took John's remains to the East, and reaching Ascalon, and realizing that "the tyrannical insurrection of those called Hagarenes" prevented the passage to Sinai, came to Jerusalem "at the beginning of the eighth

---

*Anonymous Chronicle to 1234* 108; Agapius, *Universal History* [Vasiliev 454, 468–69]; with Hoyland (2011) 93f. It is possible that this Muslim victory is identified with the battle of Ajnadayn described in Arab sources; see the authorities collected in Caetani (1912–23) vol. 1, 148. It should be noted that Shoemaker (2012a) came to my attention too late to be given proper consideration here.

20. For the curious passage see Maximus Confessor, *Letters* 8 [*PG* 91, 444A], which refers to "the many bites of the wolves of Arabia: that is to say, of the West [*toutesti tōn Dusmōn*]" as part of a pastoral metaphor rather than referring to a real situation. Hence the later reference within the same letter to actual, as opposed to metaphorical, *barbaroi* (*phobos barbarōn aisthētōn*) [*PG* 91, 445A]. For those scholars who nevertheless wish to read it as evidence for a Muslim threat in 632: see, e.g., Kaegi (2003) 218 (confusing Maximus's *Letters* 8 and 14); Boudignon (2004) 18–20. Hoyland (1997) 77 n. 75 and Jankowiak (2009) 109 n. 355 offer the correct reading.

indiction": that is, in September 634.²¹ Thus, between intervening on the *Pact of Union* in June 633 and interring Moschus in September 634, Sophronius had traveled from Alexandria via Constantinople to Rome, and thence eastward to Jerusalem. Enrica Follieri, in supporting her case that Moschus died in Constantinople rather than in Rome, suggested that this vigorous itinerary was impossible,²² but as Andrew Louth has noted in an important rebuttal, it is in fact entirely feasible, especially if Sophronius traveled by sea.²³

At Jerusalem, the biographical prologue to the *Spiritual Meadow* reports, Sophronius found "in the *xenodochium*" the higoumen of Theodosius, George the Priest, and having revealed to him his master's wishes, he and the monks of Theodosius whom he found in the town, along with the aforementioned co-disciples of Moschus, transported the latter's remains and placed them in the coenobium's resting place, "having spent the remaining time in this monastery" (*ton hupoloipon chronon en autēi tēi monēi dianusas*). What "the remaining time" signifies is

---

21. *Prologue to the Spiritual Meadow* [Usener 92f.]. For various reasons the date of September 634 is to be preferred to the alternative, September 619 (of which the most prominent supporter is Schönborn [1972] 69–72): first, the mention at *Prologue to the Spiritual Meadow* 55 of the "tyrannical insurrection of those called Hagarenes" (*tēn turannikēn epanastasin tōn legomenōn Agarēnōn*) [Usener 93] preventing the passage from Ascalon to Sinai, most obviously read as a reference to the Muslim incursion into southern Palestine; second, John Moschus's reported coauthorship of a *Life of John the Almsgiver*, which included the patriarch's death in 620 (see the information at *Epitome of the Life of John the Almsgiver* 16); third, the reference to the African prefecture of George at John Moschus, *Spiritual Meadow* 196, a tenure that began in the late 620s (see above p. 110); and fourth, a further reference within the *Prologue to the Spiritual Meadow* to the "superior of the great monastery of our sainted Father Theodosius, George the Presbyter" (58f.), seemingly that same George, archimandrite of Theodosius, mentioned in the correspondence of Pope Martin. (See Pope Martin, *Letter to George of Theodosius*.) The weight of evidence thus points to the later date. We should also note that the evidence of the *Prologue to the Spiritual Meadow* precludes Sophronius's election as patriarch late in 633 or early in 634, as in Schönborn (1972) 85.

22. Follieri (1988) 19–23, citing Eutychius, *Annals (Alexandrian Recension)* 31 [Breydy 134], which indeed claims that Sophronius arrived in Palestine from Constantinople. Eutychius's narrative of this period is, however, notoriously muddled in its details and sequencing, and it is by far preferable to prioritize the evidence of the *Prologue to the Spiritual Meadow*.

23. Louth (1998). A problem nevertheless remains in supposing that Sophronius traveled to Rome to meet with Moschus upon his deathbed, for Pope Honorius in the *First Letter to Sergius* (winter 634/5) knows of Sophronius's imminent election but is somewhat hostile to him and does not seem to know the man himself (the implication also of comparison between the Roman and Constantinopolitan versions of Sophronius's *Synodical Letter*); for the former see Sansterre (1983) vol. 2, 112f. n. 65; for the latter R. Riedinger (1982a). Unless Moschus's remains were carried with Sophronius and interred in Palestine some length of time after his actual death—which would allow greater chronological flexibility—we must assume either that Sophronius and Pope Honorius simply did not meet, or that each (perhaps through mutual dislike or suspicion) dissembled in order to disguise his acquaintance with the other, or else that later editors have altered Pope Honorius's letter in order to protect Sophronius's reputation from association with a prominent monothelete.

unclear, although it perhaps indicates a simple moratorium between arrival in Jerusalem and the actual burial.[24] (Hence the aorist participle rather than the present.) Nevertheless, one feature of the passage is striking: the monks of Theodosius, including their higoumen George, seem to have been present not in the coenobium itself, but rather in Jerusalem.[25] The reason, no doubt, was the presence of Muslim armies in Palestine, which now threatened Jerusalem itself.

The precise circumstances in which the aged monk Sophronius was elevated to the patriarchal throne of Jerusalem are obscure.[26] In his aforementioned *Letter to Honorius*, Sergius of Constantinople, when he first mentioned Sophronius in connection with his intervention at Alexandria, added "who now has been elevated to the throne of Jerusalem, as we have learned from simple rumor alone [*ex akoēs kai monēs*], for we have until now not yet received his customary synodical."[27] As we have seen, for the period between the death of Modestus and Sophronius's succession, later sources point to "irregular" consecrations carried out at the hands of a *locum tenens*, elected through "secular power."[28] That *locum tenens*, Sergius of Joppa, was perhaps now dead or deposed, although it should be noted that later sources also refer to irregular consecrations that occurred during the patriarchate of Sophronius.[29] It appears, therefore,

---

24. For different interpretations see, e.g., Vailhé (1902) 384f., "the rest of his life," and Schönborn (1972) 71 n. 64, "the rest of the time" (both placing the return of Moschus's remains in 619). "The remainder of the year"—as in Chadwick (1974) 53—seems excluded by Sophronius's election as patriarch before Christmas, when he delivered his famous oration *On the Nativity*; see below n. 64. Jankowiak (2009) 113 suggests "the remainder of the time" before Sophronius's election.

25. On George, who appears in other texts of the period, see also n. 21 above.

26. For the identification of the Sophronius of John Moschus's *Spiritual Meadow* and Sophronius the Patriarch see Vailhé (1902) and (1903); Schönborn (1972) 239–42; Déroche (1995) 31–36. To the latter arguments I would add the observation of striking similarities in theme, theology, and vocabulary between the *Prologue* to Sophronius Sophista's *Miracles of Cyrus and John* 11–13 [Bringel 32–36] and Sophronius of Jerusalem's sermon *On Saints Peter and Paul* 1–4 [*PG* 87:3, 3356A–60C]. As an impediment to that identification some scholars have pointed to the conspicuous silence of the *Prologue to the Spiritual Meadow* and Leontius of Neapolis over Sophronius's later elevation to the patriarchate. For the *Prologue to the Spiritual Meadow* see above p. 108 n. 82; for Leontius see, e.g., Chadwick (1974) 51, who suggests that Leontius "simply did not realise the identity of biographer and patriarch"; also Follieri (1988) 26 n. 121. But an obvious explanation for the silence presents itself: Sophronius's patriarchate was later associated with antimonenergist, and thus also anti-imperial, dissidence, and its overt celebration in a context of official monotheletism might have invited censure; for this suggestion see Déroche (1995) 33; cf. Jankowiak (2009) 112f.

27. Sergius of Constantinople, *First Letter to Honorius* [Riedinger 538; repr. Allen (2009) 186]. Cf. Pope Honorius's response in the *First Letter to Sergius* [Riedinger 548; repr. Allen (2009) 194], also referring to Sophronius's election. *Pace* Winkelmann (2001) 77–80 nos. 43 and 44, the references require that the letters be dated to late 634 or early 635 and not earlier in the year as he suggests there.

28. See *Acts of the Lateran Council* [Riedinger 46].

29. Pope Martin, *Letter to John of Philadelphia* [*PL* 87, 159A–B]. Cf. also idem, *Letter to Pantaleon* [*PL* 87, 172B–D] and above p. 187.

that Sophronius's election, even if it represented the definitive conclusion of the patriarchal interregnum that had occurred after the death of Modestus, did not put an end to the interfactional conflict that had informed it.[30] Indeed, the author of the Syriac *Life of Maximus*, who describes himself as a bishop and disciple of Sophronius, was nevertheless an opponent of his doctrine.[31]

In the *Synodical Letter* that Sophronius circulated to Sergius of Constantinople and Honorius of Rome subsequent to his election, he stated that the patriarchate had come upon him "through the great compulsion and force of the God-loving clerics and pious monks and faithful laymen, all the citizens of this holy city of Christ, our God, who forced me by hand and acted upon me tyrannically . . . with what judgments I do not know or understand."[32] Whatever the extent of clerical, monastic, and popular approval for Sophronius's elevation to the patriarchal throne—the *nolo episcopari*, along with claims to universal assent, are of course standard rhetorical stances for bishops-elect—those who aided that same elevation cannot have been ignorant of his recent status as the principal antagonist of the emperor's doctrinal initiatives. Whereas following the death of Modestus the religious establishment of Jerusalem had been content, it appears, at least to tolerate the *locum tenens* Sergius of Joppa, whom critics regarded as an imperial stooge (and thus, we must imagine, as a supporter of the emperor's doctrinal program), now elements within that same establishment ensured the accession to the patriarchate of a celebrated opponent of Constantinopolitan doctrine.[33] It was, no doubt, a controversial choice.[34]

We must nevertheless assume that Sophronius's election occurred with imperial approval.[35] But if Heraclius and Sergius hoped that the aged ascetic would now adhere to the terms of the *Psēphos* and disregard the discussion on the energies, both would soon be disappointed. In his *Synodical Letter* Sophronius disregarded those terms to present a robust defense of the "two operations," even if he avoided

---

30. For discussion of the monenergist/monothelete party in Palestine see esp. Schönborn (1972) 85–89; Flusin (1992b) vol. 2, 359–62; Levy-Rubin (2001) 291–98.

31. See esp. George of Resh'aina, *Life* 5–6, attributing Sophronius's doctrinal position to the influence of Maximus.

32. Sophronius, *Synodical Letter* 2.1.5 [Riedinger 414; repr. Allen (2009) 70]. As Sophronius was not in communion with Cyrus, and the patriarchate of Antioch remained vacant, he sent it only to Sergius and Honorius. On the differences between the two letters and the telling adaptations made in later recensions, see R. Riedinger (1982a), (1984), and (1994); also Conte (1971) 415f. no. 58; Allen (2009) 63f.

33. This, we should note, is the reason given in Eutychius, *Annals (Alexandrian Recension)* 31 [Breydy 134f.]. For a further potential context for Sophronius's election see the report of an earthquake in Palestine, which Michael the Syrian, *Chronicle* 11.4, dates precisely to September 634: i.e., in the very same month as Sophronius's arrival. For the same (undated) cf. Theophanes, *Chronicle* A.M. 6124; Agapius, *Universal History* [Vasiliev 454, 469].

34. Cf. Schönborn (1972) 83–89; Van Dieten (1972) 37f.; Allen (2009) 20, 34.

35. So also Brandes (2003) 106.

the explicit phrase.[36] In his Christological profession, Sophronius acknowledged that Christ was both one and two: one in terms of hypostasis and of person, and two in terms of nature and of natural properties. "Hence the same one," he continued, "remaining one Christ and Son and only-begotten, is seen to be undivided in both natures, and performs [*eirgazeto*] the deeds of both natural essences according to the essential quality or natural property that is present in both." If he had a single nature, Sophronius states, he would not have performed the deeds of each nature perfectly: "For when did Godhead, which has no share in a body, perform the deeds of a body naturally, or when did a body, devoid of God, operate actions that are known to be essentially of Godhead?"[37]

Thus Christ, "being one and both in the same—that is, both God and human being—truly performed [*edra*] what belongs to each nature, operating [*energōn*] what was done according to one or the other, the same [operating] divine acts as God and human acts as a human, and because of this the same does both divine and human things ... and no other performed the miracles, and no other produced human things and suffered the passions ... but the one and same Christ and Son, who performed divine and human things according to one or the other." Sophronius then returned to that passage of the *Tome* of Leo that we have encountered so often above: "For just as in Christ each nature preserves its property intact [*anellipōs*], thus also each form operates [*energei*] in communion with the other what is proper to it: with the Word effecting what is of the Word, in manifest communion with the body, and with the body completing what is of the body, with the Word, of course, communing in the act [*praxis*] with it."[38]

Like Leo, Sophronius explicitly presents operation (*energeia*) as a property of nature (so that two natures demand two operations): "We know that each operation of each nature—I mean the essential and natural and correspondent [operation]—proceeds indivisibly from each essence and nature according to the innate natural and essential quality, and the indivisible and simultaneously unconfused cooperation [*sunergeia*] of the other essence that it brings with it. For this it is that differentiates between the operations [*tōn energeiōn poiei to diaphoron*] in Christ, just as also the existence of the natures [differentiates] the natures. For divinity and humanity are not the same according to the property that is naturally present in each, even if they came together with each other inexpressibly into one hypostasis, and were composed into one person without confusion. ... And because of this they neither have the same operation indistinguishably from each other after the

---

36. Cf. *Synodicon Vetus* 131 (reporting a synod on the basis of Sophronius's *Synodical Letter* as embedded in the *Acts of the Sixth Ecumenical Council*).

37. Sophronius, *Synodical Letter* 2.3.7 [Riedinger 440–42; repr. Allen (2009) 96–98].

38. Sophronius, *Synodical Letter* 2.3.8 [Riedinger 442; repr. Allen (2009) 98]. It should be noted that Hovorun (2008) 138 here misreads the imperfect verb *edra* in the edition as the noun *hedra*.

natural and unconfused union that is the true and hypostatic, nor do we speak of one and a single operation of them [*mian kai monēn autōn tēn energeian*], nor of one that is essential and natural and completely indistinguishable, lest also we drive them together into one essence and one nature."[39] (We note the explicit condemnation of "one operation.")

Sophronius now adds a significant complication to his position in distinguishing the kind of actions that Christ performed and ascribing them to either nature (or to both). Thus growth, hunger, thirst, fatigue, walking, suffering, and the like—these all demonstrated his willing and salvific condescension to the experiences of human nature, "for when he wished he gave to his human nature the occasion to operate and suffer what was proper to it [*kairon energein kai paschein ta idia*]."[40] To be contrasted with these human actions, Sophronius claims, are "the miraculous and the marvelous, and the procession of wondrous deeds": that is, conception without seed, the transformation of water into wine, the healing of the sick, the banishment of demons, resurrection, and so on. These were "confessedly witnesses of the divine essence and nature of God's Word, even if they were worked [*enērgeito*] through the flesh and body and not performed without the rationally ensouled flesh."[41] The *Synodical Letter* thus proceeds to claim that divine acts were performed according to the divine nature, and that human acts were performed according to the human nature.[42] There is, however, still a third kind of action that Sophronius wishes to distinguish, "a kind of middle rank" (*mesēn tina taxin*), "the so-called new and theandric operation, which is not one but heterogeneous and differentiated."[43]

Sophronius thus repeated the ambiguities contained within the famous formula from the *Tome* of Leo: although he upheld the principle of the *communicatio operationum,* and acknowledged that some operations were theandric, it nevertheless appears that he could also conceive of purely divine and purely human operations.[44] At the same time, he departed from Leo's formula—though not, it should be said, from Leo's broader thought within the *Tome*—in attributing operation both to the natures and to the person of the Logos.[45] Indeed, he defended this position as a

---

39. Sophronius, *Synodical Letter* 2.3.10 [Riedinger 444–46; repr. Allen (2009) 102].
40. Sophronius, *Synodical Letter* 2.3.12–13 [Riedinger 448–50; repr. Allen (2009) 104–6].
41. Sophronius, *Synodical Letter* 2.3.14 [Riedinger 452–54; repr. Allen (2009) 108–10].
42. Sophronius, *Synodical Letter* 2.3.15 [Riedinger 454–56; repr. Allen (2009) 110–12].
43. Sophronius, *Synodical Letter* 2.3.16 [Riedinger 456; repr. Allen (2009) 112–14]. For discussion of Sophronius's use of "new theandric operation" see also above p. 211f. It should be noted that there is a variation in four manuscripts, which read *koinēn* rather than *kainēn* [Riedinger 456]; see also Allen and Neil (2002) 11 n. 33.
44. For comment see Hovorun (2008) 120–22, although his claim that Sophronius distinguishes Christ's action according to a grammatical metaphor (active, middle, and passive) disrupts the text and is not proper to it. In this threefold distinction Sophronius repeats the position adopted by John of Scythopolis when commenting on Ps.-Dionysius's fourth epistle at *PG* 4, 536A.
45. See Bathrellos (2004) 179 with nn. 17 and 18.

guard against Nestorianism: "Even if we teach two forms operating in communion [*duo tas koinōs energousas morphas*], each according to its natural property, still we say that one and the same Son and Christ it was who naturally worked both the lofty and the lowly [*ton ta hupsēla kai ptōcha phusikōs ergazomenon*] according to the natural and essential quality of each of his two natures."[46] As Demetrios Bathrellos has observed with reference to this position, "it seems that Sophronius treads a middle way between identifying (only) the natures as subjects of the actions and identifying (only) the person as such, without yet explaining how we are to distinguish between the two on that score."[47]

Thus, whereas in 633 Sophronius had agreed with Sergius to remain silent on the contested doctrine, in 634 he set out a position that proved somewhat ambiguous in its concept of the Christological operations but nevertheless unequivocal in its refutation of the "one operation" formula.[48] At the same time, he added to his Christological profession a long heresiological catalogue that included the condemnation of the protagonists within two prominent ecclesial discussions: first, the union at Alexandria in 617 between the Antiochene and the Alexandrian anti-Chalcedonians (which Sophronius himself perhaps witnessed), and second, that attempted union at Mabbug between Athanasius the Camel Driver and the emperor Heraclius.[49] As Marek Jankowiak has underlined, therefore, Sophronius's *Letter* constituted an assault both on the "one operation" formula of Constantinople and at the same time the spirit of accommodation and ecumenicism that underpinned it.[50] Little wonder, then, that Sergius refused it.[51]

Other sources indeed support the notion that Sophronius continued to defend the principle of doctrinal exactitude (*akribeia*) and thus to agitate against the Constantinopolitan position, even after the publication of Sergius's *Psēphos*. According to the *Acts* of the Roman council that convened to condemn monotheletism in 649—to which we shall return below—during the council's second session one

---

46. Sophronius, *Synodical Letter* 2.3.8–9 [Riedinger 444; repr. Allen (2009) 98–100].

47. Bathrellos (2004) 179f. Hovorun (2008) 138–42 argues that both for Leo and the dyenergists/dyotheletes there is "a hierarchy within the subject of the activities. The person of Christ appears to be a primary subject, whereas the natures are secondary." Hovorun includes Maximus within this (esp. 142f., nn. 255 and 256), but cf. Bathrellos (2004) 181–85. The latter regards Maximus as resolving this ambiguity in always presenting the person of the Logos as the subject of the two operations. See also Bausenhart (1992) 168–71.

48. For analysis of the doctrinal content of Sophronius's *Synodical Letter* cf. Schönborn (1972) 209–24; Allen (2009) 44–46.

49. See above p. 105 n. 66 and p. 205 n. 73.

50. Jankowiak (2009) 138.

51. See *Acts of the Sixth Ecumenical Council* [Riedinger 398]: *ta sunodika Sōphroniou... mē prosdochthenta de para tou autou Sergiou*. Jankowiak (2009) 144 suggests that Honorius also refused to recognize Sophronius's letter.

Stephen of Dora, a Palestinian bishop and disciple of Sophronius, submitted a petition to the council in which he described the "wild waves" (*kumata agria*) that were crashing upon the orthodox faith in the East as successive patriarchs of Constantinople continued to disseminate the Christological doctrines of the one operation and one will. He recalled how the late patriarch of Jerusalem Sophronius had dispatched him to Rome in order to inform the pope of the dangerous doctrinal innovations threatening the faith, first binding him in a solemn oath at the site of Christ's crucifixion. "And so go quickly from one end of the earth to the other [Sap. 8:1]," Sophronius is reported to have said, "until you come to the apostolic throne, where are the foundations [*krēpides*] of pious dogmas, and make known to the all-sacred men there—not once, not twice, but again and again—all the things that have been set in motion here for sake of exactitude [*di' akribeias*]. And do not cease from vigorously exhorting and begging them, until out of apostolic wisdom they bring their judgment to a victorious end and pronounce a final, canonical refutation of the alien dogmas."[52]

On the basis of Stephen's account within the Lateran *Acts* it is impossible to ascertain the precise date of his Roman mission. If accurate, however, the account indicates once again that as patriarch Sophronius—despite his nominal adherence to Sergius's *Psēphos*—continued to agitate against his Eastern counterparts, and furthermore that he exerted especial diplomatic pressure upon the Roman pope, pressure that aimed, we must assume, to gain full acceptance of the "two operations" formula. Indeed, it is notable that although Pope Honorius, in his *First Letter to Sergius*—dispatched soon after Sophronius's election—spoke of the new patriarch in rather dismissive terms and supported the position of Sergius's *Psēphos* both in disallowing discussion of the operations and in asserting that Christ was the agent of both the divine and the human acts, in his *Second Letter to Sergius*, dispatched after the reception of Sophronius's *Synodical Letter*, he shifted his position. While maintaining that "one Christ and Lord operates in both natures" (the position of the *Psēphos*), he also demanded the confession that "both natures are united in Christ in natural union, operating and effective with the communion of the other" (the position of Leo's *Tome*). Thus, he claimed, "we should not define or proclaim one or two operations, but instead of the one operation of which some speak, we should in truth confess the one Christ Lord operating [*energounta*] in both natures; and instead of two operations—with the expression 'double operation' excluded—people should pronounce with us two natures ... each operating its respective things [*energousas ta idia*]"—a Christological position that is far closer to that of Sophronius's *Synodical Letter*. The extant excerpt then concludes with the pope's statement that, "We have in particular instructed those whom our

---

52. *Acts of the Sixth Ecumenical Council* [Riedinger 40–42]. On Stephen of Dora see below pp. 269, 273, 295f.; also *PmbZ* "Stephanos" 6906; Winkelmann (2001) 267f.

aforementioned brother and fellow bishop Sophronius sent to us, so that he not in future keep on pronouncing the expression 'two operations,' which they wholly announced that the aforesaid man would do, if indeed Cyrus our brother and fellow bishop distance himself from speaking the phrase 'one operation.'"[53] Sophronius's emissaries—among whom, perhaps, we should place Stephen of Dora—thus failed to convince the pope to support his position; but a subtle alteration in Honorius's stance perhaps indicates that their supplications had not been entirely in vain.

Sophronius's sustained resistance to monenergism was soon to result in a quasi-ecumenical council. This council—at which the patriarch was silenced—would have been effaced from the historical record, however, if it were not for the survival of George of Resh'aina's Syriac *Life of Maximus*.[54] Therein George alleges that as patriarch Sophronius, under the pernicious influence of Maximus, sent a letter to Arcadius of Cyprus (the same archbishop with whom he had earlier corresponded on the question of the theopaschite addition to the Trisagion) to request that he convene a council to discuss the recent doctrinal dispute.[55] Arcadius complied, and soon—most probably in the first half of 636 and thus coterminous, as we shall see, with the final battle for control of the Near East—forty-six delegates gathered on Cyprus for a council.[56] Among those delegates were representatives of the four active patriarchal thrones: Cyrus of Alexandria with five of his bishops, the Roman

---

53. Pope Honorius, *Second Letter to Sergius* [Riedinger 624; repr. Allen (2009) 208]. Cf., however, later in the same letter, the statement that we should profess "one Christ Lord, who operates both divine and human things in both natures" (closer again to the earlier position). For the apparent shift in emphasis nevertheless see the observations of Schönborn (1972) 91f.; Bathrellos (2004) 180f.

54. There is a possible allusion to the council in Maximus Confessor, *Opuscula* 12 [*PG* 91, 142B].

55. See George of Resh'aina, *Life* 7-8 [Brock 305f. trans. 315], where Maximus reminds Sophronius of a letter in which "Arcadius the archbishop of Cyprus showed you contempt" and then Sophronius writes to Arcadius requesting a general council. Because of the limited Christological content of Sophronius's *Letter to Arcadius*, along with Brock (1973) 322 and Jankowiak (2009) 142f., I would associate the letter in which Arcadius showed Sophronius contempt with a lost response to it rather than thinking of the *Letter to Arcadius* itself as a fragment of the invitation to convene the council; *pace* Albert and Schönborn (1978) 170-75; followed by Winkelmann (2001) 69 no. 30. George of Resh'aina, *Life* 10, makes it appear that Sophronius was patriarch not only at the time of the Cypriot council, to which he takes some of his bishops, but also at the time of writing, when he writes through a notary and a deacon. It should also be noted that ibid. 9 claims that Maximus, at the time of the Cypriot council, was agitating also against the theopaschite addition to the Trisagion, confirming its status as an adjunct to the immediate Christological issue; see above p. 221. For its reappearance in the controversy see also Sophronius, *On the Annunciation* [*PG* 87:3, 3221D-3224B]; Anastasius of Sinai, *Hodegos* 12.1; the extracts from the *Anagnosticon* of Constantine of Ḥarran published in Van Roey (1972) 143f.; and the analysis of Michael the *Syrian, Chronicle* 11.20 and BL Oriental 8606 (the manuscript containing Sophronius's *Letter to Arcadius*) in Tannous (2006) 14-21.

56. For the date see Jankowiak (2009) 146-49, who also detects in Pope Honorius's *Second Letter to Sergius* [Riedinger 624; repr. Allen (2009) 208] the pope's intention to convene a council (145).

deacon Gaius, the Constantinopolitan archdeacon Peter, and several bishops from Palestine, not least Sophronius and George, the author of the Syriac *Life*. (Maximus himself, according to George, was fearful of attending in person and instead sent his disciple, the aforementioned Anastasius.) A heated discussion ensued, but when participants failed to reach an agreement, "the doctrine of Maximus" was sent to the emperor for assessment, who composed an edict in which he repudiated the doctrine and ordered all those who upheld it to be deposed.

As Jankowiak has argued in his recent doctoral thesis, this edict appears to be none other than the famous *Ekthesis*, a document that repeated (nearly verbatim) the *Psēphos*'s suppression of discussion of the operations and promoted the notion of the single will.[57] The pope Honorius had first suggested an explicit monothelete formula in his *First Letter to Sergius* (ca. 634/5), in response to the statement of his correspondent that "it is impossible for two identical wills [*thelēmata*] to subsist at the same time and in one and the same subject" (perhaps, in fact, a quotation from the *Psēphos*).[58] Therein the pope had approved of Sergius's suppression of Sophronius's "new quests for words"—instead claiming, in a new twist within the argument, that Christ's operations were neither one nor two but manifold—and furthermore added that "we confess one will of the Lord, Jesus Christ," thus perhaps prompting the official recognition of the same formula in the *Ekthesis* (rather than the neutral and uncontroversial disavowal of two opposed wills).[59] Sophronius, isolated from the other patriarchs, and at the receiving end of both a quasi-ecumenical referral and imperial condemnation, appears to have agreed once again to uphold the principle of doctrinal silence.[60]

---

57. The text of the *Ekthesis* is given at *Acts of the Lateran Council* [Riedinger 156–62] (with the document's full title in the Latin). On its identification with the "edict" of Cyprus see Jankowiak (2009) 149–60, *contra* Brock (1973) 323f., who associates it with the *Psēphos* (but notes the problems with that identification).

58. Sergius of Constantinople, *First Letter to Honorius* [Riedinger 542; repr. Allen (2009) 190]. The *Psēphos* is summarized ibid. [Riedinger 542–44; repr. Allen (2009) 188–90], the words of which are repeated nearly verbatim in the text of the *Ekthesis*, as read out in the *Acts of the Lateran Council* [Riedinger 158–60]. It appears that Sergius's position within the *Letter to Honorius* on the impossibility of two contrary wills in Christ—which is also repeated in the reported text of the *Ekthesis*, but with the addition of an explicit statement as to "one will"—was included in the *Psēphos* itself, as suggested in Sherwood (1952a) 38f. and supported in *Disputation with Pyrrhus* [PG 91, 305A]. Van Dieten (1972) 33f. n. 111 (with 47f. n. 161) argues that Maximus's failure to mention the "one will" in his letter to Pyrrhus precludes any such statement in the document, but it is also possible that a statement on the will—and in particular on the impossibility of two contrary wills—was not at this stage considered problematic. Cf. Bathrellos (2004) 72f. n. 63, suggesting that Maximus's silence may be explained by "diplomatic reasons." For a useful comparison of the *Psēphos* and *Ekthesis* see Murphy and Sherwood (1973) 306–8.

59. Honorius, *First Letter to Sergius* [Riedinger 548–58; repr. Allen (2009) 194–204]. For Honorius's unique position on the operations here see Hovorun (2008) 119f.

60. As implied in George of Resh'aina, *Life* 15–16, with the claim that the "four" patriarchs recognized the imperial edict (perhaps excluding Antioch, where the Chalcedonian throne still was vacant).

Although he may well have perceived the renewed suppression of discussion on the energies as an effective stalemate and determined in private to continue the diplomatic pressure now (or soon to be) applied through Stephen at Rome, his apparent recognition of the *Ekthesis* would later prove a cause of acute discomfort for his allies—hence, we must suppose, the pervasive and for the most part successful attempt later to expunge the Cyprus synod from orthodox memory.[61]

## JERUSALEM FROM ROMAN TO ISLAMIC RULE

Although Sophronius seems in the end to have bowed to the collective will of the other patriarchs, the brief period between Sergius's *Psēphos* in 633 and the Cypriot council in 636 witnessed a distinct hardening of doctrinal attitude on his part. That hardening of attitude is no doubt to be explained in one simple fact: the presence of the armies of Islam within Palestine. In the conclusion to the *Synodical Letter*, Sophronius referred to this threat and to his hope that the emperor, God willing, might rise up to remove it, showing care, in a letter destined for the capital, to reinforce a rhetoric of imperial restoration: the presence of the "Saracens" within Roman lands was the product of divine punishment for sin (and not of imperial misdeeds); and God, nevertheless, might be appeased and grant to the emperor victories over his enemies.[62] Sophronius, therefore, had not abandoned the notion of the pious Christian empire guided under pious Christian rulers, but given his outspoken opposition to the Constantinopolitan initiative of reconciliation with anti-Chalcedonians, one must wonder if he considered Heraclius capable of reversing the political disasters that had unfolded in the wake of his trumpeted program of doctrinal rapprochement.[63]

Sophronius's hopes for imperial restoration, if real, were nevertheless soon to fade. When the patriarch delivered his sermon *On the Nativity* on 25 December

---

See also the title to the document preserved in the Latin *Acts of the Lateran Council* [Riedinger 157], stating that "cum multa satisfactione et gratia exciperunt patriarchi‹cis› cum sedibus praesules." The problem is noted in Hovorun (2008) 74, suggesting Sergius of Joppa was the signatory—however, he could never have been called a patriarch.

61. For this important revision see esp. Jankowiak (2009) 150–62, arguing convincingly that the later dating of the *Ekthesis* to the twelfth indiction [638/9] (in, e.g., *Acts of the Lateran Council* [Riedinger 12]) attempts to dissociate it from Sophronius and the Cypriot synod. He points also to the chronological inconsistencies within the letter of Cyrus describing his receipt of a copy of the *Ekthesis* from the general Eustathius, at *Acts of the Lateran Council* [Riedinger 172]. For further chronological indications that the *Ekthesis* predated 638/9 see also below nn. 133 and 136. On Sophronius's apparent acceptance of the "one will" formula within the *Ekthesis*, see also below p. 264f.

62. Sophronius, *Synodical Letter* 2.7.3 [Riedinger 490–92; repr. Allen (2009) 152–54].

63. For comment on this passage cf. Olster (1994) 101.

634,[64] the Muslims were in effective control of Jerusalem's hinterland, and in August 636 their armies followed up a previous triumph in the field and inflicted a final, crushing defeat upon the Romans, either at the Yarmuk or (according to James Howard-Johnston's recent revision) between Damascus and Emesa.[65] According to the famous but perhaps fictional account contained within Arabic sources—and within the *Chronicle* of Theophilus of Edessa—Jerusalem itself surrendered when the inhabitants demanded to negotiate with the caliph himself, and the patriarch Sophronius then came to terms with 'Umar in person.[66] Although the capitulation of Jerusalem itself was of course a momentous historical event, it is nevertheless difficult to date with precision. The earliest Arabic sources offer various dates in the

---

64. Sophronius's sermon *On the Nativity* is securely dated, since the title refers to the fact that the sermon was delivered on a Sunday (*en hagiai kuriakēi* [Usener 501]). Christmas Day fell on a Sunday in 634.

65. The derivatives of Theophilus of Edessa describe two Roman defeats, one under Theodore, Heraclius's brother, in the region of Damascus and Emesa (see Theophanes, *Chronicle* A.M. 6125; Michael the Syrian, *Chronicle* 11.5; *Anonymous Chronicle to 1234* 109; Agapius, *Universal History* [Vasiliev 454, 469]); and another under the sacellarius Theodore at the Yarmuk (Theophanes, *Chronicle* A.M. 6126; Michael the Syrian, *Chronicle* 11.6; *Anonymous Chronicle to 1234* 110; Agapius, *Universal History* [Vasiliev 453, 470]). It is traditional to regard the latter as the second and more serious conflict, but Howard-Johnston (2010) esp. 211–13, 373f., associates the battle of the Yarmuk with the defeat of the emperor's brother and the more decisive battle between Emesa and Damascus with that under the sacellarius—as at Nicephorus, *Short History* 20; *Khuzistan Chronicle* [Guidi 37]. For the battle of the Yarmuk in Arab sources see Caetani (1912–23) vol. 1, 179f. It is also presented as the decisive conflict in *Anonymous Chronicle to 819* [Chabot 11] (dated here to August 636); *Anonymous Chronicle to 741* 16; *Fragment on the Arab Conquest* [Brooks 60]. The final two sources locate the battle at Gabitha, near Bostra, as also at Michael the Syrian, *Chronicle* 11.6; *Chronicle of Zuqnin* [Chabot vol. 2, 150]. But Theophanes, *Chronicle* A.M. 6121, 6125, distinguishes it from the Yarmuk and associates Gabitha with the defeat of Theodore, the emperor's brother. It seems clear that there were two Roman defeats in close geographical and chronological proximity, both under different generals called Theodore; hence the considerable confusion in the sources. The defeat of Heraclius's brother T'ēodos is also referred to in Ps.-Sebēos, *History* 42. See also the useful notes in Hoyland (2011) 96–103; also Kaegi (1992) 112–46.

66. For the various Islamic accounts see Caetani (1905–26) vol. 3, 932–50, and (1912–23) vol. 1, 200f.; for the derivatives of Theophilus see Hoyland (2011) 114–17. For the same encounter of caliph and patriarch see also *Chronicle of Seert* 104 [Scher 623f.] and Eutychius, *Annals (Alexandrian Recension)* [Breydy 139–41]. Busse (1986) argues that Jerusalem was in fact surrendered to 'Amr ibn al-'Āṣ and that the caliph's visit was later invented for narrative and ideological purposes (and somehow adopted by Theophilus); see also Howard-Johnston (2010) 380f. On the basis of the Arab sources Al-Tel (2003) 117–69 defends the historicity of 'Umar's visit as the culmination of 'Amr's campaign within Palestine. His position perhaps finds some confirmation in the *Passion of the Sixty Martyrs*, in which the main commander in the region is *Ambrus* (as per the Greek *Ambros*), who is perhaps subordinate to a separate *ammiras* (emir) at Jerusalem. Guillou (1957) 399 suggests this *ammiras* designates the caliph 'Umar, although the identification is challenged in Woods (2003b) 142f. For the narrative dynamics of the encounter of 'Umar and Sophronius as represented in the sources see Sahas (2006). I regret that I have not had access to Hendrickx (2002).

range 15–17 A.H.: that is, 636–38.[67] In similar vein, the collection of sources that here depend upon the lost *Chronicle* of Theophilus of Edessa claim that Jerusalem capitulated in Heraclius's twenty-sixth year (October 635 to September 636) but add various conflicting dates in the range 634–37.[68] Theophanes, however, adds the extra detail that the surrender occurred after a two-year siege and in Sophronius's third year as patriarch. If we accept this part of Theophanes' evidence—which complements the contention of Arabic sources that the capitulation of Jerusalem occurred after Yarmuk—then the surrender should be placed late in 636 or early in 637, a date that accords well with the recent conclusion of Othman Ismael Al-Tel (based on an exacting review of the Arabic sources) that it occurred in March or April 637.[69] But this date, it must be emphasized, is far from secure.

We should note that Theophanes makes the further claim that Sophronius died in the same year as the city's surrender.[70] Two sources nevertheless describe him as active in the period of Muslim rule. First, a tale within the *Georgian Appendix to the Spiritual Meadow*—placed after another recording how in front of Sophronius as patriarch a miracle revealed the fornication of a deacon when he approached the altar in sin—reports that when the "impious Saracens" entered into Jerusalem "with the permission of God to castigate our sins" and seized certain men to build a place of worship, "which is called a *mijgit'a* [mosque]," "Saint Sophronius" upbraided a deacon who had sold his services as a sculptor.[71] (He also, we should note, comes unstuck at the altar, having failed to defer to his clerical superior.) And second, two Latin recensions of the *Passion of the Sixty Martyrs of Gaza* describe Sophronius

---

67. See Al-Tel (2003) 110f.

68. See Theophanes, *Chronicle* A.M. 6127 (A.D. 635/6); Michael the Syrian, *Chronicle* 11.7, adding the extra dates A.G. 948 (A.D. 636/7) and 15 A.H. (A.D. 636/7); Agapius, *Universal History* [Vasiliev 454, 475]; *Anonymous Chronicle to 1234* 120 [Chabot vol. 1, 254f.], adding the dates A.G. 946 (A.D. 634/5) and 15 A.H. (A.D. 636/7). With Hoyland (1997) 64 n. 31 I am doubtful of the claim of Busse (1984) that Jerusalem surrendered to the Muslims on 2 April 635, recently supported by Howard-Johnston (2010) 381 with n. 69, and thence in Sarris (2011) 269. Busse's dating is complex and ingenious but based on several questionable suppositions (see esp. 113f.), not least that a Seleucid-era date given in the *Anonymous Chronicle to 1234* is to be preferred to other, contradictory dates given not only in that text but in other non-Arab sources (when it finds no other support). On the basis of the *Passion of the Sixty Martyrs* Guillou (1957) esp. 400f. argues that Jerusalem must have fallen by December 637, but the text contains so many contradictory dates that it cannot provide a confident chronology; see also below n. 74.

69. Al-Tel (2003) 113–17. This date also corresponds with that suggested for Sophronius's sermon *On the Theophany* (6 Jan. 637); see below p. 248f.

70. Theophanes, *Chronicle* A.M. 6127. This, however, is difficult to square with his simultaneous assertion that Sophronius acted against the Constantinopolitan patriarch Pyrrhus (elected in December 638).

71. See *Georgian Appendix to the Spiritual Meadow* 18–19 [Garitte 414–16; Latin trans. from Georgian]. For comment see also Hoyland (1997) 62–64. On the striking eucharistic content of this collection see below p. 329 n. 3.

under Muslim occupation, one of which even claims that the patriarch (here called "Florianus") was executed, having baptized some apostate Muslims in the wake of a (perhaps identical) "temple" collapsing.[72] Although the latter claim is in all likelihood erroneous,[73] traditions concerning Sophronius's survival encourage us to place his death at a later date (ca. 638)—greater precision is impossible—and perhaps suppose that Theophanes or his source wished to disguise the period of Sophronius's collaboration with or existence under the new Muslim authorities.[74]

Soon after his election as patriarch, at the Church of the Theotokos in Jerusalem, Sophronius delivered his aforementioned sermon *On the Nativity*.[75] Therein he expressed his urgent desire "to go to the God-bearing manger" at Bethlehem, "to approach the heavenly grotto," and "to see the mystery that appeared in it"; but, he added, "through our sins we have become unworthy of seeing such things, and we look to travel there but are forced to stay at home, not constrained by chains of the body but bound by fear of the Saracens."[76] Sophronius compared the alienation of his congregation from Bethlehem to Moses' destined failure to enter Israel (Deut. 3:27); to David's powerlessness to drink from the pool at Bethlehem (II Sam. 23:15); and to the expulsion of Adam from Paradise. For just as the exiled Adam saw "a flaming and wheeling sword watching the entrance to Paradise," so

---

72. For the two recensions see *BHL* 5672m, *BHL* 3053b, with the study of Woods (2003b). Woods connects the report of a collapsed "temple" to the collapsing building reportedly erected on the Temple Mount and described (although under a later date) in Theophanes, *Chronicle* A.M. 6135; Michael the Syrian, *Chronicle* 11.8; *Anonymous Chronicle to 1234* [Chabot vol. 1, 260f.]; also *Chronicle of Seert* 104 [Scher 624]; Eutychius, *Annals (Alexandrian Recension)* [Breydy 139f.]; Ps.-Sebēos, *History* 31; Anastasius of Sinai, *Tales* C3. For comment see Mango (1992); Flusin (1992a); Hoyland (1997) 64f. and (2011) 126f.; for the Arab sources Al-Tel (2003) 173–207.

73. *Pace* Woods (2003b) 139, if that martyrdom had occurred it surely would have been exploited or mentioned in the huge corpus of Maximus and his circle.

74. Schönborn (1972) 97 n. 136 argues that Sophronius died on 11 March (the date on which Sophronius is commemorated in the liturgical calendar) in 639, but the amassed evidence is too insecure to be conclusive. Based on an interpretation of the dates given the *Passion of the Sixty Martyrs* Woods (2003b) prefers a date early in 640, but despite his solid reasoning the recensions of that text are so replete with contradictory dates that it is difficult to be certain. If (*pace* Woods) we prefer the regnal dating over the indictional, Sophronius's execution is instead placed between December 637 and September 638 (Heraclius's 28th year) rather than December 639 to August 640 ("13th indiction"). For the same text see the observations of Hoyland (1997) 347–51; Jankowiak (2009) 163f. A possible clue is provided in the date later ascribed to the *Ekthesis* (twelfth indiction), for if this was indeed a sleight of hand designed to mask Sophronius's recognition of it—see above n. 61—then he must have died before that date.

75. For Sophronius's sermons in modern translation see Gallico (1991); Ferrière and Congourdeau (1999; *non vidi*). To the works discussed in Schönborn (1972) 99–109 and at CPG 7635–81 we can now add fragments of a sermon *On the Circumcision*; see Duffy (2011). Studies of the patriarchal sermons are few, but see Hoyland (1997) 67–76; and esp. Olster (1994) 99–115.

76. Sophronius, *On the Nativity* 3 [Usener 506]. For this equation of Christian sin and Muslim invasion see also Maximus Confessor, *Letters* 14 [*PG* 91, 541B–C] as below p. 278.

the Christians of Jerusalem see "that of the Saracen, wild and barbarous and full of all diabolic savagery, which threatens us with fear and death and makes us exiles from the blessed sight, and forces us to stay at home and does not allow us to go forth."[77] Sophronius, therefore, repeats once again that equation between temporal disaster and collective Christian sin that he had earlier established in relation to the Persian occupation. The scheme is nevertheless more elaborate, for here that same sin has inaugurated a new Fall, manifested in the inability of the Jerusalemites to experience Christ both physically at Bethlehem and spiritually in their lives. The Muslim occupation is the terrestrial manifestation of Christian sin, a physical expression of the soteriological barrier between Christ and mankind.

Sophronius thus summons his audience to "join faith with deeds and never reckon it aught apart from the deeds to which it is joined, so that as mighty in faith we stand firm and never be harmed by the grace of God." "If we shall do his [Christ's] will, which is that of his Father," Sophronius claims, "having true and orthodox faith we will blunt the Ishmaelite sword, turn away the Saracen knife, and break the Arab bow; then in no short time we shall see the heavenly Jerusalem and behold the miracles in it, and look upon the thaumaturge Christ himself."[78] Later he returns to the same theme: "Therefore I summon and urge and beseech you to desire for Christ God, so that, whatever our power, we may reform ourselves and take pride in repentance, and in that atonement purify and curb the flow of deeds that are hateful to God. For if we live thus, as dear and pleasant to God, we may laugh at the fall of the Saracens who oppose us, soon make their ruin feeble, and know their final destruction. For their blood-loving swords will enter into their own hearts, their bow will be shattered [cf. Ps. 37:15], and their own weapons will ensnare them, and they will provide for us a way free from fears."[79]

Sophronius here imagines a destruction of the Muslims achieved not in military action—as he had hoped in the *Synodical Letter*—but in the doctrinal and moral restitution of the Christian collective. At the same time, he mitigates his congregation's inability to visit Bethlehem through substituting the physical encounter with Christ in the manger for a spiritual encounter with Christ through the virtues: "God is displayed in a manger and gives himself into food for us who are deprived of reason and starving. Who would not delight in the divinity and be made full of heavenly wisdom, and send away irrational luxury as unworthy of the banquet and grace of God?" In place of the gifts of the Magi, Sophronius summons his congregation to celebrate Christ with the virtues: "I want to walk with [the Magi]," he says, "and to offer gifts to the newborn, even if he does not want those who offer gifts to him now to bring gold, myrrh, and frankincense, for he

---

77. Sophronius, *On the Nativity* 3 [Usener 507].
78. Sophronius, *On the Nativity* 3 [Usener 508].
79. Sophronius, *On the Nativity* 3 9 [Usener 508f.].

himself, called the creator of all things, instead furnishes the things that we need, desiring instead of gold the brightness of faith, and wanting instead of myrrh the incorruptibility of the soul and of the body, but also of dogma, proclamation, and orthodox mind toward the faith; and in respect of frankincense he longs to receive from us the sweet smell and fragrance of good deeds, in order not that he may be enriched in receiving these things but that he may make us rich through them."[80] Sophronius imagines, therefore, a reciprocal enrichment through which the spiritual advancement of the Christian is rewarded in the exaltation realized through Christ.

*On the Nativity* is the sole sermon that can be dated with confidence to the period before Jerusalem's capitulation—indeed in the remaining sermons explicit reference to the Muslim presence occurs only in the sermon *On the Theophany*. Throughout those remaining sermons—at least some of which must have been delivered during the period of Muslim control—Sophronius nevertheless continued to emphasize the same urgent need for Christian purification and to repeat the themes we have seen in *On the Nativity*.

He conceives that purification through three means: doctrinal, moral, and liturgical. The moral integrity of the community first of all presupposes a strict Chalcedonian orthodoxy, primarily defined in opposition to a vast catalogue of heretical groups and their respective doctrines. In the sermon *On the Hypapante*, in particular, Sophronius summons up a range of heresiarchs "all who impiously rave like them," in order to declare that they be "chased away from the divine meeting with Christ, in order that we who are right-minded and celebrate this festival today may meet Christ God with no blemish of any of the manifold heresies."[81] For Sophronius, therefore, the orthodox worshipping community is beset from all sides by the manifold errors of the heretics.

Throughout the patriarchal homilies there is moreover a consistent emphasis upon the reciprocal interaction of individual virtue and liturgical rite, where the spiritual effect of that rite is relativized according to the moral condition of the participant (as in Maximus's *Mystagogy*). Thus the sermon *On the Exaltation of the Cross* calls upon its audience to celebrate such things "finely and piously," for anyone who does differently "will ever be turned away and made loathsome if he cultivates himself in a manner unbecoming to them and does those things that are entirely hateful to them." "Thus," Sophronius says, "I summon and I urge you to hate and shun such things, which hate our rites [*sebasmia*], and to love and do those things that we know are pleasing to them. But they know also how to please

---

80. Sophronius, *On the Nativity* 3 2 [Usener 505f.].

81. Sophronius, *On the Hypapante* 6 [Usener 13f.]. Cf. also the vast catalogue of heretics set out in Sophronius's *Synodical Letter* [Riedinger 476–84; Allen (2009) 136–48], with the analysis of Allen (2009) 54–62.

and to give pleasure, and elevate the doer toward salvation, leading the way toward eternal life."[82]

For Sophronius, therefore, the context within which moral effort is ultimately made relevant is the ecclesiastical liturgy, and throughout his sermons he insists upon the regular participation of all Christians within the rites of the Church (as, again, in Maximus's *Mystagogy*).[83] The efficacy of liturgical acts in effecting the illumination to be realized fully in the *eschaton* is a constant theme, in particular in the sermon *On the Hypapante*.[84] "Let us rightfully be initiated [*telōmetha*] in these things," the sermon proclaims. "For they are the mystic rites [*teletai*] and mysteries of God, which although accomplished [*ekteloumena*] by man, mystically bring the initiated [*ton teloumenon*] to perfection [*teleiounta*]."[85] And again: "But let us all run to meet him, thus piously honoring his mystery; let us all enthusiastically proceed. Who shall meet him first? Who shall first behold God with their eyes? Who shall first welcome God? Who shall first carry God in their arms? Let nobody shrink from the divinely inspired course; let nobody become lame in the face of the earnest walk; let nobody halt the pious procession; let nobody be seen who has not tasted the festival; let nobody be seen who has not shared in the mysteries [*mēdeis painesthō tōn mustēriōn ametochos*]; let nobody be deprived of the light-bearing joy."[86] Other routes to enlightenment are, in comparison, ineffective: "Do service to the mysteries of Christ as something dear to Christ. For he does not come forth to those who hasten to meet him by different means, nor does he suffer to see them with his eyes, but he makes them exiles from his own assembly and sets them as uninitiated in meeting him."[87]

As in Maximus's *Mystagogy*, therefore—and in stark and telling contrast to his earlier *Miracles of Cyrus and John*—we encounter in Sophronius's patriarchal sermons a striking subordination of asceticism to eucharist, where the urgent need to engage with the latter trumps all temptation toward individual, withdrawn

---

82. Sophronius, *On the Exaltation of the Cross* 5 [PG 87:3, 3301C-9A, at 3308A–B]. It is notable that Sophronius in this sermon makes no mention of Heraclius or the Cross's restoration. The date is unsure, but it is possible that it was delivered after the removal of the Cross to Constantinople (ca. 636); see above p. 157 n. 74. The attribution of the sermon *De Festo Sanctae Crucis* to Sophronius at PG 87:3, 3309B-3316B is most probably incorrect; see Schönborn (1972) 110f.

83. For Sophronius's thoughts on the clerical hierarchy see his *On Saints Peter and Paul* [PG 87:3, 3356C-3357A], with the interpretation of Schönborn (1972) 227. Cf. idem (1975) 490; also Olster (1994) 105f. For the same theme of "union and distinction" in Maximus Confessor's corpus see Törönen (2007) esp. 143–48.

84. On this particular sermon see the study of Allen (2007).

85. Sophronius, *On the Hypapante* 1 [Usener 9].

86. Sophronius, *On the Hypapante* 4 [Usener 10f.].

87. Sophronius, *On the Hypapante* 5 [Usener 13]. The interest of Sophronius in liturgy is reflected also in several anacreontics on liturgical themes, certain liturgical hymns, and a liturgical prayer. (See Schönborn [1972] 99–109.)

endeavor. Nowhere else is this so clear as in the conclusion to the patriarch's sermon *On John the Baptist*. Having reflected upon and praised John's withdrawal to the desert, Sophronius nevertheless must contradict himself: "Although like you [John] I have the inclination," he proclaims, "I am restrained and seriously impeded from following up my own argument. In part this is because of human weakness (for I am not afraid to tell you the truth, which you knew in any case before my speech), but it is also because, as you see, the time of the divine liturgy [*ho tēs hieras leitourgias kairos*] is at hand and forces us all to hold back, and does not allow us to go with you to the beloved desert [*pros tēn philēn erēmon*]."[88] This sentiment, I would suggest, is much more than a simple comment on Sophronius's changed circumstances, a longing for a monastic life now lost; it is a recognition that older paradigms now belong to the past. The indulgent life of desert withdrawal must now come second to participation in the sacramental life of the Church.

In the final section of his sermon *On the Theophany* the patriarch considered the circumstances of the age: "But contrary matters force me to ponder on our life. For how is it that our enemies live their lives among us? How is it that barbarian onslaughts multiply? How is it that the ranks of the Saracens rise up against us? How is it that such destruction and plunder have increased? How is it that the flow of human blood has become unceasing? How is that the birds of heaven consume human bodies? How is it that churches are destroyed? How is it that the Cross is insulted?"[89] The patriarch continues to catalogue various (supposed) outrages committed at the hands of "the God-hating and avenging Saracens" and notes too the defeats inflicted upon Roman armies. (From these two facts, we should note, it is tempting to assume that the sermon was delivered on 6 January 637: that is, after the defeat of the summer of 636 but before the surrender of Jerusalem, when disparaging references to the Muslims would have risked retaliation.)[90] In response, Sophronius urges his audience to a new moralism: "Thus, brothers, let us hasten with all speed toward redemption, and let us incline toward this [Christ's] sympathy. For it helps us to incline toward sympathy, on account of his natural and divine goodness, rather than to be stirred up toward cruelty and the punishment of the evils done against us. And so knowing his philanthropy, let us run toward him with philanthropy, and let us delight him with good deeds, bearing clothes of light and bright garments of the soul, and being wholly bright and undimmed we see him with our eyes and wholly celebrate his most bright festival, and leading the celebration, the mother of all brightness and nurse of all splendor, so that we also

---

88. Sophronius, *On John the Baptist* [PG 87:3, 3353A–B].

89. Sophronius, *On the Theophany* 10 [Papadopoulos-Kerameus 166].

90. Sophronius, *On the Theophany* 10 [Papadopoulos-Kerameus 166f.]. For the date see Schönborn (1972) 104.

may come into his heavenly kingdom and thence have a share of the illumination, a pleasure that is truly unmoved, and alone fixed and unshaken [*apolausin tēn ontōs akradanton kai monēn statheēran kai asaleuton*]."[91] Here, then, Sophronius casts aside vengeance as an effective medium of restoration. He instead summons his audience to a new moral purity conducted through the structures of the Chalcedonian (dyenergist) Church, urging a Christian unity delimited by orthodoxy, defined by morality, and realized in liturgy.

In a compelling treatment of the patriarchal sermons, David Olster has argued that Sophronius "offered hope by dissociating the empire from the Christian community and creating a new Christian identity that was Roman no longer." Olster points to Sophronius's emphasis upon liturgy as "a social ritual that defined an extra-imperial communal, social and political identity." Thus "Sophronius's call for unity in the face of the Arab threat was not to join together in resistance, either passive or active, but to express Christian unity through the liturgy." At the same time, Olster indicates, "it should not be thought remarkable that Sophronius would shape his sermons so that the unity and integrity of the Christian community found its source in the rites of the sole remaining Christian social and political institution."[92]

One indeed senses in the patriarchal sermons something of a shift in emphasis. In all such sermons—and in perfect accord with the scheme of collective sin— Sophronius never hopes for an imperial Roman resurgence to remove the Muslim presence (such as he had at first hoped for, some decades earlier, in response to the Persian assault upon Jerusalem). Instead, he imagines restoration in the doctrinal, moral, and liturgical purification realized in and through the Church. Nevertheless, whereas in the sermon *On the Nativity* (written late in 634) Sophronius had fantasized an autodestruction of the Arabs through the restoration of divine favor, and thus a simultaneous restoration of Roman rule, in the later sermon *On the Theophany* (composed, it seems, after the Roman withdrawal) all claims to political restoration are abandoned. Instead, he there urges his audience to focus on the sustained illumination offered through the rites of the Church, "alone fixed and unshaken."

Sophronius's use of that model was of course a response to the particular circumstances with which he and his congregation were confronted. But in articulating it, he drew upon sensibilities present within the Moschan circle since his *Miracles of Cyrus and John*, composed some twenty-five years earlier. Throughout that entire period, Sophronius and his associates had emphasized time and again the importance of the eucharist and of eucharistic communion in distinguishing orthodox and heretical communities. But at the same time, whereas Sophronius

91. Sophronius, *On the Theophany* 11 [Papadopoulos-Kerameus 168].
92. Olster (1994) 99–115.

had earlier failed (or been unwilling) to situate the dominant ascetical narrative of the *Miracles* within a full liturgical or clerical narrative (so that their effectiveness as soteriological media was minimized), so had he and his associates later attempted to bridge the divide between competing ascetical and sacramental imperatives: Moschus, in elevating clerics and the eucharist within the *Spiritual Meadow*, and above all Maximus, in integrating ascetical and liturgical schemes in the *Mystagogy*. Sophronius's patriarchal insistence on engagement with the structures of the orthodox Church, and the concomitant relativization of their efficaciousness according to ascetic achievement, thus represented something far more than a platitude of his episcopal rank. It represented the public deployment of an ideological system that had evolved within his circle over several decades, and that in a context of crisis presented a unified Church immune to the vicissitudes of empire. From this final perspective, the restoration of temporal peace, at least in the form of Roman reoccupation, was an irrelevance.

## THE YEAR OF THE FOUR EMPERORS

During his tenure at Jerusalem, Sophronius had faced a quite formidable consensus of patriarchal opinion against him, culminating in the promulgation of the *Ekthesis*, a document that once again forbade discussion on the operations and at the same time promoted the doctrine of the single Christological will. The period 638–40, however, witnessed a substantial change of the patriarchal guard: as has been said, it was now that Sophronius died (and was not replaced);[93] in October 638 Honorius of Rome passed;[94] and in December, Sergius of Constantinople too was laid to rest.[95] Around 640, furthermore, the patriarch Cyrus of Alexandria fell foul of the authorities in Constantinople and—in a striking precedent for the fate that would befall Maximus—was tried in the capital on a charge of treason. According to Nicephorus's *Short History*, this deposition had occurred when the Alexandrian patriarch—ever the political diplomat—had suggested that the Romans give tribute to the Muslims and even that the emperor betroth the empress Eudocia to ʿAmr ibn al-ʿĀṣ, the Muslim general who had conquered Palestine. Nicephorus implies that the simple suggestion of both policies led to Cyrus's recall and subsequent trial in Constantinople. But from a tradition preserved in two independent lines—the sources derived from the lost *Chronicle* of Theophilus of Edessa and the *History of the Patriarchs of Alexandria*—it appears that the proposed tribute was

---

93. See the discussion above p. 243f.

94. *Book of Pontiffs* 72.

95. For the date of Sergius's death see *Book of Ceremonies* 2.30 [Reiske vol. 1, 630]; Nicephorus, *Short History* 26 and *Chronography* [de Boor 118]; with the discussion of Brooks (1897) 40; Van Dieten (1972) 51; Mango (1990) 190.

indeed implemented, and that as a result the conquest of Egypt was postponed for three years.⁹⁶ As an extant document from the Arsinoite nome presents Cyrus as patriarch in the thirteenth indiction (639/40), we must suppose that his deposition and trial occurred soon after the beginning of that year, perhaps in the first months of 640.⁹⁷ Under direction from the Caesars David and Martin—according to a unique piece of information preserved in the *Chronicle* of John of Nikiu—after Heraclius's death (in January or February 641) Cyrus was exiled to North Africa. Although there is no suggestion that the patriarch's disgrace was tied to his status as a principal architect of the controversial monenergist compromise, his trial and conviction on charges of treason—including, according to Nicephorus, an accusation of paganism for suggesting the political marriage of Eudocia to a Muslim—demonstrates once again the inseparable nexus of politics and religion in which the period's Christian leaders were implicated. At the same time, his notable disgrace cannot but have galvanized the doctrinal resistance that Maximus, in the precise same period, would launch from the West.

According to John of Nikiu, Cyrus was replaced in Alexandria with the patriarch George.⁹⁸ In Sergius's place was elected, on 20 December 638, Pyrrhus, the erstwhile correspondent of Maximus on the question of the operations.⁹⁹ Pyrrhus, who had no doubt been elevated for his pro-imperial credentials, appears soon after to have convened a council to examine the *Ekthesis*, for the *Acts of the Lateran Council* purports to contain excerpts from that council's subsequent letter, in which the Constantinopolitan patriarch praises the emperor's initiative and hopes that God will show favor to his rule and subjugate "the barbarian tribes."¹⁰⁰ According

---

96. See Hoyland (2011) 109–14; *History of the Patriarchs* "Benjamin" [Evetts 493]. This tradition is doubted by Butler (1902) 207–9; Beihammer (2000) 27f.; but see the compelling argument of Hoyland (1997) 574–90.

97. See *P.Lond.* 113.10; with Hoyland (1997) 590.

98. For George see John of Nikiu, *Chronicle* 119–20; although cf. Nicephorus, *Chronography* [de Boor 129]; Theophanes, *Chronicle* A.M. 6111–24; Eutychius, *Annals (Alexandrian Recension)* [Breydy 133]. On the basis of John of Nikiu I would place George's patriarchate during the brief deposition of Cyrus, 640–41, and presume that the latter's restoration has confused the chronographers; so also Jankowiak (2009) 85–88 (though differing on the date). Cyrus of Alexandria was restored under Heraclius Constantine or Heraclonas—see the conflicting reports in John of Nikiu, *Chronicle* 116, 119. It should be noted that the standard modern translations misrepresent the text's depiction of Cyrus's career, for while there is an obvious scribal error in one place reading "*kirs*, patriarch of Constantinople" [Zotenberg 204], both Zotenberg (1883) and Charles (1916) then repeatedly translate instances of *kirs* as "Pyrrhus" when it is clear that Cyrus of Alexandria is in fact intended. The error has resulted in much unnecessary rumination; see, e.g., Van Dieten (1972) 67 n. 34; Jankowiak (2009) 192f. Cyrus of Alexandria died soon after his restoration, dated firmly to Maundy Thursday, 21 March 642, in John of Nikiu, *Chronicle* 120.

99. For the date see Brooks (1897) 45f.; Van Dieten (1972) 58.

100. *Acts of the Lateran Council* [Riedinger 168]. It is interesting to note the apparent warning sounded at the end of the letter concerning the subscription of others to his encyclical and, with it, the

to a short excerpt contained within the same *Acts,* Pyrrhus would also write a letter to Pope John IV, the successor of Honorius's own short-lived successor Severinus, in which he repeated the earlier sentiment of Sergius, that two wills cannot exist within the same person (although, it seems, avoiding an overt statement of "one will"): "I indeed proclaim that two wills cannot coexist in one person [*en heni prosōpōi sunuphestanai*] without being completely opposed and ranged against each other [*allēlois antexagomenōn de pantōs kai antitetagmenōn*]."[101]

Following the death of Heraclius in January or February 641, Constantinople entered upon a crisis of succession.[102] In Heraclius's stead was elected his son and heir apparent, Heraclius Constantine (son of Heraclius's first wife, Eudocia), but after a little over three months he died of illness and was replaced with Heraclonas (son of Heraclius's second wife and niece, Martina).[103] Nicephorus records that Heraclonas now embarked upon a persecution of his predecessor's imperial treasurer, Philagrius, and thus incurred the wrath of the general Valentine, who, acting upon a previous agreement to favor the children of Heraclius Constantine over those of Martina, came with his troops to Chalcedon, looking to further their interests (and most of all those of Heraclius Constantine's son, the future emperor Constans). Under pressure from both the troops outside the walls and the people

---

*Ekthesis* [Riedinger 168–70]. It perhaps suggests that Pyrrhus expected some resistance, perhaps from Sophronius (if alive) but perhaps also from Rome, where in the period following Honorius's death the next pope was still not elected. For Pyrrhus's convention of a monothelete synod upon his election see also *Synodicon Vetus* 132 (with Duffy and Parker [1979] 111 n. 160). For his earliest doctrinal position see also Van Dieten (1972) 58–62.

101. *Acts of the Lateran Council* [Riedinger 338]. For the same letter to John cf. the passage in *Acts of the Sixth Ecumenical Council* [Riedinger 626]; also *Disputation with Pyrrhus* [PG 91, 328B]; with Conte (1971) 427 no. 98; Winkelmann (2001) 99 no. 70. Pyrrhus proceeds to offer in support a (much-contested) passage of Gregory of Nazianzus, *Orations* 30.12 [Gallay vol. 6, 250], interpreting John 6:38. The same text was reportedly cited by Pyrrhus's successor Paul; see *Acts of the Lateran Council* [Riedinger 196–204, 338]; cf. *Acts of the Sixth Ecumenical Council* [Riedinger 200, 608]. For the dyothelete response see n. 165 below, and for discussion Bathrellos (2004) 141–43 and esp. Hovorun (2008) 131f. We should also note that a letter of Pyrrhus to John IV referring to the *libellus* of Menas is mentioned at *Disputation with Pyrrhus* [PG 91, 328B]. See also on these exchanges Van Dieten (1972) 63–65.

102. For the different dates see *Chronicon Altinate* [Cessi 107–8] (11 January 641, derived from the *Book of Ceremonies*); Nicephorus, *Short History* 27 (11 February 641), with Mango (1990) 191. Treadgold (1990) makes a compelling case for the former.

103. For the disputed dates, dependent on the date of Heraclius's death, see Mango (1990) 191f., favoring 24 May; Treadgold (1990) 432f., favoring 23 April. For the possible antimonothelete credentials of Heraclius Constantine—as alluded to in Zonaras, *Epitome of Histories* 14.18—see Van Dieten (1972) 66 n. 32, and see also the Karshuni version of Pope John IV, *Letter in Defense of Honorius* (CPG 9383) in Schacht (1936) 235 (below n. 137). For rumors that Heraclius Constantine was killed by Pyrrhus, or Martina, or both—as reported in, e.g., Ps.-Sebēos, *History* 44, Theophanes, *Chronicle* A.M. 6132, and the chronographic tradition—see Van Dieten (1972) 71 n. 40.

within them, Nicephorus reports, the patriarch Pyrrhus, under orders from the emperor Heraclonas, crowned Constans coemperor, but in the process incurred such hatred that he was forced to remove his pallium and flee from the capital, then heading to North Africa.[104] In his stead was elected Paul, "former steward [*oikonomos*] of the Great Church"; this occurred in October of the fifteenth indiction (641).[105]

Nicephorus's account of the crisis ends with the attempts of Heraclonas and his mother, Martina, to appease Valentine and then leaps without warning to the death of Constans in 668. For the remainder of the crisis we must turn to the *Chronicle* of John of Nikiu.[106] The *Chronicle* too reports Martina's persecution of Philagrius, Valentine's subsequent revolt, and the coronation of Constans as coemperor, but where Nicephorus's text gives out it continues to claim that strife between the two coemperors soon grew, in particular when troops in Cappadocia produced a letter, alleged to be from Martina and the patriarch, urging one David to wage war upon Constans and then to take the empress as his wife. At this, and suspecting the involvement of one "Qəṭrāds, head of the people of Mūṭāns" (sometimes thought to be Kubrat, the Bulgar khagan), the soldiers and people of Constantinople rose up under one "Eutalius [*yutāliyos*] son of Constantine, who was called Theodore," who then defeated David and captured Constantinople for Constans.[107] He seized the imperial palace and mutilated Martina and her sons, sending them into exile on Rhodes. In contradiction of Nicephorus's account of the patriarch's willful withdrawal from the capital, the *Chronicle* records that Pyrrhus (*bers*) was then deposed without council and exiled to Tripoli (*'aṭrāblus*), and in his stead "they elected Paul [*pāwlos*], who was from the city of Constantinople."[108]

Amid all these political upheavals Maximus—for the first but not the last time—became involved in a significant moment of political dissent against the capital. According to the Syriac *Life*, following the quasi-ecumenical synod on

---

104. Nicephorus, *Short History* 31 [Mango 82]. We should note that the text gives "Chalcedon" as the patriarch's place of refuge, although "Carthage" is clearly intended. The confusion is common in Greek; cf. Theophanes, *Chronicle* A.M. 6108. For Philagrius see *PmbZ* "Philagrios" 6124, with Kaegi (1992) 256f.; for Valentine *PmbZ* "Ualentinos" 8545.

105. Nicephorus, *Short History* 32 [Mango 84]. For the election of Paul see Nicephorus, *Short History* 32, with Brooks (1897) 46; Van Dieten (1972) 76. On Paul see also *PmbZ* "Paulos II" 5763; Winkelmann (2001) 247–48.

106. For the relationship of the two texts see Howard-Johnston (2010) 246f. I discuss the transmission of John's text and the subsequent problems in Booth (2011b).

107. For Kubrat (*Koubratos*), chief of the Bulgars, see Nicephorus, *Short History* 22, with the discussion of Mango (1990) 177f., 188; and (for archaeological evidence for his association with the Heraclian regime) Curta (2006) 77–79. For the identification with John of Nikiu's Qəṭrāds see Beshevliev (1978), and for the general David see *PmbZ* "David" 1242.

108. John of Nikiu, *Chronicle* [Zotenberg 217].

Cyprus in 636, and the effective condemnation of speculation on the operations in Heraclius's edict (*sc.* the *Ekthesis*), Maximus "confined himself in a small cell out of fear of the emperor and the patriarchs who had anathematized his teaching" and remained in Syria with his disciples Anastasius and Sergius until the Arabs arrived and seized the region.[109] Then, the *Life* continues, in the absence of Roman power he began once again to sow his doctrine within the region, and following the successive deaths of Heraclius, Heraclius Constantine, Heraclonas, and Martina (in 641), and seeing that North Africa was in rebellion, he traveled there with Anastasius "and the other brethren." There Maximus and his monks settled in a monastery at Hippo Diarrhytus, in the company, so the *Life* alleges, of "Nestorian" monks from Nisibis, who of course much admired Maximus's doctrine.[110]

From Maximus's own *Letters* we can indeed confirm that he had once again returned to North Africa around this same period. In our previous exploration of Maximus's career we noted that he had formed an intimate bond with the prefect of Africa George, and that that bond appears to have existed from the earliest stages of his exile in the province.[111] In 641/2, however, George became involved in a serious dispute with Constantinople when he refused to observe an order of the empress Martina—an act that it is tempting to associate with the "rebellion" referred to in the Syriac *Life*.[112] The origins of the affair, which occupies a prominent position within Maximus's general correspondence, are summarized in *Letters* 12 to John Cubicularius. In November of the fifteenth indiction (641), and thus simultaneous with the coup that raised Constans to the throne, one Theodore arrived in North Africa with a letter from "our mistress Patricia" (that is, the empress Martina) ordering that the eparch release the refugee nuns from two Alexandrian monasteries—adherents, so Maximus claimed, of Severanism.[113] According to Maximus's account later in the same letter, when the nuns had first arrived in the province some time earlier the prefect George had welcomed them

---

109. George of Resh'aina, *Life* 17 [Brock 309f.; trans. 317]. It is tempting to connect this "Sergius" to the "Sergius Eukratas" who appears in Maximus's trial literature; see *Record* 6–9, and above p. 149 n. 43.

110. George of Resh'aina, *Life* 18–19 [Brock 310f.; trans. 317f.].

111. For the office of prefect (*huparchos* or *eparchos*) see Guilland (1981). George is referred to as both "prefect of Africa" and "prefect of Carthage" in contemporary literature; see *PmbZ* "Georgios" 1962, pp. 110 and 151f. above.

112. *Pace* Jankowiak (2009) 171, thinking the rebellion to be that of the exarch Gregory. Cf. Brock (1973) 325f.

113. There is no suggestion, we should note, that any of the heretics mentioned in the letter were in fact monenergists or monotheletes. The letter develops into a doctrinal refutation of miaphysitism, not monenergism or monotheletism; see Sherwood (1952a) 47. We should note that Maximus in the letter shows no awareness of Martina's fall, which occurred in November 641; see above p. 253. It is notable that Maximus here calls the empress "Patricia" and not "Augusta." Could this be a subtle indication of dissent?

with grace and offered to them a home, but when he had discovered that those same nuns were spreading heretical propaganda, and that the mass of the faithful were muttering against them, he considered it proper to seek imperial opinion and wrote to the local archbishop and notables, to the emperor (*sc.* Heraclius), and to the patriarchs of Rome and Constantinople (an equation of status that, as Christian Boudignon has noted, may have offended in the capital).[114] He then received decrees from both the emperor and the patriarchs that heretics who persisted in their error should be driven from the province, and that the nuns, if unrepentant, should be distributed among orthodox communities. Along with other heretics, one group of nuns had indeed returned to the catholic Church; the other, however, had persevered in their error and so had been distributed among orthodox communities as per the imperial decree.[115]

George may well have received this imperial command in Constantinople itself, for we ascertain from Maximus's *Letters* that he had earlier been summoned to the capital to answer unknown charges.[116] In the earlier *Letters* 18, sent to certain "apostate nuns from the Church of Alexandria," George (in whose name Maximus writes) expressed his frustration at those same nuns' continued intransigence, demanded the return of the "gifts" that he had granted them, and reported that he had written concerning their case to the emperors and patriarchs, with whom he had an impending audience.[117] (This, of course, fits well the description of initial events given in *Letters* 12.) Three more of Maximus's *Letters* indeed point to a period in which George had been summoned from North Africa to Constantinople. In *Letters* 1, written "To the Slave of God Lord George, the All-Praised Prefect [*eparchos*] of Africa," Maximus exhorts his recipient to place his faith in God and take courage, concluding with the sentiment that "With me truly all the honorable Fathers who live, because of you, within this province [*chōra*] send their greetings with one accord and beseech God with tears unceasingly day and night that our George be restored to us in health."[118]

---

114. Boudignon (2007) 253, contending also that the appeal represents "une usurpation par Georges et Maxime du pouvoir de décision dévolu à l'archevêque de Carthage."

115. Maximus Confessor, *Letters* 12 [PG 91, 464C–465B]. See also Larchet (1998c) 137f., noting that George consults Constantinople as well as Rome.

116. *Pace* Sherwood (1952a) 49–51, placing all these documents in 642 but noting that the Martina affair does not appear and cannot be the reason for George's recall. The consistent reference to "emperors" rather than "emperor" is problematic if we wish to place the letter in the reign of Constans II. I would therefore place George's period of absence in the capital before the Martina affair and date the letters that relate to it to the period ca. 634–40. Cf. Diehl (1896) 543–47; Van Dieten (1972) 67–70 with n. 37, placing the origins of the conflict under Heraclius Constantine rather than Heraclius.

117. Maximus Confessor, *Letters* 18 [PG 91, 584D–589B]. Cf. Maximus Confessor, *Letters* 12 [PG 91, 464C–D].

118. Maximus Confessor, *Letters* 1 [PG 91, 392A–B].

*Letters* 44 and 45, both to John Cubicularius in the capital, also belong to the period of George's absence from North Africa and again place the prefect in Constantinople. In the former, Maximus proclaims, "Let the God of all and our Lord Jesus Christ preserve our most pious and all-holy emperors, and empower the authority of their pious kingdom, and speak good and peaceful things about us, their humble servants, in their hearts. And if I may make so bold (for grief makes me so) and if the prayer is pleasing to God, let him forgive them for allowing the all-praised prefect [*huparchos*] of this province—who shines like a light in a miserable place, somehow liberating all from the pain of not seeing—to be recalled, even if for a moment."[119] He then launches into a long list of George's manifold virtues before invoking the sad scene of his departure and informing John that if he can see to the prefect's safe return, he will give to the emperors "a safe and unbreakable bulwark [*probolē*], for no one is a more trusted servant of their pious empire."[120] *Letter* 45 again recommends George in the strongest terms, here adding to his catalogue of virtues the fact that he is "a lover of the Church [*philekklēsios*] and more honorable than all, a most ardent zealot of pious doctrine in accordance with the orthodox faith." "I have set out these things," Maximus then states, "for the sole reason that my God-guarded master recognize the man's devotion to God, and that he receive and honor him as one under divine grace through these deeds, and commend him to our pious and all-holy emperors, who represent [*eikonizousi*] divine power on earth, and persuade them not to listen to the unjust tongues of lawless men, who use cunning as if it were a sharpened razor, and love evil over goodness."[121]

We cannot know the reasons for George's summons to Constantinople, but the reference to detractors confirms that it occurred under some accusation: Maximus's defense of the prefect's commitment to the empire hints at a political indictment (perhaps connected to the Muslim invasion of Egypt, for example); his references to his pious faith at a doctrinal one (the persecution of the aforementioned nuns, or the harboring of Maximus himself, perhaps). We can of course but speculate, although George appears to have survived his imperial audience, for he was later to return to North Africa, bearing perhaps that imperial decree to which Maximus referred in *Letters* 12. It ordered the expulsion of heretics from the province and the distribution of those Alexandrian nuns who refused to recant their doctrinal allegiance.

When Martina's subsequent letter commanding the release of those same Severan nuns arrived, therefore, it appears to have caused something of a stir. Maxi-

---

119. Maximus Confessor, *Letters* 44 [*PG* 91, 645C].
120. Maximus Confessor, *Letters* [*PG* 91, 648C].
121. Maximus Confessor, *Letters* 45 [*PG* 91, 648D–649B]. For such accusers cf. the introduction to Maximus Confessor, *Letters* 16 ("To Cosmas, Deacon of Alexandria") [*PG* 91, 576D–577A].

mus reports in *Letters* 12 that there was much muttering (*gongusmos*) among the faithful and that the empress's reputation as a protector of the orthodox Church was in doubt until the prefect proclaimed the letter to be counterfeit. He then pretended to be vexed (*aganaktein prosepoiēsato*) at its bearer, Theodore, and used the letter as a pretext (*prophasis*) to launch a persecution of exiled Alexandrian and Syrian heretics, who now claimed the empress for their own.[122] The letter admits that the heretics' bishop Thomas—otherwise unknown—was among those who had free access to the empress and that she held him in great esteem; this fact above all, so Maximus claims, was a cause of great disturbance and scandal. Indeed, this outrage was so great that Maximus himself had to cross-examine those who dared to proclaim such things and reassure his audience that neither the empress nor her deceased husband had ever been devoted to heretics. "Similarly," he adds in a tantalizing aside, "many other of the most blessed monks who live here in exile [*epixenoumenōn eulabestatōn monachōn*], and most of all the celebrated servants of God and our fathers, those surnamed Eukratades [*hoi epiklēn Eukratadēs*], said the same things and made many reject that bogus rumor."[123] This surname, we will remember, is that of Moschus and Sophronius, now long deceased but present, it appears, in the persons of their disciples. That Maximus still considered it worthwhile to highlight the Eukratades' involvement in the affair is testament, one suspects, to their masters' enduring reputation.

It is nevertheless clear that Maximus and his allies considered the letter to be genuine. George, so we are told, "pretended" to be vexed at its bearer; he used it as a "pretext" to persecute exiled heretics (perhaps monotheletes rather than anti-Chalcedonians); and Martina, furthermore, was known to associate with a heretical bishop, Thomas. Maximus indeed expressed himself "still not free from doubt [*amphibolia*]," for although he knew Martina to have "stood upon the unbreakable rock of faith from birth," nevertheless the bearer of the letter had sworn on oath that it was real. And so, Maximus warns his correspondent, if it transpires that the letter concerning the heretical nuns was indeed from the empress, he will not absolve him from blame. "For," he adds in a comment redolent with political implications, "I have heard from the teachings of divine Scripture that Josaphat, that pious and faithful king [*basileus*] of Judaea, fought alongside Achaab the king of Israel when he once launched a war against Syria, and being besmirched with many stains of idolatry was censured and indicted by God, who thus said to him through the prophet, 'Do you help the man whom I hate, and who despises the Lord God [II Chron. 19:2]?'"[124] Martina, Maximus warns, should not become like

---

122. Maximus Confessor, *Letters* 12 [*PG* 91, 460C].
123. Maximus Confessor, *Letters* 12 [*PG* 91, 461A].
124. Maximus Confessor, *Letters* 12 [*PG* 91, 461D]. Maximus leaves unsaid the subsequent biblical line: "Because of this the wrath of the Lord has descended upon you."

Roboamum son of Solomon, who in preferring the counsel of youths to elders lost the most part of his kingdom.[125]

No wonder, then, that observers might consider this a full-scale rebellion against Constantinople. Martina had requested that the prefect release some nuns suspected of being heretics.[126] Instead, George, who had before fallen under suspicion at Constantinople, declared the empress' letter to be forged and then embarked upon a persecution of those same groups whom she had attempted to protect. His principal spiritual advisor, furthermore, dispatched a veiled warning to a correspondent in Constantinople, pointing to the dire political consequences of fraternizing with heretics.[127] Once again, therefore, the specter of Constantinopolitan conciliation toward anti-Chalcedonians had fomented the anger of Maximus and his Palestinian circle, who honored their deceased masters in once again championing the cause of theological *akribeia*.

Sources for these events in North Africa are few. But it is nevertheless notable that one such source, the *Chronicle* of John of Nikiu, reports that during the period of crisis following the death of Heraclius Constantine (in April or May 641), certain rebels attempted to galvanize support against Martina and sent "to Africa and to all the places subject to Roman power" the message "Do not listen to the word of Martina, and do not obey her sons."[128] It is possible, therefore, that George and Maximus, who had refused a command of the empress in North Africa, were in fact aware of a far broader resistance to the regime and an imminent attempt to remove it.[129]

We do not know the outcome of the North African affair—Martina's regime had in fact collapsed as her letter had been received, and we hear no more of it. The dissidence of George, however, represents the first of a series of Western rebellions against the regime of Heraclius's successors, and the first in which the doctrinal

---

125. Maximus Confessor, *Letters* 12 [PG 91, 461D-464A].

126. *Pace* Sherwood (1952a) 48, arguing that the letter was indeed a fake. I see no means of assessing its truth, although we need not suppose that it represented some farther-reaching change in imperial doctrine.

127. For analysis of the affair see also Boudignon (2007) 247-56 (although retaining the traditional chronology of events given in Sherwood [1952a] 49-51).

128. John of Nikiu, *Chronicle* 120 [Zotenberg 211]. In this connection it is also notable that John's *Chronicle* reports that the leading general in Egypt, Theodore, having received the same message, then attempted but failed to reach Pentapolis, suggesting that North Africa was perceived as a safe haven for dissenters.

129. Cf. George of Resh'aina's *Life* 18, referring to a preexisting rebellion in North Africa before Maximus's arrival. The same text also refers to the fact that Maximus upon arrival in Africa promoted his cause and even deceived "the eparch there, whose name was George [*gywrgy*]" [Brock 311; trans. 318]. One may suspect a mistake for "Gregory" (the rebellious later exarch), but the Syriac gives *hūparchā* (i.e., *huparchos*), George's precise title. It is notable, therefore, that George of Resh'aina considers George the Prefect a doctrinal follower of Maximus.

intransigence of Maximus appears as influential, if not decisive. There is insufficient evidence here to decide if Constantinopolitan support for the *Ekthesis* was in part responsible for George's refusal of Martina's letter. But, as we shall now see, it occurred at a time when Maximus himself had begun to agitate against the monothelete formula contained within the *Ekthesis* and, in a spectacular diplomatic coup, had convinced the Roman popes to support his cause.

## FROM OPERATIONS TO WILLS

In his correspondence with Pope John IV, the new Constantinopolitan patriarch Pyrrhus perhaps hoped to convince his Roman counterpart to continue the papal support for the *Ekthesis*. Instead, the pope performed a quite spectacular volte-face. After the death of Pope Honorius in 638, the papal throne lay vacant for more than eighteen months, an indication perhaps of significant tensions concerning the doctrinal direction that the Romans wished to adopt (or perhaps of an imperial refusal to recognize the papal election before the pope-elect subscribed to the *Ekthesis*). The doctrinal position of Honorius's eventual successor, the pope Severinus, is unclear, but in a letter to Thalassius preserved in later Latin excerpts of Anastasius Bibliothecarius, Maximus claimed (via some informants in Constantinople) that when Severinus's *apocrisiarii* at Constantinople attempted to obtain an imperial ratification for the new pope's election, the Constantinopolitans demanded that Rome first acknowledge a doctrinal *charta*—no doubt the *Ekthesis*—and that the *apocrisiarii*, in fear of contradicting the pope, claimed such an acknowledgment to be outside their prerogatives and refused to sign until said *charta* had been submitted to the pope himself.[130]

Whatever the outcome of the affair, Severinus held the position for a little over two months before his own death and the subsequent elevation of John IV late in 640.[131] We ascertain from several sources that one of the new pope's acts was to convene a synod to condemn the *Ekthesis*.[132] Indeed, according to a text that

---

130. Maximus Confessor, *Letter to Thalassius* [PG 129, 583D–586B]. Severinus is not mentioned, but for the date see Sherwood (1952a) 43; also Conte (1971) 424 nos. 87 and 88. For Thalassius see above p. 154. The dispatch of the *Ekthesis* for Severinus's approval is also mentioned within a letter of Cyrus of Alexandria to Sergius of Constantinople read out at *Acts of the Lateran Council* [Riedinger 172]. Severinus is nevertheless presented as orthodox in Maximus Confessor, *Opuscula* 12 [PG 91, 143B]; and in *Liber Diurnus* [PL 105, 66B]. Cf. Conte (1971) 424f. no. 89.

131. See *Book of Pontiffs* 73–74. On Pope John IV see *PmbZ* "Johannes" 2689; Winkelmann (2001) 220.

132. See Pope Theodore, *Letter to Paul* [PL 87, 78A, 79A]; *Synodicon Vetus* 137; Theophanes, *Chronicle* A.M. 6121. See also Conte (1971) 427 no. 96; Winkelmann (2001) 95f. no. 67b. On the basis of *Synodicon Vetus* 137—which contains the striking statement that the synod's dyenergist/dyothelete ruling was dispatched to Heraclonas and David, the sons of Heraclius—Jankowiak (2009) 200f. places it in autumn 641, subsequent to the extant letter to the emperors Heraclius Constantine and Heraclonas (below).

purports to record Maximus's eventual trial in Constantinople, at the beginning of his tenure as pope John had written to the Constantinopolitan patriarch Pyrrhus against the *Ekthesis*—perhaps, we may assume, in response to the latter's aforementioned encyclical recognizing the same. The result, so the trial literature claims, was that the emperor Heraclius, "perceiving that some within the West [*kata tēn dusin*] were pouring blame upon him," issued a decree to the pope in which he retracted the document and blamed Sergius for demanding that he place his signature upon it.[133] This same allegation appears also in Maximus's *Opuscula* 12.[134] Although the emperor must have approved both Severinus's and John's election—and thus, in the end, disregarded the popes' doctrinal stance—we should of course be cautious in accepting reports of Heraclius's full capitulation, for it is a standard theme of antimonothelete literature that emperors themselves were blameless, and after Heraclius's death tales of his unwitting seduction and eventual recantation were no doubt intended as offering a precedent for Constans's own desired capitulation.[135] Indeed, on the basis of a fragment contained within a later iconophile florilegium, Alexander Alexakis has demonstrated that a perhaps identical letter of the emperor to John in fact proclaimed the opposite, for therein Heraclius refers to an inscription that adorned an icon of the crucified Christ in the patriarchal palace at Constantinople, which speaks of Christ operating both divine and human things "with his own authentic will" (*idiōi authentikōi thelēmati*)—an exposition that of course echoes the content and wording of the *Ekthesis*.[136]

John's opposition to monotheletism is not in doubt, however. There survives in three forms a letter to Heraclius Constantine and Heraclonas, Heraclius's sons and successors, in which he mounts a (weak) defense of his predecessor Honorius's antimonothelete credentials, claiming that the former's statement to Sergius concerning the "one will" of Christ referred to the natural human will alone, which, in

---

133. *Record* 9 [Allen and Neil 66]. It is notable that herein Heraclius claims that Sergius composed the *Ekthesis* "five years before my return from the East" and requests its publication upon his return. Heraclius returned from the East in 638, thus supporting the idea that the *Ekthesis* was published earlier than was later alleged and was for the most part a recapitulation of the *Psēphos*; see above n. 61; and cf. Jankowiak (2009) 177.

134. Maximus Confessor, *Opuscula* 12 [*PG* 91, 142D–143A; also *PL* 80, 488D; *PL* 128, 574C–575A].

135. See also Brandes (1998b) 203 n. 399; Winkelmann (2001) 96f. no. 68; Jankowiak (2009) 175–78; *contra*, e.g., Van Dieten (1972) 47f. n. 161. For the avoidance of direct condemnation of the emperor see below pp. 294, 313.

136. See Alexakis (1995–96). Cf. *Acts of the Lateran Synod* [Riedinger 158–60]. For the same iconophile text see Rizou-Couroupos (1987) and the comments of Brandes (1998b) 203 with n. 399. The fragment supports the earlier dating for the *Ekthesis*—see above n. 61—for Heraclius therein claims that the inscription was put up "three years ago" (January 638) and thus at least eight months before the traditional date for the *Ekthesis* (twelfth indiction). Alexakis (1995–96) 100 notes the problem and suggests that the inscription inspired the edict; it is of course far more probable that the inscription memorialized the edict. Cf. Jankowiak (2009) 178f.

being free from sin, precluded two opposed wills (but not two wills per se). Will, so John argued, was an attribute of nature—thus to speak of "one will" was to confuse the natures, to contradict the *Tome* of Leo, and to profess one nature of Christ. In two versions of the letter—though not in the third (Latin) version—John therefore offered an explicit statement of Christ's "two operations" and "two wills," and begged the emperors to rescind the *Ekthesis*, that infamous document to which orthodox bishops had been forced to subscribe.[137] The letter itself, of course, does not support the notion that Heraclius had earlier rescinded the *Ekthesis* in the West or elsewhere; it does, however, confirm that Rome itself had defected to the antimonothelete cause.[138]

---

137. The three versions of Pope John IV, *Letter in Defense of Honorius* (CPG 9383), are: a retranslation from Greek into Latin by Anastasius Bibliothecarius, at *PL* 80 [602C–607C]; a Karshuni translation rendered into German in Schacht (1936); and an Arabic précis in Eutychius, *Annals (Antiochene Recension)* [Cheiko 325–32]. The explicit statement concerning Christ's two wills occurs at Schacht (1936) 236 ("der Messias zwei Willen und zwei Wirkungsweisen hat"). On this letter see also Conte (1971) 387f., 427–29 no. 99; Winkelmann (2001) 97–99 no. 69; Zocca (1992) 123–29; Jankowiak (2009) 187–91. Ibid. 191 for the letter's address to both emperors (rather than Heraclius Constantine alone).

138. A letter of Sergius archbishop of Cyprus to Pope Theodore contained within the *Acts of the Lateran Synod* [Riedinger 60–64] and dated to May 643 testifies to a similar turnaround there: "For until today, while they [the monotheletes] were practicing some sort of accommodation [*oikonomian tina*], we remained silent, thinking that they would change their own teachings for the better. For thus also thought our divine Arcadius." [62]; cf. Conte (1971) 437 no. 119; Winkelmann (2001) 108 no. 83. Sergius perhaps excuses Arcadius's own opposition to Sophronius and Maximus as described in George of Resh'aina, *Life* 7–14. However, it is notable that Arcadius is treated as orthodox in Maximus Confessor, *Opuscula* 12 [*PG* 91, 143B]; cf. also *Georgian Appendix to the Spiritual Meadow* 28; Anastasius of Sinai, *Tales* B7, C15. It is also of interest to note that Leontius of Neapolis's *Life of John the Almsgiver*, in which Sophronius receives a great deal of praise for his orthodox doctrine, was composed at the instigation of Arcadius; see Festugière and Rydén (1974) 2–3, 411. At *Opuscula* 20 [*PG* 91, 245B-D] Maximus requests that his Cypriot correspondent Marinus inform Arcadius of his orthodoxy, and Jankowiak (2009) 198f. suggests that Maximus's entire correspondence with Marinus was in fact addressed to Arcadius, in an attempt to win him over via "un proche collaborateur." Like Pyrrhus, Arcadius fell foul of Constantinopolitan favor with the downfall of Martina, but he died before action could be taken; see John of Nikiu, *Chronicle* 120, suggesting, perhaps, that Arcadius in fact remained loyal to Pyrrhus to the end. For Arcadius see also Winkelmann (2001) 196–98. Maximus Confessor, *Opuscula* 19 (dated post-642) perhaps shows a battle to win over Cyprus, for he therein responds to some questions from the Constantinopolitan monothelete deacon Theodore apparently sent via his Cypriot correspondent Marinus; see also Winkelmann (2001) 109 no. 86, 273; *PmbZ* "Theodoros" 7529. See also George of Resh'aina, *Life* 23, associating the Muslim conquest of Cyprus with the island's acceptance of Maximus's doctrine. Sergius nevertheless appears later to have recanted his rejection of monotheletism, for in Theodore Spudaeus, *Narrations* 2 [Neil 166], in warning Martin not to give in, the author summons up "the shipwreck ["naufragium"] of Sergius, archbishop of the island of Cyprus." As Neil (2006c) 167 n. 31 observes, this perhaps occurred coterminous with Muslim pressure on the island, although the date of 647 that she gives is too early; see below p. 279. For Sergius see also *PmbZ* "Sergios" 6532; Winkelmann (2001) 261 (neither noting the recantation). He was in place still in December 655; see Theodore of Paphos, *Life of Spyridon* 20 [van den Ven 89].

The appointment of John's successor perhaps indicates how radical this defection was, for while Honorius, Severinus, and John had all been Western in origin—from Campania, Rome, and Dalmatia—the *Book of Pontiffs* describes their successor Theodore as "born in Greece, the son of Theodore, a bishop from Jerusalem" ("natione Grecus, ex patre Theodoro episcopo de civitate Hierusolima").[139] The Romans, therefore, had taken the remarkable step of appointing a Hellenophone pope with significant ties to Palestine, an indication, no doubt, both of the Roman desire to continue its theological agitation with the East and of the influence of the expatriated Palestinian faction now ensconced within the West.

Theodore, who ascended to the papal throne in November 642 and who was, it seems, elected without imperial approval, continued his predecessor's work.[140] In a letter to the new emperor, Constans II, now preserved in Karshuni (that is, Arabic in Syriac script), he requested the rescinding of the *Ekthesis* and expressed his surprise that the emperor had still not done so. He then demanded that the bishops who had elected the new Constantinopolitan patriarch Paul all anathematize his predecessor Pyrrhus, and that Paul himself refuse to reelect those deposed bishops who had served in the previous regime lest the latter might instead undertake to sow dissent both among his bishops and against Rome.[141] The new pope then sent a separate letter to Paul that repeated his call for the *Ekthesis* to be abandoned,[142] and a final letter to those bishops who had elected Paul, condemning his predecessor, chiding them for labeling the latter "sanctissimus" and calling for ecclesiastical union.[143] Although Theodore, unlike his predecessor John, at no point made explicit reference to the issue of the Christological wills, his vociferous condemnation of both the *Ekthesis* and its proponents, including the emperor Heraclius, was unambiguous.[144]

---

139. *Book of Pontiffs* [Duchesne vol. 1, 331]. The punctuation can of course be altered so that Theodore himself is from Jerusalem, but we know nothing more of his origins, and it is probable that he was more Lateran careerist than recent refugee.

140. See Jankowiak (2009) 204, pointing to how short the time was between the death of Pope John IV and the election of Pope Theodore.

141. Pope Theodore, *Letter to Constans*. I have here depended on the Latin translation in Mai (1852–1905) vol. 6, 510f., but the letter is also translated into German in Schacht (1936) 249–52. Cf. the version of the letter in Eutychius, *Annals (Antiochene Recension)* [Cheiko 325–32]; see also Conte (1971) 433f. no. 113; Winkelmann (2001) 103f. no. 77.

142. Pope Theodore, *Letter to Paul* [PL 87, 75C–80B]. See also the exemplar of the same at PL 87, 80B–D.

143. Pope Theodore, *Letter to the Bishops* [PL 87, 81B–82D]. It should be noted that in these letters and in the *Letter to Constans* Heraclius is presented in unambiguous terms as a heretic, contradicting the later claim that he renounced the *Ekthesis* before his death. For the same explicit condemnation see the letter of Theodore to Constans in Eutychius, *Annals (Antiochene Recension)* [Cheiko 336–39]. For these documents see also Conte (1971) 431–33, nos. 113–16; Winkelmann (2001) 103–6 nos. 77–81. For what they reveal of the content of Paul's earlier encyclical see below p. 282.

144. It is interesting to note that the lack of doctrinal reference (again in contrast to John) is reproduced in the papal letters as set out in Eutychius, *Annals (Antiochene Recension)* [Cheiko 336–39].

How, then, to explain this spectacular turnaround? We should, of course, not lose sight of the wider political context in which the volte-face occurred. While Honorius's *First Letter to Sergius*—which first asserted the monothelete formula— had been sent before 636, since then Heraclius's forces had suffered two crucial defeats within the East.[145] In the same period, as we have seen, the patriarch of Alexandria had negotiated an expensive reprieve for Egypt, but around 640 the political hawks in Constantinople gained the upper hand, refused to deliver the tribute, and thus precipitated the Muslim invasion of the Nile Delta.[146] Little wonder, then, if some in Rome associated the significant and unceasing disasters on the temporal plane with divine disfavor over doctrine.[147]

There may, of course, have been more immediate grievances. From 636, the new Lombard king, Rothari, had launched an offensive against Roman holdings in the north of the Italian Peninsula, and despite the successful resistance of the exarch Isaac—memorialized in his extant epitaph—had seized several towns along the western and eastern coasts.[148] We cannot ascertain the papal reaction, for the *Book of Pontiffs* and the letters of Honorius maintain a stubborn silence on Lombard activities in this period. The defensive effort nevertheless seems to have exhausted the public purse and to have precipitated a controversial seizure of papal monies. According to the *Book of Pontiffs*' short notice on the brief tenure of Severinus (in the middle months of 640), while he was still pope-elect one Maurice *cartularius* incited Roman soldiers to seize the Lateran Palace, spurring them on with the suggestion that Honorius had kept hidden the stipends sent to them from Constantinople. He then wrote to the Italian exarch Isaac at Ravenna, indicating that no obstacle now impeded the plundering of the papal coffers. Isaac, therefore, came to Rome, banished all the clerics who might offer resistance to his plans, and then raided the Lateran Palace, dispatching a portion of the proceeds to Heraclius in Constantinople.[149] The state's seizure of ecclesial monies—for which there are numerous precedents in Heraclius's reign—no doubt had a real economic purpose,[150] but it is also possible, of course, that the act also served as a convenient

---

145. For these two defeats see above at n. 65.

146. See above p. 250f.

147. That people did indeed think in such ways is indicated, for example, in Gregory the Great, *Letters* 2.43, admonishing "Eastern bishops" for associating temporal disaster with the condemnation of the Three Chapters.

148. For these conquests see Fredegar, *Chronicle* 4.71; Paul the Deacon, *History* 4.45. For the epitaph (CPG IV, 9869), which identifies him as an Armenian, see Bertolini (1952) 118. I have not been able to access (on the same inscription) Cosentino (1993). Cf. the peaceable relations between Isaac and Rothari's predecessor described in Fredegar, *Chronicle* 4.69; but see (for a similar tale placed earlier and with "Gregory the Patrician" as the actor) Paul the Deacon, *History* 4.38.

149. *Book of Pontiffs* 73. On Isaac see *PLRE* vol. 3, "Isaacius 8"; *PmbZ* "Isaakios"' 3466; Winkelmann (2001) 217f.

150. See Kaegi (2002) 172f.; Jankowiak (2009) 166f.

demonstration of imperial strength while Roman bishops wavered over doctrine. If so, however, it appears to have had the opposite effect.

At the same time, we must also acknowledge the sustained diplomatic pressure that the Palestinian faction around Sophronius and Maximus appears to have applied to successive popes and a simultaneous evolution that refocused the doctrinal debate not on the question of the Christological operations but on that of the wills. As we have seen above, the monothelete formula was enshrined within the imperial *Ekthesis* of 636, and in searching for the reasons behind the Constantinopolitan support for the "one will" formula, it is natural to assume, as most scholars do, that it was a simple and inextricable continuation of the failed monenergist compromise.[151] But if so, we must also explain the emperor's decision now to promote a further controversial formula, at a time both of vociferous opposition to the "one operation" and of considerable losses across the Levant (at the churches of which, we should remember, official monenergism had been aimed). It is possible that this represented a last, desperate effort to ensure the union of moderate miaphysite communities in Syria, Egypt, and Armenia,[152] but it is also possible that the monothelete formula was not yet perceived as controversial. Indeed, unlike the question of the operation (or operations), the question of the Christological will (or wills) with which the former came to be related had little pedigree in the post-Chalcedonian period (either in pro-Chalcedonian or in anti-Chalcedonian circles).[153] As we have seen above, it is probable that Sergius's earlier *Psēphos*—which Sophronius accepted and Maximus at first praised—contained alongside its suppression of discussion on the energies a statement to the effect that two opposed wills in Christ was impossible.[154] Sergius, therefore, may have assumed that the accepted principle that Christ could not contain two opposed wills was identical to the recognition of "one will."[155]

---

151. So, e.g., Hovorun (2008) 162.

152. For Severan monotheletism see, e.g., Chesnut (1976) 20–29. The Armenian connection is suggested in Greenwood (2008) 252f. (who ignores consistent Constantinopolitan repositioning on the monothelete formula in the face of Roman and Palestinian opposition).

153. Notwithstanding, of course, the mutual creation of florilegia to support either position. For monenergist/monothelete florilegia see, e.g., *Dispute at Bizya* 4, with Winkelmann (2001) 149 no. 145a; *Acts of the Sixth Ecumenical Council* [Riedinger 168, 176, 232–60, 268–74], with Winkelmann (2001) 135f. no. 127. The lack of pedigree for discussion on the will is indicated above all in the total absence of post-Chalcedonian dyothelete citations in the *Acts of the Lateran Council*. I am thus also skeptical of the attempts of some scholars to establish either dyotheletism or monotheletism as the more "natural" or widespread position prior to the 640s; see, e.g., Hovorun (2008) 164; Levy-Rubin (2001) 286–89. Nevertheless the latter, Brock (1973) 343–45, and Tannous (2006) 13–34 argue convincingly that monotheletism was the more widespread position across the Levant after ca. 650.

154. See above n. 58.

155. For Sergius's apparent assumption that "'different' means 'contrary'" see, e.g., Léthel (1979) 36–49; Doucet (1983) 58–63; Bathrellos (2004) 72–77; Price (2010) 225–28. For the same argument in a later context see, e.g., Paul of Constantinople, *Letter to Theodore* in *Acts of the Lateran Council* [Riedinger 200]; *Disputation with Pyrrhus* [*PG* 91, 292A–B]; *Dispute at Bizya* 4 [Allen and Neil 96].

(This, indeed, is presented as a popular monothelete argument.) If so, then the proclamation of "one will" within the *Ekthesis* was a continuation not so much of the doctrinal initiative represented in the *Pact of Union* as of the attempted restoration of the status quo presented in the *Psēphos*.

If Sophronius also recognized the *Ekthesis*—as some sources suggest—then it is possible that its explicit proclamation of "one will" was not at first perceived as the natural companion of "one operation."[156] Indeed, Sophronius himself demonstrated little interest in the explicit issue of the Christological will (or wills), and we should perhaps be cautious in extending to him an association of operation (or operations) and will (or wills) that we (in light of Maximus's later thought) may regard as self-evident.[157] After Sophronius's death, however, as the crisis of the Eastern empire deepened, Maximus began to agitate against the official recognition of monothelete doctrine, presenting it as a natural extension of monenergism. The doctrine of "two wills," however, which becomes so important to Maximus's thought, makes no explicit appearance in his extant corpus before about 640. (In fact, even in the late 630s, it was the *Ekthesis*'s suppression of the discussion on the operations that still appears most to rile him.)[158] From that time, however, and thus coterminously with Pope John's condemnation of the monothelete formula in his letter to Heraclius Constantine and Heraclonas, Maximus began his open opposition to monotheletism.[159]

Nevertheless, it is important that we not regard that doctrine as a simple political expedience, an artificial construct designed to frustrate once again imperial attempts to impose a Constantinopolitan consensus. Maximus's doctrine, once developed, provided a compelling solution to a genuine Christological and soteriological

---

156. For Sophronius's possible recognition of the *Ekthesis* see above at p. 240f.

157. For discussion see Schönborn (1972) 219f., with n. 132, and p. 75 n. 164 above. It should be noted that some scholars wish to read quasi-monothelete sentiments into Sophronius and Maximus's works from this period. See Sophronius, *Synodical Letter* 2.3.13 [Riedinger 450; repr. Allen (2009) 106], with Price (2010) 223, and Sophronius, *Letter to Arcadius* 44; Maximus Confessor, *Ambigua to Thomas* 5 [Janssens 24], speaking of Christ "moving the assumed nature of his own initiative [*autourgikōs*] in the same manner as the soul naturally moves the body with which it is born," with Parente (1953). Cf. the similar sentiment in the *Psēphos* at Sergius of Constantinople, *First Letter to Honorius* [Riedinger 542–44; repr. Allen (2009) 190]. For the date of Maximus's *Ambigua to Thomas* (ca. 634 "or shortly after") see Sherwood (1952a) 39. Other critics, however, have denied that this implies monotheletism; see esp. Schönborn (1972) 219f.; Larchet (1996) 292–314, esp. 312–14; also Bathrellos (2004) 165f.; Hovorun (2008) 126f.; Tollefsen (2012) 155f. Cf. the treatment of the same theme in Maximus Confessor, *Opuscula* 7 [*PG* 91, 77B].

158. See Maximus Confessor, *Letter to Thalassios* [*PL* 129, 583D–586B]. The letter survives only in the Latin translation of Anastasius Bibliothecarius and is fragmentary, so that it is possible that this critique of the operations developed into a now-lost discussion of the monothelete formula.

159. For the outpouring of antimonenergist and antimonothelete texts that occurred ca. 640–45 see the useful list in Hovorun (2008) 77f.

problem, and at the same time condensed and refined thoughts that had for some time been evident within his output. Thus, for example, in two of his earlier texts, the *Questions to Thalassius* and the *Exposition on the Lord's Prayer,* Maximus had expounded a Christological position that predicted his later stance on the two natural wills (and that underscored the soteriological basis for its defense).[160] In acknowledging the existence of these important continuities, however, we should not fall into the opposite trap of regarding Maximus's thought as somehow immune to all change. For in the precise same texts the undeveloped nature of his stance is proven both in the application of *gnōmē* or *proairesis* to Christ in a positive sense, in contrast to later thought,[161] and in the implicit (and never explicit) suggestion of two natural wills, the explication of which is not here the prevailing impulse. Indeed, the absence of a pressing concern over the will (or wills) is proven in Maximus's use throughout this period, in non-Christological contexts, of both "one will" and "single will," inconceivable in a context of resistance to monotheletism.[162] Such statements point to an obvious conclusion: that the doctrine of "two wills"—like that of "two operations"—drew from existing principles but was, at the same time, elevated and refined in relation to its doctrinal opposite.

Thus in *Opuscula* 4, which Jean-Claude Larchet regards as the earliest of Maximus's writings devoted to the explicit problem of the Christological will (and places ca. 640),[163] and which was sent to one "George the Most Holy Priest and

160. See, e.g., among various statements Maximus Confessor, *Exposition on the Lord's Prayer* 135–39 [Van Deun 34]: Christ "restores nature to itself in that, having become man, he preserved a will [*gnōmē*] that was passionless and undisturbed in regard to nature [*apathēs pros tēn phusin kai astasiastos*], and in no way was it shaken from its own movement according to nature, even in the face of his very crucifiers"; cf. Maximus Confessor, *Exposition on the Lord's Prayer* 148–53 [Van Deun 35] and 159–64 [Van Deun 35f.], with Bathrellos (2004) 150f.; Berthold (2011). See also Maximus Confessor, *Questions to Thalassius* 21 [Laga and Steel vol. 1, 129.49–50]; 42 [Laga and Steel vol. 1, 285–89]; 61 [Laga and Steel vol. 2, 95.187], with Larchet (1996) 231–43. Sherwood (1952a) 34 dates Maximus's *Questions to Thalassius* to 630–34.

161. See Maximus Confessor, *Exposition on the Lord's Prayer* 135–39 [Van Deun 34] and *Questions to Thalassius* 42 [Laga and Steel vol. 1, 7.285–89]. Maximus would later explicitly retract the earlier use of *proairesis* in the latter; see Maximus Confessor, *Opuscula* 1 [*PG* 91, 29D–31A], which Larchet (1998b) dates to ca. 645/6. For the change in the use of *gnōmē* cf. Maximus Confessor, *Opuscula* 16 [*PG* 91, 192A, 193A], which Larchet (1998b) dates to "a little after 643." For the undeveloped nature of Maximus's thought on *gnōmē* and *proairesis* in the earlier period see also Thunberg (1965) 227f.; Bausenhart (1992) 154f.; Larchet (1996) 241–43; Bathrellos (2004) 149–51.

162. For the statements of "single will" or "one will" see Maximus Confessor, *Exposition on the Lord's Prayer* 111–15 [Van Deun 33] and 181f. [Van Deun 37]. See also Maximus Confessor, *Letters* 2 [*PG* 91, 396C]: "And when [faith] persuades our judgment [*gnōmē*] to proceed according to nature so that it never rebels against the *logos* of nature, then all of us, as if with one nature, can have with God and with one another both one judgment and one will [*mia gnōmē kai thelēma hen*]"; cf. *PG* 91, 401B; Maximus Confessor, *Opuscula* 18 [*PG* 91, 213B].

163. Larchet (1998b) 27; also Léthel (1979) 65–74; Winkelmann (2001) 84 no. 48.

Higoumen,"[164] Maximus proclaims that Christ was "a perfect man, like us except for sin alone, through which we often rebel and wrestle against God, according to our will [kata tēn thelēsin].... But he, being free of all sin according to nature, since he was not a mere man but God made man, had nothing in opposition [to God]." "Whence his humanity," he continues, "differed from ours not on account of the *logos* of nature [dia ton logon tēs phuseōs] but by the novel *tropos* of creation [dia ton kainoprepē tēs geneseōs tropon].... And so just as his will [to thelein autou] is truly natural like ours, in being formed divinely it surpasses ours."[165] Christ's natural human will, in being free from sin, and thus in full accordance with the divine, surpassed ours in terms of its mode. Here, then, Maximus presents a clear challenge to the monothelete doctrine of the *Ekthesis*; at the same time, however, as Larchet has noted, his position, in comparison with his later ruminations on the will, remains somewhat underdeveloped.[166] Like Pope John IV, furthermore, he did not commit to an outright statement of "two wills."

Like Pope John IV again, Maximus in the same period mounted a defense of Honorius's dyothelete credentials. In that defense—contained within his *Opuscula* 20, composed around 641—he nevertheless adopted a different approach to John, for whereas the latter made an association between Honorius's position and the *Ekthesis*,[167] Maximus focuses instead on the *First Letter to Sergius* (a further indication, perhaps, of his distinct discomfort over the actual circumstances of the *Ekthesis*'s publication); and whereas John had argued that the "one will" contained within Honorius's letter in fact referred to the human will alone (designed to guard against two wills in opposition), Maximus argues instead that it referred to the divine will (again, however, in order to guard against two wills in opposition): "I think that

---

164. This George should perhaps be identified with the "Abba George the Sanctified" who appears in Maximus Confessor, *Letters* 29 and 31; see above pp. 165-68 n. 123. Another potential recipient is the (different) George who was higoumen of Moschus and Sophronius's Monastery of Theodosius near Jerusalem in this period; see *Prologue to the Spiritual Meadow* [Usener 58f.]; Pope Martin, *Letter to George of Theodosius* [PL 87, 167B-D]. For the identification of the latter see Follieri (1988) 18; Flusin (1992b) vol. 2, 16 n. 2, 370. For the same George Higoumen of Theodosius in the context of John Moschus's burial at Jerusalem late in 634, see above p. 232f. Cf. *PmbZ* "Georgios" 2064; Winkelmann (2001) 206.

165. Maximus Confessor, *Opuscula* 4 [PG 91, 60B-C]. Maximus in the same opusculum defends a contested passage of Gregory of Nazianzus on Christ's proclamation that he had come down from heaven to do the will of the one who sent him [PG 91, 61A-B]. It is clear that the monotheletes were citing the passage in defense of their position; see above n. 101 and p. 193 n. 27. For the dyothelete defense see also, e.g., Maximus Confessor, *Opuscula* 20 [PG 91, 233B-237C]; *Acts of the Lateran Council* [Riedinger 270]; *Disputation with Pyrrhus* [PG 91, 316C-317A]; and the frescoes of Santa Maria Antiqua discussed above at p. 189f. For discussion Bathrellos (2004) 141-43 and esp. Hovorun (2008) 131f.

166. See Larchet (1998b) 27.

167. See Pope John IV, *Letter in Defense of Honorius* [PL 80, 606B-607A].

Honorius, pope of the Roman church, did not denounce the duality of the natural wills in Christ [hē tōn emphutōn thelēmatōn epi Christou duas] when he spoke of 'one will' in the letter to Sergius but rather advocated and approved it, as is reasonable, speaking thus not for the abolition of the Savior's natural and human will but to give precedence to the absence of the will of the flesh or the impassioned thought [thelēma sarkos ē logismon empathē] from his unbegotten conjunction and uncorrupted creation."[168] Maximus then launches into a long dissection of Honorius's text, arguing that his use of "one will" has excluded "the impassioned and not the natural will in the Savior."[169] "And so to speak in sum," he concludes, "I think it is clear that through 'the one will' [was meant] the precedence of the divine will alone over creation according to the flesh, and that through 'there is no difference of will' [was meant] that it was not oppositional or conflictual but in all things went in step and in union."[170] Against all outward appearances, therefore, Honorius was not a monothelete.[171]

In a further defense of the pope, Maximus reports in the same text that his own disciple Anastasius had returned from a recent trip to Rome. There, he reports, Anastasius questioned "the most sacred men of the great church there" concerning "their letter to Sergius" (sc. that of Honorius). When he asked them how it spoke of "one will," "he found them grieved at it, and apologetic, and in addition the one who had dictated this in Latin according to [Honorius's] order—that is, the most holy Lord Abba John Symponus—affirmed that he had made no mention whatsoever of the will alongside the number one, even if this had now been invented by those who translated it into the Greek tongue."[172] Maximus, therefore, mounts a (rather desperate) double defense of Honorius's position: in proclaiming "one will," he had in fact meant "two wills"; and besides, he had not said "one will" in the first place.

---

168. Maximus Confessor, *Opuscula* 20 [*PG* 91, 237C–D]. For the date see Jankowiak (2009) 185 n. 94. To this early period also belongs *Opuscula* 7, "To the Deacon Marinus" [*PG* 91, 69B–89B]. *Contra* Larchet (1998b) 50, Sherwood (1952a) 41f., 51, Maximus's *Opuscula* 20 in fact seems to postdate *Opuscula* 7; see Léthel (1979) 74–77; Bathrellos (2004) 198 n. 114. For both texts see Winkelmann (2001) 90f. nos. 59 and 60. *Pace* Sherwood (1952a) 42, with n. 155, and Van Dieten (1972) 45, it seems to me quite inconceivable that Maximus was not now aware of the *Ekthesis*.

169. Maximus Confessor, *Opuscula* 20 [*PG* 91, 241B–C].

170. Maximus Confessor, *Opuscula* 20 [*PG* 91, 244A]. Cf. the reference to this same redactor in the *Disputation with Pyrrhus* [*PG* 91, 328B–329C].

171. For analysis see also Doucet (1983) 68–70; Zocca (1992) 130–35; Larchet (1998c) 128–33. The defenses of Honorius by John and Maximus are the first in a long series of attempts to deal with the so-called *Honoriusfrage*; see Bäumer (1961); Conte (1971) 299–304; Kreuzer (1975); Schwaiger (1977); Zocca (1987) and (1992) 110–21; and more literature in Winkelmann (2001) 213 and Bathrellos (2004) 78 n. 86. Despite Maximus's efforts, Honorius was nevertheless condemned at the Sixth Ecumenical Council; see Conte (1977) 80–103.

172. Maximus Confessor, *Opuscula* 20 [*PG* 91, 244C–D]. Cf. also the later defense of Honorius contained within the *Disputation with Pyrrhus* [*PG* 91, 328B–329C].

The visit of Maximus's disciple to Rome appears to have been part of a far wider diplomatic effort on the part of his circle in this period, an effort that aimed to secure Roman support for the antimonothelete cause. Within the *libellus* of Stephen of Dora contained within the *Acts of the Lateran Council*, the Palestinian bishop reports that his attendance at the Lateran Council was his third visit to Rome. The first, we can assume, was that aforementioned mission on behalf of Sophronius, launched from Golgotha; but the second, it seems, was undertaken to persuade one or other of Honorius's successors to abandon their support for the *Ekthesis*. For the period following his first petition, Stephen's *libellus* proceeds to allege that his opponents, "upon learning of what I had done, piled no trifling afflictions upon me, sending commands about me through places and regions that I should be arrested and sent to them in chains." Nevertheless, he then prevailed on the Roman popes to support his position: "God did not disregard the petition of his servants delivered with tears but to no small extent stirred up the previous apostolic high priests [*ēgeire tous prolabontas apostolikous archiereas*] to exhort and at the same time to beg the aforementioned [monenergists], even if they in no way mollified them."[173] Stephen's account, therefore, points once again to the intense period of diplomatic exchange between Rome and Maximus's Palestinian circle in the late 630s as well as hinting at his own prominent role in the doctrinal volte-face at Rome.

Following the death of Sophronius and the subsequent galvanization of the monothelete consensus in the East, Maximus had run the distinct risk of being remembered as a heresiarch within the Greek and Latin churches, to be counted alongside Nestorius as one who had divided Christ. The dramatic and perhaps unexpected volte-face at Rome perhaps rescued him from that fate and provided a vital and venerable medium through which to articulate the doctrinal opposition to Constantinople, now refocused on the monothelete doctrine first promoted some years earlier. With the conversion of Rome to their cause, the deposition of the arch-monothelete Pyrrhus, and continued imperial reversals under Muslim pressure, Maximus and his colleagues must have been confident that God, indeed, was on their side.

## MAXIMUS AND THE POPES

Like the "two operations" doctrine that it complemented, Maximus's development of the "two wills" cannot be detached from the charged double context within which it occurred: on the world stage, far-reaching Christian reversals in the face of the Muslim expansion, and at the personal level, Maximus's own retreat, for the second time, from the embattled eastern provinces. The "two wills" formula

173. *Acts of the Lateran Council* [Riedinger 42].

inhabited a space in which political and doctrinal perceptions were interwoven: on the one hand, Constantinopolitan failures in the terrestrial sphere fueled the notion that imperial doctrine was a cause of divine disfavor, and on the other, the articulation of a doctrinal opposition established the intellectual basis upon which political agitation could be legitimized. As Richard Price has argued, however, there was now a crucial difference: for whereas theologians of the "one operation" or "two operations" proved often inconsistent and indistinguishable in their doctrinal statements, Maximus now promulgated an innovation in the faith that provided a substantial theological difference to the stance of his opponents—the concept of the full, rational, human will in Christ.[174] He now began to develop and disseminate that concept in earnest.[175]

Maximus also now realized, no doubt, that his own political and intellectual fate depended on establishing Rome's unwavering adherence to orthodox doctrine. As we have seen, about 640 he penned a defense of Pope Honorius's use of a monothelete formula,[176] and later in the same decade he composed from Carthage a letter in which he defended the use of the Trinitarian *filioque* formula in Pope Theodore's synodical, in the face of detractors at Constantinople.[177] At the same time, throughout his writings from this period, Maximus emphasized the privileged position that Rome occupied in relation to the other patriarchates. In the aforementioned letter to Thalassius (ca. 640)— preserved in Latin alone—describing the fate of Severinus's *apocrisiarii* at Constantinople Maximus spoke of Rome

---

174. Price (2010) esp. 229–32. The departure of Maximus from previous patristic thought on the question of the wills—in particular in respect of Gethsemane—is demonstrated in Bathrellos (2004) 129–47. For Maximus's falsification of third-century to fifth-century patristic texts on the will, in a disingenuous attempt to establish the pedigree of will speculation, see Madden (1982). For Maximus's concept of the will in long perspective see also Sorabji (2003).

175. This is not the place for a full discussion of Maximus's complex concept of the will, which is the preserve proper of philosophers and theologians. The literature is now vast, but for introduction see the extensive discussions of Thunberg (1965) 220–43; Léthel (1979) 59–99; Doucet (1983) 70–76; Bausenhart (1992) 110–82; Larchet (1996) 221–382; Bathrellos (2004) 99–174; Hovorun (2008) 143–62.

176. See also the positive reference to Honorius in Maximus Confessor, *Opuscula* 12 [PG 91, 143A–B], dated in Sherwood (1952a) 52 and Larchet (1998b) 73 to 643/4. See also the praise for John IV and Honorius in *Disputation with Pyrrhus* (removed from the PG edition but present in Doucet's more recent but unpublished edition, and noted at Larchet (1998c) 129f. nn. 16 and 17).

177. Maximus Confessor, *Opuscula* 10 [PG 91, 133B–137C]. For the location at Carthage see PG 91, 137B, and for the date (ca. 645) Sherwood (1952a) 53–55. It should be noted that the *filioque* does not appear in the synodical letter of Theodore at PL 87, 75–80B—which is, however, incomplete. For the date and the identification of Theodore as "the present pope" see Sherwood (1952a) 54f.; Larchet (1998b) 76, with n. 1. I do not intend to treat the complex question of Maximus and the *filioque*; but see Larchet (1998c) 11–75; Jankowiak (2009) 210–14, and now Siecienski (2010) esp. 73–86. For the authenticity of the defense see, e.g., ibid. 78–86, to which we may also add the use of the *filioque* formula in the Hatfield Canons issued by Maximus's associate Theodore of Tarsus; see Bede, *Ecclesiastical History* 4.17, with Chadwick (1995); Bischoff and Lapidge (1994) 139–46.

as the "Ecclesiarum princeps mater et urbs" and called her ambassadors "firmae revera et immobilis petrae ministri, maximae videlicet et apostolicae quae illic est Ecclesiae."[178] From around this same period, but again preserved only in later Latin extracts, dates a letter sent to Peter the Illustrious, known as *Opuscula* 12 (ca. 643–45).[179] It is evident that Peter, in expectation of some imminent meeting or communication with Pyrrhus, had sought Maximus's opinion on the deposed patriarch, including the continued application to him of honorific titles (an issue that, we will remember, had also been raised in a letter of Pope Theodore to bishops in Constantinople). Within the letter, Maximus declares that as the Romans have condemned him, "anyone who anathematizes those who condemned Pyrrhus also anathematizes the see of Rome—that is, the catholic Church." Maximus recommends, therefore, that one not call Pyrrhus "sanctissimus," for "he has fallen from all sanctity, having in fact leapt from the catholic Church of his own accord." "For it is not right," he continues, "that he be addressed with any honor, when he has now been damned and rejected by the apostolic see of the city of Rome on account of his conception of alien opinion, until such time as he is received by her, having converted to her or rather to the Lord our God through pious confession and the orthodox faith, in which he will receive sanctification and the title 'sanctus.'" The monothelete patriarch, therefore, "should above all hasten to give satisfaction to Rome.... For he simply speaks in vain if he thinks that men like me need to be persuaded, and he does not satisfy and implore the most blessed pope of the most sacred Church of the Romans—that is, the apostolic see—which from the incarnate Word itself, but also in all the sacred synods, according to the sacred canons and definitions, has received and holds the rule, the authority, and the power of binding and loosing ["imperium, auctoritatem et potestatem ligandi et solvendi"] of the universal holy Churches of God throughout the entire world, through and in all things."[180] Maximus, therefore, here emphasizes three distinct bases for the Roman Church's preeminence: its status as the guardian of the orthodox faith; its inheritance through the promise of Christ to Saint Peter [Matt. 16:18–19]; and its recognition through conciliar and canonical decree.

A further profuse statement of Roman preeminence comes in a later text still extant in an excerpt in Greek—that is, *Opuscula* 11, composed at Rome in the

---

178. Maximus Confessor, *Letter to Thalassius* [*PL* 129, 585A, 586A]. Cf. also the apparent words of the *apocrisiarii* at *PL* 129, 585B–586A. See also Larchet (1998c) 134–37.

179. The letter (Maximus Confessor, *Opuscula* 12) dates to before Pyrrhus's recantation at Rome but after the death of Pope John IV in November 642, for the pope is referred to as "of blessed memory" [*PG* 91, 143A]. Sherwood (1952a) 52 and Winkelmann (2001) 110f. no. 88 situate it in late 643 or 644, but see Boudignon (2007) 256 n. 22, placing it after the disputation with Maximus but before Pyrrhus's recantation at Rome. For Peter the Illustrious cf. above p. 152 n. 53.

180. Maximus Confessor, *Opuscula* 12 [*PG* 91, 144B–C].

aftermath of monotheletism's condemnation at the Lateran Council.[181] It is worthwhile citing in extenso:[182]

> For the ends of the inhabited world and those everywhere upon earth who confess the Lord purely and with good doctrine look up directly to the most holy Church of the Romans and her confession as to a sun of eternal light, and receive from her the flashing sunbeam of the patristic and holy dogmas, just as the God-possessed and God-inspired holy six councils [*hagiai hex sunodoi*] have purely and all-piously established, proclaiming most explicitly the symbol of the faith. From the beginning, when the incarnate God Word descended to us, all the churches of Christians everywhere have had and still have the greatest of them, here, as their sole base and foundation [*krēpida kai themelion*], since never is it overcome, according to the promise of the Savior, by the gates of hell, but has the keys of the orthodox faith and confession in him, and opens that single piety that is true by nature onto those who approach piously; while at the same time it closes and blocks up every heretical mouth that speaks unjustly against the most high.

Once again, therefore, Maximus emphasized Rome's continuous orthodox confession as the basis both of its preeminence and of its power to bind and loose, and presented that confession as guaranteed in the promise of Christ to Saint Peter.[183]

As has often been observed, this handful of texts contains some of the strongest statements of Roman privilege contained within Greek sources: the acknowledgment of a universal power derived from the promise of Christ; the emphasis upon Rome's status as the basis and guardian of the faith; and the guarantee that it would never be overcome.[184] It is not surprising that some scholars have questioned the authenticity of such statements—not least because the *Letter to Thalassius* and *Opuscula* 12, at least, survive only in Latin excerpts, preserved in the ninth century precisely for their pro-Roman content.[185] Broader evidence nevertheless suggests that Maximus's circle did indeed celebrate Roman preeminence in this period, as the Eastern consensus over monotheletism began to crystallize and as the realization dawned, no doubt, that Rome represented the last significant medium through

---

181. For the date see Sherwood (1952a) 56; Larchet (1998b) 106f.

182. Maximus Confessor, *Opuscula* 11 [*PG* 91, 137C–140B]. On the reference to the "six councils" see also below p. 293.

183. On Saint Peter as head of the Apostles in Maximus's corpus cf. Maximus Confessor, *Questions to Thalassius* 27, 59, 61 [Laga and Steel vol. 1, 197; vol. 2, 55, 101], and *Book* 18.

184. See, e.g., Cooper (2005) 180–90.

185. Both are preserved in the *Collectanea* of Anastasius Bibliothecarius; see *PL* 129, 573–76, 583–86, with Neil (2006c) 71–79. Some doubts as to the authenticity of Maximus Confessor, *Opuscula* 11, are explored in, e.g., Larchet (1998b) 106–8; Cooper (2005) 180, 184–87 (although the latter is mistaken in believing that the text is preserved only through Anastasius Bibliothecarius). Cf. Jankowiak (2009) 263f.

which that circle might express its doctrinal (and political) opinions.[186] Thus embedded in the *Acts of the Lateran Council*—a text that, as we shall see below, Maximus and his allies assumed a decisive role in preparing—we find numerous statements of Roman preeminence placed in the mouths of Eastern supplicants. Thus in prefacing his account of the oath that he swore to Sophronius on Golgotha, Stephen of Dora calls Rome "the see that rules and presides over all others, I mean of course your principal and preeminent see" (*tēi pasōn archousēi kai huperkeimenēi kathedrai, legō dē tēi kath' humas koruphaiai kai huperphuei*). This appeal to Roman power, he continued, was a Christian ancient practice that could claim apostolic and canonical authority, since "the truly great Peter, the head of the apostles, was not only deemed worthy to be entrusted, alone among all, with the keys of [the kingdom of] heaven ... but was also the first to be entrusted with shepherding the sheep of the whole catholic Church. ... And again, of course, because to a peculiar and distinctive extent he possessed above all others a firm and unalterable faith in our Lord, [he was deemed worthy] to correct and sustain his colleagues and spiritual brethren [cf. Lk. 22:32] when shaken, since through Providence he had been adorned by God, who was incarnate for us, with power and with sacerdotal authority [*to kuros kekosmēmenos kai tēn hieratikēn authentian*]."[187] For Stephen here, therefore, the preeminence of Rome over the other sees was guaranteed in the promise of Christ to Saint Peter, in the apostle's leadership of his colleagues, and, perhaps above all, in his unwavering faith in the Lord.

In his *Synodical Letter* Sophronius had himself referred to the Roman see as "the illuminator [*phōstēr*] of all the churches under the sun," and in recounting their dramatic encounter on Golgotha, Stephen has Sophronius place at Rome "the foundations [*hai krēpides*] of pious doctrines" and claim that Roman condemnation will constitute "a complete refutation of the novel doctrines."[188] In similar vein, a delegation of Eastern monks who later petitioned the Lateran Council besought "the apostolic and preeminent see ... through canon and council to avenge the most holy faith, besieged as it is by the aforementioned men, and after God to preserve it safe for all, pure and free from innovation [*akainotomētos*] and resplendent, just as it was before, in pious word, for all the orthodox priests, laity, and monks across the whole inhabited world, since after God the hearts of all depend on you, knowing that you have been established by Christ as the preeminent head of the churches [*koruphaia tōn ekklēsiōn kephalē*]."[189] Maximus's

---

186. Cf. Boudignon (2007) 272; also idem (2002) 329 on the repeated union of Palestinian monks with Chalcedonian bishops in this period.

187. *Acts of the Lateran Council* [Riedinger 38–40].

188. See Sophronius, *Synodical Letter* 2.5.4 [Riedinger 474; repr. Allen (2009) 132]; *Acts of the Lateran Council* [Riedinger 40].

189. *Acts of the Lateran Council* [Riedinger 52].

comments in the contested *Opuscula,* therefore, have a broader context that corroborates their content.[190]

We should nevertheless beware of regarding such statements as exhibiting some anachronistic commitment to the monarchical claims of the later, post-Gregorian popes. Maximus and his colleagues acknowledged Roman preeminence from various angles, and although their rhetoric sometimes veered toward recognition of near-autocratic Roman power in matters of the faith, their overwhelming criterion for papal preeminence was, as Larchet has insisted, Rome's unwavering commitment to orthodox doctrine.[191] Despite his defense of the orthodox credentials of popes Honorius and Theodore, and his overt celebration of Roman *imperium, auctoritas,* and *potestas* within the *Opuscula,* Maximus did not believe that Rome and its popes were infallible in matters of the faith (as the examination of Honorius and Theodore, rather than their acceptance as prima-facie authoritative, of course suggests).[192] Thus, in that text that presents his later trial within the capital, and in which he is confronted with the specter of Roman communion with Constantinople, Maximus, though reluctant to believe that the Romans would ever be reconciled to monotheletism, claims in response that the Spirit "anathematizes even angels who introduce some innovation besides what is preached [*to kērugma*]";[193] while in a later letter to his disciple Anastasius, again confronted with the potential union of the patriarchates, he reinterprets the promise of Christ to Saint Peter so as to guarantee not Roman power or preeminence but rather the permanence of the orthodox faith, irrespective of a particular place or institution: "The God of all proclaimed the universal Church to be the orthodox and salvific confession of the faith in him, when he blessed Peter because of his right confession in him."[194] Although, as we shall see, this retreat from the earlier rhetoric occurred in a distinct context, Maximus and his allies never invested in a narrative of absolute Roman power over matters of doctrine. Thus in 649 the delegation of Eastern monks within the *Acts of the Lateran Council,* for all their rhetoric of papal privilege, would still warn the Romans from acting against their pious petition and defining something "harmful to the faith."[195] Rome had in the past never succumbed to heretical doctrine; this did not mean, however, that she could not.

---

190. For the recognition of papal privilege contained within these documents see in more depth Conte (1971) 372–74; also Schönborn (1975) 480–83.

191. Encapsulated in Maximus's famous response, at *Record* 11, to the question, "Why do you love the Romans and hate the Greeks?": "I love the Romans because we share the same faith [*hōs homopistous*] but the Greeks because we share the same language" [Allen and Neil 70].

192. For this flawed interpretation see, e.g., Riou (1973) 206–12; Garrigues (1976c).

193. *Record* 7 [Allen and Neil 62]. Maximus at the same time expresses his belief that Rome will not commune: "I will never be persuaded that the Romans will enter into union with those here."

194. Maximus Confessor, *Letter to Anastasius the Disciple* [Allen and Neil 120].

195. *Acts of the Lateran Council* [Riedinger 54].

It is preferable, therefore, to see the sometimes exuberant pro-Roman rhetoric of Maximus and his colleagues not as the expression of some deep-seated ecclesiological commitment to the authoritative preeminence of Rome over the other patriarchates,[196] but rather as the acknowledgment of an historical situation in which Rome had proved the sole patriarchate to denounce the monothelete innovation and in which her Palestinian allies had much to gain in emphasizing her subsequent *imperium* within the Church.[197] At the same time, however, we should avoid thinking of that rhetoric in simplistic terms, as nothing more than political expedience. Contingent and expedient it no doubt was, but it also represented a conspicuous extension of earlier emphases, when Maximus had offered an unprecedented recognition of the spiritual dependence of monks upon clerical mediation. Indeed, in respect of Maximus's thought on the Church and, thence, on the Roman popes, I can but here quote the powerful recent words of Adam Cooper:[198]

> Regarding the external criteria of the Church's catholicity, Maximus clearly accepts the headship of Peter among the Apostles, the pre-eminence of the Church of Rome on account of its living Petrine office, and communion with its bishop as a given norm. He also accepts a temporal hierarchy in which Christ is mediated through the apostles and prophets and teachers (the Church's bishops), and a local hierarchy of bishops, priests, deacons, monks and other lay orders, and initiates. There is no doubt that cut loose from its integral reference to the one Word and Spirit of God, such external specificity can only lend itself to confusion and dissolution. So we find Maximus invoking the Apostle Paul 'through whom the Holy Spirit condemns even angels who institute anything contrary to the kerygma'. Yet through the harmony created through right faith active in love, the Church's hierarchical *ordo* is the means by which each individual component in the whole structure is able to participate in its unique, unchanging centre (*kentron*). It is the means by which the whole Church with each of its members rightly confesses the true faith. It is the means by which God is manifested bodily on earth. And so it is the means also to true ecclesial communion and personal deification.

Maximus's celebration of Roman preeminence was, therefore, a political expedience assumed within a particular context of doctrinal and, indeed, personal alienation from the Eastern patriarchates. But it represented not some gross deviation

---

196. The status of Rome as the sole orthodox patriarchate also explains (better than a commitment to the notion of absolute papal authority) the later resort to Rome of the patriarch Pyrrhus and Maximus's recommendation that the emperor and patriarch Peter do likewise; see below pp. 286f., 315.

197. For strategic Eastern appeals to Rome in wider perspective (in the context of Ps.-Gregory II's letter to Leo III and of Theodore the Studite's westward appeal) see the comment of Dagron (1996) 179, calling such appeals "moins affaire d'ecclésiologie que de stratégie."

198. Cooper (2005) 189f.

from either his thought or that of his circle but rather the further elaboration both of the celebration of the popes contained within Moschus's earlier *Spiritual Meadow* and of the recognition of clerical and sacramental privilege evident above all within Maximus's own *Mystagogy*.

When the Persians first conquered Jerusalem in 614, Sophronius composed an anacreontic poem that called for the destructive vengeance of the Christian empire to descend upon the impious conquerors. It is possible that the same poem was composed in Alexandria, where in that same period he served as the most prominent doctrinal advisor to John the Almsgiver, a Heraclian appointee parachuted onto the patriarchal throne in a period of profound tension and charged, it appears, with the maintenance of peace between pro-Chalcedonians and anti-Chalcedonians. At this point there was perhaps, therefore, little indication of Sophronius's imminent emergence as Heraclius's most prominent religious critic.

Nevertheless, although within the *Miracles of Cyrus and John* Sophronius refused a pervasive emphasis upon anti-Chalcedonian heretics, there was within that text a strict sacramental differentiation between orthodox and heretic, and at the end of that same decade—when Alexandria witnessed the imperial sponsorship of an anti-Chalcedonian union, and when the Almsgiver himself appears to have fallen foul of imperial opinion—Moschus and Sophronius were celebrating, in their *Life of John the Almsgiver*, their hero's action against the usage of an anti-Chalcedonian phrase within the Trisagion.

In the two decades that separate both the poem *On the Capture of Jerusalem* and the *Miracles of Cyrus and John* from the patriarchal sermons, the geopolitical landscape of the eastern Mediterranean underwent a profound transformation, and so too did Sophronius's rhetoric. Within those sermons Sophronius disavows the imperialist stance that characterized his earlier poem, eschewing vengeance as an effective means to assuage divine wrath. Instead, he conceives of Christian restoration via three routes: the moral, the liturgical, and the doctrinal. For Sophronius as patriarch—as in his earliest text, the *Miracles*—the ascetic imperative is incumbent upon all Christians and, as in the *Miracles* again, participation in the orthodox eucharist is the central expression of membership of the orthodox Church. But whereas in that earlier period he demonstrates a profound ambivalence as to the need for continuous ecclesial communion within the Christian life, he here shifts his emphasis, insisting on the unrivaled spiritual gifts conferred through the eucharist and the subsequent need for regular participation; at the same time, whereas earlier he apologizes for his fleeting focus on heretics within the *Miracles*, in the *Synodical Letter* he appends a vast catalogue of doctrinal deviants that pronounces anathemas upon a range of anti-Chalcedonian luminaries, including those with whom the emperor entered into recent discussions.

Implicit within Sophronius's dissent from Constantinople were two principles: first, that doctrinal precision (*akribeia*) should not be sacrificed for the sake of union; and second, that doctrine could not be dictated through imperial will. It must be emphasized that Sophronius and Maximus never gave up on the ideal of a pious Christian empire under a pious Christian emperor; and if Heraclius had supported their particular vision of orthodox doctrine, the pair (like others both before and after them) might well have recognized the full religious pretensions of the imperial office.[199] But as the crisis of the empire deepened, and the irenic position of Constantinople proved insufficient to appease its critics, Sophronius's sermons resorted to a paradigm that had long been evident within the output of his circle: that is, the essential and inviolable independence of the Church, its elevation above the tides of terrestrial politics, and thus also its freedom from secular interference. On this vision, the existence of the Church within a Christian state remained a desideratum, but the expansion of Islam across former Roman territories nonetheless had no significant impact on the grand Christian narrative preserved unsullied in the rites of a Chalcedonian Church that now, both in practice and in theory, transcended the boundaries of individual states.

From the Constantinopolitan perspective, this assertion of ecclesial independence was something far more significant than the usual howl of the marginalized. For it occurred at a time when its leading proponents were ensconced within the West and had there formed a doctrinal alliance with Rome. As we have seen, the Romans had long promoted their own preeminence within the Church, and at least since the time of Gelasius the popes had counted within their rhetorical arsenal a differentiation of the secular and the sacred that threatened to exclude the emperor from religious narratives. In the past, Constantinopolitan patriarchs had been content to maintain a politic silence in respect of such claims. But now Eastern Chalcedonians in the shape of Rome's Palestinian allies were extending their rhetoric of clerical privilege to the popes, defending them against accusations of doctrinal deviation, pointing to their unerring commitment to the orthodox faith, and celebrating the *imperium* that guaranteed their preeminence within the Church. From here, it was but a short leap into something far more radical: the fomenting of full-scale Western secession from Constantinopolitan rule.

---

199. See Dagron (1996) 172f., 305, 314f., for examples of both earlier and later Christians recognizing the emperor's sacerdotal status.

# 7

# Rebellion and Retribution

In the period of Sophronius's patriarchate, Maximus in a letter to Peter the Illustrious, as his master in Palestine had done, reflected on the reversals that now racked the Roman empire: "What is more precarious than the evils now surrounding the inhabited world?" he asked his correspondent. "What is more terrible to those who have perceived what is happening? What is more pitiable or more fearful for those who are suffering? To see a barbarous, desert people [*ethnos erēmikon kai barbaron*] overrunning another's land as their own, and our civilized way of life consumed by wild and untamable beasts, who have the mere appearance of a human shape alone, and the Jewish people exulting over the blood of men." For Maximus, the turbulent times were a sign of the Antichrist's imminent reign, brought on in the sins of the people: "What, as I said, is more terrifying to the eyes or ears of Christians than these things, to see a cruel, portentous race conniving to stretch out its hands against the divine inheritance? But these things happened because of the great number of our sins, for we did not live our lives worthily according to the Gospel of Christ."[1]

As Wolfram Brandes has insisted in an unrivaled article on the eventual trials of Pope Martin and Maximus in Constantinople, it is crucial that we place the entire monothelete crisis against the background of imperial losses to the Muslims.[2] As

---

1. Maximus Confessor, *Letters* 14 [*PG* 91, 540A–541B, with specific reference to the Antichrist at 540B]. For the date (634–39/40) see Sherwood (1952a) 40f.; Larchet (1998a) 52. On Maximus and the Antichrist see also *Dispute at Bizya* 3 [Allen and Neil 86] and the comment of Dagron (1996) 182.

2. See Brandes (1998b) 146–51, calling monotheletism "die theologische Begleitmusik zum Untergang des spätantiken Oströmischen Reiches" (147).

the doctrinal crisis deepened in the course of the 640s, so too did Muslim aggression continue to threaten the remaining territories of the now reduced empire in the East. In 643 and 644 raids were made into Transcaucasia and Anatolia, while a mutual arms race in naval construction anticipated the battle for the Mediterranean.[3] According to the Arabic tradition, it was in this period that Constans launched a naval expedition that achieved a brief reoccupation of the Nile Delta, but the province's original conqueror, the now deposed governor ʿAmr ibn al-ʿĀṣ, was dispatched to recapture it, and from there the Muslims launched, in 647, an assault upon North Africa.[4] In the East, raids were now made into Armenia and Cappadocia, while 649 and 650 witnessed the first significant action at sea, with a significant naval battle and two Muslim raids upon Cyprus.[5] Soon after, the Muslim fleet captured the Roman island fortress of Aradus, off the coast of Phoenicia.[6]

At the same time, the emperor faced significant challenges from within his own regime. The general Valentine, who as we saw above had assisted Constans's elevation to the throne, now looked to assume the purple himself. John of Nikiu's *Chronicle* reports that soon after the emperor's accession, "there was great trouble on account of Valentine [wāləndyānos], for he assumed the imperial regalia and wanted to become emperor." When the people of Constantinople protested, however, Valentine set aside his ambition and swore to the emperor that he had not intended evil but acted so that he might take the fight to the Muslims. Thus Constans was reconciled to him, appointed him "head of the troops" (*r'əsa ḥarā*), and

---

3. See the reconstruction in Howard-Johnston (2010) 474f. On the program of naval construction see esp. Theophanes, *Chronicle* A.M. 6146; Ps.-Sebēos, *History* 45, with Zuckerman (2005) 114–17; Cosentino (2008) 583–85; also Foss (2009a, b) for the papyrological evidence.

4. For the Arab sources for the reoccupation see Caetani (1912–23) vol. 2, 289, with Butler (1902) 465–75, placing the expedition in 645/6. Howard-Johnston (2010) 153f. links the Roman mission with a naval expedition mentioned in *Anonymous Miracles of Saint Demetrius* 4 and thus dates it to 646. Otherwise non-Arab sources are (suspiciously) silent. For the Muslim assault upon North Africa see below p. 288f.

5. Raids into Armenia and Cappadocia: Michael the Syrian, *Chronicle* 11.10. Naval battle: Ps.-Sebēos, *History* 45, with Howard-Johnston (1999b) 259–62, identifying this, probably incorrectly, with the later battle of Phoenix (as also Kaplony [1996] 33–36); but cf. Zuckerman (2005) 114–17. Cyprus: Theophanes, *Chronicle* A.M. 6140; Michael the Syrian, *Chronicle* 11.10; *Anonymous Chronicle to 1234* 131–32; Agapius, *Universal History* [Vasiliev 455]; *Chronicle of Zuqnin* [Chabot vol. 2, 151]. In Arab sources Caetani (1912–23) vol. 2, 301, 308. The existence of two separate raids is confirmed in two inscriptions at Soloi; see Feissel (1987). For comment see Beihammer (2004); Howard-Johnston (2010) 477f.; Hoyland (2011) 131–34. It should be noted that a far earlier but largely unacknowledged Muslim raid on Cyprus (*qopros*) is reported in John of Nikiu, *Chronicle* 118, following the capture of Caesarea and Ascalon (*kilunās*).

6. See Theophanes, *Chronicle* A.M. 6141; Michael the Syrian, *Chronicle* 11.10; *Anonymous Chronicle to 1234* 132; Agapius, *Universal History* [Vasiliev 480f.]; *Chronicle of Zuqnin* [Chabot vol. 2, 151]. The conquest is the subject of a detailed study by Conrad (1992).

married his daughter.[7] Under Constans's second year (642/3) Pseudo-Sebēos too reports Valentine's attempt to elevate himself to the purple—again "so that having crowned himself he might thus exercise his military command"—but then reports that under "the burden of subjection" (*sc.* increased taxation) the capital's inhabitants rose up and executed him. This report no doubt conflates two episodes—first, the elevation of Valentine to a significant Eastern command soon after Constans's accession (as in John of Nikiu); and second, his later rebellion and subsequent death, which Theophanes and the *Anonymous Chronicle to 1234* report around 644.[8] As we shall see, later references in the trial literature of Pope Martin suggest that the emperor's opponents in the West were aware of this disturbance.[9] It was the first of a series of domestic rebellions that rocked Constans's reign.

It is perhaps unsurprising, therefore, to discover that the emperor's new regime had little enthusiasm for stoking the fires of doctrinal dispute. For most of the 640s, the emperor and patriarch made repeated attempts to defuse the burgeoning crisis over the Christological will or wills, but persistent Constantinopolitan repositioning did little more than confirm their critics' opposition. Maximus continued to develop the doctrinal opposition to the *Ekthesis*, and toward the end of the same decade, as the Western opposition to Constantinople intensified, Pope Theodore made a quite remarkable move: the convocation of a pan-Italian council to condemn the doctrine of the capital. The proceedings of the subsequent Lateran Council were recorded in a set of *Acts* that the new pope, Martin, distributed to correspondents across the Mediterranean, including the emperor. But the true nature of those *Acts* was disguised beneath a lie, for their authors presented them as a composition in Latin, thence translated into Greek. In fact, the Greek had been the original, and the *Acts*' authors had been none other than Maximus and his allies. There can be no better indication of the Eastern orientation of papal doctrine in this period and of the remarkable implication of Roman and Palestinian politics that it witnessed.

It is perhaps ironic that the Muslim conquests that so drove the imperial desire for domestic union seem also to have guaranteed the perception that the regime and its doctrine were corrupt. Hitherto, however, the opposition to Constantinople had been vocal but nonviolent. The rebellion of Maximus's North African protector George against the will of Martina had, as we have seen, proved a minor

---

7. John of Nikiu, *Chronicle* 120 [Zotenberg 218]. It is perhaps this first challenge to Constans that is referred to in Theophanes, *Chronicle* A.M. 6133 (A.D. 641/2), where Valentine is counted next to Martina and Heraclonas as those whom the senate ousted. For Valentine's (unsuccessful) action against the Muslims cf. *Chronicle of Zuqnin* [Chabot vol. 2, 151], placed in A.G. 955 (A.D. 643/4).

8. Theophanes, *Chronicle* A.M. 6136 (A.D. 644/5); *Anonymous Chronicle to 1234* 126 (A.G. 955, A.D. 643/4). For the revolt of Valentine see also Kaegi (1981) 156–59; Howard-Johnston (1999b) 253–55; *PLRE* vol. 3, "Valentine 5"; *PmbZ* "Ualentinos" 8545.

9. See below p. 304.

incident, overshadowed in the empress's dramatic fall from grace. But it nevertheless pointed to a future pattern and portended the province's full-scale rebellion later in the decade. Indeed, from the time of his emergence as the leading antimonothelete, Maximus would witness a series of political rebellions through which high-profile Western administrators with whom he was associated set themselves in opposition to the capital. The concurrence of his presence with significant expressions of political dissent against Constantinopolitan rule is too consistent to be coincidental.

The implication was not lost on Maximus's opponents in the capital. When peace with the caliph granted Constans a brief reprieve from Eastern warfare, he ensured the final arrest of Martin and Maximus in Rome and thence brought them to face trial for treason before the senate in Constantinople. Under questioning, Maximus is there said to have challenged imperial aspirations to quasi-sacerdotal status and thus to have denied that the emperor had a claim to debate or to define doctrine. In this, he drew upon a separation of the secular and the sacred that derived from the same ecclesiological vision that he had first elucidated within the *Mystagogy*. But where in the earlier period that vision had served above all to protect against Christian defeatism, it was now used for a new, more polemical purpose: the refusal of the emperor's special religious status and, with it, the dramatic exposure of the fundamental fault lines of Christian imperial rule.

From the time of Constantine, a profound ambiguity had characterized the emperor's relation to the Church, an ambiguity revealed above all within the liturgy. On the one hand, the elevated position of the emperor in various ecclesial rituals expressed his exalted position as God's vicegerent on earth; but on the other, as Gilbert Dagron has emphasized, those rituals also laid bare his ambiguous sacerdotal status, for while granting him quasi-priestly privileges they nevertheless proclaimed his ultimate dependence on the clerical mediation of the eucharist.[10] "An emperor is nothing if he is not everything," Dagron states, "and in particular if he is not the providential mediator between his people and God. But on this point—and this point alone—an effective resistance could be organized."[11] In the imperial capital, this tension between imperial and clerical prerogatives could be constantly played out through the inclusion of the emperor in the liturgy. But in the provinces, where imperial power was increasingly ineffective, and where bishops were assuming an ever more prominent position as the leaders of local communities, Christian commentators now looked to the rites of the Church both as the foundation for the construction of a new, post-Roman identity and as the basis for a renegotiation of the relationship of Church and state.

10. Dagron (1996) esp. 106–29.
11. Ibid. 129.

## MAXIMUS FROM AFRICA TO ROME

From the outset of his rule late in 641, and in the face of persistent territorial losses to the caliphate, the new emperor, Constans, renewed imperial attempts to appease the capital's Western critics, now in open dissent against the monothelete formula. In the process he offered considerable concessions. According to the narrative contained within the *Annals* of the Christian Arab historian Eutychius, in an exchange of letters with the popes John IV and Theodore, the new emperor had at the beginning of his reign recognized the use of "two operations" and "two wills."[12] We might of course dismiss this as the wishful thinking of a later Melkite historian if it were not for the survival of a cache of three letters extant in Karshuni and dependent, perhaps, upon an Arabic prototype from which Eutychius too derived his account.[13] The first two letters within that cache we have encountered in the previous chapter: that is, the letter of John IV in defense of Honorius and that of Theodore to Constans requesting that the *Ekthesis* be rescinded.[14] But the third letter purports to be from Constans himself to John. Therein the emperor speaks of "the contradiction into which our predecessors and ancestors ran, the God-elected emperors, whose mind the common enemy had deceived and repulsed from the orthodox faith that had been built upon that rock ["super illam petram aedificata"] against which the gates of hell will not prevail until the end of times." "We have thought it necessary," Constans continues, "that the letter of your Paternity be recognized in this great convention, in the presence of Paul, patriarch of this God-protected Constantinople." Constans reports that the new patriarch, Paul, has dispatched an encyclical "conforming to your words" and then proclaims that all the provinces of West and East now profess the same faith and suffer no novelties.[15]

The letter reads like an exercise in antimonothelete (and pro-Roman) propaganda. But from an aforementioned letter that Theodore sent to Paul—preserved in Latin and purporting to be a response to Paul's own encyclical—it does in fact appear that the pope's Constantinopolitan counterpart had therein condemned his predecessor Pyrrhus but at the same time eschewed reference to the *Ekthesis*.[16] It is

---

12. See Eutychius, *Annals (Antiochene Recension)* [Cheiko 335–39].

13. The dependence is indicated, for example, in Eutychius's reproduction of all three letters and the shared corruption of the name of the *apocrisiarius* Sericus to "Barsika," as at Constans, *Letter to Pope John* [Latin trans. Mai 511]. For discussion of the relation of the texts see Conte (1971) 387f.

14. See above pp. 260–62.

15. Constans, *Letter to Pope John*. I translate here from the Latin translation of Mai (1852–1905) vol. 6, 511f.; but see also Schacht (1936) 246–49 for a parallel German translation. For the letter see also Conte (1971) 431f. no. 111; Winkelmann (2001) 102 no. 75; Jankowiak (2009) 206–8.

16. Pope Theodore, *Letter to Paul* [PL 87, 78A–B]. For this same letter cf. above p. 262 n. 142. For Paul's synodical, which does not survive, see also Conte (1971) 431 no. 110; Winkelmann (2001) 103 no. 76. Accompanying it was a letter from the bishops who had consecrated Paul that explained the

more than probable, of course, that the imperial and patriarchal condemnation of Pyrrhus had more to do with the machinations of domestic politics in the capital than with doctrinal attitudes toward the West. Nevertheless, the Constantinopolitan silence on monothelete doctrine—evidenced in the extant letters both of Constans and of Theodore—must at least indicate the new regime's simultaneous unwillingness to spoil for a fight with Rome.[17] Constans, of course, faced more pressing challenges from the nascent caliphate, which had seized Egypt and now threatened to overrun Asia Minor.[18]

If at the start of his tenure, however, the patriarch Paul had adopted an irenic position in his correspondence with Pope Theodore, for a short time in the mid-640s continuous Western provocation appears to have pushed him into a more assertive position. Contained within the *Acts* of the Lateran and Sixth Ecumenical councils we encounter a *Letter to Pope Theodore* that is dated, in the Latin of the former, to May, third indiction (i.e., 645).[19] Therein the patriarch refers to the calumnies that he has suffered from the pope and ignored for the sake of peace. Now he declares the time for silence to have passed. Theodore's *apocrisiarii*, following various "irreconcilable discussions," have demanded from the patriarch an explanation of the "one will," which he now intends to give. There follows a long profession of faith in which the patriarch asserts that "the whole divine and human operation proceeds from one and the same Word, God enfleshed" without division or confusion, and he then proceeds to defend the "one will," "lest we ascribe to one and the same person of our Lord, Jesus Christ, an opposition [*enantiōsis*] or difference of wills, or present as dogma that he is at war with himself, or introduce two willing agents."[20]

From the aforementioned *Opuscula* 10 of Maximus—in which he defended, about 645, Theodore's use of the *filioque* formula—we know that the pope's own position had come under criticism from Constantinople.[21] Paul's *Letter to Theodore* does not refer to the same charge but instead lends the impression of a patriarch who has been forced into a more combative position following continuous

---

resignation of Pyrrhus; see Pope Theodore, *Letter to the Bishops*, with Van Dieten (1972) 76f., Jankowiak (2009) 208–10, and above p. 262 n. 143.

17. See also Van Dieten (1972) 76–79. The latter's contention, however, that in these years Paul prepared for a future fight with Rome through falsifying the *libellus* of Menas is based upon a rather credulous reading of the tale of its interpolation at *Acts of the Sixth Ecumenical Council* [Riedinger 652–54]. For the status of Menas's *libellus* see above p. 198 n. 50.

18. For the situation in Egypt see Morelli (2010); Booth (2013b).

19. *Acts of the Lateran Council* [Riedinger 205].

20. See *Acts of the Lateran Council* [Riedinger 198–202], excerpted again in *Acts of the Lateran Council* [Riedinger 338]. Cf. *Acts of the Sixth Ecumenical Council* [Riedinger 608]. On the patriarch Paul's position in general see Bathrellos (2004) 82–84.

21. See above p. 270.

provocation in (lost) papal letters and at the hands of the Roman *apocrisiarii*.²²
That new, more assertive position, however, seems to have had an unintended consequence, for a mere two months after the dispatch of Paul's letter there occurred in North Africa a dramatic event that the Constantinopolitan patriarch could not have predicted—the dramatic defeat of his deposed predecessor in a high-profile theological debate with Maximus.

As we have seen in the previous chapter, Nicephorus's *Short History* and John of Nikiu's *Chronicle* differ as to Pyrrhus's departure from Constantinople: in the former, during disturbances following the coronation of Constans as coemperor, the patriarch resigns and flees of his own accord, then traveling to North Africa; whereas in the latter, he is deposed and exiled following the fall of Heraclonas and Martina, and then banished to Tripoli.²³ Although it seems clear that Pyrrhus resigned rather than being deposed, he does not appear to have gone into immediate exile.²⁴ In that aforementioned Karshuni letter of Pope Theodore to Constans, dated after the pope's election in November 642, the pope decries that the electors of Paul still call the deposed Pyrrhus "pious" ("religiosus") and do not judge him guilty of blame;²⁵ and in the contemporaneous letter to Paul the pope voices his concerns over Pyrrhus's resignation and informs his Constantinopolitan counterpart that should the partisans of the former patriarch obstruct a formal council in the capital to examine him, then he should be sent instead to Rome.²⁶ It thus appears that, following his resignation from the patriarchate, Pyrrhus remained within the East for some time—Theodore, at least, shows no awareness of his exile. From this perspective, therefore, his eventual presence in North Africa appears not as a spontaneous action of the patriarch himself, nor as an immediate consequence of his deposition, but rather as a further potential component of the attempted imperial appeasement of the West in the early 640s. If so, however, North Africa was not a prudent choice of destination. For while the province had of late proved popular with emperors as a

---

22. For this view see also Van Dieten (1972) 90f., 102f.; Jankowiak (2009) 214–16.

23. See above p. 252f. Cf. Theophanes, *Chronicle* A.M. 6121, in which Pyrrhus is again deposed alongside Martina and her sons (much as in John of Nikiu; cf. also *Greek Life of Maximus* (Recension 2) [*PG* 90, 81B]) and *Synodicon Vetus* 138, where the hostility of the Constantinopolitan people forces Pyrrhus to seek refuge in North Africa (much as in Nicephorus).

24. See esp. Pope Theodore, *Letter to the Bishops* [*PL* 87, 81B], referring to a *libellus* of resignation. For the argument in favor of resignation see the full discussion in Van Dieten (1972) 74 with n. 48, citing a patriarchal catalogue (*kai staseōs de genomenēs dedōkōs libellon pareitēsato*).

25. Pope Theodore, *Letter to Constans* [Latin trans. Mai 511]. Cf. Schacht (1936) 251. This precise same issue appears also in Pope Theodore, *Letter to the Bishops* [*PL* 87, 81B–82D], and again after Pyrrhus's second patriarchate; see Theodore Spudaeus, *Narrations* 32 and p. 305.

26. Pope Theodore, *Letter to Paul* [*PL* 87, 79B]. For the same anxieties over Pyrrhus's resignation see Pope Theodore, *Letter to the Bishops* [*PL* 87, 81B]. See also Van Dieten (1972) 79–82; Schönborn (1975) 486f.

place of exile for their enemies, the ex-patriarch's presence there would soon aggravate tensions even further.[27]

Although the circumstances in which it was organized (or even allowed to occur) are unclear, Maximus and Pyrrhus soon engaged in a dramatic doctrinal disputation at Carthage.[28] According to the text that purports to record that disputation, the rivals met "in the month of July in the third indiction [645]," under the presidency of "the most holy patrician Gregory," the new exarch and, perhaps, a relative of the emperor.[29] The *Disputation with Pyrrhus* constitutes an extensive doctrinal dialogue between Maximus and the ex-patriarch of Constantinople on the question of the Christological wills and operations. Despite a (no doubt deliberate) impression that it was penned in the immediate aftermath of the event itself, it appears to derive from at least a decade later, from the pen of either Maximus or a close disciple.[30] In intellectual terms, nevertheless, it recreates something of the earlier reports of Sophronius's confrontations with Cyrus and Sergius, for within it Maximus, like his master before him, refuses all summons to doctrinal silence or accommodation for the sake of peace (positions which, as we have seen, seem to have characterized Constantinopolitan doctrinal policy in the earliest stages of Constans's regime).[31]

Elsewhere in the *Disputation*, Pyrrhus argues for the simultaneous use of monadic and dyadic language in respect of the wills, recognizing "a single composite" (*hen ti suntheton*) from the two wills, in order that those who speak of two wills (on account of the natural difference of natures in Christ) and those who speak of one (on account of the absolute union) would no longer be at variance with each other "on account of mere phrases" (*psilōn lexeōn heneken*).[32] As stated in our examination of Maximus's thought on the operations, he himself had once recognized as

---

27. For recent exiles to North Africa see, e.g., Cyrus of Alexandria (John of Nikiu, *Chronicle* 116: "An island in the west of Africa"); Philagrius (John of Nikiu, *Chronicle* 116: "To the province of Africa, where Cyrus had previously been in exile"; Nicephorus, *Short History* 30: "To the fortress called Septai, which lies toward the setting sun opposite the Pillars of Hercules, next to Libya").

28. Cf. Nicephorus, *Short History* 31; also *Synodicon Vetus* 138; Theophanes, *Chronicle* A.M. 6121. For speculation on Pyrrhus's motive in engaging Maximus see Van Dieten (1972) 88 and Boudignon (2007) 260f., both suggesting that the deposed patriarch may have hoped to regain the Constantinopolitan patriarchate should the exarch's rebellion have proved a success.

29. *Disputation with Pyrrhus* [PG 91, 288A]. On onomastic grounds Diehl (1896) 525 n. 7 makes the tantalizing suggestion that Gregory was a member of the Heraclian dynasty and probably the son of Nicetas; see also *PLRE* vol. 3, "Fl. Gregorius 19."

30. See the discussion in Noret (1999) pointing to *Record* 6, which shows no awareness of the text in 655/6. Besides Noret's arguments we may also note the text's clear but anachronistic anticipation of the position of the *Typos*, esp. at *Disputation with Pyrrhus* [PG 91, 300C] and perhaps also the position of Constantinople in 658; see n. 32 below. For an extensive theological and historical commentary on the text see Bausenhart (1992) 236–316.

31. See *Disputation with Pyrrhus* [PG 91, 300C, 305D–308A].

32. *Disputation with Pyrrhus* [PG 91, 296A–B].

legitimate the same approach—that is, that when speaking of the union (but not the natures) it was appropriate to speak of "one" in order to avoid the implication of division—and, as a result, had faced an accusation that he in fact recognized three operations (two at the level of nature and one at the level of the union). In the course of the 640s, however, he came indeed to abandon this position and (as in the subsequent section of the *Disputation with Pyrrhus*) to condemn those who upheld it.[33] In the *Disputation*, therefore, we can detect a double resonance, for while the presentation of Maximus's position reflects a genuine transformation in his thought around 645, at the time of the text's composition it perhaps had a more immediate purpose. For as we shall see below, the double use of "one" and "two" would in the subsequent decade become the official position of Constantinople.

For all its stubborn politics, the *Disputation with Pyrrhus* is a profound and compelling meditation on the Christological wills and operations. Therein the figure of Maximus sets out a comprehensive refutation of his opponent's alleged position and indeed is so successful that the latter recants his previous thought and requests that he may go to Rome to worship at the tombs of the heads of the apostles and to submit a *libellus* before the pope. The author of the *Disputation* thus enacts an implicit conception of the proper relationship between representatives of monasticism, Church, and state. Despite holding no clerical position, Maximus debates the faith in open, reasoned dialogue with a (deposed) patriarch; his eventual triumph, however, is not definitive but requires the ratification of Rome; and the exarch, for his part, facilitates and presides over the debate but does not attempt to interfere in discussions. The *Disputation* constitutes, therefore, both a cogent defense of the 'two operations' and 'two wills,' and an implicit condemnation of the comparative doctrinal authoritarianism and secularism of Constantinople.

The *Disputation* concludes with Pyrrhus at Rome, where he "condemned the dogmas of the impious *Ekthesis* while uniting himself through orthodox confession to the holy, catholic, and apostolic Church."[34] We cannot, of course, know how the African disputation itself proceeded—a point that theologians too often forget[35]— but the dramatic recantation of Pyrrhus at Rome is nevertheless corroborated in the Roman *Book of Pontiffs*, which records how, under Theodore, Pyrrhus came to Rome and offered a *libellus* renouncing his error. In return, he received from the pope recognition "as the *sacerdos* of the imperial city."[36] Theodore, therefore, appears

---

33. See above p. 217.

34. *Disputation with Pyrrhus* [PG 91, 353A–B].

35. See, e.g., Bathrellos (2004) 80–82 and Hovorun (2008) 150, both treating Pyrrhus's position within the *Disputation* as though he had composed it himself.

36. *Book of Pontiffs* 75 [Duchesne vol. 1, 332]. This same *libellus* is referred to in *Acts of the Lateran Council* [Riedinger 69, 72]; see also Van Dieten (1972) 85f. n. 37. For the import of Pyrrhus's communion in the context of papal ideology see Conte (1971) 324–27. For further evidence for Pyrrhus's recognition as archbishop in Rome see Theodore Spudaeus, *Narrations* 24.

to have taken the remarkable step of recognizing Pyrrhus as the patriarch proper of Constantinople, an act both of flagrant provocation towards Paul and of gross defiance against imperial will.

In the wake of Maximus's confrontation with the deposed patriarch and the latter's retreat to Rome, the North African opposition to monotheletism appears to have intensified. According to the *Acts of the Lateran Council*, during the council's second session a series of four letters sent from African bishops to Pope Theodore, to the emperor, and to Paul of Constantinople was read out to the assembled bishops.[37] From those letters we ascertain that during the fourth indiction (September 645 through August 646) two large councils, representing the bishops of Byzacena and Africa Proconsularis, met to condemn monotheletism. To these conciliar letters were added two more, both dispatched to Pope Theodore: in the first, the bishops of Numidia, Byzacium, and Mauretania report their opposition to Constantinopolitan doctrine, subsequent to Pyrrhus's appeal to Rome, and in the second, dated to July 646, the newly elected bishop of Carthage, Victor, confirms his adherence to dyothelete doctrine.[38]

It should be noted that the two letters to Theodore report considerable tensions with Constantinople. Both request that a letter to Paul be sent via the papal *apocrisiarii* in Rome rather than directly to the capital, for (according to Victor of Carthage) "wicked men have made false claims that our African province could be committing certain offenses, which in truth do not exist";[39] or (according to the bishops of Numidia, Byzacium, and Mauretania) "malevolent men within the aforesaid royal city have mentioned our Africa with a degree of suspicion ["in quandam suspectionem"]." The latter, furthermore, continue to make certain furtive references to a significant domestic disturbance that prevented the convention of an actual council.[40] It is possible that this same disturbance was a Muslim raid

37. See *Acts of the Lateran Council* [Riedinger 66–103]. Although the Council's *acta* were composed in Greek (see below p. 293), the Latin text of these letters was the original; see esp. R. Riedinger (1979) 10–11 n. 3 and (1980) 37–50, arguing that the African letters were shaped around a "Blancoformular" composed in Rome using the *Collectio Vaticana* and again under the influence of Maximus and his Eastern colleagues. Cf. the discussion in Conte (1989) 54–59. For these North African councils cf. Theophanes, *Chronicle* A.M. 6121; *Synodicon Vetus* 133–36. See also Van Dieten (1972) 87f., with Conte (1971) 437–39 nos. 120, 121; Winkelmann (2001) 117–19 nos. 98–101.

38. On Victor's letter see Jankowiak (2009) 223–25, who points to the fact that Fortunius, his predecessor as bishop of Carthage, is said in the *Acts of the Sixth Ecumenical Council* [Riedinger 652] to have visited Paul in Constantinople and there to have attended mass in Hagia Sophia. In regard to the Palestinian monks now ensconced within Carthage, it is difficult to imagine a more provocative act; at the least, Fortunius's communion with Paul demonstrates that the North African opposition to Constantinople was not universal.

39. *Acts of the Lateran Council* [Riedinger 103].
40. *Acts of the Lateran Council* [Riedinger 71].

preceding the main invasion,[41] but if so, one must wonder at both the reason for the letter's furtive reference to it and, as Marek Jankowiak has pointed out, the fact that bishops farther East were able to convene.[42] I would suggest, therefore, that the disturbance was not invasion from without but rebellion from within. As we have seen, tensions between North Africa and the capital had been a notable feature of the tenure of the prefect George, and it appears that disturbances continued at the time of the councils. Soon, however, the province would enter upon a full-scale secession from Constantinopolitan rule.

According to the group of sources that depend on the lost *Chronicle* of Theophilus of Edessa, soon after presiding over the disputation between Maximus and Pyrrhus, the African patrician and exarch Gregory launched a rebellion against the emperor Constans.[43] Muslim sources also record the event—thus Ibn ʿAbd al-Ḥakam, for example, notes that "The seat of rule in Africa at that time was a city called Qarṭājenna, where was reigning a king whose name was Jurjīr. He had originally been appointed vice-gerent there by Heraclius, but had revolted and coined dīnārs in his own name. His domain extended from Iṭrābulus [i.e., Tripoli] to Ṭanja. So when ʿAbd Allah [ibn Saʿd] approached, Jurjīr met him and a battle was fought, in which the latter was killed and his army put to flight."[44] There is, however, some disagreement as to the exarch's fate: whereas Agapius and the Syriac chroniclers claim that he traveled to the emperor Constans and did obeisance to him, the Muslim accounts claim that he was killed.[45] Latin sources support the latter version.[46]

---

41. For the existence of such raids see, e.g., John of Nikiu, *Chronicle* 120 [Zotenberg 214f.]. Cf. in Arab sources Caetani (1912–23) vol. 2, 240f., 254, 261.

42. Jankowiak (2009) 230f.

43. See Theophanes, *Chronicle* A.M. 6138 (A.D. 646/7), placing the Muslim invasion in the subsequent year. The entry also includes Constans's fifth year (A.D. 646/7), Uthman's first (A.D. 644/5), Paul of Constantinople's sixth (A.D. 647/8), and Peter of Alexandria's third (A.D. 644/5). Cf. Agapius, *Universal History* [Vasiliev 479], who places the revolt coterminous with Uthman's first year (A.D. 644/5), Constans's fifth (A.D. 646/7) and A.G. 958 (A.D. 646/7); Michael the Syrian, *Chronicle* 11.10, who places it in A.G. 958 (A.D. 646/7) and A.H. 25 (A.D. 645/6); *Anonymous Chronicle to 1234* [Chabot vol. 1, 260], which places it in A.G. 956 (A.D. 644/5). For Gregory see *PLRE* vol. 3, "Fl. Gregorius 19"; *PmbZ* "Gregorios" 2345; Winkelmann (2001) 208f. He appears in several Latin inscriptions; see *CIL* vol. 8, 2389; 10965a, b; 22652 no. 23.

44. Ibn ʿAbd al-Ḥakam, *Futūḥ Miṣr* [trans. Torrey 301f.]. For (somewhat speculative) analysis of the battle see Kaegi (2010) 123–44.

45. See Agapius, *Universal History* [Vasiliev 479]; Michael the Syrian, *Chronicle* 11.10; *Anonymous Chronicle to 1234* 126. Theophanes, *Chronicle* A.M. 6139, states simply that Gregory was driven from Africa. For the Arabic sources see Caetani (1905–26) vol. 7, 180–208, and (1912–23) 302f. On the (false) accusation that Gregory minted his own coins see Guery (1981).

46. See esp. Fredegar, *Chronicle* 4.81 [Wallace-Hadrill 69]; also *Anonymous Chronicle to 741* 24 [Mommsen 344]; *Anonymous Chronicle to 754* 38 [Mommsen 344]. The final two sources appear to draw from the earliest Muslim accounts of the conquest.

It is difficult to assess the precise nature or purpose of the rebellion—it is possible, of course, that it represented nothing more than "regional self-help," an attempt at more efficient local organization as Muslim raids grew ever more threatening and Constantinopolitan reinforcements proved lacking; or, given the witness of the North African bishops within the Lateran *Acts*, we may also wonder whether it represents one final manifestation of that classic North African pattern through which a late-antique Western administrator was forced into revolt because of dangerous rumors of secession circulating in the distant eastern capital.[47] Nevertheless, the striking coincidence of the rebellion both with the exarch's reported supervision of the disputation between Maximus and the deposed Constantinopolitan patriarch, and with the subsequent antimonothelete agitation of bishops across North Africa, suggests that disenchantment with Constans's regime was more complex than a simple dissatisfaction over defensive arrangements or scurrilous rumors. The exarch, it appears, was attempting to create nothing less than a separatist state with an ideological underpinning in the antimonothelete resistance.[48]

As we shall see below, opponents regarded Maximus as the éminence grise of the North African rebellion. Whether or not he was indeed its inspiration, he had at least helped to provide it with a distinct ideological prop, and it is quite possible that he had indeed harbored hopes for the realization of a new state that recognized his doctrine. Following the dramatic defeat of the deposed Constantinopolitan patriarch, the apparent unification of the entire North African Church around the antimonothelete cause, and the rebellion of the exarch from Constantinople, that new state was indeed beginning to take shape. But if, in committing to open battle with the Muslims, the exarch hoped to demonstrate the divine favor in which his new regime was held—and that had been such a conspicuous absence in the East—then in his defeat he collapsed the comfortable equation of orthodox doctrine and political success. In light of the loss of North Africa, the monotheletes were indeed swift to draw that same association of disaster and doctrine that appears to have informed Maximus's vision. "For," the latter's hostile biographer observed of the Muslim conquest of Africa, "following the wicked Maximos, the wrath of God punished every place which had accepted his error."[49] Henceforth, the North African Church fades from our sources for the conflict, its resistance to the capital made irrelevant, one suspects, through the advent of Muslim dominion.[50]

---

47. On the earlier period see the comment of Shaw (2011) 37.
48. Cf. Van Dieten (1972) 84, with n. 32; also Jankowiak (2009) 220f. See also the wider analysis of Western dissidence in Boudignon (2004) 40f., speaking of "un jeu de connivence entre des forces centrifuges: le pouvoir civil et militaire de l'Afrique byzantine, le pouvoir religieux de Rome, une intelligentsia monastique de Palestine."
49. George of Resh'aina, *Life* 23 [trans. Brock 318].
50. See the absence of African bishops from the Lateran Council noted in Jankowiak (2009) 255, 258. Pope Martin, *Letter to the Church of Carthage*, nevertheless informed the African Church of its outcome.

## THE ROMAN-PALESTINIAN ALLIANCE

Before the outbreak proper of the North African rebellion, according to George of Reshʿaina, Maximus and Anastasius relocated to Rome, perhaps there to witness the dramatic recantation of Pyrrhus.[51] In their wake, it seems, came "the students who had been in the monastery of Hippo Diarrhytus": that is, the aforementioned "Nestorian" monks whom the Syriac *Life of Maximus* claims to have fled the East in the face of the Muslim expansion. Upon arrival in Rome, George reports, Pope Martin granted them a monastery—none other than the one that was "called in the Latin tongue 'Cellae Novae.'"[52] As has been argued above, this appears to have been a foundation of Pope Gregory the Great and was perhaps the erstwhile Roman residence of Moschus. Now it provided a home for Maximus's "Nestorian" allies and would soon be renamed, as we have seen, for the Palestinian monastic hero Saint Sabas and populated with monks from Sabaitic institutions in North Africa and Palestine.[53] We must wonder, then, if George's "Nestorians" are not in fact Maximus's Palestinian supporters, disguised under a clichéd doctrinal slur.

Soon after his submission to the pope in Rome—perhaps following the exarch's failed rebellion in North Africa, from which he had perhaps hoped to benefit—the patriarch Pyrrhus traveled to the Italian exarch Plato and there, in the memorable words of the *Book of Pontiffs*, "returned once again like a dog to his own vomit of impiety." (Cf. Prov. 26:11.) He thence returned to "the regions of the East."[54] Confronted with the patriarch's dramatic return to monotheletism, Pope Theodore convoked a Roman council that anathematized him and once again imposed upon him the punishment of deposition—later accounts would claim that the pope had signed the council's decree in ink mixed with the eucharistic blood.[55] According to the subsequent account within the *Book of Pontiffs*, Pope Theodore then wrote to Paul, and when the pope and his *apocrisiarii* failed to convince him to renounce his doctrinal error, the Romans issued upon Paul a provocative papal deposition.[56]

---

51. George of Reshʿaina, *Life* 19 [Brock 311, trans. 318], attributing the move to "fear of the Arabs." That Maximus and his disciples witnessed Pyrrhus's recantation is implied in the concluding statement of the *Disputation with Pyrrhus* [PG 91, 353A], "And so having come to this celebrated city of the Romans with us . . ."; cf. also *Record* 2, placing Maximus in Rome on the eve of, or during, Gregory's rebellion. It is possible that here the doctrinal confrontation of Maximus and Pyrrhus was repeated, for *Record* 6 [Allen and Neil 60] refers to "the dispute over doctrine [*peri tōn dogmatōn kinēsis*] that occurred between you and Pyrrhus in Africa and Rome."
52. George of Reshʿaina, *Life* 24 [Brock 313, trans. 318].
53. See above p. 111.
54. *Book of Pontiffs* 75 [Duchesne vol. 1, 332].
55. See *Synodicon Vetus* 138 and Theophanes, *Chronicle* A.M. 6121 [de Boor 331], both repeating the line from Proverbs, and thence 2 Peter 2:22, likening Pyrrhus to a dog that returns to its vomit. For the latter cf. also *Greek Life of Maximus (Recension 2)* [PG 91, 85C].
56. *Book of Pontiffs* 75 (Theodore) [Duchesne vol. 1, 333]. For Theodore's actions see also Van Dieten (1972) 85–87; for the exchange of letters ibid. 88–91, with Conte (1971) 439f. nos. 124 and 125;

The return of Pyrrhus to the monothelete fold was, no doubt, a significant coup for Constantinople. But confronted with the North African councils condemning monotheletism, the apparent deposition issued upon Paul from Rome, and the revolt of the African exarch against Constantinople, the position of the capital once again mollified and returned to advocating the principle of doctrinal silence first supported within Sergius's *Psēphos*. The so-called *Typos* was published in 647/8,[57] and is cited in toto within the *Acts of the Lateran Council*. The document opens with an acknowledgment of the recent strife over the Christological wills and operations, and the reasons for supporting either position: one side wishing to preserve the "one person"; the other the "two natures."[58] For the sake of peace, it then attempts to suppress discussions on the operations and wills, advocating instead a faith based on Scripture, the five councils, and the "openly simple statements and pronouncements of the accepted holy fathers." Dire consequences, however, await those who attempt to transgress the new commands: clerics will be deposed, monks will be excommunicated and removed from their monasteries, members of government will be stripped of their titles, nobles will have their properties confiscated, and commoners will be beaten and sent into permanent exile.[59]

It is possible that the emperor and patriarch, seeing the dramatic defeat of the exarch in North Africa, expected a change of attitude on the part of their Western critics. Knowledge of the resolute intransigence of Maximus's circle, however, ought to have taught Constans that the attempt to impose doctrinal silence and somehow to pretend that the controversies had not occurred would, like Sergius's *Psēphos*, prove unsuccessful.[60] The emperor dispatched embassies to the West to attempt to gain support for the new initiative, but those embassies failed, and before his death in the middle of 649 Pope Theodore had begun preparations for the convocation of a pan-Italian council to discuss monotheletism.[61] In his place

---

Winkelmann (2001) 120–22 nos. 103 and 104. The sequencing of the *Book of Pontiffs* suggests that the Theodore's letter was sent in 647/8, after the retreat of Pyrrhus to the East but before the publication of the *Typos*. The letter of Paul and his subsequent deposition are also referred to in *Acts of the Lateran Council* [Riedinger 18].

57. For the date ("sixth indiction") see *Record* 6 [Allen and Neil 60]; Theodore Spudaeus, *Hypomnesticum (Greek)* 6 [Allen and Neil 156]. In *Acts of the Lateran Council* it is said to have been published "in the year just past" [Riedinger 196], which points to the *Acts*' preparation in advance. Cf. Winkelmann (2001) 123 no. 106.

58. See *Acts of the Lateran Council* [Riedinger 208].

59. *Acts of the Lateran Council* [Riedinger 208–10].

60. On the principle of accommodation in the *Typos* see esp. Ohme (2008) 317–21.

61. For the mission to Rome see *Record* 44 describing the visit to Rome of one Gregory son of Photinus, bearing an imperial gift for Saint Peter and a *keleusis* for the pope, begging him to be reconciled with Paul. The occasion for Gregory's visit to Rome appears to have been the issuing of the *Typos*, which Gregory discusses with Maximus; see Conte (1971) 440f. no. 127; Van Dieten (1972) 94f., placing the same visit before Theodore's death. For an imperial letter to Africa see Pope Martin, *Letter to*

was elected (with unusual speed and without imperial approval) an Italian, Martin, a former *apocrisiarius* in Constantinople to whom Pope Theodore had once entrusted a no doubt controversial investigation into the deposition of Pyrrhus.[62] He was, then, a man long schooled in conflict with the eastern capital. Under its notice on Martin, the *Book of Pontiffs* points to heightening tensions with Rome when its *apocrisiarii* refused to recognize the *Typos* (647/8), which Paul had persuaded the emperor to publish, and in which he "determined that one confess neither 'one' nor 'two' wills or operations in Christ, our Lord." The same text claims that Paul "went so far as to overthrow and tear out the altar of our holy see that had been consecrated in the venerable oratory in the House of Placidia, so as to prevent our *apocrisiarii* from offering to God the adorable and immaculate host and from receiving the sacraments of communion." In return for their censure concerning his "heretical purpose," the same text continues, Paul unleashed a persecution upon the *apocrisiarii* "and other orthodox men and venerable priests, forcing some of them into prison, sending others into exile, and submitting others to the lash."[63]

Concomitant with the publication of the *Typos* in 648, it does indeed appear that several prominent antimonotheletes in the capital were sent into exile. The most important of these was Anastasius Apocrisiarius, a bilingual priest and *apocrisiarius* of Rome, said in later sources to be a disciple of Maximus.[64] In a later

---

Constans [*PL* 87, 144B]. That the preparations occurred under Theodore is implicit in his death in May (*Book of Pontiffs* 75) and the meeting of the council in October (*Acts of the Lateran Council* [Riedinger 2]). The intervening period is too short to organize a major council (or to compose in advance its *Acts*; see below p. 293f.). For Theodore's involvement see also Ekonomou (2007) 116f., pointing to a possible hint at *Record* 12.

62. For Martin's former status see the words of Constans in *Book of Pontiffs* 76 [Duchesne vol. 1, 337]. For the investigation into Pyrrhus's deposition see Pope Theodore, *Letter to Paul* [*PL* 87, 78D], in which he refers the case to the archdeacon Sericus and the *apocrisiarius* Martin, with Conte (1971) 273–75; for Sericus, cf. the references to one Barsika (surely the same) in Constans, *Letter to Pope John* [Latin trans. Mai 511], and the parallel text in Eutychius, *Annals (Antiochene Recension)* [Cheiko 335f.]. Sericus also appears in Honorius, *Second Letter to Sergius* [Allen 204]. That Martin was elected without the necessary imperial approval is suggested in the charge of Theodore Calliopas at Theodore Spudaeus, *Narrations* 7; see below p. 303. See also George of Resh'aina, *Life* 21 [trans. Brock 318]: "For it was not at Konstans' orders that he became patriarch but through the fraudulence of some documents he had forged." See also Jankowiak (2009) 242 pointing also to the absence of an exarch in Ravenna who might otherwise have ratified the election.

63. *Book of Pontiffs* 76 [Duchesne vol. 1, 336]. Cf. the account given in *Acts of the Lateran Council* [Riedinger 18–20], also referring to the overturning of the altar "in our holy chapel in the house of those of Placidia [*en tōi oikōi tōn Plakidias*]."

64. See, e.g., *Dispute at Bizya* 3, 13. Anastasius is said to be bilingual in *Dispute at Bizya* 4 [Allen and Neil 98], but it is unclear whether he was Eastern in origin and likewise when he first met Maximus. He is in several places described as priest and *apocrisiarius* of Rome; see, e.g., Theodore Spudaeus, *Hypomnesticum (Greek)* 4, 6 [Allen and Neil 152, 156]. This *apocrisiarius* Anastasius is the author of the *Letter to Theodosius of Gangra*; see Conte (1989) 217–20. Winkelmann (2001) 153f. no. 151; Allen

text written about 669 to commemorate Martin, Maximus, and their followers, it is said that Anastasius was first exiled in "the sixth indiction of the past cycle": that is, in 647/8. Thereafter, the same text claims, "his disciples, Theodore and Euprepius, who were truly noble and holy brothers, the sons of Plutinus the most blessed imperial miller," made huge distributions of "alms and offerings" and then attempted to flee to Rome but were arrested at Abydus, deprived of their properties and offices, whipped, and sent into exile in Cherson.[65] It is tempting, of course, to see this as the simple application of the punishments for noncompliance outlined in the text of the *Typos*.

The first session of the Italian bishops gathered for the Lateran Council met on 5 October 649.[66] As we saw in the previous chapter, Maximus would proclaim it the "sixth" ecumenical council, but unlike previous ecumenical councils it had been not been convened under the auspices of the emperor. The (somewhat forced) claim to ecumenical status also underscored, therefore, a blatant usurpation of imperial prerogative that did not, it seems, go unnoticed farther East.[67] Its *Acts*, which we have encountered throughout this book, purport to record the precise sequence and content of events, to have been composed in Latin, and then to have been translated into Greek. In a series of important studies, however, Rudolf Riedinger has demonstrated that the opposite is true: that the text was in fact prepared in Greek—but integrating certain Latin documents—and then translated as a whole into Latin.[68] Furthermore, he has argued, the *Acts* exhibits the pervasive theological fingerprints of Maximus, who thus appears to have prepared, or

---

and Neil (2002) 40f. It is regrettable that his *Letter to the Monks of Ascalon* (CPG 7734) has not been published except in a brief description at *PG* 89, 1191, and in two brief excerpts identified within the *Doctrina Patrum* [Diekamp 262, 264]; cf. Winkelmann (2001) 152f. no. 150. For Anastasius Apocrisiarius see also *PmbZ* "Anastasios Apokrisiarios" 238; Winkelmann (2001) 188–90.

65. See Theodore Spudaeus, *Hypomnesticum (Greek)* 6 [Allen and Neil 156]; also *Hypomnesticum (Latin)* 4. On the text see Brandes (1998b) 156–58 esp. n. 96; Winkelmann (2001) 155–57 no. 154; Allen and Neil (2002) 41–43. The same text refers to three exiles of Anastasius: the first of these was to Trebizond after the publication of the *Typos*; the second was to Mesembria after the trial of Maximus (see *Dispute at Bizya* 3, 13); and the third was to Lazica after his final condemnation and mutilation alongside Maximus—see, e.g., Theodore Spudaeus, *Hypomnesticum (Greek)* 5. Cf. *PmbZ* "Anastasios Apokrisiarios" 238. From the *Hypomnesticum (Greek)* we learn that Theodore and Euprepius were men of considerable means, for Theodore Spudaeus refers to their possession of "vast wealth and various offices" [*ploutōi polutelei kai axiōmasin diaphorois*, Allen and Neil 156]; cf. *PmbZ* "Euprepios" 1721, "Theodoros" 7301; Winkelmann (2001) 203, 273f.

66. *Acts of the Lateran Council* [Riedinger 2]. For a detailed discussion of the bishops in attendance—demonstrating the limited number of non-Italians and the notable absence of some Italian sees—see Jankowiak (2009) 251–59.

67. See the words of Theodosius of Bithynia in *Dispute at Bizya* 4 [Allen and Neil 88] and *Record* 12 for further doubts cast on its validity. See also the analysis of Ekonomou (2007) 117–19.

68. See esp. R. Riedinger (1980), (1981), and (1983).

co-prepared, the *Acts*, with the intention that it be distributed afterward as a faithful record of what occurred.[69] It is therefore difficult to appreciate how representative the *Acts* may be of the proceedings themselves—that is, whether it was in fact a script to be read out or a preemptive or retrospective fabrication.[70] (Similar methodological problems, of course, beset all conciliar *Acts*.) What should not be doubted, however, is the occurrence of the council itself and the profound influence of Maximus and his Greek-speaking colleagues in controlling its image and official content.[71] At the same time, we should not suppose that Martin and his bishops were but passive actors in events—whatever the council's actual content, the pope himself convened it, presided over it, and conspired in the fiction of a Latin original, signing the council's letter to the emperor in his own hand.[72]

Although the council appears to have avoided the direct condemnation of Heraclius and his successors,[73] within the *Acts* Martin nevertheless likened "those who wage war upon the celestial Jerusalem—that is, the catholic Church" to "those who

---

69. R. Riedinger (1982b), (1985). For the influence of Maximus Confessor (esp. *Opuscula* 15) on the council's florilegia see also the earlier studies of Caspar (1930–33) vol. 2, 553–54; Pierres (1940). A "Maximus monachus" appears among the signatories of the Eastern monastic *libellus* submitted in the council's second session, next to one "Anastasius monachus"; see *Acts of the Lateran Council* [Riedinger 57]. The inconspicuous position (thirty-fourth of thirty-six) perhaps disguises his considerable influence.

70. See the discussion in Conte (1989) 36–38, 105–48; also Ekonomou (2007) 131–34; Jankowiak (2009) 246–51; Cubitt (2009) 135–38. For the same issue from a broader perspective see the papers collected in Price and Whitby (2009).

71. See esp. Conte (1989) 105–48, *contra* R. Riedinger, who in some studies leans toward seeing the council as a fiction, e.g., (1976) 37; (1982b) 118–21. Among Maximus's colleagues we should count Theodore of Tarsus, perhaps that "monk Theodore" who appears as an Eastern signatory in the *Acts of the Lateran Council* [Riedinger 57]. The presence of Theodore at proceedings is corroborated in the *Acts of the Sixth Ecumenical Council* [Riedinger 132f.], where Pope Agatho expresses his hope that "Theodore, our co-servant and co-bishop from Britain, archbishop and philosopher of the great island of Britain," would assist in expounding as an expert the theological issues surrounding monotheletism. On this passage see Lapidge (1995b) 23. For Theodore's recognition of the Lateran Council at the Council of Hatfield in 679 see Chadwick (1995). For his links to Moschus, Sophronius, and Maximus cf. above p. 114f.

72. The original Latin subscription still survives in the codex Vaticanus gr. 1455, fol. 145r; see Conte (1989) 135–37, with 189 and the plate; also Jankowiak (2009) 266–68. For the active role of Martin see also Conte (1989) 142–48; Zocca (1992) 135–40; Cubitt (2009) 142–43. For Martin's dissemination of the *Acts* see his own encyclical at *Acts of the Lateran Council* [Riedinger 412]; also Anastasius Apocrisiarius, *Letter to Theodosius* 10; Theodore Spudaeus, *Hypomnesticum (Greek)* 8; Pope Martin, *Letter to John of Philadelphia* and *Letter to Amandus*. R. Riedinger (esp. 1996) came to regard the latter as a translation from an original Greek composition that integrated sections from an existing papal letter of Leo; cf. Cremascoli (1992) 245–47; also Conte (1971) 446 no. 145; Winkelmann (2001) 128 no. 112.

73. Thus for example the *Ekthesis* is repeatedly said to be "in the name of" Heraclius, who was "induced" or "prompted" by Sergius to publish it; see esp. *Acts of the Lateran Council* [Riedinger 150, 382]. On the *Typos* cf. *Acts of the Lateran Council* [Riedinger 54]. On this theme within the *Acts*—which contrasts with later descriptions of Constans as its co-author—see Van Dieten (1972) 92f. n. 67.

have waged war upon the terrestrial Jerusalem," meaning, of course, the Persians and the Muslims. He thus establishes an equivalence between imperial doctrine and foreign invasion as the twin evils now besetting the Christian faith.[74] At the same time, the council pronounced anathemas on both the monenergist and monothelete doctrines that Heraclius and his successors had supported, on the successive Constantinopolitan patriarchs through whom these were propagated, and on the principle of accommodation adopted in the *Typos*.[75] Pope Martin then dispatched a letter to Emperor Constans in which he made an explicit association between the crisis of empire and the dogmatic innovation represented in monotheletism, predicting that Christ would subdue the emperor's enemies when the proper faith was again adopted.[76]

The appointment of Pope Theodore, the settlement of Maximus and his allies within Rome, and their evident control over the Lateran's *Acts* are but three of several indications of the ever-increasing implication of Palestinian and Roman politics in this period. Within the *libellus* that Stephen of Dora is said to have submitted to the Lateran Council, he claims that when he communicated to Pope Theodore the continued presence in Palestine of those bishops who had been consecrated under the aforementioned Sergius of Joppa, and who had now appealed for ratification from Constantinople, Theodore "through his own apostolic letters established me as his representative [*topotērētēs*]," with instructions to convert or to depose the same bishops.[77] The witness of the *libellus* first of all indicates the still fractious nature of the Palestinian doctrinal scene, where the factional conflict set in motion through the Heraclian program of doctrinal reunification continued to divide the episcopate; but it also indicates the remarkable extent to which Pope Theodore felt compelled to interfere in the doctrinal politics of Palestine, where the patriarchal throne had lain vacant since Sophronius's death (ca. 638).

It is difficult to overstate how remarkable this appointment was.[78] Although papal intervention in the politics of the East was of course well established, such intervention had for the most part been limited to the manipulation of local monastic communities or the dispatch of reproving letters. The *Acts of the Lateran Council*, however, reports that Theodore had invested Stephen with the full power of the

---

74. *Acts of the Lateran Council* [Riedinger 142].

75. See esp. *Acts of the Lateran Council*, Canon 18 [Riedinger 378–82].

76. Pope Martin, *Letter to Constans* [PL 87, 138D–146C, at 146A–B]. Once again R. Riedinger (e.g., 1977: 254f.) doubts the authorship; cf. Winkelmann (2001) 130f. no. 114.

77. *Acts of the Lateran Council* [Riedinger 46]. It is this same role of *topotērētēs* that, Stephen alleges, Sergius had presumed to assume (*tēn topotērēsian tou en Hierosulumois thronou labōn* [ibid.]); cf. Conte (1971) 202f. Pace Van Dieten (1972) 96f. (placing it ca. 648), it does not seem possible to date Stephen's appointment with precision.

78. For this appointment and the subsequent appointment of John of Philadelphia in the context of papal ideology see esp. Conte (1971) 68–72, 211–18, also 441 no. 128, 447 no. 148.

apostolic see, and Stephen, so he claimed within the *libellus*, proceeded to examine the "irregular" bishops and approve those who repented and submitted a confession of the "orthodox" faith.[79] From a series of letters that Martin dispatched in the wake of the Lateran Council, it nevertheless seems that Stephen's mission met with considerable resistance.[80] In a letter to one Pantaleon (who seems to have been in Palestine), Martin complained that certain people had prevented Stephen from realizing his commission and commanded that those bishops appointed during the patriarchate of Sophronius be deposed and that those appointed before or after it (when conditions excused irregular consecrations) be compelled to submit a doctrinal confession.[81] In a contemporaneous letter to one John of Philadelphia (in Jordan), Martin once again referred to the obstruction of Stephen and transferred onto John the status of papal *vicarius* across the East, charging him with the same examination or deposition of "irregular" bishops. At the same time, he sanctioned the appointment of clerics throughout the patriarchates of Antioch and Jerusalem, a pastoral and sacramental mission that "the strain of our age," "the pressure of barbarians," and "the tribulations because of our sins" made all the more pressing.[82]

Martin composed four further letters to individual figures recommending the new *vicarius* John. That three of those figures were also in the Transjordan perhaps indicates how marginalized Stephen and his allies had become within Palestine proper;[83] but at least one bastion of Palestinian resistance remained. That bastion

---

79. *Acts of the Lateran Council* [Riedinger 46]. Stephen reports that he has brought these confessions to the council, and it is possible that the repentant bishops who signed them are those of Transjordan to whom Martin would then write; see *PL* 87, 154B–167A, with Conte (1971) 443–45 nos. 137–39 and 142. If so, Stephen's failure to secure important signatories within Palestine proper points to the considerable marginalization of him and his allies there; see below n. 83. For the importance of Stephen in this period see also Maximus Confessor, *Opuscula* 15, a spiritual and dogmatic tract addressed to Stephen ca. 646/7. For the date Sherwood (1952a) 55; Larchet (1998b) 104; Winkelmann (2001) 122 no. 105. As Jankowiak (2009) 235 points out, Maximus hardly needed to convince Stephen, and it is thus probable that the tract was intended for use against the latter's Eastern opponents.

80. R. Riedinger, in *Acts of the Lateran Council* x f., regards these letters as forgeries compiled by the same hand (or hands) as the *Acts of the Lateran Council*, although doubts over authorship do not negate the precise historical information or the purpose that the same letters exhibit. Cf. Winkelmann (2001) 131–33, nos. 116–22; also Conte (1971) 388–90, 445–49 nos. 148–54; Cremascoli (1992) 253–55; and the convincing defense of them in Jankowiak (2009) 269–77.

81. Pope Martin, *Letter to Pantaleon* [esp. *PL* 87, 169A–C, 172B–D]. This same letter was given in response to a previous communication that complained against Stephen; see Conte (1971) 445 no. 143. This Pantaleon has sometimes been identified with the otherwise unknown Pantaleon, "priest of the Monastery of the Byzantines [at Jerusalem]," who authored the sermon *On the Exaltation of the Cross* (CPG 7915) [*PG* 98, 1265B–1269D]; see esp. Honigmann (1950); Halkin (1986); with *PmbZ* "Pantaleon" 5864.

82. Pope Martin, *Letter to John of Philadelphia* [*PL* 87, 155A–159B]. For the activities of Stephen and the appointment of John of Philadelphia see also Flusin (1992b) vol. 2, 359–65.

83. *Pace* Schönborn (1975) 487–90 suggesting (against the evidence) the considerable success of Stephen and the marginalization of Sergius of Joppa and his allies. For the Transjordanian bishops see

was none other than the monastic alma mater of Moschus and Sophronius. In his *Letter to John of Philadelphia*, Martin referred to the presence, with Stephen of Dora, of certain monks from the Palestinian coenobium of Theodosius and stated that three of those same monks—named as John, Stephen, and Leontius—had attended the Lateran Council and would now bear its decisions to the East.[84] Therefore in his *Letter to George, Archimandrite of the Monastery of Saint Theodosius*—perhaps that same George, archimandrite of Theodosius, who is said in the *Prologue to the Spiritual Meadow* to have received the remains of Moschus—he both recommended the new *vicarius* John and thanked his correspondent for protecting with his own monks the former *vicarius* Stephen as he returned from the Lateran Council to Palestine.[85]

If the letters of Pope Martin provide some invaluable insight, from the papal perspective, of the ever-increasing implication of papal politics with those of the Palestinian faction that opposed monotheletism, then the *Acts of the Lateran Council* provides further evidence of the Palestinian role within that same alliance. During the council's second session, after the reading of Stephen of Dora's *libellus*, the *Acts* claims that a convention of Eastern monks submitted a petition to the bishops for the condemnation of both monenergism and monotheletism, and their proponents. Among the list of monastic signatories—which survives in Latin but not in Greek—we discover three Johns, two Stephens, and one Leontius—among whom, perhaps, we should count the aforementioned monks of Theodosius.[86]

The monastic delegation comprised "pious higoumens and monks from among those Greeks who have resided [in Rome] for a long time and those who have settled here of late [*tōn te palai paroikountōn kai tōn endedēmēkotōn artiōs enthade Graikōn*]."[87] Their leaders were:[88]

---

Pope Martin, *Letter to Theodore*; *Letter to Antony*; and *Letter to Peter the Illustris*. That the latter was from the same region is established in the conclusion to the *Letter to John of Philadelphia* [PL 87, 163A], where he is called *Adraensis*. This "Peter the Illustrious" is distinct from Maximus's correspondent of the same name; see, e.g., Winkelmann (2001) 250f. For Martin's correspondents see *PmbZ* "Antonios" 526; "Iohannes" 2696; "Petros" 5940; "Theodoros" 7304.

84. Pope Martin, *Letter to John of Philadelphia* [PL 87, 154B, 162A].

85. Pope Martin, *Letter to George of Theodosius* [PL 87, 167B]. See also Pope Martin, *Letter to the Churches of Jerusalem and Antioch*. For George see above pp. 232f., 297. For this series of letters to Palestine, see also Jankowiak (2009) 274–77.

86. See *Acts of the Lateran Council* [Riedinger 57]. The list does not survive in Greek. For the petition itself see also Conte (1971) 444 no. 140; Winkelmann (2001) 124 no. 108.

87. *Acts of the Lateran Council* [Riedinger 48]. *Pace* Jankowiak (2009) 233f., I follow the interpretation of Boudignon (2007) 268, treating the genitive *tōn Graikōn* as partitive and thus avoiding the need to distinguish more recent Greek settlers among the signatories themselves (*contra* Sansterre [1983] vol. 1, 12). As Boudignon notes, this neat solution allows us to comprehend several phenomena: the reference to the monks' shared retreat to North Africa at *Acts of the Lateran Council* [Riedinger 52];

John, presbyter and higoumen of the venerable laura of the sainted Sabas, which lies in the desert next to the holy city of Christ our God [*en tēi erēmōi tēi kata tēn hagian Christou tou Theou hēmōn polin*]; Theodore, presbyter and higoumen of the venerable laura that lies in the Christ-loving province of Africa; Thalassius, presbyter and higoumen of the venerable monastery of the Armenians that resides here in the monastery called Renatus; and George, presbyter and higoumen of the venerable monastery of the Cilicians that resides here in the monastery called Aquae Salviae.

Among the signatories of the petition that that delegation submitted was the same "Theodorus gratia Dei abba presbyter monasterii venerandae labrae"—here, however, with the addition "sancti Sabbae."[89] Two Sabaitic monasteries were thus represented at the proceedings: first, the Palestinian Great Laura under the higoumen John; and second, an offshoot of that same institution under the higoumen Theodore. Rome thus counted among its allies the two most celebrated of Jerusalem's monastic communities—Theodosius and Sabas—as well as a satellite of the latter in North Africa.[90]

Little is known of the Armenian monks of the Renatus monastery, although it is tempting to associate its leader, Thalassius, with that same Thalassius whom we earlier encountered as the leader of the monks at Carthage and a recipient of several works of Maximus.[91] Those of Aquae Salviae, however, had their own special connection with Palestine, and indeed with the coenobium of Theodosius. For it was here in Rome where the head of the Heraclian saint Anastasius the Persian was deposited—an apostate soldier turned Palestinian ascetic transported to Ctesiphon and murdered under Khusrau II. None other than Modestus—higoumen of Theodosius, *locum tenens* of Zachariah, and thence patriarch of Jerusalem—had ordered the composition of the saint's *Acts*,[92] and as Bernard Flusin has argued in his masterful monograph on Anastasius, it was in this same period that the saint's head was transported from Palestine to Rome, no doubt in the hands of the aforementioned refugees.[93] From here, we should note, the cult

---

the mention of Thalassius as higoumen of the Armenians; and the association of Aquae Salviae with the (Palestinian) cult of Anastasius the Persian. We need not assume, of course, that the Armenian and Cilician monks were resident in those regions themselves (as Moschus himself demonstrates).

88. *Acts of the Lateran Council* [Riedinger 50]. For the identification of the "holy city of Christ, our God," as Jerusalem see the observations of Sansterre (1983) vol. 1, 24.

89. *Acts of the Lateran Council* [Riedinger 57]. The list of signatories survives only in Latin.

90. Cf. Flusin (1992b) vol. 2, 366–70.

91. See above p. 154; for the Renatus monks see Sansterre (1983) vol. 1, 12–13.

92. On Modestus's annotation of the text see *Acts of Anastasius the Persian* 5 [Flusin 45, with n. 8]. The Latin translation adds "scribere iussus sum ego Modestus archiepiscopus sanctae dei civitatis," which Flusin (1992b) vol. 2, 191–93, following Franklin and Meyvaert (1982) 112–15, explains as a marginal note added by the patriarch himself.

93. On the importation of the head see Flusin (1992b) vol. 2, 354–56. On the monastery and its connection with Anastasius see also Sansterre (1983) vol. 1, 13–17; Boudignon (2007) 269f.

of Anastasius was also transported to England, under the influence, we can assume, of the future archbishop Theodore of Tarsus, that associate of Sophronius and Maximus who retreated from the East to Rome in this same period, and who may of course have settled among his fellow Cilicians at Aquae Salviae.[94] The monks of Aquae Salviae, therefore, shared intimate connections both to Palestine and to the Moschan circle.

In the preceding chapters, we observed how all three of our protagonists—Moschus, Sophronius, and Maximus—appear to have spent some time as exiles in North Africa, and how Moschus himself had thence settled in Rome. Within their petition as presented in the *Acts*, the Eastern monks too refer to their previous presence in the province ("when we settled in the province of Africa") and, from there, their petitioning of Rome to intervene against the innovation of the faith in the East—another indication, it seems, of Palestinian diplomatic pressure applied upon the post-Honorian popes.[95] At the time of the Lateran Council itself, however, the same communities are presented as settlers in Rome, and it is possible that both Sabaitic communities were now more or less permanent residents there, with their former origins nevertheless retained within the titles of their higoumens (perhaps to lend the council "an ecumenical aspect").[96] Indeed, in the aftermath of the council it is certain that a number of those monks decided to remain.[97] As we have seen in our examination of Moschus's *Spiritual Meadow*, it was in this precise period that the monastery bearing the name Cella Nova—perhaps the former residence of Moschus and now the home for Maximus and his allies—was renamed for the Palestinian hero Saint Sabas.[98] The rededication of course suggests that it was now populated with those same Sabaitic monks whom John and Theodore represented at the Lateran Council. The Palestinian presence in Rome, of which

---

94. On Theodore's association with Moschus, Sophronius, and Maximus see above p. 114f. For his possible attendance at the Lateran Council and influence upon it see above n. 71. For his involvement in the cult of Anastasius see Vircillo Franklin (1995) and (2004); also Lapidge (1995b) 19–21.

95. See *Acts of the Lateran Council* [Riedinger 52].

96. So Sansterre (1983) vol. 1, 28f., pointing also to the fact that Martin's *Letters* to the East fail to mention the Laura of Sabas. It is notable, however, that two Johns are listed as successive higoumens of the Great Laura in this same period; see the *Palestinian-Georgian Liturgical Calendar* [Garitte 124], with Flusin (1992b) vol. 2, 367f.

97. For the return of at least some monks cf., however, Martin, *Letter to the Church of Carthage* [PL 87, 147C–D], referring to one Theodore and one Leontius "of the holy laura" (we presume of Sabas in North Africa). As only one Leontius signed the monastic petition presented to the Lateran (*Acts of the Lateran Council* [Riedinger 57]), this would again suggest a larger presence of Eastern monks than the *Acts* itself reveals.

98. See Sansterre (1983) vol. 1, 22–30. Flusin (1992b) vol. 2, 371; Coates-Stephens (2007) 224–31. Against the commonly held notion that Saint Sabas's necropolis demonstrates distinct Palestinian influences, however, see ibid. 238–44; *contra*, e.g., Sansterre (1983) vol. 1, 22.

Moschus had been such a striking pioneer, was thus now recognized in the dedication of an established monastic house to Palestine's most prominent ascetic star.

### REBELLION AND TRIAL

The North African pattern of political sedition—in which the convocation of antimonothelete councils was followed with the rebellion of the exarch—was now repeated at Rome. Earlier, after the election of Theodore in November 642 but before the death of the exarch Isaac in 643/4, the *Book of Pontiffs* reports that Maurice, the aforementioned *cartularius*, launched an unsuccessful Roman rebellion against Isaac, a rebellion it is tempting to associate with the provocative stance that the pope adopted in correspondence with Constantinople.[99] Now under Martin, and coterminous with the Lateran Council, the emperor Constans is said to have dispatched a new Italian exarch, the cubicularius Olympius, with instructions to enforce the *Typos* and, if possible, to arrest the dissident Martin. Upon the new exarch's arrival, the text reports, Olympius first attempted to arrest the pope through force, and when that scheme floundered in the face of clerical opposition, launched a failed attempt to assassinate him during the eucharistic celebration. Seeing that the hand of God protected the pope, so the *Book of Pontiffs* claims, the new exarch revealed his orders to Martin, reconciled himself to him, and then set out to Sicily to campaign "against the Saracen people who were living there."[100] Like the African exarch Gregory before him, Olympius was defeated and died soon after.[101]

Modern scholarship places the reconciliation of exarch and pope in 651.[102] The extant sources do not permit us to assess how complicit the pope and his

---

99. *Book of Pontiffs* 75 [Duchesne vol. 1, 331f.]. Cf. *PmbZ* "Mauricius" 4894. For the potential association with Theodore's stance see Jankowiak (2009) 204–6.

100. The existence of this campaign is denied in Stratos (1976); also Lo Jacono (1988) 7f.; but cf. Jankowiak (2009) 278f. Islamic sources on the conquest of Sicily are for the most part silent, but Balādhurī, *Conquest of the Lands* [de Goeje 235], places it at least a decade later, under Muʿāwiya; see Caetani (1912–23) vol. 2, 340. Evidence for the period, however, is severely limited, and there is no need to doubt an earlier occupation, given the recent conquest of North Africa and the striking coincidence with significant Arab naval action farther east. On this issue see also Woods (2003a) arguing ingeniously but to my mind unnecessarily that the "Saracens" of the *Book of Pontiffs* are in fact the Zarakianoi of Mauretania.

101. *Book of Pontiffs* 76 [Duchesne vol. 1, 337f.]. We should note that within the imperial order to the new exarch the emperor demands the subscription to the *Typos* of "foreigners" ("peregri" [i.e., "peregrini"])—a reference, no doubt, to the exiled monks under Maximus. On the *Book of Pontiffs'* account see also Neil (2006c) 115–17. On Olympius see Brandes (1998b) 168–73 (with further literature at n. 171); *PmbZ* "Olympios" 5650; Winkelmann (2001) 246f. It has sometimes been suggested (unconvincingly) that Olympius minted his own coins; see, e.g., O'Hara (1985) 121, with the comments of Brandes (1998b) 169 n. 171; Rubery (2011) 26 n. 95.

102. T. S. Brown (1984) 159 n. 25.

Palestinian allies may have been in the exarch's rebellion, but it is difficult to ignore that same coincidence—earlier manifested in North Africa—of an antimonothelete council and the exarch's secession from Constantinople. Once again, a Western exarch rebelled in the face of Muslim pressure, but once again that rebellion occurred in a context of religious dissent from the emperor's rule. Little wonder that in Constantinople, at least, his actions were perceived as nothing less than a full-scale usurpation—in which, moreover, the pope was complicit.[103]

Events in the East were soon to provide Constans with an occasion for more decisive action. If continued war with the caliphate had in the 640s checked the hand of the emperor, a reprieve from Muslim pressure now provided him with the political breathing space to act against the principal antagonists in Rome. Under sustained pressure from Muslim raids at sea and into eastern Asia Minor, in 651 Constans sued for peace and negotiated a three-year treaty that allowed him to consolidate his own position within the empire.[104] He committed himself to three crucial acts: first, and perhaps as part of a more general purge within the capital, he suppressed the rebellion of the *magister* George, a prominent general in the region of Constantinople;[105] second, he led an imperial expedition to Armenia to secure the region after the defection of its governor and brought the Armenian Church back into communion after its separation at the Council of Dvin in 649;[106] and third, and most important for our purposes, he sent a new exarch to Rome to arrest Pope Martin and Maximus.

The continuation of the notice on Martin within the *Book of Pontiffs* reports that the emperor now sent one Theodore Calliopas as Italian exarch, who then seized Martin from the Church of the Savior and transported him to Constantinople, there to be banished into exile in "Chersona" (where also were located

---

103. So also Brandes (1998b) 171f., pointing also to the specter of the rebellion of the eunuch Eleutherius in Italy in 619, described at *Book of Pontiffs* 70; *Auctarii Havniensis Extrema* [Mommsen 339]; Paul the Deacon, *History* 4.34. See *PLRE* vol. 3, "Eleutherius"; also Jankowiak (2009) 123f.

104. For the raids see, e.g., Theophanes, *Chronicle* A.M. 6142; cf. Michael the Syrian, *Chronicle* 11.11. For the peace: Theophanes, *Chronicle* A.M. 6142; Michael the Syrian, *Chronicle* 11.11; *Anonymous Chronicle to 1234* 133; Agapius, *Universal History* [Vasiliev 481f.]; Ps.-Sebēos, *History* 45; cf. also Fredegar, *Chronicle* 4.81. For detailed discussion of the peace and its terms see Kaplony (1996) 23–32.

105. See Ps.-Sebēos, *History* 47, referring also to a general purge in Constantinople; see Howard-Johnston (1999b) 263f.; Kaegi (1981) 160f. It is no doubt this same George who is referred to in the trial literature of Pope Martin; see below p. 304.

106. For the defection of the Armenian governor see Ps.-Sebēos, *History* 48; Theophanes, *Chronicle* A.M. 6143; Agapius, *Universal History* [Vasiliev 482]. Theophanes calls the defector "Pasagnathes," who should be identified with the rebellious governor Theodore Raštuni described in Ps.-Sebēos, *History* 48–49, as per Peeters (1933); Howard-Johnston (1999b) 267f. and (2010) 220; *PmbZ* "Pasagnathes." For the Council of Dvin see Ps.-Sebēos, *History* 45–46. There is no indication that monotheletism was discussed.

Anastasius Apocrisiarius and his disciples).[107] No more details are provided, but the account of Martin's arrest is verified in a text that relates his fate in far greater detail. The so-called *Narrations Concerning the Exile of the Holy Pope Martin*—which survives not in the Greek original but in the Latin translation of Anastasius Bibliothecarius—comes from the pen of one Theodore Spudaeus and is addressed to those aforementioned disciples of Anastasius Apocrisiarius, Theodore and Euprepius.[108] Theodore Spudaeus and his brother Theodosius of Gangra were admirers of the circles of Martin and Maximus, and both brothers corresponded with and visited them in exile.[109] Theodore, at least, is responsible for much of our impression of events, for alongside the *Narrations* he also authored the *Hypomnesticum*, a celebration of the later lives of Martin, Maximus, and their disciples.[110] Both he and his brother were, it appears, Palestinian monks,[111] and they had spent some time in Rome around the time of the Lateran Council.[112]

---

107. *Book of Pontiffs* 76. For Theodore see *PmbZ* "Theodoros" 7295; Brandes (1998b) 159 n. 113.

108. On the text see Conte (1989) 221–24; Chiesa (1992); Brandes (1998b) 153 n. 77; Neil (2006c) 95–103, dating it to ca. 655–62. I have elevated its lengthier account over that of the *Greek Life of Pope Martin*, which appears to epitomize the same Greek original (and in places preserves a reading preferable to the Latin). For the relation of the two texts see Brandes (1998b) 154f.; Neil (2006c) 94, 110–15.

109. For the visit of Theodore Spudaeus to Theodore, disciple of Anastasius Apocrisiarius, to Anastasius himself, and to Maximus see Theodore Spudaeus, *Hypomnesticum (Greek)* 7–8, 10, and *Hypomnesticum (Latin)* 4, 7.

110. One Theodore is identified as the author at Theodore Spudaeus, *Hypomnesticum (Greek)* 3 [Allen and Neil 150]. For discussion of the text see esp. Conte (1989) 224–28; Brandes (1998b) 156–58; also Devreesse (1935); Allen and Neil (2002) 41–43; Neil (2006c) 104f. It dates to ca. 669.

111. Theodore Spudaeus, the author of the *Hypomnesticum* and the *Narrations*, calls himself the brother of Theodosius at *Hypomnesticum (Greek)* 10 and *Hypomnesticum (Latin)* 7, perhaps that same Theodosius of Gangra who is presented in the Latin preface as the recipient of Anastasius Apocrisiarius's *Letter to Theodosius* (ibid. 1) and is said to be "in sancta Christi nostri civitate constitutum" [Allen and Neil 132]. *Contra* Devreesse (1955), Noret (2000) convincingly argues that both monks were ensconced within Jerusalem rather than Constantinople and indeed were associated with its Church of the Resurrection (which Theodore Spudaeus mentions but does not locate at *Hypomnesticum (Greek)* 10; cf. Anastasius Apocrisiarius, *Letter to Theodosius* 8). Allen and Neil (2002) 42 n. 174 and Neil (2006c) 129 nevertheless point out that Theodore Spudaeus's *Narrations* has the subtitle *Ex His Quae a Theodoro Spudeo Sanctae Sophiae Scripta Sunt* [PL 129, 586D], suggesting a Constantinopolitan connection. "Sancta Sophia," however, need not refer to the capital, since there was of course a famous Church of Holy Wisdom in Jerusalem also; see, e.g., Piacenza Pilgrim, *Itinerary* 9, 23; Strategius, *On the Fall* 23. For the term "Spudaeus" in association also with the Church of the Resurrection at Jerusalem see, e.g., Cyril of Scythopolis, *Life of Theodosius* 1 and *Life of Sabas* 31; with Pétridès (1901). Cf. *PmbZ* "Theodoros Spudaios" 7439; "Theodosios" 7816; Winkelmann (2001) 272f., 275. Theodosius of Gangra was also the recipient of an unpublished text of Maximus Confessor (*Responses to Theodosius of Gangra*); see CPG (Suppl.) 7707.

112. See the brief allusion at Theodore Spudaeus, *Hypomnesticum (Greek)* 10 [Allen and Neil 164], referring to "the saint and apostolic head Martin, pope of Rome, when we attended upon him face to face in the same city of great name . . . [*autoprosōpōs pros auton en tēi autēi megalōnumōi polei paragenomenōn*]."

Theodore's *Narrations* as it stands consists of two letters of Martin to the author appended with an independent narrative of his arrest, trial, and exile—the so-called *Commemoration*—and two more of the pope's letters.[113] In the first two letters, in which Martin describes his arrest in Rome (in June 653) and transportation to the Eastern capital, he gives some impression of the charges laid before him.[114] The immediate pretext for his arrest, it appears, was his failure to secure imperial approval before his election ("quod irregulariter et sine lege episcopatum subripuissem"),[115] but it is nevertheless evident that further (quite remarkable) "false slanders" circled around him: first, that he had communicated via letters with "the Saracens" and sent to them both "a book on what they should believe" ("tomus qualiter credere debeant") along with certain monies; second, that he had slandered the Virgin (an accusation also later leveled, we should note, at Maximus);[116] and third, that upon the arrival of the exarch Olympius he could have resisted him with force but did not.[117]

Within that same passage Martin refers to Olympius as "infamous," "a certain vain ["vanus"] man."[118] The dismissal serves to distance the pope from the exarch himself, but there can be little doubt that Martin coalesced in his rebellion. The question—and that explored during his subsequent trial in the capital—is instead whether he did so under duress. The aforementioned *Commemoration*—which is attributed to "a most Christian man" and dispatched "to those orthodox fathers who are in the West or in Rome and Africa"—purports to record a firsthand account of Martin's arrival and trial in Constantinople, held in December 653.[119]

---

113. For this separate text—and the contradictions it contains in respect to Theodore Spudaeus's wider *Narrations* in which it is embedded—see Chiesa (1992) 212–22; Neil (2006c) 96–99, 126–28. For the letters cf. Conte (1971) 452f. nos. 167–71; Winkelmann (2001) 146f. nos. 139–42; and the discussion of Cremascoli (1992) 250–53. For the letters as "exilic literature" see now also Neil (2010).

114. See Theodore Spudaeus, *Narrations* 3–7; cf. *Greek Life of Pope Martin* 3–6, and the complementary account from the *Commemoration* at *Narrations* 12–13. Theodore Spudaeus, *Narrations* 9, and the *Greek Life of Pope Martin* both claim that Martin was arrested on Wednesday 17 June, but the day (at least) cannot be correct, since 17 June fell on a Wednesday only in 649 and 655. The indiction is given as the tenth (A.D. 652), furthermore, but should be corrected to the eleventh; see Neil (2006c) 181 n. 55.

115. See Theodore Spudaeus, *Narrations* 7 [Neil 176]. For discussion of the charge see Brandes (1998b) 165–67.

116. Theodore Spudaeus, *Narrations* 3 [Neil 168–70]. Cf. *Dispute at Bizya* 14 and below p. 317f.

117. Theodore Spudaeus, *Narrations* 6. The text refers to the fact that Theodore Calliopas and his entourage "claimed that I could have repelled him [Olympius] with arms" ("cum armis me hunc potuisse repellere faterentur") [Neil 176]. Neil (2006c) 111 and 176 n. 4 negates the phrase with the addition of "non" (after the *Greek Life of Pope Martin* 4), but it seems to me unwarranted. For the same accusation cf. Theodore Spudaeus, *Narrations* 17.

118. Theodore Spudaeus, *Narrations* 6 [Neil 176].

119. Theodore Spudaeus, *Narrations* 14–15 [Neil 188–92]. Cf. *Greek Life of Pope Martin* 6–7. For the chronology of Martin's arrest, transportation, and trial in more detail see Brandes (1998b) 159f.

We cannot of course know how the trial itself proceeded—but if the purpose of the *Commemoration*'s account is to vindicate Martin before its immediate audience, then we must assume that it reflects something of the actual substance of the charges put before him. We might expect the Lateran Council's repudiation of monotheletism to have been prominent among such charges. But when the pope himself attempts to raise the issue of the faith, one Troilus shouts him down. This trial, as the *Commemoration* presents it, was not about the faith but about usurpation ("non . . . de fide, de duellio").[120]

The most prominent accusation is, therefore, Martin's complicity in Olympius's rebellion. Various former followers of the exarch are produced to condemn the pope,[121] but when the aforementioned Troilus then presses Martin over his failure to prevent the exarch's rebellion, the pope offers a cutting response, pointing to his accuser's inaction during the aforementioned revolts of the *magister* George and the general Valentine.[122] We will never know, of course, if Martin did indeed offer this clever defense, which drew a parallel between his own situation and that of members of the court in Constantinople during those revolts. But at the least it demonstrates his circle's awareness of the significant rebellions that had rocked Constans's regime from within and in which his highest dignitaries had, for better or worse, coalesced.

The *Commemoration* reports that at the end of his trial Martin was sentenced to death, remitted to exile in Cherson after the dramatic intervention of the

---

120. Theodore Spudaeus, *Narrations* 17 [Neil 196]. Cf. *Greek Life of Pope Martin* 7 [Peeters 259]. For Troilus cf. *Record* 6, 9, 11–12; *Dispute at Bizya* 10–15. Nevertheless Troilus's precise position is unclear. Brandes (1998b) 162 suggests that he was *eparchos tēs poleōs* (with some reservations expressed at n. 130). Neil (2006c) 203 n. 98, however, suggests that the *eparchos tēs poleōs* was in fact the "Gregory the prefect, a eunuch from the cubicularii" mentioned in Theodore Spudaeus, *Narrations* 22 [Neil 206], *Hypomnesticum (Greek)* 8, and *Hypomnesticum (Latin)* 5, where he is called *eparchos tēs athlias ontōs eirēmenēs poleōs* [Allen and Neil 160] and "praefectus miserae illius urbis" [Neil 246]. If so, a eunuch's elevation as urban prefect was unprecedented; cf. Brandes (1998b) 174 n. 203, suggesting that Gregory was in fact "praepositus sacri cubiculi."

121. Theodore Spudaeus, *Narrations* 16–17 [Neil 194–96]. Chief among these is "Dorotheus, patrician of Sicily." The text in fact reads "patricius Ciliciae" but should be emended to "Siciliae," as in Brandes (1998b) 170 with n. 179, Neil (2006c) 195 n. 86 (both with previous literature). The former suggests a potential link between the appearance of Dorotheus and Olympius's reported Sicilian mission at *Book of Pontiffs* 76 (which would support the latter's authenticity); see above p. 300.

122. Theodore Spudaeus, *Narrations* 17 [Neil 196–98]; for the identification of this George with George *magister* in Ps.-Sebēos, *History* 47 (above n. 105), see also Neil (2006a) 81. In respect of Troilus's political inclinations and potential splits within the Constantinopolitan court over doctrinal policy we may also note that Theophanes, *Chronicle* A.M. 6160, calls Constans's later murderer "Andreas son of Troilus" [de Boor 351]. Such splits are also suggested in the sympathetic attitude of the eunuch Gregory (see above n. 120) to Martin, expressed at Theodore Spudaeus, *Narrations* 22, and that of Theodore, "protosecretary of the praetorian prefect of Constantinople" (*ho prōtosekretarios tou praitōriou tou huparchou Kōnstantinoupoleōs*), toward Maximus. For splits within the Constantinopolitan court over Maximus's fate see also Brandes (1998b) 209f. with n. 444.

patriarch Paul on his deathbed.[123] Here the pope would soon die—either on 16 September 655 or on 13 April 656.[124] After Paul's death in December 653, however, and before Martin's exile was enforced, the *Commemoration* stages a remarkable scene in which Martin is questioned over the reception in Rome of the former patriarch Pyrrhus, now returned to the capital and pressing, it appears, for his own reinstatement.[125] From Martin's inquisition it is evident that that reinstatement met with considerable opposition from within the capital,[126] but nevertheless Pyrrhus was reelected in January 654, dying soon afterward in June.[127] He thus did not live to witness an event from which he would, one can perhaps assume, have derived some pleasure—the trial of Maximus Confessor.

Maximus's trial was convened under the tenure of the new patriarch, Peter, at some point in 655.[128] Since the trial of Martin, the empire had once again been plunged into conflict with the caliphate. The peace of 651–53 had lapsed, and the Muslims had launched a vast naval expedition from Phoenician Tripoli. At the battle of Phoenix, off the coast of southwestern Asia Minor in 654, the fleet defeated a Roman force under the command of Constans himself, who was fortunate to escape with his life.[129] Thereafter the Muslims converged upon Constantinople on

123. For the intervention see Theodore Spudaeus, *Narrations* 23; *Greek Life of Pope Martin* 10, with Van Dieten (1972) 101f.

124. For the latter date see *Greek Life of Pope Martin* [Peeters 261]: "The thirteenth of the month of April, fourteenth indiction." The date coincides with the Western feast of Saint Euphemia, to which other texts appear to reconcile the date of Martin's death according to their own calendars; thus Theodore Spudaeus, *Narrations* 28 [Neil 218–20], *Hypomnesticum (Greek)* 8, and *Hypomnesticum (Latin)* 5 [Neil 248] give 16 September 655 ("fourteenth indiction"). For discussion see Neil (2006c) 117–20.

125. For the date of Paul's death see Van Dieten (1972) 102 with n. 95.

126. Theodore Spudaeus, *Narrations* 24; *Greek Life of Pope Martin* 10. For the importance of Pyrrhus's actions in Rome see also the outburst that an anonymous attendee voices against Maximus in *Record* 11 [Allen and Neil 70]. Both Maximus and Anastasius the Disciple are questioned over their treatment of Pyrrhus at *Record* 5–6.

127. For these dates see Van Dieten (1972) 104f., based on, e.g., Nicephorus, *Chronography* [de Boor 118]; Theophanes, *Chronicle* A.M. 6145. Cf. also Theodore Spudaeus, *Narrations* 32, for Pyrrhus's reelection and his posthumous recognition under Peter. From Pope Agatho, *Letter to Constantine* [PL 87, 1205A; also *Acts of the Sixth Ecumenical Council* (Riedinger 110)], we may suppose that Pyrrhus in this short period ratified the *Typos* (although perhaps confused with the *Ekthesis*; see Jankowiak [2009] 298 n. 56).

128. For the date—which cannot be offered with better precision—see Allen and Neil (2002) 35. The date of May offered in, e.g., Van Dieten (1972) 108 and Brandes (1998b) 155 is based upon the misdating of Maximus Confessor's *Letter to Anastasius the Disciple* to 655. For Peter's election see Van Dieten (1972) 106.

129. See the accounts in Theophanes, *Chronicle* A.M. 6146; Michael the Syrian, *Chronicle* 11.11; *Anonymous Chronicle to 1234* 134; Agapius, *Universal History* [Vasiliev 483f.]. For the chronology see Zuckerman (2005) 114f., Cosentino (2008) 592; *contra* Howard-Johnston (1999) 259–62. For the (no doubt identical) "Battle of the Masts" in the Islamic tradition see Caetani (1912–23) vol. 2, 360, with Christides (1984); Cosentino (2008) 586–93. The push into the Aegean coincided with the attempted

both land and sea: the fleet seized Rhodes, Crete, and Cos, while a Muslim force pressed overland through Anatolia.[130] In 654, Constantinople was, for the second time within three decades, submitted to a siege. Once again, however—and perhaps with the aid of a violent storm that scattered the Muslim ships—it survived.[131]

For our purposes, the most important aspect of this narrative is the close chronological intersection of the siege with Maximus's trial—it suggests, perhaps, that the miraculous salvation of the capital from the Muslim assault encouraged the Constantinopolitan authorities at last to pursue the punishment of their most vocal religious critic. The various recensions of Maximus's Greek *Life*—which are more reliable for Maximus's later career than for his origins—claim that he was, like Martin, arrested at Rome with his disciples (June 653) and thence brought to face trial in the capital.[132] He must, however, have been detained elsewhere for some considerable time, for his trial did not occur until 655, and the so-called *Record of the Trial*—which Maximus himself, or a close disciple, composed soon after the trial itself—claims that it did so upon his arrival in the capital.[133]

As with the *Commemoration* of Martin's trial, we cannot read the *Record of the Trial* as its usual English name implies—it is, above all, a hagiographic piece and has more in common with the *Apology* of Plato than a modern legal transcript.[134]

---

reassertion of Muslim control over Armenia; see Theophanes, *Chronicle* A.M. 6145; Agapius, *Universal History* [Vasiliev 483]; Michael the Syrian 11.10; Ps.-Sebēos, *History*, 51, with Howard-Johnston (1999) 277–79. For the Islamic sources see Caetani (1912–23) vol. 2, 330.

130. Capture of the islands: Michael the Syrian, *Chronicle* 11.10. Theophanes, *Chronicle* A.M. 6145, and Agapius, *Universal History* [Vasiliev 482], report the conquest of Rhodes and the destruction of the Colossus, on which see Bosworth (1996); Conrad (1996). For the conquest of Cos and Crete see Michael the Syrian, *Chronicle* 11.10. For the Anatolian force see Theophanes, *Chronicle* A.M. 6146; Agapius, *Universal History* [Vasiliev 482]; Ps.-Sebēos, *History* 50.

131. See Ps.-Sebēos, *History* 50. The siege is corroborated in Arabic sources; see Caetani (1912–23) vol. 2, 338, and (1905–26) vol. 7, 516; also Brooks (1898) 184, citing Ibn al-Athīr for a raid of Muʿāwiya upon "the straits of Al-Kustantiniyya" in A.H. 32 (A.D. 652/3). For discussion of this campaign see also O'Sullivan (2004) placing the siege before Phoenix; Cosentino (2008) 589–93 demonstrating that it was after.

132. See *Greek Life of Maximus Confessor (Recension 3)* 23; and cf. Theophanes, *Chronicle* A.M. 6121, where Constans is also said to bring Martin and Maximus to the capital from Rome—*pace* Brandes (1998b) 177f., who (on the basis of the Syriac *Life*) places Maximus's arrival after Martin's. For the contested passage see below p. 324f.

133. *Record* 1 [Allen and Neil 48]. On the location and the attendees in more detail see the full discussion of Brandes (1998b) 180–83. A precedent for Maximus's detention elsewhere is perhaps Martin's reported sojourn on Naxos, en route to the capital under arrest; see Theodore Spudaeus, *Narrations* 13; *Greek Life of Pope Martin* 5. For the date of the *Record*—after the trial in 655 but before Maximus's transference from Bizya to Perberis in September 656—see *Record* 13. For discussion of the text and its authorship see Conte (1989) 207–12; Brandes (1998b) 155 n. 90; Winkelmann (2001) 140 no. 132; Allen and Neil (2002) 35f. The *Greek Life of Maximus (Recension 2)* attributes the *Record* to "the fine disciple of the holy man" [*PG* 90, 88D].

134. Cf. Brandes (1998b) 155: "Sie gibt sich den Anschein einer protokollarischen Aufzeichnung" (with n. 92).

Nevertheless, if we can again be confident that the text rebuts something of the actual charges leveled at Maximus, it must at least preserve what the author (Maximus or a close disciple) considered to be the ideal responses to those same charges, if not the responses themselves. As we have seen, the literature associated with Martin's trial presents it as a nonreligious affair in which the pope's attempts to discuss monotheletism are refused and in which he is condemned under the charge of political sedition alone. This is of course a forced and artificial distinction, which perhaps reflects the disingenuous nature of the prosecution (or the author's attempt to characterize it as such). But in the *Record of the Trial* there is no such distinction, and the text instead embraces the proper implication of the political and the religious that we have seen to dominate the discourse of the period. It thus affords us an invaluable window not only onto the perceived transgressions of Maximus and his allies but also onto the conceptual framework within which that same circle constructed and legitimized its dissidence.

Maximus's Constantinopolitan accusers indicted him under several charges, the foremost of which was politicoreligious sedition. In the trial's opening part, according to the *Record*, the (unnamed) imperial sacellarius stated, "From the things that you have done, it is apparent to everyone that you hate the emperor and his empire [*politeia*]. For alone you have betrayed Egypt, Alexandria, Pentapolis, Tripolis, and Africa to the Saracens." Maximus then requested some proof of these charges, at which point the sacellarius produced one John, former sacellarius of Peter "who had been general of Numidia in Africa"; John claimed that "twenty-two years ago [in 633] the emperor's grandfather [Heraclius] ordered the late Peter to take an army and to go into Egypt against the Saracens." Peter, however—in a striking statement of Maximus's importance within North Africa and of his implication within its highest elites—is said then to have written to Maximus and asked whether he should execute the emperor's command, and was told in response "to do nothing of the sort, since God did not deign that the empire of the Romans be assisted under the reign [*basileia*] of Heraclius and his kin [*genos*]." John claimed "at that time all those in the camp were discussing these things," but he could not produce Maximus's letter itself.[135]

In the subsequent section of the text one Sergius Magoudas brings forward another accusation. He relates that he had heard from one Abba Thomas that when the latter was in Rome, Pope Theodore sent him to the rebellious exarch Gregory to reassure him of imminent success, for "the servant of God Abba Maximus has seen in a dream [*onar*] that there were crowds of angels in the heavens in

---

135. *Record* 1 [Allen and Neil 48–50]. On these charges see also Brandes (1998b) 183–85. We can perhaps presume that the sacellarius is the same Boukoleon who presided over Martin's trial in 653; see Theodore Spudaeus, *Hypomnesticum (Greek)* 8 and *Hypomnesticum (Latin)* 5, with Brandes (1998b) 161. For Peter the General of Numidia see above p. 152 n. 53; also Brandes (1998b) 183 n. 268.

East and West. Those in the East were crying out, 'Constantine Augustus, you will be victorious [*tou binkas*],' while those in the West were shouting, 'Gregory Augustus, you will be victorious [*tou binkas*].' And the voices in the West overpowered those in the East." Maximus in response lamented that the protagonists within his accuser's indictment were no longer alive to establish his innocence. Even so, he added in a perhaps telling aside, even if he had related such a dream to Theodore, the guilt would in fact be the pope's for acting upon it, "for a dream is not a matter that is premeditated [*apoaireton*]," and thus not punishable in law.[136] Even within the apologetic *Record of the Trial*, therefore, Maximus hints as to the dream's actual occurrence.

As Brandes has demonstrated in his brilliant exegesis of the charge, Maximus's reported dream in fact engages in a sophisticated subversion of imperial propaganda.[137] First of all, it draws upon the language of Constantinopolitan imperial ceremonial, for the exclamation *toumbikas* appears in an acclamation offered to the emperor Heraclius and his household and preserved within the *Book of Ceremonies*.[138] At the same time it echoes, of course, certain accounts of Constantine's conversion at the Milvian Bridge, with the transliterated Latin *tu vincas* paralleling the famous proclamation *en toutōi nika* or *in hoc vince*.[139] This is significant, for the same Constantinian slogan also appears within the official propaganda of Constans's regime, which attempted to associate the emperor with his illustrious predecessor and namesake.[140] From the earliest stages of Constans's rule mints had issued a series of copper folles that drew upon the same accounts, inscribed EN TOYTO NIKA and intended, one presumes, to proclaim the imminent triumph of the Christian over the Muslim faith.[141] Maximus's dream thus struck at the heart of Constans's image: in subverting a slogan proclaimed within Heraclian ceremonial and echoed upon the emperor's coins, it reappropriated for his usurper the legitimizing weight of the imperial and Constantinian traditions, while reestablishing

---

136. *Record* 2 [Allen and Neil 50–52]. Boudignon (2004) 28f. suggests that the Thomas referred to may be the addressee of Maximus Confessor, *Ambigua to Thomas* and *Second Letter to Thomas*; and the Thomas who appears in Maximus Confessor, *Letters* 40 [*PG* 91, 636A]. On Sergius Magoudas—whose name points to an origin on the Euphrates—see Brandes (1998b) 185.

137. Ibid. 185–92.

138. See *Book of Ceremonies* 2.29 [Reiske vol. 1, 629f.].

139. For the exclamation see, e.g., Sozomen, *Ecclesiastical History* 1.3 [Bidez and Hansen 11]: *Ō Kōnstantine, en toutōi nika*; Rufinus, *Ecclesiastical History* 9.9 [Winkelmann vol. 2, 829]: "Constantine, *Toutōi nika*, quod est: In hoc vince."

140. For the wider imperial attempt to appropriate Constantine in this period see Haldon (1994). On the specific place of Constantine within the monothelete crisis, I regret that I have not been able to access Brandes (2001).

141. See, e.g., Grierson (1982) 113f., 127 (with further literature at Kaegi [1992] 218 n. 39; Brandes [1998b] 188 n. 298). According to Grierson, this coin was minted in Constantinople from 641 to 657/8 but in Carthage only 641–43.

the pregnant resonances of civil (rather than interconfessional) strife inherent within the original Constantinian tradition. At the same time, it appears to have intersected with a wider attempt to destabilize Constans's regime through the inversion of the precise same slogan: thus Theophanes (via Theophilus of Edessa) reports a not dissimilar tale in which, on the eve of the crucial battle of Phoenix, the emperor Constans has a dream in which he sees himself in Thessalonica. When he awakes he reports this dream to an interpreter, who proclaims, "Emperor, would that you had not slept and seen this dream. For your presence in Thessalonica means 'Give the victory to another [thes allōi nikēn]': that is, the victory belongs to your enemy."[142]

It is of course impossible to ascertain the truth of these accusations, even if Maximus's association with the main protagonists is attested elsewhere.[143] Modern commentators, however, have tended to regard those accusations as utter fabrications designed to deflect attention from imperial failings in a context of Muslim expansion within the Near East.[144] However, while the extent of the subversion is no doubt exaggerated—Maximus cannot, of course, be held responsible for the entire capitulation of North Africa—we should not dismiss out of hand the accusation of support for political sedition. Although the smoking-gun letter to Peter the general of Numidia does not survive, the political opinions expressed in Maximus's *Letters* 10, in which he informed John Cubicularius that a corrupt emperor would drag his entire empire to destruction, are at least comparable; and even if the truth of the dream and its consequences cannot be established, the exarch to whom it referred nevertheless presided over a disputation and several councils that anathematized Constantinopolitan doctrine and then launched a full-scale rebellion. Indeed, as we have seen, Maximus and his master Sophronius had in the past demonstrated a marked ambivalence toward Heraclius and his household, and it would be unsurprising if he indeed went one step further and encouraged a simultaneous political rebellion against the heretical rule of Heraclius's successors. Some time earlier, the affair between Martina and the African prefect George had perhaps presaged an imminent rebellion, and now both the African and Italian exarchs had rebelled against Constantinople while Maximus resided in their provinces, agitating against Constantinopolitan doctrine. From this perspective one can better appreciate the Constantinopolitan decision to scapegoat him as the single cause of imperial reversals in North Africa.

---

142. Theophanes, *Chronicle* A.M. 6146 [de Boor 346]. Cf. Michael the Syrian, *Chronicle* 11.1, and *Anonymous Chronicle to 1234* 134. For the same subversion of official imperial propaganda in broader perspective see, e.g., Scott (1985).

143. For this Peter (distinct from Peter the Illustrious, and the recipient of Maximus Confessor's *Comptus Ecclesiasticus*) see above p. 152 n. 53; also Brandes (1998b) 184.

144. See, e.g., Haldon (1985) 89; Brandes (1998b) 212; Sahas (2003) 110–16.

Two subsequent witnesses within the *Record of the Trial* both make accusations concerning Maximus's attitude toward the emperor: the first, one Theodore Chila, son-in-law of the former Italian exarch Plato, alleges that "During an interview between us in Rome concerning the emperor, he ridiculed what was said, making sounds of contempt and derision [*muttia kai laimia*]";[145] the second, one Gregory son of Photinus, contends that "I went to Abba Maximus's cell in Rome, and when I said that the emperor is also a priest [*hoti kai hiereus estin ho basileus*], Abba Anastasius, his disciple, said, 'He should not be deemed worthy to be a priest [*Mē axiōthēi einai hiereus*].'"[146] The reported conversation follows a familiar pattern— Gregory advocates doctrinal silence in order to achieve peace, and Maximus proclaims that "silence is also annulment" (*esti siōpē kai anairesis*)[147]—but progresses into an elucidation of Anastasius's apparent pronouncement on the emperor's sacerdotal status:[148]

> [And I said:] "None of the emperors was able through equivocal pronouncements [*mesais phōnais*] to persuade the God-conversing Fathers to be reconciled with the heretics of their age. They instead used ones that were clear and authoritative, and that corresponded to the dogma that was being inquired into, clearly proclaiming that it was the prerogative of priests to make inquiries and definitions concerning the salvific dogmas of the universal Church." And you said, "And what? Is every Christian emperor not also a priest?" And I said, "No, he is not. For he does not stand beside the altar [*thusiatērion*] and after the consecration of the bread [*meta ton hagiasmon tou artou*] raise it and say: *Holy things for the holy* [*ta hagia tois hagiois*]; nor does he baptize or carry out the ritual of anointment [*murou teletēn epitelei*], nor

---

145. *Record* 3 [Allen and Neil 52]. As noted in Allen and Neil (2002) 177 n. 14, *muttia* and *laimia* are *hapax legomena*. The Greek at *PG* 91, 114C, has instead *butia . . . kai laibia*, perhaps equivalent to the Latin "vitia" and "levia"; see Brandes (1998b) 193, and cf. Anastasius Bibliothecarius's "mutiens et subsannationes faciens" at *PL* 129, 606D. I have followed the translation of Allen and Neil (2002) 53. The exarch Plato appears to have suffered some reproach for allowing Maximus to live under his rule—see the exclamation at *Record* 4—and his son-in-law perhaps hoped to restore his reputation. Cf. the *Book of Pontiffs* 76, which claims Plato instigated the arrest of Martin. For the association of his brother with Maximus see above p. 152 n. 54; also on Plato see Brandes (1998b) 192 n. 316; Jankowiak (2009) 289–91; *PmbZ* "Platon" 6266.

146. *Record* 4 [Allen and Neil 54]. The occasion for Gregory's visit to Rome appears to have been the issuing of the *Typos*; see above n. 61. For both accusations within the *Record* and Maximus's responses see also Brandes (1998b) 192–96.

147. *Record* 4 [Allen and Neil 54]. For this tension in the episode see Ohme (2008) 318f. In the subsequent conversation Maximus refers to the Fathers' refusal of Arian appeals to *oikonomia* and states "in this Constantine the Great joined in attacking those who proposed these things [*sunepitithemenou tois tauta proteinousi*]." Both Dagron (1996) 180 and Allen and Neil (2002) 56 translate *sunepitithēmi* as "agree," which would indicate a further attempt to destabilize the Constantinian tradition to which Constans aspired. But LSJ, at least, gives not "agree" but "join in attacking."

148. *Record* 4 [Allen and Neil 56–58].

does he perform ordinations and make bishops and priests and deacons; nor does he anoint temples, nor does he bear the symbols of the priesthood [*ta sumbola tēs hierōsunēs*], the pallium and the Gospel, as of the imperial office, the crown and purple." And you said, "How is it that Scripture says Melchizedek is emperor and priest?" And I said, "Melchizedek was one type of the one king by nature, God of all, who became archpriest by nature for the sake of our salvation. So if you say that another is king and priest "according to the order of Melchizedek" [Heb. 5:6], dare then to say the rest, the "without father, without mother, without lineage, with no beginning of days and no end of life" [Heb. 7:8], and observe the evil that arises from this. For such a person will be another God incarnate, effecting our salvation not according to the order of Aaron but "according to the order of Melchizedek." Besides, why do we want to continue at length? In the holy anaphora [*eis tēn hagian anaphoran*] at the holy table, after the archpriests and priests and deacons and the entire clerical order [*pan to hieratikon*], the emperors are remembered with the lay people when the deacon says: *And the lay people who have fallen asleep in faith, Constantine, Constans and the rest*. Thus he remembers also the living emperors after all the clergy [*meta tous hierōmenous pantas*].

A simultaneous refutation of the doctrinal silence advocated in the *Typos* therefore developed into a broader political point—the right of debating and defining the faith belonged to clerics; the emperor, however, had no claim to clerical status, and the biblical archetype for that dual role (the priest-king Melchizedek) was no such thing.[149] Here, then, the ambiguous relation of the secular and the sacred as realized in the imperial office was rendered black and white. The emperor did not preside over the sacraments and was therefore a simple layman.

It is of course questionable if Constans ever explicitly declared himself "emperor and priest"; but it nevertheless is quite probable that both he and some contemporaries would have assumed his quasi-sacerdotal status. (It was indeed rumored that Heraclius had become a priest.)[150] As Dagron has demonstrated, throughout the late-antique period Christian emperors constructed imperial power on the implicit Constantinian model of the emperor as "quasi priest" or "bishop of those outside."[151] The emperor's approximation to sacerdotal status was of course beset with contradictions and ambiguities. For the most part, those same contradictions and ambiguities remained implicit, their tensions enacted in a complex of rhetoric and ritual that constantly explored the boundaries of the emperor's religious power, in particular within the capital.[152] The argument that the *Record of the Trial*

---

149. On Melchizedek in the context of Byzantine political philosophy see Dagron (1996) 184–90. For Melchizedek in Maximus's corpus see also Maximus Confessor, *Ambigua to John* [Jeauneau 67-9].

150. See *Khuzistan Chronicle* [Guidi 28].

151. Dagron (1996) 141–68. For Christian authorities' recognition of the same rhetoric ibid. 314f., concluding "il n'y a rien d'anormal à affirmer que l'empereur *idéal* est aussi un prêtre" (his italics).

152. Ibid. 106–38.

attributes to Maximus nevertheless sought to expose that model's faults, to challenge the scriptural and historical basis on which it was constructed, and to sever the typological link between the emperor and Melchizedek, thence offering a direct denial of imperial pretensions to the priesthood. Maximus within the *Record* was not the first to state that debating and defining dogma was the preserve of priests, but he was perhaps the first, as Dagron notes, "to oppose this notion of the 'two powers' to the notion of sacerdotal kingship."[153]

That Maximus was the first to use this specific formulation once again underlines the reductionism of limiting our explanations of his ideological opposition to notions of strategic convenience. For although that same formulation had a clear strategic agenda, it represented a significant departure from previous anti-imperial invective and, moreover, was not constructed ad hoc. As we have seen, at least since 630 the output of Maximus and his circle demonstrates a quite remarkable investment in the rhetoric of both clerical privilege and its sacramental basis. Here that rhetoric is perhaps at its most intense, for the *Record of the Trial* presents doctrinal debate and definition as a clerical prerogative (and thus, perhaps, excludes Maximus from the same processes). While his alliance with Rome held, and while the fiction of the Lateran *Acts*' Latin composition was in place, this position remained tenable. But when confronted with the specter of a Roman communion with the capital, Maximus's aforementioned response elsewhere in the *Record*—that the Spirit "anathematizes even angels who introduce some innovation besides what is preached [*to kērugma*]"—perhaps demonstrates an awareness of the double-edged nature of his own rhetoric.

At the same time, the position that the *Record of the Trial* attributes to Maximus points toward the further evolution of his ecclesiological vision. For whereas, in the *Mystagogy*, the emphasis on the unity and integrity of the Church's sacramental system served as a brilliant expression of its extrication from the transient world of temporal politics, here that same emphasis is deployed in a new, more politicized context.[154] The ideological position developed within Maximus's circle had proceeded hand in hand with the burgeoning crisis of empire, the perception of sin as its cause, and growing disillusionment with Constantinopolitan doctrine. From this matrix of interdependent ecclesiological, political, and doctrinal concerns, therefore, it was perhaps quite natural to extend the rhetoric so as to refute the sacerdotal pretensions of the emperor, and thus to exclude him from doctrinal interference. Thus would the pollution of monenergist and monothelete doctrine be removed; thus would sin be expiated; and thus also would divine favor be restored.

---

153. Ibid. 182. See also on Maximus's response Brandes (1998b) 194–96 (with previous literature at n. 325).

154. For the importance of Maximus's earlier ecclesiological vision in shaping his later politics see also Louth (2004); Cooper (2005) 165–205.

It should be emphasized, however, that while Maximus within the *Record of the Trial* condemns the principle of doctrinal silence advocated within the *Typos*, he avoids condemning outright the emperor, shifting blame for the document onto others and disavowing the accusation that the anathematization of the *Typos* also means the anathematization of Constans himself.[155] As their association with political rebellions perhaps suggests, Maximus and his disciples never went so far as to dissociate Church and empire altogether—the emperor might still perform a crucial role, for example, in maintaining terrestrial peace, and in different circumstances, perhaps, Maximus and his allies might well have recognized the religious pretensions of an "orthodox" ruler. Nevertheless here—in the sustained context of both the emperor's perceived doctrinal error and the crisis of empire contingent upon it—the author of the *Record* attributes to Maximus a claim both to the significant limitation of imperial prerogative and to the freedom of ecclesial doctrine from secular interference. In asserting the independence of the Church from the secular, Maximus in the *Record* thus differs from Sophronius in the earlier patriarchal sermons which had begun to contemplate a more dramatic extrication of the sacred from the secular. But the intellectual materials from which both authors constructed their visions of ecclesial independence were in fact the same. In validating his challenge to the imperial ideological edifice, Maximus here draws upon sacramental reasoning: the emperor cannot inquire into or pronounce upon the dogmas of the Church, because he does not fulfill the sacramental functions of the priesthood. As with the pro-Roman rhetoric of the previous decade, this position was no doubt a strategic statement; but as with the same rhetoric again, it was not articulated ex nihilo. It was instead the apogee of political sensibilities evident within the output of Maximus's circle over several decades.

## MAXIMUS IN EXILE

Like Martin before them, Maximus and his disciple Anastasius were condemned at their trial and exiled to separate locations in Thrace, to Bizya and Perberis.[156] Here—according to a further text that is contained within the corpus of literature associated with Maximus's trials and exiles, and that again appears as the product

---

155. See the various statements at *Record* 7, 9, 11 [Allen and Neil 62–68]. Within the *Record* when Anastasius is also questioned over his anathematization of the *Typos*, he confesses to having composed a *libellus* against it (which does not survive); see ibid. 10 [Allen and Neil 68], with Winkelmann (2001) 134 no. 125. For Maximus's anathematization of the *Typos* see also *Dispute at Bizya* 12.

156. See *Record* 13. Jankowiak (2009) 318 argues that the words *hoi tēs ekklēsias epeisan ton basilea tautēn autous katakrinai tēn pikran kai apanthrōpēn exorian* [Allen and Neil 72] suggest that—in parallel with Martin—an original punishment of death was commuted to exile under the influence of the patriarchs.

of a close disciple if not of Maximus himself—the Confessor was to engage in further theological discussion with representatives of the emperor.[157] Composed soon after the event itself, the *Dispute at Bizya* records that on 24 August 656 Maximus held a conversation with one Theodosius, bishop of Caesarea in Bithynia, in the company of the Constantinopolitan consuls Paul and Theodosius, whose evident purpose was to persuade him to commune with the powers in the capital.[158] Within the subsequent dialogue we encounter several familiar themes: Maximus's tirade against the "one operation" and "one will"; Theodosius's defense of "what occurred for the sake of accommodation" (*to di' oikonomian ginomenon*); and Maximus's restatement that silence is equivalent to annulment.[159]

At the same time, we again find here that familiar denial of the emperor's religious role set out with such force within the *Record of the Trial*. Thus, when Theodosius states that the Lateran Council was not ratified "since it occurred without the order of the emperor," Maximus again returns to the controversial question of the differentiation of Church and state, recalling a series of late-antique councils that convened at imperial command but that are nevertheless considered heretical (the implication also being, of course, that monothelete councils were comparable). "What sort of canon explicitly states that only those synods are approved that are gathered on an order of an emperor or, for that matter, that synods are convened at all on an order of an emperor?" Maximus asks. "The pious canon of the Church has known those synods to be holy and accepted that the rightness of their dogmas approved."[160] Like the *Record of the Trial*, therefore, the *Dispute at Bizya* has Maximus refuse the emperor a role in the definition of doctrine, but we notice a subtle transformation in emphasis. For where the *Record* denies the imperial right to discuss and define dogma on the basis that this is a clerical privilege, here it is not so much clerical debate and definition that determines doctrine as the righteousness of doctrine itself.

In the doctrinal debate that ensues, Theodosius is presented as making some quite remarkable concessions. Earlier in the text, on behalf of the emperor, he offers to

---

157. For discussion of text and authorship see Conte (1989) 212–17; Brandes (1998b) 156, 205; Allen and Neil (2002) 36f.; Winkelmann (2001) 148f. no. 145.

158. On the authorship of the text see Brandes (1998b) 156, 205; Allen and Neil (2002) 36f. For the date *Dispute at Bizya* 2 and 9, speaking of "the recently passed fourteenth indiction" [Allen and Neil 76] and "the current fifteenth indiction" [Allen and Neil 106]: that is, 656/7. For Theodosius of Caesarea *PmbZ* "Theodosios" 7795; Winkelmann (2001) 275f. On Paul and Theodosius see *PmbZ* "Paulos" 5802, "Theodosios" 7796; Winkelmann (2001) 249, 274f.

159. See esp. *Dispute at Bizya* 3 [Allen and Neil 84]. Cf. *Dispute at Bizya* 12 [Allen and Neil 110], where one of Maximus's interrogators proclaims in regard to the *Typos*, "It was for the sake of accommodation [*di' oikonomian*] that this happened, lest the laity be harmed through such words, which are too subtle." Maximus in turn proclaims, "Silence over words is the destruction of words." For analysis of *oikonomia* in this text see esp. Ohme (2008) 322–24.

160. *Dispute at Bizya* 4 [Allen and Neil 88].

annul the *Typos* in return for Maximus's communion;¹⁶¹ but when the latter further engages him on the question of the wills and operations, and produces the florilegium of the Lateran Council to support his position, Theodosius declares that he will "at once declare in writing two natures, two wills, and two operations." His anxieties over this position are nevertheless made evident: first, he declares to Maximus that "we also confess the natures and the different operations—that is, both divine and human—and that his divinity had a will, and his humanity had a will, since his soul was not without will. But we do not say 'two,' lest we present him as warring against himself."¹⁶² Thus Theodosius here repeats the anxieties over "two" first expressed within Sergius's *Psēphos* and repeated, for example, in the *Disputation with Pyrrhus*.¹⁶³ Indeed, even after he has concurred with Maximus over the legitimate use of "two," Theodosius states that "In terms of the union of our Savior we ought always and in every way to confess one will, exactly as Sergius and Pyrrhus, as I see it, wrote with correct apprehension."¹⁶⁴ As has been said, this approach (acknowledging both monadic and dyadic phrases) was based in the same logic that Maximus himself in an earlier context had also professed. But here he maintained his new stance, refuting the recognition of "one will" as "one nature" via the back door.

Maximus's position within the text remains belligerent, but from what follows it is clear that the Constantinopolitan authorities considered a significant accord to have been reached. According to the *Dispute at Bizya*, the meeting indeed concluded in an agreement, but on Maximus's terms—the bishop Theodosius and his companions are reconciled to his doctrinal position, and the consul Theodosius consents to request from the emperor a decree of supplication (*paraklētikē keleusis*) and from the patriarch Paul a synodical entreaty (*sunodikē deēsis*) to be submitted to the pope.¹⁶⁵ Soon after their departure, the text continues, the consul Paul returns with an imperial command to bring Maximus with all due honor to Rhegium, where in September 656 there ensues a theological discussion in which the patrician Epiphanius, like Theodosius before him, offers an explicit acknowledgment of "two operations" and "two wills" but nevertheless advocates communion on the basis of the *Typos*, which was promulgated for the sake of "accommodation [*oikonomia*] . . . lest the people be harmed through rather subtle words such as these."¹⁶⁶ Throughout the crisis, as we have seen, the advocates of monenergism

---

161. *Dispute at Bizya* 4 [Allen and Neil 88].
162. *Dispute at Bizya* 4 [Allen and Neil 96].
163. See above pp. 240 n. 58, 285f.
164. *Dispute at Bizya* 5 [Allen and Neil 100]. For this same insistence (also refuted by Maximus) see *Disputation with Pyrrhus* [PG 91, 340D].
165. *Dispute at Bizya* 4 [Allen and Neil 98]. Cf. *Dispute at Bizya* 8. On the ideological position in respect of Rome see above p. 275 with n. 196.
166. Ibid. 12 [Allen and Neil 110]. On Epiphanius see also *Record* 2, 5, with Van Dieten (1972) 110–13; Brandes (1998b) 180, 201, 206; Winkelmann (2001) 201f.; also *PmbZ* "Epiphanios" 1540.

and monotheletism are said to have made consistent recourse to this same principle, and Maximus and his allies offered a consistent rebuttal. To the great frustration of his interlocutors, Maximus refuses once again to recognize it.

The *Dispute at Bizya* presents Maximus's intransigence as occurring despite the promise of considerable honors. Thus Epiphanius at Rhegium relates to him a quite remarkable offer from Constans that, if he should enter into communion and agree to doctrinal silence, the emperor himself would march out to meet him at the Chalke Gate of the imperial palace, lead him in honor to Hagia Sophia, and there partake of communion with him in the place reserved for the emperors.[167] The spectacular offer is framed, however, in terms that make clear its purpose: "Since all the West and those who are rebelling [*diastrephontes*] in the East look to you, and all enter into *stasis* because of you, since they do not want to be reconciled to us because of the faith, may God move you to be reconciled to us on the basis of the *Typos* that we published.... For we know for sure that if you commune with the holy throne of those here, all those who have separated from our communion because of you and your teaching will enter into union with us."[168] Indeed the offer, if genuine, was an intelligent one: for if Maximus not only communed with the emperor in Hagia Sophia, but also entered into the sanctuary with him, it would have provided a spectacular coup de théâtre: not only the capitulation of the figurehead of the doctrinal resistance (and his rhetoric of strict clerical privilege) but also a stunning reaffirmation of the emperor's claims to quasi-sacerdotal status.

At the same time, Constans may have feared the political fallout that the execution of Maximus might cause.[169] Indeed, the *Dispute at Bizya* attributes to Maximus's interlocutors at Rhegium an exasperated statement in which the latter offer an explicit acknowledgment of the emperor's unwillingness to punish Maximus in a context of Muslim pressure: "But just so you know, Lord Abba, if we gain some small respite from the ruin of the tribes [*ek tēs sunchuseōs tōn ethnōn*], we shall cease to accommodate you [*harmosasthai*], by the holy Trinity, and remove the present pope and all those who speak there, along with the rest of your disciples, and put you all to the flame, in a place appropriate for each, just as Martin was put to the flame."[170] It seems, therefore, that continued Muslim agitation in the East now served an ironic double function: both to

---

167. As Jankowiak (2009) 324 argues, the final discussions between Maximus and Epiphanius and Troilus is said to occur on the eve of the Festival of the Cross—that is, 13 September—see *Dispute at Bizya* 12 [Allen and Neil 114]. Thus Constans intended to be reconciled to Maximus on "ce jour symbolique d'une fête liée intimement à la dynastie héraclienne."

168. *Dispute at Bizya* 10 [Allen and Neil 108].

169. For the relative indulgence shown to Maximus and Anastasius (in comparison with Martin) see also the comments of Brandes (1998b) 200.

170. *Dispute at Bizya* 13 [Allen and Neil 114].

guarantee the continued intransigence of Maximus and his allies and to prolong the Confessor's life.

The *Dispute at Bizya* presents Maximus as offering a consistent defense of his doctrinal position, disavowing all attempts at compromise. But if his summons to Rhegium following the first encounter with Theodosius of Caesarea—and with it the evident Constantinopolitan expectation of an imminent reconciliation—perhaps suggests that Maximus had in fact been more flexible than the text itself allows, then there are indeed further indications as to the actual complexities of the situation. In a rather incongruous aside that is separated from the discussions at Rhegium, and that is perhaps an addition to the main text, the author states:[171]

> And know also this, that while staying in Rhegium Troilus said to Abba Maximus that the *consiliarius* John wrote to him about the agreement [*sumbasis*] that had been placed before and satisfied them, "although the disturbance [*ataxia*] among your disciples prevented this from happening at the time." But I think that the aforementioned *consiliarius* John wrote not to Troilus but to the monk Menas, and that the latter in turn spoke to those at court.

The precise import of this qualification remains unclear. Nevertheless, it once again suggests that Maximus's arrival at Rhegium was predicated upon some expectation of an accord (*sumbasis*), an accord then undone either in Maximus's continued intransigence or in the "disturbance" of his disciples.[172]

In the *Dispute at Bizya* the disagreement at Rhegium concludes with the arrival of the consul Theodosius, who pronounces sentence against Maximus and sends him into further exile to Perberis, to be detained in isolation from his disciple Anastasius.[173] En route to his new place of exile, however, events take a perhaps unexpected turn, for according to the *Dispute at Bizya*, Maximus was detained at a soldiers' camp in Selymbria, where a rumor circulated that he had insulted the Mother of God. Then "the general—that is, the *topotērētēs* of the general," "under compunction from God," sent to him the camp's dignitaries, and when he offered anathema on all those who insult the Virgin, the soldiers began to empathize within him and

---

171. *Dispute at Bizya* 15 [Allen and Neil 116]. The text proceeds for two more chapters that also appear to be later additions; see Allen and Neil (2002) 184 n. 57. For Menas see also *Record* 4, 5, 10, and the scholion on *Dispute at Bizya* 15 [Allen and Neil (1999) 149], with Brandes (1998a) 181f. On John see the scholion (Allen and Neil [1999] 147) equating "consiliarius" with "*symponos* or *scholastikos*"; cf. Allen and Neil (2002) 183 n. 52; Brandes (1998b) 181 n. 257.

172. On this same passage cf. Jankowiak (2009) 324–26 suggesting that the consul Theodosius's words at *Dispute at Bizya* 13 [Allen and Neil 114] that Maximus *echei* "*to krima tōn mathētōn*" may also indicate that their dissidence was behind the failure of the attempted accord. That the Anastasii were also then examined is indicated in the same passage.

173. *Dispute at Bizya* 14 [Allen and Neil 116].

to criticize his fate, forcing an imperial guard to remove him from the camp.[174] In his recent doctoral thesis Jankowiak has highlighted a scholion on the text that identifies the aforementioned general as "Theodore of Colonia, *locum tenens* [*ho topotērētēs*] of the *comes* (that is, the emperor's brother)."[175] As Jankowiak points out, this same Theodore of Colonia was later the architect of the antimonothelete Sixth Ecumenical Council, suggesting, perhaps, that the compassion that the soldiers are said to have expressed toward Maximus surpassed the rank and file, extending also to the officers.[176] Indeed, the ultimate commander of those same soldiers was Constans's brother Theodosius, soon to be murdered in 659.[177] Theophanes, Agapius, and the *Anonymous Chronicle to 1234* report the event without explanation, as does the *Maronite Chronicle*, placing it in A.G. 970 (i.e., A.D. 658/9).[178] The *Chronicle* of Michael the Syrian, however, suggests that the action was intended to secure the succession of Constans's sons, and it may well be that Constans feared his brother as a rival to the throne.[179] In 654 the emperor had raised his son Constantine as coemperor, and in 659 he elevated his remaining sons, Heraclius and Tiberius, to the same rank.[180]

Although there is no evidential support for Andreas Stratos's contention that Theodosius had been in rebellion since 655, a text associated with Maximus's circle nevertheless suggests that his murder formed part of a wider purge.[181] The *Geor-*

---

174. *Dispute at Bizya* 13–14 [Allen and Neil 114–16]. It is in the context of the latter that some scholars have placed the Georgian *Life of the Virgin* attributed to Maximus; for discussion see Shoemaker (2006) and (2012b) 6–13. I am doubtful of the (otherwise unattested) attribution, but a fruitful avenue for further research into its authenticity would no doubt be the comparison of its Mariology with that of Sophronius's poems and sermons on the same themes—e.g., *On the Annunciation*—and in particular that contained in, e.g., Maximus Confessor, *Ambigua to John* 27, and thence in *Acts of the Lateran Council* Canon 3, with Hurley (1961); Aldama (1962); Léthel (1979) 70; Conte (1989) 72 n. 63.

175. *Dispute at Bizya* [Allen and Neil (1999) 143].

176. Jankowiak (2009) 346f. For Theodore of Colonia see *PmbZ* "Theodoros" 7312, ignoring the scholion; and Michael the Syrian, *Chronicle* 11.11 [Chabot vol. 4, 431], for Theodore's role in the Sixth Ecumenical Council.

177. Little is known of Theodosius. For his reported presence at the battle of Phoenix see Michael the Syrian, *Chronicle* 11.11; *Anonymous Chronicle to 1234* 134; Agapius, *Universal History* [Vasiliev 483f.], giving "Yaqout" in place of "Theodosius." See also *PmbZ* "Theodosios" 7797.

178. *Maronite Chronicle* [Brooks 70]. Cf. Theophanes, *Chronicle* A.M. 6151; Agapius, *Universal History* [Vasiliev 490]; *Anonymous Chronicle to 1234* 134. The derivatives of Theophilus all report that the fallout from Theodosius's death was the cause of Constans's relocation to the West in 662 for strategic reasons; see for discussion Stratos (1982); Corsi (1988); Zuckerman (2005) 79–84; Ekonomou (2007) 167–81; Howard-Johnston (2010) 486.

179. Michael the Syrian, *Chronicle* 11.11, repeating the motif of the *Maronite Chronicle* [Brooks 70] that Constans was "a second Cain."

180. These dates derive from the regnal years given in *Acts of the Sixth Ecumenical Council* [Riedinger 14, etc.].

181. Stratos (1968–78) vol. 3, 191–96 (with previous speculations on the nature of Theodosius's fault); cf. Brandes (1998b) 210.

*gian Appendix to the Spiritual Meadow*—which as we have seen above appears to come from the pen of a monk close to Moschus—includes a tale set "When Constans [*kostanti*] killed his brother and the *dux* George."[182] This George is otherwise unknown, but the precious reference perhaps indicates a wider rebellion than is suggested in other sources. We cannot ascertain if opposition to the emperor's doctrine informed Theodosius's position—as perhaps hinted at in the *Dispute at Bizya*. But it is nevertheless possible, as Stratos long ago suggested, that we have here a further political rebellion associated with Maximus's doctrinal opposition.[183]

At the least, Theodosius's murder provided the emperor's enemies with an undeniable proof of his estrangement from God and was seized upon. Thus, that same aforementioned tale within the *Georgian Appendix to the Spiritual Meadow* continues to relate how one Sergius "deacon of Saint Paul" once recounted how, at the time of Theodosius's murder, all the people rushed to witness a miracle in the Church of Saints Cosmas and Damian, where the lamps placed before the altar were filling with blood. Three such lamps were dispatched to the capital: one to the emperor, one to his empress, and one to the patriarch, "who was at heart a Jacobite [i.e., a miaphysite]." "And fear seized the people on account of this miracle," it concludes, "and in their expectation of [divine] anger all were gripped with trembling and terror."[184]

Later tradition suggests that Theodosius was ordained under the patriarch Paul (and thus before December 653). Although the aforementioned scholion's description of Theodosius as *comes* seems to give the lie to that report, an anecdote associated with it is worth pausing over. After a statement on Theodosius's murder, the later *Compendium* of the chronographer Cedrenus describes how the emperor once "took offense" against his brother "and tonsured him through the patriarch Paul as a deacon." In this role, the text continues, Theodosius was no less than "the one who also passed the spotless mysteries to the emperor in the holy chalice," and after his murder he continued often to appear to the emperor in dreams and, "bearing the raiment of a deacon and offering the chalice of blood, he said, 'Drink, brother.'"[185] We cannot of course know the origins of this anecdote, which (as we have seen) relates one of several political dreams associated with the iniquities of the emperor Constans. But it

---

182. *Georgian Appendix to the Spiritual Meadow* 17 [Latin trans. Garitte 413].

183. Stratos (1968–78) vol. 3, 195f.; also Jankowiak (2009) 345–47.

184. *Georgian Appendix to the Spiritual Meadow* 17 [Latin trans. Garitte 413]. It is unclear where the Church of Cosmas and Damian is to be located. Cf. also the embedding of Theodosius's death in an antimonothelete narrative at Theophanes, *Chronicle* A.M. 6160 [de Boor 351]. From Theophanes or his source derive also *Life of the Patriarch Germanus* 3 [Lamza 202–4]; and the Sabaitic *Life of Theodore of Edessa* 21 [trans. from Arabic in Griffiths (2001) 163]. I have been unable to access the Greek edition of the latter.

185. Cedrenus, *Compendium* [Bekker vol. 1, 762]. Report of Theodosius's ordination also occurs at Leo Grammaticus, *Chronicle* [Bekker 158].

nevertheless resonates with some of the themes that we have explored here: under the pen of the author, Constans's political crime is widened out as a crime against both the Church and the sacramental dispensation to which he is subordinate. It is an anecdote that Maximus and his allies would, no doubt, have appreciated.

If Maximus's doctrinal position was indeed associated somehow with Theodosius's murder, then it was to contribute to his undoing. In the past, as we have seen, more punitive measures had been prevented through the twin pillars of Roman and Muslim agitation, but both were soon to collapse. From 656 to 661, the attentions of the Muslim elite were absorbed in the first *fitna*, granting the Roman empire a brief respite from periodic raids. In the *Record of the Trial* (set in 655), moreover, two interlocutors warn Maximus that the *apocrisiarii* of the pope had arrived in the capital and were expected to communicate with the patriarch.[186] In a letter written in December 653, soon after his arrival in Constantinople, Martin had expressed his hope that his opponents' unprecedented plan to replace him as pope would not occur, but before his death that hope was dashed, for in August 654 Eugenius I succeeded to the papal throne, some fourteen months after Martin's arrest.[187] We must assume that the considerable moratorium between Martin's deposition and the election of his successor is to be explained in the refusal of imperial approval, and thus in an impasse between Rome and the capital.[188] The eventual consent of the emperor therefore suggests that there was now a genuine hope of rapprochement.

Although the Roman Church thus seems to have accepted Martin's deposition—indeed, while in exile, and now aware of Eugenius's election, Martin complained to a correspondent that the Roman Church had in effect disowned him[189]—the expected communion with Constantinople did not occur. As Maximus's interrogators' resentful comments on "the current pope" in the *Dispute at Bizya* indicate, upon receiving imperial approval for his election Eugenius did not in fact then enter an accord with the capital for according to the *Book of Pontiffs*, the people and clergy of Rome had in fact forced the pope to anathematize the encyclical of the new Constantinopolitan patriarch Peter, which adopted the doctrinal position of the *Typos*.[190] In 657, however, Eugenius died, and the Romans performed another doctrinal reversal. His successor Vitalian was elected a month

---

186. *Record* 7.
187. For the election of Eugenius see *Book of Pontiffs* 77.
188. Jankowiak (2009) 294f.
189. See Theodore Spudaeus, *Narrations* 29–30. See also the total silence of the *Book of Pontiffs* on Martin's arrest and punishment, suggesting an official attempt to whitewash the event under his successors; see the discussion in Chiesa (1992) 225–27.
190. See *Book of Pontiffs* 77 [Duchesne vol. 1, 341]. This is the sole witness to Peter's encyclical; see Conte (1971) 455 no. 173; Winkelmann (2001) 141 no. 133. For Eugenius's election see also the allusion in the letter of Martin at Theodore Spudaeus, *Narrations* 31; and for the man himself *PmbZ* "Eugenius" 1660; Winkelmann (2001) 202; on Peter *PmbZ* "Petros I" 5941; Winkelmann (2001) 249f.

later, and thereafter dispatched a synodical to the capital that, to judge from the response of the patriarch Peter, contained no explicit condemnation of the *Typos* and thus reestablished communion.[191] The precise context in which that reversal occurred is obscure, but the *Book of Pontiffs*' celebration of a subsequent renewal of "the church's privileges" (*privilegia ecclesiae*) suggests that after the reestablishment of exarchal power Constantinople was able to impose more far-reaching sanctions than the simple arrest and punishment of the pope.[192] At some point, therefore, continued opposition to Constantinople had become untenable and the Roman faction that favored union had gained the upper hand, at considerable loss, no doubt, to the prestige of the now-resident Palestinians.

In the *Record of the Trial* Maximus expressed grave doubts that the Romans would ever enter into that communion, but now he and his disciples were confronted with the startling fact of a union of all incumbent Chalcedonian patriarchs. To the period of his second exile at Perberis dates a letter "To Anastasius, Monk and Disciple," in which Maximus reports that the Constantinopolitan patriarch—who must be Peter—had sent messengers announcing the union of the five patriarchates, ordering Maximus to be reconciled to a now united catholic Church, and threatening furthermore that "the emperor and patriarch have decided, on instruction from the Roman pope, that unless you obey you will be anathematized and suffer the death that they have determined."[193] Around the same time, that letter's recipient, Anastasius, too dispatched a letter *To the Monks of Cagliari* in which he informed his correspondents that the monothelete heretics had "forced the *apocrisiarii* of older Rome to consent to their own sect" and begged them at once to intervene at Rome itself.[194] There are here obvious parallels with the earlier appeals of Sophronius and his Palestinian colleagues, but where such appeals had

---

191. See *Book of Pontiffs* 78; with Peter's response excerpted in *Acts of the Sixth Ecumenical Council* [Riedinger 108, 110, 586, 610] and given twice in Winkelmann (2001) at 142 no. 133a and 150 no. 147. From those excerpts it is evident that Peter had in his response to Vitalian advocated the use of "one and two" in respect of the operations and wills; see below p. 322. For the exchange of letters with the capital cf. Conte (1971) 456f. nos. 178–81; Jankowiak (2009) 327–29. On Vitalian see also Van Dieten (1972) 113f.; Ekonomou (2007) 161–66; *PmbZ* "Vitalianus" 8582; Winkelmann (2001) 278f.

192. *Book of Pontiffs* 78 [Duchesne vol. 1, 343], with Jankowiak (2009) 330f.

193. Maximus Confessor, *Letter to Anastasius the Disciple* [Allen and Neil 120–22]. For the date of Maximus's letter—19 April 658—see Winkelmann (2001) 143 no. 136; Allen and Neil (2002) 37; *contra*, e.g., Van Dieten (1972) 106–9, Brandes (1998b) 158, placing it in 655. For Maximus's response see above pp. 274 and 312, and below p. 332. Cf. also the Latin subscription to the text in which the author expresses his concerns over the threatened union [Allen and Neil 122]. For discussion of the subscription's authorship see Jankowiak (2009) 339 (favoring Anastasius the Disciple); *contra* Allen and Neil (2002) 38 (favoring Theodore Spudaeus).

194. Anastasius the Disciple, *Letter to the Monks of Cagliari* [Allen and Neil 128]. For discussion of authorship and date (658) see Winkelmann (2001) 144f. no. 137; Allen and Neil (2002) 39f.; again *contra* Van Dieten (1972) 108f., Brandes (1998b) 158, 204 (both 655).

earlier been successful and served to eschew their potential isolation from the other patriarchates, now the supplications to the West fell upon deaf ears. That Maximus and Anastasius now had to resort to monastic allies on Sardinia demonstrates how much their circle's stock had collapsed within Rome itself.[195]

From the same letters it is clear that the union had been effected on the basis of a new doctrinal formula. When Maximus inquires as to its basis in the *Letter to Anastasius*, the messenger from the patriarch reports that "We profess two operations on account of the difference, and one on account of the union"; Anastasius reports to the monks of Cagliari that the monotheletes "have been carried from the impossible to the inconsistent: that is, from claiming there are neither one nor two, to pronouncing one and two—that is, three wills and operations introduced into one and the same Christ."[196] Maximus and Anastasius both ridicule this new position. But both omit two inconvenient facts: first, that Sophronius in the *Synodical Letter* approached a not dissimilar position (in distinguishing Christ's human, divine, and theandric acts), and, second, that Maximus earlier supported this precise same approach.[197] We cannot know for sure if Maximus's Constantinopolitan suitors were aware of his earlier position on the double use of "one" and "two"; but the fact that Maximus was forced earlier to explain (to his aforementioned Sicilian detractors) that position within *Opuscula* 9 of course suggests that it had not gone unnoticed elsewhere.[198] With this new formula the Constantinopolitans—who now confessed a "two" formula for the first time—perhaps hoped to have hit upon a solution acceptable to all. Maximus, however, once again refused to cooperate.

An addition to the original text of the *Dispute at Bizya* records that after Maximus's transfer to Perberis, he was brought once again with his disciples to the capital, there to face a council in which the three were anathematized alongside Martin and Sophronius before being handed over to the senate for sentencing.[199] This

---

195. For this point Jankowiak (2009) 335, 337–40, suggesting that Maximus's allies had been exiled here in the aftermath of Vitalian's volte-face. In his *Letter to Anastasius the Disciple* [Allen and Neil 122] Maximus Confessor requests that Anastasius report recent developments to "the lord Theios and our holy fathers who are there with him," whom we must presume to be an associate of Maximus on Sardinia. For speculation on this name—perhaps a corruption of "Theodore"—see Allen and Neil (2002) 185 n. 8; Jankowiak (2009) 338.

196. Anastasius the Disciple, *Letter to the Monks of Cagliari* 1 [Allen and Neil 124]. We find confirmation of this new Constantinopolitan position in the *Acts of the Sixth Ecumenical Council* [Riedinger 108–10], where a letter of Pope Agatho recalls a letter of the Constantinopolitan patriarch Peter to Pope Vitalian in which the former advocated "one and two wills and one and two operations." Cf. Winkelmann (2001) 142 no. 133a, 150 no. 147.

197. See above pp. 236 and 217, respectively.

198. See above p. 215f.

199. See *Dispute at Bizya* 16. As Jankowiak (2009) 353f. points out, the condemnation of Anastasius Apocrisiarius is here given special attention with a striking reference both to his "blasphemies" and his "rebellions" (*turannides*). The precise import of the latter is obscure but again suggests that the antimonothelete resistance fomented political dissent even in exile.

council—which must have occurred in 662—appears to be identical with one that is memorialized in the *Acts of the Sixth Ecumenical Council*. Therein, a confession of faith from the monothelete patriarch Macarius of Antioch refers to "the holy gathering [*sunathroisis*] that persecuted them [the Maximianists] and that happened here at the command of our father and master of pious memory, [where were] Peter the most all-holy ecumenical patriarch, the most blessed Macedonius, predecessor of my humbleness, and Theodore *topotērētēs* of Alexandria, and those present with them—that is, the most holy bishops gathered in synod [*endēmountōn*] and the sacred senate. And having examined his position in writing, they anathematized him and exiled him with his impious disciples."[200] The presence of representatives of Constantinople, Antioch, and Alexandria and the council's convocation at imperial command demonstrate its perceived importance to the capital.[201]

A further addition to the *Dispute at Bizya*—the so-called Third Sentence—records the punishment that the senate then passed upon the condemned: the eparch removed the three to the praetorium and there flogged the two Anastasii; then Maximus and Anastasius Apocrisiarius had their tongues cut out and their right arms removed, the impious instruments through which the pair had sown dissent. The three were then paraded through the streets of Constantinople and thence sent into lifelong exile in Lazica.[202] Soon after, on 22 or 24 July 662, Anastasius the Disciple died. Maximus departed soon after, on 13 August.[203] Therewith died the period's most prominent religious dissident, fallen some distance from the dramatic heights of power that he had realized at the time of the Lateran Council.

200. *Acts of the Sixth Ecumenical Council* [Riedinger 228–30]. For Macarius's reported monothelete output in and around this council see Winkelmann (2001) 135–38 nos. 127–30a.

201. Jankowiak (2009) 351–53, pointing also to the statement in the *Anonymous Chronicle to 1234* 130 that this was "a council of the entire Roman empire" [Chabot vol. 1, 266]. For the council see also Winkelmann (2001) 150f. nos. 148 and 148a (with further literature).

202. For this so-called Third Sentence see *Dispute at Bizya* 17 [Allen and Neil 118], with Brandes (1998b) 156; Winkelmann (2001) 151f. no. 149; and Jankowiak (2009) 355 on the possible significance of "Third." For the punishment cf. *Greek Life of Maximus (Recension 2)* [PG 90, 104D–105C]; Theodore Spudaeus, *Hypomnesticum (Greek)* 4 and *Hypomnesticum (Latin)* 2; Anastasius Apocrisiarius, *Letter to Theodosius* 1; Theophanes, *Chronicle* A.M. 6160; Michael the Syrian, *Chronicle* 11.9; *Anonymous Chronicle to 1234* 130. Some doubts as to the actual execution of the punishment are raised in the somewhat incredible insistence that Anastasius Apocrisiarius continued to write using two twigs and even that he spoke "with a divine and invisible tongue"; for the latter see Theodore Spudaeus, *Hypomnesticum (Greek)* 4 and *Hypomnesticum (Latin)* 2. For the twigs see also *Hypomnesticum (Greek)* 10, including a reference to Anastasius's "other handwritten books and tomes from after his suffering" [Allen and Neil 164].

203. For the deaths of Maximus and Anastasius the Disciple see Anastasius Apocrisiarius, *Letter to Theodosius* 4. Cf. also Theodore Spudaeus, *Hypomnesticum (Greek)* 9. For Anastasius Apocrisiarius's death (on 11 October 666) see the scholion to Anastasius Apocrisiarius, *Letter to Theodosius* 14 [Allen and Neil 146]; Theodore Spudaeus, *Hypomnesticum (Greek)* 5 and *Hypomnesticum (Latin)* 6.

The precise reason for this sudden Constantinopolitan condemnation of Maximus, after repeated efforts to secure his capitulation, is not given. Peace with the caliphate and communion with Rome no doubt provide one explanation, and potential involvement with the murdered Theodosius and his allies perhaps provides another. But it is perhaps to this period that we should also date an episode in George of Resh'aina's *Life of Maximus*, which provides a more immediate context. It reports how, following the acceptance in Rome of his "blasphemies" (*sc.* the Lateran Council), Maximus learned of the emperor's absence from the capital and traveled there to spread his heretical teaching, residing in that same "House of Placidia" that was, in the past at least, the home of the Roman *apocrisiarii*.[204] (In George's account, however, it has been transformed into a community of nuns.) The Syriac *Life* breaks off at this point, but something of the conclusion is preserved in the accounts of Michael the Syrian and the *Anonymous Chronicle to 1234*, both of which draw from George's account. They report that after Maximus's arrival in the capital, a council was convened in which he was defeated at the hands of one "Constantine of Perge" (in Michael), and then shut up within a nunnery as punishment (the same "House of Placidia," no doubt, referred to in the *Life*). Here, however, he soon convinced his hosts not to receive the sacraments from their higoumen or patriarch and was thus further punished with mutilation and exile.[205]

Although the two chronicles place the Placidia episode between Maximus's condemnation at a council and his subsequent punishment, it seems more probable to situate it before them, in line both with George's extant narrative and the wider sources for the council.[206] That episode concludes with the mutilation of Maximus—a punishment applied in 662—but most commentators have nevertheless assumed that George's *Life* and the chronicles that derive from it preserve an alternative tradition of Maximus's first arrival in the capital, one undertaken of his own volition and preceding his initial trial in 655.[207] Nevertheless, further chronological signposts contained within the Syriac *Life* indicate otherwise. The reported events occurred, so George informs us, at a time of peace between Muʿāwiya and Con-

---

204. George of Resh'aina, *Life* 25f. [Brock 313, trans. 319]; cf. *Book of Pontiffs* 76 [Duchesne vol. 1, 336]. If one assumes that Maximus was moved to this community by imperial command rather than under his own volition, it is difficult to suppose that it remained in the hands of the Roman see; cf. also Brock (1973) 329, Jankowiak (2009) 358 n. 229.

205. Michael the Syrian, *Chronicle* 11.9 [Chabot vol. 4, 426f.], and *Anonymous Chronicle to 1234* 130 [Chabot vol. 1, 264–67]. On Constantine of Perge see Brandes (1998a) identifying him with the Apergius bishop of Perge anathematized at *Acts of Sixth Ecumenical Council* [Riedinger 702].

206. See Jankowiak (2009) 354f., 358, *contra* Brock (1973) 331f.

207. See, e.g., Van Dieten (1972) 102; Brock (1973) 330f.; Winkelmann (2001) 139f. no. 131b. These support their position through pointing to the fact that Michael the Syrian, *Chronicle* 11.9, claims that the patriarch whose ministrations Maximus warns against is Paul (641–53), but this identification in fact occurs in the Arabic version of Michael alone; see Chabot vol. 2, 436 n. 2; Brock (1973) 329, 339.

stans, when the former had declared war upon "Abu Turāb" ('Ali) at Siffin and the latter was absent in Azerbaijan.[208] In interpreting this passage and attempting to reconcile it to the narrative of Maximus's arrest and trial, Brandes has argued that the peace is that of 651, and that the expedition to "Azerbaijan" is in fact that to Armenia in 652/3.[209] This is of course quite logical, but the unambiguous reference to the aborted battle of Siffin, which occurred in 657, cannot be explained on such grounds.[210] We must either assume, therefore, that George has here telescoped several events,[211] or that the reported return of Maximus occurred much later, in the period preceding his final condemnation, and that George was unaware of or ignored his previous condemnations. On this interpretation, therefore, the peace to which George refers was the peace that occurred between Muʿāwiya and Constans during the first *fitna* (and that Theophanes places in 657/8),[212] and the expedition of the emperor was that grand Transcaucasian progress, recorded in Movsēs Daskhurantsʿiʾs *History of Albania*, that occurred in 659/60.[213]

We can perhaps assume, therefore, that before his departure for the Caucasus the emperor Constans moved Maximus to a more secure location in the capital—in particular, one may imagine, if his presence in the Balkans was fomenting further rebellion. Here, however, it appears that the Confessor continued to agitate against imperial doctrine, for he soon convinced his hosts within the House of Placidia to refuse communion with Patriarch Peter. Once again, therefore, we witness the extent to which sacramental and doctrinal boundaries were, for Maximus, coterminous. But whereas earlier he and his circle insisted both on the regular participation of all Christians in the eucharist and battled for the strict exclusion of heretics from communion, in the face of the patriarchal consensus against him he now advocated a quite different end: separation from ecclesial communion altogether.[214]

---

208. George of Reshʿaina, *Life* 25f.

209. Brandes (1998b) 177–79 esp. n. 228; also Brandes (2003) 111. For the peace of 651 and the expedition to Armenia see above n. 104.

210. For the battle of Siffin see Caetani (1912–23) vol. 2, 396, 411f., with, e.g., Humphreys (2006) 79f. for context. In non-Arab sources see Theophanes, *Chronicle* A.M. 6151; Michael the Syrian, *Chronicle* 11.11; *Anonymous Chronicle to 1234* 136; *Chronicle of Zuqnin* [Chabot vol. 2, 152f.]. See also Ps.-Sebēos, *History* 52, with Howard-Johnston (1999) 284–88.

211. So Brock (1973) 329.

212. For this peace see Theophanes, *Chronicle* A.M. 6150 (A.D. 657/8); and for the later chronographers and Muslim sources Caetani (1912–23) vol. 2, 444f., with the discussion of Kaplony (1996) 37–46. Ibid. 46 places the peace in 658.

213. See Movsēs Daskhurantsʿi, *History* 2.22 [trans. Dowsett 118–20]. See also Ps.-Sebēos, *History* 52, with Howard-Johnston (1999) 281–84, on the restoration of the catholicus Narses, which perhaps occurred at the same time. For the expedition see also Zuckerman (2002c) 258–61; Jankowiak (2009) 347f.

214. This position, we should note, is attributed to Maximus in Macarius of Antioch's confession of faith at *Acts of the Sixth Ecumenical Council* [Riedinger 228]: *rhiptein to sōma Christou tou Theou hēmōn ho Hellēn edidaxe*.

When the emperor returned from his eastern progress, he at last imposed a decisive punishment. From the imperial perspective, the final removal of Maximus had now become unavoidable. Despite continuous Constantinopolitan attempts to achieve union—including the now qualified use of "two" in describing the Christological wills and operations—Maximus continued to refuse all attempts at conciliation, condemning positions that he himself had earlier adopted, challenging the ideological basis of the imperial office, and now refusing the sacramental ministrations of the Church. In the past, conditions in both East and West, and the continued hope that Maximus might convert, had checked the emperor's hand. But by 662 the specter of Western dissidence had been removed, and the first *fitna* had granted several crucial years of reprieve from Muslim pressure, even if such pressure would soon be renewed. It had now become abundantly clear that Maximus would never offer the dramatic capitulation that the Constantinopolitan authorities craved, and his continued intransigence—and the potential ideological prop that his existence offered to Constans's enemies—proved enough to ensure his effective elimination.[215] The final trial and condemnation of Maximus, therefore, was not so much a thoughtless act of aggression or political scapegoating in a context of crisis; it was rather the long-awaited consequence of continuous recalcitrance and even provocation.

Various episodes described within this chapter have once again underscored the place of the eucharist within our narratives for the period. Although those narratives for the most part emanate from the same antimonothelete circles, it appears that both sides in the conflict shared this sacramental emphasis: thus, just as Pope Theodore is said to have signed Pyrrhus's deposition in the eucharistic blood, and Maximus is said to have advised the nuns of Placidia to refuse communion with the patriarch, so too is Paul said to punish the Roman *apocrisiarii* through preventing them from offering and receiving the sacrament, and Constans is said to suggest communion with Maximus in Hagia Sophia to express their reconciliation.

If both sides did indeed place a premium on eucharistic communion as a medium of political expression—a preference that, as we shall see, forms part of a far wider pattern in Chalcedonian circles of the period—then we must nevertheless reiterate the divergent ideologies that underpinned that shared emphasis. For Maximus and his allies, committed to a principle of doctrinal *akribeia*, communion was conceived less as an inclusive and more as an exclusive act, reaffirming ritual boundaries against a mass of heretical pretenders; for the monotheletes (as for the monenergists), however, communion was conceived less as an exclusive and more as an inclusive act, expressing the wider union of the Christian faithful (against, instead, a mass of non-Christian pretenders). As we have seen, these

---

215. Cf. Howard-Johnston (2010) 485.

divergent attitudes manifest from the earliest stages of the crisis: both in antithetical responses to the union at Alexandria in 633 and in contrasting approaches to the Trisagion (approaches that, at both the doctrinal and the liturgical level, provide an obvious parallel to the two sides' sacramental ideologies).

Throughout the monenergist and then monothelete crises, the authorities at Constantinople at all times attempted to achieve consensus, advocating a principle of doctrinal accommodation (*oikonomia*) in their dealings with both anti-Chalcedonians and antimonotheletes, and experimenting with a range of doctrinal formulas in order to appease resistance. If that principle was at first intended to achieve an ecclesial union that mirrored the political reintegration achieved in Heraclius's restoration of the East to Roman control, it soon became instead a desperate bid for domestic peace in the face of a rising, energetic, expansionist Islam. We should avoid thinking of this doctrinal maneuvering as the shameless manipulation of religion for political purposes—to do so is to invest too much in the rhetoric of its opponents. Rather, it represented the consistent application of a theological principle in which the minutiae of content (or *akribeia*) were subordinated to the benefits (both spiritual and political) of mutual communion.[216] That the emperor in the end turned to violent persecution to enforce this same principle should not overshadow the considerable efforts that he and his allies had made in order to appease their opponents.

The sustained intransigence of Maximus may in contrast appear distasteful, the product of a character bent on disruption for its own sake. But to adopt that reductionist position is to ignore the theological principle that underpinned it and the context within which it was formed. Maximus, it must be acknowledged, was not from the outset an explicit opponent either of monenergism and monotheletism or of doctrinal silence—as we have seen, he at first proved diplomatic in approaching the question of Sergius's *Psēphos*, and over time his own position on the operations and wills underwent considerable revision and elaboration. This evolution accompanied the gradual application of a theological principle at odds with that of *oikonomia* but no less legitimate than it: that is, a commitment to the explicit elucidation of dogma and the relegation of union to precision in regard to theological substance.

In acknowledging this evolution within Maximus's thought, we should again not conclude that he was somehow insincere or duplicitous. Rather, that evolution represented a specific response to the particular conditions that he and his circle confronted. Earlier within this book it was argued that Sophronius's response to monenergism from June 633 should be regarded not as the unambiguous

---

216. For this conclusion cf. Boudignon (2004) 40–42 contrasting between Maximus and Heraclius two visions of the empire that are "diametrically opposed": for the former, an empire subordinated to correct faith; for the latter, a faith subordinated to the health of empire.

extension of some developed commitment to "two operations" but rather as the formation of a theological position informed as much through the peaks and troughs of Roman fortunes as through preformed intellectual commitments. Maximus's own resistance to monotheletism should be appreciated on similar grounds. As time progressed and the empire's woes multiplied—and with them the significant disruptions to Maximus's own life—he no doubt became more convinced that a direct causal relationship existed between the promulgation of the monenergist and monothelete doctrines and the spectacular reversals of the Christian empire. For Maximus (as for Sophronius), the most pressing concern of the age was to articulate a proper and explicit doctrine of Christ, and as his opponents refined their own positions in an attempt to achieve consensus, so too did Maximus refine his own opposition, creating therein a new Christological position that departed from previous patristic thought in its radical assertion of the full human will in Christ.

For a modern observer, there is perhaps a hint of the tragic about the ensuing conflict. As Muslim successes became more entrenched, so both sides intensified their positions: the monotheletes scrambled for a compromise formula that would achieve the desired union while their opponents, under Maximus's leadership, reinvigorated their calls for the specific recognition of "two operations" and "two wills." In essence, then, we are dealing with the clash both of two separate Christologies and of two separate political ideologies, and it was as much the latter as the former that rendered the positions irreconcilable. For the monotheletes, the universal communion of the faithful was the most pressing soteriological (and political) imperative; for Maximus and his allies, it was the defense of the full human nature in Christ and the subordination of union to theological substance. Both sides in the conflict shared the desire for union, the desire to reverse repeated Christian disasters; but both sides' diagnoses of those disasters' cause, and their appropriate antidote, were quite different. In the final analysis, therefore, it is difficult not to sympathize with the exasperated words of two of Maximus's interlocutors within the *Record of the Trial*: "The whole thing is difficult and insoluble" (*Holē duscherē kai anekbata*).[217]

---

217. *Record* 9 [Allen and Neil 66].

# Conclusion

Throughout this book we have on occasion encountered the so-called *Georgian Appendix to the Spiritual Meadow*, a short collection of spiritual tales appended to a Georgian manuscript of the *Meadow*, compiled in its final form before 668 and derived from the pen of a person close to Moschus. Like Moschus, the author was, it appears, a Palestinian monk who had traveled to Rome, and like Moschus again, he demonstrates a notable interest both in the popes and in the sacraments.[1] As we have seen, the *Georgian Appendix* is conspicuous for its implication within the earliest cult of Gregory the Great, for it includes a miracle (told through one "Abba Paul the Scribe, from Cilicia") associated with the pope, and notable for its pro-Roman rhetoric.[2] But we also encounter within the collection a quite remarkable (and indeed overwhelming) emphasis upon the eucharist, extending once again the various sacramental themes explored within the *Spiritual Meadow*.[3] There is

---

1. For the author and the text in more detail see above chap. 3 at nn. 107ff.

2. See esp. the opening and closing remarks of *Georgian Appendix to the Spiritual Meadow* 12 [Latin trans. Garitte 406, 408], the latter of which reads, "Now therefore you see the faith of the Romans, and that the chosen Apostle [Paul] does not bear witness to them in vain [cf. Rom. 1:8]. Because of this they have been until now, by the will of God, the unmoved protectors against all heretics."

3. See *Georgian Appendix to the Spiritual Meadow* 13 (monks in the desert being nourished for weeks with a small morsel of eucharistic bread), 14 (a celebrating priest killed at the hands of Slavs to see if the bread had passed into his stomach—it had not), 16 (a monk receives the host from the Virgin when he refuses to commune with monks who recognize a heretic emperor), 18 (a deacon is struck with illness when he approaches the altar as a sinner), 19 (a disobedient deacon paralyzed at the altar), 22 (children enact the liturgical celebration and transform the bread), 27 (a priest refuses to interrupt the liturgy even though wolves have stolen his son), 28 (a sorcerer-priest sees a man in white

here, however, something quite distinct, for where the *Meadow* maintained a resolute silence on the emperor Heraclius, the *Georgian Appendix* contains two striking tales that condemn Constans II, under whom it appears to have been written. The first is that tale of the bleeding lamps encountered above; and the second too revolves around several of the themes that we have explored here.[4] Therein one Abba Stephan, archpriest of the coenobium of Saint Theodosius—that is, the same monastery to which Moschus and Sophronius had once belonged—tells how he once did not wish to communicate with his fellow monks, who named the iniquitous emperor Constans in their prayers. The archimandrite cuts him off from communion, but because of illness Stephan is unable to leave the confines of the monastery. Disbarred from the eucharist, the monk despairs, but one night he has a dream in which the Virgin visits him in church. When he explains to her his problem, she commands him to fetch the box in which he keeps his hosts, fills it, and then tells him, "Take this, and do not despair. But see to it that you do not communicate with any of those who commemorate the name [of the emperor]; for he who communicates with them communicates with demons."[5]

Like several tales within Moschus's *Spiritual Meadow*, the tale revolves around the practical problems for those ascetics wishing to receive the eucharist while suspecting the credentials of the priest or coparticipants; and like Moschus's *Meadow* again, it maintains the importance of communion proper while offering a miraculous solution. (Here, the dispensation of the host through the Virgin.) Nevertheless, the conditions in which that same narrative occurs are here quite distinct. The reason for Stephen's excommunication is not some vague anxiety over a sinful celebrant but concrete concerns over the emperor's doctrine and his recognition in the diptychs. At the same time, the short vignette expresses what must have been, at the time of its composition, a real and urgent danger to those who still refused monotheletism: that is, the patriarchal consensus that now threatened to sever them from all communion. The solution—to continue to underline the importance of eucharistic communion while nevertheless elevating ascetics above the constraints of submission to a priest—may appear paradoxical. But it is nevertheless familiar from the anti-Chalcedonian tradition, where in a comparable situation of political and ecclesial exclusion, John Rufus's *Plerophoriae* adopted a quite similar position.[6]

---

celebrating the mass in his place and is revealed when he pretends to communicate), 30 (an aged monk dies having received the eucharist as his final act). For the eucharistic emphasis of this collection see also Déroche (2002) 172.

4. See above chap. 7 at nn. 181ff.

5. See *Georgian Appendix to the Spiritual Meadow* 16 [Latin trans. Garitte 412f.]. The tale suggests that the monks of Theodosius in this period went over to monotheletism; see Jankowiak (2009) 345, with ibid. 360f. on the position of Jerusalem in the decades after Maximus's death.

6. See above chap. 1 at nn. 162ff.

This (re)elevation of ascetic endeavor—and the concomitant devaluation of ecclesial communion—is epitomized within a further tale contained within the *Georgian Appendix*, undated but perhaps also belonging to the reign of Constans. The tale begins with a Moschus-esque chain of authorities (Orestes, priest of Saint George near Apamea, said that John of Bonita in the same region heard from an Asian deacon at Constantinople who used to be a ship's master that . . .) and concerns a former deacon whose priest excludes him from communion. The deacon then travels to a neighboring priest who again refuses him communion, and then to the local bishop who does the same, telling him he must be reconciled to his own priest. In the meantime, however, the latter has died, and so the deacon is forced to seek refuge at ever higher levels on the ecclesiological food chain. He first attends the local metropolitan, who sends him to the patriarch of Constantinople, who in turn sends him to Rome: "Believe me my son," the patriarch opines, "because you have done such damage to your soul when you did not humble yourself to him and persuade him to absolve you while he was alive, nobody is able to absolve you hereafter except the patriarch of Rome, because he is the head of all God's churches through Peter, who accepted the power to bind and loose from our God Christ." And so the deacon travels to Rome, but there the pope refuses to see him and instead sends him to the patriarch of Jerusalem, who in turn dismisses him to the fathers in the desert: "See perhaps if someone worthy can be found among them," he says, "who can pray to merciful God and absolve you from this dire bond." In the desert, the deacon meets with an advanced elder who denounces his disobedience but nevertheless orders him to supplicate God for three days outside his cave. The period complete, the deacon sees his former priest coming through the air on a couch and begs his forgiveness for his former sin. The dead priest grants his request, on three grounds: "the mercy of God, the prayer of this holy father, and his free speech ["audacia"] before God."[7]

On the face of it, then, we encounter some of the preoccupations of Maximus and his Palestinian allies in the same period: the insistence on communion, the importance of obedience to priests, and the recognition of papal preeminence. Here, however, we also observe a subtle but nevertheless striking inversion of those same themes: although Rome is placed above Constantinople in the chain of appeal, it is noticeable that the (at the time perhaps nonexistent) patriarch of Jerusalem is placed above the pope; and although "the word of the priest" is presented as sacrosanct, it is nevertheless a Palestinian ascetic who is the sole religious figure capable of interceding with God to remove the most grievous of charges, in effect usurping the clerical prerogative to bind and loose. At the same time, the tale presents a Christian world in which the patriarchates have been reconciled, and thus

---

7. *Georgian Appendix to the Spiritual Meadow* 20 [Latin trans. Garitte 417–19]. A mutilated Greek version of the tale is published in Canart (1966) 18–20.

perhaps condenses the anxieties of those whom the rapprochement realized after 657 now excluded. In the face of the patriarchal monolith, new, less formal authorities could be sought.

Here we have retreated somewhat from the prosacramental and pro-Roman rhetoric that distinguishes something of our circle's output before Maximus's trial. We will remember that during his trial and in its aftermath Maximus is said to have been confronted with the same specter of patriarchal consensus. In the *Record of the Trial*, when an interlocutor reports the arrival of Pope Eugenius's *apocrisiarii* in the capital and the expectation of imminent communion, Maximus responds that the Spirit "anathematizes even angels who introduce some innovation besides what is preached"; in a later letter to his disciple Anastasius, when confronted with the actual reestablishment of communion under Pope Vitalian, Maximus reinterprets the rock on which Christ founded the Church not as a the Roman Church but as the orthodox faith (in effect liberating that faith from the confines of a particular institution).[8] In these later texts, therefore, both Maximus and the author of the *Georgian Appendix to the Spiritual Meadow* upheld the essential independence of the faith from the vagaries of patriarchal politics, presenting the righteous ascetic as the ultimate guardian of Christian truth. In asserting this same independence, both authors were attempting to undo an ideological matrix that their immediate circle had in fact done much to create.

In the course of the fourth, fifth, and sixth centuries, ascetic communities were brought within ecclesial structures through various means: through the creeping stigmatization of ascetic practices that clerics deemed threatening, through the promotion of an ideal of clerical monasticization, and through processes of legal and economic subordination. But in all this, one conspicuous intellectual issue remained unaddressed—that is, the traditional ascetic (and hagiographic) indifference to the eucharist, and with it the implication that ascetics, in fact, might still be self-sufficient. In the period after Chalcedon, numerous Christian authors attempted to negotiate this tension. Hagiographers—in particular, anti-Chalcedonian hagiographers—began to propagate more sacramentalized visions of the saint, and the Pseudo-Areopagite, for the first time, set out a cosmological vision that attempted to place ascetical narratives within an ecclesial context. From their earliest writings, the circle of Moschus, Sophronius, and Maximus demonstrated a profound and ever-deepening interest in this same tension. For the same group, the Chalcedonian eucharist had from the outset been the central icon of the orthodox faith; but as time progressed, so too did the group come to express its spiritual as well as social aspects. Sophronius in the *Miracles of Cyrus and John* saw the eucharist as a glorious precursor to the ascetic

---

8. See *Record* 7 [Allen and Neil 62]; Maximus Confessor, *Letter to Anastasius the Disciple* [Allen and Neil 120]; with chap. 6 at n. 194 and chap. 7 at nn. 153ff. above.

life; Moschus in the *Spiritual Meadow* presented regular eucharistic participation as essential to the life of virtue; and Maximus in the *Mystagogy*—and Sophronius again in his patriarchal sermons—presented the eucharistic rite as the summation of Christian existence. Our three protagonists, therefore, were the impresarios of a new ascetic culture that emphasized the essential coinherence of the ascetic and clerical vocations, and the continued uprightness of a Church beset on all sides with terrestrial disasters and potential pollutants.

I have emphasized here how dependent the articulation of that same vision was upon the political and material context in which it occurred. It is perhaps unsurprising, therefore, to discover comparable processes of cultural renegotiation across a range of Chalcedonian authors of the same period. Two such authors should hold our attention here: first, Leontius of Neapolis (fl. 640s) and, second, Anastasius of Sinai (fl. ca. 650–700). We have on several occasions encountered the derivatives of Moschus and Sophronius's *Life of John the Almsgiver*, a text that in its celebration of a patriarch perhaps predicts the celebration of the clerical vocation so evident in Moschus's *Spiritual Meadow*. It is, however, Leontius of Neapolis's continuation of that *Life* that provides the most obvious parallel to Moschus's work, demonstrating as it does the parallel attempts of some Chalcedonian contemporaries to transcend established paradigms of hagiographic holiness. As Vincent Déroche has demonstrated in a magisterial monograph on Leontius and his hagiographies, John the Almsgiver's holiness here consists not in rigorous asceticism, nor even in the performance of miracles, but in the simple but often paradoxical application of Gospel precepts, and in an active urban engagement that does not wait to be prompted. Leontius's *Life*, like the Moschan-Sophronian text on which it was based, is little concerned with the niceties of hagiographic cliché. It presents a patriarch denuded of the traditional markers of holiness but nevertheless sanctified through social integration and an active engagement in the salvific mission of the Church.[9]

Like Moschus, Leontius demonstrates an acute interest in the potential for concealed urban holiness.[10] Thus in the *Life of John the Almsgiver* we read about a destitute servant giving a beggar his prized possession, a precious silver cross;[11] in a later chapter the hagiographer recounts a tale—an apparent favorite of his hero— in which a customs officer, following a revelation of Christ, sells himself as a slave in Jerusalem and flees when some former associates recognize him as he serves at his master's table (as he leaves the house his mere presence heals the deaf-mute gatekeeper).[12] Next to these vignettes concerning pious *kosmikoi*, Leontius, like

9. For John as "more holy than nearly all those who spend time in asceticism and the desert" see Leontius of Neapolis, *Life of John the Almsgiver* 47 [Festugière 397f.]. For John's redefinition of holiness see Déroche (1995) 227–38.
10. See Déroche (1995) 264–69, 297–301.
11. Leontius of Neapolis, *Life of John the Almsgiver*, prologue.
12. Ibid. 20–21.

Moschus again, also explores the possibilities of an urban asceticism that inverts the traditional hagiographic emphasis on the desert. Two stories concern wandering mendicant monks who scandalize the Alexandrians through associating with women; but in both cases the same monks are revealed to be pious, and their detractors mistaken. Indeed, both contain the same striking sentiment as to the potential for concealed urban holiness: thus in one the enlightened Alexandrians extol God's "hidden servants" (*kruptous doulous*) and in the other the patriarch himself exclaims (to John and Sophronius, no less), "Bless me! How many hidden servants God has, yet we in our simplicity do not know them! [*Babai, posous kruptous doulous echei ho Theos kai ouk oidamen hēmeis hoi tapeinoi*]."[13] This much-repeated exclamation, we should note, also appears in that tale of a bishop turned laborer that we encountered above within the *Spiritual Meadow*.[14]

Perhaps the most striking tale of concealed urban holiness in Leontius's *Life of John the Almsgiver* concerns, however, a *salos*, or fool for Christ's sake, who adopts a scandalous life within Alexandria as a form of radical self-abasement.[15] Although the tale of the fool Vitalius occupies a single tale within the *Life of John*, Leontius would develop this theme in his subsequent hagiographic masterpiece, the *Life of Symeon the Holy Fool*. Drawing inspiration from a number of sources, not least from Moschus's *Spiritual Meadow*, Leontius therein described the unusual life of one Symeon of Emesa, another *salos*.[16] Symeon operates in an urban context, pretending to be a fool and associating with prostitutes, while all the time practicing asceticism in private and attempting to convert those prostitutes to a better life. Before embarking upon this urban existence, Symeon retreats to a monastery and thence to more elevated endeavors in the desert. Telling, however, is his reported reason for entering into Emesa: "Brother," he asks his companion John, "what future benefit do we earn from spending time in this desert? But if you will listen to me, get up, let us leave and save others as well. For as things are we benefit no one except ourselves and earn no reward for anyone else."[17]

It has sometimes been observed that Leontius's *saloi* to some extent recreate the spirituality of the "Messalians": that is, in their radical spiritual and material

---

13. See, respectively, ibid. 50 [Festugière 401] and 23 [Festugière 375].

14. Cf. John Moschus, *Spiritual Meadow* 37 [PG 87:3, 2888C]: *Posous kruptous doulous echei ho Theos, kai monōi autōi gnōrimoi eisin*. For variations of this same phrase cf. *Greek Life of Daniel of Scetis* 3, 5 [Dahlman 126, 146]; also Festugière and Rydén (1974) 175f., 588.

15. Leontius of Neapolis, *Life of John the Almsgiver* 38.

16. For Leontius's sources see the discussion in Déroche (1995) 96–116. For parallels with John Moschus, *Spiritual Meadow* see Leontius of Neapolis, *Life of Symeon the Holy Fool* 22, 29; cf. *Spiritual Meadow* 3, 72. These parallels are discussed in Palmer (1997a). For the use of the *Spiritual Meadow* for Leontius's *Life of John the Almsgiver* see Kresten (1977) 161–62, 170 n. 45; Déroche (1995) 125–28, 132.

17. Leontius of Neapolis, *Life of Symeon the Holy Fool* 10 [Rydén 76]. For Symeon's imitation of Christ's salvific mission in Jerusalem, see Krueger (1996) 108–25.

detachment, urban presence, and apparent indifference to the Church and its representatives.[18] Although part of Leontius's purpose is no doubt to undermine that normative paradigm of monastic practice that served both to present the deserts as the "proper" context for asceticism, and thence to suppress the Messalian paradigm of more active social engagement, there are nevertheless crucial differences.[19] As we have seen, a central component of the Messalian profile was the group's indifference to the sacraments, in particular the eucharist. Leontius, however, is careful to represent the prosacramental credentials of his protagonists, despite their own apparent independence of the sacramental order. Thus in the *Life of John* the vignette concerning the fool, though short, nevertheless contains an explicit statement that the monk resides in a cell next to the Church of Saint Metras, where he celebrates mass with the prostitutes whom he is instructing;[20] in the *Life of Symeon* the eponymous hero denounces those who do not engage in frequent communion and praises those who approach the eucharist with simple virtue.[21]

Leontius, of course, differs from Moschus in certain of his emphases: his holy fools (unlike Moschus's urban ascetics), for example, are not simply present in the city but actively engaged within it;[22] and Symeon, though insistent that others must participate in the eucharist, seems himself to transcend the demands of the sacramental system.[23] We nevertheless discover in Leontius's hagiographies some striking parallels with the *Spiritual Meadow*: downgrading the desert as the sole "proper" context for monastic practice, exploring new paradigms of holiness outside traditional monasticism, and insisting on regular and pious participation in the eucharist.

Those parallels are not limited to Leontius, however—who had, after all, read at least some of Moschus's narratives. Thus in the corpus of Anastasius of Sinai we discover, alongside the celebration of Sinaitic desert asceticism in what is called "collection A" of his *Tales*—spiritual narratives akin to those of Moschus—a broader insistence that monasticism is not the sole route to salvation. Thus in a sermon *On the Holy Synaxis* Anastasius has an imagined interlocutor ask, "'Alas! How can I be saved? I am not able to fast; I do not know how to perform a vigil; I

---

18. See, e.g., P. Brown (1988) 331–37; Escolan (1999) 122f.; also Déroche (1995) 249–54 on the "miraculous economy" of Leontius's text.

19. See ibid. 221–25.

20. Leontius of Neapolis, *Life of John the Almsgiver* 38 [Festugière 390]. On the eucharist in the *Life of John the Almsgiver* see also ibid. 12, 15 (both on not bearing grudges before communion), 45 (on not leaving church to gossip after the Gospel reading). The latter reports that John "also gave much thought to the holy synaxis and took great pains over it" [Festugière 397].

21. See Leontius of Neapolis, *Life of Symeon the Holy Fool* 32, 40, with the discussion of Déroche (1995) 194f. Déroche also points to an instance where Symeon disrupts the liturgy (chap. 12) and argues that a vignette in which he dips sausages into mustard (chap. 30) is a parody of eucharistic communion.

22. See the detailed discussion of the spirituality of Leontius's holy fools in Déroche (1995) 154–225.

23. See ibid. 194.

am not able to be continent; I cannot bear to withdraw from the world. How then can I be saved? How?' I say to you, 'Forgive, and it will be forgiven unto you.' Yield, and it will be yielded to you. See, there is one short road to salvation. And so I shall show to you a second. What? 'Do not judge,' it says, 'and you will not be judged." [Cf. Lk. 6:37]. See, this other path is without fasting, without vigil, without labor."[24] This same theme recurs in another important text, the *Questions and Answers*, where Anastasius criticizes as a work of the devil the concept that "It is impossible to be saved unless you renounce life and become a monk [*ei mē tou biou apotaxēi kai monasēis*], and go into the deserts," and asserts in place of asceticism a simple Christian virtue based in a lack of pride.[25] As Déroche, again, has observed, Anastasius like Leontius asserts a basic Christian virtue in which the monastic monopoly on ascetic holiness is undone, and where the potential for virtuous Christians of all vocations to enter heaven is made explicit.[26]

As the title to the sermon *On the Holy Synaxis* makes evident, Anastasius also demonstrates a profound interest in issues of eucharistic procedure and thought. Thus a dominant theme of the "B" and "C" collections, as they are called, of Anastasius's *Tales*—collections that, like the *Spiritual Meadow*, broaden the perspective to transcend the desert focus of "collection A"—is the power of the eucharist, with numerous stories concerning the host functioning either to establish the continued truth of the Christian faith against heretical outsiders (skeptics, heretics, pagans, Jews, Muslims, et al.) or, in the continued absence of advanced theological speculation on the subject, to explore some unresolved problem of liturgical procedure.[27]

The Moschan circle's expansion of asceticism outside the circles of monastics and its simultaneous elevation of the eucharist therefore form part of a far wider

---

24. Anastasius of Sinai, *On the Holy Synaxis* 18 [PG 89, 845A]. Cf. the conclusion to the sermon: *On the Holy Synaxis* 22.

25. Anastasius of Sinai, *Questions and Answers* 88 [Richard and Munitiz 140–43]. For the parallels between Anastasius's texts on this point see also Haldon (1992) 133f.

26. See further Déroche (1995) 271–76, 283–88, noting the striking insistence in both authors on not judging others. See, e.g., Leontius, *Life of John the Almsgiver* 38; Anastasius of Sinai, *On the Holy Synaxis* 18–22. Cf. Anastasius of Sinai, *Questions and Answers*, appendix 18.

27. For the *Tales* of Anastasius of Sinai see CPG no. 7758, which divides them into three collections: for collection A (1–40) see Nau (1902a); for collection B (1–9) Nau (1903a) 56–75 (nos. 43–51). The C collection (1–18) has been published only in part: for C4 and C11 see ibid. 87–89, 78–79; for C9 Dobschütz (1899) 226**–32**; for C15 Halkin (1945) 62–64. On the unity of the collections see Flusin (1991) esp. 393–96 containing also a useful précis of the C collection. A critical edition of the *Tales* by André Binggeli is much anticipated. For those anecdotes that concern the eucharist see Anastasius of Sinai, *Tales* A30, B1, B5–9, C1, C2, C12, C18. Similar issues of eucharistic protocol are dealt with by Anastasius of Sinai in his *Questions and Answers* 39–41, 64, 67, and *Hodegos* 23 (on eucharistic symbolism versus eucharistic realism). Anastasius of Sinai, like Leontius of Neapolis, thinks that some monks may attain to such holiness that they have no need of the eucharist; see *Questions and Answers* 6. For Anastasius of Sinai's interest in the eucharist see also Déroche (2002) 172f.; Binggeli (2009) 441.

pattern.[28] In itself, as we have seen, that heightened interest in the eucharist is not new: it is anticipated in anti-Chalcedonian texts of the preceding period, texts that demonstrate a similar desire to reaffirm the ritual and doctrinal boundaries of orthodox communities in the face of external pollutants.[29] What is new, therefore, is not the elevation of the sacramental system per se but rather the more advanced Chalcedonian attempt at social and theological integration around it. For these seventh-century authors, the power of the host proclaimed the continued truth of the orthodox faith, irrespective of political reversals, as communion within the orthodox Church, furthermore, defined the ritual boundaries of the orthodox group against a mass of heretical outsiders, providing a powerful shared icon around which all orthodox Christians could assemble in the face of dramatic political, social, and economic change.[30] Thus as Chalcedonian observers began to emphasize the basic components that comprised Christian virtue and to point to the Church and its rites as the sole medium through which universal salvation could be achieved, those same observers also began to challenge or deemphasize the central place of monasticism to concepts of Christian virtue, asserting in its place more unified visions of their communities, visions that pointed to a less exclusive ascetic virtue and a dependence on the eucharist as the principal route to redemption.[31]

It is therefore possible to situate the ideological program of Moschus, Sophronius, and Maximus within a far broader cultural narrative, as a constituent of a wider "ideological reorientation" (in John Haldon's phrase) or "mental adjustment" (in Averil Cameron's) through which Chalcedonian contemporaries attempted to respond to and make sense of the shifting circumstances of their age.[32] In exploring this tension, Moschus and his associates were, like other Chalcedonians in the same period, responding to the crisis of empire and its consequences, emphasizing the sustained accord and righteousness of the orthodox Church in a context of profound Christian reversals. Within the same group's immediate context, however, this same emphasis assumed or came to complement three further positions that posed a fundamental challenge to the political and

---

28. On the heightened interest in the eucharist in this period see the characteristically comprehensive treatment in Déroche (2002) 167–80.

29. See above chap. 1 at nn. 147ff.

30. I make no claim to the effectiveness of this program in practice. Liturgical historians in fact point to this period as one of "diminished liturgical participation by the people" and "liturgical disintegration"; see, respectively, Schulz (1964, trans. O'Connell 34); Ware (1988) 27. See also Caseau (2002) on the decline of autocommunion and communion from the hand in this same period.

31. For this crisis in asceticism see also, on the shift away from contemporary subjects within seventh-century hagiography, Rapp (1995); and, on the failure of traditional monastic political paradigms within the eighth-century *Life of Stephen the Younger*, Hatlie (1999).

32. Haldon (1986) and (1990) esp. 403–36; Averil Cameron (1992a, d).

doctrinal policies of Constantinople: first, an absolute refusal to contemplate compromise or communion with heretics (against the advocates of *oikonomia*); second, a recognition of papal preeminence within the Church (against the dictatorial stance of the capital); and third, the exclusion of the emperor from religious narratives (against the political culture of the Christian empire).

It is again essential to situate these same developments within the context of the fluctuating geopolitics of the eastern Mediterranean. After his dramatic triumph over the Persians and the reintegration of the conquered eastern provinces under Constantinopolitan rule, it was quite natural for Heraclius to attempt a simultaneous doctrinal union to mirror on the celestial plane his achievement on the terrestrial. The stunning success of those unions—which, for a fleeting moment, realized the reunification of several Eastern churches—must in part reflect the cultural and political capital that the emperor's triumph bestowed. But Sophronius and Maximus, who had spent much of the preceding period as refugees in the West, and who had (with other Palestinian authors) pointed to collective sin as the cause of disaster, greeted the emperor's achievement with distinct ambivalence. As Heraclius entered into communion with a series of anti-Chalcedonian communities, and as his success was proved ephemeral in the conquests of Islam, it therefore seems less surprising that the pair began to oppose the imperial will and to focus on the quest for proper doctrine as the most pressing imperative of the age.

From the first emergence of the group into the full gaze of the historian—in Sophronius's *Miracles of Cyrus and John*—one at once encounters a strict sacramental differentiation between Chalcedonian and anti-Chalcedonian communities, an emphasis that reflects a wider reorientation of Christian cultures in the charged doctrinal contexts of the post-Chalcedonian period (and evident, in particular, in anti-Chalcedonian texts). But in this earliest text, the strident assault on heretics so evident in the same author's later output is less pronounced—a reflection, perhaps, of his status as the leading doctrinal disputant of a prominent Heraclian appointee. Moschus's later *Spiritual Meadow*, however, adopts a quite different stance, further expanding the importance of the orthodox sacraments but with a far more pervasive emphasis on the iniquities of heretics, in particular the Severans. Indeed, in the same period when Moschus set down his pen, Sophronius himself emerged as the most vociferous advocate of the principle of *akribeia* and with it the maintenance of the sacramental pureness of the Chalcedonian Church. Thus, as the emperor and patriarch at Constantinople first attempted a spectacular union of the anti-Chalcedonians through a compromise formula (monenergism) and then struggled to maintain Chalcedonian peace through a series of further formulas, Sophronius and Maximus refused all attempts at accommodation and instead developed an explicit doctrinal opposition.

In that same opposition, Sophronius, Maximus, and their allies convinced the Roman popes to defect to their cause and thence began the circle's explicit celebration of Roman preeminence within the Church. It must be emphasized that this pro-Roman rhetoric never went so far so as to recognize the monarchic powers that would characterize later papal doctrine, but neither was it a simple strategic machination; for while no doubt expedient in political terms, it also served as an obvious extension to the celebration of clerical and sacramental mediation set out within an earlier context. Indeed, the circle's marked respect for Rome in fact preceded the opening salvos of the doctrinal crisis, for it is a conspicuous presence in the *Spiritual Meadow* of Moschus.

At the same time, the ecclesiological emphasis explored within an earlier context now served a further purpose, for it provided the intellectual basis for a denial of the sacerdotal pretensions of the emperor and thence his right to interfere in matters of the faith. Maximus, we must again note, never goes so far as Sophronius's patriarchal sermons, which, confronted with the realities of Muslim rule, begin to relativize the Christian empire as an effective soteriological medium. The most consistent political aim of Maximus and his colleagues, still operating within the Roman empire, was not the full extrication of ecclesial and secular life, but rather the reign of an emperor who endorsed their particular vision of orthodox doctrine. Hence it was perhaps no contradiction that Maximus became associated with and was even said to have supported several political rebellions against Constans's reign. If a compliant "orthodox" emperor had ascended to the throne, we might have supposed a significant alteration in his rhetoric. But over several decades, as the Constantinopolitan emperors continued to lend their weight to monadic Christological expressions, and as Muslim success became ever more entrenched, so did Maximus's circle further extend the more integrated ecclesiological paradigm through which it had first responded to Christian reversals, asserting a vision of ecclesial independence that assumed a more patent political dimension in its claim to the Church's absolute right to self-determination and in its explicit denial of the emperor's aspiration to sacerdotal status.

It will perhaps come as little surprise that some scholars have seen in Maximus the last of the great late-antique ascetics, wielding free speech (*parrhēsia*) before the emperor and fearless in the face of the combined might of the secular and ecclesial authorities. In his classic treatment of the period, for example, Haldon has seen Maximus's resistance as the quintessential expression of a devolution of the sacred through which, in the face of the crisis overwhelming the Roman state, more established poles of spiritual power (the emperor and the cleric) lost ground to less formal rivals who offered alternative claims to divine favor—the ascetic and the icon;[33] and in a compelling recent reflection on Maximus's thought, Christian

---

33. See Haldon (1985) and (1990) 304–12.

Boudignon has spoken of Maximus's transformation of the universal Church into an orthodox confession, thus detaching it from a "historic, concrete institution" and limiting it to an "intellectual position."[34]

As we have seen, there is much to commend this perspective. Toward the end of his life, when threatened with the universal communion of the patriarchates, Maximus indeed expressed a classic monastic position: that is, the ascetic as outsider, wielding spiritual power from the edges of the settled world and its institutions, and presenting correct doctrine as the prime measure of virtue. At the same time, when confronted with that same communion, he is said to have advised refusal of the eucharist and thus to have repudiated the (heretical) Church's sacramental order. Thus, an ascetic who had invested so much intellectual effort in recognizing clerical structures and in celebrating the spiritual power offered in the eucharist was reduced, in the final instance, to once again relegating the importance of the Church within the Christian life.

This was nevertheless a position adopted in extremis, when the consistent emphasis that Maximus and his circle had placed upon the terrestrial forms of the Church, its clerical and sacramental structures, returned to haunt them. This alternative emphasis indeed had deep roots within the thought of Maximus and his circle. Although our three protagonists never went so far as to invest in a rhetoric of absolute clerical—and thence Roman—power over the Church and its doctrine, Moschus, Sophronius, and Maximus from about 630 placed a consistent emphasis upon the mediating function of the priesthood and the absolute need for regular submission to the eucharist. Maximus was above all, therefore, a man not of the desert but of the Church. In the late 650s, however, as the patriarchal consensus solidified around the "one and two" formula advocated from Constantinople, he and his allies faced the unpalatable prospect of being excluded from all communion and thence the illumination offered in the sacraments. Hence the late emphasis upon proper faith as the principal criterion of righteousness, and hence also the strange contradictions of the *Georgian Appendix to the Spiritual Meadow*, which cannot abandon the now embedded narratives of monastic communion and submission to the Church, but which nevertheless attempts to reestablish the essential moral independence of ascetics.

It is therefore difficult to see Maximus's resistance to the emperor as the simple continuation of the noble tradition of ascetic *parrhēsia*. It was not his status as an alternative, charismatic source of spiritual power that posed the real threat to Constantinople. It was, instead, the dangerous coincidence of Roman and Palestinian doctrinal agendas that he represented and, at a fundamental level, the simultaneous coincidence of papal and ascetic ideologies. Indeed, as the Moschan circle

---

34. Boudignon (2007) 272. For an extreme expression of this same perspective see Athanassiadi (2010) 125–31.

invested in a new, more unified ecclesiological vision and used that vision to underscore papal preeminence, so was the papal rhetoric of ecclesiological privilege becoming more strident, drawing upon comparable notions of *communio* that also elevated eucharistic union as the ultimate expression of the peace of the Church.[35] Thus, in the same manner as the papal differentiation of the "two powers" became more potent, in the Latin West, in its intersection with the Augustinian thesis of the "two cities," so too did it become more potent, in the Greek East, in its intersection with the thought of Maximus and his circle.[36]

This intersection of ideas presented a far more profound threat to the emperor than a simple assertion of charismatic power. At least since the pontificate of Pope Gelasius in the late fifth century, the Roman popes carried within their rhetorical arsenal a strict differentiation of the secular and the sacred, but now the Eastern circle of Maximus was expounding comparable ideas, using that same differentiation as the basis for a radical repudiation of the imperial ideological edifice. The immediate context for that same repudiation was the promulgation of monenergism and monotheletism, but it was no coincidence that it was voiced, and became more vociferous, as the crisis of the Eastern Roman empire deepened. As the emperor Constans was beset with continued Muslim aggression in the East, Maximus led a movement of protest against his irenic religious policies, challenging the emperor's right to promulgate doctrine, and perhaps even fostering a series of political rebellions. Subsequent to his arrest in Rome, it is perhaps surprising that Constans did not at once execute Maximus, the period's most prolific, persistent, and pervasive dissident. But that he did not do so points to the capital's clear caution over the potential repercussions of such an action and, moreover, to the importance that it attached to the monk's desired submission.

Even if the same submission never came, the eventual defection of Rome under Pope Vitalian marked the effective end of Maximus's resistance. That defection meant more to Maximus than his political and doctrinal isolation: it meant a fundamental challenge to the ideological basis on which he had constructed his dissidence. From the earliest stages of the doctrinal crisis, it was crucial to the Palestinian faction gathered around Sophronius to secure a patriarchal mouthpiece for their doctrine, as much for the stage that it provided as for the sanction that it offered their position. Moschus, Sophronius, and Maximus came to construct themselves as ecclesial ascetics, respectful of the priesthood, mindful of the Church's rites, and devoted to the sacraments. When pushed, it was still possible for Maximus and his allies to revert to an older paradigm, of the ascetic as outsider, transcending the political machinations of terrestrial institutions. But he and his masters had, in contrast to previous generations of Chalcedonian ascetics, done

---

35. Conte (1971) esp. 305, 324–27.
36. For that Western intersection see Dagron (1996) 311f.

much to promote a new model, in which the ascetic was placed not on the edges of the Church but at its beating heart. It was in this guise—not as mere charismatics but as institutionalized charismatics—that the Moschan circle was at its most original, most radical, and most subversive. As the crisis of empire destabilized traditional conceptions of monastic holiness, Moschus, Sophronius, and Maximus helped to forge a less exclusive, less introspective asceticism, broadening its social base and situating it within a wider sacramental, hierarchical, and ecclesial context. Indeed, along with the doctrines of the "two wills" and "two operations," recognized as orthodox at Constantinople some decades later, it was this same, more integrated model of ascetic practice, and the blueprint for political dissidence that accompanied it, that were to be their most enduring and most significant contributions to the culture of the Greek Christian East. Far from being the last of the late-antique holy men, Maximus was instead the first of a new type of Byzantine ascetic, wielding power not from without but from within the Church, and no less powerful for that.

# BIBLIOGRAPHY

## PRIMARY SOURCES

Abū Ṣāliḥ. [Pseudo-Abū Ṣāliḥ.] *Churches and Monasteries of Egypt*. Trans. B. T. A. Evetts, *Churches and Monasteries of Egypt and Some Neighbouring Countries*. Oxford, 1895.

*Acts of Anastasius the Persian*. Ed. B. Flusin in *Saint Anastase le Perse et l'histoire de la Palestine au début du VII<sup>e</sup> siècle*, vol. 1, 41–91. Paris, 1992.

*Acts of the Council of 536*. Ed. E. Schwartz in *Collectio Sabaitica contra Acephalos et Origeniastas destinata: Insunt Acta synodorum Constantinopolitanae et Hierosolymitanae anno 536*, ACO, ser. 1, tom. 3, 25–186. Berlin, 1940.

*Acts of the Council of Chalcedon*. Ed. E. Schwartz. 6 vols. ACO, ser. 1, tom. 2. Berlin, 1983–87.

*Acts of the Council of Gangra*. Ed. P.-P. Joannou in *Discipline générale antique (IV<sup>e</sup>-IX<sup>e</sup> s.)*, vol. 1, part 2, *Les canons des synods particuliers*, 85–99. Rome, 1962.

*Acts of the Council of Saragossa*. Ed. F. Rodríguez, "Concilio I de Zaragoza: Texto crítico," in *Primero Concilio Caesaraugustano: MDC aniversario*, 9–25. Saragossa, 1981.

*Acts of the Fifth Ecumenical Council*. In J. Straub and E. Schwartz, eds., *Concilium universale Constantinopolitanum sub Iustiniano habitum*, ACO, ser. 1, tom. 4, vols. 1 and 2. Berlin, 1971.

*Acts of the Lateran Council*. Ed. R. Riedinger, *Concilium Lateranense anno 649 celebratum*. ACO, ser. 2, tom. 1. Berlin, 1984.

*Acts of the Sixth Ecumenical Council*. Ed. R. Riedinger, *Concilium universale Constantinopolitanum tertium*. 2 vols. ACO, ser. 2, tom. 2. Berlin, 1990–92.

Adamnan. *On the Holy Places*. Ed. L. Bieler in P. Geyer et al., eds., *Itineraria et alia geographica*, CCSL 175, 178–234. Turnhout, 1965.

*Against the People of Constantinople*. In P. Allen and B. Neil, eds., *Scripta saeculi VII vitam Maximi Confessoris illustrantia*, CCSG 39, 230–32. Turnhout, 1999. [Reprint: Allen and Neil (2002) 172–74.]

Agapius. *Universal History*. Ed. A. A. Vasiliev, *Kitab al-'Unvan: Histoire universelle, écrite par Agapius de Menbidj*. Part 2.2. PO 8.3. Paris, 1912.
ʿAmr ibn Mattā. *The Tower*. Ed. H. Gismondi, *Maris, Amri, et Salibae: De patriarchis Nestorianorum commentaria*. Vol. 1. Rome, 1896.
Anastasius I of Antioch. *Definitions*. Ed. K.-H. Uthemann, "Die 'philosophischen Kapitel' des Anastasius I. von Antiochen (559–598)," *OCP* 46 (1980) 343–60.
Anastasius Apocrisiarius. *Letter to Theodosius of Gangra*. In P. Allen and B. Neil, eds., *Scripta saeculi VII vitam Maximi Confessoris illustrantia*, CCSG 39, 173–89. Turnhout, 1999. [Reprint: Allen and Neil (2002) 132–46.]
Anastasius of Sinai. *Against the Monotheletes*. Ed. K.-H. Uthemann in *Sermones duo in constitutionem hominis secundum imaginem Dei*, CCSG 12, 35–83. Turnhout, 1985.
———. *Hodegos*. Ed. K.-H. Uthemann, *Anastasii Sinaitae Viae dux*. CCSG 8. Turnhout, 1981.
———. *On the Holy Synaxis*. PG 89, 825–49.
———. *Questions and Answers*. Ed. M. Richard and J. A. Munitiz, *Anastasii Sinaitae Quaestiones et responsiones*. CCSG 59. Turnhout, 2006.
———. *Tales*. Ed. F. Nau. [A.] "Le texte grec des Récits utiles à l'âme du moine Anastase sur les saints pères du Sinai," *OC* 2 (1902) 58–89; [B.] *OC* 3 (1903) 56–75. [The C collection remains unpublished but is summarized in Flusin (1991) 386–88.]
Anastasius the Disciple. *Letter to the Monks of Cagliari*. In P. Allen and B. Neil, eds., *Scripta saeculi VII vitam Maximi Confessoris illustrantia*, CCSG 39, 166–69. Turnhout, 1999. [Reprint: Allen and Neil (2002) 124–30.]
*Anonymous Chronicle to 724*. Ed. E. W. Brooks in *Chronica minora*, vol. 2, CSCO 3, SS 3, 75–156. Paris, 1960.
*Anonymous Chronicle to 741*. Ed. T. Mommsen in *Chronica minora saeculorum IV. V. VI. VII.*, vol. 2, MGH, AA 11, 334–59. Berlin, 1894.
*Anonymous Chronicle to 754*. Ed. T. Mommsen in *Chronica minora saeculorum IV. V. VI. VII.*, vol. 2, MGH, AA 11, 334–68. Berlin, 1894.
*Anonymous Chronicle to 819*. Ed. A. Barsaum in J.-B. Chabot, ed., *Chronicon anonymum ad annum Christi 1234 pertinens*, CSCO 81, SS 36, 3–22. Louvain, 1916–20.
*Anonymous Chronicle to 1234*. Ed. J.-B. Chabot, *Chronicon anonymum ad annum Christi 1234 pertinens*. 2 vols. CSCO 81–82, SS 36–37. Louvain, 1916–20.
*Anonymous Life of John the Almsgiver*. Ed. H. Delehaye, "Une vie inédite de saint Jean l'Aumonier," *AB* 45 (1927) 19–25.
*Anonymous Miracles of Saint Demetrius*. Ed. P. Lemerle in *Les plus anciens recueils des Miracles de saint Démétrius*, vol. 1, 167–241. Paris, 1979.
Anonymous of Whitby. *Life of Gregory the Great*. Ed. B. Colgrave, *The Earliest Life of Gregory the Great*. Lawrence, Kans., 1968.
*Anthologia Graeca*. Ed. H. Beckby. 4 vols. Munich, 1957–58.
Antiochus Monachus. *Confession*. PG 89, 1849–56.
———. *Letter to Eustathius*. PG 89, 1421–28.
———. *Pandects*. PG 89, 1428–1849.
Antony of Choziba. *Life of George of Choziba*. Ed. C. Houze, "Sancti Georgii Chozebitae confessoris et monachi vita auctore Antonio eius discipulo," *AB* 7 (1888) 97–144, 336–59.

———. *The Miracles of the Blessed Theotokos at Choziba*. Ed. C. Houze, "Miracula Beatae Virginis Mariae in Choziba eodem Antonio Chozebita auctore," *AB* 7 (1888) 360–70.
*Apophthegmata Patrum (Alphabetical)*. PG 65, 72–440.
*Armenian Version of Dionysius the Areopagite*. Ed. R. W. Thomson, *The Armenian Version of the Works Attributed to Dionysius the Areopagite*. Vol. 1. Louvain, 1987.
Athanasius. *Life of Antony*. PG 26, 837–976.
*Auctarii Havniensis Extrema*. Ed. T. Mommsen in *Chronica minora saeculorum IV. V. VI. VII.*, vol. 1, MGH, AA 9, 304–33. Berlin, 1892.
Balādhurī. *Conquest of the Lands*. Ed. M. J. de Goeje, *Liber expugnationis regionum*. Leiden, 1870.
Barsanuphius and John. *Questions and Answers*. Ed. F. Neyt and P. de Angelis–Noah, *Barsanuphe et Jean de Gaza: Correspondance*. 5 vols. SC 426, 427, 450, 451, 468. Paris, 1997–2002.
Bede. *Ecclesiastical History*. Ed. B. Colgrave and R. A. B. Mynors, *Bede's Ecclesiastical History of the English People*. Oxford, 1969.
Benjamin. *Sermon on the Feast of Cana*. Ed. H. De Vis, "Sermon de Benjamin sur les Noces de Cana," in *Homélies coptes de la Vaticane*, 53–106. Louvain, 1990.
*Bohairic Life of Pachomius*. Ed. L. T. Lefort, *Sancti Pachomii vita Bohairice scripta*. CSCO 89, SC 7. Louvain, 1925.
*Book of Ceremonies*. Ed. I. Reiske, *Constantini Porphyrogeniti Imperatoris De ceremoniis aulae Byzantinae libri duo*. 2 vols. Bonn, 1829–30.
*Book of Pontiffs*. Ed. L. Duchesne, *Le Liber pontificalis*. 2 vols. Paris, 1886–92.
*Book of the Consecration of the Sanctuary of Benjamin*. Ed. R.-G. Coquin, *Livre de la consécration du Sanctuaire de Benjamin*. Cairo, 1975.
Bordeaux Pilgrim. *Travels*. Ed. P. Geyer and O. Cuntz, *Itinerarium Burdigalense*. In P. Geyer et al., eds., *Itineraria et alia geographica*, CCSL 175, 1–26. Turnhout, 1965.
*Canons of the Council of Chalcedon*. Ed. P.-P. Joannou in *Discipline générale antique (IV$^e$–IX$^e$ s.)*, vol. 1.1, *Les canons des conciles œcuméniques*, 66–97. Rome, 1962.
Canterbury Commentator. *First Commentary on the Pentateuch*. Ed. B. Bischoff and M. Lapidge in *Biblical Commentaries from the Canterbury School of Theodore and Hadrian*, 298–384. Cambridge, 1994.
———. *Second Canterbury Commentary on the Gospels*. Ed. B. Bischoff and M. Lapidge in *Biblical Commentaries from the Canterbury School of Theodore and Hadrian*, 396–422. Cambridge, 1994.
Cedrenus. *Compendium of Histories*. Ed. I. Bekker, *Georgius Cedrenus Ioannis Scylitzae ope*. 2 vols. Bonn, 1838–39.
*Chronicle of Seert*. Ed. A. Scher, *Histoire Nestorienne: Chronique de Séert*. 4 vols. PO 4.3, 5.2, 7.2, 13.4. Paris, 1908–19.
*Chronicle of Zuqnin*. Ed. J.-B. Chabot, *Chronicon anonymum pseudo-Dionysianum vulgo dictum*. 2 vols. CSCO 91, 104, SS 43, 53. Paris, 1927–65.
*Chronicon Altinate*. Ed. R. Cessi, *Chronicum Venetum: Origo civitatum Italie seu Venetiarum (Chronicon Altinate et Chronicon Gradense)*. Rome, 1933.
*Codex Justinianus*. Ed. P. Krueger. Berlin, 1877.
*Codex Theodosianus*. Ed. T. Mommsen, *Theodosiani libri xvi cum constitutionibus Sirmondianis et Leges Novellae ad Theodosianum pertinentes*. 2 vols. Berlin, 1905.

Constans. *Letter to Pope John IV.* Trans. Schacht (1936) 246–49 (German from Karshuni); also Latin trans. A. Mai in *Noua Patrum bibliotheca*, vol. 6 (Rome, 1954), 511–12.

Cyril of Scythopolis. *Lives.* Ed. R. Schwartz, *Kyrillos von Skythopolis*. TU 49.2. Leipzig, 1939.

Cyrus of Alexandria. *First Letter to Sergius.* Ed. R. Riedinger in *Acts of the Sixth Ecumenical Council* [q.v.], 588–92. [Reprint: Allen (2009) 160–62.]

———. *Second Letter to Sergius* Ed. R. Riedinger in *Acts of the Sixth Ecumenical Council* [q.v.], 592–94. [Reprint: Allen (2009) 174–76.]

*De Persica Captivitate Opusculum.* PG 86:2, 3236–40.

*Disputation against the Jews.* PG 89, 1204–81.

*Disputation with Pyrrhus.* PG 91, 288–353.

*Dispute at Bizya.* In P. Allen and B. Neil, eds., *Scripta saeculi VII vitam Maximi Confessoris illustrantia*, CCSG 39, 73–151. Turnhout, 1999. [Reprint: Allen and Neil (2002) 76–119.]

*Doctrina Patrum.* Ed. F. Diekamp, *Doctrina Patrum de incarnatione Verbi: Ein griechisches Florilegium aus der Wende des 7. und 8. Jahrhunderts*. Münster, 1907.

*Doctrine of Jacob the Recently Baptized.* Ed. V. Déroche, "Juifs et Chrétiens dans l'Orient de VIIe siècle," in T&MByz 11, 71–219. Paris, 1991.

*Ecclesiastical Canons That Were Given by the Holy Fathers during the Time of Persecution.* Ed. A. Vööbus, *The Synodicon in the West Syrian Tradition*, CSCO 367, SS 161, 159–63. Louvain, 1975.

Egeria. *Travels.* Ed. A. Franceschini and R. Weber, *Itinerarium Egeriae*, in P. Geyer et al., eds., *Itineraria et alia geographica*, CCSL 175, 37–103. Turnhout, 1965.

*Egyptian Miracles of Cosmas and Damian.* Ed. E. Rupprecht, *Cosmae et Damiani sanctorum medicorum vita et miracula e codice Londiniensi*. Berlin, 1935.

*Epitome of the Life of John the Almsgiver.* Ed. E. Lappa-Zizicas, "Un épitomé de la Vie de saint Jean l'Aumônier par Jean et Sophronius," *AB* 88 (1970) 265–78.

Eubulus of Lystra. *Against the "Libellus" of Athanasius to the Emperor Heraclius.* [Fragments.] In F. Diekamp, ed., *Doctrina Patrum de incarnatione Verbi: Ein griechisches Florilegium aus der Wende des 7. und 8. Jahrhunderts*, 141–48. Münster, 1907.

Eustathius Monachus. *Letter on the Two Natures.* Ed. P. Allen, *Eustathii Monachi Epistula de duabus naturis*, in J. H. Declerck et al., eds., *Pamphilus theologus: Diversorum capitum seu Difficultatum solutio; Eustathius Monachus, Epistula de duabus naturis*, CCSG 19, 391–474. Turnhout, 1989.

Eustratius Presbyter. *The Life of Golinduch.* Trans. G. Garitte, "La passion géorgienne de sainte Golindouch," *AB* 74 (1956) 405–40. [Latin trans. from Georgian.]

———. *On the State of Souls after Death.* Ed. P. Van Deun, *Eustratii Presbyteri Constantinopolitani De statu animarum post mortem* (CPG 7522). CCSG 60. Turnhout, 2006.

Eutychius. *Annals (Alexandrian Recension).* Ed. M. Breydy, *Das Annalenwerk des Eutychios von Alexandrien*. CSCO 471, SA 44. Louvain, 1985.

———. *Annals (Antiochene Recension).* Ed. L. Cheiko, *Eutychii patriarchae Alexandrini Annales.* 2 vols. CSCO 50, 51, SA 6, 7. Beirut, 1906–9.

Evagrius Ponticus. *Commentary on Ecclesiastes.* Ed. P. Géhin, *Évagre le Pontique: Scholies à l'Écclésiaste.* SC 397. Paris, 1993.

———. *The Gnostic.* [Greek fragments.] In A. Guillaumont and C. Guillaumont, eds., *Évagre le Pontique: Le Gnostique.* SC 356. Paris, 1989.

———. *Gnostic Centuries*. Ed. A. Guillaumont, *Les six Centuries des "Kephalaia Gnostica" d'Évagre le Pontique*. PO 28.1. Paris, 1958.
———. *Letter of Faith*. Ed. Y. Courtonne in *Saint Basile: Lettres*, vol. 1, 22–37. Paris, 1957.
———. *The Monk*. In A. Guillaumont and C. Guillaumont, eds., *Évagre le Pontique: Traité Pratique; ou, Le Moine*. Vol. 2. SC 171. Paris, 1971.
———. *On Malign Thoughts*. PG 79, 1200–1233.
———. *On the Eight Evil Spirits*. PG 79, 1145–64.
———. *To Monks*. Ed. H. Greßmann, "Nonnenspiegel und Mönchsspiegel des Euagrios Pontikos," in TU 39.4, 152–65. Leipzig, 1913.
Evagrius Scholasticus. *Ecclesiastical History*. Ed. J. Bidez and L. Parmentier, *The Ecclesiastical History of Evagrius, with the Scholia*. London, 1898.
*Fifteen Canons against Origen or the Origenists*. Ed. J. Straub in *Concilium universale Constantinopolitanum sub Iustiniano habitum*, ACO, ser. 1, tom. 4, vol. 1, 248–49. Berlin, 1971.
*First Greek Life of Pachomius*. Ed. F. Halkin in *Sancti Pachomii Vitae Graecae*, SH 19, 1–96. Brussels, 1932.
*Fragment on the Arab Conquest of Syria*. Ed. E. W. Brooks in *Chronica minora*, vol. 2, CSCO 3, SS 3, 75. Paris, 1960.
Fredegar. *Chronicle*. Ed. J. M. Wallace-Hadrill, *The Fourth Book of the Chronicle of Fredegar, with Its Continuations*. London, 1960.
George of Pisidia. *Against Severus*. PG 92, 1373–84.
———. *The Avar War*. Ed. A. Pertusi in *Giorgio di Pisidia: Poemi*, vol. 1, *Panegirici, Epici*, 176–200. Ettal, 1959.
———. *Heraclias*. Ed. A. Pertusi in *Giorgio di Pisidia: Poemi*, vol. 1, *Panegirici, Epici*, 240–92. Ettal, 1959.
———. *On the Restoration of the Cross*. Ed. A. Pertusi in *Giorgio di Pisidia: Poemi*, vol. 1, *Panegirici, Epici*, 225–30. Ettal, 1959.
———. *The Persian Expedition*. Ed. A. Pertusi in *Giorgio di Pisidia: Poemi*, vol. 1, *Panegirici, Epici*, 84–136. Ettal, 1959.
George of Resh'aina. *Life of Maximus Confessor*. Ed. and trans. S. Brock, "An Early Syriac Life of Maximus the Confessor," AB 91 (1973) 299–346.
*Georgian Appendix to the Spiritual Meadow*. Latin trans. G. Garitte, "'Histoires édifiantes' géorgiennes," *Byzantion* 36 (1966) 406–23.
Georgius Monachus. *Chronicle*. Ed. C. de Boor and P. Wirth, *Georgius Monachus: Chronicon*. 2 vols. Leipzig, 1978.
*Greek Life of Daniel of Scetis*. Ed. B. Dahlman, *Saint Daniel of Sketis: A Group of Hagiographic Texts Edited with Introduction, Translation and Commentary*. Studia Byzantina Upsaliensia 10. Uppsala, 2007.
*Greek Life of Maximus Confessor (Recension 2)*. PG 90, 68–109.
*Greek Life of Maximus Confessor (Recension 3)*. Ed. B. Neil and P. Allen, *Life of Maximus Confessor: Recension 3*. Sydney, 2003.
*Greek Life of Pope Martin*. Ed. P. Peeters, "Une vie grecque de saint Martin 1ᵉʳ," AB 51 (1933) 225–62.
Gregory of Nazianzus. *Orations*. Ed. J. Bernardi et al., *Grégoire de Nazianze: Discours*. 9 vols. SC 247, 250, 270, 284, 309, 318, 358, 384, 405. Paris, 1978–95.

Gregory of Tours. *Glory of the Martyrs*. Ed. B. Krusch in *Gregorii Turonensis opera*, vol. 2, *Miracula et opera minora*, MGH, SRM 1.2, 484–561. Berlin, 1885.

———. *History of the Franks*. Ed. B. Krusch and W. Levison, *Gregorii Episcopi Turonensis libri Historiarum X*. MGH, SRM 1.1. Hannover, 1951.

Gregory the Great. *Dialogues*. Ed. A. de Vogüé, *Grégoire le Grand: Dialogues*. 3 vols. SC 251, 260, 265. Paris, 1978–80.

———. *Letters*. Ed. D. Norberg, *Sancti Gregorii Magni Registrum epistularum libri I–VII*. CCSL 140. Turnhout, 1982.

———. *Moralia on Job*. Ed. M. Adriaen, *Sancti Gregori Magni Moralia in Iob*. 3 vols. CCSL 143, 143A, 143B. Turnhout, 1979–85.

Heraclius. *Novels*. Ed. J. Konidaris, "Die Novellen des Kaisers Herakleios," *Fontes Minores* 5 (1982) 1–106.

*History of the Monks in Egypt*. Ed. A.-J. Festugière, *Historia Monachorum in Aegypto*. SH 34. Paris, 1961.

*History of the Patriarchs of Alexandria*. Ed. B. Evetts, "History of the Patriarchs of the Coptic Church of Alexandria," parts 1–3, PO 1.2, 1.4 (Paris, 1904), 99–214, 381–518; PO 5.1 (Paris, 1910), 1–215; and PO 10.5 (Paris, 1915), 357–552.

Ibn ʿAbd al-Ḥakam. *Futūḥ Miṣr*. Ed. C. Torrey, *Futūḥ Miṣr wa-akhbāruhā* (New Haven, 1922); partial English trans. idem, "The Mohammedan Conquest of Egypt and North Africa in the Years 643 to 705 A.D.," in *Biblical and Semitic Studies: Critical and Historical Essays by the Members of the Semitic and Biblical Faculty of Yale University* (New York, 1901), 277–330.

Isaac the Presbyter. *Life of Samuel of Kalamon*. Ed. A. Alcock, *The Life of Samuel of Kalamon by Isaac the Presbyter*. Warminster, 1983.

Ishoʿyahb II, *Christological Letter* Ed. L. R. M. Sako, *Lettre christologique du patriarche syro-oriental Īšōʿyahb de Gḏālā (628–46): Étude, traduction et édition critique*. Rome, 1983.

Jacob of Edessa. *Chronicle*. Ed. E. W. Brooks in *Chronica minora*, vol. 3, CSCO 5, SS 5, 261–330. Paris, 1961.

Jacob of Serug. *Letter to Stephen bar Sudaili*. Ed. A. L. Frothingham in *Stephen Bar Sudaili the Syrian Mystic and the Book of the Holy Hierotheos*, 10–26. Leiden, 1886.

John Cassian. *Conferences*. Ed. M. Petschenig, *Iohannis Cassiani Conlationes XXIII*. CSEL 13. Vienna, 1886.

John Climacus. *The Ladder of Divine Ascent*. PG 88, 632–1164.

John Malalas. *Chronicle*. Ed. H. Thurn. Berlin, 2000.

John Moschus. *Spiritual Meadow*. PG 87:3, 2852–3112.

John of Antioch. *Chronicle*. Ed. U. Roberto, *Ioannis Antiocheni fragmenta ex Historia chronica*. Berlin, 2005.

John of Ephesus. *Ecclesiastical History*. Ed. E. W. Brooks, *Iohannis Ephesini Historiae ecclesiasticae pars tertia*. 2 vols. Louvain, 1952.

———. *Lives of the Eastern Saints*. Ed. E. W. Brooks. PO 17–19. Paris, 1923–25.

John of Nikiu. *Chronicle*. Ed. H. Zotenberg, *Chronique de Jean, évêque de Nikiou*. Paris, 1883.

John of Tella. *Canons*. Ed. A. Vööbus in *The Synodicon in the West Syrian Tradition*, vol. 1, CSCO 367, SS 161, 145–46. Louvain, 1975.

———. *Rules to Deacons*. Ed. V. L. Menze, "The 'Regula ad Diaconos': John of Tella, His Eucharistic Ecclesiology and the Establishment of an Ecclesiastical Hierarchy in Exile," *OC* 90 (2006) 44–90.

John of Thessalonica. *Miracles of Demetrius*. Ed. P. Lemerle in *Les plus anciens recueils des Miracles de saint Démétrius*, vol. 1, 47–165. Paris, 1979.
John Rufus. *Life of Peter the Iberian*. Ed. R. Raabe, *Petrus der Iberer: Ein Charakterbild zur Kirchen- und Sittengeschichte des 5. Jahrhunderts*. Leipzig, 1895.
———. *Plerophoriae*. Ed. and trans. F. Nau, *Les Plérophories de Jean, évêque de Maiouma*. PO 8.1. Paris, 1912.
John the Deacon. *Life of Gregory the Great*. PL 75, 61–242.
Justinian. *Edict against Origenism*. Ed. E. Schwartz in *Collectio Sabaitica contra Acephalos et Origeniastas destinata: Insunt Acta synodorum Constantinopolitanae et Hierosolymitanae anno 536*, ACO, ser. 1, tom. 3, 189–214. Berlin, 1940.
———. *Letter to the Synod on Origen*. PG 86, 989D–993B.
———. *Novels*. In R. Schoell and W. Kroll, eds., *Corpus Iuris Civilis*, vol. 3, *Iustiniani Novellae*. Berlin, 1928.
*Khuzistan Chronicle*. Ed. I. Guidi in *Chronica minora*, vol. 1, CSCO 1, SS 1, 15–39. Paris, 1960.
Leo Grammaticus. *Chronicle*. Ed. I. Bekker, *Leonis Grammatici Chronographia*. Bonn, 1842.
Leontius of Byzantium. *Against the Nestorians and Eutychians*. PG 86, 1267–1398.
Leontius of Neapolis. *Life of John the Almsgiver*. In A.-J. Festugière and L. Rydén, eds., *Vie de Syméon le Fou et Vie de Jean de Chypre*, 343–409. Paris, 1974.
———. *Life of Symeon the Holy Fool*. In A.-J. Festugière and L. Rydén, eds., *Vie de Syméon le Fou et Vie de Jean de Chypre*, 1–222. Paris, 1974.
Liberatus. *Breviarium*. Ed. E. Schwartz in *Acts of the Council of Chalcedon* [*q.v.*], vol. 5, 98–141.
*Liber Diurnus*. PL 105, 21–120.
*Life of Daniel the Stylite*. Ed. H. Delehaye in *Les saints stylites*, 1–94. Brussels, 1923.
*Life of John Eremopolites*. Ed. F. Halkin, "Saint Jean l'Eremopolite," AB 86 (1968) 13–20.
*Life of Marcellus Acoemeta*. Ed. G. Dagron, "La vie ancienne de Marcel l'Acémète," AB 86 (1968) 271–321.
*Life of Symeon the Younger*. Ed. P. van den Ven, *La vie ancienne de saint Syméon Stylite le Jeune (521–592)*. Vol. 1. Brussels, 1962.
*Life of Theodore of Sykeon*. Ed. A.-J. Festugière, *Vie de Théodore de Sykéon*. Brussels, 1970.
*Life of Theodore the Studite*. PG 99, [A] 113–232, [B] 233–328.
*Life of the Patriarch Germanus*. In L. Lamza, ed., *Patriarch Germanos I. von Konstantinopel (715–730): Versuch einer endgültigen chronologischen Fixierung des Lebens und Wirkens des Patriarchen, mit dem griechisch-deutschen Text der Vita Germani am Schluss der Arbeit*, 200–240. Würzburg 1975.
Mari. *History of the Nestorian Patriarchs*. Ed. H. Gismondi, *Maris, Amri, et Salibae de patriarchis Nestorianorum commentaria*. Vol. 2. Rome, 1899.
*Maronite Chronicle*. Ed. E. W. Brooks in *Chronica minora*, vol. 2, CSCO 3, SS 3, 43–74. Paris, 1960.
Maximus Confessor. *Ambigua to John*. Ed. E. Jeauneau, *Maximi Confessoris Ambigua ad Iohannem iuxta Iohannis Scotti Eriugenae Latinam interpretationem*. CCSG 18. Turnhout, 1988.
———. *Ambigua to Thomas*. Ed. B. Janssens in *Maximi Confessoris Ambigua ad Thomam una cum Epistula Secunda ad Eundem*, CCSG 48, 3–34. Turnhout, 2002.
———. *Book on the Ascetic Life*. Ed. P. Van Deun, *Maximi Confessoris Liber Asceticus*. CCSG 40. Turnhout, 2000.

———. *Centuries on Love*. Ed. A. Ceresa-Gastaldo, *Massimo Confessore: Capitoli sulla carità*. Rome, 1963.
———. *Centuries on Theology and Economy*. PG 91, 1084–1173.
———. *Exposition on the Lord's Prayer*. In P. Van Deun, ed., *Maximi Confessoris opuscula exegetica duo*, CCSG 23, 3–22. Turnhout, 1991.
———. *Letters*. PG 91, 364–649.
———. *Letter to Anastasius the Disciple*. In P. Allen and B. Neil, eds., *Scripta saeculi VII vitam Maximi Confessoris illustrantia*, CCSG 39, 160–63. Turnhout, 1999. [Reprint: Allen and Neil (2002) 120–22.]
———. *Letter to Thalassius*. PL 129, 583–86.
———. *Mystagogy*. Ed. C. Boudignon, *Maximi Confessoris Mystagogia*. CCSG 69. Turnhout, 2011.
———. *Opuscula*. PG 91, 362–649.
———. *Questions to Thalassius*. Ed. C. Laga and C. Steel, *Maximi Confessoris Quaestiones ad Thalassium*. 2 vols. CCSG 7, 22. Turnhout, 1980–90.
———. *Scholia on Pseudo-Dionysius's "On Mystical Theology."* PG 4, 416–32.
———. *Scholia on Pseudo-Dionysius's "On the Divine Names."* PG 4, 185–416.
———. *Second Letter to Thomas*. Ed. B. Janssens in *Maximi Confessoris Ambigua ad Thomam una cum Epistula Secunda ad eundem*, CCSG 48, 37–49. Turnhout, 2002.
Michael the Syrian. *Chronicle*. Ed. J.-B. Chabot. 4 vols. Paris, 1899–1910.
*Miracles of Anastasius the Persian*. Ed. B. Flusin in *Saint Anastase le Perse et l'histoire de la Palestine au début du VIIe siècle*, vol. 1, 117–53. Paris, 1992.
*Miracles of Artemius*. Ed. V. S. Crisafulli and J. W. Nesbitt, *The Miracles of St. Artemios: A Collection of Miracle Stories by an Anonymous Author of Seventh-Century Byzantium*. Leiden, 1997.
*Miracles of Cosmas and Damian*. Ed. L. Deubner, *Kosmas und Damian: Text und Einleitung*. Leipzig, 1907.
*Miracles of Thecla*. Ed. and trans. G. Dagron, *Vie et miracles de Ste. Thècle*. SH 62. Brussels, 1978.
*Miracles of Therapon*. Ed. L. Deubner in *De incubatione capita quattuor*, 120–34. Leipzig, 1900.
Movsēs Daskhurants'i. *History of Albania*. Ed. V. Arak'elyan, *Patmut'iwn Ałuanits' Ashkharhi* (Erevan, 1983). Trans. C. J. F. Dowsett, *The History of the Caucasian Albanians by Movses Dasxuranc'i* (London, 1961).
*Narration of Abbots John and Sophronius*. Ed. A. Longo, "Il testo integrale della *Narrazione degli abati Giovanni e Sofronio* attraverso le Hermêneiai di Nicone," *RSBN* 12–13 (1965–66) 223–67.
*Narration of Sophronius, Patriarch of Jerusalem, concerning Those Who Do Not Recite the Ecclesiastical Office*. Ed. S. Heid, "Eine erbauliche Erzählung des Sophronios von Jerusalem (BHG 1641b) über der kirchliche Binde- und Lösegewalt über Verstorbene," in W. Blumer et al., eds., *Alvarium: Festschrift für Christian Gnilka*, 151–72. Münster, 2002.
*Narration on Armenian Affairs*. Ed. G. Garitte, *La Narratio de rebus Armeniae*. CSCO 132, Subsidia 4. Louvain, 1952.
Nicephorus. *Chronography*. Ed. C. de Boor in *Nicephori Archiepiscopi Constantinopolitani opuscula historica*, 81–135. Leipzig, 1880.

———. *Short History.* Ed. C. Mango, *Nikephoros, Patriarch of Constantinople: Short History.* Washington, D.C., 1990.
Nicephorus Callistus. *Ecclesiastical History.* PG 147, 9–448.
*Pact of Union.* Ed. R. Riedinger in *Acts of the Sixth Ecumenical Council* [q.v.], 594–600. [Reprint: Allen (2009) 168–72.]
*Palestinian-Georgian Liturgical Calendar.* Ed. G. Garitte, *Le calendrier palestino-géorgien de Sinaiticus 34 (X$^e$ siècle).* Brussels, 1958.
Palladius. *Lausiac History.* Ed. C. Butler, *The Lausiac History of Palladius.* 2 vols. Cambridge, 1903–4.
*Paschal Chronicle.* Ed. L. Dindorf, *Chronicon Paschale.* Bonn, 1832.
*Passion of the Sixty Martyrs of Gaza.* Ed. H. Delehaye, "Passio sanctorum sexaginta martyrum," *AB* 23 (1904) 289–307.
Paul of Aegina. Ed. I. L. Heiberg, *Paulus Aegineta.* 2 vols. Leipzig, 1921–24.
Paul the Deacon. *History of the Lombards.* Ed. L. Capo, *Paolo Diacono: Storia dei Longobardi.* Verona, 1992.
Paulus Evergetinus. *Synagōgē.* Συναγωγὴ τῶν θεοφθόγγων ῥημάτων καὶ διδασκαλιῶν τῶν θεοφόρων καὶ ἁγίων πατέρων. Venice, 1783.
Philoxenus of Mabbug. *Letter to Abraham and Orestes.* Ed. Frothingham (1886) 28–48.
Photius. *Bibliotheca.* Ed. R. Henry, *Photius: Bibliothèque.* 8 vols. Paris, 1959–77.
Piacenza Pilgrim. *Itinerary.* Ed. P. Geyer, *Antonini Placentini Itinerarium,* in P. Geyer et al., eds., *Itineraria et alia geographica,* CCSL 175, 129–74. Turnhout, 1965.
Pope Gelasius. *Letters.* Ed. A. Thiel in *Epistolae Romanorum pontificum genuinae et quae ad eos scriptae sunt,* vol. 1, 287–510. Braunsberg, 1867–68.
———. *Tractates.* Ed. A. Thiel in *Epistolae Romanorum pontificum genuinae et quae ad eos scriptae sunt,* vol. 1, 510–607. Braunsberg, 1867–68.
Pope Honorius. *First Letter to Sergius.* Ed. R. Riedinger in *Acts of the Sixth Ecumenical Council* [q.v.], 548–58. [Reprint: Allen (2009) 194–204.]
———. *Letters.* PL 80, 469–82.
———. *Second Letter to Sergius.* Ed. R. Riedinger in *Acts of the Sixth Ecumenical Council* [q.v.], 620–25. [Reprint: Allen (2009) 204–8.]
Pope John IV. *Letter in Defense of Honorius.* PL 80, 602–7 (Latin retrans. from Greek); also trans. Schacht (1936) 235–46 (German trans. from Karshuni).
Pope Leo. *Letters.* PL 54, 593–1218.
Pope Martin. *Letter to Amandus.* Ed. R. Riedinger in *Acts of the Lateran Council* [q.v.], 422–44.
———. *Letter to Antony, Bishop of Bacatha.* PL 87, 165–68.
———. *Letter to Constans.* PL 87, 137–46.
———. *Letter to George, Archimandrite of the Monastery of Saint Theodosius.* PL 87, 167–68.
———. *Letter to John of Philadelphia.* PL 87, 153–64.
———. *Letter to Pantaleon.* PL 87, 169–74.
———. *Letter to Peter the Illustris.* PL 87, 173–76.
———. *Letter to the Churches of Jerusalem and Antioch.* PL 87, 175–80.
———. *Letter to the Church of Carthage.* PL 87, 145–54.
———. *Letter to Theodore, Bishop of Esbus.* PL 87, 163–66.

Pope Theodore. *Letter to Constans II.* Trans. Schacht (1936) 246–49 (German trans. from Karshuni); also Latin trans. A. Mai in *Noua Patrum bibliotheca*, vol. 6 (Rome, 1954), 510–11.

———. *Letter to Paul of Constantinople. PL* 87, 75–80.

———. *Letter to the Bishops Who Consecrated Paul Patriarch of Constantinople in Place of Pyrrhus, Ex-Patriarch. PL* 87, 81–82.

*Prologue to the Spiritual Meadow.* Ed. H. Usener in *Der heilige Tychon*, 91–93. Leipzig, 1907.

Pseudo–Abū Ṣāliḥ. *See* Abū Ṣāliḥ.

Pseudo-Dionysius. *Celestial Hierarchy.* Ed. G. Heil in G. Heil and A. M. Ritter, eds., *Corpus Dionysiacum*, vol. 2, 7–59. Berlin, 1991.

———. *Ecclesiastical Hierarchy.* Ed. G. Heil in G. Heil and A. M. Ritter, eds., *Corpus Dionysiacum*, vol. 2, 63–132. Berlin, 1991.

———. *Letters.* Ed. A. M. Ritter in G. Heil and A. M. Ritter, eds., *Corpus Dionysiacum*, vol. 2, 155–210. Berlin, 1991.

Pseudo-Macarius, *Collection I.* Ed. H. Berthold, *Reden und Briefe des Makarios/Symeon: Die Sammlung I. des Vaticanus graecus 694 (B).* 2 vols. Berlin, 1973.

Pseudo-Methodius. *Apocalypse.* Ed. G. J. Reinink, *Die syrische Apokalypse des Pseudo-Methodius.* Louvain, 1993.

Pseudo-Sebēos, *History.* Ed. G. Abgaryan, *Patmut'iwn Sebēosi* (Erevan, 1979). Trans. R. Thomson in R. Thomson and J. Howard-Johnston, eds., *The Armenian History Attributed to Sebeos*, vol. 1 (Liverpool, 1999).

Pseudo-Shapuh. *History of the Anonymous Storyteller.* Ed. M. H. Darbinjan-Melikjan, *Patmut'iwn Ananun Zruts'agri.* Erevan, 1971.

Pseudo-Zachariah of Mytilene. *Chronicle.* Ed. F. J. Hamilton and E. W. Brooks, *The Syriac Chronicle Known as That of Zachariah of Mitylene.* London, 1899.

*Record of the Trial.* In P. Allen and B. Neil, eds. and trans., *Scripta saeculi VII vitam Maximi Confessoris illustrantia*, CCSG 39, 14-51. Turnhout, 1999. [Reprint: Allen and Neil (2002) 48-74.]

*Regulations of Horsiesius.* Ed. L.-T. Lefort in *Œuvres de saint Pachôme et ses disciples*, CSCO 160, 82–99. Louvain, 1956.

*Return of the Relics of Anastasius the Persian.* Ed. B. Flusin in *Saint Anastase le Perse et l'histoire de la Palestine au début du VII$^e$ siècle*, vol. 1, 99–107. Paris, 1992.

Rufinus. *Ecclesiastical History.* Ed. E. Schwartz and T. Mommsen, *Eusebius, Werke: Die Kirchengeschichte.* 3 vols. GCS 9.1-3. Berlin, 1903-9. [2nd ed. F. Winkelmann. GCS, n.F., 6.1-3. 3 vols. Berlin, 1999.]

*Rules of Saint Pachomius.* Ed. A. Boon in *Pachomiana Latina: Règle et épîtres de saint Pachôme épître de saint Théodore et "Liber" de saint Orsiesius*, 11–52. Louvain, 1932.

Sebēos. *History of Heraclius.* Fragments 1 and 2. Ed. G. Abgaryan in *Patmut'iwn Sebēosi*, 429-33. Erevan, 1979.

Sergius of Constantinople. *First Letter to Cyrus.* Ed. R. Riedinger in *Acts of the Sixth Ecumenical Council* [*q.v.*], 528–30. [Reprint: Allen (2009) 162–66.]

———. *First Letter to Honorius.* Ed. R. Riedinger in *Acts of the Sixth Ecumenical Council* [*q.v.*], 534–46. [Reprint: Allen (2009) 182–94.]

———. *Second Letter to Cyrus.* Ed. R. Riedinger in *Acts of the Sixth Ecumenical Council* [*q.v.*], 592–94. [Reprint: Allen (2009) 174–76.]

Sergius of Resh'aina. *On the Spiritual Life.* Ed. P. Sherwood, "Mimro de Serge de Rešayna sur la vie spirituelle," part 1, *OrSyr* 5 (1960) 433-57; part 2, *OrSyr* 6 (1961) 95-115, 121-56.

Severus of Antioch. *Against the Additions of Julian.* Ed. R. Hespel, *Sévère d'Antioche: La polémique antijulianiste*, II A. CSCO 295, SS 124. Louvain, 1968.

———. *Against the Apology of Julian.* Ed. R. Hespel, *Sévère d'Antioche: La polémique antijulianiste*, II B. CSCO 301, SS 126. Louvain, 1969.

———. *Against the Impious Grammarian.* Ed. J. Lebon, *Severi Antiocheni Liber contra impium grammaticum.* 3 vols. CSCO 93, 101, 112, SS 45, 50, 59. Louvain, 1929-38.

———. *First Letter to Sergius.* Ed. J. Lebon in *Severi Antiocheni Orationes ad Nephalium, eiusdem ac Sergii Grammatici epistulae mutuae*, CSCO 119, SS 64, 73-96, 103-44, 157-77. Louvain, 1949.

———. *Letters.* Ed. E. W. Brooks, *A Collection of Letters of Severus of Antioch from Numerous Syriac Manuscripts.* 2 vols. PO 12.2, 14.1. Paris, 1919-20.

———. *Select Letters.* Ed. E. W. Brooks, *The Sixth Book of the Select Letters of Severus Patriarch of Antioch.* Vol. 1. London, 1902.

———. *Sermon on the Nativity.* Ed. and trans. M. Brière and F. Graffin in *Sancti Philoxeni episcopi Mabbugensis dissertationes*, PO 38.3, 300-302. Turnhout, 1977.

Sophronius. *Anacreontics.* Ed. M. Gigante, *Sophronii Anacreontica.* Rome, 1957.

———. *Epigrams.* PG 87:3, 3421-24.

———. *Letter to Arcadius of Cyprus.* Ed. and trans. M. Albert and C. von Schönborn, *La lettre de Sophrone de Jérusalem à Arcadius de Chypre.* PO 39.2. Turnhout, 1978.

———. *Miracles of Cyrus and John.* Ed. N. F. Marcos, *Los "Thaumata" de Sofronio: Contribución al estudio de la "Incubatio" cristiana* (Madrid, 1975). Trans. J. Gascou, *Sophrone de Jérusalem: Miracles des Saints Cyr et Jean (BHG 477-79).* Paris, 2006.

———. *On John the Baptist.* PG 87:3, 3321-53.

———. *On Saints Peter and Paul.* PG 87:3, 3356-64.

———. *On the Annunciation.* PG 87:3, 3217-83.

———. *On the Capture of Jerusalem.* Ed. M. Gigante in *Sophronii Anacreontica*, 102-7. Rome, 1957.

———. *On the Circumcision.* Ed. John Duffy, "New Fragments of Sophronius of Jerusalem and Aristo of Pella?" in D. Bumazhnov et al., eds., *Bibel, Byzanz und christlicher Orient: Festschrift für Stephen Gerö zum 65. Geburtstag*, Orientalia Lovaniensia Analecta 187, 15-28. Louvain, 2011.

———. *On the Exaltation of the Cross.* PG 87:3, 3301-9.

———. *On the Holy Cross.* Ed. M. Gigante in *Sophronii Anacreontica*, 114-17. Rome, 1957.

———. *On the Hypapante.* Ed. H. Usener, *De praesentatione Domini sermo.* Bonn, 1889.

———. *On the Nativity.* Ed. H. Usener, "Weihnachtspredigt des Sophronios," *Rheinisches Museum für Philologie* 41 (1886) 500-516.

———. *On the Theophany.* Ed. A. Papadopoulos-Kerameus in *Analekta Ierosolumitikēs stachuologias*, vol. 5, 151-68. Petroupolis, 1897. [Reprint: 5 vols. Brussels, 1963.]

———. *Prologue to the Miracles of Saints Cyrus and John.* Ed. P. Bringel, *Sophrone de Jérusalem: Panégyrique des saints Cyr et Jean.* PO 51.1. Turnhout, 2008.

———. *Synodical Letter.* Ed. R. Riedinger in *Acts of the Sixth Ecumenical Council* [q.v.], 410-94. Berlin, 1990. [Reprint: Allen (2009) 66-156.]

Sozomen. *Ecclesiastical History.* Ed. J. Bidez and G.C. Hansen, *Sozomenus: Kirchengeschichte.* Berlin, 1995.

Stephen bar Sudaili. *Book of the Holy Hierotheos.* Ed. and trans. F.S. Marsh, *The Book Which Is Called the Holy Hierotheos, with Extracts from the Prolegomena and Commentary of Theodosius of Antioch and from the "Book of Excerpts" of Gregory bar-Hebraeus.* London, 1927.

Strategius. *On the Fall of Jerusalem.* [Georgian] Ed. G. Garitte, *La prise de Jérusalem par les Perses en 614.* 2 vols. CSCO 202, 203, SI 11, 12 (Louvain, 1960). [Arabic] Ed. G. Garitte, *Expugnationis Hierosolymae, A.D. 614, Recensiones Arabicae.* 4 vols. CSCO 340, 341, 347, 348; SA 26–29 (Louvain, 1973–74).

*Synodicon Vetus.* Ed. J. Duffy and J. Parker. Washington, D.C. 1979.

*Syriac Life of Symeon Stylites.* Ed. P. Bedjan in *Acta martyrum et sanctorum,* vol. 4, 507–64 (Paris, 1984). Trans. R. Doran in *The Lives of Symeon Stylites,* 103–98 (Kalamazoo, 1989).

Ṭabarī. *Annals.* Ed. M.J. de Goeje et al., *Annales quos scripsit Abu Djafar Mohammed ibn Djarir at-Tabari.* 15 vols. Leiden, 1879–1901.

Thalassius the Libyan. *Centuries on Charity. PG* 91, 1428A–1469C.

Theodore of Canterbury. *Iudicia.* Ed. P.W. Finsterwalder, *Die Canones Theodori Cantuariensis und ihre Überlieferungsformen.* Weimar, 1929.

Theodore of Paphos. *Life of Spyridon.* Ed. P. van den Ven, *La légende de saint Spyridon, évêque de Trimithonte.* Bibliothèque de Muséon 33. Louvain, 1953.

Theodore of Petra. *Life of Theodosius.* Ed. H. Usener in *Der heilige Theodosios: Schriften des Theodoros und Kyrillos,* 1–101. Leipzig, 1890.

Theodore of Raithou. *Preparation.* Ed. F. Diekamp in *Analecta patristica,* 173–227. Rome, 1938.

Theodore of Scythopolis. *Libellus on the Errors of Origen. PG* 86, 231B–236B.

Theodore Spudaeus. *Hypomnesticum (Greek).* In P. Allen and B. Neil, eds., *Scripta saeculi VII vitam Maximi Confessoris illustrantia,* CCSG 39, 197–227. Turnhout, 1999. [Reprint: Allen and Neil (2002) 148–70.]

———. *Hypomnesticum (Latin).* Ed. B. Neil in *Seventh-Century Popes and Martyrs: The Political Hagiography of Anastasius Bibliothecarius,* Series Antiqua Australiensia, 234–64. Turnhout, 2006.

———. *Narrations concerning the Exile of the Holy Pope Martin.* Ed. B. Neil in *Seventh-Century Popes and Martyrs: The Political Hagiography of Anastasius Bibliothecarius,* Series Antiqua Australiensia, 166–232. Turnhout, 2006.

Theodore Syncellus. *On the Siege of Constantinople.* Ed. L. Sternbach, *Analecta Avarica,* 298–320. Krakow, 1900. [Reprint: F. Makk, *Traduction et commentaire de l'homélie écrite probablement par Théodore le Syncelle sur le siège de Constantinople en 626.* Szeged, 1975.]

———. *On the Virgin's Robe.* Ed. F. Combefis in *Novum actuarium,* vol. 2, 751–86. Paris, 1648.

Theodoret. *Compendium of Heretical Doctrines. PG* 83, 336–556.

———. *Ecclesiastical History.* Ed. L. Parmentier, *Theodoret: Kirchengeschichte.* Berlin, 1954. [2nd ed. G.C. Hansen. Berlin, 1998.]

———. *Religious History.* Ed. P. Canivet and A. Leroy-Molinghen, *Théodoret de Cyr: L'histoire des moines de Syrie.* SC 234. Paris, 1977.

Theodorus Lector. *Tripartite History.* Ed. G.C. Hansen, *Theodoros Anagnostes: Kirchengeschichte.* Berlin 1995.

Theodosius. *On the Topography of the Holy Land*. Ed. P. Geyer in *Itineraria et alia geographica*, CCSL 175, 115–25. Turnhout, 1965.
Theophanes. *Chronicle*. Ed. C. de Boor, *Theophanis Chronographia*. Leipzig, 1883.
Theophylact Simocatta. *History*. Ed. C. de Boor and P. Wirth, *Theophylacti Simocattae historiae*. Stuttgart, 1972.
Thomas Artsruni. *History of the House of the Artsrunik'*. Ed. K. Patkanean. St. Petersburg, 1887. [Reprint: *Thomas Artsruni, History of the House of Artsrunik': A Facsimile Reproduction with an Introduction by Robert W. Thomson*. Delmar, N.Y., 1991.]
Thomas of Marga. *Book of Governors*. Ed. E. A. Wallis Budge, *The Book of Governors: The "Historia Monachorum" of Thomas, Bishop of Margâ, A.D. 840*. Vol. 1. London, 1883.
*Translation of the Relics of Anastasius the Persian*. Ed. B. Flusin in *Saint Anastase le Perse et l'histoire de la Palestine au début du VII<sup>e</sup> siècle*, vol. 1, 99–107. Paris, 1992.
*Trophies of Damascus*. Ed. G. Bardy, "Les trophées de Damas: Controverse judéo-chrétienne du VII<sup>e</sup> siècle," PO 15, 169–291. Paris, 1927.
Zachariah. *Letter to the Jerusalemites*. PG 86, 3228–33.
Zonaras. *Epitome of Histories*. Ed. L. Dindorf, *Ioannis Zonarae Epitome Historiarum*. 6 vols. Leipzig, 1868–75.

### SECONDARY SOURCES

Abicht, R., and H. Schmidt. 1896. "Quelle achweise zum Codex Suprasliensis." *Archiv für Slavische Papyrologie* 18: 138–55.
Abuladze, I. 1960. *Ioane Moshi, Limonari: Tek'sti gamokvlevit'a da lek'sikonit' gamosc'a*. Tiflis.
Agosti, G. 2011. "Le brume di Omero: Sofronio dinanzi alla *paideia* classica." In L. Cristante and S. Ravalico, eds., *Il calamo della memoria: Riuso di testi e mestiere letterario nella tarda antichità*, vol. 4, 33–50. Trieste.
Albert, M., and C. von Schönborn, eds. 1978. *La lettre de Sophrone de Jérusalem à Arcadius de Chypre*. PO 39.2. Turnhout.
Aldama, J. A. de. 1962. "El canon terciero del concilio lateranense de 649." *Marianum* 24: 65–83.
Alexakis, A. 1995–96. "Before the Lateran Council of 649: The Last Days of Herakleios the Emperor and Monotheletism." In R. Bäumer et al., eds., *Synodus: Beiträge zur Konzilien- und allgemeinen Kirchengeschichte—Festschrift für Walter Brandmüller*, Annuarium Historiae Conciliorum 27–28, 93–101.
Alexander, P. J. 1985. *The Byzantine Apocalyptic Tradition*. Berkeley and Los Angeles.
Allen, P. 1985. "Blue-print for the Edition of Documenta ad Vitam Maximi Confessoris Spectantia." In C. Laga, J. Munitiz, and L. van Rompay, eds., *After Chalcedon: Studies in Theology and Church History*, Orientalia Lovanensia Analecta 18, 11–21. Louvain.
———. 2007. "The Greek Homiletic Tradition of the Feast of the Hypapante: The Place of Sophronios of Jerusalem." In K. Belke et al., eds., *Byzantina Mediterranea: Festschrift für Johannes Koder zum 65. Geburtstag*, 1–12. Vienna.
———. 2009. *Sophronius of Jerusalem and Seventh-Century Heresy: The Synodical Letter and Other Documents: Introduction, Texts, Translations and Commentary*. Oxford.
Allen, P., and B. Neil, eds. 2002. *Maximus the Confessor and His Companions: Documents from Exile*. Oxford.

Al-Tel, O. I. 2003. *The First Islamic Conquest of Aelia (Islamic Jerusalem): A Critical Analytical Study of the Early Islamic Historical Narratives and Sources.* Dundee.

Altheim-Stiehl, R. 1992a. "The Sasanians in Egypt: Some Evidence of Historical Interest." *Bulletin de la Société d'Archéologie Copte* 31: 87–96.

———. 1992b. "Wurde Alexandreia im Juni 619 n. Chr. durch die Perser erobert? Bemerkungen zur zeitlichen Bestimmung der sāsānidischen Besetzung Ägyptens unter Chosrau II. Parwēz." *Tyche* 6: 3–16.

———. 1992c. "Zur zeitlichen Bestimmung der sasanidischen Eroberung Ägyptens: Ein neuer terminus ante quem für Oxyrhynchos ist nachzutragen." In O. Brehm and S. Klie, eds., Μουσικὸς ἀνήρ· *Festschrift für Max Wegner zum 90. Geburtstag*, 5–8. Bonn.

Alwis, A. 2012. "Men in Pain: Masculinity, Medicine and the *Miracles* of St. Artemios." *BMGS* 36: 1–19.

Amundsen, D. W. 1982. "Medicine and Faith in Early Christianity." *Bulletin of the History of Medicine* 56: 326–50.

Argárate, P. 2003. "Maximus Confessor's Refutation of Origenism." In L. Perrone et al., eds., *Origeniana octava: Origen and the Alexandrian Tradition*, 1037–41. Louvain.

Arras, V., ed. 1967. *Patericon Aethiopice.* Vol. 2. CSCO 278, SAe 54. Louvain.

Arthur, R. A. 2001. "A Sixth-Century Origenist: Stephen bar Sudhaili and His Relationship with Ps.-Dionysius." *SP* 35: 369–73.

———. 2008. *Pseudo-Dionysius as Polemicist: The Development and Purpose of the Angelic Hierarchy in Sixth-Century Syria.* Aldershot.

Athanassiadi, P. 2010. *Vers la pensée unique: La montée de l'intolérance dans l'antiquité tardive.* Paris.

Auzépy, M.-F. 1994. "De la Palestine à Constantinople: Étienne le Sabaïte et Jean Damascène." In T&MByz 12, 183–218. Paris.

Avi-Yonah, M. 1954. *The Madiba Mosaic Map, with Introduction and Commentary.* Jerusalem.

Avni, G. 2010. "The Persian Conquest of Jerusalem (614 C.E.): An Archaeological Assessment." *BASOR* 357: 35–48.

Baars, W. 1968. *New Syro-Hexaplaric Texts.* Leiden.

Baguenard, J.-M. 1988. *Les moines Acémètes: Vies des saints Alexandre, Marcel et Jean Calybite.* Maine-et-Loire.

Bathrellos, D. 2001. "The Relationship between the Divine Will and the Human Will of Jesus Christ according to Saint Maximus the Confessor." *SP* 37: 346–52.

———. 2004. *The Byzantine Christ: Person, Nature and Will in the Christology of Maximus the Confessor.* Oxford.

Bäumer, R. 1961. "Die Wiederentdeckung der Honoriusfrage im Abendland." *RQ* 56 (1961) 200–214.

Bausenhart, G. 1992. *"In allem uns gleich außer der Sünde": Studien zum Beitrag Maximos' des Bekenners zu altkirchlichen Christologie.* Mainz.

Baynes, N. H. 1947. "The *Pratum Spirituale.*" *OCP* 13: 404–14. [Reprint: idem, *Byzantine Studies and Other Essays*, 261–70. London, 1955.]

Beihammer, A. D. 2000. *Quellenkritische Untersuchungen zu den ägyptischen Kapitulationsverträgen der Jahre 640–646.* Vienna.

———. 2004. "The First Naval Campaigns of the Arabs against Cyprus (649, 653): A Reexamination of the Oriental Source Material." In G. K. Livadas, ed., *Festschrift in Honour of V. Christides*, Graeco-Arabica 9–10, 47–68. Athens.
Ben-Ami, D., and Y. Tchekhanovets. 2008. "A Hoard of Golden Coins from the Givati Parking Lot and Its Importance to the Study of Jerusalem in the Late Byzantine Period." In E. Meyron, ed., *City of David: Studies of Ancient Jerusalem, the Tenth Annual Conference*, 35*–44*. Jerusalem.
Ben-Ami, D., Y. Tchekhanovets, and G. Bijovsky. 2010. "New Archaeological and Numismatic Evidence for the Persian Destruction of Jerusalem in 614 CE." *IEJ* 60: 204–21.
Benevitch, G. 2009. "Maximus the Confessor's Polemics against Anti-Origenism: *Epistulae* 6 and 7 as a Context for the *Ambigua ad Iohannem*." *RHE* 104: 5–15.
Berthold, G. C. 2011. "Free Will as a Partner of Nature: Maximus the Confessor on the *Our Father*." *SP* 51: 173–79.
Bertolini, O. 1952. "Il patrizio Isacio, esarca d'Italia." In *Atti del secondo Congresso Internazionale di studi sull'alto medioevo, Grado, Aquileia, Gorizia, Cividale, Udine, 7–11 settembre 1952*, 117–20. Spoleto.
Beshevliev, V. 1978. "Zur Chronik des Johannes von Nikiu CXX 46–49." *Byzantinobulgarica* 5: 229–36.
Bijovsky, G. 2010. "A Single-Die Hoard of Heraclius from Jerusalem." In *Mélanges Cécile Morrisson*, T&MByz 16, 55–92. Paris.
Binggeli, A. 2009. "Les stylites et l'eucharistie." In N. Bériou et al., eds., *Pratiques de l'eucharistie dans les églises d'Orient et d'Occident (Antiquité et Moyen Âge)*, vol. 1, *L'institution*, 421–44. Paris.
Binns, J. 1994. *Ascetics and Ambassadors of Christ: The Monasteries of Palestine, 314–631*. Oxford.
Bischoff, B., and M. Lapidge, eds. 1994. *Biblical Commentaries from the Canterbury School of Theodore and Hadrian*. Cambridge.
Bitton-Ashkelony, B., and A. Kofsky. 2000. "Gazan Monasticism in the Fourth–Sixth Centuries: From Anchoritic to Cenobitic." *Proche-Orient Chrétien* 50: 14–62.
———, eds. 2004. *Christian Gaza in Late Antiquity*. Leiden.
———. 2006. *The Monastic School of Gaza*. Leiden.
Blaudeau, P. 2006. *Alexandrie et Constantinople (451–491): De l'histoire à la géo-ecclésiologie*. Rome.
Blowers, P. M. 1995. *Exegesis and Spiritual Pedagogy in Maximus the Confessor*. Notre Dame.
Booth, P. 2009. "Saints and Soteriology in Sophronius Sophista's *Miracles of Cyrus and John*." In T. Claydon and P. Clarke, eds., *The Church, the Afterlife and the Fate of the Soul*, Studies in Church History 45, 52–63. Woodbridge, Suffolk.
———. 2011a. "Orthodox and Heretic in the Early Byzantine Cult(s) of Saints Cosmas and Damian." In P. Sarris, M. Dal Santo, and P. Booth, eds., *An Age of Saints? Power, Conflict and Dissent in Early Medieval Christianity*, 114–28. Leiden.
———. 2011b. "Shades of Blues and Greens in the *Chronicle* of John of Nikiou." *BZ* 104: 555–601.
———. 2013a. "Gregory and the Greek East." In M. Dal Santo and B. Neil, eds., *Brill Handbook of Gregory the Great*. Leiden.

———. 2013b. "The Muslim Conquest of Egypt Reconsidered." In *Le septième siècle*, T&MByz 17, 1–32. Paris.

Borkowski, Z. 1981. *Inscriptions des factions à Alexandrie*. Warsaw.

Bornert, R. 1966. *Les commentaires byzantins de la divine liturgie du VII<sup>e</sup> au XV<sup>e</sup> siècle*. Paris.

Bosworth, C. E. 1996. "Arab Attacks on Rhodes in the Pre-Ottoman Period." *JAS*, ser. 3, 6: 157–64.

Boudignon, C. 2002. "Maxime le Confesseur et ses maîtres: À propos du 'bienheureux ancien' de la *Mystagogie*." In G. Filoramo, ed., *Maestro e discepolo: Temi e problemi della direzione spirituale tra VI secolo a.C. e VII secolo d.C.*, 326–30. Brescia.

———. 2004. "Maxime le Confesseur: Était-il constantinopolitain?" In B. Janssens, B. Rosen, and P. Van Deun, eds., *Philomathestatos: Studies in Greek Patristic and Byzantine Texts Presented to Jacques Noret*, 11–43. Louvain.

———. 2007. "Le pouvoir de l'anathème; ou, Maxime le Confesseur et les moines palestiniens du VII<sup>e</sup> siècle." In A. Camplani and G. Filoramo, eds., *Foundations of Power and Conflicts of Authority in Late-Antique Monasticism: Proceedings of the International Seminar, Turin, December 2–4, 2004*, 245–74. Louvain.

Bousset, W. 1923. *Apophthegmata: Studien zur Geschichte des ältesten Mönchtums*. Tübingen.

Bowersock, G. 2009. "Old and New Rome in the Late Antique Near East." In P. Rousseau and M. Papoutsakis, eds., *Transformations of Late Antiquity: Essays for Peter Brown*, 37–49. Farnham, Surrey.

———. 2012. *Empires in Collision in Late Antiquity*. Waltham, Mass.

Brakke, D. 1995. *Athanasius and the Politics of Asceticism*. Oxford.

Brandes, W. 1998a. "Apergios von Perge: Ein Phantomhäretiker." *JÖByz* 48: 35–40.

———. 1998b. "'Juristische' Krisenbewältigung im 7. Jahrhundert? Die Prozesse gegen Martin I. und Maximos Homologetes." *Fontes Minores* 10: 141–212.

———. 1998c. "Die melkitischen Patriarchen von Antiocheia im 7. Jahrhundert: Anzahl und Chronologie." *Le Muséon* 111: 37–58.

———. 2001. "Konstantin der Große in den monotheletischen Streitigkeiten des 7. Jahrhunderts." In E. Kuntura-Galaki, ed., *The Dark Centuries of Byzantium (7th–9th c.)*, 89–107. Athens.

———. 2003. "Orthodoxy and Heresy in the Seventh Century: Prosopographical Observations on Monotheletism." In Averil Cameron, ed., *Fifty Years of Prosopography: The Later Roman Empire, Byzantium and Beyond*, 103–18. Oxford.

Brock, S. 1973. "An Early Syriac Life of Maximus the Confessor." *AB* 91: 299–346.

———. 1981. "The Conversations with the Syrian Orthodox under Justinian." *OCP* 47: 87–121. [Reprint: Brock (1992) XIII.]

———. 1985. "A Monothelete Florilegium in Syriac." In C. Laga et al., eds. *After Chalcedon: Studies in Theology and Church History Offered to Professor Albert van Roey for His Seventieth Birthday*, 35–45. Louvain. [Reprint: Brock (1992) XIV.]

———. 1986. "Two Sets of Monothelete Questions to the Maximianists." *OLP* 17: 119–40. [Reprint: Brock (1992) XV.]

———. 1992. *Studies in Syriac Christianity: History, Literature and Theology*. Aldershot.

Brooks, E. W. 1897. "On the Lists of Patriarchs of Constantinople from 638–715." *BZ* 6: 33–54.

———. 1898. "The Arabs in Asia Minor (641–750), from Arabic Sources." *JHS* 18: 182–208.

Brown, P. 1971. "The Rise and Function of the Holy Man in Late Antiquity." *JRS* 61: 80–101.
———. 1976. "Eastern and Western Christendom in Late Antiquity: A Parting of the Ways." In D. Baker, ed., *The Orthodox Churches and the West*, Studies in Church History 13, 1–24. Oxford.
———. 1981. *The Cult of the Saints: Its Rise and Function in Latin Christianity*. Chicago.
———. 1988. *The Body and Society: Men, Women and Sexual Renunciation in Early Christianity*. New York.
Brown, T. S. 1984. *Gentlemen and Officers: Imperial Administration and Aristocratic Power in Byzantine Italy, A.D. 554–800*. Rome
Browning, R. 1983. "The 'Low Level' Saint's Life in the Early Byzantine Period." In S. Hackel, ed., *The Byzantine Saint*, 117–27. London.
Brubaker, L. 1998. "Icons before Iconoclasm?" In O. Capitani, ed., *Morfologie sociali e culturali in Europa fra tarda antichità e alto medioevo*, Settimane di Studio del Centro Italiano di Studi sull'Alto Medioevo 45.1, 1215–54. Spoleto.
Bunge, G. 1989. "Hénade ou monade? Au sujet de deux notions centrales de la terminologie évagrienne." *Le Muséon* 102: 69–91.
Bunge, G., and A. de Vogüé. 1994. *Quatre ermites égyptiens: D'après les fragments coptes de l'Histoire Lausiaque*. Bégrolles-en-Mauges.
Burrus, V. 1995. *The Making of a Heretic: Gender, Authority and the Priscillianist Controversy*. Berkeley and Los Angeles.
Busse, H. 1984. "Omar b. al-Ḫaṭṭāb in Jerusalem." *JSAI* 5: 73–119.
———. 1986. "Omar's Image as the Conqueror of Jerusalem." *JSAI* 8: 149–68.
Butler, A. J. 1902. *The Arab Conquest of Egypt and the Last Thirty Years of the Roman Dominion*. Oxford.
Caetani, L. 1905–26. *Annali dell'Islam*. 10 vols. Milan.
———. 1912–23. *Chronographia Islamica*. 3 vols. Paris and Rome.
Callam, D. 1996. "Early Monasticism and Ps.-Denys." In P. Allen and E. Jeffreys, eds., *The Sixth Century: End or Beginning?* Byzantina Australiensia 10, 112–17. Brisbane.
Cameron, Alan. 1976. *Circus Factions: Blues and Greens at Rome and Byzantium*. Oxford.
———. 1983. "The Epigrams of Sophronius." *CQ*, n.s., 33: 284–92.
———. 2007. "Poets and Pagans in Byzantine Egypt." In R. S. Bagnall, ed., *Egypt in the Byzantine World, 300–700*, 21–46. Cambridge.
Cameron, Averil. 1978. "The Theotokos in Sixth-Century Constantinople: A City Finds Its Symbol." *JThS*, n.s., 29: 79–108. [Reprint: eadem (1981) XVI.]
———. 1979a. "Images of Authority: Elites and Icons in Late Sixth-Century Byzantium." *P&P* 84: 3–35. [Reprint: eadem (1981) XVIII.]
———. 1979b. "The Virgin's Robe: An Episode in the History of Early Seventh-Century Constantinople." *Byzantion* 49: 42–56. [Reprint: eadem (1981) XVII.]
———. 1981. *Continuity and Change in Sixth-Century Byzantium*. London.
———. 1982. "Byzantine Africa: The Literary Evidence." In J. H. Humphrey, ed., *Excavations at Carthage 1978*, 1–51. Ann Arbor. [Reprint: Averil Cameron (1996) VII.]
———. 1991. "The Eastern Provinces in the Seventh Century AD: Hellenism and the Emergence of Islam." In S. Said, ed., *"Hellenismos": Quelques jalons pour une histoire de l'identité grecque, Actes du Colloque de Strasbourg, 25–27 octobre 1989*, 287–313. Leiden. [Reprint: Averil Cameron (1996) IV.]

———. 1992a. "Byzantium and the Past in the Seventh Century: The Search for Redefinition." In J. Fontaine and J. N. Hillgarth, eds., *The Seventh Century: Change and Continuity*, 250–76. London. [Reprint: Averil Cameron (1996) V.]

———. 1992b. "Cyprus at the Time of the Arab Conquests." *Cyprus Historical Review* 1: 27–49. [Reprint: eadem (1996) VI.]

———. 1992c. "The Language of Images: The Rise of Icons and Christian Representation." In D. Wood, ed., *The Church and the Arts*, Studies in Church History 28, 1–42. Oxford. [Reprint: Averil Cameron (1996) XII.]

———. 1992d. "New Themes and Styles in Greek Literature, 7th–8th Centuries." In Averil Cameron and L. Conrad, eds., *The Byzantine and Early Islamic Near East*, vol. 1, *Problems in the Literary Source Material*, Studies in Late Antiquity and Early Islam 1, 81–105. Princeton.

———. 1993. "The Byzantine Reconquest of North Africa and the Impact of Greek Culture." *Graeco-Arabica* 5: 153–65. [Reprint: eadem (1996) X.]

———. 1996. *Changing Cultures in Early Byzantium*. Aldershot.

———. 2002. "Blaming the Jews: The Seventh-Century Invasions of Palestine in Context." In V. Déroche, ed., *Mélanges Gilbert Dagron*, T&MByz 14, 57–78. Paris.

———. 2004. "The Cult of the Virgin in Late Antiquity: Religious Development and Myth-Making." In R. N. Swanson, ed., *The Church and Mary*, Studies in Church History 39, 1–21. Oxford.

Canart, P. 1966. "Trois groupes de récits édifiants byzantins." *Byzantion* 36: 5–25.

Caner, D. 2002. *Wandering, Begging Monks: Spiritual Authority and the Promotion of Monasticism in Late Antiquity*. Berkeley and Los Angeles.

Canivet, P. 1977. *Le monachisme syrien selon Théodoret de Cyr*. Paris.

Carcione, F. 1985a. "Energheia, thelema e theokinetos nella lettera di Sergio, patriarcha di Constantinopoli, a papa Onorio primo." *OCP* 51: 263–76.

———. 1985b. *Sergio di Constantinopoli ad Onorio I nella controversia monotelita del VII secolo*. Rome.

Caseau, B. 2002. "L'abandon de la communion dans le main (IVᵉ–XIIᵉ siècles)." In V. Déroche, ed., *Mélanges Gilbert Dagron*, T&MByz 14, 79–94. Paris.

Caspar, E. 1930–33. *Geschichte des Papsttums von den Anfängen bis zur Höhe der Weltherrschaft*. 2 vols. Tübingen.

———. 1932. "Die Lateransynode von 649." *ZKG* 51: 75–137.

Cerulli, E. 1946. "La 'Conquista persiana di Gerusalemme' ed altre fonti orientali cristiane di un episodio dell''Orlando Furioso.'" *Orientalia*, n.s., 15: 439–81.

———. 1947. "Nuovi testi sulla 'Conquista persiana di Gerusalemme' come fonte di un episodio dell''Orlando Furioso.'" *Orientalia*, n.s., 16: 377–90.

Chadwick, H. 1951. "Eucharist and Christology in the Nestorian Controversy." *JThS*, n.s., 2: 145–64.

———. 1974. "John Moschus and His Friend Sophronius the Sophist." *JThS*, n.s., 25: 41–74.

———. 1995. "Theodore of Tarsus and Monotheletism." In Lapidge (1995a) 88–95.

Charles, R. 1916. *The Chronicle of John, Bishop of Nikiou*. London.

Chesnut, R. C. 1976. *Three Monophysite Christologies: Severus of Antioch, Philoxenus of Mabbug, and Jacob of Serug*. Oxford.

Chiesa, P. 1992. "Le biografie greche e latine di papa Martino I." In *Martino I papa (649–53) e il suo tempo*, 211–41. Spoleto.
Chirban, J. T. 2010. "Understanding the Importance of Epistemologies and Methodologies in Holistic Healing." In idem, ed., *Holistic Healing in Byzantium*. Brookline, Mass., 37–71.
Chitty, D. J. 1966. *The Desert a City: An Introduction to the Study of Egyptian and Palestinian Monasticism under the Christian Empire*. Oxford.
Christides, V. 1984. "The Naval Engagement of Dhāt aṣ-Ṣāwarī, A.H. 34/A.D. 655–6: A Classic Example of Naval Warfare Incompetence." *Byzantina* 13: 1329–45.
Clark, E. A. 1992. *The Origenist Controversy: The Cultural Construction of an Early Christian Debate*. Princeton.
Clugnet, L. 1905. "Vies et récits d'anchorètes, II: Textes grecs inédits." *ROC* 10: 39–56.
Coates-Stephens, R. 2007. "S. Saba and the Xenodochium de via Nova." *RAC* 83: 223–56.
Conrad, L. I. 1992. "The Conquest of Arwad: A Source-Critical Study in the Historiography of the Early Medieval Near East." In Averil Cameron and L. I. Conrad, eds., *The Byzantine and Early Islamic Near East*, vol. 1, *Problems in the Literary Source Material*, Studies in Late Antiquity and Early Islam 1, 317–401. Princeton.
———. 1996. "The Arabs and the Colossus." *JAS* 3.6: 165–87.
Constas, N. 2002. "An Apology for the Cult of the Saints in Late Antiquity: Eustratius Presbyter of Constantinople, *On the State of Souls after Death* (CPG 7522)." *JECS* 10: 267–85.
Conte, P. 1971. *Chiesa e primato nelle lettere dei papi del secolo VII*. Milan.
———. 1977. "Il significato del primato papale nei padri del VI concilio ecumenico." *Archivum Historiae Pontificiae* 15: 7–111.
———. 1989. *Il Sinodo Lateranense dell'ottobre 649: La nuova edizione degli atti, a cura de Rudolf Riedinger*. Vatican City.
Conybeare, F. 1910. "Antiochos Strategos' Account of the Sack of Jerusalem in A.D. 614." *EHR* 25: 502–17.
Cooper, A. G. 2005. *The Body in St Maximus the Confessor: Holy Flesh, Wholly Deified*. Oxford.
Cormack, R. 1985. *Writing in Gold: Byzantine Society and Its Icons*. New York.
Corsi, P. 1988. "La politica italiana di Costante II." In *Bisanzio, Roma e l'Italia nell' alto Medioevo*, Settimane di studio del Centro Italiano di Studi sull'Alto Medioevo 34, 751–96. Spoleto.
Cosentino, S. 1993. "L'iscrizione ravennate dell'esarco Isacio e le guerre di Rotari." In *Atti e Memorie della Deputazione di Storia Patria per le Antiche Province Modenesi* 11.15: 23–43.
———. 2008. "Constans II and the Byzantine Navy." *BZ* 100: 577–603.
Cremascoli, G. 1992. "Le lettere di Martino I." In *Martino I papa (649–653) e il suo tempo*, 243–58. Spoleto.
Crisafulli, V. S., and J. W. Nesbitt, eds. 1997. *The Miracles of St. Artemios: A Collection of Miracle Stories by an Anonymous Author of Seventh-Century Byzantium*. Leiden.
Crislip, A. T. 2005. *From Monastery to Hospital: Christian Monasticism and the Transformation of Health Care in Late Antiquity*. Ann Arbor.
Csepregi, I. 2002. "The Miracles of Saints Cosmas and Damian: Characteristics of Dream Healing." *Annual of Medieval Studies at CEU* 8: 89–121.
———. 2006. "Mysteries for the Uninitiated: The Role and Symbolism of the Eucharist in Miraculous Dream Healing." In I. Perczel et al., eds., *The Eucharist in Theology and*

*Philosophy: Issues of Doctrinal History in East and West from the Patristic Age to the Reformation*, 97–130. Louvain.

Cubitt, C. 2009. "The Lateran Council of 649 as an Ecumenical Council." In M. Whitby and R. Price, eds., *Chalcedon in Context: Church Councils 400–700*, 133–47. Liverpool.

Curta, F. 2006. *Southeastern Europe in the Middle Ages, 500–1250*. Cambridge.

Dagron, G., ed. 1968. "La vie ancienne de Marcel l'Acémète." *AB* 86: 271–321.

———. 1970. "Les moines et la ville: Le monachisme à Constantinople jusqu'au concile de Chalcédoine (451)." In T&MByz 4, 229–76. Paris.

———, ed. 1978. *Vie et miracles de Ste. Thècle*. SH 62. Brussels.

———. 1990. "La règle de exception: Analyse de la notion d'économie." In D. Simon, ed., *Religiöse Devianz: Untersuchungen zu sozialen, rechtlichen und theologischen Reaktionen auf religiöse Abweichung im westlichen und östlichen Mittelalter*, Studien zur Europäischen Rechtsgeschichte 48, 1–18. Frankfurt.

———. 1992. "L'ombre d'un doute: L'hagiographie en question, VI$^e$–XI$^e$ siècle." *DOP* 46: 59–68.

———. 1996. *Empereur et prêtre: Étude sur le "césaropapisme" byzantine*. Paris.

Dagron, G., and V. Déroche. 1991. "Juifs et Chrétiens dans l'Orient de VII$^e$ siècle." In T&MByz 11, 17–274. Paris.

Dahlman, B., ed. and trans. 2007. *Saint Daniel of Sketis: A Group of Hagiographic Texts Edited with Introduction, Translation and Commentary*. Studia Byzantina Upsaliensia 10. Uppsala.

Daley, B. 1976. "The Origenism of Leontius of Byzantium." *JThS*, n.s., 27: 333–69.

———. 1982. "Apokatastasis and 'Honourable Silence' in the Eschatology of Maximus the Confessor." In F. Heinzer and C. von Schönborn, eds., *Maximus Confessor: Actes du Symposium sur Maxime le Confesseur, Fribourg, 2–5 septembre 1980*, 309–39. Freiburg.

———. 1995. "What Did 'Origenism' Mean in the Sixth Century?" In G. Dorival and A. le Boulluec, eds., *Origeniana sexta: Origène et la Bible / Origen and the Bible*, 627–38. Louvain.

———. 2002a. "Divine Transcendence and Human Transformation: Gregory of Nyssa's Anti-Apollinarian Christology." *Modern Theology* 18: 497–506.

———. 2002b. "'Heavenly Man' and 'Eternal Christ': Apollinarius and Gregory of Nyssa on the Personal Identity of the Savior." *JECS* 10: 469–88.

Dalmais, I.-H. 1961. "Saint Maxime le Confesseur et la crise de l'Origénisme monastique." In *Théologie de la vie monastique: Études sur la tradition patristique*, 411–21. Paris.

———. 1962. "La place de la *Mystagogie* de saint Maxime le Confesseur dans la théologie liturgique byzantine." *SP* 5: 277–83.

———. 1966. "L'héritage évagrienne dans la synthèse de saint Maxime le Confesseur." *SP* 6: 356–62.

———. 1982. "La vie de Saint Maxime le Confesseur reconsiderée." *SP* 17: 26–30.

Dal Santo, M. J. 2009a. "Gregory the Great and Eustratius of Constantinople: The *Dialogues on the Miracles of the Italian Fathers* as an Apology for the Cult of the Saints." *JECS* 17: 421–57.

———. 2009b. "Philosophy, Hagiology and the Byzantine Origins of Purgatory." In P. Clarke and T. Claydon, eds., *The Church, the Afterlife and the Fate of the Soul*, Studies in Church History 45, 52–63. Woodbridge, Suffolk.

———. 2012. *Debating the Saints' Cult in the Age of Gregory the Great*. Oxford.
Davis, S. J. 2001. *The Cult of Saint Thecla: A Tradition of Women's Piety in Late Antiquity*. Oxford.
Degórski, B. 2009. "San Leone Magno e San Gregorio Magno nel *Pratum Spirituale* di Giovanni Mosco." In E. López Tello García and B. S. Zorzi, eds., *Church, Society and Monasticism: Acts of the International Symposium, Rome, May 31–June 3, 2006*, Studia Anselmiana 146, 403–21. Rome.
Dekkers, E. 1957. "Les anciens moines cultivaient-ils la liturgie?" *La Maison-Dieu* 51: 31–54.
Delehaye, H. 1904. "S. Grégoire le Grand dans l'hagiographie grecque." *AB* 23: 449–54.
———. 1923. *Les saints stylites*. Brussels.
———. 1925. "Les recueils antiques des miracles des saints." *AB* 43: 5–85, 305–25.
———, ed. 1927. "Une vie inédite de saint Jean l'Aumonier." *AB* 45: 5–75.
Den Heijer, J. 1989. *Mawhūb ibn Manṣūr ibn Mufarriǧ et l'historiographie copto-arabe: Étude sur la composition de l'"Histoire des Patriarches d'Alexandrie."* Louvain.
Déroche, V. 1993. "Pourquoi écrivait-on des recueils de miracles? L'exemple des Miracles de Saint Artémios." In C. Jolivet-Lévy, M. Kaplan, and J.-P. Sodini, eds., *Les saints et leur sanctuaire à Byzance: Textes, images et monuments*, 95–116. Paris.
———. 1995. *Études sur Léontios de Néapolis*. Studia Byzantina Upsaliensia 3. Uppsala.
———. 1996. "Quelques interrogations à propos de la *Vie de Syméon Stylite le Jeune*." *Eranos* 94: 65–83.
———. 1999. "Polémique anti-judaïque et émergence de l'Islam (7ᵉ–8ᵉ siècles)." *RÉB* 57: 141–61.
———. 2000. "Tensions et contradictions dans les recueils de miracles de la première époque byzantine." In D. Aigle, ed., *Miracle et Karāma*, Bibliothèque de l'École des Hautes Études, Sciences Religieuses 109, 145–66. Turnhout.
———. 2002. "Représentations de l'Eucharistie dans la haute époque Byzantine." In V. Déroche, ed., *Mélanges Gilbert Dagron*, T&MByz 14, 167–80. Paris.
———. 2006. "Vraiment anargyres? Don et contredon dans les recueils de miracles proto-byzantins." In B. Caseau et al., eds., *Pèlerinages et lieux saints dans l'Antiquité et le Moyen Âge : Mélanges offerts à Pierre Maraval*, 153-58. Paris.
Déroche, V., and B. Lesieur. 2010. "Notes d'hagiographie byzantine: Daniel le Stylite—Marcel l'Acémète—Hypatios de Rufinianes—Auxentios de Bithynie." *AB* 128: 283–95.
Devreesse, R. 1935. "Le texte grec de l'Hypomnesticon de Théodore Spoudée." *AB* 53: 49–80.
———. 1937. "La fin inédite d'une lettre de Saint Maxime: Un baptême forcé de Juifs et de Samaritans à Carthage en 632." *RSR* 17: 25–35.
———, ed. 1955. "La lettre d'Anastase l'Apocrisiaire sur la mort de saint Maxime le Confesseur et de ses compagnons d'exil: Texte grec inédit." *AB* 73: 5–16.
Diehl, C. 1896. *L'Afrique byzantine: Histoire de la domination byzantine en Afrique, 533–709*. Paris.
Diekamp, F. 1899. *Die origenistischen Streitigkeiten in sechsten Jahrhundert und das fünfte allgemeine Concil*. Münster.
Dobschütz, E. von. 1899. *Christusbilder: Untersuchungen zur christlichen Legende*. Leipzig.
Donner, F. M. 1981. *The Early Islamic Conquests*. Princeton.
Donner, H. 1981. *Die anakreontischen Gedichte Nr. 19 und Nr. 20 des Patriarchen Sophronius von Jerusalem*. Heidelberg.

Doucet, M. 1983. "Est-ce que le monothélisme a fait autant d'illustres victimes? Réflexions sur un ouvrage de F. M. Léthel." *Science et Esprit* 35: 53–83.

Drijvers, H. J. W. 1981. "The Byzantine Saint: Hellenistic and Oriental Origins." In S. Hackel, ed., *The Byzantine Saint*, 25–33. London.

———. 2002. "Heraclius and the *Restitutio Crucis*: Notes on Symbolism and Ideology." In G. J. Reinink and B. H. Stolte, eds., *The Reign of Heraclius (610–641): Crisis and Confrontation*, 175–90. Louvain.

Driver, S. D. 2002. *John Cassian and the Reading of Egyptian Monastic Culture*. London.

Duchesne, L. 1910. "Le sanctuaire d'Aboukir." *Bulletin de la Société Archéologique d'Alexandrie* 12: 3–14.

Duffy, J. 1984a. "Byzantine Medicine in the Sixth and Seventh Centuries: Aspects of Teaching and Practice." *DOP* 38: 21–27.

———. 1984b. "Observations on Sophronius' *Miracles of Cyrus and John*." *JThS*, n.s., 35: 71–90.

———. 1987. "The *Miracles of Cyrus and John*: New Old Readings from the Manuscript." *ICS* 12: 169–77.

———. 2011. "New Fragments of Sophronius of Jerusalem and Aristo of Pella?" In D. Bumazhnov et al., eds., *Bibel, Byzanz und christlicher Orient: Festschrift für Stephen Gerö zum 65. Geburtstag*, Orientalia Lovaniensia Analecta 187, 15–28. Louvain.

Duffy, J., and J. Parker, eds. and trans. 1979. *Synodicon Vetus: Text, Translation and Notes*. Washington, D.C.

Duval, Y. 1971. "Le patrice Pierre, exarque d'Afrique?" *AntAfr* 5: 209–14.

Dvornik, F. 1964. *Byzance et la primauté romaine*. Paris.

———. 1966. *Early Christian and Byzantine Political Philosophy: Origins and Background*. Washington, D.C.

Echle, H. A. 1945. "The Baptism of the Apostles: A Fragment of Clement of Alexandria's Lost Work *Hypotyposeis* in the *Pratum Spirituale* of John Moschus." *Traditio* 3: 365–68.

Ekonomou, A. J. 2007. *Byzantine Rome and the Greek Popes: Eastern Influences on Rome and the Papacy from Gregory the Great to Zacharias, A.D. 590–752*. Plymouth.

Elert, W. 1951. "Theodor von Pharan und Theodor von Raithu." *ThLZ* 76: 67–76.

Ericsson, K. 1968. "Revising a Date in the *Chronicon Paschale*." *JÖByz* 17: 17–28.

Esbroeck, M. van. 1981. "La diffusion orientale de la légende des saints Cosme et Damian." In *Hagiographie, Cultures et Sociétés: IV$^e$–XII$^e$ siècles*, Études Augustiniennes, 61–77. Paris.

———. 1993. "Peter the Iberian and Dionysius the Areopagite: Honigmann's Thesis Revisited." *OCP* 59: 217–27.

———. 1995. "Le discours du Catholicos Sahak III en 691." In G. Nedungatt and M. Featherstone, eds., *The Council in Trullo Revisited*, 323–451. Rome.

Escolan, P. 1999. *Monachisme et église: Le monachisme syrien de IV$^e$ au VII$^e$ siècle—Un ministère charismatique*. Paris.

Evans, D. B. 1970. *Leontius of Byzantium: An Origenist Christology*. Washington, D.C.

———. 1980. "Leontius of Byzantium and Dionysius the Areopagite." *Byzantine Studies/Études Byzantines* 7: 1–34.

Feissel, D. 1987. "Inscriptions chrétiennes et byzantines 532: Chypre, Soloi." *RÉG* 100: 380–81.

Ferrière, J. de la, and M. H. Congourdeau. 1999. *Sophrone de Jérusalem: Fêtes chrétiennes à Jérusalem*. Paris.
Festugière, A.-J., ed. 1971. *Sainte Thècle, Saints Côme et Damien, Saints Cyr et Jean (extraits), Saint Georges*. Paris.
Festugière, A.-J., and L. Rydén, eds. 1974. *Vie de Syméon le Fou et Vie de Jean de Chypre*. Paris.
Fiori, E. 2011. "Mystique et liturgie: Entre Denys l'Aréopagite et le Livre de Hiérothée: Aux origines de la mystagogie syro-occidentale." In A. Desreumaux, ed., *Les mystiques syriaques*, 27–44. Paris.
Fitschen, K. 1998. *Messalianismus und Antimessalianismus: Ein Beispiel ostkirchlicher Ketzergeschichte*. Göttingen.
Flusin, B. 1983. *Miracle et histoire dans l'œuvre de Cyrille de Scythopolis*. Paris.
———. 1991. "Démons et Sarrasins: L'auteur et le propos des Diêgêmata stêriktika d'Anastase le Sinaïte." In T&MByz 11, 380–409. Paris.
———. 1992a. "L'esplanade du Temple à l'arrivée des arabes d'après deux récits byzantins." In J. Raby and J. Johns, eds., *Bayt al-Maqdis: 'Abd al-Malik's Jerusalem*, Oxford Studies in Islamic Art 9, 17–31. Oxford.
———. 1992b. *Saint Anastase le Perse et l'histoire de la Palestine au début du VII<sup>e</sup> siècle*. 2 vols. Paris.
Follieri, E. 1988. "Dove e quando morì Giovanni Mosco?" *RSBN*, n.s., 25: 3–39.
Foss, C. 1975. "The Persians in Asia Minor and the End of Antiquity." *EHR* 90: 721–47.
———. 2003. "The Persians in the Roman Near East (602–630 AD)." *JAS*, ser. 3, 13.2: 149–70.
———. 2009a. "Egypt under Mu'āwiya, Part I: Flavius Papas and Upper Egypt." *BSOAS* 72: 1–24.
———. 2009b. "Egypt under Mu'āwiya, Part II: Middle Egypt, Fusṭāṭ and Alexandria." *BSOAS* 72: 259–78.
Frankfurter, D. 1990. "Stylites and *Phallobates*: Pillar Religions in Late Antique Syria." *VChr* 44: 168–98.
Franklin, C., and P. Meyvaert. 1982. "Has Bede's Version of the 'Passio S. Anastasii' Come Down to Us in 'BHL' 408?" *AB* 100: 373–400.
Frazee, C. 1982. "Late Roman and Byzantine Legislation on the Monastic Life from the Fourth to Eighth Centuries." *Church History* 51: 263–79.
Frend, W. H. C. 1976. "Eastern Attitudes to Rome during the Acacian Schism." In D. Baker, ed., *The Orthodox Churches and the West*, Studies in Church History 13, 69–81. Oxford.
Frothingham, A. L. 1886. *Stephen Bar Sudaili the Syrian Mystic and the Book of the Holy Hierotheos*. Leiden.
Frøyshov, S. S. 2000. "La réticence à l'hymnographie chez les anchorètes de l'Égypte et du Sinaï du 6<sup>e</sup> au 8<sup>e</sup> siècles." In A. M. Triacca and A. Pistoia, eds., *L'hymnographie: Conférences Saint-Serge—XLVI<sup>e</sup> semaine d'études liturgiques, Paris, 29 juin–2 juillet 1999*, 229–45. Rome.
Gallico, A., ed. 1991. *Sofronio di Gerusalemme: Le omelie*. Rome.
Gariboldi, A. 2009. "Social Conditions in Egypt under the Sasannian Occupation." *PP* 64: 321–53.
Garitte, G., ed. 1952. *La Narratio de Rebus Armeniae*. CSCO 132, Subsidia 4. Louvain.

———. 1964. "La version géorgienne du 'Pré spirituel.'" In *Mélanges Eugène Tisserant*, vol. 2, ST 232, 171–85. Vatican City.
———, trans. 1966. "'Histoires édifiantes' géorgiennes." *Byzantion* 36: 396–423.
Garrigues, J.-M. 1976a. "Le martyre de saint Maxime le Confesseur." *Revue Thomiste* 76: 410–52.
———. 1976b. *Maxime le Confesseur: La charité, avenir divin de l'homme*. Théologie Historique 38. Paris.
———. 1976c. "Le sens de la primauté romaine chez saint Maxime le Confesseur." *Istina* 21: 6–24.
Gascou, J., ed. 2006. *Sophrone de Jérusalem: Miracles de saints Cyr et Jean (BHG 477–79)*. Paris.
———. 2007. "Les origines du culte des saints Cyr et Jean." *AB* 125: 241–81.
Goddard Elliott, A. 1987. *Roads to Paradise: Reading the Lives of the Early Saints*. Hannover.
Goddio, F. 2007. *Underwater Archaeology in the Canopic Region in Egypt: The Topography and Excavation of Heracleion-Thonis and East Canopus (1996–2006)*. Oxford.
Goddio, F., and M. Clauss, eds. 2006. *Ägyptens versunkene Schätze / Egypt's Sunken Treasures*. Munich and New York.
Goehring, J. 1993. "The Encroaching Desert: Literary Production and Ascetic Space in Early Egyptian Egypt." *JECS* 1: 281–96. [Reprint: idem, *Ascetics, Society and the Desert: Studies in Early Egyptian Monasticism*, 73–88. Harrisburg, 1999.]
———. 2005. "The Dark Side of Landscape: Ideology and Power in the Christian Myth of the Desert." In D.B. Martin and P. Cox Miller, eds., *The Cultural Turn in Late Ancient Studies: Gender, Asceticism and Historiography*, 136–49. Durham, N.C.
Golitzin, A. 1994. *Et introibo ad altare Dei: The Mystagogy of Dionysius Areopagita, with Special Reference to Its Predecessors in the Eastern Christian Tradition*. Thessalonica.
Golysenko, V.S., and V.F. Dubrovina. 1967. *Sinajskij paterik*. Moscow.
Gray, P. 1979. *The Defense of Chalcedon in the East*. Studies in the History of Christian Thought 20. Leiden.
———. 2005. "From Eucharist to Christology: The Life-Giving Body of Christ in Cyril of Alexandria, Eutyches and Julian of Halicarnassus." In I. Perczel et al., eds., *The Eucharist in Theology and Philosophy: Issues of Doctrinal History in East and West from the Patristic Age to the Reformation*, 23–36. Louvain.
Greenwood, T.W. 2008. "'New Light from the East': Chronography and Ecclesiastical History through a Late Seventh-Century Armenian Source." *JECS* 16: 197–254.
Gribomont, A. 1957. "Le monachisme au IV$^e$ siècle en Asie Mineure: De Gangres au Messalianisme." *TU* 64, 400–415. Berlin.
Gribomont, J. 1980. "Saint Basile et le monachisme enthousiaste." *Irenikon* 53: 123–44.
Grierson, P. 1950. "The Consular Coinage of 'Heraclius' and the Revolt against Phocas of 608–10." *Numismatic Chronicle* 6.10: 71–93.
———. 1982. *Byzantine Coins*. London.
Griffiths, S.H. 2001. "The *Life of Theodore of Edessa*: History, Hagiography and Religious Apologetics in Mar Saba Monastery in Early Abbasid Times." In J. Patrich, ed., *The Sabaite Heritage in the Orthodox Church from the Fifth Century to the Present*, 147–70. Louvain.
Grillmeier, A., and T. Hainthaler. 1995. *Christ in Christian Tradition*, vol. 2, *From the Council of Chalcedon (451) to Gregory the Great (590–604)*, part 2, *The Church of Constantinople in the Sixth Century*. Trans. P. Allen and J. Cawte. London.

Grossmann, P. 1998. "The Pilgrimage Centre of Abū Mīnā." In D. Frankfurter, ed., *Pilgrimage and Holy Space in Late Antique Egypt*, Religions in the Graeco-Roman World 134, 281–302. Leiden.
Grumel, V. 1958. *La chronologie*. Traité d'Études Byzantines 1. Paris.
Guery, R. 1981. "Le pseudo-monnayage de l'usurpateur Grégoire." *Bulletin de la Sociéte Française de Numismatique* 36: 60–68.
Guidi, I. 1900–1901. "Vie et récits de l'abbé Daniel le Scétiote (VI$^e$ siècle), III: Texte copte." *ROC* 5: 535–64 ; and *ROC* 6: 51–53.
Guilland, R. 1981. "Études sur l'histoire administrative de l'Empire Byzantine—L'éparque, II: Les éparques autres que l'éparque de la ville." *Byzantinoslavica* 42: 186–96.
Guillaumont, A. 1961a. "Étienne bar Soudaïli." In M. Viller et al., eds., *Dictionnaire de spiritualité: Ascétique et mystique, doctrine et histoire*, vol. 4.2, 1481–88. Paris.
———. 1961b. "Évagre et les anathématismes antiorigénistes de 553." *SP* 3: 219–26.
———. 1962. *Les "Kephalaia Gnostica" d'Évagre le Pontique et l'histoire de l'origénisme chez les Grecs et chez les Syriens*. Patristica Sorbonensia 5. Paris.
———. 1969–70. "Justinien et l'église de Perse." *DOP* 23–24: 39–66.
———. 1989. "Anachorèse et vie eucharistique dans le monachisme." In A. Caquot and P. Canivet, eds., *Ritualisme et vie intérieure*, 83–93. Paris.
Guillaumont, A., and C. Guillaumont, eds. 1971. *Évagre le Pontique, Traité pratique; ou, Le moine*. SC 356. Paris
Guillou, A. 1957. "Prise de Gaza par les Arabes au VII$^e$ siècle." *BCH* 81: 396–404.
Gvaramia, R. 1965. *Al-Bustāni: X saukunis sinuri xelnaceris mixedvit'*. Tiflis.
Haase, F. 1915. "Die armenischen Rezensionen des syrischen Chronik Michaels des Großen."*OC*, n.s., 5: 60–82, 211–84.
Hage, W. 2004. "Athanasios Gammala und sein Treffen mit Kaiser Herakleios in Mabbug." In M. Tamcke, ed., *Syriaca*, vol. 2, *Beiträge zum 3. Deutschen Syrologen-Symposium in Vierzehnheiligen, 2002*, 165–74. Münster.
Hainthaler, T. 2005. "Perspectives on the Eucharist in the Nestorian Controversy." In I. Perczel et al., eds., *The Eucharist in Theology and Philosophy: Issues of Doctrinal History in East and West from the Patristic Age to the Reformation*, 3–22. Louvain.
Haldon, J. F. 1985. "Ideology and the Byzantine State in the Seventh Century: The 'Trial' of Maximus the Confessor." In V. Vavrinek, ed., *From Late Antiquity to Early Byzantium*, 87–91. Prague.
———. 1986. "Ideology and Social Change in the Seventh Century: Military Discontent as a Barometer." *Klio* 68: 139–90.
———. 1990. *Byzantium in the Seventh Century: The Transformation of a Culture*. Cambridge.
———. 1992. "The Works of Anastasius of Sinai: A Key Source for the History of Seventh-Century East Mediterranean Society and Belief." In Averil Cameron and L. Conrad, eds., *The Byzantine and Early Islamic Near East*, vol. 1, *Problems in the Literary Source Material*, Studies in Late Antiquity and Early Islam 1, 107–47. Princeton.
———. 1994. "Constantine or Justinian? Crisis and Identity in Imperial Propaganda in the Seventh Century." In P. Magdalino, ed., *New Constantines: The Rhythm of Imperial Renewal in Byzantium, 4th–13th Centuries*, 95–107. Aldershot.
———. 1997. "Supplementary Essay: The *Miracles of Artemios* and Contemporary Attitudes—Context and Significance." In Crisafulli and Nesbitt (1997) 33–75.

———. 2008. "'Tortured by My Conscience': The *Laudatio Therapontis*—A Neglected Source of the Seventh or Eighth Centuries." In H. Amirav and B. ter Haar Romeny, eds., *From Rome to Constantinople: Studies in Honour of Averil Cameron*, 263–78. Louvain.
Halkin, F. 1945. "La vision de Kaioumos et le sort éternel de Philentolos Olympiou." *AB* 63: 56–64.
———. 1955. "Le pape saint Grégoire le Grand dans l'hagiographie byzantine." *OCP* 21: 109–14.
———, ed. 1986. "Un discours inédit du moine Pantaléon sur élévation de la Croix, *BHG* 427p." *OCP* 52: 257–70.
Halleux, A. de. 1963. *Philoxène de Mabbog: Sa vie, ses écrits, sa théologie*. Louvain.
Harb, P. 1969. "L'attitude de Philoxène de Mabboug à égard de la spiriualité 'savante' d'Évagre le Pontique." In *Mémorial Mgr. Gabriel Khouri-Sarkis, 1898–1968*, 135–55. Louvain.
Harvey, S. A. 1984. "Physicians and Ascetics in John of Ephesus: An Expedient Alliance." *DOP* 38: 87–93.
———. 1988. "The Sense of a Stylite: Perspectives on Simeon the Elder." *VChr* 42: 376–94.
———. 1990. *Asceticism and Society in Crisis: John of Ephesus and the Lives of the Eastern Saints*. Berkeley and Los Angeles.
———. 1998. "The Stylite's Liturgy: Ritual and Religious Identity in Late Antiquity." *JECS* 6: 523–39.
Hatch, W. H. P. 1937. "The Subscription in the Chester Beatty Manuscript of the Harclean Gospels." *HThR* 30: 141–55.
Hathaway, R. F. 1969. *Hierarchy and the Definition of Order in the Letters of Pseudo-Dionysius*. The Hague.
Hatlie, P. 1999. "Spiritual Authority and Monasticism in Constantinople during the Dark Ages (650–800)." In J. W. Drijvers and J. W. Watt, eds., *Portraits of Spiritual Authority: Religious Power in Early Christianity, Byzantium and the Christian Orient*, 195–222. Leiden.
———. 2002. "A Rough Guide to Byzantine Monasticism in the Early Seventh Century." In G. Reinink and B. H. Stolte, eds., *The Reign of Heraclius (610–641): Crisis and Confrontation*, Groningen Studies in Cultural Change 2, 205–26. Louvain.
———. 2007. *The Monks and Monasteries of Constantinople, ca. 350–850*. Cambridge.
Hausherr, I. 1933. "L'influence du 'Livre de Saint Hiérothée.'" *OC* 30: 176–211.
Havener, I. 1988. "Two Early Anecdotes concerning Gregory the Great from the Greek Tradition." In M. J. Chiat and K. L. Reyerson, eds., *The Medieval Mediterranean: Cross-Cultural Contacts*, 19–24. St. Cloud, Minn.
Heid, S., ed. 2002. "Eine erbauliche Erzählung des Sophronios von Jerusalem (BHG 1641b) über der kirchliche Binde- und Lösegewalt über Verstorbene." In W. Blumer et al., eds., *Alvarium: Festschrift für Christian Gnilka*, 151–72. Münster.
Hendrickx, B. 2002. "The 'Abominatio Desolationis': Standing in the Holy Place." *APB* 13: 165–76.
Hendy, M. 1985. *Studies in the Byzantine Monetary Economy, c. 300–1450*. Cambridge.
Hesse, O. 2001. "Das altkirchliche Mönchtum und die kaiserliche Politik am Beispiel der Apophthegmen und der Viten des Symeon Stylites und des Daniel Stylites." *SP* 34: 88–96.
Hesseling, D. C. 1931. *Morceaux choisis du "Pré spirituel" de Jean Moschos, avec un aperçu sur l'auteur, une introduction à l'étude de la koinê, une traduction, des notes et un index*. Paris.

Hevelone-Harper, J. L. 2005. *Disciples of the Desert: Monks, Laity and Spiritual Authority in Sixth-Century Gaza*. Baltimore.

Hirschfeld, Y. 1990. "List of the Byzantine Monasteries in the Judean Desert." In G. C. Bottini et al., eds., *Christian Archaeology in the Holy Land: New Discoveries—Archaeological Essays in Honour of V. C. Corbo*. Jerusalem.

———. 1992. *The Judaean Desert Monasteries in the Byzantine Period*. New Haven.

———. 2001. "The Physical Structure of the New Laura as an Expression of Controversy over the Monastic Lifestyle." In J. Patrich, ed., *The Sabaite Heritage in the Orthodox Church from the Fifth Century to the Present*, Orientalia Lovaniensia Analecta 98, 323–46. Louvain.

Holman, S. R. 2008. "Rich and Poor in Sophronius of Jerusalem's *Miracles of Saints Cyrus and John*." In eadem, ed., *Wealth and Poverty in Early Church and Society*, 103–26. Grand Rapids.

Hombergen, D. 2001. *The Second Origenist Controversy: A New Perspective on Cyril of Scythopolis' Monastic Biographies as Historical Sources for Sixth-Century Origenism*. Studia Anselmiana 132. Rome.

———. 2004. "Barsanuphius and John of Gaza and Origenism." In B. Bitton-Ashkelony and A. Kofsky, eds., *Christian Gaza in Late Antiquity*, 173–82. Leiden.

Honigmann, E. 1950. "La date de l'homélie du prêtre Pantaléon sur la fête de l'Exaltation de la Croix (VII$^e$ siècle) et l'origine des collections homiliaires." *Bulletin de la Classe des Lettres et des Sciences Morales et Politiques, Académie Royale de Belgique* 36: 547–59.

Horden, P. 1982. "Saints and Doctors in the Early Byzantine Empire: The Case of Theodore of Sykeon." In W. J. Sheils, ed., *The Church and Healing*, Studies in Church History 19, 1–13. Oxford.

———. 1985. "The Death of Ascetics: Sickness and Monasticism in the Early Byzantine Middle East." In W. J. Sheils, ed., *Monks, Hermits and the Ascetic Tradition*, Studies in Church History 22, 41–52. Oxford.

Horn, C. 2006. *Asceticism and Christological Controversy in Fifth-Century Palestine: The Career of Peter the Iberian*. Oxford.

Horrocks, G. 1997. *Greek: A History of the Language and Its Speakers*. London.

Hovorun, C. 2008. *Will, Action and Freedom: Christological Controversies in the Seventh Century*. Leiden.

———. 2010. "Controversy on Energies and Wills in Christ: Between Politics and Theology." *SP* 48: 217–20.

Howard-Johnston, J. 1994. "The Official History of Heraclius' Persian Campaigns." In E. Dąbrowa, *The Roman and Byzantine Army in the East*, 57–87. Krakow. [Reprint: Howard-Johnston (2006) IV.]

———. 1995. "The Siege of Constantinople in 626." In C. Mango and G. Dagron, eds., *Constantinople and Its Hinterland*, 131–42. Aldershot. [Reprint: Howard-Johnston (2006) VII.]

———. 1999a. "Heraclius' Persian Campaigns and the Revival of the East Roman Empire." *War in History* 6: 1–44. [Reprint: Howard-Johnston (2006) VIII.]

———. 1999b. *Historical Commentary*. Volume 2 of R. Thomson and J. Howard-Johnston, eds., *The Armenian History Attributed to Sebeos*. Liverpool.

———. 2004. "Pride and Fall: Khusro II and His Regime, 626–8." In G. Gnoli, ed., *La Persia e Bisanzio*, 93–113. Rome. [Reprint: Howard-Johnston (2006) IX.]

———. 2006. *East Rome, Sasanian Persia and the End of Antiquity: Historiographical and Historical Studies*. Aldershot.

———. 2010. *Witnesses to a World Crisis: Historians and Histories of the Middle East in the Seventh Century*. Oxford.

Hoyland, R. G. 1997. *Seeing Islam as Others Saw It: A Survey and Evaluation of Christian, Jewish and Zoroastrian Writings on Early Islam*. Princeton.

———. 2011. *Theophilus of Edessa's Chronicle and the Circulation of Historical Knowledge in Late Antiquity and Early Islam*. Liverpool.

Huber, M. 1913. *Iohannes Monachus: Liber de miraculis*. Heidelberg.

Humphreys, R. S. 2006. *Mu'awiya ibn Abi Sufyan: From Arabia to Empire*. Oxford.

Hunt, E. D. 1982. *Holy Land Pilgrimage in the Later Roman Empire, A.D. 312–460*. Oxford.

Hurley, M. 1961. "Born Incorruptibility: The Third Canon of the Lateran Council, A.D. 649." *The Heythrop Journal* 2: 216–26.

Janin, R. 1953. *La géographie ecclésiastique de l'empire byzantin*, vol. 1, *Le siège de Constantinople et le patriarcat œcuménique*, part 3, *Les églises et les monastères*. Paris.

———. 1975. *La géographie ecclésiastique de l'empire byzantin*, vol. 2, *Les églises et les monastères des grands centres byzantins: Bithynie, Hellespont, Latros, Galèsios, Trébizonde, Athènes, Thessalonique*. Paris.

Jankowiak, M. 2009. "Essai d'histoire politique du monothélisme à partir de la correspondance entre les empereurs byzantins, les patriarches de Constantinople et les papes de Rome." Unpublished PhD thesis. Paris and Warsaw.

Jansma, T. 1974. "Philoxenus' Letter to Abraham and Orestes concerning Stephen Bar Sudaili: Some Proposals with Regard to the Syriac Text and the English Translation." *Le Muséon* 87: 79–86.

Johnson, S. F. 2006. *The Life and Miracles of Thekla: A Literary Study*. Cambridge, Mass.

Kaegi, W. E. 1973. "New Evidence on the Early Reign of Heraclius." *BZ* 66: 308–30.

———. 1981. *Byzantine Military Unrest, 471–843: An Interpretation*. Amsterdam.

———. 1992. *Byzantium and the Early Islamic Conquests*. Cambridge.

———. 2000. "A Misunderstood Place-name in a Poem of George of Pisidia." *ByzF* 26: 229–30.

———. 2003. *Heraclius: Emperor of Byzantium*. Cambridge.

———. 2010. *Muslim Expansion and Byzantine Collapse in North Africa*. Cambridge.

Kaplan, M. 2001. "L'espace et le sacré dans la Vie de Daniel le Stylite." In idem, ed., *Le sacré et son inscription dans l'espace à Byzance et en Occident*, 199–217. Paris.

Kaplony, A. 1996. *Konstantinopel und Damaskus: Gesandtschaften und Verträge zwischen Kaisern und Kalifen, 639–750*. Berlin.

Khoperia, L. 2000. "The Old Georgian Translations of Saint Maximus the Confessor's Works." *Annual of Medieval Studies at the CEU* 6: 225–31.

———. 2001. "Maximus the Confessor in Ancient Georgian Sources." *SP* 36: 134–39.

———. 2003. "Old Georgian Sources concerning Maximus the Confessor's Life." *Le Muséon* 116: 395–414.

Klein, H. A. 2001. "Niketas und das wahre Kreuz: Kritische Anmerkungen zur Überlieferung des Chronicon Paschale ad annum 614." *BZ* 94: 580–87.

Konstantinovsky, J. 2009. *Evagrius Ponticus: The Making of a Gnostic*. Farnham, Surrey.

Kouli, M. 1996. "Life of St. Mary of Egypt." In A.-M. Talbot, ed., *Holy Women of Byzantium: Ten Saints' Lives in English Translation*, 65–93. Washington, D.C.

Kresten, O. 1977. "Leontios von Neapolis als Tachygraph? Hagiographische Texte als Quellen zu Schriftlichkeit und Buchkultur im 6. und 7. Jahrhundert." *S&C* 1: 155–75.
Kreuzer, G. 1975. *Die Honoriusfrage im Mittelalter und in der Neuzeit.* Stuttgart.
Krueger, D. 1996. *Symeon the Holy Fool: Leontios's Life and the Late Antique City.* Berkeley and Los Angeles.
———. 2004. *Writing and Holiness: The Practice of Authorship in the Early Christian East.* Philadelphia.
———. 2005. "Christian Piety and Practice in the Sixth Century." In M. Maas, ed., *The Cambridge Companion to the Age of Justinian*, 291–315. Cambridge.
———. 2009. "The Unbounded Body in the Age of Liturgical Reproduction." *JECS* 17: 267–79.
———. 2011. "Between Monks: Tales of Monastic Companionship in Early Byzantium." *Journal of the History of Sexuality* 20: 28–61.
Lackner, W. 1967. "Zu Quellen und Datierung der Maximosvita (BHG³ 1234)." *AB* 85: 285–316.
———. 1971. "Der Amtstitel Maximos des Bekenners." *JÖB* 20: 63–65.
———. 1982. "Zwei membra disiecta aus dem Pratum Spirituale des Joannes Moschos." *AB* 100: 341–50.
Laga, C. 1990. "Judaism and Jews in Maximus Confessor's Works: Theoretical Controversy and Practical Attitudes." *Byzantinoslavica* 51: 183–88.
Lampe, G. W. H. 1961. *A Patristic Greek Lexicon.* Oxford.
Lange, C. 2012. *Mia Energeia: Untersuchungen zur Einigungspolitik des Kaisers Heraclius und des Patriarchen Sergius von Constantinopel.* Tübingen.
Lane Fox, R. 1986. *Pagans and Christians.* Harmondsworth.
———. 1997. "The *Life of Daniel.*" In M. J. Edwards and S. Swain, eds., *Portraits: Biographical Representation in Greek and Latin Literature of the Roman Empire*, 175–225. Oxford.
Lapidge, M., ed. 1995a. *Archbishop Theodore: Commemorative Studies on His Life and Influence.* Cambridge.
———. 1995b. "The Career of Archbishop Theodore." In Lapidge (1995a) 1–29. Cambridge.
Lappa-Zizicas, E., ed. 1970. "Un épitomé de la Vie de saint Jean l'Aumônier par Jean et Sophronius." *AB* 88: 265–78.
Larchet, J.-C. 1991. *Théologie de la maladie.* Paris. [Trans. J. Breck and M. Breck, *The Theology of Illness.* Crestwood, N.Y.]
———. 1996. *La divinisation de l'homme selon Maxime le Confesseur.* Paris.
———. 1998a. "Introduction." In J.-C. Larchet and E. Ponsoye, eds., *Saint Maxime le Confesseur: Lettres*, 7–62. Paris.
———. 1998b. "Introduction." In J.-C. Larchet and E. Ponsoye, eds., *Saint Maxime le Confesseur: Opuscules théologiques et polémiques*, 7–108. Paris.
———. 1998c. *Maxime le Confesseur, médiateur entre l'Orient et l'Occident.* Paris.
———. 2005. "The Question of the Roman Primacy in the Thought of Saint Maximus the Confessor." In W. Kasper, ed., *The Petrine Ministry: Catholics and Orthodox in Dialogue*, 188–209. Mahwah, N.J.
Lavagnini, B. 1979. "Sofronio: Compianto per Gerusalemme occupata dai Persiani (614)." *BBGG*, n.s., 33: 3–8.

Layerle, B. 2005. "Monks and Other Animals." In D. B. Martin and P. Cox Miller, eds., *The Cultural Turn in Late Ancient Studies: Gender, Asceticism and Historiography*, 150–74. Durham, N.C.

Lemerle, P., ed. 1979–81. *Les plus anciens recueils des Miracles de saint Démétrius*. 2 vols. Paris.

Lesieur, B. 2011. "Le monastère de Séridos sous Barsanuphe et Jean de Gaza: Un monastère conforme à la législation impériale ou ecclésiastique?" *RÉB* 69: 5–47.

Léthel, F. M. 1979. *Théologie de l'agonie du Christ: La liberté humaine du fils de Dieu et son importance sotériologique mises en lumière par saint Maxime le Confesseur*. Paris.

Levi della Vida, G. 1946. "Sulla versione araba di Giovanni Mosco e di Pseudo-Anastasio Sinaita secondo alcuni codici Vaticani." In *Miscellena G. Mercati*, vol. 3, *Letteratura e storia bizantina*, ST 123, 104–15. Rome.

Levy-Rubin, M. 2001. "The Role of the Judean Desert Monasteries in the Monothelete Controversy in Seventh-Century Palestine." In J. Patrich, ed., *The Sabaite Heritage in the Orthodox Church from the Fifth Century to the Present*, Orientalia Lovaniensia Analecta 98, 283–300. Louvain.

Llewellyn, P. 1974. "The Roman Church in the Seventh Century: The Legacy of Gregory I." *JEH* 25: 363–80.

Lo Jacono, C. 1988. "Gli Arabi in Sicilia." In *Testimonianze degli Arabi in Italia: Giornata di studio, Roma, 10 dicembre 1987*, 5–33. Rome.

Longo, A. 1965–66. "Il testo integrale della *Narrazione degli abati Giovanni e Sofronio* attraverso le Hermêneiai di Nicone." *RSBN* 12–13: 223–67.

Lourié, B. 2010. "Peter the Iberian and Dionysius the Areopagite: Honigmann—van Esbroeck's Thesis Revisited." *Scrinium* 6: 143–212.

Louth, A. 1989. *Denys the Areopagite*. London.

———. 1996. *Maximus the Confessor*. London.

———. 1997. "St. Maximus the Confessor: Between East and West." *SP* 32: 332–45.

———. 1998. "Did John Moschus Really Die in Constantinople?" *JThS*, n.s., 49: 149–54.

———. 2003. "The 'Collectio Sabaitica' and Sixth-Century Origenism." In L. Perrone, ed., *Origen and the Alexandrian Tradition: Papers of the 8th International Origen Congress, Pisa, 27–31 agosto 2001*, 1167–75. Louvain.

———. 2004. "The Ecclesiology of St Maximos the Confessor." *International Journal for the Study of the Christian Church* 4: 109–20.

———. 2007. *The Origins of the Christian Mystical Tradition: From Plato to Denys*. 2nd ed. Oxford.

———. 2009. "Eucharist and Church according to St Maximus the Confessor." In T. Hainthaler, ed., *Einheit und Katholizität der Kirche: Forscher aus dem Osten und Westen Europas an den Quellen des gemeinsamen Glaubens*. Innsbruck, 319–30.

Lucius, E. 1904. *Die Anfange des Heiligenkults in der christlichen Kirche*. Tübingen.

Luongo, G. 1997. "Il 'dossier' agiografico dei santi Cosma e Damiano." In S. Leanza, ed., *Sant'Eufemia d'Aspromonte*, 33–89. Soveria Mannelli.

Lynch, J. J. 1975. "Leontius of Byzantium: A Cyrillian Christology." *ThS* 36: 455–71.

MacCoull, L. 1986. "Coptic Egypt during the Persian Occupation: The Papyrological Evidence." *SCO* 36: 307–13.

———. 1998. "George of Pisidia, 'Against Severus': In Praise of Heraclius." In R. Dahood, ed., *The Future of the Middle Ages and the Renaissance: Problems, Trends and Opportunities for Research*, 69–79. Turnhout.

Madden, J. D. 1982. "The Authenticity of Early Definitions of Will (*thelēsis*)." In F. Heinzer and C. von Schönborn, eds., *Maximus Confessor: Actes du Symposium sur Maxime le Confesseur, Fribourg, 2–5 septembre 1980*, 61–79. Freiburg.

Magdalino, P. 1993. "The History of the Future and Its Uses: Prophecy, Policy and Propaganda." In R. Beaton and C. Roueché, eds., *The Making of Byzantine History: Studies Dedicated to Donald M. Nicol*, 3–34. Aldershot.

Magness, J. 2011. "Archaeological Evidence for the Sasanian Persian Invasion of Jerusalem." In K. G. Holum and H. Lapin, eds., *Shaping the Middle East: Jews, Christians and Muslims in an Age of Transition*, 85–98. Bethesda.

Mahé, J.-P. 1984. "Critical Remarks on the Newly Edited Excerpts from Sebēos." In T. J. Samuelian and M. E. Stone, eds., *Medieval Armenian Culture*, 218–39. Chico, Calif.

Mai, A., ed. 1852–1905. *Nova Patrum bibliotheca*. 10 vols. Rome.

Maisano, R. 1982. *Il Prato*. Naples.

———. 1984. "Tradizione orale e sviluppi narrativi nel Prato di Giovanni Mosco." *BBGG*, n.s., 38: 3–17.

Mango, C. 1973. "La culture grecque et l'Occident au VIII$^e$ siècle." In *I problemi dell'Occidente nel secolo VIII*, Settimane di studio del Centro Italiano di Studi sull'Alto Medioevo 20, 683–719. Spoleto.

———. 1984. "A Byzantine Hagiographer at Work: Leontius of Neapolis." In I. Hutter, ed., *Byzanz und der Westen*, 25–41. Vienna.

———. 1985. "Deux études sur Byzance et la Perse sassanide." In T&MByz 9, 91–117. Paris.

———. 1990. *Nikephoros, Patriarch of Constantinople: Short History*. Washington, D.C.

———. 1991. "Greek Culture in Palestine after the Arab Conquest." In G. Cavallo, G. de Gregorio, and G. Maniaci, eds., *Scritture, libri e testi nelle aree provinciali di Bisanzio*, 149–60. Spoleto.

———. 1992. "The Temple Mount, AD 614–638." In J. Raby and J. Johns, eds., *Bayt al-Maqdis: 'Abd al-Malik's Jerusalem*, Oxford Studies in Islamic Art 9, 1–16. Oxford.

Maraval, P. 1981. "Fonction pédagogique de la littérature hagiographique d'un lieu de pèlerinage: L'exemple des Miracles de Cyr et Jean." In *Hagiographie, Cultures et Sociétés: IV$^e$–XII$^e$ siècles*, Études Augustiniennes, 383–97. Paris.

Marcos, N. F., ed. 1975. *Los "Thaumata" de Sofronio: Contribución al estudio de la "Incubatio" cristiana*. Madrid.

Markus, R. 1990. *The End of Ancient Christianity*. Cambridge.

Marsh, F. S., ed. and trans. 1927. *The Book Which Is Called the Holy Hierotheos, with Extracts from the Prolegomena and Commentary of Theodosius of Antioch and from the "Book of Excerpts" of Gregory bar-Hebraeus*. London.

Maspero, J. 1923. *Histoire des patriarches d'Alexandrie*. Paris.

Mazza, E. 1989. *Mystagogy: A Theology of Liturgy in the Patristic Age*. Trans. M. J. O'Connell. New York.

Menze, V. L. 2003. "Die Stimme von Maiuma: Johannes Rufus, das Konzil von Chalkedon und die wahre Kirche." In B. Aland et al., eds., *Literarische Konstituierung von Identifikationsfiguren in der Antike*, 215–32. Tübingen.

———. 2004. "Priest, Laity and the Sacrament of the Eucharist in Sixth-Century Syria." *Huyoge* 7: 129–46.

———, ed. 2006. "The 'Regula ad Diaconos': John of Tella, His Eucharistic Ecclesiology and the Establishment of an Ecclesiastical Hierarchy in Exile." *OC* 90: 44–90.

———. 2008. *Justinian and the Making of the Syrian Orthodox Church*. Oxford.

Michelson, D. 2008. "'Though He Cannot Be Eaten, We Consume Him': Appeals to Liturgical Practice in the Christological Polemic of Philoxenos of Mabbug." In G. A. Kiraz, ed., *Malphono w-Rabo d-Malphone: Studies in Honor of Sebastian P. Brock*, 439–76. Piscataway, N.J.

Mihevc-Gabrovec, E. 1960. *Études sur la syntaxe de Joannes Moschos*. Ljubljana.

Milazzo, A. M. 1992. "Σύντονος χαρακτὴρ e ἀνειμένος χαρακτὴρ nella teoria retorica tardoantica." *SicGymn* 45: 71–82.

Miller, T. S. 1985. *The Birth of the Hospital in the Byzantine Empire*. Baltimore.

Mioni, E. 1950. "Le Vitae Patrum nella traduzione di Ambrogio Traversari." *Aevum* 24: 319–31.

———. 1951. "Il Pratum Spirituale di Giovanni Mosco." *OCP* 17: 61–94.

Montserrat, D. 1998. "Pilgrimage to the Shrine of SS Cyrus and John at Menouthis in Late Antiquity." In D. Frankfurter, ed., *Pilgrimage and Holy Space in Late Antique Egypt*, Religions in the Graeco-Roman World 134, 257–79. Leiden.

———. 2005. "'Carrying on the Work of the Earlier Firm': Doctors, Medicine and Christianity in the *Thaumata* of Sophronius of Jerusalem." In H. King, ed., *Health in Antiquity*, 230–42. London.

Moorhead, J. 1981. "The Monophysite Response to the Arab Invasions." *Byzantion* 51: 579–91.

Moreira, I. 2000. *Dreams, Visions and Spiritual Authority in Merovingian Gaul*. Ithaca.

Morelli, F. 2010. "'Amr e Martina: La reggenza di un'imperatrice o l'amministrazione araba d'Egitto." *ZPE* 173: 136–57.

Mueller-Jourdan, P. 2005. *Typologie spatio-temporelle de l'ecclesia byzantine*. Leiden.

Müller, C. D. G. 1968. *Die Homilie über die Hochzeit zu Kana und weitere Schriften des Patriarchen Benjamin I. von Alexandrien*. Heidelberg.

Munitiz, J. 1983. "The Link between Some Membra Disiecta of John Moschos." *AB* 101: 295–96.

Murphy F.-X., and P. Sherwood. 1973. *Constantinople II et III*. Paris.

Nau F., ed. 1902a. "Le texte grec des Récits utiles à l'âme du moine Anastase sur les saints pères du Sinai." *OC* 2: 58–89.

———. 1902b. "Vies et récits d'anchorètes (IVe–VIIe siècles), I: Analyse du ms. grec de Paris 1596." *ROC* 7 : 604–17.

———, ed. 1903a. "Le texte grec des Récits utiles à l'âme d'Anastase (le Sinaïte)." *OC* 3: 56–90.

———. 1903b. "Vies et récits d'anchorètes (IVe–VIIe siècles), II: Analyse du ms. grec de Paris 1596." *ROC* 8: 91–100.

Neil, B. 1998. "The *Lives* of Pope Martin I and Maximus the Confessor: Some Reconsiderations of Dating and Provenance." *Byzantion* 68: 91–109.

———. 2001. "The Greek *Life* of Maximus Confessor (*BHG* 1234) and Its Three Recensions." *SP* 36: 46–53.

———. 2006a. "Commemorating Pope Martin I: His Trial in Constantinople." *SP* 39: 77–82.
———. 2006b. "The *Miracles of Saints Cyrus and John:* The Greek Text and Its Transmission." *Journal of the Australian Early Medieval Association* 2: 183–93.
———. 2006c. *Seventh-Century Popes and Martyrs: The Political Hagiography of Anastasius Bibliothecarius.* Series Antiqua Australiensia 2. Turnhout.
———. 2009. *Leo the Great.* London.
———. 2010. "From *Tristia* to *Gaudia:* The Exile and Martyrdom of Pope Martin I." In J. Leemans, ed., *Martyrdom and Persecution in Late Antique Christianity: Festschrift Boudewijn Dehandschutter,* 179–94. Louvain.
Neil, B., and P. Allen. 2003. *The Life of Maximus Confessor—Recension 3.* Early Christian Studies 6. Sydney.
Nesbitt, J. W. 1997. In Crisafulli (1997) 1–30.
Nevo, Y. D., and J. Koren. 2003. *Crossroads to Islam: The Origins of the Arab Religion and the Arab State.* Amherst, N.Y.
Nichols, A. 1993. *Byzantine Gospel: Maximus the Confessor in Modern Scholarship.* Edinburgh.
Nissen, T. 1938. "Unbekannte Erzählungen aus dem Pratum sprituale." *BZ* 38: 351–76.
Nöldeke, T. 1878. *Geschichte der Perser und Araber zur Zeit der Sassaniden.* Leiden.
Noret, J. 1999. "La rédaction de la Disputatio cum Pyrrho (CPG 7698) de saint Maxime le Confesseur serait-elle postérieure à 655?" *AB* 117: 291–96.
———. 2000. "À qui était destiné la lettre *BHG* 1233d d'Anastase l'Apocrisiaire?" *AB* 118: 37–42.
O'Hara, M. D. 1985. "A Find of Byzantine Silver from the Mint of Rome for the Period A.D. 641–752." *Revue Suisse de Numismatique* 64: 105–40.
Ohme, H. 2008. "Oikonomia im monenergetisch-monotheletischen Streit." *ZAC* 12: 308–43.
Olster, D. 1985. "Chalcedonian and Monophysite: The Union of 616." *Bulletin de la Société d'Archéologie Copte* 27: 93–108.
———. 1993a. "The Construction of a Byzantine Saint: George of Choziba, Holiness, and the Pilgrimage Trade in Seventh-Century Palestine." *GOTR* 38: 309–22.
———. 1993b. *The Politics of Usurpation in the Seventh Century: Rhetoric and Revolution in Byzantium.* Amsterdam.
———. 1994. *Roman Defeat, Christian Response and the Literary Construction of the Jew.* Philadelphia.
O'Sullivan, S. 2004. "Sebeos' Account of an Arab Attack on Constantinople in 654." *BMGS* 28: 67–88.
Palmer, J. S. 1991. "Materielle Kultur im Pratum spirituale vom Johannes Moschos." In *XVIth International Congress of Byzantine Studies: Summaries of Communications,* vol. 2, 1068–70. Washington, D.C.
———. 1993a. "Latinismos en el léxico del Pratum spirituale de Juan Mosco." In P. Bádenas and J. M. Egea, eds., *Oriente y Occidente en la Edad Media: Influjos bizantinos en la cultura occidental,* 9–21. Vitoria-Gasteiz.
———. 1993b. *El monacato oriental en el* Pratum spirituale *de Juan Mosco.* Madrid.
———. 1994a. "Demonología en el Pratum spirituale de Juan Mosco." In *Actas del VIII Congreso español de estudios clásicos,* vol. 3, 304–8. Madrid.

———. 1994b. "El monje y la ciudad en el Pratum spirituale de Juan Mosco." In R. M. Aguilar, M. López Salvá, and I. Rodríguez Alfageme, eds., *Caris Didaskalis: Studia in honorem Ludovici Aegidii*, 495–504. Madrid.

———. 1997a. "John Moschus as a Source for the *Lives* of St. Symeon and St. Andrew the Fools." *SP* 32: 366–70.

———. 1997b. "Juan Mosco y la defensa del dogma de Calcedón." In M. Morfakidis and M. Alganza, eds. *La religión en el mundo griego: De la Antigüedad a la Grecia moderna*, 289–97. Granada.

Papathanassiou, M. 2006. "Stephanos of Alexandria: A Famous Byzantine Scholar, Alchemist, and Astrologer." In P. Magdalino and M. Mavroudi, eds., *The Occult Sciences in Byzantium*, 163–203. Geneva.

Paramelle, J. 1996. "Morceau égaré du *Corpus Dionysiacum*; ou, Pseudo–pseudo Denys? Fragment d'une *Lettre à Tite* inconnue." In Y. de Andia, ed., *Denys l'Aréopagite et sa postérité en Orient et en Occident*, 235–66. Paris.

Parente, P. 1953. "Uso e significato del termine θεοκίνητος nella controversia monotelistica." *RÉB* 11: 245–48.

Pasini, C. 1985. "Il monachesimo nel Prato di Giovanni Mosco e i suoi aspetti popolari." *VetChr* 22: 331–79.

Patrich, J. 1995. *Sabas, Leader of Palestinian Monasticism: A Comparative Study in Eastern Monasticism, 4th to 7th Century*. Dumbarton Oaks Studies 32. Washington, D.C.

Pattenden, P. 1975. "The Text of the *Pratum Spirituale*." *JThS*, n.s., 26: 38–54.

———. 1982. "Who Was the Father of St. John the Almoner?" *JThS*, n.s., 33: 191–94.

———. 1984. "The Editions of the *Pratum Spirituale*." *SP* 15: 16–19.

———. 1989. "Some Remarks on the Newly Edited Text of the 'Pratum' of John Moschus." *SP* 18: 45–51.

Peeters, P. 1933. "Pasagnathes-Persogenes." *Byzantion* 8: 405–23.

Pelikan, J. 1987. "The Odyssey of Dionysian Spirituality." In C. Luibheid et al., *Pseudo-Dionysius: The Complete Works*, 11–24. London.

Penkett, P. 2003. "Palestinian Christianity in the *Spiritual Meadow* of John Moschos." *Aram* 15: 173–84.

Perczel, I. 1999a. "Le pseudo-Denys, lecteur d'Origène." In W. Bienert, ed., *Origeniana septima*, 673–710. Louvain.

———. 1999b. "Une théologie de lumière: Denys l'Aréopagite et Évagre le Pontique." *RÉAug* 45: 79–120.

———. 2000a. "Once Again on Dionysius the Areopagite and Leontius of Byzantium." In T. Boiadjiev et al., eds., *Die Dionysius-Rezeption im Mittelalter*, 41–85. Turnhout.

———. 2000b. "Sergius of Reshaina's Syriac Translation of the *Dionysian Corpus*: Some Preliminary Remarks." In C. Baffioni, ed., *La diffusione dell'eredità classica nell'età tarodantica e medievale: Filologia, storia, dottrina*, 79–94. Alessandria.

———. 2001. "Pseudo-Dionysius and Palestinian Origenism." In J. Patrich, ed., *The Sabaite Heritage in the Orthodox Church from the Fifth Century to the Present*, Orientalia Lovaniensia Analecta 98, 261–82. Louvain.

———. 2006–7. "Finding a Place for the *Erotapokriseis* of Pseudo-Caesarius: A New Document of Sixth-Century Palestinian Origenism." *Aram* 18–19: 49–83.

———. 2008. "The Earliest Syriac Reception of Dionysius." *Modern Theology* 24: 557-71. [Reprint: S. Coakley and C. M. Stang, eds., *Re-thinking Dionysius the Areopagite*, 27-41. Chichester, 2009.]

Perrone, L. 1980. *La chiesa di Palestina e le controversie christologiche: Dal concilio di Efeso (431) al secondo concilio di Costantinopoli (553)*. Brescia.

———. 2001. "Palestinian Monasticism, the Bible and Theology in the Wake of the Second Origenist Controversy." In J. Patrich, ed., *The Sabaite Heritage in the Orthodox Church from the Fifth Century to the Present*, Orientalia Lovaniensia Analecta 98, 234-60. Louvain.

Pertusi, A. 1958. "L'encomio di S. Anastasio martire Persiano." *AB* 76: 5-63.

Pétridès, E. 1901. "Le monastère de Spoudaei à Jérusalem et les Spoudaei de Constantinople." *ÉO* 4: 225-31.

Petrina [née Stolz], Y. 2012. "Das Gold von Kyros und Johannes: Eine Goldschmiedewerkstatt in der Bucht von Abuqir in Ägypten. " *ActaArch* 63: 407-16.

Pierres, J. 1940. *S. Maximus confessor, princeps apologetarum synodi Lateranensis a. 649*. Rome.

Pinggéra, K. 2002. *All-Erlösung und All-Einheit: Studien zum 'Buch des heiligen Hierotheos' und seiner Rezeption in der syrisch-orthodoxen Theologie*. Wiesbaden.

Pitra, I.-B. 1868. *Iuris ecclesiastici Graecorum historia et monumenta*. 2 vols. Rome.

Plested, M. 2004. *The Macarian Legacy: The Place of Macarius-Symeon in the Eastern Christian Tradition*. Oxford.

Pourshariati, P. 2008. *Decline and Fall of the Sasanian Empire: The Sasanian-Parthian Confederacy and the Arab Conquest of Iran*. London.

Price, R. 2010. "Monotheletism: A Heresy or a Form of Words?" *SP* 48: 221-32.

Price, R., and M. Whitby. 2009. *Chalcedon in Context: Church Councils 400-700*. Liverpool.

Rapp, C. 1995. "Byzantine Hagiographers as Antiquarians, Seventh to Tenth Centuries." *ByzF* 21: 31-44.

———. 2004. "All in the Family: John the Almsgiver, Nicetas and Heraclius." *Nea Rhome: Rivista di Ricerche Bizantinistiche* 1: 121-34.

———. 2006. "Desert, City, and Countryside in the Early Christian Imagination." In J. Dijkstra and M. van Dijk, eds., *The Encroaching Desert: Egyptian Hagiography and the Medieval West*, 93-112. Leiden.

Reinink, G. J. 2002. "Heraclius, the New Alexander: Apocalyptic Prophecies during the Reign of Heraclius." In G. J. Reinink and B. H. Stolte, eds., *The Reign of Heraclius (610-641): Crisis and Confrontation*, 81-95. Louvain.

Richard, M. 1947. "Léonce de Byzance était-il origéniste?" *RÉB* 5: 31-66.

———. 1966. "Une faux dithélite: Le traité de saint Irénée au diacre Démétrius." In P. Wirth, ed., *Polychronion: Festschrift Franz Dölger zum 75. Geburtstag*, 431-40. Heidelberg.

———. 1970. "Le traité de Georges Hiéromoine sur les hérésies." *RÉB* 28: 239-69.

Riedinger, R. 1976. "Aus den Akten der Lateran-Synode von 649." *BZ* 69: 17-38. [Reprint: idem (1998) I.]

———. 1977. "Griechische Konzilsakten auf dem Wege ins lateinische Mittelalter." *AHC* 9: 253-301. [Reprint: idem (1998) V.]

———. 1979. *Lateinische Übersetzungen griechischer Häretikertexte des siebenten Jahrhunderts*. Vienna.

———. 1980. "Zwei Briefe aus den Akten der Lateransynode von 649." *JÖByz* 29: 37–59. [Reprint: idem (1998) VI.]
———. 1981. "Sprachschichten in der lateinischen Übersetzung der Lateranakten von 649." *ZKG* 92: 180–203. [Reprint: idem (1998) VIII.]
———. 1982a. "Die Epistula synodica des Sophronios von Jerusalem im Codex Parisinus BN graecus 1115." *Byzantiaka* 2: 143–54. [Reprint: idem (1998) XI.]
———. 1982b. "Die Lateransynode von 649 und Maximos der Bekenner." In F. Heinzer and C. von Schönborn, eds., *Maximus Confessor: Actes du Symposium pour Maxime le Confesseur, Fribourg, 2–5 Sept. 1980*, 111–21. Freiburg. [Reprint: R. Riedinger (1998) X.]
———. 1983. "Papst Martin I. und Papst Leo I. in den Akten der Lateran-Synode von 649." *JÖByz* 33: 87–88. [Reprint: idem (1998) XIII.]
———. 1984. "Die Nachkommen der Epistula synodica des Sophronios von Jerusalem (c. 634)." *RömHM* 26: 91–106. [Reprint: idem (1998) XIV.]
———. 1985. "Die Lateransynode von 649: Ein Werk der Byzantiner um Maximos Homologetes." *Byzantion* 13: 519–34. [Reprint: idem (1998) XV.]
———. 1994. "Die lateinischen Übersetzungen der Epistula encyclica Papst Martins I. (CPG 9403) und der Epistula synodica des Sophronios von Jerusalm (CPG 7635)." *Filologia Mediolatina: Rivista della Fondazione Ezio Franceschini* 1: 45–69. [Reprint: idem (1998) XX.]
———. 1996. "Wer hat den Brief Papst Martins I. an Amandus verfaßt?" *Filologia Mediolatina: Rivista della Fondazione Ezio Franceschini* 3: 95–104. [Reprint: idem (1998) XXI.]
———. 1998. *Kleine Schriften zu den Konzilsakten des 7. Jahrhunderts*. Instrumenta Patristica 34. Turnhout.
Riedinger, U. 1956. "Ps.-Dionysius, ps.-Kaisarios, und die Akoimeten." *BZ* 52: 276–96.
Riou, A. 1973. *Le monde et l'église selon Maxime le Confesseur*. Paris.
Rizou-Couroupos, S. 1987. "Un nouveau fragment de la keleusis d'Héraclius au pape Jean IV." In J. Drummer, ed., *Texte und Textkritik*, 531–32. Berlin.
Roosen, B. 2010. "Maximi Confessoris Vitae et Passiones Graecae: The Development of a Hagiographic Dossier." *Byzantion* 80: 408–61.
Roques, M. R. 1961. "Éléments pour une théologie de l'état monastique selon Denys l'Aréopagite." In *Théologie de la vie monastique: Études sur la tradition patristique*, Théologie 49, 283–314. Paris.
Rorem, P. E. 1989. "Moses as the Paradigm for the Liturgical Spirituality of Pseudo-Dionysius." *SP* 18: 275–79.
Rorem, P. E., and J. C. Lamoreaux. 1998. *John of Scythopolis and the Dionysian Corpus: Annotating the Areopagite*. Oxford.
Rozemond, K. 1977. "Jean Mosch, patriarche de Jérusalem en exil (610–634)." *VChr* 31: 60–67.
———. 1984. "La lettre De hymno trisagio du Damascène ou Jean Mosch, patriarche de Jérusalem." *SP* 15: 108–11.
Rubery, E. 2011. "Papal Opposition to Imperial Heresies: Text as Image in the Church of Santa Maria Antiqua in the Time of Pope Martin I (649–54/5)." *SP* 50: 3–30.
Rushforth, G. 1902. "The Church of Santa Maria Antiqua." *PBSR* 1: 1–123.
Sahas, D. J. 2003. "The Demonizing Force of the Arab Conquests: The Case of Maximus (ca. 580–662) as a Political 'Confessor.'" *JÖByz* 53: 97–116.

———. 2006. "The Face-to-Face Encounter between Patriarch Sophronius of Jerusalem and the Caliph 'Umar Ibn al-Khaṭṭāb." In E. Grypeou et al., eds., *The Encounter of Eastern Christianity with Early Islam*, 33–44. Leiden.
Sako, L. R. M., ed. 1983. *Lettre christologique du patriarche syro-oriental Īšō'yahb de Gḏālā (628–46): Étude, traduction et édition critique*. Rome.
Sánchez Valencia, R. 2003. "The Monophysite Conviction in the East versus Byzantium's Political Convenience: A Historical Look to Monotheletism in Palestine." *Aram* 15: 151–57.
Sansterre, J.-M. 1983. *Les moines grecs et orientaux à Rome aux époques byzantine et carolingienne (milieu du VI<sup>e</sup> s.–fin du IX<sup>e</sup> s.)*. 2 vols. Brussels.
———. 1989. "Les saints stylites de V<sup>e</sup> au XI<sup>e</sup> siècle: Permanence et évolution d'un type de sainteté." In J. Marx, ed., *Sainteté et martyre dans les religions du livre*, 33–45. Brussels.
———. 1991. "Apparitions et miracles à Ménouthis: De l'incubation païenne à l'incubation chrétienne." In A. Dierkens, ed., *Apparitions et miracles*, Problèmes d'Histoire des Religions 2, 69–83. Brussels.
Sarris, P. 2006. *Economy and Society in the Age of Justinian*. Cambridge.
———. 2011. *Empires of Faith: The Fall of Rome to the Rise of Islam, 500–700*. Oxford.
Sauget, J.-M. 1973. "Saint Grégoire le Grand et les reliques de saint Pierre dans la tradition arabe chrétienne." *RAC* 49: 301–9.
Sayed, G. G. A. 1984. *Untersuchungen zu den Texten über Pesyntheus Bischof von Koptos (569–632)*. Bonn.
Scarborough, J. 1984. "Early Byzantine Pharmacology." *DOP* 38: 213–32.
Schacht, J. 1936. "Der Briefwechsel zwischen Kaiser und Papst von 641/2 in arabischer Überlieferung." *Orientalia*, n.s., 5: 235–46.
Schick, R. 1995. *The Christian Communities of Palestine from Byzantine to Islamic Rule: A Historical and Archaeological Study*. Princeton.
Schmidt, A. 1996. "Die zweifache armenische Rezension der syrischen Chronik Michaels des Großen." *Le Muséon* 109: 299–319.
Schönborn, C. von. 1972. *Sophrone de Jérusalem: Vie monastique et confession dogmatique*. Théologie Historique 20. Paris.
———. 1975. "La primauté romaine vue d'Orient pendant la querelle du monoénergisme et du monothélisme (VII<sup>e</sup> siècle)." *Istina* 20: 476–90.
Schulz, H.-J. 1964. *Die byzantinische Liturgie: Vom Werden ihrer Symbolgestalt*. Freiburg. [Trans. M. J. O'Connell, *The Byzantine Liturgy: Symbolic Structure and Faith Expression*. New York, 1986.]
Schwaiger, G. 1977. "Die Honoriusfrage: Zu einer neuen Untersuchung des alten Falles." *ZKG* 88: 85–97.
Scott, R. 1985. "Malalas, the *Secret History*, and Justinian's Propaganda." *DOP* 39: 99–109.
Shaw, B. D. 2011. *Sacred Violence: African Christians and Sectarian Hatred in the Age of Augustine*. Cambridge.
Sherwood, P. 1952a. "An Annotated Date-List of the Works of Maximus Confessor." *Studia Anselmiana* 30: 1–64.
———. 1952b. "Sergius of Reshaina and the Syriac Versions of the Pseudo-Denis." *SEJG* 4: 174–83.

———. 1955. *The Earlier Ambigua of Saint Maximus the Confessor and His Refutation of Origenism*. Rome.

Shoemaker, S. 2006. "The Georgian *Life of the Virgin* Attributed to Maximus the Confessor: Its Authenticity(?) and Importance." In A. Muraviev and B. Lourié, eds., *Mémorial R. P. Michel van Esbroeck, S.J.*, 307–28. St. Petersburg.

———. 2012a. *The Death of a Prophet: The End of Muhammad's Life and the Beginnings of Islam*. Philadelphia.

———, ed. 2012b. *Maximus the Confessor: The Life of the Virgin*. New Haven.

Siecienski, A. E. 2010. *The Filioque: History of a Doctrinal Controversy*. Oxford.

Sivan, H. 2000. "From Byzantine to Persian Jerusalem: Jewish Perspectives and Jewish/Christian Polemics." *GRBS* 41: 277–306.

Skedros, J. C. 1999. *Saint Demetrios of Thessaloniki: Civic Patron and Divine Protector, 4th–7th Centuries C.E.* Harvard Theological Studies 47. Harrisburg.

Sodini, J.-P. 1998. "Les inscriptions de l'aqueduc de Kythrea à Salamine de Chypre." In *Eupsychia: Mélanges offerts à Hélène Ahrweiler*, 691–33. Paris.

Sorabji, R. 2003. "The Concept of the Will from Plato to Maximus the Confessor." In T. Pink and M. Stone, eds., *The Will and Human Action: From Antiquity to the Present Day*, 6–28. London.

Sotinel, C. 1992. "Autorité pontificale et pouvoir impérial sous le règne de Justinien: Le pape Vigile." *MÉFR* 104: 439–63.

———. 2005. "Emperors and Popes in the Sixth Century: The Western View." In M. Maas, ed., *The Cambridge Companion to the Age of Justinian*, 267–90. Cambridge.

Spain Alexander, S. 1977. "Heraclius, Byzantine Imperial Ideology and the David Plates." *Speculum* 52: 217–37.

Speck, P. 1997. *Varia*, vol. 6, *Beiträge zum Thema byzantinische Feindseligkeiten gegen die Juden im frühen siebten Jahrhundert*. Bonn.

———. 2000. "Zum Datum der Translation der Kreuzreliquien nach Konstantinopel." In idem, *Varia*, vol. 7, 166–79. Bonn.

Stannard, J. 1984. "Aspects of Byzantine Materia Medica." *DOP* 38: 205–12.

Steppa, J. E. 2002. *John Rufus and the World Vision of Anti-Chalcedonian Culture*. Piscataway, N.J.

Sterk, A. 2004. *Renouncing the World Yet Leading the Church: The Monk-Bishop in Late Antiquity*. Cambridge, Mass.

Stewart, C. 1991. *Working the Earth of the Heart: The Messalian Controversy in History, Texts and Language to AD 431*. Oxford.

Stolz, Y. 2008. "Kanopos oder Menouthis? Zur Identifikation einer Ruinenstätte in der Bucht von Abuqir in Ägypten." *Klio* 90: 193–207.

———. 2012. *See* Petrina [née Stolz], Y.

Stoyanov, Y. 2011. *Defenders and Enemies of the True Cross: The Sasanian Conquest of Jerusalem in 614 and Byzantine Ideology of Anti-Persian Warfare*. Vienna.

Stratos, A. 1968–78. *Byzantium in the Seventh Century*. 5 vols. Amsterdam.

———. 1976. "The Exarch Olympius and the Supposed Arab Invasion of Sicily in A.D. 652." *JÖByz* 25: 63–73.

———. 1982. "Expédition de l'empereur Constantin III surnommé Constant en Italie." In *Bizanzio e l'Italia: Raccolta di studi in memoria di Agostino Pertusi*, 348–57. Milan.

Suchla, B. R. 1980. *Die sogenannten Maximus-Scholien des Corpus Dionysiacum Areopagiticum*. Göttingen.
Taft, R. 1986. *The Liturgy of the Hours in East and West: The Origins of the Divine Office and Its Meaning for Today*. Collegeville, Minn.
———. 2000. "The βηματίκιον in the 6/7 c. Narration of the Abbots John and Sophronius (*BHGNA* 1438w): An Exercise in Comparative Liturgy." In H.-J. Feulner et al., eds., *Crossroad of Cultures: Studies in Liturgy and Patristics in Honour of Gabriele Winkler*, 675–92. Rome.
———. 2003. "Home-Communion in the Late Antique East." In C. V. Johnson, ed., *Ars Liturgiae: Worship, Aesthetics and Praxis: Essays in Honour of Nathan D. Mitchell*, 1–26. Chicago.
Tannous, J. 2006. "Monotheletism: The View from the Edge." Unpublished paper.
Temkin, O. 1991. *Hippocrates in a World of Pagans and Christians*. Baltimore.
Thacker, A. 1998. "Memorializing Gregory the Great: The Origin and Transmission of a Papal Cult in the Seventh and Early Eighth Centuries." *EME* 7: 59–84.
Thierry, N. 1997. "Héraclius et la vraie croix en Arménie." In J.-P. Mahé and R. W. Thomson, eds., *From Byzantium to Iran: Armenian Studies in Honour of Nina G. Garsoïan*, 165–86. Atlanta.
Thunberg, L. 1965. *Microcosm and Mediator: The Theological Anthropology of Maximus the Confessor*. Uppsala.
———. 1985. *Man and the Cosmos: The Vision of St. Maximus the Confessor*. Crestwood, N.Y.
Tollefsen, T. T. 2008. *The Christocentric Cosmology of St Maximus the Confessor*. Oxford.
———. 2012. *Activity and Participation in Late Antique and Early Christian Thought*. Oxford.
Törönen, M. 2007. *Union and Distinction in the Thought of St Maximus the Confessor*. Oxford.
Treadgold, W. 1990. "A Note on Byzantium's Year of the Four Emperors." *BZ* 83: 431–33.
Tyler-Smith, S. 2004. "Calendars and Coronations: The Literary and Numismatic Evidence for the Accession of Khusrau II." *BMGS* 28: 33–65.
Ullmann, W. 1960. "Leo I and the Theme of Papal Primacy." *JThS*, n.s., 11: 26–28.
———. 1981. *Gelasius I. (492–96): Das Papsttum an der Wende Spätantike zum Mittelalter*. Stuttgart.
Urbainczyk, T. 2002. *Theodoret of Cyrrhus*. Ann Arbor.
Usener, H., ed. 1907. *Der heilige Tychon*. Leipzig and Berlin.
Uthemann, K.-H. 1980. "Die 'philosophischen Kapitel' des Anastasius I. von Antiochen (559–598)." *OCP* 46: 306–60.
———. 1997. "Der Neuchalkedonismus als Vorbereitung des Monotheletismus: Ein Beitrag zum eigentlichen Anliegen des Neuchalkendonismus." *SP* 29: 373–413.
Vailhé, S. 1902. "Sophrone le sophiste et Sophrone le patriarche." Part 1. *ROC* 7: 360–85.
———. 1903. "Sophrone le sophiste et Sophrone le patriarche." Part 2. *ROC* 8: 32–69, 356–87.
Van Bekkum, W. J. 2002. "Jewish Messianic Expectations in the Age of Heraclius." In G. J. Reinink and B. H. Stolte, eds., *The Reign of Heraclius (610–641): Crisis and Confrontation*, 95–113. Louvain.
Van Dam, R. 1993. *Saints and Their Miracles in Late Antique Gaul*. Princeton.

van den Ven, P., ed. 1962. *La vie ancienne de saint Syméon Stylite le Jeune (521–592)*. 2 vols. Brussels.

Van Dieten, J. L. 1972. *Geschichte der Patriarchen von Sergios I. bis Johannes VI. (610–715)*. Amsterdam.

Van Roey, A. 1972. "Trois auteurs chalcédoniens syriens: Georges de Martyropolis, Constantin et Léon de Ḥarran." *OLP* 3: 125–53.

Vircillo Franklin, C. 1995. "Theodore of Tarsus and the Passio S. Anastasii (*BHL* 410b)." In Lapidge (1995a) 175–203.

———. 2004. *The Latin Dossier of Anastasius the Persian: Hagiographic Translations and Transformations*. Toronto.

Vivian, T. 2003. "Witness to Holiness: Abba Daniel of Scetis." *Coptic Church Review* 24 (2002) 2–52.

Voicu, S. J. 1995. "Cesaria, Basilio (*Ep.* 93/4) e Severo." *Augustinianum* 35: 697–703.

von Balthasar, H. U. 1961. *Kosmische Liturgie: Das Wiltbeld Maximus' des Bekenners*. Einsiedeln. [English trans. B. E. Daley, *Cosmic Liturgy: The Universe according to Maximus Confessor*. San Francisco, 2003.]

Ware, K. 1988. "Teaching the Faith: The Meaning of the Divine Liturgy for the Byzantine Worshipper." In R. Morris, ed., *Church and People in Byzantium*, 7–28. Birmingham.

Watt, J. W. 1980. "Philoxenus and the Old Syriac Version of Evagrius' Centuries." *OC* 64: 65–81.

Wessel, S. 2001. "Literary Forgery and the Monothelete Controversy: Some Scrupulous Uses of Deception." *GRBS* 42: 201–20.

———. 2008. *Leo the Great and the Spiritual Rebuilding of a Universal Rome*. Leiden.

Whitby, Mary. 1994. "A New Image for a New Age: George of Pisidia on the Emperor Heraclius." In E. Dąbrowa, ed., *The Roman and Byzantine Army in the East*, 197–225. Krakow.

———. 1998. "Defender of the Cross: George of Pisidia on the Emperor Heraclius and His Deputies." In eadem, ed., *The Propaganda of Power: The Role of Panegyric in Late Antiquity*, 247–73. Leiden.

———. 2002. "George of Pisidia's Presentation of the Emperor Heraclius and His Campaigns: Variety and Development." In G. J. Reinink and B. H. Stolte, eds., *The Reign of Heraclius (610–641): Crisis and Confrontation*, 157–74. Louvain.

Whitby, Michael, and Mary Whitby. 1989. *Chronicon Paschale, 284–628 AD*. Liverpool.

Widengren, G. 1961. "Research in Syrian Mysticism: Mystical Experiences and Spiritual Exercises." *Numen* 8: 161–98.

Wijk, N. van. 1933. "Einige Kapitel aus Johannes Moschos." *ZSlPh* 10: 60–66.

Wilken, R. L. 1992. *The Land Called Holy: Palestine in Christian History and Thought*. New Haven.

Wilkinson, J. 2002. *Jerusalem Pilgrims before the Crusades*. Warminster.

Winkelmann, F. 1987. "Die Quellen zur Erforschung des monenergetisch-monotheletischen Streites." *Klio* 69: 515–69.

———. 2001. *Der monenergetisch-monotheletische Streit*. Frankfurt.

Wipszycka, E. 1970. "Les confréries dans la vie religieuse de l'Égypte chrétienne." In D. H. Samuel. ed., *Proceedings of the Twelfth International Congress of Papyrology*, American Studies in Papyrology 7, 511–24. Toronto.

———. 1988. "La christianisation de l'Égypte aux IV$^e$ et VI$^e$ siècles." *Aegyptus* 68: 117–65.

Wolska-Conus, W. 1989. "Stéphanos d'Athènes et Stéphanos d'Alexandrie: Essai d'identification et de biographie." *RÉB* 47: 5-89.
Wood, P. 2010. *"We Have No King but Christ": Christian Political Thought in Greater Syria on the Eve of the Arab Conquest (c. 400-585)*. Oxford.
Woods, D. 2000. "On St. Artemios as 'Deacon.'" *BMGS* 24: 230-33.
———. 2003a. "Olympius and the 'Saracens' of Sicily." *BMGS* 27: 262 -65.
———. 2003b. "The Sixty Martyrs of Gaza and the Martyrdom of Bishop Sophronius of Jerusalem." *Aram* 15: 129-50.
———. 2007. "Adomnán, Arculf, and the True Cross: Overlooked Evidence for the Visit of the Emperor Heraclius to Jerusalem *c*. 630?" *Aram* 19: 403-13.
Wortley, J. 2001. "'Grazers' (βοσκοί) in the Judean Desert." In J. Patrich, ed., *The Sabaite Heritage in the Orthodox Church from the Fifth Century to the Present*, Orientalia Lovaniensia Analecta 98, 37-48. Louvain.
Zaborowski, J. R. 2003. "Egyptian Christians Implicating Chalcedonians in the Arab Takeover of Egypt: The Arabic Apocalypse of Samuel of Qalamun." *OC* 87: 100-115.
Zocca, E. 1987. "Onorio I e la tradizione occidentale." *Augustinianum* 27: 571-615.
———. 1992. "Onorio e Martino: Due papi di fronte al monotelismo." In *Martino I papa (649-653) e il suo tempo*, 103-47. Spoleto.
Zotenberg, H., ed. 1883. *Chronique de Jean, évêque de Nikiou*. Paris.
Zuckerman, C. 1995. "La petite Augusta et le Turc: Epiphania-Eudocie sur les monnaies d'Héraclius." *RN* 150: 113-26.
———. 2002a. "La haute hiérarchie militaire en Afrique byzantine." *AntTard* 10: 169-75.
———. 2002b. "Heraclius in 625." *RÉB* 60: 189-97.
———. 2002c. "Jerusalem as the Center of the Earth in Anania Širakac'i's Ašxarhac'oyc'." In M. Stone et al., eds., *The Armenians in Jerusalem and the Holy Land*, 255-74. Louvain.
———. 2005. "Learning from the Enemy and More: Studies in 'Dark Centuries' Byzantium." *Millennium* 2: 79-135.

# INDEX

Abū Bakr, caliph, 230
Acacius, patriarch of Constantinople, 35, 226
Acephali, 131
Acoemetae, 226
Aeliotes, laura of, 45
Agapetus, pope, 124, 136
Agapius of Manbij, 220, 288, 318
*akribeia*, 219, 222, 237–38, 258, 277, 326–27, 338
Alexakis, Alexander, 260
Alexander, patriarch of Antioch, 124
Al-Tel, Othman Ismael, 243
'Ali, caliph, 325
Ambrose of Milan, 13
Amos, patriarch of Jerusalem, 92
'Amr ibn al-'Āṣ, 250, 279
Anastasius Apocrisiarius, 292–93, 302, 323
Anastasius Bibliothecarius, 259, 302
Anastasius, disciple of Maximus, 153–54, 240, 254, 268, 274, 290, 310, 313, 317, 321–23, 332
Anastasius, emperor, 126, 227
Anastasius of Sinai: on monasticism, 335–36; on the eucharist, 335–36
Anastasius, patriarch of Alexandria, 104
Anastasius I, patriarch of Antioch, 36, 192–94
Anastasius II, patriarch of Antioch, 202
Anastasius the Persian, 127, 298
*Anonymous Chronicle to 1234*, 280, 318, 324
Antichrist, 204, 278
Antiochus Monachus, 95–97, 142, 204

Antony of Choziba, 96, 100, 137
apocalypse, expectation of, 158–59, 171, 278
*apocrisiarii*, Roman, 124, 129, 225, 259, 283–84, 287, 290, 292, 321, 324, 326
Apollinarius of Laodicea, 88, 189, 204
Apollinarius, patriarch of Alexandria, 124, 209
Aquae Salviae, 111, 298–99
Arcadius of Cyprus, 219–20, 239, 261n138
Ardashir III, 156
Aristotle, 211
Aspagurius, general, 102–3
Athanasius, patriarch of Alexandria, 8, 13, 124
Athanasius the Camel Driver, patriarch of Antioch, 104, 202–5, 221
Augustine, 341
Avars, 108, 140–41, 164

Barsanuphius and John, 19, 23
Basiliscus, emperor, 35, 38
Basil of Caesarea, 7–8, 189–90
Bathrellos, Demetrios, 196, 217, 237
battle: of Gaza in 634, 230; of Nineveh in 627, 141; of Phoenix in 654, 305, 309; of Siffin in 657, 325; of Yarmuk in 636, 242
Bedouin, raids of, 95–96, 142, 165, 168, 204
Benjamin, patriarch of Alexandria, 206
Binns, John, 119–20
Bonosus, 50
*Book of Ceremonies*, 308

## INDEX

*Book of Pontiffs*, 263, 286, 290, 292, 300, 320
Boran, 200–201
Boudignon, Christian, 147, 150, 152–53, 155, 165, 255, 339–40
Bousset, Wilhelm, 93
Brandes, Wolfram, 278, 308, 325
Brock, Sebastian, 144, 192–93, 198
Brown, Peter, 37

Calamon, 96
Cameron, Averil, 162, 337
Caner, Daniel, 8–9
Canopus, 48
Cedrenus, 319
Cella Nova, 111–12, 115, 290, 299
Chadwick, Henry, 107
Chalcedon, council of: doctrinal dissent over, 38–40; legislation of, 8–9, 227. *See also* Monenergism; Monotheletism; *Tome* of Leo; union
Choziba, Monastery of, 137
*Chronicle of Seert*, 201, 203
Clement of Alexandria, 114
Climacus, John, 183
Coates-Stephens, Robert, 111
collective sin, 99–100, 116–17, 138, 161, 185, 245, 249, 278, 296, 338
Comitas, catholicus of Armenia, 97
*Commemoration*, 303–6
Constans I, 311
Constans II, emperor: Caucasian progresses of, 325; doctrinal politics of, 260, 262, 280, 282–85, 291, 300, 313–17, 322, 325–27, 338–40; Muslims and, 279, 281, 283, 301, 305–6, 316, 320, 341; political propaganda of, 308, 312; political rebellion and, 279–81, 287–89, 300–301, 318–19, 339; relation to Maximus, 153; succession of, 252–54, 284.
Constantine I, emperor, 160–61, 281, 308–9, 311–12
Constantine IV, emperor, 318
Constantine of Perge, 324
Constantine Sacellarius, 150, 162
Constantinople: Avar-Persian siege of, 108, 141, 164; council of in 662, 322–23; first ecumenical council at, 227; Muslim attack upon, 305–6; relations with North Africa, 254–59, 287–88; relations with Rome, 209, 225–28, 238–40, 259–64, 282–85, 291–92, 294–95, 320–21, 324, 326.
Cooper, Adam, 169, 176, 275
Cosmas and Damian, saints, 121, 319. *See also* *Miracles of Cosmas and Damian*

Cyprus, council of in 636, 239–41
Cyril, patriarch of Alexandria, 47–48
Cyril of Jerusalem, 13
Cyril of Scythopolis: compared to Moschus, 117, 119–20; John of Scythopolis and, 32–33; on asceticism, 16–17; on Evagrius Ponticus, 18, 20–22; ordination of monks in, 22, 34–35, 37; Origenism and, 18–22, 31.
Cyrus and John, saints: assimilated to doctors, 64–65; imitators of Christ, 71–72; martyrdom of, 47; sponsors of Sophronius, 57–58; translation of, 47. *See also* Menuthis; *Miracles of Cyrus and John*
Cyrus of Nikiu, 206
Cyrus of Phasis, patriarch of Alexandria: support for monenergism, 197–99, 202, 205–10, 239, 285; trial and exile of, 250–51, 263

Dagron, Gilbert, 226, 281, 311–12
Daley, Brian, 20
Damian, patriarch of Alexandria, 104
Daniel of Scetis, 92
Daniel the Stylite, 34–35, 37
David, king, 160–61
David, son of Heraclius, 251
Democritus, 60, 63, 65–66
Déroche, Vincent, 51, 102, 333, 336
Didymus the Blind, 18
Dioscorus, patriarch of Alexandria, 40
*Disputation with Pyrrhus*, 196–98, 285–86, 315
*Dispute at Bizya*, 314–17, 322
*Doctrina Patrum*, 203
Dvin, Council of in 649, 301

*Ekthesis*, 240–41, 250–51, 254, 259–62, 265, 267, 269, 280, 282, 286
Elert, Werner, 191
Elias, patriarch of Jerusalem, 128
emperor: church councils and, 314; sacerdotal status of, 310–12, 339
Ennaton, 53n44, 92, 118, 129
Ephraim, patriarch of Antioch, 121, 131–32
Epiphanius, patrician, 315–16
Eubulus of Lystra, 203
eucharist: Anastasius of Sinai and, 335–36; anti-Chalcedonians and, 38–42, 139, 337; ascetic participation in, 13–14, 33–42; *Dispute at Bizya* and, 316; *Georgian Appendix to the Spiritual Meadow* and, 329–32; hagiography and, 13–15, 34–42; House of Placidia and, 292, 324; indiscriminate participation in, 39–41, 85, 133–34, 221, 330; John Rufus and,

38–41; Leontius of Neapolis and, 85, 335; Maximus's *Mystagogy* and, 178, 180–81, 333; minimalist attitudes towards, 9–12, 14–15, 23, 29–30, 33, 38, 49, 76, 87, 171–73, 181, 332; miracle collections and, 81–82; *Miracles of Cyrus and John* and, 43, 54–55, 76–79, 132–33, 332–33; monenergist unions and, 200–3, 206–7, 221; monothelete crisis and, 326–27; place of in Second Origenist Crisis, 22–25; Pseudo-Dionysius the Areopagite and, 28–29; *Record of the Trial* and, 310–11; Roman deposition of Pyrrhus and, 290; sectarian identity and, 38, 40–43, 49, 79, 85, 131–33, 185, 222, 244–50, 276, 325–26, 336; seventh-century Chalcedonians and, 336–37; Severus of Antioch and, 41; Sophronius's patriarchal sermons and, 247–50, 333; *Spiritual Meadow* and, 128–38, 333; stylites and, 34–37, 43; Theodosius, brother of Constans II, and, 319; *Tome* of Gelasius and, 227
Eudocia, wife of Heraclius, 153, 252
Eudocia, daughter of Heraclius, 250–51
Eugenius I, pope, 320, 332
Eukratas, 106, 149–50, 163, 170, 256
Eulogius, patriarch of Alexandria, 128–30, 218–19
Euprepius, son of Plutinus, 292, 302
Euripides, 126
Eusebius of Caesarea, 223
Eustathians, 7–8, 10–11
Eusturgius, Monastery of, 119
Euthymius, Monastery of, 118
Eutyches, 204
Eutychius, historian, 282
Evagrius Ponticus, 11–12, 14, 16, 18–25, 29, 31–33, 49, 171, 178, 183
Evans, David, 20
Ezr, catholicus of Armenia, 200, 221

Fifth Ecumenical Council, 18, 21
*Filioque*, 270
Fiori, Emiliano, 30
*fitna*, first, 320, 325
Flavian, patriarch of Constantinople, 128–29
florilegia, 191–94, 198, 211, 260, 315
Flusin, Bernard, 16–17, 21, 32, 161, 298
Follieri, Enrica, 106–7, 232

Gaianites, 88, 218
Galen, 60–61, 63, 65–66
Gangra, Council of, 7–8, 10–11
Garitte, Gérard, 113,

Gascou, Jean, 47–48, 58
Gelasius, pope, 226–27, 277, 341
Gennadius, patriarch of Constantinople, 35, 128
George Arsas, 197
George of Choziba, 96, 127
George of Pisidia, 159–62
George of Resh'aina, 144, 150, 153, 234, 239–41, 289–90, 324
George, higoumen of Theodosius, 232–33, 297
George, *magister*, 301, 304
George, patriarch of Alexandria, 251
George, prefect of Africa, 110, 137, 151–52, 254–59, 280, 288, 309
*Georgian Appendix to the Spiritual Meadow*: asceticism and, 330–32, 340; authorship of, 113, 329; Constans II and, 318–19, 330; eucharist and, 329–31, 340; Gregory the Great and, 113–14, 329; Rome and, 329; Sophronius and, 243
Golitzin, Alexander, 30
Gregory, exarch of Africa, 285, 288–89, 300, 307
Gregory of Nazianzus, 189–90
Gregory, patriarch of Antioch, 128
Gregory the Great, pope, 111–15, 124, 128–29, 290
Guillaumont, André, 18

Hagia Sophia, 316
Haldon, John, 67, 337, 339
Harvey, Susan Ashbrook, 37, 117–20
Hausherr, Irénée, 23
Heid, Stefan, 228
Heptastomus, Laura of, 92
Heraclianus of Chalcedon, 217
Heraclius, emperor: acclamation of, 308; communion with anti-Chalcedonians, 200–201, 203; death of, 251–52, 254; defeats to Muslims, 230, 242, 263, 307; doctrinal politics of, 105, 185, 187–88, 194–208, 210, 220, 224–25, 231, 234, 255, 260, 295, 327, 338–39; economic crisis under, 109–10, 263; peace with Shahrbaraz, 156–57; Persian campaigns of, 88–89, 140–42, 199, 208, 327, 338; revolt of, 50; True Cross and, 155–59, 185–86, 204
Heraclius Constantine, emperor, 51, 153, 252, 254, 258, 260, 265
Heraclius, son of Constans II, 318
Heraclonas, emperor, 252–54, 260, 265, 284
Hippocrates, 60–61, 63, 65–66
*History of the Monks in Egypt*, 14–15,
*History of the Patriarchs of Alexandria*, 103, 206–7, 250
holy fools, 121, 334–35

Hombergen, Daniel, 20–22
Honorius, pope, 209–11, 214, 219, 233–34, 238–40, 250, 259–60, 262–63, 267–70, 282
Horn, Cornelia, 39
Horrocks, Geoff, 126
Hovorun, Cyril, 195, 201, 218
Howard-Johnston, James, 242
*Hypomnesticum*, 302

Ibn 'Abd al-Ḥakam, 288
icons, 260, 339
Isaac, exarch of Italy, 263, 300
Isaac, general, 102, 104
Isaiah, prophet, 72
Isho'yahb, Nestorian catholicus, 201, 221
Isis, cult of at Menouthis, 47
Islam, conquests of, 106, 139, 158, 223, 228, 230–31, 233, 241–43, 250–51, 263, 269, 277–80, 283, 288–90, 300, 305–7, 309, 316, 320, 324, 326–28, 338–39

Jacob Baradaeus, 204
Jacob, prophet, 39
Jankowiak, Marek, 104–5, 216, 219, 240, 288, 318
Jerusalem: doctrinal scene at, 187, 204–5, 233–34, 295; fall to Muslims, 239–41; fall to Persians, 94–95; Heraclius at, 158–59, 186.
Jews: forced baptism of in 632, 110, 170–71; polemical texts against, 184–85, 278
Job, 70
John Chrysostom, 13, 124, 189–90
John Cubicularius, 147, 150, 152, 162, 222, 254, 256, 309
John IV, pope, 252, 259–62, 265, 267, 282
John of Cyzicus, 146–47, 167–68
John of Ephesus, 117
John of Nikiu, 50, 103, 251, 253, 258, 279–80, 284
John of Philadelphia, 296–97
John of Scythopolis, 31–33
John Rufus, 38–41, 86, 131, 330
John the Almsgiver, patriarch of Alexandria: association with Heraclius and Nicetas, 50–51, 101–5, 153; doctrinal stance of, 51–54, 102, 104, 197–98; election of 50; Leontius of Neapolis's presentation of, 333–34; surrender of Alexandria and, 102–4; union of 617 and, 104–5
John the Baptist, 39
John the Deacon, biographer of Gregory the Great, 113
John the Faster, patriarch of Constantinople, 36
Judas, 29, 79, 207

Julianists, 88
Justin I, emperor, 42
Justin II, emperor, 35
Justinian I, emperor: legislation of, 16–17; on the Christological operations, 192–93, 195; Origenism and, 18–19, 25, 31

Kavadh Shiroe, 155–56
Khusrau II, 88, 111, 140–41, 155–56, 158, 161, 298
*Khuzistan Chronicle*, 95, 103
Kubrat, 253
Kurisikios, 147, 165–69, 187

Larchet, Jean-Claude, 182, 266–67, 274
Lateran Council of 649, 187, 189, 198, 212, 237, 251, 269, 273–74, 280, 283, 287, 289, 291, 293–300, 302, 304, 312, 314–15, 323–24
Leo I, emperor, 34
Leontius of Byzantium: Christological operations and, 196; Origenism and, 19–20
Leontius of Jerusalem, 196
Leontius of Neapolis: eucharist and, 85, 335; *Life of John the Almsgiver* of, 50, 52–53, 85, 102–4, 109, 152–53, 332; *Life of Symeon the Holy Fool* of, 334–35; urban holiness and, 333–35.
Leo, pope, 124, 129–30, 189–90, 210, 219, 227, 235–36. See also *Tome of Leo*
*Life of Antony*, 8, 13
Lithazomen, 92, 125
liturgy, monks and, 15, 36–7, 84–85, 228–30. See also eucharist
Lombards, 263
Louth, Andrew, 106, 183, 232

Macarius, patriarch of Antioch, 323
Macarius, patriarch of Jerusalem, 136
Macedonius, patriarch of Antioch, 323
Maisano, Riccardo, 91
Mango, Cyril, 159
*Maronite Chronicle*, 318
Martin, pope: anathematisation of, 322; arrest of, 301–3; association with Theodore Spudaeus and Theodosius of Gangra, 302; exile of, 303–5, 313, 319; Lateran Council and, 294–97, 304; *Letters* of, 187, 295–97, 303, 319; *Life* of, 145–46; Olympius and, 300–301, 303; pontificate of, 292–301; trial of, 278, 280–81, 303–7
Martin, son of Heraclius, 251
Martina, wife of Heraclius, 252–54, 256–59, 280, 284, 309

INDEX    389

Maurice, *cartularius*, 263, 300
Maurice, emperor, 121, 186
Maximus Confessor: *Acts of the Lateran Council* and, 293–95; *akribeia* and, 327–28, 332; Anastasius I of Antioch and, 194; *Ambigua* of, 213; apocalypse and, 171, 278; association with Alexandria, 148, 150; association with Moschus and Sophronius, 149–51, 153, 163–64; association with political rebellion, 254–59, 280–81, 287–89, 300–301, 309, 319, 325, 339, 341; association with secular elite, 148, 151–55; association with Theodore Spudaeus and Theodosius of Gangra, 302; as the last late antique holy man, 339–42; at Rome, 289, 293–95; *Book on the Ascetic Life* of, 171; *Centuries on Love* of, 171–72; commentary on Pseudo-Dionysius, 174; Council of Cyprus in 636 and, 240, 253–54; Cyzicus and, 146–47; death of, 323; defence of Pope Honorius, 267–68, 270, 274; defence of Pope Theodore, 270, 274; disputation with Pyrrhus and, 285–86, 288–89; doctrinal silence and, 213, 264, 285, 291, 310, 313–16; dyotheletism and, 225, 265–70, 280, 285–86, 314, 338; early life of, 142–51, 155, 164–65; early pronouncements on the operations, 213–17, 285–86; early pronouncements on the wills, 266; emperor and, 222–23, 228, 231, 281, 293, 307, 309, 310–14, 339, 341; eucharist and, 143, 170–73, 178, 180–81, 221, 250, 276, 310–12, 324–26, 340; eucharistic minimalism within, 171–73; exile of, 313–18, 321–23, 325–26; *Exposition on the Lord's Prayer* of, 171–72, 266; final punishment of, 323–26; flight from the East, 164–65, 167–68; Greek *Life* of, 143–46; in Syria, 254; Islam and, 231, 278; *Letter to Anastasius* of, 274, 321–22, 332; *Letter to Thalassius* of, 259, 270–72; *Letters* of, 147, 149–52, 162–70, 187, 213–15, 222–23, 231, 254–59, 309; North Africa and, 149, 151–55, 163, 170–71, 254–59, 299; on Cyprus, 150; *Opuscula* of, 110, 191, 213, 217, 260, 266–67, 271–72, 274, 283, 322; *Passiones* of, 145–46; *Questions to Thalassius* of, 266; reaction to forced baptism of Jews in 632, 170–71; respect for clerical vocation, 143, 166–67, 169–70; Roman pre-eminence and, 225, 270–76, 278, 293, 312; Syriac *Life* of, 144, 148–49, 234, 239–41, 253–54, 289–90, 324; trial of, 152, 260, 274, 281, 305–13, 324–25; triumph of Heraclius and, 162–63, 223, 225; Virgin and, 303, 317, 318n174. See also *Mystagogy* of Maximus Confessor

medicine: late-antique healing culture and, 67; *Miracles of Cyrus and John* and, 59–69
Menas, patriarch of Constantinople, 193, 196–98, 210
Menas, saint, 54
Menuthis, shrine of Cyrus and John at: history of, 47–48; impresarios within, 48; reported clientele of, 46, 48, 54–55; strategies of resistance within, 54–55
Menze, Volker, 41
Messalianism, 10–11, 334–35
Michael the Syrian, 104, 202–3, 205, 318, 324
Mioni, Elpidio, 92
*Miracles of Artemius*, 67–69, 80–84, 86
*Miracles of Cosmas and Damian*, 80–82, 86
*Miracles of Cyrus and John*: anti-Chalcedonians within, 54–56, 76–78, 88, 276, 338; as analogies for the spiritual life, 48–49, 69–73; clerical mediation and, 80, 84–85; compared to Sophronius's patriarchal sermons, 247, 249–50; composition of, 45, 57; designation of 'Rome' within, 107–8; dyenergism within, 197–98, 211–12; eucharist and, 43, 76–9, 84–85, 132–33, 135, 139, 171, 183, 221, 249–50, 332, 338; healing power of, 58; healing within, 45, 48–49; heretics and, 87–88, 276, 338; Hippocratic medicine and, 59–69; purpose of, 58–59; recommendation of asceticism in, 73–76; Sophronius as author of, 55–58. See also Sophronius of Jerusalem
*Miracles of Demetrius*, 68, 80
*Miracles of Thecla*, 80–82, 86
*Miracles of Therapon*, 68
Modestus, patriarch of Jerusalem, 96–97, 142, 159, 169, 186, 188, 204, 233–34, 298
monasticism: ecclesial subordination of, 7–9, 15, 25–28, 33–35, 42–43, 121, 143, 332; economy of in Palestine, 97, 186; imperial subordination of, 17, 43
monenergism: Constantinopolitan suppression of, 210, 213, 240–41; *Disputation with Pyrrhus* and, 285–86; imperial support for, 194–206, 224, 264; in Armenia, 200, 221; in Egypt, 205–9, 219, 221–22, 327; in Palestine, 187–88; in Persia, 200–202, 221; in Syria, 202–5, 221; intellectual origins of, 188–96; Lateran Council and, 295, 297; relation to monotheletism, 264–65; Sophronius's florilegium against, 211; Sophronius's resistance to, 209–22, 234–41
monotheletism: *Disputation with Pyrrhus*, 285–86; florilegium of, 192–94; intellectual

monotheletism *(continued)*
  origins of, 188–96; imperial promotion of, 225, 240, 260, 264, 282–83; Lateran Council and, 295, 297; Maximus's opposition to, 265–68; North African resistance to, 287–89; Paul II of Constantinople and, 283; relation to monenergism, 264–65; Roman opposition to, 259–64
Moschus, John: as priest, 123; as possible patriarch of Jerusalem, 168–69; at Alexandria under John the Almsgiver, 49–53, 85, 105, 131, 152–53, 205, 334; at Rome, 111–15, 290, 299; burial in Jerusalem, 231–33; death at Rome, 231; date of death, 232n21; early life of, 44–45; in North Africa, 110–11, 151, 299; *Life of John the Almsgiver* by, 50–52, 101–4, 110, 332; on Cyprus, 100–101; retreat from Alexandria, 98, 101; retreat to the West, 106–10; Stephanus the Sophist and, 63–64. See also *Spiritual Meadow*
Mount Sinai, 45, 135, 231
Movsēs Daskhurants'i, 325
Mu'āwiya, caliph, 324
Muhammad, prophet, 230
Muslims. See Islam
Mystagogical treatises, 12–13, 173
*Mystagogy* of Maximus Confessor: active and contemplative Christians within, 178–83; church unity within, 174–5; compared to Sophronius's patriarchal sermons, 246–47; compared to the *Spiritual Meadow*, 183–84; context of, 183–84; date of, 173–74; ecclesial symbolism and, 175–77; eucharist and, 178, 180–81, 221, 250, 276; Pseudo-Dionysius and, 173, 182; purpose of, 173; structure of, 174; symbolism of the liturgy within, 177–81. See also Maximus Confessor

*Narration of the Abbots John and Sophronius*, 229
*Narrations Concerning the Exile of the Holy Pope Martin*, 302–3
Nau, François, 92, 154
Nea Laura, 45
Nestorius, 200–201, 269
Nestorianism, 195, 200–201, 206, 226
Nicephorus, 109, 160, 216, 250–53, 284
Nicetas, cousin of Heraclius, 50–51, 101–5, 109, 153–55
Nicetas, son of Shahrbaraz, 157, 159
Nissen, Theodor, 93
North Africa: George, prefect of, 110, 137, 151–52, 254–59, 280, 288, 309; Gregory, exarch of, 285, 288–89, 300, 307; John Moschus in, 110–11, 151, 299; Laura of Sabas in, 290, 298; Maximus Confessor in, 149, 151–55, 163, 170–71, 254–59, 299, 307; Muslim conquest of, 279, 289, 307; Nicetas and, 153–54; political rebellions of, 254–59, 288–89, 300; relations with Constantinople, 254–59, 278–88; Pyrrhus and, 252–53, 284–86; resistance to monotheletism, 287–89; Sophronius in, 110–11, 151, 299

Ohme, Heinz, 218
*oikonomia*, 218–19, 222, 295, 310, 314–16, 327, 338
Olster, David, 249
Olympius, exarch of Italy, 300–301, 303–4
ordination, of monks, 8, 22, 33–35, 37, 123, 332
Origenism: anathemas against, 18–19, 25, 31; John of Scythopolis and, 32–33; Maximus Confessor and, 149; Pseudo-Dionysius and, 25–26, 30; second crisis over, 18–22, 31–32, 43; Stephen bar Sudaili and, 24

*Pact of Union*, 205–6, 211–12, 218, 231, 265
Palaia Laura, 133, 144
Palladius, 14–15
Pantaleon, 296
papacy. See Rome
*parrhēsia*, 339–40
*Paschal Chronicle*, 50, 94
*Passion of the Sixty Martyrs of Gaza*, 243–44
Pattenden, Philip, 91, 93, 107
Paul, consul, 314–15
Paul of Samosata, 227
Paul II, patriarch of Constantinople, 253, 262, 282–84, 287, 292, 305, 315, 319, 326
Paul, saint, 40, 111–12, 227
Paul the One-eyed, 196, 199, 220
Penthus, coenobium of, 119
Perczel, István, 21
Persians: after deposition of Khusrau, 155–57; at Jerusalem, 94–95, 98–100, 116, 138, 276; invasions of, 45, 49–50, 88–89, 94–95, 98–99, 102–4, 108, 140–42, 165, 168, 171, 197; provincial reactions to, 184
Peter, general of Numidia, 152, 307, 309
Peter III, patriarch of Antioch, 104
Peter, patriarch of Constantinople, 305, 319–23, 325
Peter, saint, 111–14, 129, 227, 271–74
Peter the Fuller, patriarch of Antioch, 38
Peter the Iberian, 38, 41
Peter the Illustrious, 271
Pharon, laura of, 45, 128

Philagrius, 252–53
Philoxenus of Mabbug, 23–24
Phocas, emperor, 49–50, 162
Photius, patriarch of Constantinople, 218–19
pilgrimage, 97
Pinggéra, Karl, 26
Placidia, House of, 292, 324–26
Plato, *Apology* of, 306
Plato, exarch of Italy, 152, 290, 310
Porphyry, 78
Price, Richard, 218, 270
*Prologue to the Spiritual Meadow*: authorship of, 107–8; on Moschus and Sophronius, 101, 123, 297
*Psēphos*, 213–16, 218, 220, 230, 234, 238, 240, 240n58, 241, 264–65, 291, 315, 327
Pseudo-Dionysius the Areopagite: John of Scythopolis and, 31–33; Maximus's commentary on, 174; Maximus's *Mystagogy* and, 173, 182; on the ecclesial hierarchy, 26–28; on the eucharist, 28–29; on monasticism, 26–28, 43; Origenism and, 25–26, 30; relation to Stephen bar Sudaili, 25–26, 29–30; Sergius of Resh'aina and, 31; theandric operation in, 206, 212
Pseudo-Macarius, 11–12, 16, 49, 172
Pseudo-Sebēos, 94–95, 97, 159–60, 289
Pyrrhus, patriarch of Constantinople, 196, 213–16, 251–53, 259–60, 262, 269, 271, 282–88, 290–92, 305, 315, 326

Rapp, Claudia, 51
*Record of the Trial*, 152, 260, 274, 306–14, 320, 328, 332
Renatus, monastery of, 298
Riedinger, Rudolf, 293
Romanus the Melodist, 84
Rome: claims to pre-eminence, 227–28, 341; differentiation of secular and sacred, 226–28; *Dispute at Bizya* and, 315; Maximus's celebration of, 270–76, 278, 332, 338–41; monotheletism and, 240, 259–64, 282–87; Moschus at 111–15; Palestinian celebration of, 112–14, 124, 129–30, 139, 270–76; patronage of eastern ascetics, 112–15, 225–26, 295, 299–300; political rebellion and, 300–301; Pyrrhus and, 286–87, 305; relations with Constantinople, 209, 225–28, 238–40, 259–64, 282–85, 291–92, 294–95, 320–21, 324, 326; relations with Palestinians, 262, 264–76, 295–300, 321, 332, 338–40
Roosen, Bram, 145–46
Rothari, 263

Rozemond, Keetje, 106, 168–69
Rubery, Eileen, 190

Sabas, North African Laura of, 290, 298
Sabas, Palestinian Laura of, 95–96, 107, 113, 119, 124, 142, 230, 290, 298
Sabas, Roman Monastery of, 115, 290, 299
Samuel of Kalamon, 207
Sansterre, Jean-Marie, 113
Santa Maria Antiqua, 189
Scholarii, coenobium of, 133, 137
Sergius Eukratas, 149, 254n109
Sergius Magoudas, 307
Sergius of Arsinoe, 191, 196, 198
Sergius of Joppa, 187, 204–5, 233–34, 295
Sergius of Resh'aina, 31
Sergius, patriarch of Constantinople, 158, 191, 194, 196–99, 202, 206, 209–11, 213–14, 216–21, 231, 233–34, 237–38, 240, 250–51, 260, 263, 267–69, 285, 313, 327
Severans, 52, 76, 88, 130–34, 196, 199, 205, 220, 254, 256, 338. *See also* Theodosians
Severinus, pope, 252, 259–60, 262–63
Severus of Antioch, 41, 76, 131, 134, 195, 206
Shahrbaraz, 94, 141–42, 156, 159, 200
Sherwood, Polycarp, 217
Sixth Ecumenical Council, 198, 200, 205–6, 283, 318, 323
Sophronius of Jerusalem: active under Muslim rule, 243–44, 246; anathematisation of, 322; Arcadius of Cyprus and, 219–20; as author of *Prologue to the Spiritual Meadow*, 106–8; as impresario of Cyrus and John, 55–58; as patriarch of Jerusalem, 187, 228–29, 233–50; association with Maximus Confessor, 149–51, 163–69; at Alexandria in 633, 209, 285; at Alexandria under John the Almsgiver, 49–53, 85, 105, 152–53, 162, 205, 209, 212, 334; at Constantinople in 633/4, 209–11, 219, 285; at Rome to collect Moschus's remains, 231; death of, 243–44, 250; doctrinal dissidence of, 188, 196–97, 205, 208–24, 231, 234–41, 327–28, 338; dyenergism of, 234–37; early commitment to dyenergism, 211–13, 216–17, 220–21; Council of Cyprus and, 239–41; early life of 44–45; election as patriarch, 233–34; eucharist and, 79, 84–87, 247–8, 312, 340; heresiological catalogue of, 237, 246–47; in North Africa, 110–11, 151, 299; *Life of John the Almsgiver* by, 50–52, 101–4, 110, 332; medical education of, 63–64; on Cyprus, 100–101; monotheletism and, 265; on Hippocratic

Sophronius of Jerusalem *(continued)*
  medicine, 59–69; *oikonomia* and, 219–22, 285; on the Cross, 160–62; on the Muslims, 241, 244–45, 248–49; patriarchal sermons of, 107–8, 241–50, 276, 339; poems on Jerusalem, 98–100, 127, 160–62, 276; recourse to Cyrus and John, 45–46; retreat from Alexandria, 98, 101; return to the East, 163; Rome and, 237–39, 273, 321; *Synodical Letter* of, 234–38, 241, 273, 322; Trisagion and, 220–21; union at Hierapolis and, 205; union of 617 and, 105. See also *Miracles of Cyrus and John*

*Spiritual Meadow*: admiration for Rome, 112–14, 124, 129–30, 276, 329, 339; chronological frame of, 118–19; compared to Maximus's *Mystagogy*, 174, 183–84; composition of, 90–91, 116; designation of 'Rome' within, 107–8; doctrinal politics of, 93, 130–38, 338; focus on eucharist in, 93, 131–39, 143, 171, 183, 221, 250, 312, 329–30, 335, 338, 340; given to Sophronius, 231; language and structure of, 93, 126–7; manuscript tradition of, 91–92, 107; modern approaches to, 117–20; on clerics, 123–24, 139, 143, 170, 183, 250, 332, 335, 341; on Gregory the Great, 112–13; on lay people, 117, 119, 124–25, 138, 183, 335; paradisiacal themes within, 116–18; social breadth within, 93, 116–17, 119–27, 184; urban asceticism and, 121–23, 333–35. See also Moschus, John

Stephanus the Sophist, 63–64
Stephen bar Sudaili, 23–26, 30
Stephen of Dora, 187, 237, 241, 269, 273, 295–97
Strangers, Monastery of, 125
Strategius, 92, 94–96, 99–100, 127
Stratos, Andreas, 219, 318
stylites, 34–37, 131–32
Symeon the Holy Fool, 334–35
Symeon the Stylite (the Elder), 34
Symeon the Stylite (the Younger), 35–37, 136, 193

Ṭabarī, 95
Thacker, Alan, 114
Thalassius the Libyan, 154, 259, 298
Theocharistus, 152
Theodore Calliopas, 301
Theodore, *locum tenens* of Alexandria, 323
Theodore of Colonia, 318
Theodore of Mopsuestia, 13, 201
Theodore of Pharan/Theodore of Raithou, 191–92, 196–98
Theodore of Scythopolis, 31

Theodore of Tarsus, archbishop of Canterbury: association with Moschus and Sophronius, 114, 299; cult of Anastasius the Persian and, 299; life of, 114–15; on Gregory the Great, 114–15
Theodore, patriarch of Alexandria, 50
Theodore, pope, 262, 280, 282–84, 286–87, 290–91, 295, 300, 326
Theodore, son of Plutinus, 292, 302
Theodore Spudaeus, 302
Theodoret of Cyrrhus, 10
Theodosians, 53, 88, 205–7, 209, 218. See also Severans
Theodosius, bishop of Caesarea, 314–15, 317
Theodosius, brother of Constans II, 318–19, 324
Theodosius, coenobium of, 44–45, 107, 169, 231–33, 297–98, 330
Theodosius, consul, 314–15, 317
Theodosius II, emperor, 47
Theodosius of Gangra, 302
Theodosius, patriarch of Alexandria, 76
Theodotus of Antioch, 123, 126
Theophanes, chronicler, 109, 202, 204, 243–44, 280, 309, 318, 325
Theophilus of Edessa, 94, 242–43, 250, 288, 309
Theophilus, patriarch of Alexandria, 48
Theophylact Simocatta, 158
Thomas Artsruni, 94
Three Chapters, 227
Thunberg, Lars, 181
Tiberius II, emperor, 45
Tiberius, son of Constans II, 318
Timothy Aelurus, patriarch of Alexandria, 39
*Tome* of Leo, 129, 188, 190, 195, 198, 203, 206–7, 210, 235–36, 238, 261. See also Leo, pope
Tribonian, 16
Trisagion, 51, 82, 180, 220–21, 239, 239n55, 327
Troilus, 304, 307
True Cross: capture of, 94–95, 99n37; George of Pisidia on, 159–62; return to Jerusalem, 142, 155–62, 185–86; Sophronius on, 160–62
Turks, 141
*Typos*, 291–93, 295, 311, 313, 315–16, 320

'Umar, caliph, 242
union: attempted between Heraclius and Athanasius the Camel Driver ca. 629/30, 202–5, 221, 237; between Cyrus of Phasis and the Egyptian Severans in June 633, 205–9,

214, 219, 221–22, 327; between Heraclius and the Armenian catholicus in ca. 631, 200, 221; between Heraclius and the Nestorian catholicus in ca. 630, 200–202, 221; between the Alexandrian and Antiochene Severans in 617, 104–5, 237
Uthemann, Karl-Heinz, 196

Valentine, general, 252–53, 279–80, 304
Victor, archbishop of Carthage, 287
Victor of Fayyūm, 206
Vigilius, pope, 193

Virgin, the, 118, 141, 303, 317, 330
Vitalian, pope, 321, 332, 341
von Balthasar, Hans Urs, 12, 176, 180, 183
von Schönborn, Christoph, 59

*Whitby Life of Gregory the Great*, 114
Wolska-Conus, Wanda, 64

Zachariah of Mytilene, 47
Zachariah, patriarch of Jerusalem, 94–95, 99, 142, 169, 298
Zeno, emperor, 227